Risk Management Handbook

American Society for Healthcare Risk Management

Series Editor: Roberta Carroll

Volume II Editor: Sylvia M. Brown

JB JOSSEY-BASS

Risk Management Handbook

FOR HEALTH CARE ORGANIZATIONS

Fifth Edition

VOLUME II

Clinical Risk

1807
WILEY
2007

John Wiley & Sons, Inc.

American Hospital Publishing, Inc.
An American Hospital Association Company
Chicago

Library of Congress Cataloging-in-Publication Data

Risk management handbook for health care organizations. — 5th ed.
    p. ; cm.
  Includes bibliographical references and index.
  ISBN-13: 978-0-7879-8672-8 (v. 1 : alk. paper)
  ISBN-10: 0-7879-8672-0 (v. 1 : alk. paper)
  ISBN-13: 978-0-7879-8708-4 (v. 2 : alk. paper)
  ISBN-10: 0-7879-8708-5 (v. 2 : alk. paper)
  ISBN-13: 978-0-7879-8724-4 (v. 3 : alk. paper)
  ISBN-10: 0-7879-8724-7 (v. 3 : alk. paper)
 1. Health facilities—Risk management. I. Nakamura, Peggy. II. Carroll, Roberta.
  [DNLM: 1. Health Facilities—economics. 2. Health Facilities—organization & administration.
 3. Risk Management. WX 157 R59533 2006]
  RA971.38.R58 2006
  362.11'068—dc22   2006023722

FIFTH EDITION
HB Printing   10 9 8 7 6 5 4 3 2 1

Contents

List of Exhibits, Figures, Tables, Photos, and Appendices

EXHIBITS

FIGURES

TABLES

PHOTOS

APPENDICES

About the Contributors

Joyce H. Benton, RN, MSA, ARM, CPHRM, DFASHRM, LHRM, Risk Control Consulting Director for CNA HealthPro. Before joining CNA HealthPro, Benton served as the Director of Quality Management and Safety at Henry General Hospital, an acute care hospital in the suburbs of Atlanta. In that role, she developed the risk management and infection control programs and assisted in restructuring the safety, workers' compensation, and quality improvement programs at the facility. Benton began her career as a registered nurse in surgical pediatrics at Grady Memorial Hospital in Atlanta and newborn nursery and childbirth education at Henry General Hospital. Benton is an active member of the American Society for Healthcare Risk Management (ASHRM), served on ASHRM's 2003–2004 Board of Directors, and is also an active member of the Georgia Society for Healthcare Risk Management and North Carolina ASHRM. She was awarded the Fellow designation (FASHRM) from ASHRM in 1992, and the Distinguished Fellow designation (DFASHRM) in 1998. Benton completed ASHRM's Healthcare Risk Management Certificate Program in 1996. She also received the Certified Professional in Healthcare Risk Management (CPHRM) designation from ASHRM in 2000. Benton was also the recipient of ASHRM's Excellence in Writing Award in 1999. In 2005, Benton was awarded ASHRM's highest honor, the Distinguished Service Award (DSA). In addition, Benton received the 1995–1996 Georgia Healthcare Risk Manager of the Year Award, the 2002 Distinguished Service Award for outstanding contributions in the advancement of the profession of risk management and service to the Georgia Society for Healthcare Risk Management (GSHRM), and 2004 GSHRM Lifetime Achievement Award. Benton is a frequent speaker on health care risk management topics at the local, state, and national level, and she has written several articles. She was a contributing author to the 4th Edition of the Risk Management Handbook. She has served as faculty for ASHRM's Healthcare Risk Management Certificate Program, CPHRM Study Course, and Insurance 101 program.

Sylvia M. Brown, RN, JD, Vice President, Risk Management Premier Insurance Management Services. Brown received her baccalaureate degree in English and nursing from Stanford University, and a juris doctorate degree from The Washington College of Law at the American University. She has more than twenty-five years of experience in health care risk management. Her accomplishments include development of a total quality management program for a 100-hospital system, presentation of numerous education programs to clients, implementation of an international newsletter, and numerous ASHRM publications. She also worked with the Virginia Hospital Association to develop and implement risk management education seminars for hospital boards of directors. As the Vice President of Risk Management for Premier Insurance Management Services, Brown provides a variety of risk management services to Premier members, including seminars, newsletters, and Web site resources.

Robert F. Bunting, Jr., MT (ASCP), MSA, DFASHRM, CPHRM, CPHQ,   Clinical Research Manager for WellPoint, the nation's leading health benefits company. Bunting received clinical training as a laboratory scientist. His Bachelor of Science in Medical Technology and Master of Science in Administration in Health Care were awarded by Columbus State University in Columbus, Georgia. He has more than twenty years of health care experience, including ten years as the director of quality and risk management for a comprehensive health care system. He was the instructor of a graduate school risk management course for more than ten years. He has written several health care books and articles, and he has served on the Editorial Board of the Journal of Nursing Risk Management, published by the Armed Forces Institute of Pathology since 2002. He is a frequent speaker on the state and national levels. He is a past president (1994–1995) of the Georgia Society for Healthcare Risk Management (GSHRM), and he received GSHRM's 1996–1997 Risk Manager of the Year Award. He served as chair of ASHRM's Certification Education Task Force in 1999–2001 and 2002–2003. He has been the editor of ASHRM's A Study Guide for the Certified Professional in Healthcare Risk Management (CPHRM) Examination since its inception. Bunting earned the Distinguished Fellow of the American Society for Healthcare Risk Management (DFASHRM) designation in 1998, won ASHRM's Excellence in Writing Award in 1999, earned his CPHRM designation in 2000, and received GSHRM's first Distinguished Service Award in 2001. He was awarded ASHRM's Distinguished Service Award in 2003.

Robin Burroughs,   Risk Control Consulting Director with CNA HealthPro, based in their New York City regional offices. She has been with CNA since 1995. Burroughs is responsible for providing risk management consulting services to the health care industry. While at CNA HealthPro, in addition to providing direct client consulting services, Burroughs has participated in the analysis of claims, including the long-term care claims studies and nurse practitioner claims study published by CNA HealthPro. In addition to co-authoring the chapter in the American Society of Healthcare Risk Management's Risk Management Handbook, *Risk Management for Behavioral Health,* along with a self-assessment checklist for facilities, she recently wrote an article on fall prevention that appeared in the May 2, 2005 edition of AAHSA's *Weekly Perspective.* Before joining CNA HealthPro, Burroughs was Acting Assistant Vice President, Quality Management, and Corporate Risk Manager for New York City's public health care system, Health and Hospitals Corporation (HHC). Before joining the New York City Health and Hospital Corporation, Robin was Assistant Vice President, Risk Management, for Interfaith Medical Center, another multi-hospital integrated health care delivery system in New York City. Burroughs is a registered nurse and a certified professional health care risk manager. Her clinical and administrative nursing experience includes medical, oncology research, geriatric, and psychiatric specialties. She has also consulted to several New York City law firms in the assessment and investigation of medical malpractice and negligence cases. A graduate of the Buffalo General Hospital School of Nursing, Burroughs also attended the State University of New York at Buffalo and D'Youville College. She is a graduate of the Institute of Medical Law, where she earned certification as a health care risk manager (CHRM). She has achieved ASHRM designation as a certified professional health care risk manager

(CPHRM), and is licensed in Texas as a Field Safety Representative—Specialty in Hospitals, and a Loss Control Representative—General Liability, Professional Liability, Commercial and Auto. Burroughs is a member of the adjunct faculty of New York University's School of Professional and Continuing Education.

Christine L. Clark, MT (ASCP), JD, CPHRM   Director of Risk Management at Resurrection West Suburban Medical Center in Oak Park, Illinois. She has held several positions in claims and risk management experience and has quality- and performance-improvement experience in various health care settings including academic hospitals, community hospitals, insurance companies, and the College of American Pathologists. She is a Medical Technologist and former paramedic with thirteen years of clinical experience in hospital and reference laboratories and on a municipal fire department. She has published several articles on health care regulation, home health care, claims management, and patient safety-related topics. She serves on the ASHRM Journal Task Force and Pearls Task Force. Clark has also served as chair of the ASHRM Nominating Committee and the On-line Education Task Force, and as a member of the Safety/Security Special Interest Group, Video Education Task Force, and the Bloodborne Pathogens Task Force. She is currently Treasurer of the Chicagoland Healthcare Risk Management Society and has served on the Executive Board, the Bylaws Committee, and as chair of the Program Committee. She has also chaired the Health Law Committee for the Women's Bar Association of Illinois; served on various Chicago Bar Association Committees, and the Chicago Area Nurse Attorneys' Association. She holds a Bachelor of Science in Medical Technology from Eastern Illinois University and a Juris Doctor from Loyola University Chicago School of Law. Clark is an Illinois licensed attorney. She also holds a Healthcare Leadership Certificate through Loyola University's School of Business Administration.

Hedy Cohen, RN, BSN, MS,   Vice President for the Institute for Safe Medication Practices (ISMP). She received an Associate of Arts in Nursing from Bucks County Community College in Newtown, Pennsylvania, a BSN from LaSalle University in Philadelphia, a Masters Degree in Health Systems Administration from Rochester Institute for Technology, in Rochester, New York, and is presently is a Ph.D. candidate in health policy at the University of the Sciences in Philadelphia. Her clinical nursing background of more than eighteen years was focused in critical care and nursing management. She is a frequent speaker for health care organizations on current issues in medication safety, and has written numerous articles on improving the medication-use process. She also edits ISMP's monthly newsletter *Nurse Advise-ERR,* co-wrote a handbook on high-alert drugs, and is on the National Advisory Board for the *Nursing Advance Journal* and *Davis's Drug Guide for Nurses.* Cohen has been appointed Adjunct Associate Professor at Temple School of Pharmacy and Faculty Fellow in the Executive Patient Safety Fellowship, which is offered through Virginia Commonwealth University in Richmond. She also serves as a medication error clinical analyst for the Pennsylvania Safety Authority's reporting program.

Mary Lynn Curran, RN, MS, CPHRM, FASHRM   Director of Clinical Risk Management for Thilman Filippini, Chicago. Curran has been working in the health care risk management field as a consultant to health care organizations and insurance companies for many years. Her background includes nursing practice in acute and clinical settings. Before working at Thilman Filippini, Curran was a consultant with AIG Consulting, Inc.—Healthcare Management Division, Chicago, where she worked as consultant to hospitals, long-term care organizations, and miscellaneous health care facilities. She also worked for Premier, Inc., Chicago, in the insurance division and hospital relations division. Currently, she is responsible for working directly with Thilman Filippini's health care and senior housing clients as a consultant to their risk management and safety programs. Specifically, Curran is responsible for development of prevention and control programs; education and training of client staff, and onsite consultation surveys with the agency's clients. She served on the executive board of the Chicago Healthcare Risk Management Society (CHRMS) in 2002–2004 and serves on various committees. She has sat on various committees of the American Society for Healthcare Risk Management (ASHRM), including bylaws and editorial review. She is a contributing author of numerous risk management-related articles for CHRMS and ASHRM publications, including *Pearls—Risk Management Advice for the Long Term Care Organization, Pearls For Physicians,* and a chapter on "Healthcare Enterprise Organizational Staffing" for the fourth edition of *Risk Management Handbook for Healthcare.* Curran earned her nursing degree from St. Francis School of Nursing, Evanston, Illinois, and her bachelors in science and masters in health care administration from the University of St. Francis, Joliet, Illinois. She earned the designation of Certification in Professional Healthcare Risk Management (CPHRM) in 2002 and in 2005. Curran was awarded the Designation of Fellow from the American Society of HealthCare Risk Management (FASHRM) in 2005.

Bruce Dmytrow, BS, MBA, CPHRM,   Vice President, CNA HealthPro, for Chicago-based CNA. He has been with CNA since 1995. Dmytrow is responsible for leading the risk management business unit of CNA HealthPro. The business unit is composed of a group of consultants with diverse backgrounds who provide risk management consulting services to health care clients. Clients include hospitals, medical group practices, long-term care facilities, advanced medical technology companies, allied health care facilities, risk retention groups, and captives. Before joining CNA, Dmytrow was a manager and health care consultant at MMI Companies, Inc. and Bio-Med Associates. Before his career in the insurance industry, Dmytrow served as a clinician at the University of Chicago Hospitals and Northwestern Memorial Hospital. Within the profession, Dmytrow provides education programs to health care professionals and participates in panel discussions for major insurance and health care-related associations. He is widely published and often quoted in industry journals. Dmytrow serves as an active member on several health care organization boards of directors and advisory boards. Dmytrow graduated *cum laude* from Boston College with a bachelor of science degree. He received a postgraduate degree in medical dosimetry from Yale University Medical School/Yale–New Haven Hospital and a master of business administration degree in entrepreneurship, with highest distinction, from DePaul University in Chicago.

David Bryan Earle, MD,   Director of Minimally Invasive Surgery (MIS) and Director of the MIS Fellowship at Baystate Medical Center in Springfield, Massachusetts. Earle is Assistant Professor of Surgery for Tufts University School of Medicine (TUSM) in Boston. Baystate Medical Center is the Western Campus for TUSM. Previously, Dr. Earle was Assistant Professor of Surgery and Director of Laparoscopic Surgery with State University of New York, Health Science Center at Brooklyn, and was an attending physician with Kings County Hospital and Kingsbrook Jewish Medical Center, both in Brooklyn. Earle is a member of the Society of American Gastrointestinal Endoscopic Surgeons; Chair of the Guidelines Committee (2004); a member of the Fundamentals of Laparoscopic Skills Committee; and a member of the International Relations Committee. In addition, he is a member of the Society of Laparoendoscopic Surgeons; the American College of Surgeons,

Fellow; American Hernia Society (Charter Member); and a member of Premier physician advisory committees (regarding endomechanical products (FY2002–03). He received the Resident Achievement Award from the Society of Laparoendoscopic Surgeons (1995).

Alice Epstein, LHRM, CPHQ, CPHRM,   Risk Control Consulting Director with CNA HealthPro. She holds a Masters in Hospital and Healthcare Administration from the University of Alabama in Birmingham. She holds the following honorary designations: Fellow of the National Association of HealthCare Quality and Distinguished Fellow of the American Society of Healthcare Risk Management. Epstein has received the following professional certifications and licenses: Certified Professional in Healthcare Risk Management from the American Society for Healthcare Risk Management, Certified Professional in Healthcare Quality from the Healthcare Quality Professional Board, Certified Professional Environmental Auditor from the Health & Safety, Board of Environmental Auditing, Field Safety Representative with Specialty in Hospitals for the State of Texas, Loss Control Representative for Commercial Auto, General Liability and Professional Liability for the State of Texas, Licensed Health Care Risk Manager for the State of Florida, and Continuing Education Insurance Instructor for the South Carolina Department of Insurance.

Frank Federico, R.Ph.,   Director at the Institute for Healthcare Improvement in Cambridge, Massachusetts. His primary areas of focus include patient safety, application of reliability principles in health care, and the *Idealized Design of Perinatal Care.* He is also a faculty member for the Patient Safety Officer Training Program. Federico has worked with the Institute for Healthcare Improvement since 1996 as a faculty member and co-chair of several Patient Safety Collaboratives. Before joining IHI, Federico was the Program Director of the Office Practice Evaluation Program and a Loss Prevention/Patient Safety Specialist at Risk Management Foundation (RMF) of the Harvard Affiliated Institutions in Cambridge, Massachusetts. He, along with a team of nurse surveyors, developed a compendium of effective practices to reduce risk and harm in the office setting. Federico is one of the executive producers of *First, Do No Harm, Part 2: Taking the Lead.* He served as Director of Pharmacy at Children's Hospital, Boston. While in that position, he was co-chair of a quality improvement team charged with revamping the medication system and chaired the Adverse Drug Event Committee. Federico has worked with the Institute for Healthcare Improvement in Boston since 1996 as a faculty member and co-chair of several Patient Safety Collaboratives. He is co-author of a chapter in *Achieving Safe and Reliable Healthcare, Strategies and Solutions.* Federico lectures extensively, nationally and internationally, on patient safety.

Gary Harding,   Director of Technical Services for Greener Pastures LLC. and a career professional biomedical engineer. He received a *magna cum laude* biomedical engineering technology degree from Temple University College of Engineering and has postgraduate experience in law and social policy. He has direct experience in medical device and health care worker safety while a senior consultant and senior project engineer at ECRI, the manager of the National Clinical Risk Management program for Johnson & Higgins, and a national practice manager in the Health Care Risk Advisory Services offered by Laventhol & Horwath. Harding has reviewed, discussed, and published articles on such subjects as back injury, accidental needlesticks, exposure to hazardous materials, emergency medical systems, risk management, laser technology, and the evaluation of medical devices. He is experienced in reviewing and analyzing health care policies and procedures for a wide range of medical clients, including medical device manufacturers, acute and chronic care facilities, insurers, and psychiatric services. He is well experienced in OSHA requirements related to bloodborne pathogens. He has provided accident investigation and expert witness services throughout the country related to medical device-acquired infections and injuries for health care workers and others such as sanitation workers, police, and firefighters, and for several high technology and other devices. He has discussed methods to perform such investigations and methods to use to procure safer products.

Kathryn Hyer, PhD, MPP, Associate Professor in the School of Aging Studies at the University of South Florida and Director of the Training Academy on Aging, a program sponsored by the University to promote geriatric and gerontological training for health care professionals. Hyer is a nationally recognized leader in geriatric and gerontological education and holds joint faculty appointments in The College of Public Health's Health Policy and Management Department and the Division of Geriatric Medicine in the College of Medicine. Hyer played a key role in Florida's Nursing home reform bill of 2001, the legislation that mandates all Florida nursing homes to report adverse incidents and create risk management programs. She is the course director for a state-approved licensed health care risk management program that emphasizes risk management in long-term care. Hyer holds a Masters degree in Public Policy from the Kennedy School of Government at Harvard University and Doctorate in Public Administration from Arizona State University. She is a member of ASHRM, Gerontological Society of America, American Geriatrics Society, a Fellow in the Association for Gerontology in Higher Education, has testified before the Federal Physician Payment Review Commission, and has contributed more than forty publications to the literature in the fields of geriatrics care, the education of health care professionals, and policy issues relating to the quality of long-term care.

Brenda K. Johnson, RN, MS, ARM, Risk Management Consultant and a principal with Benedict and Associates, Inc. and Murex Risk Services LLC. Her education includes a master of science and bachelor of science in nursing from the University of Illinois, Champaign, Illinois. She is a registered professional nurse in Florida and holds an associate in risk management designation. Johnson has been the director of cardiovascular/surgical nursing services for an acute care medical facility and an assistant vice president for critical care, surgical, and cardiac and pulmonary rehabilitation programs. She has provided risk management for health care consulting firms, acute and long-term care facilities, and has testified as an expert witness in numerous malpractice cases. Johnson is a member of the Risk and Insurance Management Society, the American Association of Legal Nurse Consultants, and Sigma Theta Tau International. Johnson has also written and published several articles and educational materials. She was primary author for the risk management licensure program at the University of South Florida.

Trista Johnson, Ph.D., MPH, Director of Performance Measurement and Analysis for Allina Hospitals & Clinics. In this role, she works to provide coordinated, accurate analysis and results to drive organizational improvement. Previously, she served as the Director of Patient Safety and coordinated initiatives and measurements across the eleven-hospital, forty-four-clinic Allina system. She helped create a standard data collection tool and taxonomy for patient safety events, and continues to work with this system, analyzing the data and using the results in safety collaboratives. Collaboratives conducted while leading patient safety include falls prevention, teamwork and patient safety, insulin safety, and the IHI trigger tool analysis. Johnson serves as a member of the Minnesota Alliance for Patient

Safety (MAPS), which is helping to implement the mandatory state-wide reporting of the twenty-seven National Quality Forum events. She completed her doctoral work on the application of epidemiology to the study of medical errors.

Eric Knox, MD,   Professor of OB-GYN at the University of Minnesota, Minneapolis, and the former Director of Patient Safety and Risk Management, Children's Hospitals and Clinics, Minneapolis and St. Paul. While at Children's he led the developmental team that created and implemented the organization's anonymous and story-based patient safety reporting network. Under his leadership, Children's Hospitals and Clinics was a finalist for the AHA McKesson award for building a culture of safety in 2002. Before joining Children's, Dr. Knox was president and chief medical officer of Obstetrix Medical Group, Inc., a for-profit publicly traded national group practice of Maternal-Fetal Medicine Specialists. Before Obstetrix, he founded Minnesota Perinatal Specialists and actively practiced Maternal-Fetal Medicine for twenty-two years. His research and consulting has focused on High Reliability and Teamwork in preventing Perinatal Injury and malpractice claims. He has published over 100 articles concerning clinical practice and management of clinical risk. Currently, he is doing multidisciplinary qualitative research on patterns of nurse-physician communication and their effect on patient injury in obstetrics. From 1985–1997, Dr. Knox served as the Medical Director of MMI Companies, Inc., a medical malpractice insurer and clinical risk management group that served hospital, physician and health plan clients throughout the United States, the United Kingdom, Germany, and Australia. He has given more than 200 lectures and seminars to nurses, physicians, and governing boards on all aspects of managing clinical risk and creating patient safety. He was a founding board member of the National Patient Safety Foundation. He currently consults actively with TIG, MCIC Vermont (a university-based medical malpractice insurance captive,) and large health care organizations throughout the United States.

Nancy Lagorio, RN, MS, CCLA,   Consultant with CNA HealthPro with more than twenty years of health care experience. Lagorio has a diverse background that encompasses marketing, business development, physician relations and recruitment, medical office management, and clinical operations. Her accomplishments include planning and implementing a reproductive health center, developing and administering a multi-specialty medical group, and directing marketing and strategic planning for a multi-hospital system. She has also led change management and reengineering efforts, and has negotiated managed care contracts on behalf of both physicians and hospitals. Lagorio is a registered nurse, has the designation of Casualty Claims Law Associate, and received her Master of Science in Health Care Administration from the University of St. Francis in Joliet, Illinois. Lagorio is a member of the American Society for Healthcare Risk Management and the Society of Claim Law Associates. Consulting clients include, hospitals, long-term care communities, medical practices, ambulatory surgical centers, and laboratories.

June Leigh, RN, MS, ARM, CPHRM, DFASHRM   provides health care consulting services for physicians, nurses, medical group practices, hospitals, long-term care and assisted living facilities, and other health care providers. Leigh has more than twenty years experience in the health care industry, including experience in acute care settings, medical group practices, managed care, and peer review organizations. She provides consulting services that include risk assessments, development of risk management tools and resources, and educational presentations. Leigh has several years experience in regulatory compliance. She has been a member of the American Society for Healthcare Risk

Management (ASHRM) since 1986 and is a current member of the American College of Healthcare Executives, the Chicagoland Healthcare Risk Management Society, and the Assisted Living Federation of America. She currently is serving on ASHRM's Board of Directors. Leigh attended the University of Kentucky, where she earned a Bachelor of Science in Nursing and received a Master of Science in Health Services Administration from the College of St. Francis in Joliet, Illinois. She has earned the Associate in Risk Management (ARM) designation from the Insurance Institute of America and the designation of Certified Professional in Healthcare Risk Management (CPHRM) from ASHRM. Leigh also received a Certificate of Completion by ASHRM for the Health Care Risk Management Certificate Program. She was recognized as a Distinguished Fellow of the American Society for Healthcare Risk Management (DFASHRM) in April 2005.

David Lickerman, MD, FACEP, ABIM, CHQM,   Emergency Physician at St. Luke's Hospital in Chesterfield, Missouri. Previously he was Associate Director of Emergency Medical Services at Christian Hospitals NE-NW for twenty-three years in St. Louis. He is a graduate of Indiana University School of Medicine. His residency training was in Primary Care Internal Medicine at St. Luke's Hospital–Washington University in St. Louis. His board certifications include Internal Medicine, Emergency Medicine, and Quality Improvement. In 1993, he founded MeduLogic, LLC, to produce and distribute computer-based continuing medical education materials. Software written by Dr. Lickerman and published by MeduLogic include *Clinical Communication* and *Risk Management Strategies for Emergency Medicine, The Many Faces of Family Violence*, and *Risk Management & the Art of Primary Care*. He has also published CME courses on the Internet at the Virtual Lecture Hall [www.vlh.com]. Current course offerings include *EMTALA: An ER Law that Affects All Physicians* and *Risk Management and the Art of Medicine*. While at Christian Hospital, he was chair of the Emergency Department's Quality Improvement Committee for twenty-one years and developed and edited the *QI Notes* and *QI FlashNotes* newsletters. He has served as an ED risk management consultant for the Medical Protective Company and Farmers Insurance Company Professional Liability Division. Dr. Lickerman is a well-known legal expert in ED medical-legal and risk management issues. He has written and lectured nationally on the subjects of ED quality improvement, risk management, ED redesign, family violence, and physician-patient communication.

Stephanie Lickerman, EMT, RN, BSN,   Director of Community Education for the Melanoma Hope Network, St. Louis. A graduate of St. Luke's School of Nursing and St. Louis University, she has been editor of the Christian Hospital *QI Notes* newsletter since 1989. Additionally, she has edited three medical education software packages: *Clinical Communication and Risk Management Strategies for Emergency Medicine, The Many Faces of Family Violence*, and *Risk Management and The Art of Primary Care*. Previously, Lickerman served as Chairman of the Planning Commission, Wildwood, Missouri (1995–97), co-authored the master plan, ordinances, and natural resource matrix; was one of the original founders of the city; and served as City Science Coordinator (1997–2003). Her medical background is in cardiothoracic, cardiac medicine, neuro and surgical intensive care, and inservice, ACLS, and CPR instructing (both in-hospital and corporate). She has received the following awards: Recognition of Outstanding Service, Southern Illinois University, Edwardsville, 1996; Resolution 97–13, Stephanie Lickerman month, December 1997, for public service and city development; Melanoma Hope Network service award, 2004; Rose award, Rockwood School District's highest honor, 2005, for outstanding service in education. Lickerman has spoken on the national level regarding her city science work and is well known in her community for educational outreach in the environmental and medical sciences.

Peggy Berry Martin, MS, ARM, Med,   Senior Risk Management Coordinator for Lifespan Risk Services of the Lifespan Corporation, Providence, Rhode Island. She assists risk managers from member hospitals to proactively identify areas of potential risk, and designs interventions and educational programs to address them. Martin has held several positions in health care facilities and captive insurance companies during her twenty-five years of experience, the most recent as the director of education for the Risk Management Foundation of the Harvard Medical Institutions. She was elected president of the American Society for Healthcare Risk Management for the 2006 term and was previously on the Board of Directors. Martin has received the designation of Distinguished Fellow of the American Society for Healthcare Organizations and has served as chair of several ASHRM committees. She was instrumental in developing the first ASHRM Patient Safety Training Modules and continues as faculty for that program. On the state level, Martin was the first president and one of the founding members of the Massachusetts Society for Healthcare Risk Management and was the recipient of their first Distinguished Service Award in 2000.

Denise Murphy, RN, BSN, MPH, CIC,   Chief Patient Safety and Quality Officer at Barnes-Jewish Hospital at Washington University Medical Center in St. Louis. Before taking that position, she spent seven years as Director of Healthcare Epidemiology and Patient Safety for BJC HealthCare. Murphy went to nursing school in Philadelphia, received her BSN in Portland, Maine, and a Master of Public Health degree from St. Louis University, School of Public Health. Murphy's early nursing experience was in pediatric ICUs, surgical nursing, and nursing management. She entered the field of Infection Control in 1981, sitting for the first certification in infection control (CIC) exam in 1983. She has been an ICP in hospitals ranging from 100–1200 beds, in rural and urban settings. Her presentations and publications are numerous on prevention of surgical site infections, bloodstream infections and ventilator-associated pneumonia, on re-designing infection control services, the business of infection control, and establishment of patient safety programs. Murphy is an active member of The Association for Professionals in Infection Control and Epidemiology (APIC), the Society for Healthcare Epidemiology of America (SHEA), and the American Society for Healthcare Risk Managers (ASHRM). She is a past president of the APIC Greater St. Louis chapter, and currently serves as a director on the APIC national board and chair of Strategic Planning. Murphy was a four-year member of the APIC annual conference task force, and is currently the ICP representative on the SHEA educational conference planning committee. She graduated from the first AHA/National Patient Safety Foundation-sponsored Leadership Fellowship training program in August, 2003.

Peter Pronovost, MD, PhD, FCCM,   anesthesiologist and critical care physician, a lecturer, a patient safety researcher, and leader. He is a professor in the Departments of Anesthesiology and Critical Care Medicine and Surgery in the School of Medicine, Nursing in the School of Nursing, and Health Policy and Management in the Bloomberg School of Public Health at the Johns Hopkins University. Dr. Pronovost is the director of the Quality and Safety Research Group, director of the Division of Adult Critical Care Medicine, co-director of the Cardiac Surgical Intensive Care Unit, and medical director for the Center for Innovation in Quality Patient Care at Johns Hopkins. Dr. Pronovost holds a doctorate in clinical investigation from the Johns Hopkins Bloomberg School of Public Health. He has written more than 130 articles and chapters in the fields of patient safety, ICU care, quality health care, and evidence-based medicine. Nationwide, he is chair of the ICU Advisory Panel for Quality Measures with JCAHO, chair of the ICU Physician Staffing Committee for the Leapfrog Group, and is on the National Quality Forums Quality Measures Work Group. He has won several national awards for his research including the 2004 John Eisenberg Patient Safety Research Award. Dr. Pronovost is currently leading multiple large nationwide safety projects, funded by the U.S. Agency for Healthcare Research and Quality. He has developed innovative yet feasible tools to improve quality of care and patient safety that are being used by thousands of hospitals.

Gina Pugliese, RN MS, Vice President of the Safety Institute, Premier Inc., Chicago. She holds associate faculty appointments at the University of Illinois School of Public Health, Division of Epidemiology and Biostatistics and Rush University College of Nursing, Chicago. Pugliese is on the Editorial Advisory Board of the Joint Commission Journal on Quality and Safety and is the Senior Associate Editor of *Infection Control and Hospital Epidemiology.* She is the co-director of the international Healthcare Epidemiology Training Program that is co-sponsored by the Society for Healthcare Epidemiology of America (SHEA) and the Centers for Disease Control and Prevention (CDC). For eight years, Pugliese was the Director of Safety of the American Hospital Association, Chicago. She was a founding board member and past president of the national Certification Board of Infection Control (CBIC) and has served as a board member of the national Association for Professionals in Infection Control and Epidemiology (APIC). She is the author of more than 130 publications and has served on the faculty in more than 300 educational conferences (thirteen countries) and appeared in more than thirty videotape, television, and teleconference programs. Pugliese currently serves on several national committees including the expert panel for the CMS National Surgical Infection Prevention (SIP) and Surgical Care Improvement Projects (SCIP), AHRQ's Patient Safety Research Coordinating Center Steering Committee, and FDA's Medical Product Surveillance Network (MEDSUN) Advisory Group. Pugliese is the 2001 recipient of the APIC Carole DeMille outstanding achievement award in safety and epidemiology. In 2004, the Gina Pugliese Scholarship was established for five clinicians to attend each of the SHEA/CDC international Healthcare Epidemiology Training Courses, held bi-annually, in recognition of her contributions to health care epidemiology.

Fay A. Rozovsky, JD, MPH, DFASHRM, has more than twenty years experience as a health care risk management consultant and attorney. She has lectured extensively and has written or co-authored numerous articles and books including *Consent to Treatment: A Practical Guide, Clinical Trials and Human Research* (with Rodney Adams, Esq.) and *What Do I Say? Communicating Intended or Unanticipated Outcomes in Obstetrics* (with Dr. James R. Woods). She co-edited with Dr. Woods *The Patient Safety Compliance Handbook: A Practical Guide for Healthcare Organizations*, published in March 2005. Rozovsky's expertise in consent law has been recognized by several courts, including the U.S. Supreme Court and appellate courts in Hawaii, Kentucky, West Virginia, and several other states. Rozovsky received a J.D. from Boston College Law School and an M.P.H. from the Harvard School of Public Health. She is an Affiliate Associate Professor in the Department of Legal Medicine at Virginia Commonwealth University School of Medicine. Rozovsky is admitted to the practice of law in Florida and Massachusetts. Rozovsky is a Distinguished Fellow and Past President of the American Society for Healthcare Risk

Management and a recipient of the Distinguished Service Award, the highest honor bestowed on a member of ASHRM. Currently, she is the chair of the Professional Technical Advisory Committee for Hospitals of the Joint Commission on Accreditation of Healthcare Organizations.

Jeffrey M. Sconyers, JD,   Vice President and General Counsel of Children's Hospital and Regional Medical Center, Seattle, the regional pediatric referral and teaching center for Washington, Alaska, Idaho, Montana, and Wyoming. Sconyers received his law degree from Yale Law School and has practiced health law for more than twenty years. He is a past president of the Washington State Society of Healthcare Attorneys and its program czar in perpetuity. He was a founding co-editor of the *Washington Health Law Manual,* published by WSSHA and the Washington State Hospital Association. He is a member of the Executive Committee of the Board of Directors of the American Health Lawyers Association and chair of its Professional Resources Committee. At Children's Hospital, he chairs the Compliance Committee, staffs the Governance and the Audit and Corporate Responsibility Committees, and oversees the departments of safety, security, risk management, compliance, and legal affairs.

Katrina A. Shannon, B.A., J.D.,   Risk Management Coordinator for Barnes-Jewish Hospital in St. Louis, and an adjunct professor at Maryville University in St. Louis. Shannon received her B.A. in Business Management and her Certificate in Health Information Management from Saint Louis University. She received her Juris Doctor from Saint Louis University School of Law and a Health Law Certificate from the Saint Louis University School of Law Center for Health Law Studies. She is licensed to practice in Missouri. Shannon is a former law clerk for the BJC Health System, Armstrong Teasdale, LLP, and a former Associate Attorney for Lashly & Baer, P.C. In these roles, Shannon practiced corporate, government, education, and health care law. Shannon is a member of the Missouri Bar Association, the Mound City Bar Association, the St. Louis Area Health Law Association, the St. Louis Association for Health Care Risk Managers, and the American Society for Healthcare Risk Management.

Laurence A. Sherman, BA, BS, MD, JD, FACP, FCAP,   Professor Emeritus of Pathology at Northwestern Medical School, Chicago, and board certified in Internal Medicine, Clinical Pathology, and Blood Banking. Sherman consults part-time in medical legal, compliance, and billing areas, including for the Northwestern faculty, and is part of the Northwestern Transplantation Ethics group. He also intermittently surveys for JCAHO. Previously at Northwestern, he was Director of Clinical Laboratories and Blood Bank at Northwestern Memorial and Director of the Blood Bank at Childrens' Memorial. His earliest clinical laboratory experience was as a medical technologist in the army. Prior academic positions include Professor of Pathology and Medicine at Washington University in St. Louis, and Director of its (NHLBI) National Heart, Lung, and Blood Institute Institutional Training Program in Blood Banking, Associate Director of its NHLBI Specialized Center of Research in Thrombosis, and Director of the Blood Bank at Barnes Hospital. Nationally he held many offices in the American Association of Blood Banks, including president, and received its Quinn Jordan award for contributions in transfusion medicine and government affairs. Sherman received his Bachelor of Science degree from the University of Chicago, his Doctor of Medicine from Albany Medical College, and Juris Doctor from Loyola (Chicago). He has served on committees of the American Society of Hematology, American Society of Clinical Pathology, American Heart Association, College of

American Pathologists, and National Veterans Administration, and also served in local and regional groups. He has written or edited books in Clinical Pathology and Coagulation Research, and has published more than 100 journal articles and book chapters on blood transfusion, coagulation and thrombosis, clinical pathology, medical legal matters, and medical ethics, and given many presentations around the country.

Kathleen M. Shostek, RN, ARM, BBA, FASHRM,   Senior Risk Management Analyst with ECRI, an independent, nonprofit health service research agency in Plymouth Meeting, Pennsylvania. Shostek researches and authors risk analyses, educational resources, and assessment tools on several patient safety topics and health care risk management issues for ECRI's print and online Healthcare Risk Control System, Continuing Care Risk Management, Risk Management Reporter newsletter, INsight software, and HRC Alerts. She also provides telephonic, Internet, and on-site consultative and educational services to a wide range of health care providers and institutions, including hospitals, ambulatory surgery centers, physician groups, and continuing care facilities. She was previously risk management director for a large multi-specialty physician group, and consultant for a national malpractice insurance company. Shostek received ASHRM's Excellence in Writing Award in 1998, and served on several ASHRM committees and task forces including the nominating, journal, and monographs committees. She chaired the Professional Ethics Committee in 2003 and has been an Editorial Review Board member for the *Journal of Healthcare Risk Management* since 1999. A registered nurse, Shostek attained a bachelor's degree in Business Administration at Wilkes University, Wilkes-Barre, Pennsylvania, and was designated an ASHRM Fellow in 2001.

Kathleen Rice Simpson, PhD, RNC, FAAN,   Perinatal Clinical Nurse Specialist at St. John's Mercy Medical Center in St. Louis. Simpson is responsible for perinatal nursing practice and research, and consultation on clinical issues for the antepartum, intrapartum, and obstetric triage units. She coordinates the perinatal nursing fellowship program, and orientation, continuing education, and competence validation for the professional nursing staff. Simpson is a fellow in the American Academy of Nursing and a member of the Association of Women's Health, Obstetric, and Neonatal Nurses, the Association of Critical Care Nurses, Sigma Theta Tau, and Alpha Sigma Nu, the Jesuit Honor Society. She is the chair of the National Certification Corporation (NCC) Obstetric Content Team for the In-Patient OB and Electronic Fetal Monitoring Certification Examinations. Simpson is the editor of *AWHONN's Perinatal Nursing* and *AWHONN's Competence Validation for Perinatal Care Providers* and the author of *AWHONN's Practice Monograph Cervical Ripening and Induction and Augmentation of Labor.* She is a member of the National Nurse Advisory Council of the March of Dimes and a member of the editorial boards of the *Journal of Perinatal Neonatal Nursing* and *MCN The American Journal of Maternal-Child Nursing.* She is the author of many articles and text chapters on perinatal patient safety and has been principal investigator on numerous research studies about safe care during labor and birth. She has provided perinatal risk management consultation to many hospitals and health care systems across the country and has been a labor and delivery nurse for more than twenty years.

David M. Stallings, MHA, CPHQ, FASHRM,   Director of Risk Management of Children's Hospital and Regional Medical Center, Seattle, the regional pediatric referral and teaching center for Washington, Alaska, Idaho, Montana, and Wyoming. Stallings received his bachelor of science degree from San Jose State University and a master of health administration degree from the University of Southern California. He is the former director of risk management and quality assessment at UCLA Medical Center/UCLA Health Network and has more than sixteen years experience managing risk in community, tertiary, and academic medical centers. Stallings is an active member, and former board member, of the Washington Health Care Risk Management Society. He has served in various member and leadership capacities with ASHRM and is a current member of the ASHRM Board of Directors. He has been a Certified Professional in Healthcare Quality since 1994 and was awarded the Fellow of ASHRM designation in 2003.

Nancy Tuohy, RN, MSN,   Medication Safety Specialist at ISMP. She is also the Assistant Editor for ISMP Nurse Advise-ERR and a contributor to the other ISMP Medication Safety Alert! publications. Tuohy's interests include patient safety and health care systems analysis, including the evolution of health care informatics. Her prior work experiences cover a broad range of health care settings, including pediatrics, critical care, outpatient clinic, elementary school settings, pharmaceutical research, and pre-hospital care as an emergency medical technician. Tuohy obtained her BSN at the University of North Carolina at Chapel Hill and her MSN at University of Pennsylvania. She also holds a bachelor's degree in psychology from Wake Forest University.

Sally T. Trombly, RN, MPH, JD, DFASHRM,   Executive Director of the Dartmouth-Hitchcock Risk Management Program, based at Dartmouth-Hitchcock Medical Center in Lebanon, New Hampshire, and an adjunct instructor in community and family medicine at Dartmouth Medical School. Dartmouth-Hitchcock's risk management and self-insured liability insurance program covers tertiary care services and graduate medical education at Mary Hitchcock Memorial Hospital, a network of more than 900 Dartmouth-Hitchcock Clinic specialty and primary care physicians practicing throughout New Hampshire and Vermont, and an affiliated group of regional hospitals and related health care organizations. Her background includes extensive risk management experience in several health care delivery sites, including fourteen years at the Risk Management Foundation working with the institutions participating in Harvard's self-insured liability insurance program. Trombly has served on ASHRM's board of directors, its legislative committees, various ASHRM task forces, and has participated at the state chapter level. Since 1995, she has been on the board of directors of the Anesthesia Patient Safety Foundation (APSF) and participates in review of research grant proposals as a member of the APSF's Scientific Evaluation Committee. She also serves on the editorial advisory review board for ECRI. She has written and lectured on several risk management and health law topics.

Kelley Woodfin RN, BS, CPHRM,   Vice President, Risk Management Consulting Services, Southern California Presbyterian Homes, Executive Director, LTC Risk Consulting Services. Woodfin has a diversified background as a registered nurse, having worked in all levels of health care delivery systems. Her primary clinical nursing background was in pediatric and adult critical care and emergency services, with additional service on the board of directors of Torrance Home Health Care Services. In addition, she has had extensive experience with developing and implementing proactive, fully integrated Risk Management programs in several health care settings, including acute care, ambulatory care, managed care, and long term care. She graduated with honors from the Los Angeles County/USC Medical Center School of Nursing, and has a Bachelor of Science degree, with honors, in Business Administration from the University of Phoenix. Woodfin is a member of ASHRM and the Southern California Association for Healthcare Risk

Management (SCAHRM), where she served both on the board of directors and as president of the Association. She was also an elected member of the ASHRM Nominating Committee and a participant in ASHRMs Module I Task Force. She completed the ASHRM certificate program in Risk Management, and is a Certified Professional in Healthcare Risk Management (CPHRM).

Sheila Cohen Zimmet, BSN, JD,   Associate Dean (Research Compliance) at Weill Medical College of Cornell University, where she serves as the course director for the Tri-Institutional Responsible Conduct of Research course for Weill Cornell Medical College, Rockefeller University, and Memorial Sloan-Kettering Institute. She previously served as Director of Research Assurance and Compliance and as senior counsel for Georgetown University Medical Center. She started her professional career as a neonatal intensive care nurse after earning her undergraduate nursing degree from Georgetown University in 1971. After she received her law degree (JD) from Georgetown in 1975, Zimmet pursued a legal career with the federal government in the fields of occupational and mine safety and health. She returned to Georgetown University in 1984, where her health law practice focused on clinical, bioethical and biomedical research issues, professional liability and risk management, and other hospital and higher education legal issues involving patients, students, faculty, and staff that are common to academic medical centers. Zimmet also serves as a member of the National Advisory Research Resources Council of the National Institutes of Health.

Preface

As health care risk management continues to evolve as a profession, the opportunities abound for astute risk management professionals to advance their careers while adding value to their organizations. Risk management professionals are in a unique position to enhance organizational efforts to ensure patient safety and minimize risk, while creating an atmosphere that is conducive to teaming and trust. They work within an environment that is complex, changing, and burdened with increasing regulations and laws. They have never been more needed.

Health risk management today requires a well-seasoned, dedicated professional with the requisite skill set to recommend and facilitate change. These committed professionals are valued by their organization for the strategies and solutions that they offer to enhance the culture of the work environment, and by initiating techniques to reduce the exposures to risk inherent in all health care operations. Risk management professionals are generalist; and while not expert in all areas, they are familiar with all aspects of the organization and readily see the "big picture" of how risks interact and are synergistic. *The risk management professional understands how risk represents not only the potential for loss but also the opportunity for gain and profit.*

Enterprise risk management, while slow for health care to grasp, is nonetheless making headway. An analogy can be made to current efforts in patient safety. Both are organization-wide initiatives requiring the commitment and attention of every employee, and both emanate from the top of the organization. Neither of these initiatives is easily accomplished. Both represent a life commitment on the part of the organization if they are to be successful.

The fifth edition of the *Risk Management Handbook for Health Care Organizations* has tried to capture that essential knowledge crucial for the risk management professional in health care today and translate the information into a useful reference resource. Very little in risk management ever seems to go away. We just keep adding to this vast wealth of information by way of new requirements, statutes, standards, best practices, and so on. What has changed is how we evaluate organizational risks, the impact that one risk has on another, and our approach to eliminate or manage those risks.

Our goal with this handbook is to educate the risk management professional on an enterprise-wide basis offering discussion on a variety of risk topics, both clinical and non-clinical, representative of different care settings. Where possible, we have discussed the risk issue, developed a strategy to eliminate or minimize specific risks, and offered solutions. We have continued, as with other editions, to offer an extensive variety of tools such as policies and procedures, checklists, tables, graphs, figures, and the like. It is anticipated that this information will be supplemented by material from the Internet, an invaluable resource for any risk management professional. Many contributing authors have suggested Web sites and readings to augment their chapter information.

The sheer volume of information that was felt to be important to communicate to the health care risk management professional (or other interested parties) necessitated that we revise the format. No longer could the information be contained in one book. Therefore, this edition has been written as a three-volume series. Although many chapters are new to this edition, others have simply been updated or revised. Many of the chapters refer the reader to other chapters within the series. We have highlighted those references for you to make it easier to find additional information within the series. The three volumes in the series are:

Volume I   The Essentials
Volume II   Clinical Risk
Volume III Business Risk: Legal, Regulatory, & Technology Issues

New chapters on medication safety, risk management information systems, risk in the operating room, pediatrics, ICU, radiology, and emergency departments, and chapters on Enterprise Risk Management ~ The Basics, and Basic Claims Administration represent just some of the new material presented in this fifth edition.

This series embodies the collective work of eighty-seven authors and fifty-eight chapters, and represents the better part of two years to finalize from the initial author contact until publication. It was no easy feat on an all-volunteer basis. I want to thank all the contributing authors for their dedication and their willingness to give up personal time to advance the profession of risk management. They all have an abiding commitment to our educational efforts, for which we are appreciative. Please give a resounding and well-deserved "thank you" the next time you see one of the authors. Each volume has a beginning section, "About the Contributors," where you will see every author listed with a brief biographical sketch. I think you will agree that the diversity and expertise of our author panel is unsurpassed by any other risk management text. In this edition we have also added the writing of several new physician authors and experts from the ISMP, IHI, and many other organizations dedicated to risk management and patient safety, all adding to the credibility of this reference series.

An undertaking of this magnitude requires the assistance of a dedicated team. I want to personally express my gratitude and thanks to each volume editor for an outstanding job. Without them this project would not have been done.

Volume I   Peggy Nakamura and Roberta Carroll
Volume II   Sylvia Brown
Volume III Glenn Troyer

Peggy, Sylvia, and Glenn each worked with a dedicated task force to assist with their specific volume. Please take a moment to look in the "About this Book" section in the front of each volume for a listing of those individuals. Again, they are entitled to a well-deserved "thank you" and our gratitude.

The support of ASHRM staff with our publication efforts is very much appreciated. We anticipate that this new series will quickly be a best seller and a big hit with the attendees at the 2006 ASHRM annual educational conference.

Even with the best of intentions not to compete with the holiday season, this series was prepared for the publisher by the beginning of 2006. I want to thank my family for their patience while I disappeared into my office over the holidays to read and edit. A special thank you, once again, to my brother Terrance (Red) Carroll for his production assistance in preparing the manuscript for the publisher. I'll make him a risk manager yet!

We hope you find this series easy to use, thorough, convenient, and an invaluable resource that becomes a mainstay in your risk management library. Share it with others in your organization, so that they can better understand and support the role of the health care risk management professional.

Thank you,
Roberta Carroll
Series Editor

About This Book

In this volume of the ASHRM Handbook's Fifth Edition, the Volume II Editorial Task Force endeavored to accomplish three goals.

The first was to update information published in previous handbooks concerning rapidly evolving clinical environments such as long-term care and key clinical risk management topics such as informed consent. This could not have been done without the support of fourteen returning authors (Joyce Benton, Robert Bunting, Robin Burroughs, Bruce Dmytrow, Alice Epstein, Gary Harding, Kathryn Hyer, Brenda Johnson, Peggy Martin, Fay Rozovsky, Jeff Sconyers, David Stallings, Sally Trombly, and Sheila Zimmet).

The second was to add new clinical area-specific chapters. In this regard, the Task Force acknowledges the substantive input of five new physician authors—David Earle, Eric Knox, David Lickerman, Peter Pronovost, and Larry Sherman—who added invaluable perspective and credibility to the chapters on surgical services, obstetrics, emergency services, intensive care, and laboratory. Nine other new authors who wrote about specific clinical areas were Christine Clark, Hedy Cohen, Stephanie Lickerman, Kathy Shostek, Kathleen Simpson, Nancy Tuohy, and Kelley Woodfin.

The third goal was to help risk management professionals internalize the many resources that derive from the patient safety movement, including situational briefing techniques like SBAR and FMEA (failure mode effect analysis). In this regard, the Task Force particularly acknowledges the valuable participation of six new authors, Denise Murphy, Katrina Shannon, June Leigh, Nancy Lagorio, Frank Federico, and Gina Pugliese.

The reader will note that this volume has two parts. The first contains chapters on generic risk management resources and issues that pertain to all clinical areas, such as patient safety, performance improvement, and medication safety. The second contains chapters on risk management issues and solutions for specific clinical environments. These chapters are intended to be primers that address complex risks, in terms that can be quickly internalized by anyone unfamiliar with the particular clinical area.

The work of the Volume II Task Force, Petra Berger, Mary Lynn Curran, Sheila Hagg-Rickert, Cristyn Chandler, and Rebecca Price, is also gratefully acknowledged.

Submitted by:

Sylvia Brown
Editor, Volume II

1

Patient Safety and the Risk Management Professional: New Challenges and Opportunities

Denise M. Murphy
Katrina Shannon
Gina Pugliese

Risk management has been practiced in business for more than 100 years, beginning with the fields of engineering and economics. In the 1960s, risk management became associated with insurance strategies aimed at minimizing or financing predictable business losses.[1] Philosophically, risk management aims to bring order from chaos and to facilitate certainty in an environment of uncertainty.

The field of health care risk management grew out of the insurance crisis of the 1970s, when professional liability premiums skyrocketed in part from the dissolution of the doctrine of charitable immunity, which once shielded a hospital's assets from malpractice lawsuits.[2]

The Joint Commission on Accreditation of Healthcare Organizations (JCAHO) defines risk management as "clinical and administrative activities undertaken to identify, evaluate, and reduce the risk of injury to patients, staff, and visitors, and the risk of loss to the organization itself."[3] Thus, health care risk management is committed to reducing loss associated with patient safety-related events in health care settings.

Like the malpractice crisis of the 1970s, the patient safety movement today is forcing a great deal of change in health care risk management. One of the greatest catalysts has been the Institute of Medicine's 1999 report, "To Err Is Human" (The IOM Report),[4] which shed light on the growing problem of medical errors.

The problems exposed by the IOM Report have since given rise to mounting regulations and government scrutiny. However, despite the significant challenges, the health care industry has responded to the crisis in many innovative ways.

Most important, risk managers today must assist health care professionals in meeting an unprecedented high standard of care. Providers must prove that they acted as another reasonably prudent provider would have in malpractice lawsuits. Today, however, the evidence determining "reasonableness" now includes highly prescriptive JCAHO standards, such as the requirement that every procedure be preceded by a "time out." Even more challenging, to help providers *implement* new approaches, the risk management professional must work with other managers to transform a traditionally hierarchical health care environment into a "culture of patient safety." Risk management professionals today have additional responsibilities to help their employers satisfy patient safety reporting requirements and to stay abreast of new patient safety-related legislation such as the recent Patient Safety and Quality Improvement Act.[5]

The recent evolution fueled by the patient safety movement has also created tremendous opportunities for risk management professionals. Not only are they gaining a broader understanding of the dynamics of error from patient safety theory, but they are also learning from new tools, such as electronic incident reporting, designed to capture relevant information, help providers learn from these errors, and implement processes to prevent them in the future. Armed with additional information on the frequency and nature of errors, risk managers are in a better position to receive resources and support from organizational leaders to enhance safety programs. Health care executives also better understand why keeping patients safe from harm protects market share, reimbursement levels, organizational reputation, and accreditation status. Safety has become a top priority today in every health care organization. Most important, through patient safety efforts, the risk management professional participates in efforts that can help restore societal trust in a health care system whose safety track record is being closely scrutinized by decision-makers, legislators, payers, and consumers.

This chapter will discuss the scope of medical errors in health care, provide an overview of patient safety theory and related safety guidelines, and highlight strategies to leverage patient safety concepts to reduce loss and improve care.

••••••••••••

THE SCOPE OF MEDICAL ERRORS

In the IOM Report, an adverse event is defined as an injury caused by medical management rather than by the underlying disease or condition of the patient. Some but not all adverse events are the result of medical errors. The IOM Report also defines *medical error* as the failure of a planned action to be completed as intended, or the use of a wrong plan to achieve an aim.[6] Two studies of large samples of hospital admissions, one in New York known as the Harvard Medical Practice Study, which uses 1984 data,[7] and another in Colorado and Utah using 1992 data,[8] found that adverse events occurred in 2.9 and 3.7 percent of hospitalizations, respectively. Data from these two studies were extrapolated in the IOM Report to the more than 33.6 million admissions to U.S. hospitals in 1997. They imply that at least 44,000 to 98,000 patients in U.S. hospitals die each year as a result of medical errors. Figure 1.1 provides details on the types of adverse events found in the Harvard Medical Practice Study among 30,000 randomly selected discharges from 51 randomly selected hospitals in New York.

The accuracy of the IOM's near-100,000 death estimate was challenged at the time it was published, but subsequent data indicate that there might be even *more* deaths from medical errors.[9] Estimates about the financial impact of medical errors are no less alarming. The Agency for Healthcare Research and Quality (AHRQ) estimates that medical

FIGURE 1.1   **Most Frequent Adverse Events in Hospitalized Patients**

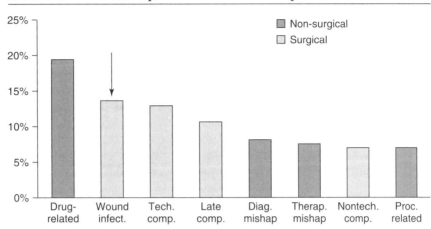

errors cost a typical large hospital about $5 million per year; all totaled, medical errors cost the U.S. health care system between $17 billion and $29 billion per year. These costs include follow-up and additional medical treatment of any adverse outcomes, and any expenses related to lost income and household productivity and potential long-term or permanent disability. Virtually none of these costs can later be recouped for proactive health initiatives.

Viewed in the larger context of medical errors, medication errors have become an increasing area of concern for risk managers. According to the IOM report, medication errors alone, either in or outside of the hospital, have been estimated to account for over 7,000 deaths a year. Moreover, a study referenced by the IOM concluded that about two out of every 100 admissions experience a preventable adverse drug event, resulting in average excess hospital costs of $4,700 per admission or about $2.8 million in additional costs for a typical 700-bed teaching hospital.[10] If these findings are generalizable, the IOM Report points out, the increased hospital costs alone of preventable adverse drug events affecting inpatients are $2 billion for the nation as whole.[11]

The IOM Report enumerates and expands upon the categorization of the types of medical errors that were reported by Leape in 1993.[12] These categories are: diagnostic; therapeutic; preventive; or related to failures of communication, equipment, or other systems. Diagnostic errors are further defined as those related to error or delay in diagnosis, failure to perform indicated tests, use of outmoded tests or therapy, or failure to act on results of monitoring or testing.

Treatment-related errors are defined as those that occur in performance of an operation, procedure or test, in administering treatment, or in the dose or method of using a drug and can be the result of an avoidable delay in treatment or in responding to an abnormal test result or inappropriate (not indicated) care.

Preventive errors were found to include failure to provide prophylactic treatment or inadequate monitoring or follow-up of treatment.

According to AHRQ, the most common adverse events that patients experience while receiving health care services include medication and transfusion errors, infections, complications of surgery (including wrong-site surgery), suicide, restraint-related injuries, falls, burns, pressure ulcers, misidentification, delays, and wrong diagnosis or treatment.

Health care-associated infections are an important patient safety issue. The CDC estimates that 2 million patients a year are infected in U.S. hospitals, and approximately 90,000 die as a result of those infections. Health care-associated infections cost the U.S. health care system an estimated $6.7 billion annually (based on 2002 data).[13] In New York hospitals alone, for example, surgical site infections were found to be the second-most common adverse event, according to the Harvard Medical Practice study.[14] Recent studies have shown that up to 350,000 hospitalized patients acquire bloodstream infections each year at a minimum cost of about $38,703 per episode[15] and with a mean attributable mortality of 15–20 percent.[16]

Studies have shown that most medical errors occur among women and infants in hospital intensive care units, operating rooms, and emergency departments. Further detail on medical errors in specific populations will be provided in other chapters in this text.

The health care system bears the additional costs for treatment related to medical errors. Nowhere is this more evident than in rising insurance rates and malpractice premiums. Clinicians in many parts of the country have been forced to abandon their medical practices because of increasing malpractice premiums.

Finally, two of the most overlooked effects of medical errors are the unquantifiable expense of psychological damage to patients, families, and providers, and the erosion of public trust in our health care system.

....

SEEKING SOLUTIONS: WHAT ARE THE CAUSES OF MEDICAL ERRORS?

The financial and societal implications of medical errors only reveal part of the overall problem for the health care industry. The contributing or underlying causes of medical errors must be identified to adequately address them.

Of equal concern for risk management professionals today is an understanding of the underlying causes of medical errors. According to the Agency for Healthcare Research and Quality (AHRQ), medical errors are caused by:[17]

- Communication problems
- Inadequate information flow
- Human factors-related problems
- Patient-related issues
- Organizational transfer of knowledge
- Staffing patterns and workflow
- Technical failures
- Inadequate policies and procedures

Theories on Accident Causation

Health care professionals are reaching out to other industries to understand and address the causes of medical errors. Although there might not be total agreement on how to apply non-health care industry strategies, everyone understands that health care, like aviation, is a complex environment in which people may suffer as a result of systems failure.

FIGURE 1.2   Swiss Cheese Model of Accident Causation

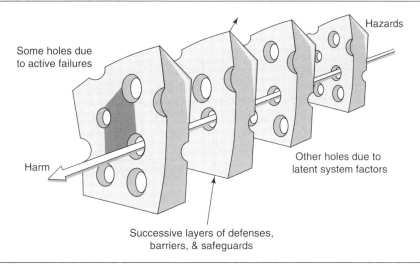

Some holes due
to active failures

Hazards

Harm

Other holes due to
latent system factors

Successive layers of defenses,
barriers, & safeguards

Reprinted with the permission of Cambridge University Press.
Source: Modified from James Reason, 1990.

Following are some of the leading theories about systems failure and how they can be applied to medical errors in a health care setting.

"Swiss Cheese" Model   Two commonly used models of accident causation in the patient safety literature are found in the work of James Reason and David D. Woods. Reason's "Swiss Cheese Model"[18] makes it easy to visualize how complex systems fail because of the combination and timing of multiple small failures. Reason contends that any one failure or situation alone would be insufficient to cause an accident, but the combination and timing of small failures look much like the alignment of holes in a piece of Swiss cheese (Figure 1.2). A practical example of this model is an ICU nurse who was "floated" to an oncology unit due to short staffing and administered a wrong dose of chemotherapy. In a subsequent review of the circumstances, it is learned that the ICU nurse failed to follow the standard protocol of having an experienced oncology nurse double-check the physician's order against the prepared medication before giving it to the patient. The experienced oncology nurse, who was anticipating being asked to assist with the double check, was unexpectedly involved in a crisis and forgot to "check in" with the float nurse before the incident occurred. The holes in the Swiss cheese lined up and the patient was harmed.

Active versus Latent Failures   Following the same example, the *active failure* was that the nurse did not comply with the medication administration policy, and therefore administered the wrong dose of a chemotherapeutic agent to the patient. Other second-layer failures, or holes in the Swiss cheese, are considered *latent* or hidden. For example, it is not immediately apparent in the circumstances of this error that the recent budget cut that led to the staffing shortage was responsible for the float situation in the first place. The inability of administrative staffing mechanisms to compensate for the budget cut is a good example of latent failure.

FIGURE 1.3   Blunt End/Sharp End Model of Accident Causation

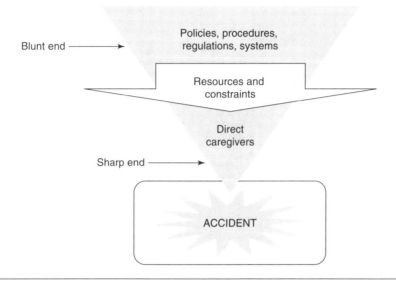

Source: Cook. Cognitive Technologies Laboratory, 2000.
Adapted from Woods, 1991.

"Blunt End/Sharp End" Model   David Woods wrote about a second model of accident causation called the "Blunt End/Sharp End" model.[19] This model assumes that health care workers at the sharp end, where patient care is delivered, are affected by decisions, policies, and regulations made at the blunt end, or hospital administration side, of the system. This administrative end generates resources, and generates constraints and conflicts that shape the environment in which the technical work takes place, and thereby may produce latent failures (Figure 1.3). At the sharp end, constraints place stresses on providers, who respond with appropriate coping mechanisms, such as letting senior management know about their perception, or unsafe shortcuts that increase the risk of medication error, like storing medications in their pockets as a time-saving strategy.

Hindsight Bias   Richard Cook, an anesthesiologist who has extensively studied causes of, and reaction to, accidents in health care, notes that investigations into accidents frequently stop with identifying the human error and designating the practitioners as the "cause" of the event. Often this determination is made without any evaluation of systems or processes that might have contributed to the error. According to Cook, this limited type of investigation can lead to solutions characterized by a phenomenon he calls "hindsight bias."[20] Such bias occurs when the investigators work backward from their knowledge of the outcome of the event. This linear analysis makes the path to failure look as though it should have been foreseeable, or predictable, although this is not the case.

These theories and models raise our awareness of the complexity of the system in which patients receive care and in which providers work. They make clear that organizational leaders must become "systems thinkers" who demand in-depth analyses of safety concerns. Health care leaders must also advocate a culture of safety that replaces punitive reactions to mistakes with an open environment that encourages staff to bring errors to light, so that the error can be dissected and addressed. Only when staff members are confident that their leaders will proactively address any risks that they divulge will there be an opportunity to build safer health care organizations.

Creating a Just Culture of Safety

To envision a culture of safety, it is important to understand the concept of "organizational culture." *Organizational culture* can be described as the set of values, guiding beliefs, or ways of thinking that are shared among members of an organization. It is the *feel* of an organization that is quickly picked up by new members. Culture is "the way we do things around here." Culture is powerful, and is likely to become particularly visible, when an organization tries to implement new strategies that are not "in step" with the status quo. It is human nature for people to resist changing the way they do things. Similarly, it is human nature for people to change the culture in which they live or work.

So what is the definition of a culture of safety? Dr. Tom Hellmich, a physician member of the Patient Safety Council at Children's Hospital and Clinics in Minneapolis, described it this way: "The medical culture that silently taught the ABCs as Accuse, Blame, and Criticize is fading. Rising in its place is a safety culture emphasizing blameless reporting, successful systems, knowledge, respect, confidentiality, and trust."[21]

In schools of medicine, nursing, and allied health, providers have traditionally been taught, through incident reporting procedures and behavior of other staff members, that when things go wrong they should find out, "Who did it?" The focus has been on individual failures. On the other hand, a safety culture asks, "What happened?" Safety culture looks at the system, the environment, the knowledge, the workflow, the tools, and other stressors that may have affected provider behavior.

When the patient safety movement began in the United States, a *non-punitive culture* was seen as a solution to medical errors. This raised concerns that people who acted recklessly would not be held accountable. Lucien Leape, the Harvard surgeon who is sometimes referred to as the father of the patient safety movement, introduced the term "just culture" and noted that having a safety culture "doesn't mean there is no role for punishment. Punishment is indicated for willful misconduct, reckless behavior, and unjustified, deliberate violation of rules . . . but not for human error."[22]

David Marx, an attorney who specializes in human resources and organizational development, also differentiates between a non-punitive and a just response to error, by describing a just culture of safety in terms of a set of beliefs and a set of duties. According to Marx, providers in a just culture must:

- Recognize that professionals make mistakes
- Acknowledge that even professionals will use shortcuts
- Support zero tolerance for reckless behaviors

  Marx adds that staff members in this culture must:

- Openly admit that "I have made a mistake"
- Call out when they see risk
- Participate in a learning culture (where information about mistakes and near-misses is shared with others so they can prevent similar situations)[23]

  Participants in a just safety culture are sensitive to risk, as they try to identify where and how the next mistake might occur, and then work to prevent it from happening. Staff members share information about mistakes and errors to prevent them from recurring somewhere else or to someone else, and they are constantly seeking best practices. These behaviors are characteristic of a *learning organization.* This type of organization also values *reciprocal accountability.* In other words, everyone holds each other accountable for patient safety. Leadership can expect staff members to call out or "stop the line" when they see risk, and the staff can expect leadership to listen and act, even if that means dealing with problem professionals who display intentionally reckless behaviors. Patients and family members are respected partners and understand their own responsibility to keep themselves safe while in a health care organization. Examples of patient responsibilities include keeping written records of medications and allergies and reminding busy health care workers to perform hand hygiene.

The National Patient Safety Foundation outlines several attributes of a safety culture that all health care organizations should strive to operationalize through the implementation of strong safety management systems.[24] These include a culture that:

- Encourages all workers (including front-line staff, physicians, and administrators) to accept responsibility for the safety of themselves, their co-workers, patients, and visitors
- Prioritizes safety above financial and operational goals
- Encourages and rewards the identification, communication, and resolution of safety issues
- Provides for organizational learning from accidents
- Allocates appropriate resources, structure, and accountability to maintain effective safety systems
- Absolutely avoids reckless behaviors

In a just safety culture, top-down communication must be replaced by bi-directional communication that flows to the front line from leadership and back to leadership from those providing patient care on the front line. Similarly, silence about harmful events must be replaced with open, honest disclosure about serious patient safety events.

Communication and Teamwork

We know that the failure to communicate effectively is responsible for the vast majority of avoidable accidents. During the 2004 National Patient Safety Foundation Conference, a comment from a representative of the Joint Commission on Accreditation of Healthcare Organizations (JCAHO) helps to illustrate the complex issues related to inadequate communication among members of the health care team that contribute to many adverse outcomes. According to this individual, in 100 percent of root cause analyses (RCAs) submitted for wrong-site surgery, someone in the room at the time of the error admitted knowing that something wrong was about to happen, but was too intimidated to speak up. Many factors contribute to communication-related patient safety issues. The following are a few of the most important, accompanied by associated patient safety strategies.

Traditionally Complex Hierarchical Approach   When nurses perceive that a physician or other senior clinician is using an unsafe clinical approach, they traditionally access the "chain of command" to resolve the question. In many health care organizations, the chain of command is cumbersome, and it requires the nurse to contact two to three people at minimum, based on existing reporting relationships and formal interfaces between the nursing and medical staff.

If patient safety is at stake, the most knowledgeable resolution must be achievable in a short time, and there is no time for the traditional chain of command. Many successful malpractice suits have involved circumstances in which a question about care, or need for expert intervention, was not addressed promptly.

Analogously, the aviation industry recognized that hierarchy-associated communication failures were at the root of 70 to 80 percent of all the jet transport accidents over a twenty-year period. The industry made significant improvements in its poor safety record through a strategy called "crew resource management" (CRM) training. One important tenet of this strategy is that every team member has a responsibility to point out a perceived risk. This places the pilot and crew on equal footing, when safety of the craft or passengers is in question.

Empirical proof of the value of such team training in health care has been demonstrated only in small sample studies to date, but evidence from emergency department operations and obstetric settings is proving that it reduces risk.[25] Still another strategy from outside the health care industry comes from manufacturing assembly lines. Some health care organizations have "stop the line" policies that empower everyone to respectfully call out and stop any risky process or procedure until all preventable risks are removed.[26]

Simplifying the hierarchy is a key patient safety strategy to resolving patient safety-related communication issues. Empowering charge nurses to facilitate rapid resolution of care questions is one approach that some organizations are developing.

Personal Style of Providers   Hierarchy has one additional undesirable ramification; it may legitimize intimidating behavior. One JCAHO surveyor observed, for example, that intimidation is a significant factor in wrong-site surgery. For more information, please refer to the Institute of Safe Medical Practice study on intimidation, discussed in Chapter 6 of this volume.

Solutions to address an intimidating personal style range from simple training to disciplinary action within the parameters of appropriate human resources protocols and medical staff bylaws. Long-term resolution often requires the strong support of senior administrative and clinical leaders.

At the other end of the spectrum is lack of assertiveness by frontline staff. This timidity is sometimes a response to another provider's intimidating behavior. This unassertive personal style may be equally dangerous because important issues are simply never raised. When the nurse calls a physician in the middle of the night, but does not clearly explain the reason for the call, the nurse well might not get the response that is needed to address an urgent clinical issue at hand.

Situational Briefing Model: S–B–A–R[27]   One means of facilitating clear communication between providers in crisis is a standardized situational briefing model. For example, S-B-A-R (Situation, Background, Assessment, and Recommendation) is an approach used increasingly in health care settings to facilitate effective communication of issues in an impending crisis by support staff to physicians.

A summary of key steps in S-B-A-R follows.

BEFORE using S-B-A-R Communication and Calling a Physician, It Is Important to:

- Assess the patient.
- Review the chart to determine the appropriate physician to call.
- Know the admitting diagnosis.
- Read most recent progress notes and assessments from clinicians on prior shifts.
- Have *available* when speaking with the physician the medical record, patient allergies, medications, IV fluids, and laboratory and other diagnostic test results.

  The following are the essential components of S-B-A-R communication:

Situation

- State your name, position, and unit.
- "I am calling about . . ." (patient name and room number).
- "The problem I am calling about is . . ."

Background

- State the admission diagnosis and date of admission.
- State the pertinent medical history.
- A brief synopsis of the treatment to date.

Assessment   Begin with outlining any changes from prior assessments. Include changes in:

- Mental status
- Pain
- Respiratory rate or quality; retractions or use of accessory muscles
- Pulse and blood pressure rate and quality; rhythm changes
- Skin color; wound drainage
- Neurological changes
- Gastrointestinal, genitourinary, or bowel changes (nausea, vomiting, diarrhea, increased or decreased output)
- Musculoskeletal weakness, joint deformity

Recommendation   State clearly what you think the patient needs urgently. Examples might include:

- Transfer the patient to ICU or PICU.
- Come to see the patient immediately.
- Talk to the patient or family about the code status.
- Ask for a consultant to see the patient now.
- Suggest tests or laboratory studies needed (for example, chest X-ray, arterial blood gases, EKG).

If a change in treatment is ordered, ask how often vital signs should be checked and when the physician would like to be contacted again. Document any changes in patient status, what intervention was completed, and whether or not the intervention was effective. Also document any contact you have had with the physician.

Lack of Common Language　　Barriers to communication might stem from language, ethnic, cultural, age, and gender differences. Even among providers with similar genetic and cultural backgrounds, there might be a lack of familiarity with terminology, including jargon and abbreviations. Refer to the discussion of issues surrounding unclear medication orders in Chapter 6 on Medication Safety. One example of a solution to standardizing communication among providers is the National Institute of Child Health and Human Development's (NICHHD) adoption of common definitions for fetal monitor interpretation discussed in Chapter 13.

JCAHO has built several strategies to improve provider communication into its National Patient Safety Goals (Exhibit 1.1). These include read-backs on verbal orders and critical lab values, identification of patients using two sources, site marking using the word "YES" on operative or procedure sites, checklists to verify correct patient, site, and procedure, and calling a "time out" before procedures and operations begin to ensure that all health care team members are comfortable that safety preparations for the procedure are complete.

Other principles that can help providers avoid communication breakdowns include the following:

- Just because someone said and understands something doesn't mean that others did.

- Communication is not accomplished unless both parties are on the same page.

- A standard method of communication gives the right amount and type of useful information that is critical to patient safety.

- Assertiveness is necessary if you have concerns about safety, because patients are counting on you.

- It is necessary to ask clarifying questions if you don't understand.

- Information about problems and mistakes must be shared appropriately to help improve systems and prevent recurrence of medical errors.

Human Factors and Patient Safety

Mistakes made by humans are reportedly responsible for most serious accidents in non-health care industries. For example, they are responsible for 80 percent of industrial and airline accidents and 50 to 70 percent of nuclear power accidents.[28]

Human factors engineering, human factors analysis, and ergonomics are among the disciplines developed to address risk in non-health care industries. These fields of study have much to offer patient safety initiatives.

The goal of *human factors engineering (HFE)* is the design of tools, machines, and systems that take into account human capabilities and limitations. To support this goal, human factors engineers research human psychology, social, physical, and biological characteristics. The risk management professional and others addressing patient safety can use human factors engineering principles to analyze the relationship between human beings and machines, the breakdown of which often plays a part in medical errors. Among patient safety-oriented approaches based on human factors engineering principles are strategies that eliminate the use of dangerous shortcuts that lead to medical errors.[29] For example, staff must follow manufacturers' directions in testing defibrillators. *Human factors analysis* is the systematic study

EXHIBIT 1.1   The 2006 National Patient Safety Goals

In May 2005, the Joint Commission's Board of Commissioners approved the 2006 National Patient Safety Goals. This year, the Joint Commission developed program-specific goals for all accreditation programs. Below are the 2006 NPSGs, which include continuing 2005 goals.

Goal: Improve the accuracy of patient/resident/client identification. [All programs]

• Use at least two patient identifiers (neither to be the patient's room number) whenever administering medications or blood products; taking blood samples and other specimens for clinical testing, or providing any other treatments or procedures. [Ambulatory, Assisted Living, Behavioral Health Care, Critical Access Hospital, Disease-Specific Care, Home Care, Hospital, Laboratory, Long Term Care, Office-Based Surgery]
• Prior to the start of any invasive procedure, conduct a final verification process to confirm the correct patient, procedure, site, and availability of appropriate documents. This verification process uses active—not passive—communication techniques. [Assisted Living, Disease-Specific Care, Home Care, Laboratory, Long Term Care]

Goal: Improve the effectiveness of communication among caregivers. [All programs]

• For verbal or telephone orders or for telephonic reporting of critical test results, verify the complete order or test result by having the person receiving the order or test result "read-back" the complete order or test result. [All programs]
• Standardize a list of abbreviations, acronyms and symbols that are not to be used throughout the organization. [All programs]
• Measure, assess and, if appropriate, take action to improve the timeliness of reporting, and the timeliness of receipt by the responsible licensed caregiver, of critical test results and values. [Ambulatory, Behavioral Health Care, Critical Access Hospital, Disease-Specific Care, Home Care, Hospital, Laboratory, Office-Based Surgery]
• All values defined as critical by the laboratory are reported directly to a responsible licensed caregiver within time frames established by the laboratory (defined in cooperation with nursing and medical staff). When the patient's responsible licensed caregiver is not available within the **time** frames, there is a mechanism to report the critical information to an alternative response caregiver. [Laboratory]
• Implement a standardized approach to "hand off" communications, including an opportunity to ask and respond to questions. [Ambulatory Health Care, Assisted Living Facility, Behavioral Health Care, Critical Access Hospital, Disease Specific Care, Hospital, Laboratory, Long Term Care, Office Based Surgery, Home Care]

Goal: Improve the safety of using medications. [Ambulatory, Behavioral Health Care, Critical Access Hospital, Disease-Specific Care, Home Care, Hospital, Long Term Care, Office-Based Surgery]

• Remove concentrated electrolytes (including, but not limited to, potassium chloride, potassium phosphate, sodium chloride >0.9%) from patient care units. [Ambulatory, Critical Access Hospital, Disease-Specific Care, Home Care, Hospital, Long Term Care, Office-Based Surgery]
• Standardize and limit the number of drug concentrations available in the organization. [Ambulatory, Behavioral Health Care, Critical Access Hospital, Disease-Specific Care, Home Care, Hospital, Long Term Care, Office-Based Surgery]
• Identify and, at a minimum, annually review a list of look-alike/sound-alike drugs used in the organization, and take action to prevent errors involving the interchange of these drugs. [Ambulatory, Behavioral Health Care, Critical Access Hospital, Home Care, Hospital, Long Term Care, Office-Based Surgery]
• Label all medications, medication containers (e.g. syringes, medicine cups, basins), or other solutions on and off the sterile field in perioperative and other procedural settings. [Ambulatory Health Care, Critical Access Hospitals, Hospitals, and Office Based Surgery]

Goal: Eliminate wrong-site, wrong-patient, wrong-procedure surgery. [Disease-Specific Care]

• Create and use a preoperative verification process, such as a checklist, to confirm that appropriate documents (e.g., medical records, imaging studies) are available. [Disease-Specific Care]
• Implement a process to mark the surgical site and involve the patient in the marking process. [Disease-Specific Care]

Goal: Improve the safety of using infusion pumps. [Ambulatory, Assisted Living, Behavioral Health Care, Critical Access Hospital, Disease-Specific Care, Home Care, Hospital, Long Term Care, Office-Based Surgery]

• Ensure free-flow protection on all general-use and PCA (patient controlled analgesia) intravenous infusion pumps used in the organization. [Ambulatory, Assisted Living, Behavioral Health Care, Critical Access Hospital, Disease-Specific Care, Home Care, Hospital, Long Term Care, Office-Based Surgery]

Goal: Improve the effectiveness of clinical alarm systems. [Disease-Specific Care]

• Implement regular preventive maintenance and testing of alarm systems. [Disease-Specific Care]
• Assure that alarms are activated with appropriate settings and are sufficiently audible with respect to distances and competing noise within the unit. [Disease-Specific Care]

EXHIBIT 1.1 (*Continued*)

Goal: Reduce the risk of health care-associated infections. [All programs]

• Comply with current Centers for Disease Control and Prevention (CDC) hand hygiene guidelines. [All programs]
• Manage as sentinel events all identified cases of unanticipated death or major permanent loss of function associated with a health care-associated infection. [All programs]

Goal: Accurately and completely reconcile medications across the continuum of care. [Ambulatory, Assisted Living, Behavioral Health Care, Critical Access Hospital, Disease-Specific Care, Home Care, Hospital, Long Term Care, Office-Based Surgery]

• Implement a process for obtaining and documenting a complete list of the patient's/resident's/client's current medications upon the patient's/resident's/client's admission to the organization and with the involvement of the patient/resident/client. This process includes a comparison of the medications the organization provides to those on the list. [Ambulatory, Assisted Living, Behavioral Health Care, Critical Access Hospital, Disease-Specific Care, Home Care, Hospital, Long Term Care, Office-Based Surgery]
• A complete list of the patient's medications is communicated to the next provider of service when it refers or transfers a patient to another setting, service, practitioner or level of care within or outside the organization. [Ambulatory, Assisted Living, Behavioral Health Care, Critical Access Hospital, Disease-Specific Care, Home Care, Hospital, Long Term Care, Office-Based Surgery]

Goal: Reduce the risk of patient/resident/client harm resulting from falls. [Assisted Living, Critical Access Hospital, Home Care, Hospital, Long Term Care]

• Assess and periodically reassess each patient's risk for falling, including the potential risk associated with the patient's medication regimen, and take action to address any identified risks. [Assisted Living, Critical Access Hospital, Home Care, Hospital, Long Term Care]
• Implement a fall reduction program, and evaluate the effectiveness of the program. [Assisted Living Facility, Critical Access Hospitals, Disease Specific Care, Hospitals, Long Term Care, Home Health]

Goal: Reduce the risk of influenza and pneumococcal disease in institutionalized older adults. [Assisted Living, Disease-Specific Care, Long Term Care]

• Develop and implement a protocol for administration and documentation of the flu vaccine. [Assisted Living, Disease-Specific Care, Long Term Care]
• Develop and implement a protocol for administration and documentation of the pneumococcus vaccine. [Assisted Living, Disease-Specific Care, LTC]
• Develop and implement a protocol to identify new cases of influenza and to manage an outbreak. [Assisted Living, Disease-Specific Care, Long Term Care]

Goal: Reduce the risk of surgical fires. [Ambulatory, Office-Based Surgery]

• Educate staff, including operating licensed independent practitioners and anesthesia providers, on how to control heat sources and manage fuels, and establish guidelines to minimize oxygen concentration under drapes. [Ambulatory, Office-Based Surgery]

Goal: Implementation of applicable National Patient Safety Goals and associated requirements by components and practitioner sites. [Integrated Delivery System, Managed Care Organizations, Preferred Provider Organizations]

• Inform and encourage components and practitioner sites to implement the applicable National Patient Safety Goals and associated requirements. [Integrated Delivery System, Managed Care Organizations, Preferred Provider Organizations]

Goal: Encourage the active involvement of patients and their families in the patient's own care as a patient safety strategy.

• Define and communicate the means for patients and their families to report concerns about safety, and encourage them to do so. [Assisted Living Facility, Disease Specific Care, Laboratory, Home Care]

Goal: Prevent health care-associated pressure ulcers (decubitus ulcers).

• Assess and periodically reassess each patient's risk for developing a pressure ulcer (decubitus ulcer) and take action to address any identified risks. [Long Term Care]

©2006 Joint Commission Resources: National Patient Safety Goals. www.jcaho.org. Last accessed December 12, 2005.

FIGURE 1.4   Human Machine Interface

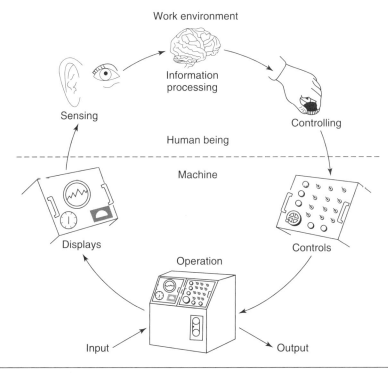

Source: McCormick, E.J. and Sanders, M.S. *Human Factors in Engineering and Design*, pg. 14, 15th edition, New York: McGraw-Hill (1982).

of the human-machine interface, with the intent of improving working conditions or operations. Refer to Figure 1.4 for an illustration.

Ergonomics professionals study people at work, and then design tasks, jobs, information, tools, equipment, facilities, and the working environment to be safe, effective, productive, and comfortable. In health care, understanding how humans interface with highly complex technology and the surrounding environment is crucial to preventing errors. For example, medication stations must have sufficient space around them for nurses to work without getting in each other's way at times that many medications are due, and there must be sufficient light for them to see what they are doing.

To evaluate the safety of a work environment and applying human factors and ergonomics principles, Carayon, Alvarado, and Hundt recommend asking the following questions:[30]

- What are the characteristics of the individual performing the work? Does the individual have the musculoskeletal, sensory, and cognitive abilities to do the required tasks? If not, can any of these gaps in ability be accommodated in the design of the task?

- What tasks are being performed, and what characteristics of those tasks might contribute to unsafe patient care? What in the nature of the tasks allows the individual to perform them safely or assume risks in the process?

- What tools and technology are being used to perform the tasks, and do they increase or decrease the likelihood of untoward events?

- What aspects of the physical environment can be sources of error and which promote safety? What in the environment ensures safe behavior or allows unsafe behavior to occur?

FIGURE 1.5   Components of Human Factors Assessment

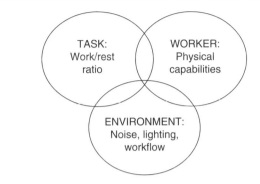

Source: Potter P, Boxerman S, Wolf L, Marshall J, Grayson D, Sledge J, Evanoff B. Mapping the Nursing Process: A New Approach for Understanding the Work of Nursing. *JONA* Vol. 34, No. 2, 101–09. February 2004. Reprinted with permission.

Human factors assessment should also include:

- Evaluating the work—what is the work-to-rest ratio?
- Evaluating the workers—what are their physical and mental capabilities?
- Evaluating the environment—are noise levels, lighting, and workflow potential barriers or facilitators to successful task completion? (Figure 1.5).

Another illustration of the importance of evaluating the "human machine" is a recent study of the working memory of a nurse, which found that a nurse is thinking of an average of ten things simultaneously during a work shift.[31] It is not hard to imagine errors of omission when the typical human working memory becomes taxed if asked to hold more than a seven-digit telephone number.

The mental capabilities of health care workers should be evaluated, as should physical characteristics, such as:

- Physical size (anthropometry)
- Endurance/fatigue (physiology)
- Force (biomechanics)
- Hand and arm coordination (kinesiology)
- Sensory (hearing, vision, touch)

Environmental issues that affect safe care delivery include

- Noise, light (glare), vibration, temperature, force
- Work space or supplies layout
- Equipment-environment compatibility issues

The safety-related implications of the interface between humans and their physical environment are starkly illustrated by the potential for desensitization of the intensive-care staff to the significance of one alarm in an environment in which numerous alarms are sounding all the time. This issue is clearly exacerbated by other employee-related safety issues such as fatigue. Biomedical and human factors engineers should seek solutions in each individual environment.

FIGURE 1.6   Poorly Designed Paper Towel Dispenser/Disposal Unit

Reprinted with permission. BJC Corporate Health Services, St. Louis, MO.

A simpler, but equally important, example of the unsafe effect that comes from ignoring human factors and ergonomics principles is the poorly designed paper towel dispenser found in many hospital bathrooms. The mechanism that holds clean towels is connected to the dirty paper towel disposal unit. This design makes it easy for freshly washed hands to be contaminated by dirty towels overflowing from the dispenser (Figure 1.6).

Human factors and ergonomics principles can help prevent equipment-related medical errors. Proactively, these disciplines can also "mistake-proof" the environment so that providers will find it hard to do the wrong thing.

Systems Thinking

Another industrial concept useful to patient safety experts is the notion of "systems thinking." A *system* may be defined as a combination of elements organized in a structure to achieve goals and objectives. System elements can be seen as the interaction of:

- Elements (personnel, equipment, procedures)
- Environment (physical, social, organizational)
- Inputs and outputs
- Structure
- Purpose and goals

The objectives of system evaluation must include reliability of the system and the human using it. System reliability depends on the reliability of each individual component. Components can be in series, parallel, or a combination of the two. Parallel systems are redundant and can increase reliability. Parallel redundancy is often helpful to human functions, because the human component in a system is the least reliable.

The best way to assess the likelihood of human error is through a failure modes and effects analysis (FMEA). In FMEA, a team analyzes a process in detail to determine possible system failures and brainstorm solutions before the process goes into effect.[32]

Reporting

It is impossible to reduce medical errors and adverse outcomes by focusing only on any one aspect of the health care system. As Wood's "blunt end and sharp end" model of accident causation implies, patient safety must be analyzed from the national level, where health policy and legislation are created, down to the front line of patient care delivery.

The aviation industry illustrates the positive effect of reporting on safety. In the 30 years since its inception, the Federal Aviation safety reporting system has logged more than 500,000 confidential "near miss" reports. Today, there are more than 30,000 incidents reported per year.[33]

AHRQ defines "near misses" as "events in which the unwanted consequences were prevented because there was a recovery by planned or unplanned identification and correction of the failure." The effectiveness of a patient safety program can, to some degree, be measured by increased near-miss reporting, because the data provide important insight into problems that need to be addressed.

The recently passed Patient Safety and Quality Improvement Act is a major step toward creation of a national voluntary system of incident reporting and medical error information. Key among the provisions of the Act are the creation of patient safety organizations. These will be responsible for developing a network of patient safety databases, which will collect and analyze voluntarily reported medical errors to use for identifying patient safety improvement strategies. The law ensures that what is reported cannot be used against the provider in court or in disciplinary proceedings. This provision is intended to encourage providers to identify and correct medical errors.

Event Reporting Systems

In addition to providing information about individual events, event reporting systems enable the organization to prioritize resources through analysis of trends. The greatest challenge has always been the fear of punishment. This single factor is often the cause of lost valuable information that could help to address system problems.

It is important for the risk management professional to be aware of common "myths" or unspoken rules that staff members might use to justify not reporting. Some examples of unspoken rules include:[34]

"If I can make it right, it is not an error."   If a dose was omitted, a nurse changes the subsequently scheduled drug administration scheduled to "get back on track."

"If it's not my fault, it is not an error."   Late administration or an omission occurred when the prescribed drug was not available on the unit.

"If another patient's needs are more urgent than accurate medication or treatment, it is not an error."   Delayed or omitted medication delivery was caused by dealing with urgent situations arising with another patient.

"A clerical error is not a real medical error."   A nurse on a previous shift failed to document drug administration or documented in the wrong section of the record.

"If my actions prevent something worse, it is not an error."   Nurses know that they will be busy later due to planned admissions, discharges, and so on, and administer medication early rather than risk omitting doses.

"If everyone knows (or does it), it is not an error."   Nurses sometimes give medications early or withhold medications at night so that patients suffering from sleep deprivation can rest uninterrupted for longer periods of time.

The most common barriers to reporting include lack of knowledge about what to report or how to report, lack of trust, extra work, skepticism about the likelihood that things will change, desire to forget the event, and fear of reprisal or punishment.[35]

The most important resource to counter obstacles to reporting is a just culture of safety. If providers feel confident that their senior managers will support them, they will point out risk and report medical errors. Other strategies to facilitate reporting include:

- New online reporting options that include telephone hotlines or that enable staff members to input medical error data more easily and facilitate analysis
- Paper reports (if they are used) that are readily accessible by all members of the health care team
- Highly effective reporting programs that keep the identity of the reporter confidential

Any risk trending analysis must assess types of errors, people, systems, and processes involved, place and time of occurrence, and risk factors identified. This information should be shared with key stakeholders and used to drive improvements that reduce risk of harm to patients (and employees).

JCAHO, State, and Federal Medical Error Reporting Requirements

After an adverse event occurs, the risk management professional and leadership must determine whether an event must be reported externally. The Centers for Medicaid and Medicare Services (CMS) has designated Patient Safety Indicators (for example, third-degree lacerations during a vaginal birth), as those that must be reported by licensed organizations receiving Medicare and Medicaid. Additionally, organizations that are accredited by the JCAHO must evaluate a sentinel event and determine whether to report it, because sentinel event reporting to JCAHO is voluntary. The following are examples of sentinel events that are voluntarily reportable under the Joint Commission's Sentinel Event Policy:

- Any individual death, paralysis, coma, or other major permanent loss of function associated with a medication error
- Any suicide of a patient in a setting where the patient is housed around the clock, including suicides following elopement from such a setting
- Any elopement, that is, unauthorized departure, of a patient from an around-the-clock care setting resulting in a temporally related death (suicide or homicide) or major permanent loss of function
- Surgery on the wrong patient, wrong side of the individual's body, or wrong organ
- Any intrapartum (related to the birth process) maternal death

- Any perinatal death unrelated to a congenital condition in an infant having a birth weight greater than 2,500 grams
- The abduction of an individual from the organization where that patient receives care, treatment, or services
- Assault, homicide, or other crime resulting in individual death or major permanent loss of function
- A fall that results in death or major permanent loss of function as a direct result of the injuries sustained in the fall
- Hemolytic transfusion reaction involving major blood group incompatibilities
- A foreign body, such as a sponge or forceps, left in an individual after surgery[36]

  In contrast, the following are events that are *not* reportable to the JCAHO:

- Any "near miss" event
- Full or expected return of limb or bodily function to the same level as prior to the adverse event by discharge or within two weeks of the initial loss of said function
- Any sentinel event that has not affected an individual
- Medication errors that do not result in death or major permanent loss of function
- Suicide other than in an around-the-clock care setting or following elopement from such a setting
- A death or loss of function following a discharge "against medical advice" (AMA)
- Unsuccessful suicide attempts
- Minor degrees of hemolysis not caused by a major blood group incompatibility and with no clinical sequelae[37]

Most health care organizations have established committees responsible for peer review that can be used if an event involves questionable practice or behavior of a licensed professional. These committees may consist of peers from medicine, nursing, pharmacy, or other allied health professions that review a case and determine the appropriateness of the provider's activities related to that case. The risk management professional should be formally accountable for referring an event to the organization's peer review committee as necessary.

State Requirements

Individual states, such as Florida, Minnesota, New York, and Pennsylvania, have created mandatory reporting programs. Risk management professionals must stay current with the requirements of these programs and must facilitate staff members' understanding of their implications. Similarly, they must be aware of requirements and must facilitate federal reporting requirements such as those associated with the Safe Medical Devices Act (SMDA).

············
CONCLUSION

The patient safety movement has brought numerous challenges and opportunities to risk management professionals. By collaborating with other members of the management team, risk management professionals can use these new strategies to solve the ongoing challenge of medical errors.

Endnotes

1. Orlikoff, J., W. Fifer, and H. Greeley, *Malpractice Prevention and Loss Control for Hospitals*. Chicago, Illinois: American Hospital Association, 1981.

2. *Darling v. Charleston Community Memorial Hospital*, 33 Ill.2d 326, 211 N.E.2d 253 (1965), cert. denied, 383 U.S. 946 (1966).

3. Joint Commission on Accreditation of Health Care Organizations. Sentinel Event Glossary of Terms, 2005. Available at: www.jcaho.org/accredited+organizations/sentinel+event/glossary.htm]. Accessed December 12, 2005.

4. Kohn, L. T., J. M. Corrigan, M. S. Donaldson, eds. *To err is human: Building a safer health system*. Washington, D.C.: National Academy Press, 2000. Available at: [www.ahrq.gov/news/focus/ptsafety.pdf]. Accessed December 12, 2005.

5. Public Law 109-41, 2005.

6. Kohn, *op. cit.*

7. Leape, L. L., T. A. Brennan, N. Laird, A. G. Lawthers, B. A. Barnes, L. Herbert, J. P. Newhouse, P. C. Weiler, and H. Hiatt. "The Nature of Adverse Events in Hospitalized Patients: Results of the Harvard Medical Practice Study II." *New England Journal of Medicine*. 1991 Feb 7; 324 (6): 377–84.

8. Thomas, E. J., D. M. Studdert, J. P. Newhouse. "Costs of Medical Injuries in Utah and Colorado." *Inquiry*, 1999; 36 (3): 255–64.

9. Leape, L. L., "Institute of Medicine error figures are not exaggerated." *JAMA 2000*; 284 (1): 95–97.

10. Bates, D. W., N. Spell, D. J. Cullen et al., "The cost of adverse drug events in hospitalized patients." *JAMA 1997*; 277: 307–311.

11. *Ibid.*

12. Leape, L. L, A. G. Lawthers, T. A. Brennan, et al., "Preventing Medical Injury." *Quality Review Bulletin*. 19 (5): 144–49; 1993.

13. Graves, N. "Economics and preventing hospital-acquired infection." *Emerging Infectious Diseases* [serial online] 2004 Apr [date cited]. Available from: [www.cdc.gov/ncidod/EID/vol10no4/02-0754.htm]. Accessed December 12, 2005.

14. Brennan, T. A., L. L. Leape, N. M. Laird, L. Hebert, A. R. Localio, A. G. Lawthers, J. P. Newhouse, P. C. Weiler, H. H. Hiatt, "Harvard Medical Practice Study I." *Quality and Safety in Health Care*. 2004 Apr; 13(2):145–51; discussion 151–2.

15. Stone, P. W., E. Larson, L. N. Kawar. "A systematic audit of economic evidence linking nosocomial infections and infection control interventions: 1990-2000." *American Journal of Infection Control*. 2002 May; 30 (3): 145–52.

16. Wenzel, R. P. and M. B. Edmond. "The Impact of Hospital-Acquired Bloodstream Infections." *Emerging Infectious Diseases*. 7(2) Mar–Apr 2001. Available at: [www.cdc.gov/ncidod/eid/vol7no2/wenzel.htm]. Accessed December 12, 2005.

17. Agency for Healthcare Quality and Research: Patient Safety Initiative: Building Foundations, Reducing Risk. Available at: [www.ahrq.gov/qual/pscongrpt/psini2.htm#RootCauses]. Accessed December 12, 2005.

18. Reason, J. "Human error: Models and management." *British Medical Journal* 2000; 320:768–770. 18 March.

19. Cook, R.I. and D. D. Woods. "Operating at the sharp end: the complexity of human error." In: Bogner, M.S., *Human Error in Medicine*. Hinsdale, NJ: Lawrence Erlbaum Associates; 1994: pp 255–310 [Available at: www.ctlab.org/]. Accessed December 12, 2005.

20. *Ibid.*

21. Morath, J. Presentation at BJC Healthcare, Patient Safety Forum, St. Louis, Mo. February, 2003.

22. Leape, L. L. Presentation at Missouri Hospital Association, Patient Safety Seminar. St. Louis, Mo. 2002.

23. Marx, D. *Patient Safety and the "Just Culture": A Primer for Healthcare Executives.* New York, NY: Columbia University; 2001. Available at: [www.mers-tm.net/support/Marx_Primer.pdf]. Accessed March 20, 2003.

24. National Patient Safety Foundation: Safety Culture. Available at: [search.freefind.com/find.html?id=28648537&t=s&nsb=&pageid=r&mode=ALL&s=definitions&query=Safety+Culture]. Accessed December 12, 2005.

25. Baker, et al. *Medical Team Training Programs in Healthcare.* 2005 Advances in Patient Safety: From Research to Implementation, Vol. 4, p. 260. Rockville, MD, Agency for Healthcare Research and Quality (AHRQ).

26. *Ibid.*

27. Kaiser Permanente's SBAR Communication model has been adapted with permission from copyrighted material of Kaiser Foundation Health Plan, Inc., California Regions.

28. Potter P., S. Boxerman, L. Wolf, J. Marshall, D. Grayson, J. Sledge, B. Evanoff. "Mapping the Nursing Process: A New Approach for Understanding the Work of Nursing." *Journal of Nursing Administration,* Vol. 34, No. 2, 101–09. February 2004.

29. Gosbee, J. "Human Factors Engineering and Patient Safety." *Quality and Safety in Health Care* 2002; 11: 352–354. Available at [qhc.bmjjournals.com/cgi/content/full/11/4/353]. Accessed September 6, 2004.

30. Carayon, P., C. Alvarado, A. Hundt, 2003. Center for Quality and Productivity Improvement and the Department of Industrial Engineering, University of Wisconsin-Madison. "Reducing Workload and Increasing Patient Safety through Work and Workspace Design." Paper Commissioned by the Institute for Medicine Commission on the Work Environment for Nurses and Patient Safety. In Keeping Patients Safe: Transforming the Work Environment for Nurses. Ann Page, Editor. 2004.

31. *Ibid.*

32. Wolf, L. BJC HealthCare, Patient Safety Curriculum. Human Factors Module. 2004. Statistics on aviation accidents available at [aviationtoday.com/cgi/am/show_mag.cgi?pub=am&mon=0501&file=0501workforce.htm] Statistics on industrial accidents available at [http://www.processcooling.com/CDA/ArticleInformation/Safe_Haven_Item/0,6582,112320,00.html]. Accessed December 12, 2005.

33. Baker, S. P., B. O'Neill, M. Ginsburg, L. Guohua. *The Injury Fact Book,* 2nd edition. New York: Oxford University Press, 1992.

34. Caleca, B. BJC HealthCare Patient Safety Curriculum. Importance of Reporting Module. 2004.

35. Leonard, M. Director of Patient Safety, Kaiser Permanente. Presentation. BJC HealthCare, Patient Safety Forum, St. Louis, Mo. September 2002.

36. Joint Commission on Accreditation of Healthcare Organizations. Voluntarily Reportable Sentinel Events, 2005. Available at [www.jcaho.org/accredited+organizations/sentinel+event/voluntarily+reportable+sentinel+events.htm]. Accessed December 12, 2005.

37. *Ibid.*

2

Risk Management's Role in Performance Improvement

Peggy Berry Martin
Frank Federico

An effective performance improvement (PI) program is one that facilitates communication among patient safety, performance improvement, and risk management. Although these functions are often separate within a health care organization, each offers a different view of issues and data that together comprise a fuller picture of the performance of systems in the organization. Each also brings perspective on innovative approaches generated in response to the 1999 publication of the Institute of Medicine Report, "To Err is Human,"[1] which concluded that between 44,000 and 98,000 individuals die every year due to medical error.

For example, research on human factors, errors, and system defects has provided new insight into why and how humans make mistakes. These efforts to understand the nature of human errors, minimize their harmful effects, and revise health care systems to incorporate safeguards will benefit patient safety initiatives, improve quality, and minimize risk of liability to the organization and its practitioners.

All performance improvement team members are learning new techniques resulting from this research. However, the risk management professional's knowledge and prior experience in managing medical error brings a critical perspective.

For example, process failures such as lack of adherence to standard treatment protocols present risk management staff with opportunities to lead or participate in efforts to eliminate the root causes of these problems. In this way, risk management can reduce the likelihood of process failures, and of their loss-generating potential, and can inform and supplement the PI efforts of any health care organization. Examples from claims files show the cost of process failure and illustrate the importance of the risk management professional's involvement:

- Patient's death due to delay in diagnosis of epidural abscess, $1.3-million settlement (Failure to adhere to standard treatment)

- Tonsillectomy performed on wrong child, $350,000 settlement (Inadequate patient identification process)

- Patient's death from kidney tumor that was missed on pre-operative X-ray five years earlier, $2-million settlement (No procedure to follow-up on abnormal "routine" X-rays)

- Chest tube placed on wrong side of critically injured man, $250,000 settlement (Inadequate procedure-site identification)[2]

This chapter discusses the continuing evolution of PI efforts in health care and emphasizes the essential role of the risk management professional in organizational and provider performance improvement.

....

THE EVOLUTION OF PERFORMANCE IMPROVEMENT

Efforts to understand and improve care have been goals of health care providers since the beginning of health care. The early days of health care in the United States were characterized by formal efforts, such as those of Dr. Ernest Codman, a surgeon at Massachusetts General Hospital in the early 1900s, which led to the creation of the American College of Surgeons (ACS) Hospital Standardization Program in 1918. This program performed hospital evaluation surveys, using pre-established standards, and granted accreditation for recognized compliance with the standards. The basic elements of the ACS program were incorporated by the Joint Commission on Accreditation of Healthcare Organizations (JCAHO), when it established an accreditation program, decades later.[3] Over time, different terms have been used, and improvement processes, techniques, and tools have become more sophisticated. In the 1970s, the ACS again took the lead and published the first Patient Safety Manual, in which the term "patient safety system" is used to describe a hospital-wide program that coordinates quality assurance, risk management, and medical staff credentialing and peer review.[4]

In the 1980s, the JCAH (Joint Commission on the Accreditation of Hospitals, the predecessor of the JCAHO) defined quality assurance as "a formal, systematic program by which care rendered to patients is measured against established criteria."[5] The 1980s and 1990s brought variations on the organizational quality efforts developed from concepts introduced by Shewhart[6], Deming,[7] Juran,[8] and others. The term "total quality management" (TQM) was introduced to help reduce organizational silos and encourage a communicative environment in which quality efforts could thrive. The concept of continuous quality improvement (CQI) was added at about the same time, to promote a systematic, team-based approach to process and performance improvement. Both terms came to health care from other industries.[9]

In the 1990s, the emphasis placed by health care organizations on the value of a TQM environment represented a significant philosophical change in the environment of health care. In some ways, it foreshadowed the current patient safety movement, which stresses the complexity of systems in health care and raised concerns about the effect that malfunctioning systems may have on provider and organization performance.

A review of essential TQM program characteristics demonstrates their kinship with current patient safety concepts:

- Establishment of a non-punitive atmosphere in which staff are unafraid to question the status quo, openly and frankly discuss problems and opportunities for improvement, and freely share information vital to understanding and improving important clinical, management, and governance processes. It is noteworthy that the recently introduced concept of a "just culture," in which individuals know how they will be held accountable when there is a serious adverse event, can contribute to an environment in which discussion of adverse events and near misses is used to enhance performance improvement.[10,11]

- Staff-wide understanding of, and access to, a formal, team-based process improvement mechanism.

- Staff-wide recognition of internal and external customer-supplier relationships, and the value of customer satisfaction as a driving force behind improving performance.

- Visible executive leadership of, and support for, ongoing efforts to measure and improve organizational performance. For example, including updates on performance improvement projects on the agendas of committee and board meetings is one way to demonstrate leaders' involvement.

- Hold staff members accountable and empower them to take actions that are essential to achieving optimal performance.

- Focus on looking at performance issues proactively rather than reactively.

- Focus on discovering common causes of problems inherent to a process, rather than blaming individuals for aberrant performance.

- Focus on a systematic, organized method of problem solving that uses data and statistical quality control tools as integral components of the problem identification, analysis, and resolution processes.[12]

While many models of quality improvement (QI) or performance improvement (PI), such as TQM, are adapted from the quality literature and the standards enumerated by accrediting bodies, they share five essential steps:

- Design a process.
- Monitor performance through data collection.
- Analyze current performance.
- Design changes that will result in improvement.
- Improve and sustain improved performance.[13]

THE RISK MANAGEMENT—PERFORMANCE IMPROVEMENT INTERFACE

The increased emphasis on patient safety by accrediting bodies makes the connection between patient care quality initiatives and the risk management function an obvious one. For the past several years, the chapter on "Improving Organization Performance" in the JCAHO Accreditation Manual has included language acknowledging "quality-control and risk-management findings" to be an important source of data for monitoring performance.[14] In July 2001, JCAHO created additional Patient Safety Standards[15] that address the role of leadership in creating a culture of safety, implementation of patient safety programs in organizations, how to respond to an adverse event, prevention of accidental harm, and the responsibility to disclose adverse events to patients and families. Similar standards went into effect for behavioral health care and long-term care organizations in 2003 and for ambulatory care and home care organizations in 2004. These standards speak to the involvement of risk management, not just as a data source for performance improvement and patient safety, but as a resource for policy making and guidance in the development of procedures to comply with policies.

The best example of the interface between risk management and performance improvement may be the JCAHO's Sentinel Event Policy, published in 1996. In the policy, a *sentinel event* is defined as "an unexpected occurrence involving death or serious injury—including loss of limb or function—or psychological risk thereof." "Risk thereof" means that although no harm has occurred at this time, any recurrence would carry a significant chance of a serious adverse outcome.[16] In other words, sentinel events prioritize performance improvement intervention for those occurrences most likely to lead to patient injury and malpractice action.

In addition, the similarities between steps in the PI process and in the traditional risk management process make risk management professionals logical choices to lead or provide coaching for patient safety and quality initiatives. One has only to compare the five steps in the QI/PI process with that of the traditional view of the risk management process espoused by George Head of the Insurance Institute of America to see the similarities:

- Identify and analyze the exposures to loss.
- Examine the feasibility of alternative techniques, such as risk control to stop losses, risk financing to pay for losses, and so on.
- Select the apparent best technique.
- Implement the apparent best technique.
- Monitor and improve the risk management program.[17]

It is clear that there is significant overlap between PI activities, current patient safety requirements, and the risk management professional's effort to protect the institution and its providers from financial loss. How can this overlap be translated into synergy? By assuming a leadership role in risk management-related performance improvement activities and by supporting the use of risk data to prioritize performance improvement activities, the risk management professional can facilitate the performance improvement effort.

The following example uses the components of a PI process to address a problem identified from traditional risk management information. Awareness of the problem-solving models and analytical tools referred to can help the risk manager effectively lead resolution of such issues.

Identify a Goal

Describe in objectively verifiable terms the known or suspected problem that represents an opportunity to prevent patient injury, reduce potential liability exposure, and improve an aspect of the organization's performance.

Example: Four claims in the emergency department in three years with allegations of failure to diagnose an acute myocardial infarction (AMI). One of the contributing causes was found to be lack of evidence of written discharge instructions for these patients.

Clearly state what undesired situation or event(s) the project will seek to reduce or eliminate.

Example: Lack of condition-specific discharge instructions, including timeframes in which the patient is instructed to seek care, make "failure to diagnose" malpractice claim allegations difficult to defend.

State how much the problem is expected to be reduced within a specified timeframe in response to (corrective) intervention.

Example: The goal is that within one year, 100 percent of patients who present to the ED receive condition-specific discharge instructions, including timeframes within which they should seek care.

Analyze Systems and Processes

Specify the baseline data needed to demonstrate how frequently or severely the undesired situation or event is being seen within a specified timeframe and the causes (that is, malfunctioning processes, functions, or parts thereof) that are contributing to it. Knowledge of the current problem's extent is necessary to determine if any change in the data is an improvement.

State the measures, for example, indicators, that have been or will be used to collect the baseline data and to monitor performance for signs of improvement subsequent to taking action.

Example: Compliance with and documentation of ED generic screening elements.

Collect the specified data and use appropriate graphic display tools to review and analyze data.

- To display frequency or volume of occurrences, use run charts, control charts, pie charts, or histograms.
- To display causes, use cause-and-effect (fishbone) diagrams, flowcharts, or Pareto charts.[18]

Plan Appropriate Action

Propose corrective intervention based on the team's analysis of findings concerning the problem's frequency and severity and causes. Tools that may be used include:

Flowcharts: By graphically depicting the steps in any process, teams can identify failure points and redundant steps. However, use of flow charting must be skilled, to prevent the PI team from spending more time developing the flow diagram than testing changes.

Example: Triage process, discharge process.

Cause-and-effect diagram—Known also as the Fishbone or Ishikawa diagram, this method helps link relationships between problems and their possible causes.

Example: Why do patients leave without being seen by a physicians? Why are there delays in triage?

Force-field analysis—This tool helps teams to identify the forces and factors in place that support or work against the solution so that the positives can be reinforced and the negatives eliminated or reduced.

Nominal group technique—This tool allows a team to quickly come to consensus on the relative importance of issues, problems, or solutions by allowing every team member to rank issues.

Test the selected action(s) for a specified period and monitor performance to determine whether it has had a desired effect, a negative effect, or no effect.

Example: The Institute of Healthcare Improvement's (IHI's) Model for improvement was developed by Associates in Process Improvement (www.apiweb.org) and is based on Shewhart's work. The model asks three basic questions: What are we trying to accomplish? How will we know that a change is an improvement? What changes can we make that will result in improvement?[19]

The model is based on small tests of change that build on each other, leading to dramatic improvement. Plsek explains that a measured pace is crucial to success in this model. The value derives from the principle that each cycle provides information that can be the basis for future learning.[20]

Monitor Performance to Sustain Improvements

Solidify or implement the solutions (that is, make them permanent) if data reveals that performance has improved. A well-designed change will produce desired results.

Continue to monitor performance until it is within acceptable levels and the problem's causes have been eliminated permanently or otherwise brought under control. Thereafter, monitor performance as needed to make sure the desired improvement is being sustained. If the actions taken are not followed by evidence of improved performance, revisit the team's analysis of the problem to see whether any causes have been overlooked.

Reassess the performance indicator(s). Are the data being generated truly reflective of actual performance? Identify and implement alternative intervention. Continue monitoring performance for signs of improvement.

The Role of Data

An important role for risk management is helping to prioritize the organization's goals through the use of risk data. Ongoing analysis of malpractice data, risk issues, quality improvement data, and information from peers are all essential to meeting this objective.

Health care risk management professionals see the role that systems problems and individual provider performance play in the quality and safety of care, in the context of the malpractice claims information. They continually seek to understand the relationship between human process problems and the frequency and severity of claims. Although there is a scarcity of studies to prove it, liability is likely to be decreased by addressing performance issues proactively.

Quality and patient safety initiatives, including those based on regulations, such as accreditation standards, should be designed to address the very issues that lead to malpractice claims. To contribute maximally to the resolution of quality initiatives, the risk management professional must define the problem to be addressed from the information sources that are most under control—incident reports, potential and actual claims, compliance data, occurrence trends, and perhaps patient complaints.

Through collaboration with performance improvement professionals, this data should be analyzed with data from other sources that are important in evaluating the effectiveness of a system's quality improvement processes, such as:

- Voluntary reporting—Many organizations have focused on developing or improving voluntary reporting of errors, facility-wide or in individual departments. These reports can be useful in targeting areas for improvement. The advantages and disadvantages of a voluntary reporting system are discussed in Chapter 1 of this volume of the series.

- Focus groups—These provide qualitative information about how a system is functioning. Although this method does not provide a reliable way to quantify frequency of events, it can uncover areas of concern that might be suitable for further exploration.

- Chart reviews—Chart reviews collect data using specific criteria to determine compliance with procedures, clinical processes, or desired outcomes.

- Trigger tools[21]—These are used in chart review. They focus reviewers on specific indicators in the medical record.

- Direct observation[22]—This can be used to evaluate compliance with institutional requirements such as handwashing, or with steps in a process such as medication administration. *sponge counts*

- Inspection points—These are used to check for errors at specific points in a production process, such as a review of physicians' orders by a pharmacist.

Combining risk management data, particularly medical malpractice claim information, with data from any or all of these sources will yield a rich source of information that can be used to drive performance improvement.

Implications for Accreditation

As previously discussed, accrediting and regulatory bodies require evidence of a PI process that is closely aligned with patient safety initiatives. By participating actively in process improvement activities, the risk management professional can help lead facilities or practices toward compliance and also can address issues that drive patient injury and liability. Such activities also help avoid non-compliance with regulatory bodies and the risk of financial loss and damage to reputation often associated with such non-compliance.

The Risk Management Professional as Change Agent

One more way in which the risk manager should routinely interact with performance improvement concerns the role of the risk management professional as a change agent. The current process of health care is extremely complex. Compounding this is the current unprecedented rate of change in the delivery of health care. These influences exacerbate stress, distraction, turmoil, inefficiency, and discontent among providers, administrators, and patients. The resultant atmosphere can breed unpredictable adverse outcomes, additional liability, provider frustration, uncertain budgets, and patient dissatisfaction. Downsizing, mergers, the performance of more complicated procedures in less-controlled environments, and increasing demands by regulators add to the likelihood that care will become even more fragmented, patients will be displeased, and mistakes will be made.[23]

Risk management professionals have a vested interest in helping all parties cope effectively with change. Through performance improvement initiatives, risk management professionals can help identify issues associated with proposed change and with solutions. They can also play an active part in improvement projects that assess how changes are affecting care. Risk management professionals can recommend adjustments in data collection tools, to assess new risks, and can identify potential issues created by new organizational structures. The risk management professional can also identify necessary areas of training, an intervention which tends to alleviate staff anxiety over a new venture, while reducing potential liability.

Use of the PI Process for Risk Management

Risk management departments themselves are certainly affected by changes in the health care delivery system. Risk management professionals can use the PI process to look closely at their own operations on a periodic basis.

Openly using the PI process for the risk management program, including involving other health care providers in an assessment of risk management functions, can spread the word that the PI process is a valued practical resource which should be used on a day-to-day basis. It also conveys that the risk management professional is interested in improving department performance. Moreover, results of the initiatives can be shared with other providers to help them improve their own systems. For example, if the goal of the risk management function is to have a zero-percent surprise rate (meaning, knowing about all potential claims before they become real claims or suits), periodically reviewing timeliness of risk management data reporting is a useful strategy. Such a process can facilitate greater overall efficiencies in what is reported to whom and also identify opportunities for capturing information that can be fed back into other quality and patient safety initiatives.

If the risk management professional's duties have increased as a result of mergers or other organizational changes, using performance improvement tools to review routine processes might help ensure that there is no loss of program efficiency. For example, change in organizational structure may prompt a review of claims and litigation management to ensure efficient allocation of claim management responsibilities, seamless communication with defendants during the litigation process, and appropriate monitoring of defense attorneys.[24]

Managing the Risk of Performance Improvement

The risk management professional should also identify risk management and patient safety-related issues in performance improvement projects and point them out constructively.

Implementation of an inappropriate solution due to organizational arrogance is often manifested by implementation of a process change at the direction of an individual (most commonly a powerful person within the organization) who thought it was a great idea, even though there has been no research to see how others manage the issue that the change is intended to address. Staff and senior managers need to understand that taking time to solicit the experience of other organizations, and assessing any applicable benchmark data, is a valuable step in implementing process change. Such additional information is not meant to stifle true creativity or innovation, but rather to allow evaluation of new ideas in the light of prior knowledge and experience. It might be helpful for the risk management professional encountering this inappropriate use of PI processes to suggest use of Failure Mode and Effects Analysis (FMEA) to assess the potential risk of proposed solutions before they leave the pilot (or testing) stage. (Please see discussion of FMEA in Chapter 3 in this volume of the series.)[25]

A variant on this is implementation of an inappropriate solution due to a "damn the torpedoes, full speed ahead" mentality, which is characterized by the rush to implement solutions, without any form of pilot (or small-scale) testing to work out the kinks before full-scale implementation is attempted. Whereas performing small-scale tests is sometimes seen as a delaying tactic, it actually has been shown to make implementation quicker and easier, because potential risks and barriers to implementation on a wider scale will be known, and their influence can be diffused ahead of time.

Indeed, if small-scale testing has not been done first and defects in the solution are later identified, it might be very difficult to convince staff members who have invested time and energy in implementation that more change is necessary.

Still another issue that can impede successful performance improvement projects is promotion—rather than minimization—of silo mentality, by redesigning a process without considering its effect on related processes or personnel. One hallmark of silo mentality is a design team that excludes key players. Another example is the selection of performance measures that focus only on process efficiency, without including measures of clinical quality or customer satisfaction. As health care evolves into a team-based model, it is necessary to bring all stakeholders into the process, including patients when possible.

Introduction of a new risk by implementing a solution whose implications have not been fully assessed is another concern. Excessive reaction to anecdotal occurrences happens most often when reliable data are not available or not used well. For example, a risk management professional might easily be tempted to advocate a specific process change on the basis of one disastrous occurrence, without assessing whether the circumstances indicate evidence of a "special cause variation." A special cause variation is a rare event that needs to be analyzed and treated differently than an occurrence that has happened several times before and is likely to happen again (a "common cause" event). The latter is usually much more amenable to PI efforts. This does not mean that root cause analysis of a critical systems failure that resulted in a sentinel event and is due to a "special cause" should not be studied further. However, when routine processes are changed without sufficient analysis, new risks can be introduced by an inadequately researched solution. To avoid this issue, it is essential to think through the effect of the solution on the every aspect of the system involved. Again, FMEA may be a helpful strategy.

Engaging Physicians in the PI Process

As previously noted, including the appropriate stakeholders is key to success of any organizational project. In health care, this means engaging physicians in almost every effort, because they are at the heart of patient care. Paul Plsek describes "the need for widespread staff involvement and unprecedented cooperation across traditional boundaries as key principles of quality improvement."[26] However, involvement of physicians in the PI process has been and continues to be a challenge to many. To successfully engage physicians, one must understand broad concepts of physician culture and the needs and expectations of both the organization and clinicians. At the outset, it is critical to understand the differences between the culture and needs of physicians and managers. In brief, managers see the system as a whole, responding to the needs of a larger population, while physicians see the patient as an individual who needs help.

To serve the patient's needs, physicians have been trained to be autonomous and to be problem solvers. As noted by Leape and Berwick ". . . the culture of medicine is deeply rooted, both by custom and by training, in high standards of autonomous individual performance, and a commitment to progress through research."[27] As health care has changed from a single provider to a team-based approach involving not only other physicians but also other disciplines, physicians must now learn to work in teams.

Another physician concern relates to the concept of standardization. Although this principle is important to improving consistency of care, reducing errors, and optimizing outcomes, physicians might view it as a threat to their authority and autonomy. For example, standardization in the form of clinical guidelines might be viewed as cookbook medicine and thus a restriction on the skills of a physician. In addition, there might be fear that guidelines increase the risk of liability, even though studies have shown that "they are at worst a neutral factor" in malpractice actions.[28] The risk management professional can explain how standardization for the sake of the patient will improve outcomes.

Another concern of physicians may be that the term "performance improvement" implies that there is indeed room for improvement. And this, in turn, might imply that the existing quality of (their) care is poor.

Beyond these fears, many physicians do not have the tools nor have they been taught the skills needed to participate in performance improvement and quality improvement efforts. Donabedian noted that we ask clinicians to solve system problems when they have not received any training in systems thinking or in the use of tools to solve these problems.[29]

Because physicians are an important part of the functioning of any health care system, and because the quality of their performance is a major driver of the quality of patient care, risk management professionals must actively work to bring the physicians into the PI process. One way to accomplish this is for risk managers to use potential or actual claims data to motivate physicians to become directly involved in PI efforts. However, essential prerequisites to this approach include getting the buy-in of physician leaders and using the most credible and objective data available (for example, from a source other than the risk managers' own health care system). In a survey of 1,000 Colorado physicians and 500 Colorado households, it was determined that most physicians believe "that the fear of malpractice litigation is a barrier to successful error reduction," versus being a motivating factor. The survey also showed that while most physicians believed "that reduction of medical errors should be a national priority," they were "much less likely than the public to believe that the quality of care is a problem."[30]

Remember that physicians can become disillusioned quickly with projects that are initiated without supporting data or that seem irrelevant to improving the quality of the care that they render to their patients. Literature on how physicians learn confirms that they are more motivated to learn a new concept, treatment, or procedure if it directly relates to a patient care question that is important to them in their own daily practice. Research has also found that regulations, or the threat of regulatory or legal sanctions, is the least motivating way for physicians to acquire new knowledge.[31] Therefore, emphasis on patient care issues may be very helpful in engaging physicians in developing or implementing a PI solution to a risk management issue.

In addition, physicians might hesitate to engage in PI efforts if they feel they do not understand the process or what role they could play in it. Berwick reports that many physicians lack the knowledge and training in the system of health care delivery or the tools necessary to improve the system. Sharing with physicians the series of articles in the 1998 *Annals of Internal Medicine* entitled "Physicians as Leaders in Improving Healthcare," edited by Berwick and Nolan, might help to begin discussions with them.

There are many other ways to interest physicians in patient safety and health care improvement. Selecting what to improve is critical. Selecting a topic that is relevant, crosses many functional areas, can be associated with improved patient outcomes, and is measurable will assist in engaging all stakeholders, not only physicians. Because physicians direct a large part of patient care, it is essential to gain physician engagement and even leadership of PI initiatives.

Proactively improving systems that physicians rely on can help them to deliver better patient care and can help them better defend that care, should claims arise.

As customers of the hospitals' systems, physicians often correctly perceive that they have only limited input into how those systems are designed. A good example is the hospital's documentation system. By encouraging physician input at key junctures, for example, purchase of a new electronic medical record, and working closely with health information professionals to make the record easier to use, the risk management professional can improve the substance of documentation and gain physician good will.

Systematically obtaining and distributing outcomes data that can be used to modify and enhance physician practice can get and keep the physicians' attention. Physicians tend to be very responsive to data if it is presented in a relevant and credible context. By presenting claims or incident reporting data that is well organized and focused on clinical relevance, risk management professionals can interest the physician in PI efforts. By showing physicians how such information can improve the quality of care, the risk management professional can also gain their support in prevention of liability. Working with key physician opinion leaders to analyze and distribute such data is usually a very effective approach.

Physicians can be encouraged to be involved in PI efforts if information on best practices is shared with them in a non-judgmental way. Physicians are likely to be most interested in PI teams organized to address either specific diseases or specific clinical pathways. With the increased accessibility of information on best practices, whether through formal benchmarking programs, literature searches, or personal experiences, risk managers now can get this information into the hands of the appropriate physician leaders and committees.

In general, it is very helpful for physicians to see risk management professionals as facilitators who help providers deal with change-related concerns, such as training issues, communication lapses, ambiguous policy and procedures, and low morale. Even more important to the physicians and the organization, the risk manager can help design solutions to problems that are identified.

············

CONCLUSION

Opportunities to prevent patient injury, control risk, decrease losses, and enhance performance through improvement of processes and systems make risk management professionals important stakeholders in the success of their organizations' quality and patient safety initiatives. By guiding the use of risk management data as a priority setter in the performance improvement process and leading efforts to resolve liability-related patient safety issues, risk management professionals play an important role on a performance improvement team vested in addressing medical error.

Conversely, risk management professionals who choose not to participate limit their organizations' ultimate success and significantly marginalize their own roles. Ultimately their functions may become irrelevant and expendable.

Endnotes

1. "To Err is Human: Building A Safer Health System, Crossing the Quality Chasm: The IOM Health Care Quality Initiative." Published on November 1, 1999.
2. Examples from closed claims of Lifespan.
3. Meisenheimer, C. G. *Quality Assurance.* Rockville, Md.: Aspen Systems Corp., 1985.
4. *Patient Safety Manual.* Chicago: American College of Surgeons, 1979.
5. Meisenheimer, *op. cit.*
6. Shewhart, W. A. *Economic Control of Quality of Manufactured Product.* Washington, DC: Ceepress, The George Washington University, 1986 (reprinted from the American Society for Quality Control, 1980, and Van Nostrand, 1931).
7. Walton, M. *The Deming Management Method.* New York: Dodd, Mead, 1986.
8. Juran, J. *Juran on Leadership for Quality: An Executive Handbook.* New York: The Free Press, 1989.
9. Tan, M. W. "TQM in Healthcare: a Time of Transition." *RMF Forum,* 1991, 12(5), 1.
10. Marx, D. *Patient Safety and the "Just Culture": A Primer for Healthcare Executives.* Funded by a grant from the National Heart, Lung, and Blood Institute, National Institutes of Health (Grant RO1 HL53772, Harold S. Kaplan, MD, Principal Investigator), April 17, 2001.
11. Reason, J. *Managing the Risks of Organizational Accidents.* Chapter 9 (culpability algorithm). Aldershot: Ashgate Publishing, 1997.
12. Weber, D. R. "Incorporating Quality Improvement Strategies and Benchmarking into Risk Management." In Youngberg, B. (ed.), *The Risk Manager's Desk Reference.* Rockville, Md.: Aspen Systems Corp., 1994.
13. Tan, *op. cit.*
14. "Improving Organization Improvement." In *Comprehensive Accreditation Manual for Hospitals: The Official Handbook.* CAMH, Chicago: JCAHO, 2005. "Facts about Patient Safety." Retrieved June 9, 2005. Available at: [www.jcaho.org/accredited+orgqanization/patient+safety].
15. "Sentinel Events." In *Comprehensive Accreditation Manual for Hospitals: The Official Handbook CAMH,* Chicago: JCAHO, 2001.
16. Head, G. L., and S. Horn, *Essentials of Risk Management* (vol. 1, 2nd ed.). Malvern, Pa.: Insurance Institute of America, 1991.
17. One source for description and explanation of such standard PI tools is The Memory Jogger. GOAL/QPC, 13 Branch St., Methuen, MA 01844-1953.
18. Langley, G. L., et al. *The Improvement Guide: A Practical Approach to Enhancing Organizational Performance.* San Francisco: Jossey-Bass, 1996.
19. Plsek, P. "Section I: Evidence-based Quality Improvement, Principles, and Perspectives." *Pediatrics,* January 1999, 103(1), 203–214.
20. Knox, G. E., et al. "Downsizing, Reengineering, and Patient Safety: Numbers, Newness, and Resultant Risk." *Journal of Healthcare Risk Management,* 1999, 19(3), p. 19.
21. Rozich, J. D., C. R. Haraden, R. K. Resar. "Adverse Drug Event Trigger Tool: A Practical Methodology for Measuring Medication-related Harm." *Quality and Safety in Healthcare,* 2003, 12, 194–200.

22. Barker, K. N., E. A. Flynn, G. A. Pepper. "Observation Method of Detecting Medication Errors." *American Journal of Health-System Pharmacy*, 2002, 59(23), 2314–2316.

23. Knox et al, *op. cit.,* 17.

24. "Hospitals Tackle New JCAHO Requirement with Failure Mode and Effects Analysis (FMEA) Risk Management Reporter," *ECRI*. April 2002, 1, 3–7.

25. Plsek, P. "Section I: Evidence-based Quality Improvement, Principles, and Perspectives." *Pediatrics*, January 1999, 103(1), 203–214.

26. Leape, L., Berwick, D. "Five Years After To Err is Human." *JAMA*, 2005, 293(19), 2384–90.

27. Reinertsen, J. L., MD. "Zen and the Art of Physician Autonomy Maintenance." *Annals of Internal Medicine* 2003; 138:992–995.

28. Mullan, F. A. "Founder of Quality Assessment Encounters a Troubled System Firsthand." *Health Affairs* 2001; 20(1):137–141.

29. Robinson, A. R., et al. "Physicians and Public Opinions on Quality of Healthcare and the Problem of Medical Errors." *Archives of Internal Medicine*, 2002, 162(19), 2186–2190.

30. Fox, R. D., et al. (eds.). *Changing and Learning in the Lives of Physicians*. New York: Prager, 1989.

31. Berwick, D. M., T. W. Nolan. "Physicians as Leaders in Proving Healthcare." Series in *Annals of Internal Medicine*, 1998, 128(4), 289–298; 128(10), 833–838; 128(12), 1004–1009.

3

Clinical Crisis Management

June Leigh
Nancy Lagorio

In 1999, the Institute of Medicine report "To Err is Human: Building a Safer Health System" focused the nation's attention on medical errors in hospitals. However, despite subsequent efforts by the nation's hospitals to reduce errors and improve quality, a 2004 survey of more than 2,000 adults found that nearly half were concerned about the safety of the medical care they receive, and 55 percent said they were dissatisfied with quality of care—up from 44 percent when the survey had been conducted four years earlier.[1]

With the public's confidence in health care at an all-time low, health care organizations must redouble their efforts. This chapter will suggest strategies for proactively managing clinical crises, an arena where potential medical error and public perception may converge very visibly.

A clinical crisis can be defined as an urgent situation in which an action or omission by a care provider might have deviated beyond safe limits of practice, subsequently contributing to an adverse patient outcome.

The following principles can be helpful in developing a plan which will improve patient outcomes, and patient and public perception of clinical crisis management.

PREVENTING THE CRISIS

Obviously, the best crisis management is to prevent a clinical crisis from happening at all. Steps in crisis prevention include conducting a failure mode effect analysis to evaluate the possibility of a crisis taking place and implementing strong staff communication processes to promote safety.

Failure Mode Effect Analysis

Failure Mode Effect Analysis (FMEA) involves the proactive and thorough examination of a process to determine what *could* go wrong. FMEA thus enables us to address the problem before a breakdown in patient safety occurs. Failure modes can be thought of as anything that could go wrong, or a weakness in any part of a process, that has the potential to adversely affect patient safety.

The FMEA process originated in industry. More recently, Healthcare Failure Mode Effect Analysis (HFMEA™) was developed for use in health care by the Veterans Administration National Center for Patient Safety with assistance from Tenet Healthcare.

The HFMEA process comprises the following steps:

- Select a high-risk process to study.
- Assemble a multidisciplinary team.
- Diagram and graphically describe the process and all subprocesses.
- Brainstorm to identify all potential failure modes, and prioritize them.
- Identify the causes of the potential failures, determine the probability of occurrence, and evaluate the effect or severity if the failure does occur. Probability and severity levels can be assigned numerically from 1 through 5.
- Develop and implement actions for each failure mode cause, and assign responsibility for completing each action.
- Assess new processes to ensure that they are effective, and do not create additional potential failure modes. [2]

Safety-Oriented Staff Communication: Safety Briefings

Another important communication approach that can help prevent a clinical crisis is to use safety briefings in patient care areas. Where possible, the briefing should encompass the expanded health care team—interns and residents, respiratory therapists, and others. Safety briefings also benefit other clinical areas, such as the departments of pharmacy and radiology. Safety briefings are held for a maximum of five minutes at the beginning of each shift with full staff participation. They are used to share information on potential patient safety issues on the unit,[3] for example, two patients with the same name, or a new IV pump in use.

A safety briefing also may occur before the start of a procedure. For example, a briefing in the operating room could emphasize that a patient had a prior right mastectomy and explain the need to avoid right arm compression. Another briefing might discuss ways to avoid potential problems with the OR table that is about to hold a particularly obese patient.

Successful safety briefings should be:

- Non-punitive
- Brief
- Intended to identify an initial list of safety issues for discussion
- Open and encouraging of active participation, so that staff will feel comfortable in raising additional points

Debriefing at the end of each shift also may let staff members raise observations of potential or actual safety lapses that could have led to an adverse patient outcome.

Safety-Oriented Staff Communication: Leadership Safety Rounds

In addition to safety briefings, senior leadership safety rounds can help strengthen a culture of patient safety, foster reporting of patient safety failures or near misses, and help reduce the number of adverse events.[4] During these rounds, senior leadership representatives visit clinical areas, such as patient care units, the operating room, radiology, and the pharmacy, to engage employees in discussion about patient safety and how to prevent a clinical crisis from occurring.

Examples of formats are one-on-one discussions with clinical staff members in private areas of patient care units, or small group discussions including those with similar job functions.

Sample questions might include:

- Have you observed any actions or omissions that could have caused patient harm, but didn't? Tell me about it.

- Do you feel comfortable in speaking to other care providers if you feel they are jeopardizing a patient's safety? Do you feel comfortable reporting lapses you observe in patient safety? Why or why not?

- Can you tell me about a time when a patient was harmed? Tell me how you think that happened and your ideas on how we could prevent it from happening again.

Clearly, success of this strategy depends upon convincing employees that the organization is committed to a non-punitive environment and confidentiality of individual responses. Rounds should be made regularly and routine participation of senior staff should be required. Actions taken as a result of employee input should be communicated to staff members.

MANAGING THE CRISIS

Despite health care professionals' best efforts to prevent clinical crises, those crises occur, and they must be managed. Successful crisis management requires effective communication methods and programs, teamwork in response to crises, and well-developed disclosure, follow-up, and analysis procedures.

Communication Among Health Care Providers

Between 1995 and 2004, the Joint Commission on Accreditation of Healthcare Organizations (JCAHO) received nearly 3,000 reports of sentinel events. Patient death was the outcome in 75 percent of the cases. Communication failure was identified as a root cause of the sentinel event about 65 percent of the time.[5] Clearly, improving communication among health care providers is an important step in reducing the likelihood of errors.

In particular, it is important to address the hesitancy many non-physician providers feel about communicating with the medical staff, at the first sign of an impending clinical crisis.

SBAR Communication Method

The SBAR technique has been adapted from the aviation industry and the military. It is a structured, systematic method of organizing communication, especially concerning urgent events. It can be used by all providers of care as they communicate with each other and with the patient and family. The acronym stands for:

- **S**ituation—description of the current patient status
- **B**ackground—summary of the clinical context
- **A**ssessment—synopsis of the problem as you see it
- **R**ecommendation—statement of actions you believe are indicated

Preparation is the key to the success of SBAR communication. An example of the SBAR technique is as follows:

S	Dr. Jones, this is Nancy Smith, the nurse on 4 north. I am calling about Ann King. She is currently diaphoretic; her pulse is 120, blood pressure 80/50, respirations 28 and shallow. Her O_2 saturation is 84 percent. She is difficult to rouse.
B	She was admitted yesterday with a diagnosis of CHF. Her prior vital signs ranged from a BP of 140/90 to 130/82, pulse 88 to 98 with skin warm and dry. She is on oxygen 2 L/M. Blood work and the EKG from yesterday were within normal limits.
A	Breath sounds are absent on right side and I think she has had a pneumothorax.
R	I think we should get a stat chest x-ray, and the patient needs to be seen now.

As in all aspects of patient care, communication is a team effort. Implementing the SBAR technique requires commitment from administrative, clinical, and medical staff leadership. Multidisciplinary education sessions provide opportunities to learn and practice this skill.

Rapid Response Team

Most hospitals have created "code" teams to respond when a patient suffers a catastrophic emergency, such as a cardiac arrest. Unfortunately, the code is often called too late for the patient.

Rapid Response Teams (RRT) are designed to prevent codes and other medical crises from happening at all by "rescuing" the patient at the first sign of trouble, rather than attempting to resuscitate them afterwards. Hospitals that have implemented RRT have experienced the following results:

- Decrease in the number of cardiac arrests
- Decrease in deaths from cardiac arrests
- Decrease in hospital deaths overall
- Decrease in number of ICU days
- Decrease in codes per 1,000 discharges and in codes outside the ICU
- Decrease in post-operative complications, including respiratory failure, stroke, severe sepsis, and renal failure[6]
- Increase in survival-to-discharge of coded patients[7]

Team Structure

Different team models have been used successfully. Generally, an ICU RN and a respiratory therapist are the foundation of the RRT. Depending upon a hospital's patient milieu, the RRT also may include a hospitalist, intensivist, physician assistant, or resident.

Staff members must feel comfortable in calling the RRT. Therefore, care should be exercised in selecting members with excellent clinical and assessment skills. RRT members also should exhibit strong interpersonal, communication, collaboration, and coaching skills. Because RRT members must be available to respond promptly when called, staffing considerations must be addressed.

When to Call the RRT

Staff members should not hesitate to call the RRT if their instincts tell them the patient could be in trouble. Even if physical symptoms are not present, the RRT should be contacted. Triggers for calling the RRT include:

- Changes in vital signs
- Shortness of breath
- Chest pain
- Decreased oxygen saturation
- Alteration in consciousness level
- Changes in skin color or temperature
- Change in urinary output

The Role of the RRT

The RRT joins and supports the care provider who has called for assistance, assesses the patient, and initiates appropriate interventions. The patient's physician is informed, using the SBAR approach. The team can help transfer the patient to a higher level of care if necessary, and should take time to provide the staff with feedback. A standard method of documenting the reason for the RRT call, the assessment, interventions performed, and notification of the primary care physician should be used.

The Aftermath of the Clinical Crisis

After caring for the patient, the most immediate need following a clinical crisis is to manage the aftermath. This includes disclosure to the patient and family of what is known about what happened and gathering appropriate professionals, including the risk management professional, to investigate and interview involved staff members, conduct medical record reviews, sequester equipment if malfunction might have contributed to the outcome, report to appropriate external regulatory agencies, and prepare for media communications.

By formalizing the steps necessary to manage the aftermath of a clinical crisis, the health care organization can optimize management of such situations. Tools, such as outlines, checklists, assessment documents, and so on, should be developed to help the response team ensure that key crisis plan components are addressed. See Exhibit 3.1 for a sample Critical Event Response Checklist.

The communications encompassed in managing a clinical crisis, including disclosure discussions, must be well prepared and professionally conceived to support the health care organization's patient safety philosophy and positive reputation. Awareness and appropriate implementation of the response plan by the organization's leadership and staff will drive the success of the response.

EXHIBIT 3.1   Critical Event Response Checklist

1. Determine what should be investigated. This is usually based on the level of actual or potential severity or harm. See chart below:

Severity/Sensitivity (high public awareness)	Level of Investigation
Low to Moderate	• Capture event type • Job function of staff involved • Description of what happened • Contributing factors • Action taken Include event in appropriate reports and determine if data set reveals a trend. If so, consider RCA.
High to Catastrophic	• All of above The patients and providers as applicable should be involved in and/or informed of the investigation, and a full RCA is to be conducted.

2. Assure that appropriate notification of senior leadership and management has occurred.*
3. Call together a critical response team as appropriate (for situations where serious injury or unexpected death are involved to develop a response plan).*
4. Determine and communicate roles of managers in process.*
5. Learn why the incident happened and the capacity to prevent reoccurrence.*
6. Consider facts to determine how detailed the investigation should be (actual or potential risk of severe harm often guides scope of investigation).*
7. Prepare detailed timeline from medical record, department records, and interviews.
8. Determine if an investigation will be conducted under the auspices of peer/professional review/the quality committee and/or anticipation of litigation or work product.*
9. Notify legal counsel and insurance carrier when applicable.*
   • Evaluate claim potential
   • Invoke claims handling
   Determine if the event has happened before or is an isolated case.
10. Determine/involvement of other appropriate disciplines, i.e. infection control.*
11. Determine what barriers, if any, are in place to prevent the event and why they were ineffective.
12. As the investigation progresses, identify potential solutions for use in corrective action.
13. Prioritize events for a RCA in regards to severity and resources with the guide below:

Full RCA	Consider RCA or Rapid Cycle Improvement
• Unexpected deaths related to the event • Suspected permanent injury/loss of function related to the event • JCAHO reviewable sentinel events	• Patient needed further medical/surgical/intervention related to the event • Near misses worth an in-depth review • All events that trigger external investigations such as medical examiners' inquest, complaints, legal claims, and criminal investigations • Public awareness

14. Identify RCA members.
    • Include all applicable staff involved
    • Use a multidisciplinary approach to review the event—have an expert facilitator present.
15. Collect evidence and gather information including:*
    • Medical records (secure them)—review documentation for accuracy and completeness, have staff consult Risk Management if incident not entered into the medical record
    • Diagnostics—lab, x-ray, etc. (secure them)
    • Policies, guidelines, protocols, etc.
    • Event reports
    • Staff involved—Compile job descriptions, competency checklists for all staff roles involved in event.
    • Equipment—preserve it (Ensure date in machine is stored.), sequester, establish chain of custody, obtain equipment documentation including purchase information

(Continued)

EXHIBIT 3.1   Critical Event Response Checklist (*Continued*)

- • Switchboard or other records response time such as beeper records, phone calls, etc.
- • Audit reports or meeting minutes
- • Services and maintenance records
- • Risk assessments

16. Interviews*
  - • Determine appropriate course of action in union setting.
  - • Explain to staff why the interview is conducted and explain pertinent confidentiality principles.
  - • Advise staff to document recollection of incident on appropriate occurrence report
  - • Advise staff to not complete personal notes.
  - • Conduct the interview one on one in private. It should be supportive and non-judgmental
  - • Record chronology of events and ask:
    1. What happened—describe events that took place
    2. What knowledge or information was used in making decisions and goals?
    3. Contributing factors
  - • Use responses to compare with other staff members to identify gaps.

17. Site visits
  - • Evaluate site to determine if physical environment was contributing factor.
  - • Consider reconstruction of event. (This is particularly useful when staff is unclear on what happened.)

18. Anticipate media involvement*
  - • Prepare a written statement/script.
  - • Identify and communicate who will be the "point person" for media inquiries.

19. Analyze information
  - • Identify underlying causes and lessons.
  - • Use accountability determination model.
  - • Avoid hindsight bias.

20. Consider peer review referral or HR involvement.

21. Anticipate that the state licensing body (or JCAHO) will conduct a survey.

22. Consider need for involving other authorities, i.e. law enforcement.

23. Patient involvement
  - • Recognize level of severity—level of involvement depends on the nature of the incident
  - • Contact and follow-up
  - • Disclosure of event
  - • Inform about review process and action
  - • Ask for their perceptions
  - • Involve in post-investigation findings

24. Map the event based on the interview findings.

25. Compile literature search for "best practices", industry standards and other background information for all aspects of event.

26. Identify lessons learned about the investigation process itself.

General Considerations

1. Remain flexible when using this checklist. Order of priority will depend on the event type/timeframe.
2. Realize that several of the action steps may occur simultaneously.
3. Determine the focus of the review—peer/professional review—under the quality umbrella, as work product or in anticipation of litigation. Each requires a certain method of handling, and more than one process may be occurring simultaneously

*Consider within the first 24 hours post event

· · · · · · · · · · ·

DISCLOSURE

Studies have found that poor communication among providers of care, patients, and families is a significant factor in the decision to consult an attorney following an unexpected adverse outcome.[8] Perceptions of cover-up, failure to answer questions, lack of an empathic and humane approach when conveying bad news, little or no assurance of follow-up, resolution, and prevention of similar events are all predictors of a lawsuit.[9]

Therefore, if the outcome is not what was anticipated, and there might be medical error involved, communication is an essential liability avoidance measure.

On July 1, 2001, the JCAHO issued a new standard requiring that patients and their families, when appropriate, should receive information about outcomes of care, including unanticipated outcomes.[10] The National Patient Safety Foundation and the American Medical Association Code of Medical Ethics also support the concept of ensuring that patients understand their medical treatment and any adverse events that might occur during that treatment.

After much consternation and debate about the meaning of disclosure, and potential liability related to disclosure, health care organizations began to recognize that disclosure, like informed consent, represents an effective mode of patient communication. Not only do disclosure discussions help health care providers enhance patient relations, but they also promote ongoing communication with patients and their families throughout the course of medical treatment.

Planning the disclosure discussion, ensuring that questions and concerns of the patient and the family are addressed, and providing follow-up communication and support to the patient, family, and staff, are vital to effective communication and management of the aftermath of an adverse event.

Also note that the disclosure process has become a core element in the management of clinical crises, adverse outcomes, unanticipated events, medical errors, and medical mishaps. To promote consistency in an approach that serves so many purposes, the health care organization needs to establish and use similar terms and nomenclature for the disclosure process. Including the disclosure process in a crisis response plan, in particular, will reinforce its importance to the staff.

Developing the Disclosure Process

Implementing any new process effectively often requires organizations to overcome significant challenges. In the case of disclosure, maximally effective implementation requires that the organization change from a culture that associates blame with medical error, to one that concentrates on patient safety. To achieve this change, the leadership team must demonstrate support through its mission statement and must process improvement initiatives.

Therefore, a disclosure process that communicates adverse outcomes effectively is a hallmark of an organization which has mastered proactive culture change. Even if such a cultural transformation has only just begun, however, the organization must work to achieve effective disclosure. The process is much too critical to the communication of adverse outcomes to await a perfect cultural environment.

In brief, the steps that should be included in a disclosure process include the following:

- Who will be involved in disclosure discussions?
- What information will be disclosed?
- When it is appropriate to disclose information?
- Where is the proper location for disclosure discussions?
- How is the disclosure discussion best communicated?

Another important step is the development of staff education programs that relate to disclosure and communication. Education should occur at all levels within the organization. Programs should address such topics as:

- Philosophy of patient safety
- Disclosure process, including apology
- Roles and responsibilities
- Barriers to disclosure
- Communication skills

Disclosure Models

Health care organizations should determine the disclosure model that best incorporates their levels of comfort and sophistication in discussions with patients and families. There are four basic communication models:

- The *One-Person Model* usually involves the risk manager or other designated, effective communicator. The disadvantages of this model are the lack of shared responsibility with others in the organization and the absence of back-up processes and resources if the designated communicator is unavailable or has left the organization.

- The *Team Model* includes a group of individuals (usually multidisciplinary) designated or trained as effective communicators. This model includes shared responsibility for effective disclosure discussions throughout the organization. The disadvantage of this model is that several members might be away from their daily responsibilities at unpredictable times, potentially leading to operational inefficiencies and deficiencies.

- The *Train-the-Trainer Model* uses learned communication and interpersonal skills of identified individuals in the organization to educate others to become skilled communicators in disclosure discussions. This allows the organization to expand the group of trained physicians and staff members who promote the culture of patient safety through open communications with patients and families. The primary disadvantage of this model is that it places responsibility on one individual for coordinating the entire training and scheduling process.

- The *Just-in-Time Coaching Model* allows for practitioners to conduct the disclosure discussion at the point of care or adverse event. When the organization has truly established a culture of patient safety and trained all levels of staff to communicate effectively and conduct disclosure discussions, this model should be implemented. If practitioners at the point of care do not have effective communication skills or did not receive communication training, the model might be difficult to implement.[11]

A combination of the models also can be used to ensure that two or three key individuals who have successfully completed communication training are selected to disclose the medical error or adverse event. A contact person should be identified to handle ongoing communication with the patient or family. Whenever possible, the primary communicator should be the attending physician. In addition, the patient or family may have individual preferences for discussion participants. The family, however, should not be outnumbered by the disclosure team.

Disclosure Strategies

The critical information in disclosure discussions includes:

- An acknowledgement that an adverse event or medical error occurred
- Communication of regret about the event

- An apology (appropriate to the organization's policy)
- Objective statement of facts
- Statement that the event is being investigated
- Statement that when all facts are determined, steps will be taken to avoid future recurrences

The timing of a disclosure discussion is critical to its success. The adverse event should be acknowledged as soon as possible. Often, the facts are not available, but the patient or family should be assured that an investigation is ongoing. The designated individual or team responsible for conducting the discussion should establish the appropriate time when sufficient facts are available to initiate discussions with the patient or family. If the discussion occurs too early and not enough facts are known about the adverse event, the patient or family may be confused and angry that nothing is being done to address the situation. If the discussion occurs too late, the patient or family might feel that the health care providers and organization do not have a caring attitude or are hiding information.

The location of the disclosure discussion is also essential to success. It is preferable to have the discussion in a comfortable, private room away from telephone and staff interruptions. Patients and families will feel more supported by the organization and staff if undivided attention is provided during these discussions.

Many health care providers and organizations have shared effective communication strategies to help others enhance their disclosure processes. The following have been identified as effective strategies in the disclosure process:

- Allow adequate time for the discussion and questions from the patient or family.
- Prohibit cell phones, pagers, and other interruptions.
- Assess the readiness of the patient or family to be able to absorb and understand the information, and adjust the length and depth of the discussion accordingly.
- Recognize cultural, religious, and socioeconomic factors of the patient or family.
- Plan for special communication needs such as interpreters, sign language specialists, learning disability instructors, and so on.
- Speak in short, simple sentences and avoid medical jargon.
- Provide a sincere apology and regret for what happened.
- Be prepared to acknowledge the need for crying, anger, or denial.
- Be cognizant of the appropriate time to end the discussion.
- Solicit questions and answer them honestly.
- Pause and allow time for the information to be processed after all facts have been provided.
- Provide support resources for the patient or family, for example, social services, pastoral counseling, home health services, and so on, to manage individuals' emotional and psychological needs, particularly if the event was catastrophic.
- State next steps, people to contact, and accommodations.[12]

Follow-up Procedures

After the disclosure discussion takes place, follow-up measures should be implemented. First, documentation of the discussion in the medical record should reflect the essence of the discussion, the participants, the plan for additional treatment and follow-up care, next scheduled meetings if any, and the expressed understanding of the patient or family.[13]

The organization should evaluate the disclosure process and implement changes as a result of lessons learned. It should also periodically review its disclosure policy and revise that policy as appropriate to incorporate any new information or successful strategies. The leadership team should be actively involved in any critical decision-making processes that affect the organization's movement toward achieving a culture of patient safety, such as proposed revisions to the disclosure process.

ROOT CAUSE ANALYSIS

Why did a clinical crisis happen? Why was a patient harmed—or almost harmed? Root cause analysis can be defined as a problem-solving methodology which seeks to identify the causal factors of a failure or error which resulted in harm to a patient. With this methodology, solutions are implemented to prevent the failure from happening again.

Like HFMEA, the concept of root cause analysis originated in the military in collaboration with what is today called the Nuclear Regulatory Commission. Unlike HFMEA, the root cause analysis process is retrospective in nature, and seeks to answer the question "why?" Clearly, we cannot solve a problem unless we understand it thoroughly. Whereas we have learned that systems and processes are more frequent causes of failure than an individual's performance, it is imperative that root cause analysis dig deeply to determine the multiple factors underlying an error.

As an essential, continuous quality-improvement tool that helps the organization adhere to a culture of patient safety, root cause analysis should never be performed perfunctorily, merely to satisfy JCAHO requirements. It should be strongly supported by leadership and recognized by all as an approach that will foster improvement, rather than assign blame.

Root cause analysis should be conducted for all events that have resulted in serious harm to a patient and for sentinel events as defined by JCAHO, including an event that has resulted in an unanticipated death or major permanent loss of function, not related to the natural course of the patient's illness or underlying condition, and suicide of any individual receiving care, treatment, or services in a staffed round-the-clock care setting or within 72 hours of discharge. (Please see Chapter 1 of this text for a list of reportable sentinel events.)[14]

Root cause analysis should also be conducted when even though the patient was not harmed in a particular situation, the probability for harm would be high if there is a recurrence of the event. Examples include elopements from the mental health unit, an infant abduction drill that fails, or emergent Cesarean sections that do not begin within the prescribed timeframes.

Steps In the Process

There are several models for root cause analysis, both in the literature and in software systems that the risk manager may use to facilitate the process. Refer to Exhibit 3.2, Key Steps in Root Cause Analysis and Improvement Planning. The basic steps include:

- Organize a multidisciplinary team, including all those involved in the occurrence and others who were not. Remember that the team might be emotional about the event. Consider including a former patient, family member, or someone from the community.

- Define the problem by describing what happened as accurately as possible to focus analysis and interventions more clearly.

EXHIBIT 3.2   Key Steps in Root Cause Analysis and Improvement Planning

The work plan can include the following key activities with target dates for each major milestone:

- Organize a team   Completion Date: _____
- Define the problem   Completion Date: _____
  - Choose area(s) for analysis
  - Develop a plan
- Study the problem   Completion Date: _____
  - Gather information
- Determine what happened and why (proximate causes)   Completion Date: _____
  - Identify process problem(s)
  - Determine which patient care processes are involved
  - Determine factors closest to the event
  - Extract measurement data
- Identify root causes   Completion Date: _____
  - Determine which systems are involved
- Design and implement an action plan for improvement
  - Identify risk reduction strategies   Completion Date: _____
  - Formulate actions for improvement
    (consider actions, measures, responsible party, desired
    completion date, and so forth)
  - Consider the impact of the improvement action
- Design improvements   Completion Date: _____
- Implement action plan   Completion Date: _____
- Measure effectiveness   Completion Date: _____
  - Develop measures of effectiveness
  - Assure success of measurement
- Evaluate implementation efforts   Completion Date: _____
- Communicate results   Completion Date: _____

Reprinted with Permission: © Joint Commission Resources, Root Cause Analysis in Healthcare, 3ed Ed. Oakbrook Terrace, Il: Joint Commission on Accreditation of Healthcare Organizations.

- Gather as many facts and as much information as possible. Use tools such as a chronological list of events with timelines, fishbone diagrams, brainstorming, or cause-and-effect diagrams. Keep asking "why?" Identify data gaps and validate information.
- Isolate root causes by determining which systems are involved and prioritize.
- Use the process to enhance safety and quality improvement action plans. Specific related strategies include confirming ownership of solutions; defining the effect of changes; widely distributing what was learned, devising recommendations and actions; giving individual feedback when necessary to the patient, family, or others, and developing benchmark criteria.
- Measure effectiveness. Evaluate the results of the action plan(s) and modify, if necessary.

Early Offer and Acceptance of Responsibility

There might be situations where the organization, with the advice of legal counsel, has determined that negligence is the likely cause of an adverse outcome and that acceptance of responsibility might represent the best opportunity to expedite a resolution. The acceptance of responsibility may come in the form of an early offer plan.

In an early offer plan as proposed by Jeffrey O'Connell, Professor of Law, University of Virginia, the defendant in a medical malpractice claim would, within 120 days after the adverse event or filing of a claim, be given the option to provide periodic payments for economic damages (salary, medical, and rehabilitation expenses). Payments would include lower hourly attorney rates for the claimant but would not include compensation for pain and suffering.

Proponents of this proposal assert that its advantages include reduced attorneys' fees for plaintiffs and defendants, reduction in overall pain and suffering compensation awards, quicker resolution of claims, decreased time and burden of litigation, an opportunity to provide compensation to claimants more swiftly than through lengthy trials, and enhanced reporting and disclosure of adverse events.[15]

Another method of resolving potential claims following disclosure of adverse events is a pre-litigation early offer for compensation accompanied by the possibility of mediation. In the late 1980s, the Veterans Affairs Medical Center in Lexington, Kentucky, developed such a model, which includes an apology to the patient or family.

Other early mediation models have been developed that are initiated once all the facts have been determined and disclosure discussions have occurred (Pew Demonstration Mediation and Alternate Dispute Resolution Project). In the model developed by Rush University Medical Center in Chicago, mediation is initiated after the adverse event occurs and litigation commences. The goal is to settle the case promptly and with the agreement of all parties. Until recently, an apology usually occurred after the settlement, and it generally communicated sympathy rather than responsibility for the adverse event.[16]

Apologies

Physicians and health care organizations have been reluctant to include apologies in their disclosure discussions or communications with patients because of the apprehension that the apology might be brought into court against them when a malpractice case ensues. Recent legislative initiatives have begun to address this issue. As of 2005, many states have enacted medical malpractice reform laws, which include provisions that prevent apologies, expressions of regret, and other similar communications from being admitted as evidence of liability in malpractice cases. Those states with apology laws include Arizona, Georgia, Maine, Missouri, Montana, New Hampshire, South Dakota, Virginia, and West Virginia.[17] California, Massachusetts, and Texas enacted such measures several years ago. Apology laws of other states, such as Pennsylvania, include requirements for written disclosure.

As more states adopt medical liability reform and patient safety laws, health care providers and health care organizations will become more comfortable conducting disclosure discussions with patients. Patients and families will expect ongoing communication to be a routine part of their medical care and treatment.

Internal and External Communication

Internal and external communication approaches are critical to the well-being of the health care organization, and they become particularly essential when a medical error or adverse event occurs. In a study conducted by the American Association of Critical-Care Nurses (AACN), "Silence Kills: The Seven Crucial Conversations for Healthcare," it was determined that a health care organization with poor communication processes is more likely to have errors and high staff turnover. It is desirable for an organization's staff and leadership to learn communication skills in multidisciplinary training sessions which facilitate effective collaboration and decision-making, as part of the organization's patient safety culture.[18]

Media Communication

When medical errors occur, particularly those that are catastrophic and newsworthy, health care organizations must be prepared for external communication. A designated representative should be identified to communicate with the media throughout the crisis. Staff should be instructed to direct any media inquiries to the designated representative in the organization. As much information as possible should be shared with the media. However, patient or family permission is essential, with scrupulous adherence to governing state confidentiality laws and potential HIPAA violations. Expressions of concern and empathy, and commitment to investigation of the adverse event should be transmitted to the media. Statements of cooperation with regulatory agencies, accreditation organizations, and law enforcement are also important to convey to the public. Other media communication issues to consider following a clinical crisis include:

- Provide a designated area for the media.
- Schedule a press conference as appropriate to the situation.
- Be honest and admit if further investigation is required to obtain answers.
- Provide assurance that an investigation and follow-up will occur to prevent future recurrences.
- Minimize medical and highly technical terminology.
- Anticipate questions and have prepared answers as much as possible.
- Treat the media with respect and not as the enemy.

The status of media-related communication, and other communication with external parties, should also be addressed in internal communications with those staff members involved in the clinical crisis. Internal e-mail, intranet, and written communications can facilitate this process. Keeping the staff informed helps minimize any proliferation of rumors, defuses misinformation, and engages the staff in implementing the organization's crisis management communication plan.

············

CONCLUSION

Unfortunately, the complete elimination of clinical errors in the health care setting is unlikely. Thus, the risk management professional must have a firm grasp on methods to reduce the likelihood of errors and manage the consequences of error-related clinical crises. With the risk management professional's help, by studying systems and processes before such crises occur; by managing adverse events after they have occurred, including open and empathic communication with patients and families; by examining and learning from mistakes; and by educating physicians and staff, the health care organization can become a safer environment and regain the public trust.

Endnotes

1. National Survey on Consumers' Experiences with Patient Safety and Quality Information. Henry J. Kaiser Family Foundation, the U.S. Agency for Healthcare Research and Quality, and the Harvard School of Public Health. November 2004.

2. [www.patientsafety.gov/FMEA2_files/frame.htm].

3. Institute for Healthcare Improvement. "Safety Briefings." [www.ihi.org/IHI/Topics/PatientSafety/SafetyGeneral/Tools/SafetyBriefings]. 2004.

4. Institute for Healthcare Improvement. "Patient Safety Leadership Walk Rounds." [www.ihi.org/IHI/Topics/PatientSafety/SafetyGeneral/Tools/PatientSafetyLeadershipWalkRounds]. 2004.

5. Joint Commission on Accreditation of Healthcare Organizations. "Sentinel Events." [www.jcaho.org/].

6. Institute for Healthcare Improvement. "100,000 Lives Campaign: How-to Guide: Rapid Response Teams." [www.ihi.org/IHI/Programs/Campaign/].

7. Halaszynski, T. M., R. Juda, D. G. Silverman. "Critical Surgical Illness: Preoperative Assessment and Planning." *Critical Care Medicine*, 2004, 32(4), 916–921.

8. Hickson, G. B., et al. "Patient Complaints and Malpractice Risks." *JAMA*, 2002, 287(22), 2951–2957.

9. Beckman, H. B., K. M. Markakis, A. L. Suchman, and R. M. Frankel. "The Doctor-Patient Relationship and Malpractice: Lessons from Plaintiff Depositions." *Archives of Internal Medicine*, 1994, 154, 1365–1370.

10. Standard RI.1.2.2.; renumbered in 2003 to RI.2.90.

11. *Disclosure of Unanticipated Events: The Next Step in Better Communication with Patients*. No. 1. Chicago, Ill.: American Society for Healthcare Risk Management of the American Hospital Association, 2003.

12. Amori, G. "Communication with Patients and Other Customers: The Ultimate Loss Control Tool." *Risk Management Handbook for Health Care Organizations*. Fourth ed. Chicago, Ill.: Jossey-Bass Inc., 2004.

13. *Disclosure of Unanticipated Events: Creating an Effective Patient Communication Policy*. No. 2. Chicago, Ill.: American Society for Healthcare Risk Management of the American Hospital Association, 2003.

14. *Root Cause Analysis in Health Care: Tools and Techniques*. 3rd ed. Joint Commission Resources Publications, 2005.

15. O'Connell, J. "A Proposed Remedy for Medical Malpractice Miseries." Presented at the 51st Annual Meeting of the American College of Obstetricians and Gynecologists (ACOG), Apr. 28, 2003. [cgood.org/healthcare-reading-cgpubs-speeches-10.html]. Last visited April 2005.

16. Liebman, C. B., and Hyman, C. S. "A Mediation Skills Model to Manage Disclosure of Errors and Adverse Events to Patients." [medscape.com/viewarticle/483263_print]. Last visited June 2005.

17. National Conference of State Legislatures. "State Medical Malpractice Reform Action 2005." [www.ncsl.org/standcomm/sclaw/medmalreform05.htm]. Last visited June 2005.

18. Speers, C. "Breaking through the health care legacy of silence." *ASHRM Patient Safety Interest Network INsights*, 2005, 1(1), 1–3.

Additional Resources

Pines, W. L., and Lisa M. Watt. *Crisis Communications in Healthcare: A Delicate Balance*. Washington Business Information, Inc., 2001.

Crisis Communications in Healthcare: Managing Difficult Times Effectively. Society for Healthcare Strategy and Market Development, 2002.

"Media Crisis Guidelines." [www.stfrancishospitals.org].

4

Informed Consent as a Loss Control Process

Fay A. Rozovsky

communication about what physician has in mind

Securing the informed consent of a patient marks the culmination of an important step in the care provider-patient relationship. "Consent," the act of agreeing to a specific diagnostic test or treatment, is not merely the completion of a form, but rather a process[1] based on effective communication and an agreement regarding what is and is not to be done to the patient. Characterized in this way, consent to treatment is like a contract for agreed-upon services by the provider in exchange for valuable consideration (payment) by the patient or payer.[2]

In other ways, however, consent to treatment is different from other contracts. It is the bond that holds together the ongoing health care provider-patient relationship. It is the platform for communication between patient and caregiver that starts at the outset of the care-giving relationship and ends with the completion of treatment. It is also the backdrop for disclosure of both anticipated and unanticipated outcomes of tests or treatment.[3] Consent to treatment is marked by extensive case law and is guided by federal and state statutes and regulations that set forth not only the broad parameters for a valid treatment authorization,[4] but also requirements for specific diagnostic interventions and surgery. Consent to treatment is also the subject of Interpretive Guidelines[5] published by the Centers for Medicare and Medicaid Services to guide state surveyors in conducting validation and compliant based surveys of health care facilities. At the state level, a host of laws set forth specific consent requirements for a myriad of health care needs including genetic testing, HIV testing, breast cancer surgery, abortion, and end-of-life choice-making.

Despite all the judicial interpretations, statutes, and regulations, consent—or the lack of it—remains a persistent basis for claim in health professional liability lawsuits. This is true whether the consent claim is ancillary to other tort allegations or a stand-alone basis for action. Additionally, attempts continue to be made through litigation to impose a consent responsibility on health care organizations.

Consent litigation has moved beyond negligence claims and intentional torts, such as battery, to new levels of legal argument. These include "breach of contract" in situations in which patients argue that the caregiver "guaranteed" a specific outcome, and claims based on misrepresentation, deceit, or fraud. Due to state-based legislation governing unfair and deceptive trade practices, caregivers can find themselves on the receiving end of litigation that relies on such laws in lawsuits involving misrepresentation. Unlike traditional negligence litigation, consent claims based on misrepresentation may involve punitive damages.

Some state legislation ties consent litigation to laws that govern unprofessional conduct. This is an interesting risk management issue. Not only would a caregiver be exposed to a traditional negligent consent claim, the state professional licensing body might also pursue an investigation or hearing for unprofessional conduct based on the same set of facts and circumstances. Defending on "two fronts," the caregiver has new risk exposure that was not present in years past.

From a risk management perspective, it is disturbing that consent litigation persists. As a communication process and an integral part of the provider-patient relationship, a successful consent process can be used to pinpoint and address at-risk situations. To appreciate management of the consent process as a loss control or risk management technique requires an understanding of the elements of a valid treatment authorization, of the right to make an informed refusal-of-care decision, and of common problem areas that involve minors or patients whose capacity to make treatment choices is in doubt. At the same time, the risk management professional should be familiar with recurrent problems such as those emanating from compulsory treatment situations, behavioral health settings, ambulatory care, and the absence of appropriate documentation of the consent process.

Consent-to-treatment responsibilities belong to the care provider who is to conduct the proposed test or treatment. Educating providers about their respective roles and responsibilities is a function that is well suited to risk management professionals. Treating consent as a tool to avoid liability exposure, the risk manager also can use it as a means of facilitating greater trust among patients and care providers in health care systems that undergo dynamic change.

This chapter identifies the contemporary legal sources of influence for the consent process. It describes the basic elements of the consent-to-treatment process from risk management's perspective. It also discusses the principal exceptions to the consent process and suggests measures that can be taken to avoid liability exposure with regard to consent to treatment. Finally, the chapter discusses the use of the consent process as a "patient safety tool" for both avoiding liability exposure related to basic principles of informed consent, and following tests or treatment, a framework for disclosing the outcomes of care.

THE LEGAL SOURCES OF INFLUENCE IN THE CONSENT PROCESS

The Consumer Bill of Rights and Responsibilities, proposed by the President's Advisory Commission on Consumer Protection and Quality in the Health Care Industry and published in November 1997, not only reiterated the fundamental framework of consent to treatment, it set in place the cornerstone of future federal legal initiatives on the topic. The Commission said:

To ensure consumers' right and ability to participate in treatment decisions, health care professionals should:

- Provide patients with easily understood information and opportunity to decide among treatment options consistent with the informed consent process.

- Discuss all treatment options with a patient in a culturally competent manner, including the option of no treatment at all.

- Ensure that people with disabilities have effective communications with members of the health system in making such decisions.

- Discuss all current treatments a consumer may be undergoing, including those alternative treatments that are self-administered.

- Discuss all risks, benefits, and consequences to treatment or non-treatment.

- Give patients the opportunity to refuse treatment and to express preferences about future treatment decisions.

- Discuss the use of advance directives—both living wills and durable powers of attorney for health care—with patients and their designated family members.

- Abide by the decisions made by their patients or their designated representatives consistent with the informed consent process.

To facilitate greater communication between patients and providers, health care providers, facilities, and plans should:

- Disclose to consumers factors—such as methods of compensation, ownership of or interest in health care facilities, or matters of conscience—that could influence advice or treatment decisions.

- Ensure that provider contracts do not contain any so-called "gag clauses" or other contractual mechanisms that restrict health care providers' ability to communicate with and advise patients about medically necessary treatment options.

- Be prohibited from penalizing or seeking retribution against health care professionals or other health workers for advocating on behalf of their patients.[6]

The Rights and Responsibilities bill serves as the basis for a recurrent theme in subsequent sources of influence on the topic of informed consent. It also encapsulates federal requirements on informed consent that date back to the 1970s in the area of human research and more contemporary legislation and regulations that address "patient dumping" under the Emergency Treatment and Active Labor Act (EMTALA-COBRA) and its accompanying rules.[7]

There are other federal sources of influence that promote consent as a process. Some of these provisions, however, are not part of laws or regulations directly related to patient care. Instead, these are regulations designed to protect and promote civil rights. For example, the regulations under the 1964 Civil Rights Act that bar discrimination on the basis of race, color, or national origin also affect consent practices. Hospitals and other health care organizations that provide services to recipients of federally assisted programs must take reasonable steps "to provide information in appropriate languages to such persons."[8] This means that patients enrolled in federally assisted programs who do not speak English enjoy some language service protection. Failure to meet such requirements could subject a health care organization to enforcement activities through the auspices of the U.S. Department of Justice, Office of Civil Rights (OCR). The related guidance document addresses the needs of those with limited English proficiency (LEP) and the cultural needs of those seeking treatment.[9]

The Civil Rights Act is part of a body of legislation and regulations that address compliance with standards set by the federal government. Some of these standards involve consent to treatment and advance directives. Examples include the conditions of participation (COPs) for health care facilities receiving Medicare and or Medicaid dollars. The provisions for hospitals state in part that:

Patients or their representatives (as allowed under state law) have the right to make informed decisions regarding their care. Patients' rights include being informed of their health status, being involved in care planning and treatment, and being able to request or refuse treatment.[10]

Health care organizations involved in corporate compliance activities purport to adhere to such requirements. Evidence of non-conformity with the COPs, EMTALA, or the Civil Rights Act of 1964 might constitute non-compliance under the entity's corporate standards of conduct. The subsequent failure to take corrective action for non-conforming consent practices may cast doubt on the corporate compliance plan. In some instances involving billing or coding issues or patient complaints, it might trigger a regulatory investigation. Hence, corporate compliance, a voluntary program for health care organizations, might actually be a "federal driver" in the area of informed consent. (Refer to Chapter 19 in Volume III of this series for further information on corporate compliance.)

As noted elsewhere in this book, there are very specific federal requirements governing end-of-life choice-making under the terms of the Patient Self-Determination Act[11] and rules governing consent to participate in human subject research trials.[12] These are important requirements that are quite specific in their application. Additionally, the HIPAA Privacy Standards provide direction for securing not a consent but an "acknowledgement" of a privacy notice with respect to certain uses of protected health information (PHI).[13] Some federal agencies or departments have developed "informational tools" that can be used to facilitate the consent process. For example, the Centers for Disease Control and Prevention (CDC) have developed a series of informational tools to explain the benefits and possible side effects of childhood immunization.[14]

Beyond legislation and regulations, guidance documents have been issued by the Office of Civil Rights of the Department of Health and Human Services. The guidance does not have the full weight or authority of legislation or regulations. Nonetheless, it provides important insight into the regulatory mindset on two important factors that are integral to an effective consent: linguistic capability and culture.

The Office of Civil Rights of HHS characterizes the linguistic issue in terms of limited English proficiency (LEP).[15] With respect to cultural issues, the government has coined the term CLAS, an acronym that stands for *culturally and linguistically appropriate services*.[16] Whereas the LEP documentation is in the form of policy guidance, the CLAS information reflects actual standards. The point is that the government has determined that deficiencies in language accommodation and cultural sensitivity have a direct influence on the quality of communication. In the health care area, this includes the consent process.

In May 2004, the Centers for Medicare and Medicaid Services revised the *State Operations Manual (Interpretive Guidelines)* used by state surveyors to assess compliance with the Conditions of Participation in Medicare and Medicaid. Some of the changes applicable to hospitals affect consent to treatment. In particular, a requirement to inform patients of the names and responsibilities of those involved in treatment caused much concern, especially among teaching hospitals. As noted by many health care risk management professionals, hospitals might not know until the last moment which resident will participate in a patient's care. A patient might have been sedated by the time the resident is assigned to the case. This makes it very difficult to effect a complete consent process as delineated in the CMS interpretive guidelines.

The interpretation is apt to change in light of the practical issue. One idea is to tell patients that residents, interns, students, and so on, will be involved in treatment and include an explanation of the role or responsibility of these individuals. The disclosure to patients would include a statement that the names of these individuals will not be known until immediately before the procedure. In the post-procedure note, the names and roles of those participant would be documented.

Like other guidance described earlier, the *Interpretive Guidelines* do not have the effect of law. Still, from a risk management and consent perspective, the content is important for two reasons. First, the content might influence court decisions, especially in those situations in which a judge is discussing regulatory intent. Second, the *Interpretive Guidelines* offer a "window" on regulatory compliance. They are a road map that tell a hospital what to anticipate in terms of a validation or complaint survey. Turning it around, the *Interpretive Guidelines* serve as a blueprint for hospital operations. The same holds true in the consent arena. Designing consent policies and procedures to meet such guidance helps avoid regulatory risk exposure.

The cadre of federal legislation, rules, and regulations that shape patients' rights and responsibilities create legal concerns and risk exposures. The sanctions can be quite serious, including decertification from federal funding programs, civil monetary penalties, and in the case of corporate compliance, imposition of a corporate integrity program. Insurance coverages may be limited when dealing with the costs of defending a regulatory proceeding. Insurers will not reimburse health care organizations for criminal fines. Hence, there is a substantial financial loss exposure that stems from the "federal drivers" of consent. Coupled with the fallout from adverse media coverage, the reputational and financial loss exposure merits innovations in using the consent process as a loss control tool. Getting to this point requires the risk management professional to have a firm knowledge of the basic elements of the consent process.

....

BASIC ELEMENTS OF CONSENT TO TREATMENT

Although the laws vary from jurisdiction to jurisdiction, several elements generally are recognized as integral to the consent process. These elements involve not only what information should be disclosed to the patient or surrogate decision maker, but also the qualifications for who may authorize or decline treatment. These factors apply to so-called elective care situations in which there is sufficient time to obtain relevant history and to exchange pertinent information.

The law presumes that an adult is capable of making a treatment choice. Sometimes this "ability to consent" is extended to minors. This includes those minors who are emancipated, living independently from their parents or guardians. In other cases, the law has carved out certain treatment-specific exceptions that enable even unemancipated minors to authorize treatment. For example, minors who seek treatment for substance abuse, sexually transmitted diseases, and other "sensitive" types of issues may be authorized to obtain care without consent of a guardian or parent. In other situations, these procedure-specific laws enable minors to donate blood. These laws are very dependent upon the criteria found in a specific state. Some set age thresholds for when a minor is legally "capable" of making such decisions. In others, although there is not requirement to obtain consent from a guardian or parent, leeway is given to the caregiver to notify parents in some instances.

Sometimes the law removes the right of an individual to give or decline consent to treatment. A court determination may be for a specific treatment—such as court-ordered treatment for tuberculosis —or on a permanent basis, where a finding is made that the individual can no longer make treatment choices. When a court appoints a guardian of the "person" to make health care decisions on behalf of the patient it signifies a judicial determination that the person is legally incapable of making treatment choices. From a practical standpoint, however, many caregivers still involve the patient in the dialogue to the extent that is practical. The rationale is that the patient might have important information about prior treatments, allergies, and so on, that could influence the care plan recommended for the individual.

The law also assumes that every individual has the requisite mental capability to make a treatment decision. In essence, it is a belief that the person can weigh the pros and cons of recommended and alternate care to make a treatment choice. The law recognizes, however, that patients may lack such ability due to injury, egregious pain, the influence of medication, illegal drugs, or alcohol abuse. The law will not tell a caregiver who is and who is not mentally capable of making a treatment choice. This necessitates a case-by-case determination by the caregiver. Sometimes the results can be surprising. For example, a person may have a blood alcohol level that is over the legal limit for driving under the influence yet the individual has the ability to make cogent treatment choices. From a risk management standpoint, it is important to work with caregivers to develop practical criteria for making such a determination and designing a framework for documenting such an assessment. This is especially important in cases fraught with ethical implications. Care providers might be very much opposed to a patient's decision, yet they are legally and morally obliged to respect it. A clinical impression of mental incapacity may serve as a pretext to overruling the patient's choice. Such a paternalistic approach must be avoided. Risk management professionals engaged in consent education programs often appropriately reinforce the point that care providers must not insert their values in place of those of their patients. Also reinforced in these programs is the need to respect patients' rights and to make use of ethics committees in difficult cases.

Aside from legal capability and mental capacity to make a treatment choice, many jurisdictions have delineated the fundamental elements of what should be disclosed to the person making a treatment choice. These elements include:

- A disclosure of the nature and purpose of the proposed test or treatment
- A description of the probable risks and benefits of the test or treatment
- An explanation of alternate tests or treatment and the probable risks and benefits associated with these options
- An explanation of the probable risks and benefits of forgoing proposed or alternate tests or treatment
- An opportunity to ask questions and receive understandable answers
- An opportunity to make a decision free of coercion and undue influence

As a practical starting point, the consent conversation must be geared to the comprehension level of the patient. Medical jargon is unacceptable for most patients. However, talking down to a patient to the point that the patient is insulted or "turned off" is equally unacceptable.

The degree or extent of disclosure is a matter of sharp legal differences of opinion. The majority position, the "patient need" standard, requires disclosure of "material" or significant information that a reasonable person, in the same or a similar position as the patient, would want to know so as to make a treatment choice. The minority perspective is based on what the "medical community" believes the patient should know.

Whether the risk manager works in a jurisdiction that follows the patient need or the medical community standard, the risk management stand is to furnish relevant, understandable information that will prevent or eliminate any misinformation or misunderstanding. In practical terms, this means conveying to patients information regarding:

- The risk of death, disability, disfigurement, or major change in lifestyle
- The degree of pain, dysfunction, or discomfort associated with the test or treatment
- The time commitment associated with proposed and alternate treatments, including rehabilitation, physical therapy, or long-term medication management
- The urgency to undergo the test or treatment
- The consequences of deferring the test or treatment

Many care providers find it difficult to discuss certain types of risk information with patients.[17] Known risks should be discussed with the patient. Generally speaking, remote risks need not be disclosed except in a few well-defined situations. If there is a risk of death, albeit remote, associated with a contemplated procedure such risk should be discussed. The risk of death from general anesthesia is a frequently cited example. The anesthesiologist or nurse anesthetist is obliged to disclose to the patient that death is a possibility, albeit a remote one. In this instance, the risk management point to convey to care providers who are uneasy about such discussions is that their effectiveness rests on two important elements: what is said to the patient and how the message is delivered. Remote risks can be put in an appropriate context to enable patients to make informed choices. From a risk management standpoint the use of statistics should be discouraged in this regard because many patients do not have a framework for understanding what a 15-percent risk of death from anesthesia or surgery really means.

·············
EXCEPTIONS TO THE GENERAL RULES OF CONSENT

The requirements for a valid consent to treatment are not absolute. Indeed, the law recognizes several exceptions to the rule, including exceptions for emergency treatment, impracticality of consent, therapeutic privilege, compulsory treatment situations, and the recently recognized psychiatric advance directive.[18]

Emergency Treatment Exception

The emergency treatment exception is well recognized in case law[19] and in legislation.[20] Although the specifics vary from jurisdiction to jurisdiction, the basic criteria are the same:

- The patient presents with a life-threatening illness or injury that requires immediate attention.
- The patient is unable to either communicate or take part in a communication process.
- There is no time to secure a treatment authorization from someone else who might be empowered by law to act on the patient's behalf.

When these criteria are met, the law implies a treatment authorization on behalf of the patient for such diagnostic tests or treatments as are medically necessary to alleviate a life-threatening event. In doing so, the law assumes that if patients were capable of participating in the consent process, they would readily agree to the course of treatment provided.

The emergency treatment exception authorizes only care that is medically necessary to rectify the urgent situation. Medically necessary care can be quite expansive, including removal of organs, amputation of limbs, and the causing of a miscarriage. However, it does not authorize a care provider to perform tests or treatments that are not immediately required. Thus, a surgeon might be within the scope of the emergency exception in removing a patient's ruptured spleen, but not in removing a pigmented nevus on that patient's abdomen.

From a risk management perspective, it is important to understand that the law will not sanction the application of the emergency exception when a patient is temporarily incapacitated by a preoperative medication and there is neither a life- nor health-threatening event that necessitates urgent surgical intervention. A competent patient in the midst of a health-threatening event still enjoys the right to refuse treatment. The emergency exception does not preempt the competent patient's right to refuse treatment.

Caregivers often have difficulty accepting the fact that a competent person may decline life-saving care when confronted with the potential of death or serious harm from a heart attack, stroke, allergic reaction, or asthmatic attack. As health professionals trained to save life, they feel that the better approach is to intervene to provide treatment. In doing so, they minimize the power of the law and the significance of the principle of individual choice-making. Judges and juries alike are apt to react quite negatively in cases in which the patient had made clear a choice not to undergo treatment when confronted with a life- or health-threatening event. In such instances, the risk is one of a battery claim in which there need not be proof of actual harm to the individual.

Today, the right to refuse life-saving care is closely connected with end-of-life decision-making. Although there is a substantial amount of overlap between the two topics, it should be understood that the competent patient can decline treatment designed to save life or health without any requirement that the situation involve a terminal illness. This is particularly important in EMTALA-style cases and emergency department treatment decisions.

Risk management professionals know that most emergency cases are not "black and white" episodes. Indeed, many cases are filled with shades of gray that necessitate uncovering factual information to substantiate that a true emergency does exist. To this end, several steps can be taken to minimize inappropriate use of the exception including:

- Clinical pathways for declaring an emergency
- Decision trees for declaring an emergency
- Education on the emergency treatment exception for new hires and in-service for regular staff
- Mandatory training and in-service for contracted employees of the emergency and urgent care departments
- Documentation to substantiate the declaration of an emergency
- Documentation to substantiate compliance with a patient directive declining treatment in an emergency

··········

IMPRACTICALITY OF CONSENT

A variation on the emergency exception is impracticality of consent.[21] Although it is not well-defined in law, it reflects many of the treatment situations found in emergency departments and urgent care centers. Like the true emergency situation, the patient presents with a life-threatening or health-threatening event that requires *immediate treatment*. However, unlike the true emergency situation, the patient *is able* to communicate with the treatment team. The urgency of the situation, however, precludes the opportunity for a full discussion of the indications for treatment, an explanation of care, probable benefits, probable risks, and treatment alternatives.

From a risk management perspective, consent policies and procedures should include a framework for managing impracticality of consent. Care providers should be oriented to managing impracticality of consent situations. This would include:

- Situations in which the exception is applicable, for example, patients who present in shock due to a bee sting, gunshot wound, allergic reaction, *and* who are capable of communication

- What questions to ask of such cognitive and communicative patients, for example, details of current medications, allergy or drug sensitivity history, and so on

- What information to share with the patient, for example, what the team will be doing to address the life-threatening or health-threatening event

- Answering patient questions as the situation permits, noting that after the immediate event is over, a more detailed discussion will take place with the individual

- Documentation of the reason(s) for using the impracticality of consent exception

Therapeutic Privilege Exception

In comparison to the emergency treatment provision, the therapeutic exception is a far more nebulous concept. This exception usually applies in narrowly drawn circumstances in which the disclosure of certain information is believed to cause the patient a risk of significant harm (likely to be psychogenic or psychobiologic in nature).

To invoke the therapeutic privilege exception, certain criteria must be met. These include a full assessment of the facts and circumstances of the patient's case and condition and a medical opinion that a full disclosure of information will have a significant or seriously adverse effect on the patient.[22] Typically, this is done in accordance with well-delineated policy and procedure in the health care organization. Many health care entities require that the assessment be performed by a person expert in psychiatry. To be certain that the evaluation is objective, the person making the assessment is one who is not otherwise involved in the care and treatment of the patient. If the "second opinion" confirms the need for therapeutic privilege, this assessment is documented in the medical record along with the rationale for it.

From a risk management standpoint, caregivers are often encouraged to document what they disclose to the patient in the therapeutic privilege context, in addition to what was not revealed in the discussion. This may be done as a concurrent note in the medical record. If it is determined after the test or treatment that the patient's status is such that untoward harm is not likely to occur as a result of the disclosure, the caregiver may explain to the patient "why" information was withheld and the nature of the details that had not been imparted earlier. The fact that such a discussion took place should also be documented in the medical record.

The therapeutic privilege exception does not negate the obligation to inform the patient. Rather, it grants the care provider leeway in the degree of disclosure surrounding those details that are apt to cause harm to the patient. From a risk management perspective, the exception requires careful application and detailed documentation to verify that it was used appropriately.

Compulsory Treatment Exception

The compulsory treatment situation is another type of exception from the general rules of consent. In essence, the law makes a value judgment that the rights and liberties of the individual must give way for the greater good and health of the community. As such, the compulsory treatment exception is largely rooted in public health legislation, empowering officials to quarantine, test, or treat individuals with infectious illnesses.[23] Even in the context of this exception, however, there are safeguards to obviate inappropriate use of public health legislation as a mechanism for circumventing the law of consent to treatment.

············

EFFECTIVE COMMUNICATION IN THE CONSENT PROCESS

Communicating in practical terms that the patient can understand may involve use of several communication channels. In addition to face-to-face verbal explanations, media may include video displays, interactive computer programs, and printed items such as brochures, pamphlets, or information sheets. From a risk management perspective, the key point is that the message conveyed in all the media must be consistent, because discrepancies create an opportunity to challenge the integrity of the consent process. It also is important to remember that multimedia resources, though useful tools, are ancillary to the care provider-patient communication that underpins the consent process.

In today's Internet society, communication is a serious issue in terms of informed consent. Patients access the Web and may find a host of sites that offer information pertinent to their health care needs. Some of the Web sites are legitimate locations that contain valid information. Other sites, however, although crafted by well-intentioned individuals, contain personal observations or "life experiences" that cannot be validated or replicated for others. This is also true of medical "blog" sites on the Internet and consumer listservs dedicated to specific illnesses. Reliance on such information could lead to imprudent health choices by patients.

Why do patients "surf the Web" if their caregivers are furnishing them with salient information? The answer is that there is a level of distrust among today's health care consumers that they are not getting the "full story" and that they should do their own independent research lest they rely on inadequate information in making treatment decisions. Marketing by self-help and health information Web sites promotes such activity.

Confronted with a multitude of pamphlets, brochures, booklets, information sheets, and videotapes, there is a danger that patients can be confused rather than informed in making choices. Add to this abundant Internet material that contradicts or casts doubt on details provided by caregivers, and there is a shift from confusion to doubt or uncertainty. Patients are primed to confront caregivers with challenges demanding to know why they were not told about risks or treatment alternatives they found on the Internet. Indeed, enterprising plaintiffs' counsel will use such information to raise questions about the completeness of the "informed" consent process.

The role of the risk manager is to restore order to consent as a communications process. This may involve preemptive practice assessments including:

- Inventory of media used for conveying information to patients
- Consistency of information disseminated to patients
- Reviewing content of patient information Web sites sponsored by the health care entity
- Providing "sanctioned" Web addresses to patients
- Warnings that some Web addresses, blogs, and listservs may contain information that is not scientifically proven or valid, and to exercise caution in relying on treatment details at these sites

Patients today are also hearing more and more about alternate and complementary medicine. Some use herbal supplements or remedies to treat mood swings, joint pain, and the symptoms of menopause. The failure to acknowledge this practice may lead to misdiagnosis or treatments with severe adverse results. Part of the contemporary risk management consent toolkit is to ask salient questions during the communication process that reveal such treatment practices. Once the information is in hand, appropriate treatment plans can be recommended to the patient.

Another communication-related consideration is the choice of messenger. Ideally, the person who is to perform the test or treatment should secure the patient's authorization. This step does not involve the administrative or clerical act of securing the patient's signature on a treatment authorization. Rather, the focal point of the consent process is on the communication exchange—the solicitation of critical information from the patient and the dissemination of relevant details in return. Another care provider is less likely to complete a successful consent process due to being less familiar with the patient's history, needs, and desires. Thus, relying on another to fulfill this task might create information gaps that culminate in consent claims.

Sometimes missing in the communication aspect of informed consent is confirmation of the successful exchange of information. A consent form is evidence of the process; however, it typically provides little to substantiate that decisions were made with an understanding of benefits, risk, alternatives, opting for alternative and complementary therapy, and the consequences of declining all care.

The confirmation aspect of communication can occur in several ways. Establishing a consistent protocol of questions that substantiates a confirmation of communication is one method. Making it a "usual and customary practice" might suffice in some states. However, a better approach is to use a checklist or some other form of documentation. Posing confirmatory questions is a useful risk management tool. Rather than asking patients, "Do you understand what I have been saying?," the approach is to ask open-ended questions such as, "Tell me in your own words what you understand to be involved in the operation." Patient response with appropriate answers is a confirmation of the communication process. From a risk management standpoint, the use of a confirmatory dialogue is important in especially risk-prone situations, including those in which the patient has communication challenges that are accommodated by use of devices (language boards, TTY, teletype) or interpreters. Documenting that the patient gave knowledgeable responses to such questions affirms that the communication was effective. A similar process may be used with surrogate decision-makers.

Importance of an Informed Refusal of Care

Although most health care professionals recognize the importance of informed choice in leading to a patient's agreement to some type of diagnostic test or treatment, the same level of recognition is not always present in regard to informed refusals of care. Because the law has given particular recognition to the need for patients to decline tests or treatment on the basis of informed choice-making,[24] informed refusal is an important concept.

The leading case on the topic involved a patient in California who repeatedly declined recommendations from her primary care physician to undergo a pap smear.[25] Ultimately, she died of cervical cancer, leaving two minor children as survivors. The children sued the primary care physician for lack of informed refusal of care, successfully persuading the court that it was not sufficient for a care provider simply to recommend a diagnostic test. Instead, they argued, the duty to inform goes further, requiring the care provider to ensure that a patient's decision to refuse or decline tests or treatment is an informed decision.[26]

This California case has become a legal benchmark. To the extent that it is practical to do so, care providers need to discuss with their patients the consequences of declining tests or treatment and to document this phase of the consent process. In this way, patients are hard-pressed to claim later that a decision to forgo tests or treatment was based on inadequate disclosure of information. Informed refusal of care has applications beyond routine care in the physician's office. It is equally applicable in emergency department (ED) settings where decisions to forgo transfer to another facility or to decline admission for care have profound legal implications under EMTALA provisions of applicable federal and state law. (See Chapter 10 of this volume for additional information.)

For an informed refusal of care to be valid, the patient must be legally and mentally capable of making a choice. When the patient does not meet these criteria, a duly authorized surrogate decision-maker may make the determination. Like the patient, the surrogate decision-maker must be properly informed about the consequences of a refusal of care.

Once the patient (or surrogate decision-maker) has made an informed choice to refuse care, it is incumbent upon care providers to respect that determination.[27] Care providers sometimes find this concept difficult to apply. Nonetheless, the law does not permit them—however well-intentioned—to substitute their values and beliefs regarding what is "best" for those of their patients. Furthermore, the law expects that in providing patients with the requisite degree of information needed to make a treatment choice, care providers will deliver the details about the pros and cons of treatment even-handedly. Failure to do so creates a needless risk of exposure for lawsuits based on lack of informed refusal of care.

············

THE RIGHT OF THE PATIENT TO WITHDRAW CONSENT

Patients have the right to withdraw a valid treatment authorization. From a risk management standpoint, it is important to ask "when" a patient can make such a decision. A Wisconsin ruling offers an answer on the issue of "change of mind" in the informed consent process.[28]

A patient, pregnant for the third time, was informed by her doctor that although she had previously undergone Caesarean deliveries, she should have a vaginal birth after Caesarean (VBAC) this time. The doctor suggested that, if medically necessary, a Caesarean section would be performed. During admission, the patient signed both a consent form for a vaginal delivery and another regarding a Caesarean section. Several hours later, when the doctor came in to see the patient, she told him she wanted to have a Caesarean section. The doctor responded by encouraging her to stick to the original delivery plan. When the patient's labor was not proceeding as had been anticipated, the doctor broke the amniotic sac to accelerate the process. The patient suffered such severe abdominal pain that the medication did not work. Once again, the patient informed the doctor that she had changed her mind and that she wanted a Caesarean section. The doctor indicated that if he acceded to all such requests, all deliveries would be accomplished by Caesarean section.

When the baby's heart rate dropped, an emergency Caesarean section was performed. The outcome was poor. The mother's uterus had ruptured and the lack of oxygen left the child with spastic quadriplegia, unable to speak and unable to move below her neck.

In remanding the case for a determination of damages, the Supreme Court of Wisconsin reasoned that once a medical procedure has commenced, the patient does not relinquish the right to withdraw consent to treatment. Much depends on the circumstances of each case and the specific treatment alternatives in deciding when there is no turning back. In this case, Caesarean section was an alternative form of delivery and therefore, the patient was able to withdraw her consent to vaginal childbirth. By changing her mind, the patient set in motion a responsibility to complete a new informed consent discussion.

This "change of mind" case points out a critical component of risk management training on informed consent. It is imperative to sensitize caregivers to recognize consent "speed bumps" put in place by patients or substitute decision makers. As long as the point of no return has not been reached and there are treatment options, the patient has the right to opt out of an agreed-upon course of care.

············
NEEDS OF SPECIFIC PATIENTS IN THE INFORMED CONSENT PROCESS

Many states have singled out specific categories of patients for special consideration under the law of consent to treatment. These categories include minors, elderly patients, mentally disabled or challenged persons, and those undergoing tests or treatment for certain diseases such as HIV, blood transfusion therapy, or breast cancer.

Care should be exercised in generalizing about the requirements for consent with regard to specific patient groups or types of tests or treatment. Much of the law is quite state-specific, necessitating specific legal advice and policy and procedure to address these matters.

Although state law is quite specific in this area, remember the basic requirements for a valid consent process. The law presumes that a patient possesses both legal competency and mental capability to make a treatment choice. Only in certain specific situations does the law require a different approach to the consent process. Such requirements typically go into effect when:

- Legislation varies the general rules of consent
- Court orders require specific treatment or bar certain care
- The facts of a given consent trigger the need for a determination of legal competency or mental capacity to make a treatment choice

JCAHO

Aside from the law, there are very practical reasons for managing the consent process differently with certain categories of patients. These include:

- Auditory, speech, or visually impaired patients
- Culturally sensitive consent situations
- Linguistic barriers between patients and care providers

Preliminary screening of patients can eliminate the risk that the process will unravel due to the patient's inability to hear, speak, or see sufficiently to engage in a valid consent process. Indeed, this risk can be obviated by telling patients at the outset that the care provider or facility is sensitive to such needs and encourages patients to disclose them. By the same token, care providers should be trained in methods that help detect those patients who need assistive devices, such as TDD (telephone devices for the deaf) or TTY (teletype).

Most health care entities are required to make reasonable accommodation to meet the needs of patients with a disability that could impair the consent process.[29] Some states have gone further, requiring the use of interpreters for those who confront a linguistic barrier to an effective consent process.[30] These are laws that have heightened awareness about regulatory compliance. This emphasis on related regulatory compliance is also reflected in the federal initiatives dealing with LEPs, discussed earlier.

Cultural sensitivity is also an important consideration.[31] Although sometimes difficult to embrace in policy and procedure, cultural sensitivity reflects an awareness of what is disclosed to a patient and by whom. For example, discussion of urogenital anomalies or surgery by a male clinician with a female patient can be culturally charged and can cause the consent process to become derailed. In other situations, the cultural context of patients from other countries may make it difficult for them to understand such things as the meaning of over-the-counter medications, home remedies, and so on. Good risk management in this regard demands identification of the cultural needs in the catchment area served by the health care organization. In addition, the consent policy and procedure should be flexible enough to accommodate the needs of patients who object to such discussions. The content for such a policy and procedure may be influenced to some extent by the CLAS standards described earlier.

Another class of patients has been singled out for special consideration in obtaining informed consent. A number of states have enacted laws that empower patients to execute an advance directive for mental health services. Like the advance directives that take effect when a patient is incapacitated due to the effects of injury, coma, anesthesia, or terminal illness, the psychiatric advance directive comes into effect when a mental health patient is unable to participate in treatment decision-making. The statutes vary from state to state, but the goal is the same: afford mental health patients the opportunity to delineate treatment choices or preferences while they are capable of making such decisions. The statutes typically include some limitations on what a person may or may not request. Nonetheless, the exception is an important one from a risk management standpoint.

Having such tools in place can avoid a lot of confusion, misunderstanding, and delays in care in the middle of a psychiatric event. The use of a psychiatric advance directive may obviate the need for going to court and seeking a court order or the appointment of a person to act on behalf of the patient. As such, it is a tool that should be considered in consent policy and procedure. The use of the psychiatric advance directive requires orientation and in-service training for those likely to encounter patients with such documents, including personnel in the emergency department, urgent care, and behavioral services. Because the psychiatric advance directive was singled out for discussion in the preamble discussion to the Patients' Rights Standards under the Conditions of Participation for Hospitals in Medicare and Medicaid,[32] it is a topic that also merits review from a regulatory compliance perspective.

Although the law views consent as a process between patient and care provider, it is not uncommon for family members to be involved in the discussion. This "family-focused" consent process is a practice sanctioned by the Joint Commission on Accreditation of Healthcare Organizations (JCAHO). Family involvement is not necessarily a sign that the patient distrusts the care provider. Indeed, family members may facilitate the process by furnishing additional details that the patient is unable to recall. Furthermore, from a loss control perspective, family involvement affords an opportunity to set expectations and establish a strong relationship. This rapport may be beneficial in short-circuiting potential litigation if untoward consequences result from tests or treatment.

The benefit of family involvement is reflected in the ASHRM white paper, "Perspective on Disclosure of Unanticipated Outcomes of Care."[33] Consistent with the JCAHO Patient Safety Standard on disclosure of treatment outcomes, the disclosure should be directed to the patient, and when practical, the family.[34] As discussed in the ASHRM white paper, having a rapport with the patient and patient's family is important. The communication component of the consent process helps set the context for discussing adverse and unanticipated outcomes of care.[35] (For further discussion on this topic, see the ASHRM Disclosure Monograph Series available at [www.ashrm.org]. See also Chapter 3 in this text.)

From a risk management standpoint, it is critical that consent policy and procedure recognize state-specific exceptions and delineate an appropriate, practical process for securing a treatment decision in these matters. The same holds true for involving the family in the consent process, taking into account patient confidentiality and HIPAA Privacy Standards requirements (see Chapter 18 in Volume III of this series). This approach can avert needless risk exposure and potential litigation.

••••••••••••
CONSENT REQUIREMENTS ALONG THE CONTINUUM OF CARE

Consent to treatment has long been associated with hospitals. For many years "consent" has been viewed as a forms-driven necessity to substantiate in writing that the patient agreed to a specific treatment. In reality, consent *as a process* should take place in physicians' offices, clinics, ambulatory care and day surgery centers, and behavioral health units. Consent as a process is very much a part of long-term care, end-stage renal dialysis, and hospice care.

The essential elements for consent to treatment remain the same along the continuum of care. However, some differences merit recognition from a risk management perspective. For example, in the end stage renal dialysis setting in which patients may present for repetitive care three times a week, there need be only one consent process. This process is completed at the outset of care. During each repeat visit, screening questions are posed to "rule out" treatment and "rule in" the need for an assessment of the patient. Questions posed may include:

- Did you follow your renal diet?
- Did you take your medications?
- Have you seen any other care providers, including dentists who added new medications to your treatment regimen? If so, what medications were added?

- Have you had any complications, such as fever, chills, nausea?
- Have you experienced any problems with the canula site such as redness, soreness, or swelling? (The care provider doing the screening will also examine the canula site.)

If there have been changes that shift the risk-benefit analysis on which the initial consent was based, the situation calls for a new consent process. This risk management approach to consent can avoid untoward consequences in repetitive treatment settings while obviating the need for a new consent process each time the patient presents for care.

Other settings of care might warrant very specific consent procedures. For example, some states require a specific consent for patients involved in telemedicine treatment.[36] In this type of treatment setting the patient is in one location while the care provider interpreting an X-ray, CT scan, or MRI is located in another state or country. Because the doctor is *not* on location and the information is being transmitted electronically, it necessitates a different type of consent process.

Friction can occur between physicians and health care facilities regarding the proper location of the consent process. Surgeons may spend considerable amounts of time discussing surgical procedures. This discussion typically takes place in the surgeon's office or clinic. The patient may execute a consent document in the office or clinic. At the day surgery center or the acute care facility, the patient is asked to sign an additional consent for the procedure. Not only is this confusing for the patient, it presents a risk management concern. Many times the content of the facility-based consent document is inconsistent with what the patient signed in the care provider's office or clinic. Rather than cementing the treatment authorization process, this duality of consents serves as the basis for confusion. In some situations, when there is marked variation between the consent information, the integrity of the consent to treatment may be eviscerated.

All health care organizations, physician practices, and clinics might not have the same needs in the consent process. However, they have a shared purpose: quality, safe care for the patient. Risk management professionals can take steps to rectify the potential risk stemming from the duality of consent processes. This might involve a streamlined consent process, an explanation to patients of the reason for separate consent documentation, and an explanation of why the content information varies from the care provider's location to the hospital or day surgery unit setting. Education is vital for staff and physician orientation consistent with the elimination of the confusion with consent processes along the continuum of care.

. . . .
RESULTS OF A BREAKDOWN IN THE CONSENT PROCESS

Traditionally, consent litigation was premised on battery, an intentional tort that did not require proof of actual harm. In most states, patients can sue on several different legal theories for ineffective informed consent. These include:

- Negligent consent: An unintentional tort that requires actual injury emanating from failure to follow appropriate standards for completing the consent process, resulting in causally linked and reasonably foreseeable harm
- Misrepresentation or deceit: The failure to honestly disclose important information or the act of presenting details in a way that misstates such details, resulting in an authorization that otherwise would have been withheld by the patient. In many jurisdictions, this type of claim carries with it the prospect of punitive damages

- Breach of contract: A claim premised on traditional notions of contract law in which the patient asserts that the care provider guaranteed or promised a certain result that was not achieved. This is most likely to happen in elective procedures involving plastic surgery, orthodontics, or other restorative fields of medical or dental care

- Battery: The traditional basis for claims involving an unauthorized test or treatment. Battery also can be asserted in cases in which a patient has withdrawn consent and the care provider nonetheless proceeds with the test or treatment

- Corporate liability: Perhaps the least likely basis for a consent claim, but nonetheless a source of consternation for health care risk managers. Traditionally, consent responsibilities have been reviewed as a duty of care of the attending care provider. However, to the extent that health care facilities intrude into and impose conditions and requirements upon the consent process, the risk of corporate liability for defective consents has increased. Corporate liability may also follow from "constructive notice" of a flawed consent process that was known to an allied health professional who did not follow health care facility policy and procedure and inform a supervisor of the problem. Coupled with a health care facility's mission statement, bylaws, and policies and procedures that speak to the institution's responsibility to safeguard patient care and well-being, the groundwork may be in place for such a claim to be made.

- Licensure action: The failure to follow applicable laws and regulations in the consent process may form the basis for a complaint based on unprofessional conduct under state licensing laws. This may occur as an administrative proceeding stemming from the same set of facts that forms the basis for civil litigation.

- Compliance action: The Conditions of Participation for Hospitals in Medicare and Medicaid include patients' rights standards (COPs).[37] It is possible that a serious breach of the compliance standards relative to the patient's role in care planning and treatment decision making may trigger regulatory scrutiny. In some instances this might involve allegations of regulatory non-compliance or a breach of the Conditions of Participation. Because this may affect Medicare and Medicaid certification, it is a matter that should be taken seriously.

cannot be delegated physician must do

By far, the most likely basis for claim is negligent consent. It may be asserted as an ancillary claim in a professional liability lawsuit or may proceed as a separate basis for claim. The point to remember is that consent is a viable basis for litigation. With the prospect of punitive damages for battery or misrepresentation,[38] consent is an issue ripe for effective risk management treatment.

documentation will help defense — minimal documentation will hurt

COP very clear

A RISK MANAGEMENT AND PATIENT SAFETY APPROACH TO CONSENT TO TREATMENT

From a risk management perspective, several measures can be taken to avoid liability exposure involving consent to treatment. Many of these measures go to the core of patient safety initiatives. Such measures involve:

- Consent policies and procedures
- Consent clinical algorithms or pathways
- Consent risk identifiers

- Education
- Documentation

Each of these is discussed in the following sections as a component of a comprehensive approach to consent as a loss control mechanism. Taken together, these measures represent a practical, hands-on approach to lessening the risk of consent-related litigation.

Consent Policies and Procedures

Consent policies and procedures are central to a loss prevention program; they should be comprehensive, yet practical. The content should address frequently encountered problems, providing health care professionals and management with reasoned, legally appropriate responses. Consent policies and procedures should address all aspects of health care delivery reflected in health care organizations. Thus, a hospital network that merges with a group of nursing homes or purchases a home infusion company needs to expand its consent policies and procedures to address additional informed consent requirements applicable to the acquired services and practice sites.

Certain basic components should be reflected in the consent policies and procedures. Some issues to address include:

- Requirements for a valid consent to treatment
- Assessment for legal and mental capacity to give consent
- Admission requirements
- Patient self-determination requirements
- Surrogate decision-makers
- Requirements for a valid consent to participate in human experimentation
- EMTALA consent requirements
- Managed care consent requirements, for example, assuring that a patient receives information on all treatment options, regardless of whether reimbursement is available from the managed care organization (MCO)
- Documentation requirements
- Handling specific situations
- Anesthesia consents
- Advance directives
- Do-not-resuscitate orders on requests
- Organ procurement
- Authorizations for autopsies
- Handling refusals of care
- HIV testing
- Requests not to use certain types of care, such as blood transfusion therapy

As with other policies and procedures, the content should be field-tested to ensure that it is practical and understandable to end users. Further, it should be reviewed and updated periodically to make certain that any changes in federal or state law, including judicial decisions, are reflected in the policies and procedures.

FIGURE 4.1   Patient Presents

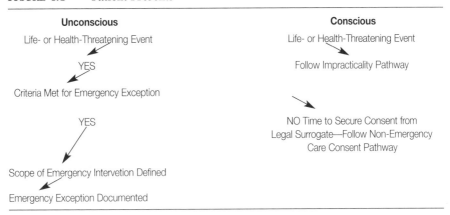

Consent Algorithms

Based on a clearly written policy and procedure clinical pathways or algorithms can help achieve compliance with consent requirements. For example, in the emergency department such an approach might be as follows: for an example of such an approach in the emergency department refer to Figure 4.1.

The pathway must permit individual variations. Such variations would be documented to explain why the process was not followed. Follow-up action would be taken to address non-compliance with the pathway to reduce potential liability risk and patient safety concerns.

Consent Risk Identifiers

A comprehensive loss program should include monitoring for consent risk exposures. A broad approach to such monitoring includes the use of quality outcome data, patient satisfaction information, and the results gleaned from incident reports, loss runs, and litigation files. In addition, personnel should be encouraged to report consent risk situations, including disputes among family members regarding appropriate treatment for an incompetent relatives, managed care-linked EMTALA problems in the ED, and refusals of care from questionably "capable" individuals. Effective patient history screening is a potent tool in identifying potential consent problems. For example, a patient or family member who presents with conflicting history information might be withholding important data that could affect the risk-benefit analysis of one form of care over another. This can happen with placement of an elderly person in an institutional care setting, when the relative selectively discloses information in the hope that the elderly patient will be situated in an assisted-living environment rather than a nursing facility or skilled nursing facility.

In other situations the information disclosed by the patient or relative might reveal unrealistic expectations of care or treatment outcome. This, too, is a risk-prone situation that should be addressed appropriately.

In some instances, potential pitfalls may be found in the way the sequence of consent processes is designed to work. For example, consent documentation for surgery might include a provision for patients to be informed of the option to participate in autologous blood donation and storage programs. If the notification is dated the same day or the day before an elective surgical procedure, the result is that the patient was not notified or informed of the autologous blood program until it was too late to participate in this transfusion plan, providing glaring evidence of an inadequate consent process.

Traditionally, incomplete consent documentation has been viewed as a sentinel indicator of risk. Although this is certainly a valid consent risk identifier, it does not relieve a health care entity of the need to ferret out other, perhaps less obvious risk exposures in the processes.

Education

Risk management professionals should never assume that health care professionals know how to properly secure a valid consent to treatment. Much is learned in clinical mentoring, including a discussion of inappropriate methods for communicating information to patients and recording a treatment authorization. To lessen the likelihood of liability exposure, it is prudent to include orientation and regular in-service education on the proper way to secure a valid consent to treatment.

Education efforts regarding informed consent have become far more expansive than was previously the case. With hospitals and other health care entities taking on increased roles in home health care, hospice, long-term care, sub-acute care, and ambulatory care, the horizon has broadened with respect to who must—and actually does—obtain consent to treatment. Therefore it is important for risk managers to think broadly about who needs education on consent to treatment processes and practices.

Documentation

Consent documentation is important as a mechanism to memorialize in writing the scope of a treatment authorization. It is not a replacement for the consent process. Selecting the best method or methods for documenting consent is a collaborative activity involving care providers, legal counsel, and the risk manager.

Some health care entities prefer the long-form consent, which delineates risks, benefits, alternatives, and additional information. Others prefer the short-form consent, which basically indicates only that a valid consent transaction occurred. A third approach calls for a detailed note in the patient record, with or without execution of a specific consent form. The note should record the time and date of the transaction and should be signed by the provider who informed the individual and secured the authorization. This customized approach is considered to be more credible and genuine than a standard "boiler plate" consent form. A fourth method is the checklist consent form, which has categories that are checked off by the care provider who secures the patient's consent. Once the consent process is completed, the form is signed by the provider and, in some locations, the patient. The form, designed to meet state law requirements, provides ample room for the care provider to detail the probable risks, probable benefits, and treatment alternatives for the patient, along with the risks of forgoing care. This approach is seen as a compromise between the traditional long-form consent and the detailed note in the record. Because it is streamlined and allows for the document to be customized to a specific patient, the checklist consent form may be seen as a reasonable approach to memorializing the consent process. Regardless of the method chosen, it is important that the process is consistent with applicable federal and state laws governing documentation.

The importance of the format of a consent form has been the subject of significant debate. Consent documentation that uses a small font might be setting the stage for risk exposure if the print is so small that it cannot be read easily by the patient or surrogate decision-maker. Indeed, provision has been made in the Medicare Carrier Manual for suggesting that the Advance Beneficiary Notice (ABN) be printed in 12-point type.[39]

Taking the lead from Medicare, it is important to develop a format that is easily read by the intended recipient. This might mean "field testing" different document styles and fonts to find the one that is best for the service population. Although the form does not replace the consent communication process, if the supporting documentation is unreadable, it does little to substantiate an effective consent process did, in fact, occur.

Another issue that often comes up with consent documentation is the matter of signatures on traditional consent forms. There are different signatures for different purposes. The physician usually signs traditional documents to verify completion of the consent process. If evidence disputes that the process was completed properly, the signature could be used against the practitioner. On the other hand, a signature by a nurse who witnesses the consent process does not attest to the content of the consent process, but rather only provides evidence that the consent process actually took place.

Consent forms, whether the documents are traditional in format or more innovative, do not replace the basic informed consent discussion requirements described in this chapter. Consent is a communication process, not a form. Written evidence that supports a successful consent process is important for purposes of billing, continuity of care, and legal defense to a consent claim. Whatever method of consent documentation is selected, the key is to use it consistently. Failure to do so might signal potential risk concerns, bringing into question why consent was not documented in a specific manner in a given case. It is important to engage health care professionals in the design and development of the documentation system to make certain that they will cooperate and use the documentation format effectively.

The Consent Patient Safety Checklist

The patient safety consent checklist [40] is another concept gaining popularity in health care organizations. As in other areas of health care risk management, typically there has been a faulty assumption that caregivers can recall all the information they need in making critical judgments about patient care. While performing many tasks at once or when fatigued, caregivers might forget certain steps or processes in developing a care plan, assessing a patient, or providing treatment. Consent is no different in this regard. Caregivers might forget to ask salient questions that could mean the difference between a patient receiving a prescription for a medication that is an appropriate addition to their regime or one that interacts severely with the decongestant they take routinely. The care provider also might forget to explain the risk of consuming certain types of foods that can have an adverse effect with respect to certain prescription medications. A checklist that reminds the care provider to ask about over-the-counter preparations, food consumption habits, and related issues can avert needless medication risk exposures.

The Consent Patient Safety Checklist is a tool that helps facilitate the consent process. It promotes patient safety by offering prompts or reminders to caregivers to make certain that key items are addressed in the consent process. These include the following:

- Evaluation of patient or surrogate decision-maker to participate in the consent process
- "Drill down" questions on consent (for example, instead of "Do you take medication?" the line of questions in the tool goes further: "Do you use over-the-counter preparations such as aspirin?"; "Do you use any natural or herbal substances or therapies?"; "Have you seen any other doctors or dentists lately who have prescribed medication for you?")
- Follow-up questions to confirm ability of patient or family to adhere to treatment plan

- Follow-up questions to confirm patient's or surrogate decision-maker's understanding of test or treatment

- Screening questions for continuing care interventions in end-stage renal dialysis, oncology, or allergy immunization, to ascertain if the underlying circumstances have changed to warrant a review before proceeding with care

The Consent Patient Safety Checklist may be customized to a specific service or health care delivery setting. Thus, the tool used in a preoperative workup may be different than the one used in an urgent care center.

The tool may be adapted to serve as "evidence of" consent. This could be done by having the caregiver who uses it sign and date the document. In this way, it substantiates that the consent process was completed. However, unlike the checklist consent form described previously, this is a patient safety tool designed specifically for caregivers.

....

CONCLUSION

Consent is a double-edged sword. When completed properly, the consent process is a potent tool for averting liability claims and the basis for a strong defense to assertions that a patient was not properly informed. However, when the consent process is inadequate or incomplete, it can be used as a weapon against a health care facility or professional.

Viewing consent as a loss control mechanism means designing a process that is both practical and used consistently. It means drawing from legal requirements at the state and federal level, and from the experience of care providers regarding what will and will not work. Further, as with other aspects of loss control, vigilance is required in terms of monitoring and managing risks that emerge, especially given the vortex of change in the health care field, where further modifications can be anticipated that are central to the consent process.

Suggested Readings

Adams, R., and F. A. Rozovsky. *Human Research: A Practical Guide to Regulatory Compliance.* San Francisco: Jossey-Bass, 2003.

"Ethical Issues and Patients' Rights Across the Continuum of Care." Oakbrook Terrace, Ill.: Joint Commission on Accreditation of Healthcare Organizations, 1998.

Rozovsky, F. A. *Consent To Treatment: A Practical Guide* (3rd ed.). Gaithersburg, Md.: Aspen Publishing, 2000 (with annual supplements, including December 2004 Supplement).

Rozovsky, F. A., and J. R. Woods, Editors. *The Handbook of Patient Safety Compliance.* San Francisco: Jossey-Bass, 2005.

Woods, J. R., and F. A. Rozovsky. *What Do I Say? Communicating Intended or Unanticipated Outcomes in Obstetrics.* San Francisco: Jossey-Bass, 2003.

Suggested Web Sites

Agency for Healthcare Research and Quality [www.ahrq.gov].

American Association of Health Plans [www.aahp.org].

American Hospital Association [www.aha.org].

American Academy on Physician and Patient [www.physicianpatient.org].

American Society for Healthcare Risk Management [www.hospitalconnect.com/desktopservlet].

Bayer Institute for Healthcare Communications [www.bayerinstitute.com].

Centers for Medicare and Medicaid Services (CMS), formerly known as the Health Care Financing Administration (HCFA) [www.cms.gov].

Food and Drug Administration [www.fda.gov].

Institute for Healthcare Improvement [www.ihi.org].

Institute for Safe Medication Practices [www.ismp.org].

Institute of Medicine [www.iom.edu].

Joint Commission Accreditation of Health Care Organizations [www.jcaho.org].

National Committee on Quality Assurance [www.ncqa.org].

National Institutes of Health [www.nih.gov].

National Forum for Health Care Quality Measurement and Reporting [www.qualityforum.org].

National Patient Safety Foundation [www.npsf.org].

Partnership for Patient Safety [www.p4ps.org].

Quality Interagency Coordination Task Force (QuIC) [www.quic.gov].

The Business Roundtable [www.brt.org].

The Buyers Health Care Action Group [www.choiceplus.com].

U.S. Pharmacopoeia [www.usp.org].

Endnotes

1. Rozovsky, F. A. *Consent to Treatment: A Practical Guide* (3rd ed.). Gaithersburg, Md.: Aspen Publishing, 2000 (with annual supplements). Consent as a process is the same throughout most of the common-law world and in jurisdictions that follow the Napoleonic Code.

2. Note, however, that payment is not necessary for consent to be informed or valid.

3. See "Perspectives on Disclosure of Unanticipated Outcomes of Care," *ASHRM*, July 2001; and J. R. Woods and F. A. Rozovsky, *What Do I Say? Communicating Intended or Unanticipated Outcomes in Obstetrics*. San Francisco: Jossey-Bass, 2003.

4. The cases most often described as the benchmarks for the contemporary approach to consent to treatment include *Canterbury v. Spence*, 464 F.2d 772 (DC Cir. 1972); *Cobbs v. Grant*, 501 P.2dl (CA 1972); and *Wilkinson v. Vesey*, 295 A.2d 676 (1972). These cases marked a watershed in the field of health law, the repercussions of which have been noted in extensive case law and statutory law on the subject of consent to treatment.

5. State Operations Manual, Interpretive Guidelines for Hospitals, May, 2004.

6. "Participation in Treatment Decisions." Taken from the Consumer Bill of Rights and Responsibilities (Ch. 4). President's Advisory Commission on Consumer Protection and Quality in the Health Care Industry, November 1997.

7. 42 USC §1395dd. The regulations are at 42 C.F.R. §498.24 (1998).

8. 28 C.F.R. §42.405 (1998).

9. "National Standards on Culturally and Linguistically Appropriate Services (CLAS) in Health Care," Fed. Reg. 65(247):pp. 80865, et seq., December 22, 2000.

10. Fed. Reg., 64(127): 36088, (July 2, 1999).

11. 42 USC §§1395cc (a) et seq., as amended (1990). See also, regulations promulgated pursuant to the statute at 57 Fed. Reg. 8,194 et seq. (1992).

12. Rozovsky, F. A., and R. A. Adams, "A Practical Guide to Regulatory Compliance," *Human Research*. San Francisco: Jossey-Bass, 2003.

13. The HIPAA Privacy Rule was first proposed in the Federal Register on November 3, 1999, in 64: 59,918, et seq. The Final Rule, first version, was published on December 28, 2000, in the Federal Register 65: 82462, et seq. The Secretary of Health and Human Services opened the Privacy Rule for additional public comment in March 2001 [See, Fed. Reg. 66 12738] and then made it effective on April 14, 2001 [Fed. Reg. 65: 12433]. On March 27, 2002, the Department of Health and Human Services issued proposed changes to the Privacy Rule [Fed. Reg. 67: 14776]. In the August 14, 2002, Federal Register, the Department issued the revised Final Rule changes with regard to privacy under HIPAA [Fed. Reg. 67(157): 53182, et seq.]

14. See the CDC forms at www.cdc.gov/nip/vacsafe that were developed pursuant to the National Childhood Vaccine Injury Pub. Law No. 99-660 as amended by Pub. Law No. 103–183.

15. "Policy Guidance on the Prohibition Against National Origin Discrimination As It Affects Persons with Limited English Proficiency." Federal Register 65(169): 52762, et seq., August 30, 2000.

16. "National Standards on Culturally and Linguistically Appropriate Services (CLAS) in Health Care," Federal Register 65(247): Pp. 80865, et seq., December 22, 2000.

17. Rozovsky, F. A., and J. R. Woods, Editors. *The Handbook of Patient Safety Compliance*, Chapter 9. San Francisco: Jossey-Bass, 2005.

18. For a detailed examination of the topic, see Rozovsky, *Consent to Treatment*, Chapter 2.

19. Case law on the topic can be found as early as 1906. See, for example, *Pratt v. Davis*, 79 N.E. 562 (Ill., 1906).

20. See, for example, GA Code 31-9-3 (1971).

21. Woods and Rozovsky, *What Do I Say?* See also Rozovsky, *Consent to Treatment*, Chapter 2.

22. Rozovsky, *Consent to Treatment*, 2.4.1.

23. *Ibid.*, 2.5.

24. *Truman v. Thomas*, 611 P.2d. 902 (Cal., 1980).

25. *Ibid.*

26. *Ibid.*

27. *Stamford Hospital v. Vegas*, P 236 Conn. 646 (1996).

28. *Schreiber v. Physicians Insurance Company of Wisconsin*, 588 NW2d 26 (Wis.,1999).

29. See 42 USC sec.12101, et seq. (1990). Title III provides the pertinent legislative requirements on the topic. Although exemptions are provided for certain religious facilities, many have chosen to follow the law.

30. See, for example, 210 ILCS 87/1, et seq. (Smith-Hurd 1994). (Language assistance is required if 5 percent of the population served by a health care facility on an annual basis do not speak English or are limited in their ability to speak English.)

31. For an interesting insight on the topic, see Gostin, L. "Informed Consent, Cultural Sensitivity, and Respect for Persons." *Journal of the American Medical Association*, 274(10), Sept. 13, 1995, pp. 844–845.

32. Fed. Reg. 64: 36070, et seq., July 2, 1999.

33. "Perspective on Disclosure of Unanticipated Outcome Information," *ASHRM*, July 2001.

34. [RI.1.2.2] states: "Patients, and when appropriate, their families are informed about the outcomes of care, including unanticipated outcomes." Comprehensive Manual on Accreditation of Hospitals, 2002 Standards.

35. Woods and Rozovsky, *What Do I Say?*

36. See, e.g. Ariz.Rev.Stat. 36-3602. (2004); Cal. Business & Professional Code § 2290.5. (1998) and Vernons Texas Insurance Code Annotates Art. 21.53F. (2001).

37. Fed. Reg. 64: 36070, et seq., July 2, 1999.

38. See, for example, *Lunsford v. Regents, University of California*, No. 837936 (Superior Ct., San Francisco County, Cal., Apr. 19, 1990).

39. Medicare Carrier Manual, CMS-R-131-G.

40. See Rozovsky, *Consent to Treatment;* see also Woods and Rozovsky, *What Do I Say?*

5

Clinical Research—Institutional Review Boards

Sheila Cohen Zimmet

The successful conduct of medical research in a free society depends on trust between the scientific enterprise and the public, trust in the integrity of the discovery process, and especially trust in the safety of patients and health volunteers who participate in the process. Maintaining strong safeguards for the safety of human subjects in medical research is a paramount obligation of clinical investigators and their institutions. Institutional Review Boards (IRBs) are the heart of the protection regime; they are responsible for reviewing all clinical and translational research conducted at their respective institutions and for making ethical determinations that risks to human subjects have been minimized to the greatest extent possible; risks are reasonable in relation to anticipated benefits, if any; and the risks, benefits, and alternative options are clearly communicated to the potential participants in the informed consent process.[1]

J.J. Cohen
Academic Medical Centers and Medical Research

Governmental vigilance regarding research is intensifying, and noncompliance with pertinent regulations can result in significant loss of dollars, organizational reputation, and community trust, and also potential civil liability. This chapter provides an overview of the history, mandated structure, and regulatory authority for IRBs. The complex requirements that accompany IRBs and risk management strategies also will be addressed.

••••••••••••••

ETHICAL PRINCIPLES

The central concept of the modern system of human subject protection in biomedical research is the primacy of the human subject.[2] It has its roots in the ethical principles of respect for persons, beneficence, and justice, the hallmarks of the Belmont Report issued in 1979 by the National Commission for the Protection of Human Subjects in Biomedical and Behavioral Research. (Refer to Appendix 7.1 in Volume I, Chapter 7 in this series for more information on the Belmont Report. See also the Nuremberg Code [Appendix 7.3 in Volume I, Chapter 7 in this series] and the Declaration of Helsinki at [www.wma.net/e/policy/b3.htm], which provide the accepted ethical standards for international human subject research.)

The underlying ethical principles for the current regulations governing human biomedical research that derive from the Belmont Report are defined in the Report as follows:

● *Respect for persons* means a recognition of the personal dignity and autonomy of individuals, and special protection of those persons with diminished autonomy . . . an affirmative obligation to protect vulnerable populations.

● *Beneficence* involves an obligation to maximize benefits and minimize risks of harm (non-maleficence).

● *Justice* requires a fair distribution of the benefits and burdens of research.

Adherence to these basic ethical concepts ensures that the disadvantaged are not used as research subjects for the benefit of the advantaged, and that the goal of social progress resulting from human research does not take precedence over the rights of the individual subject.[3]

The federal research requirements are founded on respect for the autonomy of the research subject, evidenced by stringent informed consent requirements, the protection of vulnerable populations, the absence of coercion, and the reasonable balance of benefits and burdens of the proposed research for the individual subject, not for society at large. An individual's decision not to participate in research may not in any way affect the ability of the individual to receive medical care or other benefits to which the individual otherwise would be entitled. It is the role of the IRB to review and monitor the conduct of research and to educate the research community about the proper conduct of research.

Is It Human Subject Research?

The human subjects regulations (45 CFR Part 46) define research as "a systematic investigation, including research development, testing, and evaluation, designed to develop or contribute to generalizable knowledge" [45 CFR 46.102(d)]. A human subject is "a living individual about whom an investigator (whether professional or student) conducting research obtains (1) data through intervention or interaction with the individual or (2) identifiable private information" [45 CFR 46.102(f)].

Is It Research or Is It Treatment?

The Belmont Report distinguishes between research and clinical practice in discussing which activities require special review. Research is defined as an activity designed to test a hypothesis, permit conclusions to be drawn, and thereby to develop or contribute to generalizable knowledge (expressed, for example, in theories, principles, and statements of relationships). Clinical practice includes interventions which are designed to enhance the well-being of a patient through diagnosis or treatment, and have a reasonable expectation of success. A departure from standard practice or the institution of a novel or innovative treatment is not viewed as research. This distinction is incorporated into the regulatory definition of human subject research noted above.[4]

For a helpful tool to determine whether an activity is research involving human subjects, see OHRP's (Office of Human Research Protection) Human Subjects Regulations Decision Charts at [www.hhs.gov/ohrp/humansubjects/guidance/decisioncharts.htm].

Applicable Federal Regulations

Following publication of the Belmont Report, both the Department of Health, Education and Welfare (formerly the DHEW, now the Department of Health and Human Services [DHHS]) and the Food and Drug Administration (FDA) strengthened their human subject protections, increasing but not altering the role of the Institutional Review Boards (IRBs). The DHHS human research regulations, including IRB requirements, are codified at Code of Federal Regulations Title 45, Part 46. This includes the federal policy known as the "Common Rule," which encompasses the human subject protections followed by all federal agencies that sponsor research. (See also Appendix 7.4 in Volume I of this series, "On the Protection of Human Subjects".) FDA regulations on human research are codified at CFR Title 21 Parts 50 (informed consent), 56 (Institutional Review Boards), 312 (Investigational New Drug Application), 812 (Investigational Device Exemptions), and 860 (Medical Device Classification Procedures).

Each health care institution that receives federal funding for human research from a department or agency covered by the Federal Policy or "Common Rule," or that conducts research that is regulated by the FDA, must have one or more IRBs with authority to prospectively review, monitor, require modification of, approve, or disapprove the research. The IRB may be established by the institution or, less often, may be an independent IRB under contract to the institution to provide IRB services.[5] A document assuring compliance with human subject protection regulations must be negotiated between the institution and DHHS before DHHS-funded research may be conducted. The document, known as an Assurance, may be for a single project or, more often, may be a Federal-Wide Assurance (FWA) which applies to the pertinent activities of the institution. Applicable regulations are codified at 45 CFR. 46.103.

DHHS and FDA have the authority to conduct compliance inspections of institutions engaged in research, including the activities of IRBs, and to halt or restrict federally funded or FDA-regulated research if institutions are found out of compliance with applicable human subject protections.

Institutional Review Boards

For Dr. Gary B. Ellis, who was director of the former federal Office for Protection from Research Risks (OPRR),[6] the relationship between subject and researcher is one based on trust, and that trust must be respected. Ellis said:

In the final analysis, research investigators, research institutions, and federal regulators are stewards of a trust agreement with the people who are research subjects. For research subjects who are safeguarded by the federal regulations, we have a system in place that (1) minimizes the potential for harm, (2) enables and protects individual, autonomous choice, and (3) promotes the pursuit of new knowledge. By doing so, we protect the rights and welfare of our fellow citizens who make a remarkable contribution to the common good by participating in research studies. We owe them our best effort.[7]

It is the role of the IRBs to safeguard that trust and to assess research in terms of risks and benefits, the adequacy of informed consent, the adequacy of safeguards to protect the privacy and confidentiality of subjects,[8] and the equitable selection of subjects. Maintaining strong safeguards for the safety of human subjects in medical research is a paramount obligation of clinical investigators and their institutions.

IRB Membership and Quorum

IRBs must be composed of at least five members with diverse backgrounds, including at least one scientific member, one non-scientist, and one non-affiliated member. IRBs relied on under an Assurance must be registered with the Office for Human Research Protection (OHRP). IRB registration requires a listing of members, their affiliations, and whether they serve as scientist or non-scientist members.

No IRB member may participate in any IRB review of a study with which the member has a conflict of interest. It is useful to remind IRB members at the beginning of each meeting of the need to recuse on any matter in which they might have a conflict and to include the following (or similar) reminder on all IRB agendas:

No member of the IRB may participate in the review of any project in which the IRB member is an investigator, has a financial conflict of interest, or has any other interest which has an adverse impact on the IRB member's ability to exercise independent judgment. Under such circumstances, the IRB member shall not be present during IRB deliberations, except to provide information requested by the IRB.

To satisfy quorum requirements, a majority of IRB members that include a non-scientist member must be present and voting. In other words, a non-scientist member must always be present and voting for the IRB to take official action. Many institutions include at least two non-scientist members on their IRBs to ensure that at least one non-scientist is present whenever the IRB convenes. For IRB action to be taken on research involving minors, prisoners, or mentally impaired individuals, an IRB member with expertise in the particular area involved (for example, pediatrician, prisoner activist, mental health professional) must be present and voting.

IRB Review

If an institution subject to the Common Rule is engaged in human subject research, prospective and ongoing IRB review is required, unless the research qualifies for an exemption under 45 CFR 46.101(b). (See the sample Request for Exemption with listing of eligible categories at [med.cornell.edu/research/for_pol/ins_rev_boa.htlm]. See also Human Subject Regulations Decision Charts at [www.hhs.gov/ohrp/humansubjects/guidance/decisioncharts/htm].

IRB review is classified as either full board or expedited review, based on the nature of the proposed research. Research activities that present no more than minimal risk and involve only procedures listed in one or more expedited review categories, as specified by the FDA, may be reviewed by the IRB through expedited procedures. (See sample Request for Expedited Review that lists categories of research eligible for expedited review at [med.cornell.edu/research/for_pol/ins_rev_boa.html]. See also Human Subject Regulations Decision Charts cited previously.)

IRB review and approval of research must be conducted "at intervals appropriate to the degree of risk, but not less than once per year." (See OHRP Guidance on Continuing Review, [www.hhs.gov/ohrp/humansubjects/guidance/contrev2002.htm].)

IRB approval lapses after one year, resulting in administrative suspension. Accordingly, unless the IRB schedules annual continuing review sufficiently in advance of the annual approval date to accommodate delays in IRB meetings, requests for additional information, modifications to consent forms, and so on, IRB approval of research may expire, and all research activity must cease. In the event of an administrative suspension, the IRB may determine and inform the investigator that it is in the best interest of enrolled subjects to continue research activities. However, new enrollment must cease. (See OHRP Guidance on Continuing Review cited previously.)

Note that HHS regulations require that the IRB review the actual application or proposal when reviewing proposed HHS-funded human subject research, to verify that the application or proposal is consistent with the proposed IRB protocol (45 CFR 46.103[f]). Many IRBs have been required to re-review all previously approved HHS-funded research because of a failure to review the grant application as part of the initial IRB review and approval.

Investigators are also responsible for notifying the IRB of adverse events and unexpected risks to human subjects, and for seeking IRB approval for any amendments or modifications to protocols and to consent forms before they are instituted.

Required IRB Findings

To approve research on human subjects, the IRB must (1) identify risks of the research, (2) determine that the risks will be minimized to the extent possible, (3) identify probable benefits of the research, (4) determine that the risks are reasonable in relation to the benefits to the subject and the knowledge to be gained, (5) ensure that research subjects are provided with an accurate and fair description of the risks, discomforts, and anticipated benefits, (6) ensure that research subjects are offered the opportunity to voluntarily accept or reject participation in the research, or discontinue participation, without coercion or fear of reprisal or deprivation of treatment to which the patient is otherwise entitled,[9] and (7) determine intervals of periodic review and, when necessary, determine the adequacy of mechanisms for monitoring data collection. OHRP not only requires that these findings be made; it requires that the findings and actions be documented in IRB minutes and that information necessary to support the determinations be included in the records of the IRB. Approval of research involving minors requires specific IRB determinations that must be documented in the minutes of the IRB (see 45 CFR 46.404–46.407). A useful IRB tool is a protocol review form that includes a checklist of required findings, which can be incorporated into IRB minutes. (See sample IRB Protocol Review Form for Reviewers at [med.cornell.edu/research/for_pol/forms/policies.pdf] and sample Request for IRB Approval of Investigation Involving Use of Human Subjects at [med.cornell.edu/research/for_pol/forms/IRB_protocol_Jan_06.pdf].)

Informed Consent

A human being may be included as a subject in research only if the "investigator has obtained the legally effective informed consent of the subject or the subject's legally authorized representative."[10] Required individual elements of informed consent, which must be documented in an informed consent form, and the circumstances under which certain elements or documentation may be waived, are set forth at 45 CFR 46.116 and 45 CFR 46.117. To ensure inclusion of all required information, it is recommended that each IRB have an informed consent template that includes both the required elements and preferred local boilerplates (such as the institution's policy on compensation for research-related injury). These are available online at [med.cornell.edu//research/for_pol/forms/irbcf.pdf]. To help develop an informed consent template, refer to the Informed Consent Checklist—Basic and Additional Elements at [www.hhs.gov/ohrp/humansubjects/assurance/consentckds.htm].

Informed Consent in Emergency Settings

The FDA regulations and The Common Rule provide a mechanism to waive informed consent requirements for studies conducted in certain emergency settings. For example, informed consent may be waived for human subjects in need of emergency medical intervention, for which available treatments are unproven or unsatisfactory and where it is not possible to obtain informed consent. (See the relevant FDA Information Sheet at [fda.gov/oc/ohrt/irbs/except.html] and OHRP Guidance at [www.hhs.gov/ohrp/humansubjects/guidance/hsdc97–01.html].)

Exculpatory Language in Consent Forms

Both the Common Rule and FDA regulations preclude use of exculpatory language in consent forms by which the subject is deemed to have waived any right or benefit. This has been interpreted to preclude often-used consent form provisions related to tissue donation or ownership of tissue and derived inventions with commercial potential, and so on. Refer to: [www.hhs.gov/ohrp/humansubjects/guidance/exculp.htm] for examples of impermissible exculpatory language and examples of acceptable language.

Clinical Trial Web Sites

Information that is provided to potential human research subjects must be approved by the IRB and must be non-coercive in the manner that it is conveyed, as in content. This requirement for IRB review and approval also applies to recruitment material, including clinical trial Web sites.[11]

Reporting Incidents to OHRP and Other Federal Oversight Bodies

DHHS regulations require that institutions have written procedures to ensure reporting to the institutional official, funding department or agency head, and OHRP of (a) unanticipated problems involving risks to subjects or others, (b) any serious or continuing noncompliance with the Common Rule or determinations of the IRB, and (c) any suspension or termination of IRB approval. See Guidance and Decision Tree at [www.hhs.gov/ohrp/policy/incidreport_ohrp.html].

For gene transfer protocols, notification must also be provided to the National Institutes of Health Office of Biotechnology Activities. For more information, see [www4.od.nih.gov/oba].

Note that there is an additional reporting requirement for gene transfer protocols conducted in NIH-supported General Clinical Research Centers (GCRC); namely, whenever a gene transfer protocol conducted through the GCRC results in a report to the FDA of a serious unexpected adverse event or a report to the IRB of an unanticipated problem involving risks to subjects or others, a copy of that report should be sent to NCRR's Division of Clinical Research Resources, which funds the GCRC.

These reporting obligations are in addition to the FDA reporting obligations of the investigator who has been authorized to conduct work under an IND (Investigational New Drug) or IDE (Investigational Device Exemption).

Compliance

Government oversight compliance activities have increased significantly since 1999 and are expected to continue at increased intensity, signaling an increase in public interest in the ethical and procedural propriety of biomedical research. This intensified oversight is occurring at a time of declining clinical revenue, when there might be increased pressure from principal investigators and administrators to cut corners and speed up the approval process for sponsored research. Such an approach places the welfare of the researcher and the research institution ahead of the welfare of the subject and is inconsistent with the ethical foundation of biomedical research and the derivative regulatory framework. The results of research, whether in terms of scientific recognition or financial reward, may never take priority over the research subject. Compliance activities of federal regulatory bodies have shown that an approach to research that minimizes protection of the subject can ultimately prove very costly, both in revenue and reputation.

At the 2002 Fraud and Compliance Forum sponsored by the American Health Lawyers Association and the Health Care Compliance Association, Dr. Melody Lin, of the OHRP Office of Research Compliance, identified common findings and deficiencies associated with compliance oversight activities. These included:

- Initial and continuing review issues
- Inadequate IRB review, particularly with respect to issues affecting vulnerable populations
- IRB review without sufficient information
- Contingent approval with no system for follow-up
- Inadequate continuing annual review, including failure to review at least once per year
- Informed consent and informed consent documentation issues
- Language that is too complex
- Use of impermissible exculpatory language
- Standard consent forms inadequate for certain procedures
- Reliance on standard surgical consent form to collect tissue samples
- Inappropriate boilerplates
- Failure to minimize possibility of coercion or undue influence
- IRB membership and expertise issues
- Lack of researcher diversity

- Lack of IRB expertise for research
- Lack of IRB expertise for research involving children and prisoners
- Lack of sufficient understanding of regulations
- Designation of an additional IRB without OHRP approval
- Documentation of IRB activities
- Inappropriate application of exemption (not in six categories) (Explain what the six categories are)
- Inappropriate use of expedited approvals
- Failure to document consideration of additional safeguards
- Inadequate minutes (meaning votes not recorded, no summary of important issues, inability to reconstruct what was approved)
- Poorly maintained files
- IRB convened without a quorum
- Non-scientist absent
- Majority not present
- Conflict of interest issues
- IRB members
- Office of sponsored research
- Institutional officials
- Inappropriate waiver of informed consent
- Lack of written standard operating procedures
- Failure to report unanticipated problems to OHRP
- Inadequate IRB resources and overburdened IRBs

OHRP posts its compliance actions on its Web site, including the text of Determination. Letters sent to research institutions operating under OHRP Assurances. These letters, posted at [ohrp.osophs.dhhs.gov/detrm_letrs/lindex.htm], provide a good source of information for risk managers on OHRP compliance and enforcement priorities.

A review of the posted 2005 OHRP Determination Letters reveals a pattern of common deficiencies: (1) Consent form deficiencies, such as language that is not understandable to the public, inadequate explanation of potential risks, failure to address all required elements of informed consent, and failure to describe all research procedures; (2) IRB procedural and process deficiencies, such as inadequate written policies and procedures; improper use of expedited review for research not within permissible categories; inadequate information available to the IRB to support required risk-benefit determinations (particularly with respect to research involving pediatric subjects, for which specific documented findings are required); substantive changes to protocols and consent forms without full board re-review; failure of documentation of IRB actions, including attendance, specific votes on actions taken, and summary of IRB discussions; (3) Lapsed IRB approval (as previously noted, IRB approval is valid for no greater than one year; therefore, study approval expires after one year and the study administratively terminates when the approval expires); 4) Failure to report unanticipated problems involving risks to subjects, serious or continuing noncompliance, and suspensions and terminations to OHRP.

The risk manager should review the OHRP Determination Letters, Informed Consent Checklist, guidance documents, and decision charts on the OHRP Web site [www.hhs.gov/ohrp/] for a more detailed analysis and useful tools for compliance with the IRB's obligations in each of these areas. Comprehensive, mistake-proof IRB application forms, consent form templates, and IRB reviewer forms that elicit all required information, address all necessary informed consent elements, and contain required IRB findings are important tools in maximizing the safety of human subjects and minimizing institutional liability.

It is the responsibility of each research institution and its IRB to educate investigators, to monitor the conduct of research (for example, through random and "for cause" audits) and to ensure that the IRB members are adequately and continually trained in human research protection. Ultimately, the expectation is that there will be increasing institutional support for the research compliance infrastructure, including adequate staff resources that incorporate a research compliance officer function for implementation and monitoring of research activities and for management of research funds.

Conflict of Interest

The failure of some IRBs to consider whether the investigator and institution have a potential conflict of interest and to determine how to manage or eliminate that conflict, along with the failure to inform the subject of these potential conflicts of interest, has resulted in significant public condemnation and increased regulatory scrutiny of clinical research efforts. It is essential that each research institution establish its own policies and procedures for the reporting and managing of investigator and institutional conflicts of interest. Does an investigator, for example, have an impermissible financial conflict of interest because of a paid consultancy or an equity interest in the sponsor? Can the conflict be managed with an independent oversight committee to verify the integrity of the data? (For more information, see the conflict of interest resource available at [grants1.nih.gov/grants/policy/coi/index.htm] and the recommendations of the Association of American Medical Colleges at [www.aamc.org/members/coitf/].)

Gene or Recombinant DNA Research

Research involving recombinant DNA or gene therapy that receives any federal funding requires additional levels of review and approval at the institutional level by an Institutional Biosafety Committee and at the federal level by the Recombinant DNA Advisory Committee [RAC] of the Office of Biotechnology Activities [OBA]. The RAC was established to respond to public concerns about the safety of research that involves gene manipulation. See "Frequently Asked Questions" on the OBA Web site at [www4.od.nih.gov/oba/RAC/RAC_FAQs.htm]. Refer also to the new OBA Web-based resource on informed consent in gene transfer research that can be accessed at [www4.od.nih.gov/oba/rac/ic/].

Additional Areas of Research Interest

For "Issues to Consider in the Research Use of Stored Data or Tissues and Human Genetic Mutant Cells" see [www.hhs.gov/ohrp.humansubjects/guidance/reposit.htm]. For information on "Guidance on Research Involving Human Embryonic Stem Cells, Germ Cells, and Stem Cell-Derived Test Articles" see [www.hhs.gov/ohrp/humansubjects/guidance/stemcell.pdf]. See also the "Institute of Medicine, Guidelines for Human

Embryonic Stem Cell Research," published April 26, 2005, at [www.iom.edu/report.asp?id=26661].

Registration of Clinical Trials

The stated policy of the International Committee of Medical Journal Editors (ICMJE) is that member journals will consider a clinical trial for publication, only if the study was registered on a public registration site before enrollment of the first subject:

> (The Committee's) goal . . . is to foster a comprehensive, publicly available database of clinical trials. A complete registry of trials would be a fitting way to thank the thousands of participants who have placed themselves at risk by volunteering for clinical trials. They deserve to know that the information that accrues from their altruism is part of the public record, where it is available to guide decisions about patient care, and they deserve to know that decisions about their care rest on all of the evidence, not just the trials that authors decided to report and that journal editors decided to publish.[12] Legislation is pending in the U.S. Congress that would require publication of clinical trials in a national registry as a precondition to IRB approval.[13]

Summary of Risk Management Implications

Each research institution should review its own policies and procedures and its IRB records for compliance with federal regulations to determine whether it is vulnerable to an adverse action. Does the institution have an internal "for cause" and random monitoring and audit program to verify that investigators are complying with research protocols? Are signed research consent forms available for all research subjects? Do IRB policies and procedures satisfy federal requirements? Are minutes of IRB meetings maintained and do they adequately document IRB findings and actions? Does training of IRB members and investigators address regulatory emphasis on education? Risk managers should assess whether and how they, or research compliance officers or similar officials, can help the institution meet its obligations in the area of human biomedical research. Risk managers should also assess coordination of the activities of their research regulatory bodies—the IRB, the Institutional Biosafety Committee for Recombinant DNA and biohazards, and the Radiation Safety Committee (which is required by the institution's Nuclear Regulatory Commission license).

If compliance is not adequate, the loss to the institution, in terms of funding and reputation, could be enormous. Institutions must be vigilant in their review and monitoring of the activities of the IRB and investigators and mindful of their own institutional financial conflicts of interest and those of their researchers. If they are not, they can expect that federal oversight, investigative, or prosecutorial bodies will be.

Risk managers also should be mindful of the potential for costly civil and criminal litigation growing out of regulatory non-compliance. Numerous well-publicized instances of death or serious injury to human subjects in clinical trials have given rise to costly litigation against institutions, investigators, and individual IRB members. In virtually all instances, civil litigants have raised non-disclosure of prior adverse effects experienced by research subjects, or non-disclosure of conflicts of interest as bases of their causes of action. It is advised that the risk manager ensure that IRB procedures and audit mechanisms provide for full disclosure to the IRB and research subjects of all potential risks and complications and all conflicts of interest associated with the research. It is further advised that the risk manager investigate whether coverage for personal injury and death arising out of administrative actions, such as actions of IRB chairs and members, is included in its insurance portfolio, whether through its professional and general liability coverage or its directors' and officers' (D&O) insurance. It is important that D&O policies traditionally do not include coverage for personal injury and death.

An additional area of potential risk arising out of regulatory non-compliance relates to enforcement activities of the DHHS Office of the Inspector General (OIG) and the U.S. Department of Justice. The risk manager should be aware that obtaining federal funds in a fraudulent manner—for instance, through billing of the federal government for health care services provided pursuant to a clinical trial for which service billing is not permitted, engaging in scientific misconduct (fabrication, falsification, or plagiarism) in a federally funded research proposal, or improper time and effort and cost reporting in federally funded grants—can all serve to support both civil and criminal charges under the federal fraud and abuse laws, including the False Claims Act.[14] In the civil context, the government is entitled to treble damages for successful prosecution.

Federal prosecutors have indicated that non-compliance with IRB requirements, such as false information or a failure to provide required information to the IRB regarding adverse events, can serve as a basis for prosecution under the fraud and abuse laws. In a press release announcing civil settlements in an enforcement action relating to the death of a subject in a gene therapy trial at the University of Pennsylvania, the U.S. Department of Justice, Eastern District of Pennsylvania, stated:

> Perhaps most significant is the impact that these settlements will have on the way clinical research on human participants is conducted throughout the country . . . This action covers two major research centers which (sic) have instituted important changes in the conduct and monitoring of clinical research on human participants. We hope that these settlements will now serve as a model for similar research nationwide.
>
> The government has alleged, among other allegations, that the study had produced toxicities in humans that should have resulted in termination, but the study continued. Reports were submitted to FDA, NIH, and to the Institutional Review Boards (IRBs) charged with oversight of this study that misrepresented the actual clinical findings associated with the study. Additionally, the consent form and process did not disclose all anticipated toxicities.[15]

The Fiscal Year 2006 Work Plan of the DHHS Office of the Inspector General lists several research related areas earmarked for scrutiny, including compliance by grant recipients with the financial conflict of interest disclosure and conflict management requirements of the FDA and NIH for clinical investigators, accuracy of university representations as to investigator time commitments when applying for grants (Has a university over-committed faculty researchers to obtain federally funded grants?), adequacy of cost accounting and monitoring/audit programs by grantees, and charges for university administrative and clerical salaries.

Federal enforcement of regulatory requirements as they apply to research has been and will continue to be aggressive, whether through agency enforcement activities or application of civil or criminal penalties. The risk management professional plays a key role in ensuring that the institution avoids the considerable risk of non-compliance.

Endnotes

1. Cohen, J. J., "Academic Medical Centers and Medical Research," *JAMA*, 2005, 294(11), 1367–1372.

2. In discussing the policy of the *New England Journal of Medicine* not to publish the results of unethical research, then Executive Editor Dr. Marcia Angell wrote, "Denying publication even when the ethical violations are minor protects the principle of the primacy of the research subject. . . . [R]efusal to publish unethical work serves notice to society at large that even scientists do not consider science the primary measure of a civilization. Knowledge, although important, may be less important to a decent society that the way it is obtained." Angell, M., "The Nazi Hypothermia Experiments and Unethical Research Today," *NEJM*, 1990, 322146–64.

3. Jonsen, A. R. "The Ethics of Research with Human Subjects: A Short History." In Jonsen, A. R., R. M. Veatch, and L. Walters. *Source Book in Bioethics*. Georgetown: Georgetown University Press, 1998, pp. 5–9.

4. In distinguishing between research, which requires adherence to human subject protection regulations, including prospective IRB review, and innovative therapeutic intervention, which does not, consider whether the primary intent is to develop generalizable knowledge or treat an individual patient; consider also whether the intent is to publicly present or publish results or whether the activity is for internal quality improvement purposes. See Baruch, A. B., L. B. McCullough, R. R. Sharp. "Consensus and Controversy in Clinical Research Ethics," *JAMA*, 2005, 294(11), 1411–1414.

5. The National Cancer Institute Central IRB (CIRB) initiative is an effort to reduce the administrative burden of multiple local IRB reviews of multi-site cancer trials sponsored by the NCI and Cooperative Groups. Institutions that join the CIRB may rely on the CIRB as the IRB with primary jurisdiction to review these studies, and use a local facilitated review mechanism in lieu of local full board review. See [www.ncicirb.org/].

6. OPRR is the former federal office with human subject research oversight authority. The office relocated from the National Institutes of Health (NIH) to the Office of Public Health and Science, DHHS, and is now called the Office for Human Research Protection (OHRP). The move was generally accepted as a means to increase the visibility of federal oversight of human subject protection and access to the secretary of DHHS.

7. Ellis, G. "Protecting the Rights and Welfare of Human Research Subjects." *Academic Medicine*, 74(9), September 1999, pp. 1008–1009.

8. There is a mechanism for protection of data for particularly sensitive research, such as genetic research, when there is a concern that the release of information regarding the results of research could lead to discrimination in the workplace or in the ability of individuals who are found to be carriers of genetic diseases to obtain life or health insurance. The Secretary of DHHS, or the Secretary's designee, may issue a Certificate of Confidentiality "to protect the privacy of research subjects by withholding their identities from all persons not connected with the research. . . . Persons so authorized to protect the privacy of such individuals may not be compelled in any Federal, State, or local civil, criminal, administrative, legislative, or other proceedings to identify such individuals." 42 USC 241(d), Section 301(d) of the Public Health Service Act, Protection of Identity, Research Subjects. For further information, call NIH at (301) 402-7221 or see the Certificate of Confidentiality Kiosk at [grants1.nih.gov/grants/policy/coc/].

9. For example, is the amount of compensation offered so excessive as to be coercive? Is the subject compensated only at the end of a six-month clinical trial so that the subject cannot withdraw during the trial without loss of all compensation? Or is the compensation pro-rated for the amount of time the subject participated?

10. 45 CFR 46.116

11. www.hhs.gov/ohrp/policy/clinicaltrials.html

12. DeAngelis, C., J. M. Drazen, F. A. Frizelle, C. Haug, J. Hoey, R. Horton, R., et al., "Clinical trial registration: a statement from the International Committee of Medical Journal Editors," *Annals of Internal Medicine*, 2004, 141: 477–8). See [www.clinicaltrials.gov/].

13. H. R. 3196, June 30, 2005; S. 470, Feb. 28, 2005.

14. 31 USC sec 3729 et seq.

15. Press Release, U. S. Dept of Justice, Eastern District of Pennsylvania, "U.S. Settles Case of Gene Therapy Study That Ended With Teen's Death," Sept. 9, 2005.

Appendix 5.1

```
┌──────────────────────────────────┐
│ Protocol No. _____   │
│                                  │
│ Receipt Date _____   │
└──────────────────────────────────┘
```

**The New York Presbyterian Hospital—Weill Medical
College of Cornell University
Institutional Review Board (IRB)**

Request for Exemption

> The human subjects regulations (45 CFR Part 46) define **research** as "a systematic investigation, including research development, testing, and evaluation, designed to develop or contribute to generalizable knowledge" [45 CFR 46.102(d)]. A **human subject** is "a living individual about whom an investigator (whether professional or student) conducting research obtains (1) data through intervention or interaction with the individual or (2) identifiable private information" [45 CFR 46.102(f)].

Some research involving human subjects may be exempt from the regulations. The categories below describe these exemptions. Please note that an exemption can be invoked only if **all** components of the research fit the category as described. You might find the following decision charts helpful: www.hhs.gov/ohrp/humansubjects/guidance/decisioncharts.htm

If you believe that your research may fall into one of the exempt categories, please indicate the relevant category in the space next to the category number below, and the IRB Chairperson or IRB designee will review your research to determine if an exemption can be granted. If granted, your exemption request will be returned to you with an approval signed by the IRB Chairperson or IRB designee, and you may begin your research. You must notify the IRB if your research changes in any way, because the exemption may no longer apply. The IRB may request periodic follow-up. If an exemption cannot be granted, your exemption request will be returned to you with the reason stated, and your research will be reviewed by the IRB. Please direct questions to the IRB Office at (212) 821-0577.

Read instructions carefully and then type and complete each item. If an item is not applicable, indicate this by "NA". Obtain required signatures. Submit original and 3 copies to Room A-128.

1. Principal Investigator _____   Degree _____

2. Academic Title _____

3. Telephone_____   FAX _____

4. Department _____   Division _____

5. Mailing Address _____

   _____

6. Email Address _____

7. Project title (if applicable, use title of externally-funded research)

   _____

8. Inclusive dates of study _____ to _____   Expected duration of study on individual subjects (days/months) _____

9. Source of funds (agency and/or institutional) _____

10. Proposal   □ will not be;   □ will be;   □ has been submitted to funding agency

    (Date) _____

11. If project will be funded to another investigator, give Principal Investigator's name and grant title

    _____

    _____

12. Co-Investigators: name, degree, department, extension

    a. _____

    b. _____

    c. _____

    d. _____

13. Student Research   □ No   □ Yes   Student Name _____

Section One: Categories Eligible for Exemption (Please indicate the relevant category in the space next to the category number. Categories continue on the next page.):

NOTE: These exemptions do not apply to research involving prisoners, pregnant women, human fetuses, or human in vitro fertilization.

1. ____   Research conducted in established or commonly accepted educational settings, involving normal educational practices. Examples include:

       a) Research on regular and special education instructional strategies, **OR**

b) Research on the effectiveness of or the comparison among instructional techniques, curricula, or classroom management methods.

2. ___ Research involving the use of educational tests (cognitive, diagnostic, aptitude, or achievement), survey procedures, interview procedures, or observation of public behavior. *NOTE: Except as noted above, this exemption applies to all such research involving ADULT subjects unless BOTH of the following conditions apply:*

a) Information obtained is recorded in such a manner that human subjects can be identified, directly or through identifiers linked to the subjects (NOTE: Codes constitute identifiers.); **AND**

b) Any disclosure of the subjects' responses outside of the research could reasonably place the subjects at risk of criminal or civil liability or be damaging to the subjects' financial standing, employability, or reputation.

NOTE: This exemption applies to research involving CHILDREN EXCEPT that (i) research involving survey or interview procedures with children is NOT EXEMPT, and (ii) research involving observation of the public behavior of children is NOT EXEMPT if the investigator(s) participate(s) in the actions being observed.

3. Research involving the use of educational tests (cognitive, diagnostic, aptitude, achievement), survey procedures, interview procedures, or observation of public behavior that is not exempt under category 2 above, IF:

___ a) The human subjects are elected or appointed public officials or candidates for public office; **OR**

___ b) Federal statute(s) require(s) without exception that the confidentiality of the personally identifiable information will be maintained throughout the research and thereafter.

4. Research involving the collection or study of existing data, documents, records, pathological specimens, or diagnostic specimens (**existing** means research materials are already on the shelf or archived when the research is proposed; e.g., blood samples already taken from patients or subjects for other clinical or research purposes). This exemption applies if:

___ a) These sources are publicly available; **OR**

___ b) The information is recorded by the investigator in such a manner that individual subjects cannot be identified, directly or through identifiers linked to the subjects.

5. ___ Research and demonstration projects that are designed to study, evaluate, or otherwise examine:

a) Public benefit or service programs;

b) The procedures for obtaining benefits or services under such programs;

c) Possible changes in or alternatives to such programs or procedures; or

d) Possible changes in methods or levels of payment for benefits or services under such programs.

NOTE: This exemption applies ONLY to research and demonstration projects studying FEDERAL programs, and its use must be authorized by the Federal Agency supporting the research. As with all exemptions, IRBs and institutions retain the authority not to invoke the exemption, even if so authorized by the relevant Federal Agency. Studies of state and local public service programs require IRB review. Waiver of informed consent is possible for such programs under 45 CFR 46.116(c).

6. Taste and food quality evaluation and consumer acceptance studies, which meet any of the following conditions:

____ a) If wholesome foods without additives are consumed; **OR**

____ b) If a food is consumed that contains a food ingredient at or below the level and for a use found to be safe, or agricultural chemical or environmental contaminant at or below the level found to be safe, by the Food and Drug Administration or approved by the Environmental Protection Agency or the Food Safety and Inspection of the U.S. Department of Agriculture.

Section Two: Additional Information and Materials

A: NON-TECHNICAL RESEARCH PLAN

State concisely the aims and specific objectives of the research and the procedures to be used to accomplish these aims. Describe what will happen to subjects and what they will be expected to do. State why you believe the research involves no more than minimal risk to subjects. *(If additional space is needed, attach a separate sheet.)*

B: Please attach the following materials:

1. Informed consent document (if applicable)
2. Any survey tools or questionnaires.

_____   _____

Signature of Investigator   Date

FOR IRB USE ONLY

Comments:

☐ Exemption allowed (Category _____)

☐ Exemption Not Allowed (Please see comments)

_____

Signature of IRB Chair

_____

Date

Appendix 5.2

REQUEST FOR EXPEDITED REVIEW
OF INVESTIGATIONS

RASP-202-3-95

Protocol No. _____
Receipt Date _____

The New York Presbyterian Hospital—Weill Medical
College of Cornell University
Institutional Review Board (IRB)

Request for Expedited Review of Investigation
Involving Use of Adult Human Subjects

The human subjects regulations (45 CFR Part 46) define **research** as "a systematic investigation, including research development, testing, and evaluation, designed to develop or contribute to generalizable knowledge" [45 CFR 46.102(d)]. A **human subject** is "a living individual about whom an investigator (whether professional or student) conducting research obtains (1) data through intervention or interaction with the individual or (2) identifiable private information" [45 CFR 46.102(f)].

Medical Center and Federal Policies require review of each protocol with respect to the: (1) rights and welfare of subjects; (2) adequacy of methods used to secure informed consent; and (3) risk and potential benefits of the research to the subject. Read instructions care fully and then type and complete each item. If an item is not applicable, indicate this by "NA". Obtain required signatures. Submit original and 3 copies to Room A-128.

1. Principal Investigator _____ Degree _____

2. Academic Title _____ Telephone_____

3. Department _____ Division _____

4. Mailing Address _____

5. ☐ New Protocol ☐ 3-Year Renewal Prior Protocol No._____

6. Project Title (if applicable, use same title of externally funded research; limit to 60 spaces)

   _____

7. Inclusive dates of study _____ to _____ Expected duration of study on individual subjects (days/months) _____

8. Source of funds (agency, institutional, or industry sponsor)_____

9. Proposal ☐ will not be; ☐ will be; ☐ has been submitted to funding agency (date) _____

10. If project will be funded to another investigator, give Principal Investigator's name and grant title

    _____

    _____

11. Co-Investigators: name, degree, department, extension

    a. _____

    b. _____

    c. _____

    d. _____

12. Student Research ☐ No ☐ Yes Student Name _____

If yes, indicate the role of the student(s) and who will supervise the students:_____

_____

_____

SECTION A. **EXPEDITED REVIEW**
(Minimal Risk Procedures)

Check procedures applicable to this research and complete additional information as necessary.

Research activities that (1) present no more than minimal risk to human subjects and (2) involve only procedures listed in one or more of the Eligible Categories for Expedited Review below may be reviewed by the IRB through the expedited review procedure. *Minimal risk* means that the risks of harm anticipated in the proposed research are not greater, considering probability and magnitude, than those ordinarily encountered in daily life or during the performance of routine physical or psychological examinations or tests. Use of clinical patients must have the approval of the attending physician.

You might find the following decision charts helpful:

http://www.hhs.gov/ohrp/humansubjects/guidance/decisioncharts.htm

If you believe that your research falls into one of the following categories, please indicate which category or categories you believe is or are appropriate. The IRB Chairman or his designee will review your research to determine if expedited review is warranted. If granted, the form will be returned to you with an approval stamp along with the signature of the IRB Chairman, and you may begin your research. You must notify the IRB if your proposed research changes in any way. The IRB will request periodic updates. If expedited procedures cannot be used, the reason will be explained, and your research must be reviewed during a convened IRB meeting. Please direct questions to the IRB Office at (212) 821-0577

Categories Eligible for Expedited Review (Please indicate one or more category, as appropriate, in the space next to the category numbers below.)

1.   Clinical studies of drugs and medical devices only when condition (a) or (b) is met:

___   (a)   Research on drugs for which an investigational new drug application is not required. (*Note:* Research on marketed drugs that significantly increases the risks or decreases the acceptability of the risks associated with the use of the product is not eligible for expedited review.) **OR**

___   (b)   Research on medical devices for which (i) an investigational device exemption application is not required or (ii) the medical device is cleared/approved for marketing and the medical device is being used in accordance with its cleared/approved labeling.

2.   Collection of blood samples by finger stick, heel stick, ear stick, or venipuncture from:

___   (a)   Healthy, nonpregnant adults who weigh at least 110 pounds. For these subjects, the amounts drawn may not exceed 550 ml in an 8-week period and collection may not occur more frequently than 2 times per week; **OR**

___   (b)   Other adults and children, considering the age, weight, and health of the subjects, the collection procedure, the amount of blood to be collected, and the frequency with which it will be collected. For these subjects, the amount drawn may not exceed the lesser of 50 ml or 3 ml per kg in an 8-week period and collection may not occur more frequently than 2 times per week.

Note: *"Children" in (b) above is defined in the HHS regulations as "persons who have not attained the legal age for consent for treatments or procedures involved in the research, under the applicable law of the jurisdiction in which the research will be conducted" [45 CFR 46.402(a)].*

3. ___   Prospective collection of biological specimens for research purposes by noninvasive means.

Examples:

(a)   Hair and nail clippings in a nondisfiguring manner

(b)   Deciduous teeth at time of exfoliation or if routine patient care indicates a need for extraction

(c)   Permanent teeth if routine patient care indicates a need for extraction

(d) Excreta and external secretions (including sweat)

(e) Uncannulated saliva collected either in an unstimulated fashion or stimulated by chewing gumbase or wax or by applying a dilute citric solution to the tongue

(f) Placenta removed at delivery [must complete Sec. B – Human Tissue]

(g) Amniotic fluid obtained at the time of rupture of the membrane prior to or during labor

(h) Supra- and subgingival dental plaque and calculus, provided the collection procedure is not more invasive than routine prophylactic scaling of the teeth and the process is accomplished in accordance with accepted prophylactic techniques

(i) Mucosal and skin cells collected by buccal scraping or swab, skin swab, or mouth washings

(j) Sputum collected after saline mist nebulization

4. ____ Collection of data through noninvasive procedures (not involving general anesthesia or sedation) routinely employed in clinical practice, excluding procedures involving X-rays or microwaves. Where medical devices are employed, they must be cleared/approved for marketing. (Studies intended to evaluate the safety and effectiveness of the medical device are not generally eligible for expedited review, including studies of cleared medical devices for new indications.)

Examples:

(a) Physical sensors that are applied either to the surface of the body or at a distance and do not involve input of significant amounts of energy into the subject or an invasion of the subject's privacy

(b) Weighing or testing sensory acuity

(c) Magnetic resonance imaging

(d) Electrocardiography, electroencephalography, thermography, detection of naturally occurring radioactivity, electroretinography, ultrasound, diagnostic infrared imaging, doppler blood flow, and echocardiography

(e) Moderate exercise, muscular strength testing, body composition assessment, and flexibility testing where appropriate given the age, weight, and health of the individual

5. Research involving materials (data, documents, records, or specimens) that:

____ (a) have already been collected for some other purpose **OR**

____ (b) will be collected for non-research purposes (such as medical treatment or diagnosis).

6. ____ Collection of data from voice, video, digital, or image recordings made for research purposes.

7. Research on:

____ (a) individual or group characteristics or behavior (including, but not limited to, research on perception, cognition, motivation, identity, language, communication, cultural beliefs or practices, and social behavior) **OR**

___ (b) research employing survey, interview, oral history, focus group, program evaluation, human factors evaluation, or quality assurance methodologies.

8.   Continuing review of research previously approved by the convened IRB as follows:

___ (a) Where:

    (i) The research is permanently closed to the enrollment of new sub-jects, and

    (ii) All subjects have completed all research-related interventions, and

    (iii) The research remains active only for long-term follow-up of subjects, **OR**

___ (b) Where no subjects have been enrolled and no additional risks have been identified, **OR**

___ (c) Where the remaining research activities are limited to data analysis.

9. ___ Continuing review of research, not conducted under an investigational new drug application or investigational device exemption, where categories 2 through 8 do not apply, but the IRB has determined and documented at a convened meeting that the research involves no greater than minimal risk and no additional risks have been identified.

SECTION B. **HUMAN TISSUE**

Is human tissue, as identified below, being used in this study? ___ Yes ___ No

If YES, complete this section.

1. Human tissue from surgical or autopsy procedures includes ALL DIAGNOSTIC AND PATHOLOGICAL SPECIMENS (including placentas, umbilical cords, umbilical cord blood, bone marrow aspirates, fine needle aspirates, cytologic specimens, and all other tissue removed from the body but not blood or amniotic fluid at the time of rupture of mem-branes prior to or during labor).

2. Surgical or autopsy tissue excludes "surgical waste" which is specifically defined as subcutaneous tissue removed to facilitate wound closure and tissues significantly altered or diluted by the procedure such as lens phakoemulsifications, vitrectomy specimens, and liposuction specimens.

3. No surgical or autopsy tissue can be released for research or clinical purposes without the express permission of an attending pathologist or designee.

4. Surgical or autopsy tissue can be released by Pathology for research purposes **only** after sufficient tissue has been reserved for any and all diagnostic and pathological procedures.

5. Written consent of the Department of Pathology and Laboratory Medicine must be obtained in all cases where human tissue is used for research. This includes protocols in which tissue is taken solely for research purposes and those involving tissue (such as a bone marrow aspirate) that normally is not submitted to Pathology. In these situations an exception to the Tissue Submission Policy must be granted (see next page).

6. A copy of the approved and stamped "IRB Tissue Request Form" will be kept on file in Pathology (see page 7 of this document for the form).

7. If fetal tissue is requested and the gestational age is greater than 12 weeks, a completed and signed autopsy consent (Form #41160) must be submitted, attached to the Surgical Pathology requisition (attach copy of standard hospital form).

8. Which consent form will be obtained permitting disposition of surgical or autopsy tissue for research?

_____None needed (placenta, umbilical cord, and umbilical cord blood only)

_____Authorization for surgery form (#45350) or autopsy form (#41160)

_____ Study specific consent form

9. Are all investigators totally disassociated from those responsible for the surgical procedure which produces the surgical tissue? _____ Yes _____ No. If **no**, explain on a continuation page.

10. Will **only** that tissue or fluid normally taken for therapeutic or diagnostic purposes be used (i.e., no additional material will be taken for research purposes only)? _____ Yes _____No. If **no**, you must use Full rather than Expedited review.

Is an **EXCEPTION** to the Tissue Submission Policy being requested? _____ Yes _____ No

If YES, Please explain in detail the basis of your exception request, and obtain the additional signature of approval by the Department of Pathology and Laboratory Medicine.

Tissue Submission Policy: Surgical tissue removed during a diagnostic or therapeutic procedure must be submitted to Surgical Pathology intact and may not be incised, opened, or damaged in any way. In addition, tissue **may not** be removed from the specimen prior to receipt in Surgical Pathology. Any exceptions must be detailed below and specifically approved by the Department of Pathology and Laboratory Medicine.

Exception Approval:

_____   _____   _____
Department of Pathology and   Signature   Date
     Laboratory Medicine

IRB Tissue Request Form

Principal Investigator _____

Name of Protocol _____

_____

Persons authorized to obtain tissue _____

_____

Type of tissue required (fresh, sterile, frozen, sections from paraffin-embedded tissue)

_____

Organ/site of tissue required _____

Minimum tissue required/patient (cc's, sections from blocks, slides, cells, etc.)

_____

"Normal" tissue required/patient (cc's, sections from blocks, slides, cells, etc.)
_____

Estimated number of patients _____

Protocol Number_____

IRB Approval Stamp
With start & end dates

A copy of this stamped form will be kept on file in the Department of Pathology and Laboratory Medicine. Tissue will not be released without this form.

If technical work will be requested from Pathology (histology, flow cytometry, immuno-histochemistry, etc.), please complete the "Clinical Research Protocol" form that may be downloaded from the Department of Pathology and Laboratory Medicine's website, http://www.cornellpathology.org/research/. Please note that paraffin-embedded tissue blocks may not be released from Pathology; however, unstained slides from tissue blocks can be provided.

SECTION C. **ADDITIONAL REGULATORY INFORMATION**

3. **RADIOACTIVE MATERIALS.**

☐ Yes   ☐ No

Will this study involve use of radioisotopes or other sources of ionizing radiation?
If Yes, expedited review does not apply. The investigator must complete a Request for Approval of Investigation Involving Use of Human Subjects.

4. **RECOMBINANT DNA AND/OR GENE THERAPY**

Does this project involve the use of recombinant DNA and/or gene therapy? If so, Institutional Biosafety Committee (IBC) approval must be obtained. [*Note*: Recombinant DNA studies that are exempt from RAC review under Appendix M, are not exempt from local IBC review.]

☐ Yes   ☐ No

Not sure if IBC approval is required? Contact 212-746-6201

Need help filing an IBC application?
Forms are available at: http://intranet.med.cornell.edu/research/ibc.html or call 212-821-0668.

5. **CONFLICT OF INTEREST**

Do any investigators or co-investigators have a conflict of interest as defined in the Conflicts of Interest and Commitment Policy and Instruction of Weill Medical College and Graduate School of Medical Sciences of Cornell University (Fourth Edition 2004)?

☐ Yes   ☐ No

A copy of the WMC Study Specific Financial Disclosure Form for each investigator and Co-Investigator involved with this study must be attached to this application.

If you answered yes above, have you included a disclosure of the conflict of interest in the informed consent document?

☐ Yes   ☐ No

If no, please explain why you believe that disclosure to potential subjects is not necessary or not appropriate.

6. **NON-SIGNIFICANT RISK MEDICAL DEVICE**

Does this study involve the experimental use of medical and surgical diagnostic or therapeutic devices of unproven safety and efficacy?

☐ Yes   ☐ No

If Yes, the investigator must determine the applicability of the Investigational Device Exemption federal regulations to the study. If this study involves a "Significant Risk" Device, expedited review does not apply. The investigator must complete a Request for Approval of Investigation Involving Use of Human Subjects.

a. Name of device: _____

b. Sponsor of device: _____

c. Will device be custom-built?   ☐ Yes   ☐ No

d. Non-Significant Risk Device

    (1) Is this previously "banned" device?   ☐ Yes   ☐ No

    (2) Describe the device and how it will be used, and explain why it does not pose "significant risk" as defined by FDA:

SECTION D. **NON-TECHNICAL RESEARCH PLAN**

State concisely the aims and specific objectives of the research and procedures to be used to accomplish these aims. Because Committee includes laypersons, avoid highly technical language. Specify criteria for inclusion and exclusion in the study. Describe what will happen to subjects and what they will be expected to do. State specific interventions, which would not be performed except for purposes of this study. Assess potential benefits to subjects and to society that may accrue as a result of this research. Analyze risk-benefit ratio and explain why benefits to be gained outweigh the risks.

SECTION E. **SUBJECT POPULATION**

1. Number: Male [ ]   Female [ ]   Age Range_____to_____

2. [ ] Inpatients   [ ] Patient controls

    [ ] Outpatients   [ ] Normal volunteers

    [ ] Special racial or ethnic group   [ ] Students and/or employees
        (specify)

    _____

3. Subject's state of physical health. Indicate if seriously or terminally ill.

    _____

    _____

4. Location of subjects (hospitals, clinics, industry, unions, other; specify and give locations):

    _____

    _____

5. Will NYH-CMC Clinical Research Center be used? [ ] Yes   [ ] No
    Pediatric Unit [ ] and/or Adult Unit [ ]   If Yes, complete special CRC Protocol Form.

6. Indicate how subjects are a) initially identified (medical records, physician referral, canvassing, classes, etc.; be specific); b) and/or recruited (bedside or clinic interview, ads, telephone, letter, etc; be specific).

7. Will subjects receive any inducements before, or rewards or compensation after study:
    [ ] Yes   [ ] No   If Yes, how much and in what form? (Cash, taxi fares, medical care, gifts, etc.):

SECTION F. **CONFIDENTIALITY OF DATA**

What specific safeguards will be employed to protect confidentiality of data, such as coding or removal of identifiers as soon as possible, limitation of access to data, use of locked file cabinets, etc.? Will data which identify individual subjects be published or in any way disclosed to third parties other than project personnel?
If so, explain, here:

SECTION G. **INFORMED CONSENT**

Informed consent is necessary for all research involving human subjects and must be documented. For this Expedited Review of research, an oral presentation of the elements of informed consent is acceptable, but the Committee reserves the right to require alternative or more stringent means of securing consent.

1. Describe procedures, used to obtain informed consent, including how and where consent will be obtained. (See Instructions, page 3.)

    _____

    _____

    _____

    _____

2. Will you obtain **written** consent: ☐ Yes   ☐ No

    Sample Consent Form must be completed and attached.

3. Will you obtain **oral** consent: ☐ Yes   ☐ No

    NOTE: Oral consent is sufficient in the case of minimal risk to the subject. Subject must be informed of basic elements of consent as outlined in the Instructions. A **SUMMARY** of the information to be imparted to the subject must be submitted and approved by the Committee. This method of obtaining consent is approved **ONLY** for NO RISK or MINIMAL RISK procedures.
    SAMPLE OF SUMMARY MUST BE ATTACHED TO THIS PROTOCOL

Assent of Minors

The federal regulations require that adequate provision must be made for soliciting the assent of children when in the judgment of the IRB the children are capable of providing assent, taking into consideration the ages, maturity, and psychological state of the children involved. Generally the assent of a child could be sought when the child is seven years of age or older, on an assent form that is written in language understandable to a child in the age group involved.

PRINT:
PI Name ———————————— **Protocol Title** ————————————

SECTION H. **SIGNATURES**

1. I certify that the above information concerning procedures to be taken for protection of human subjects is correct. I will seek and obtain prior approval for substantive modification of this protocol and will report promptly to the Committee on Human Rights in Research any unexpected or otherwise significant adverse effects encountered in the course of the study.

————————————   ————————————   ————————————
Investigator   Signature   Date

This protocol has been reviewed and approved for submission to the Committee on Human Rights in Research.

————————————   ————————————   ————————————
Department Chairperson   Signature   Date

2. If subjects covered under this research protocol are administratively the responsibility of another department, approval is required:

a. Department: ————————————————————————

————————————   ————————————   ————————————
Department Chairperson   Signature   Date

b. Department: ————————————————————————

————————————   ————————————   ————————————
Department Chairperson   Signature   Date

3. Will your research involve the use of human tissue(s)?

☐ Yes   ☐ No   If Yes, approval is necessary by the Chairperson, Department of Pathology:

————————————   ————————————   ————————————
Department of Pathology   Signature   Date

The International Committee of Medical Journal Editors (ICMJE) has established a requirement that all clinical trials be entered in a public registry before the onset of patient enrollment as a condition of consideration for publication. Additional information may be found at: http://clinicaltrials.gov/ and at http://www.icmje.org/clin _ trialup.htm

Please contact the Protocol Registration System (PRS) administrator by e-mail at: ICR@med.cornell.edu to set up a PRS user account to register new and ongoing clinical trials. The e-mail should contain the PI's full name, department, phone number, and e-mail address.

Attachments

Please attach the following for the IRB to review your research:

Original Request for Approval of Investigation Involving Use of Human Subjects (IRB Protocol) plus 3 copies for Expedited Review, including the consent form (and assent form if applicable)

4 copies of any supplemental material:

- Sponsor's Protocol
- Investigator's Brochure
- Data Collection Sheets
- Study Specific Financial Disclosure Form for each investigator
- NIH grant application (if applicable)
- HIPAA research forms
- Any recruitment notices or advertisements
- Any survey instruments, psychological tests, interview forms, or scripts
- Any communication from the FDA regarding IND, IDE, or Humanitarian Use applications related to this submission

Appendix 5.3

IRB PROTOCOL REVIEW FORM
FOR REVIEWERS

IRB Number:_____

Weill Medical College of Cornell University
IRB Protocol Review Form for Reviewers

PI Name:		Reviewer:	
Title of Protocol:			

Reviewer: Please check the following sections and detail all changes to be made below.

Type of Review (check one):	Recommendation (check one):
❑ Full Board Initial Review ❑ Full Board Reactivation ❑ Full Board Amendment (not necessary to answer all questions for an amendment) ❑ Full Board Amendment Expedited Initial Review* (not necessary to answer all questions) * If **expedited**, list appropriate category below by referencing the Expedited Review Form:	❑ Approve as submitted ❑ Approvable pending non-substantive changes ❑ Defer for substantive issues/changes/ additional information* ❑ Disapprove* * For **deferral** or **disapproval**, list reasons **below**.

Continuing Review Frequency (check one)	Risk Level (check one)	If only non-substantive changes, do you want to review the PI's response?
❑ 12 Months ❑ 6 Months ❑ Other	❑ Minimal risk* ❑ Greater than minimal risk	❑ Yes ❑ No

IRB Number:_____

* Minimal risk means that the probability and magnitude of harm or discomfort antici-pated are not greater in and of themselves than those ordinarily encountered in daily life or during the performance of routine physical or psychological examinations or tests (45 CFR 46.102[i]).

Changes, Modifications, Clarifications

> In the space below, please list any changes, modifications, or clarifications required to the research protocol, informed consent form, or IRB application. If the research is to be deferred or disapproved, please also provide a brief explanation.

PROTOCOL REVIEW CHECKLIST

Please check whether the following elements are adequately addressed in the materials submitted to the IRB and make comments, if necessary. Where noted throughout the checklist, make the determinations that follow the checklist.

I. Risks to Subjects Minimized

Indicate whether risks to subjects are minimized by considering the following elements of the protocol:	Yes	No	NA	Comments (If necessary)
• Does study design adequately protect the subjects involved in the research? • Background information • Data collection tools • Safety monitoring • Qualifications of personnel				

II. Risk-Benefit Ratio

Indicate whether the risks of the research are reasonable in relation to the benefits by considering the following elements in the protocol:	Yes	No	NA	Comments (If necessary)
• Types of risks: physical, psychological, sociological, economic, or legal • Risks to others (e.g., risks related to disclosure of genetic information) • Long-term effects • Clear and accurate identification of risks				

IRB Number: _____

III. Selection of Subjects	Yes	No	NA	Comments (If necessary)
Indicate whether the selection of subjects is reasonable and equitable by considering the following elements of the protocol:				

- Inclusion and exclusion criteria
- Minority and ethnic representation
- Representation of women, appropriate safeguards for women of childbearing potential
- Justification of sample size
- Recruitment methods
- Special considerations of vulnerable populations
- Inclusion of pregnant women and/or fetuses (Subpart B)
  NOTE: If pregnant women and/or fetuses are involved, make determination 6 on page 6. If the research is directed toward fetuses in utero, make determination 7 on page 6.
- Inclusion of prisoners (Subpart C)
  NOTE: If prisoners are involved, make determinations 4 AND 5 on page 6
- Inclusion of children (Subpart D)
  NOTE: If children are involved, make determination 3 on page 5
- Other vulnerable populations

IV. Obtaining Informed Consent	Yes	No	NA	Comments (If necessary)
Indicate whether the process to obtain informed consent is adequate				

NOTE: If investigator is requesting a waiver and/or alteration of the informed consent process or its documentation requirements, make determinations 1 and 2 on page 5.

	Yes	No	NA	Comments (If necessary)
Process for special populations				
• Minors: Is assent needed (generally for children over 7 years of age enrolling in non-therapeutic trials)?				
• Adults with impaired decision-making capacity: Are there mechanisms for obtaining informed consent from legally authorized representative?				
• Non-English-speaking subjects				
• Consideration of circumstances of obtaining consent (timing, place, etc.)				

IRB Number: _____

V. Informed Consent Form	Yes	No	NA	Comments (If necessary)
Indicate whether informed consent will be documented by obtaining a signed informed consent form.				
Indicate whether the informed consent form is written at an appropriate level of understanding.				
Indicate whether the informed consent form is adequate by considering whether it contains the required 8 basic elements:				
• A statement that the study involves research, an explanation of the purposes of the research and the expected duration of subject's participation, a description of what procedures will be followed, and which ones are experimental				
• A description of any foreseeable risks or discomforts				
• A description of benefits to the subject or others who may benefit				
• Disclosure of appropriate alternative procedures or treatments that may be advantageous to the subject				
• A statement describing the extent of confidentiality of records identifying the subject				
• Research involving more than minimal risk must include explanation regarding ❖ whether any compensation is available for participation ❖ whether medical treatments are available for injuries, and, if so, a description of them or where more information is available				

IRB Number:_____

• Whom to contact
  ❖ For answers to questions about research
  ❖ For answers to questions about subjects' rights
  ❖ If a research-related injury occurs				

• A statement that participation is voluntary, that refusal to participate will not penalize the subject, and consent to participate can be withdrawn at any time				
If appropriate to the research, indicate whether the informed consent form contains the following 6 additional elements:				
• That some risks to subject (embryo, fetus) may be unforeseeable				
• Outlines the circumstances where a subject's participation may be terminated by PI without regard to subject's consent				
• Whether there are any additional costs for which subjects will be responsible				
• The consequences of a subject's decision to withdraw (safety issues)				
• That new and significant findings, which may affect subject's willingness to continue, will be disclosed				
• The approximate number of subjects involved in the research at the institution and nationally				

IRB Number:_____

VI. Privacy and Confidentiality of Data and Records

	Yes	No	NA	Comments (If necessary)
Indicate whether the provisions to maintain the privacy of the subjects and confidentiality of data and research records are adequate by considering the following elements in the protocol:				
• Recording and coding of data				
• Identifiability of data				
• Storage of data				
• Sharing of data (including by electronic transmission)				
• Storage of subject samples (saliva, blood, tissue)				

VII. Investigator Conflict of Interest

	Yes	No	NA	Comments
Do any investigators or co-investigators have a conflict of interest as identified in the Conflicts of Interest and Commitment Policy and Instruction of Weill Medical College and Graduate School of Medical Sciences of Cornell University (Fourth Edition 2004)				
Is a copy of the WMC Study Specific Financial Disclosure Form for each investigator and co-investigator involved with this study attached to the application?				
If you answered Yes above, has the PI included a disclosure of the conflict of interest in the informed consent document?				
If No, has the PI explained why disclosure to potential subjects is not necessary or not appropriate?				
Is disclosure necessary?				

IRB Number:_____

Complete only if applicable
IRB DETERMINATIONS

Please complete the sections that apply in order to make determinations as required.

INFORMED CONSENT
1. **Is a waiver or alteration of consent requested or appropriate? (46.116[c])** (*ALL MUST APPLY*)
   ❑ Research involves no more than minimal risk; **AND**
   ❑ Waiver/alteration will not adversely affect rights and welfare of subjects; **AND**
   ❑ Research could not practicably be conducted without waiver/alteration; **AND**
   ❑ Whenever appropriate, subjects will be provided additional pertinent information after participation.

2. **Is PI requesting waiver of requirement to obtain signed consent form? (46.117[c]) (Either may apply)**
   ❑ The only record linking subject to research would be the consent form, and principal risk to subject would be potential harm resulting from breach of confidentiality; **OR**
   ❑ Research presents no more than minimal risk of harm to subject and involves no procedures for which written consent is normally required outside of research context.

RESEARCH WITH CHILDREN
3. **If research involves minors (Subpart D), which of the following conditions applies? The research is:**
   ❑ No greater than minimal risk, and assent of child and permission of parents are obtained (46.404); **OR**
   ❑ Greater than minimal risk, but presents the prospect of direct benefit to individual subjects (46.405). *Note:* The IRB must find that (a) the risk is justified by the anticipated benefit to the subjects; (b) the relation of the anticipated benefit to the risk is at least as favorable to the subjects as that presented by available alternative approaches; and (c) adequate provisions are made for soliciting the assent of the children and permission of their parents or guardians; **OR**
   ❑ Greater than minimal risk, and no prospect of direct benefit to individual subjects, but likely to yield generalizable knowledge about the subject's disorder or condition (46.406). *Note:* The IRB must find that (a) the risk represents a minor increase over minimal risk; (b) the intervention or procedure represents experiences to subjects that are reasonably commensurate with those inherent in their actual or expected medical, dental, psychological, social, or educational situations; (c) the research is likely to yield knowledge of vital importance; and (d) adequate provisions are made for soliciting the assent of the children and permission of parents or guardians; **OR**

IRB Number: _____

❏ Not otherwise approvable, but presents an opportunity to understand, prevent, or alleviate a serious problem affecting the health or welfare of children (46.407). *Note:* After the IRB makes this finding, the Secretary of the Department of Health and Human Services may allow the research to proceed after consultation with a panel of experts in pertinent disciplines (for example, science, medicine, education, ethics, law) and following opportunity for public review and comment.

RESEARCH WITH PRISONERS
4. If research involves prisoners, is it approvable? (46.305) (*ALL MUST APPLY*)
  ❏ Advantages to participation are not coercive; **AND**
  ❏ Risks are commensurate with what would be acceptable to nonprisoners; **AND**
  ❏ The selection procedures are fair; **AND**
  ❏ The information is presented in an understandable language; **AND**
  ❏ There is no effect on decisions related to parole; **AND**
  ❏ Provisions for follow-up are adequate.

RESEARCH WITH PRISONERS
5. If all of the previous conditions are satisfied, mark one of the following determinations (46.306):
  ❏ Research on possible causes, effects, and processes of incarceration and of criminal behavior, provided that the study presents no more than minimal risk and no more than inconvenience to the subjects; **OR**
  ❏ Research on prisons as institutional structures or of prisoners as incarcerated persons, provided that the study presents no more than minimal risk and no more than inconvenience to the subjects; **OR**
  ❏ Research on conditions particularly affecting prisoners as a class, provided that the study may proceed only after the Secretary of DHHS has consulted with appropriate experts (in penology, medicine, and ethics) and published notice in the Federal Register of the intent to approve such research; **OR**
  ❏ Research on practices, both innovative and accepted, which have the intent and reasonable probability of improving the health or well-being of the subjects; **OR**
  ❏ If the research includes the assignment of prisoners to control groups that might not benefit from the research, it may proceed only after the Secretary of HHS has consulted with appropriate experts and published a note in the Federal Register of the intent to approve the research.

RESEARCH INVOLVING PREGNANT WOMEN AND/OR FETUSES
6. If research is directed at pregnant women (46.207), which of the following conditions applies? (<u>ONE OF THE FIRST TWO CONDITIONS MUST BE MET</u>)
  ❏ The purpose of the activity is to meet the health needs of the mother, and the fetus will be placed at risk only to the minimum extent to meet such needs; **OR**
  ❏ The risk to the fetus is minimal; **OR**
  ❏ The research does not meet either of these conditions and cannot be approved as submitted.

IRB Number: _____

7. **If research is directed toward fetuses *in utero* as subjects, which of the following conditions applies? (<u>ONE OF THE FIRST TWO CONDITIONS MUST BE MET</u>)**

   ❑ The purpose of the activity is to meet the health needs of the fetus, and the fetus will be placed at risk only to the minimum extent to meet such needs; **OR**

   ❑ The risk to the fetus is minimal, and the purpose is the development of important biomedical knowledge which cannot be obtained by other means; **OR**

   ❑ The research does not meet either of these conditions and cannot be approved as submitted.

8. **If approvable under category 6 or 7 above, the following conditions must also be met:**

   ❑ Consent of both mother and father are obtained, unless the father is not reasonably available.

   ❑ Individuals engaged in the research will have no part in decisions related to terminating the pregnancy and determining viability.

   ❑ No inducements are offered to terminate pregnancy for the purposes of the research.

Appendix 5.4

⋮ REQUEST FOR APPROVAL OF INVESTIGATION

Protocol No. _____

Receipt Date _____

The New York Presbyterian Hospital-Weill Medical College of Cornell University Institutional Review Board (IRB)

REQUEST FOR APPROVAL OF INVESTIGATION INVOLVING USE OF HUMAN SUBJECTS

Medical Center and Federal Policies require review of each protocol by the Medical Center's IRB with respect to the:

1) rights and welfare of subjects; 2) adequacy of methods used to secure informed consent; and 3) risk and potential benefits of the research to the subject. Read instructions carefully and then type and complete each item. If an item is not applicable, indicate this by "NA". Obtain required signatures. Submit original and 26 copies to Room A-128 or 425 E. 61st Street, Suite 301.

1. Principal Investigator_____ Degree_____

2. Academic Title _____ Telephone_____

3. Department_____ Division_____

4. Mailing Address_____ Room_____

5. ☐ New Protocol   Prior Protocol Number:_____

6. Project title (if applicable, use same title of externally funded research; limit to 60 spaces):

_____

7. Purpose of Project (one or two sentences):

_____

_____

8. Inclusive dates of study_____ to _____

Expected duration of study on individual subjects (days/months) _____

_____

9. Source of funds
(agency, institutional, or industry sponsor) _____

10. Proposal: ☐ will not be   ☐ will be   ☐ has been submitted to funding
agency (date):_____

11. If project will be funded to another investigator, give Principal Investigator's name
and grant title

_____

12. Co-investigators:

Name	*Degree*	*Department*	*Telephone #*
a. _____	_____	_____	_____
b. _____	_____	_____	_____
c. _____	_____	_____	_____
d. _____	_____	_____	_____
e. _____	_____	_____	_____
f. _____	_____	_____	_____

13. Student Research: ☐ No   ☐ Yes, complete the items below

List Student Name(s): _____

_____

_____

Indicate the role of the student(s) and who will supervise the student(s):

_____

14. Where will study be conducted? (be specific) _____

15. **Required Summary:** Please create a brief descriptive summary of this study (200
words or less), in layman terms (8th-grade language), that would be useful as a
public awareness mechanism.

SECTION A. NON TECHNICAL RESEARCH PLAN

<u>State concisely the design, aims, and specific objectives of the research, and the procedures to be used to accomplish these aims in language that can be understood by a non-scientist. Because the Committee includes lay persons, avoid or explain highly technical language.</u> Describe what will happen to subjects and what they will be expected to do. State specific interventions which would not be performed except for the purposes of this study. Use continuation pages if necessary.

Study Design (for example, hypothesis, research question, standard and experimental procedures, special or unusual equipment of procedures):

Rationale and justification for the study (for example, historical background, investigator's personal experience, pertinent medical literature):

Primary study endpoint:

Primary objective:

Secondary objectives:

Inclusion/Exclusion criteria:

Treatment Plan:

Statistical considerations (justification for sample size or "n", poser or degree of change):

Relative importance/value of the trial, considering "standard" therapy and published/competing trials:

SECTION B. SUBJECT POPULATION

1. Number being enrolled: Male: _____   Female: _____
   Age Range _____ to _____

2. Type: ☐ Inpatients   ☐ Patient Controls
           ☐ Patient Minors (up to 18 years)   ☐ Outpatients
           ☐ Normal Volunteers   ☐ Volunteer Minors
                                              (up to 18 years)

3. Special Groups (check applicable boxes):

   ☐ Minors*   ☐ Prisoners*
   ☐ Fetuses*   ☐ Students and/or employees
   ☐ Pregnant Women*   ☐ Derived materials or data
   ☐ Special racial or ethnic group (specify):   ☐ Mentally/cognitively impaired
   _____   (mentally ill, mentally
                                                    retarded, emotionally
                                                    disturbed, senile dementia)

These special groups require additional protections under the law—see applicable sections at the end of this application.

4. Rationale for use of special groups, or subjects whose ability to give voluntary informed consent may be in question:

5. Subject's state of physical health. Indicate if seriously or terminally ill.

6. Indicate a) how subjects are initially identified (medical records, physician referral, canvassing, classes, etc.; be specific), b) and/or recruited (bedside or clinic interview, ads, telephone, letter, etc.; be specific)

7. Will WMC General Clinical   ☐ Yes   ☐ No
   Research Center be used?   ☐ Pediatric Unit   ☐ and/or Adult Unit

8. Will subjects receive any inducements before, or rewards or compensation during or after study?
   ☐ No   ☐ Yes,   How much and in what form? (Cash, taxi fares, medical care, meals, gifts, etc.):
   _____

SECTION C. HUMAN TISSUE - SURGICAL OR AUTOPSY TISSUE:

Is human tissue, as identified below, being used in this study? _____Yes _____No

If YES, complete this section.

1. Human tissue from surgical or autopsy procedures includes ALL DIAGNOSTIC AND PATHOLOGICAL SPECIMENS (including placentas, umbilical cords, umbilical cord blood, bone marrow aspirates, fine needle aspirates, cytologic specimens, and all other tissue removed from the body but not blood or amniotic fluid at the time of rupture of membranes prior to or during labor).

2. Surgical or autopsy tissue excludes "surgical waste," which is specifically defined as subcutaneous tissue removed to facilitate wound closure and tissues significantly altered or diluted by the procedure such as lens phakoemulsifications, vitrectomy specimens, and liposuction specimens.

3. No surgical or autopsy tissue can be released for research or clinical purposes without the express permission of an attending pathologist or designee.

4. Surgical or autopsy tissue can be released by Pathology for research purposes **only** after sufficient tissue has been reserved for any and all diagnostic and pathological procedures.

5. Written consent of the Department of Pathology and Laboratory Medicine must be obtained in all cases where human tissue is used for research. This includes protocols in which tissue is taken solely for research purposes and those involving tissue (such as a bone marrow aspirate) that normally is not submitted to Pathology. In these situations an exception to the Tissue Submission Policy must be granted (see next page).

6. A copy of the approved and stamped "IRB Tissue Request Form", will be kept on file in Pathology. (See page 7 of this document for the form.)

7. If fetal tissue is requested and the gestational age is greater than 12 weeks, a completed and signed autopsy consent (Form #41160) must be submitted, attached to the Surgical Pathology requisition. (Attach copy of standard hospital form).

8. Which consent form will be obtained permitting disposition of surgical or autopsy tissue for research?

_____None needed (placenta, umbilical cord, and umbilical cord blood only)

_____Authorization for surgery form (#45350) or autopsy form (#41160)

_____Study specific consent form

9. Are all investigators totally disassociated from those responsible for the surgical procedure that produces the surgical tissue? _____Yes_____No. If **no,** explain on a continuation page.

10. Will **only** that tissue or fluid normally taken for therapeutic or diagnostic purposes be used (i.e., no additional material will be taken for research purposes only)?

_____Yes_____No. If **no,** you must use Full rather than Expedited review.

Is an **EXCEPTION** to the Tissue Submission Policy being requested? _____Yes _____No

If YES, Please explain in detail the basis of your exception request, and obtain the additional signature of approval by the Department of Pathology and Laboratory Medicine.

Tissue Submission Policy: Surgical tissue removed during a diagnostic or therapeutic procedure must be submitted to Surgical Pathology intact and may not be incised, opened, or damaged in any way. In addition, tissue **may not** be removed from the specimen prior to receipt in Surgical Pathology. Any exceptions must be detailed below and specifically approved by the Department of Pathology and Laboratory Medicine.

Exception Approval:

_____   _____   _____
Department of Pathology and   Signature   Date
   Laboratory Medicine

IRB Tissue Request Form

Principal Investigator _____

Name of Protocol _____

_____

Persons authorized to obtain tissue _____

_____

Type of tissue required (fresh, sterile, frozen, sections from paraffin-embedded tissue _____

_____

Organ/site of tissue required _____
Minimum tissue required/patient (cc's, sections from blocks, slides, cells, etc.)

_____

"Normal" tissue required/patient (cc's, sections from blocks, slides, cells, etc.)

_____

Estimated number of patients _____

Protocol Number _____

IRB Approval Stamp
With start & end dates

A copy of this stamped form will be kept on file in the Department of Pathology and Laboratory Medicine. Tissue will not be released without this form.

If technical work will be requested from Pathology (histology, flow cytometry, immuno-histochemistry, etc.), please complete the "Clinical Research Protocol" form that may be downloaded from the Department of Pathology and Laboratory Medicine's website, http://www.cornellpathology.org/research/. Please note that paraffin-embedded tissue blocks may not be released from Pathology, however, unstained slides from tissue blocks can be provided.

SECTION D. RISKS

The purpose of this section is to determine if subjects will be placed "at risk"—i.e., exposed to the possibility of physical, psychological, sociological, or other harm as a consequence of any activity proposed in the research project.

Risk Classification: What is the overall risk classification of the research: (1) No more than minimal risk, or (2) greater than minimal risk.

(Circle the classification that applies.)

NOTE: According to HHS/FDA regulations, no more than minimal risk means: "The probability and magnitude of harm or discomfort anticipated in the research are not greater in and of themselves than those ordinarily encountered in daily life or during the performance of routine physical or psychological examinations or tests."

DOES THE RESEARCH PLANNED IN THIS PROJECT INVOLVE:	Yes	No
1. Any surgical process (specify):	☐	☐
2. Administration of drugs, chemical or biological agents; if yes, complete Section H.	☐	☐
3. Use of radioisotopes or other sources of ionizing radiation (e.g., x-ray machine, etc.). If yes, see Section F.	☐	☐
4. Major changes in diet or exercise (specify):	☐	☐
5. Administration of physical stimuli other than auditory and visual stimuli associated with normal classroom situations.	☐	☐
6. Deprivation of physiologic requirements such as nutrition or sleep, manipulation of psychological and/or social variables (e.g., sensory deprivation social isolation, psychological stresses, deceptions, etc.).	☐	☐
7. Use of new medical devices as defined by FDA regulations: If yes, use Section G.	☐	☐
8. Use of deceptive techniques without the knowledge of subject, (e.g., placebo single blind, double blind, or control group).	☐	☐
9. Possible invasion of privacy of subject or family, including use of personal or medical information.	☐	☐
10. Any probing of information that might be considered personal or sensitive.	☐	☐
11. Presentation to the subject of any materials that they might find to be offensive, threatening, or degrading.	☐	☐
12. Other possible risks (specify):	☐	☐

<u>IF ANY OF THE PRECEDING QUESTIONS HAVE BEEN ANSWERED YES, EXPLAIN BELOW:</u>

13. Describe risks of study medications and/or procedures in detail and assess their seriousness. Include incidence of complications, if known.
14. Explain in detail what precautions have been taken to minimize these risks, their likely effectiveness, and the data safety monitoring plan being used to follow subjects. For assistance, we have included information below about data and safety monitoring plans.

What is a Data and Safety Monitoring Plan (DSMP)?

A DSMP is a prospectively defined strategy to assess the assumptions made in the protocol design while the study is in progress. Its main purpose is to ensure the safety of participants in clinical research studies and the validity and integrity of research data collection.

Depending on the nature, size, complexity, and risk of the study, the level of monitoring can vary from a single monitor for a small trial with minimal risk to an external data and safety monitoring board (DSMB) for more complex and high-risk trials.

Key Elements

Key elements to be included in a DSMP:

- Assessment of risk and monitoring level
- Safety contact: Who is responsible?
- Safety monitoring: Who will do it? How often?
- Informed consent process; consistency with protocol
- Data collection process
- Adverse Events Monitoring: Anticipated and Unanticipated
  - Description of anticipated adverse events
  - Grading and attribution method
  - Reporting of unanticipated adverse events
  - Plans for periodic reporting
  - Impact on termination of subjects from the study and study closure

15. Describe other alternative and accepted procedures or methods of diagnosis and treatment, if any, that were considered and why they will not be used.

16. Assess potential benefits to subjects and to society that may accrue as a result of this research. Analyze risk-benefit ratio, and explain why benefits to be gained outweigh and risks.

SECTION E. CONFIDENTIALITY OF DATA

What specific safeguards will be employed to protect confidentiality of data, e.g., coding or removal of identifiers as soon as possible, limitation of access to data, use of locked file cabinets, protection of computer-based data systems, etc.? Will data which identify individual subjects be published or in any way disclosed to third parties other than project personnel? If so, explain here, and incorporate in consent form:

SECTION F. ADDITIONAL REGULATORY INFORMATION

1.   USE OF RADIATION PRODUCING EQUIPMENT AND RADIOACTIVE MATERIALS

A) Will diagnostic ionizing radiation (radionuclides, radiography, fluoroscopy, computed tomography) and/or radiation therapy be used in the course of this study?

_____Yes   _____No

B) If radionuclides are to be used the following items must be completed:

1) Name of radionuclides licensee:_____

# of License:_____Date Issued:_____Does license cover human use? _____Yes _____No

2) Radionuclide(s) to be administered:_____

3) Chemical form(s) _____

4) Activity administered per procedure (in millicuries) for each radionuclide: (Use separate sheet for each type of examination.) _____

_____

5) How many studies of each type will be performed per patient :_____

6) Will any complementary non-radioactive drugs be administered as part of the radionuclide study?

_____No_____Yes, name of drug(s) and dose schedule(s):_____

7) Dosimetry*:

Major Organ dose:_____rad   Total body dose:_____ rad

Gonadal dose: Female_____rad   Male_____rad

Other:_____

Source of dosimetry data:_____

C) If radiography, fluoroscopy, or computed tomography are to be used the following items must be completed:

1) <u>Type of examination</u>   <u>Body region exposed</u>

_____Radiography   _____

_____Fluoroscopy   _____

_____Computed   _____

2) Dosimetry*: Include entrance skin dose, gonadal dose, critical organ doses, e.g., lens of eye, bone marrow.

_____

3) How many times will each examination be done?

_____

D) If research involves radiation therapy detailed description of methodology and dosimetry should be provided on a separate page.

*Referral for assistance with dosimetry calculations may be obtained by calling Radiation Safety at 746-6964.

2. RECOMBINANT DNA AND/OR GENE THERAPY

Does this project involve the use of recombinant DNA and/or gene therapy? If so, Institutional Biosafety Committee (IBC) approval must be obtained. [*Note:* Recombinant DNA studies that are exempt from RAC review under Appendix M, are not exempt from local IBC review.]

_____Yes   _____ No

Not sure if IBC approval is required? Contact 212-746-6201

Need help filing an IBC application?
Forms are available at: http://intranet.med.cornell.edu/research/ibc.html or call 212-821-0628

3. CONFLICT OF INTEREST

Do any investigators or co-investigators have a conflict of interest as defined in the Conflicts of Interest and Commitment Policy and Instruction of Weill Medical College and Graduate School of Medical Sciences of Cornell University (Fourth Edition 2004)?

_____Yes   _____No

A copy of the WMC Study Specific Financial Disclosure Form for each investigator and co-investigator involved with this study must be attached to this application.

If you answered yes above, have you included a disclosure of the conflict of interest in the informed consent document?

_____Yes   _____No; please explain why you believe that disclosure to potential subjects is not necessary or not appropriate.

SECTION G. MEDICAL DEVICES

NOTE: If this project involves an FDA regulated drug or device, please submit any communications from the FDA regarding IND, IDE, or humanitarian use applications related to this submission.

Will any medical devices be used during the study?

☐ No, proceed to Section H

☐ Yes If this study involves the experimental use of medical and surgical diagnostic therapeutic devices of unproven safety and efficacy, the investigator must determine the applicability of the Investigational Device Exemption federal regulations to the study, and must complete the following:

1) FDA IDE# : _____

2) Name of device: _____

3) Sponsor of device: _____

4) Will device be custom-built?   _____ Yes   _____ No

5) Does the study involve a (   ) "significant risk" device, or a (   ) "non-significant risk device, as defined below?

   Significant risk device means an investigational device that:

   (a) Is intended as an implant and presents a potential for serious risk to the health, safety, or welfare of a subject;

   (b) Is purported or represented to be for use in supporting or sustaining human life and presents a potential for serious risk to the health, safety, or welfare of a subject;

   (c) Is for a use of substantial importance in diagnosing, curing, mitigating, or treating disease or otherwise preventing impairment of human health and presents a potential for serious risk to the health, safety, or welfare of a subject; or

   (d) Otherwise presents a potential for serious risk to the health, safety, or welfare of a subject.

6. Non-Significant Risk Device (Complete, if applicable)

   Is this a previously "banned" device   _____ Yes   _____ No

7. Significant Risk Device (Complete, if applicable)

   a) Does sponsor intend to apply for IDE?   _____ Yes   _____ No

   b) Have you signed an agreement with sponsor to participate in the study?

      _____ Yes   _____ No

   c) Submit on continuation page the investigational plan of sponsor and reports to prior investigations.

SECTION H. USE OF DRUGS OR BIOLOGICAL AGENTS

The Joint Commission on Accreditation of Healthcare Organizations (JCAHO) requires that the administration of investigational drugs to patients cared for within a health care organization be under the central control of the hospital pharmacy department.

All IRB-approved protocols that involve the administration of FDA-approved medications and/or investigational medications **MUST** utilize the Investigational Pharmacy to dispense the medications specified in the research protocol. Prior to submission of a new IRB application, investigators must make arrangements with the Investigational Pharmacy and must have Section H signed by an authorized member of the Department of Pharmacy. This will ensure that all medications are accounted for and that studies budget properly for the utilization of the Investigational Pharmacy.

Please complete the table below for **each** medication being administered as part of the protocol.

	Status of Medication:		
Medication Name	*Investigational*	*Off-Label Use of FDA-Approved Medication*	*Used According to FDA Labeling*
	☐	☐	☐
	☐	☐	☐
	☐	☐	☐
	☐	☐	☐
	☐	☐	☐
	☐	☐	☐

For *each* medication that is ***investigational*** or ***off-label use of an FDA-approved medication,*** please complete the form on the next page.

If any medications will be administered and/or dispensed as part of this protocol, please obtain approval from the Department of Pharmacy.

_____   _____   _____

Department of Pharmacy   **Signature**   **Date**
(Print Name)

Study Title:

Medication Name (generic name):
Medication Name (brand name, if applicable):
Synonyms for medication name:
Sponsor IND#:
Dosage Form:
Strength:
Status of medication: ☐Investigational   ☐Off-Label Use of
FDA-approved medication
Indication for Medication Use in this Protocol:

Please list co-investigators that are <u>authorized to prescribe</u> medications related to this research study:

Effects of the drug for its intended use (dosage range and efficacy data in humans plus animal studies when appropriate):

Known side effects, risks, and hazards (include incidence, if known):

Regimen being administered in this protocol:

Medication Name & Strength	Dose	Route of Administration	Frequency	Duration of Therapy

Clinically significant drug interactions:

Essential Compatibility Data:

	Dextrose-Based IV Solutions	Saline-Based IV Solutions	Lactated Ringers	Other (_____)
Compatible	☐	☐	☐	☐
Not Compatible	☐	☐	☐	☐

Reconstitution and Stability Data:

Storage, Accountability, Staff Precautions, Special Instructions, etc.:

Note: A copy of this form must be placed in the patient's medical chart along with a copy of the signed and dated informed consent.

Investigational Drug Data Sheet

Please answer all questions below.

Study Title:

Principal Investigator: Telephone: Email:

Study Coordinator: Telephone: Email:

Please specify the number of patients you expect to enroll in this study:

Please complete the table below for **each** medication being administered as part of the protocol.

Medication Name	Status of Medication:		
	Investigational	*Off-Label Use of FDA-Approved Medication*	*Labeled Use of FDA-Approved Medication*
	☐	☐	☐
	☐	☐	☐
	☐	☐	☐
	☐	☐	☐

Service(s) required from the Investigational Pharmacy (select all that apply):

☒ Storage   ☒ Inventory/Accountability   ☒ Dispensing   ☒ Labeling

☐ Re-order medication supplies   ☐ Re-pack study medication

☐ Compound study medication   ☐ Prepare intravenous medications

☐ Perform randomization   ☐ Design randomization schema

☐ Prepare placebo (single or double-blinding)   ☐ Perform dose calculations

☐ Patient drug returns   ☐ Prepare drug data sheet

☐ Other special preparation

Will Investigational Pharmacy services be required off-hours and/or on weekends?

☐ Yes   ☐ No

In addition to this form, please submit two copies of each of the following materials to the Investigational Pharmacy:
- ❏ IRB protocol submission
- ❏ Investigator's brochure/Other sponsor materials related to the protocol
- ❏ FDA Form 1572

These protocols can be dropped off to the Investigational Pharmacy in Room F-08.

SECTION I.   SPECIAL POPULATIONS OF RESEARCH SUBJECTS
PEDIATRIC SUBJECTS

Please check the category below that best represents the degree of risk and benefit to which the children in this study will be exposed. *Note: More than one category may be indicated, such as when a protocol involves both a study group and a control; in that case, please specify the group to which the category applies.*

The federal regulations divide research into different risk categories: research that is **not greater than minimal risk** to the participant and research that is **greater than minimal risk**. Under the regulations, **minimal risk** means that the probability and magnitude of harm or discomfort anticipated in the research are not greater in and of themselves than those ordinarily encountered in daily life or during the performance of routine physical or psychological examinations or tests.

CHECK ONE OF THE FOLLOWING BELOW:

(1) _____ The proposed research is **not greater than minimal risk**, as defined previously. (45 CFR 46.404)

(2) _____ The proposed research poses a **greater than minimal risk** with the **potential for direct benefit**. (45 CFR 46.405)

The risk must be justified by the benefit. Please explain:

_____

_____

_____

The risk/benefit assessment must be at least as favorable as that presented by alternative approaches. Please explain:

_____

_____

_____

(3) _____ The proposed research is **greater than minimal risk** with **no prospect for direct benefit** to individuals, but is **likely to yield generalizable knowledge** about the subjects' disorder or condition. (45 CFR 46.406) (Answer below)

NOTE: If your research is in this category, <u>consent of both parents is required</u> unless one parent is deceased, unknown, incompetent, or not reasonably available, or when only one parent has legal responsibility for and custody of the child.

This research is approvable if:

The risk represents a minor increase over minimal risk. Please justify:

_____

_____

_____

The intervention or procedure is likely to yield generalizable knowledge about the subjects' disorder or condition which is of vital importance for the understanding or amelioration of the subjects' disorder or condition. Please justify:

_____

_____

_____

(4) _____ Research involving minors that does not fit within these categories but that presents an opportunity to understand, prevent, or alleviate a serious problem affecting the health or welfare of children is approvable only with approval of the Secretary of HHS, after consultation with a panel of experts. (45 CFR 46.407) If this category applies, please consult the IRB office at 212-821-0577.

Assent of Minors

The federal regulations require that adequate provision must be made for soliciting the assent of children when in the judgment of the IRB the children are capable of providing assent, taking into consideration the ages, maturity, and psychological state of the children involved. Generally the assent of a child could be sought when the child is seven years of age or older, on an assent form that is written in language understandable to a child in the age group involved.

PREGNANT WOMEN, FETUSES, AND NEONATES

Please check the category below that best represents the degree of risk and benefit in this study.

The federal regulations divide research into different risk categories: research that is **not greater than minimal risk** to the participant and research that is **greater than minimal risk**. Under the regulations, **minimal risk** means that the probability and magnitude of harm or discomfort anticipated in the research are not greater in and of themselves than those ordinarily encountered in daily life or during the performance of routine physical or psychological examinations or tests.

1) PREGNANT WOMEN AND FETUSES

(a) When appropriate, have studies been done on animals and non-pregnant individuals? _____ Yes _____ No

If yes, please explain briefly the nature and findings of these previous studies:

_____

_____

_____

_____

_____

(b) Does the research pose a greater than minimal risk to the woman or fetus? _____ Yes _____ No

If yes, please check the appropriate category and justify:

_____ The risk to the fetus is caused solely by interventions/procedures that hold out the prospect of direct benefit for the woman or fetus. Justification:

_____

_____

_____

_____ There is no prospect of direct benefit to either the woman or the fetus, but the risk to the fetus is not greater than minimal and the purpose of the research is the development of important biomedical knowledge that cannot be obtained by any other means. Justification:

_____

_____

_____

To be approvable, the risk must be the least possible for achieving the objectives of the research. Please justify:

_____

_____

_____

If the research holds out the prospect of direct benefit to the woman and/or the fetus, or if the research presents no more than minimal risk, the **consent of the woman** must be obtained.

If the research holds out the prospect of direct benefit solely to the fetus, the **consent of the woman and the father** of the fetus must be obtained, unless the father is unavailable, incompetent, incapacitated, or if the pregnancy resulted from incest or rape.

The PI must agree that no inducements, monetary or otherwise, will be offered to terminate a pregnancy.
_____ PI agrees   _____ PI does not agree

The PI must agree that individuals engaged in the research will have no part in any decisions as to the timing, method, or procedures used to terminate a pregnancy.
_____ PI agrees   _____ PI does not agree

The PI must agree that individuals engaged in the research will have no part in determining the viability of a neonate.
_____ PI agrees   _____ PI does not agree

2) NEONATES

For the purpose of human subject protections regulations, newborns are considered neonates until they are determined to be viable. The regulations applicable to pediatric subjects would then apply. This section applies to **neonates of uncertain viability** and **nonviable neonates.**

When appropriate, have preclinical and clinical studies been conducted and have they provided data for assessing potential risks to neonates:
_____ Yes   _____ No

The PI must agree that individuals engaged in the research will have no part in determining the viability of the neonate.
_____ PI agrees   _____ PI does not agree

(a) Neonates of uncertain viability.

The research must hold out the prospect of enhancing the probability of survival of the neonate to the point of viability and any risk is the least possible for achieving that objective. Please justify:

_____

_____

_____

OR

The purpose of the research is the development of important biomedical knowledge that cannot be obtained by other means and there will be no added risk to the neonate resulting from the research. Please justify:

_____

_____

_____

Consent of either parent of the neonate of uncertain viability is required, or, if neither is able to consent, of the legally authorized representative of either parent. Consent of the father or his representative is not required if the pregnancy resulted from rape or incest

(b) Nonviable neonates. After delivery, nonviable neonates may not be involved in research unless:

_____ Vital functions of the neonate will not be artificially maintained.

_____ The research will not terminate the heartbeat or respiration of the neonate

_____ There will be no added risk to the neonate resulting from the research. and

_____ The purpose of the research is the development of important biomedical knowledge that cannot be obtained by other means.

Consent of both parents of the nonviable neonate is required, unless either parent is unable to consent due to unavailability, incompetence, or incapacity. The consent of the father is not needed if the pregnancy resulted from rape or incest. Consent of a legally authorized representative of either or both parents is not adequate.

PRISONERS

Because prisoners may be under constraints because of their incarceration which could affect their ability to make a truly voluntary and un-coerced decision about whether or not to participate as subjects in research, the federal regulations provide additional safeguards for the protection of prisoners as human subjects in research.

The federal regulations divide research into different risk categories: research that is **not greater than minimal risk** to the participant and research that is **greater than minimal risk**. Under the regulations, **minimal risk** means that the probability and magnitude of harm or discomfort anticipated in the research are not greater in and of themselves than those ordinarily encountered in daily life or during the performance of routine physical or psychological examinations or tests.

The IRB can only approve research that falls into one of the following categories and which has been approved by the Secretary of HHS after consultation with a panel of experts.

Please check the one that applies and justify the research:

_____ *Cause and Effect*: Study of the possible causes, effects, and processes of incarceration and of criminal behavior and presents no more than a minimal risk.

_____

_____

_____

_____

_____ *Institutional Structures:* Study of prisons as institutional structures or of prisoners as incarcerated persons, provided it causes no more than a minimal risk.

_____

_____

_____

_____

_____ *Conditions Affecting Prisoners as a Class:* Research on conditions particularly affecting prisoners as a class (e.g., vaccine trials and other research on hepatitis which is more prevalent in prisons; research on social and psychological problems such as alcoholism, drug addiction, and sexual assaults).

_____

_____

_____

_____

SECTION J. INFORMED CONSENT

Informed consent is necessary for all research involving human subjects and must be documented in some manner. The investigator may determine which method would best serve the interest of the subject population, but the Committee reserves the right to require alternative or more stringent means of securing consent. Use of subjects unable to give personal consent for reasons of age, mental state, legal, or other such status requires that consent or assent be secured from parents or a legal guardian.

1. Describe procedures used to obtain informed consent (and minor assent, if applicable), including how and where informed consent (and assent, if applicable) will be obtained.

2. Will you obtain <u>written</u> consent: ☐ Yes ☐ No

    NOTE: This is always required when there is a definite physical, social, or psychological risks to the subject. Document must embody all of the basic elements of informed consent. These are contained in the template IRB Consent Form.

3. Will you obtain only oral consent: ☐ Yes ☐ No

    NOTE: Oral consent may be sufficient in the case of minimal risk to the subject, specifically those procedures for normal adult volunteers as described in Section C.1 of this form. Subject must be informed of applicable basic elements of consent. No signed document is necessary on the part of the subject. However, a sample written copy of the information to be imparted to the subject must be submitted and approved by the Committee. This method of obtaining consent is usually approved ONLY for no risk or minimal risk procedures.

    Sample documentation is attached: ☐ Yes   ☐ No

PRINT:

PI Name _____ Protocol Title _____

SECTION K. SIGNATURES

1. I certify that the above information concerning procedures to be taken for protection of human subjects is correct. I will seek and obtain prior approval for any modification of this protocol and will report promptly to the Committee on Human Rights in Research any unexpected or otherwise significant adverse effects encountered in the course of the study.

_____   _____   _____

Investigator Name   **Signature**   **Date**

This proposal has been reviewed and approved for submission to the Committee on Human Rights in Research

_____   _____   _____

Department Chairperson Name   **Signature**   **Date**

2. Are subjects covered under this research protocol administratively the responsibility of another department?

☐ No   ☐ Yes, approval is required, please obtain signature below.

a) Department Name: _____

_____   _____   _____

Department Chairperson Name   **Signature**   **Date**

b) Department Name: _____

_____   _____   _____

Department Chairperson Name   **Signature**   **Date**

3. Will your research involve the use of human tissue(s)?

☐ No   ☐ Yes, approval is necessary by the Chairperson of the Department of Pathology

_____   _____   _____

Department Chairperson Name   **Signature**   **Date**

4. Does this protocol make use of Perioperative Services (which includes the OR, Endoscopy, IVF, Genetics, Anesthesia, Gastrointestinal, Bronchoscopy, and Pulmonary Function)?

☐ No   ☐ Yes, please obtain the signature of the Administrative Director of Perioperative Services

_____   _____   _____
Admin Director Name   **Signature**   **Date.**

The International Committee of Medical Journal Editors (ICMJE) has established a requirement that all clinical trials be entered in a public registry before the onset of patient enrollment as a condition of consideration for publication. Additional information may be found at: http://clinicaltrials.gov/ and at http://www.icmje.org/clin _ trialup.htm

Please contact the Protocol Registration System (PRS) administrator by e-mail at: ICR@med.cornell.edu to set up a PRS user account to register new and ongoing clinical trials. The e-mail should contain the PI's full name, department, phone number and e-mail address.

Attachments

Please attach the following for the IRB to review your research:

Original Request for Approval of Investigation Involving Use of Human Subjects (IRB Protocol), including the consent form (and assent form, if applicable) plus 26 copies for Full Board Review

4 copies of any supplemental material:

- Sponsor's Protocol
- Investigator's Brochure
- Data Collection Sheets
- Study Specific Financial Disclosure Form for each investigator
- NIH grant application (if applicable)
- HIPAA research forms
- Any recruitment notices or advertisements
- Any survey instruments, psychological tests, interview forms, or scripts
- Any communication from the FDA regarding IND, IDE, or Humanitarian Use applications related to this submission

Appendix 5.5

CONSENT FORM FOR CLINICAL INVESTIGATION: THE NEW YORK PRESBYTERIAN HOSPITAL—WEILL MEDICAL COLLEGE OF CORNELL UNIVERSITY

Date (M/D/Y)	Location Service	
Age	Doctor	If No Plate, Print Name, Sex, and History No.

(PROTOTYPE)

Consent Form for Clinical Investigation
(If necessary, translate into language of subject)

Project Title: _____

  _____

Research Project #   _____

Principal Investigator   _____

INSTITUTION: (*Name of institutions participating in this research under this IRB approval*)

INTRODUCTION

You are invited to consider participating in a research study. The study is called ("*Title of Study*"). You were selected as a possible participant in this study because (state why and how the subject was selected).

Please take your time to make your decision. It is important that you read and understand several general principles that apply to all who take part in our studies:

(a) Taking part in the study is entirely voluntary.
(b) Personal benefit to you may or may not result from taking part in the study, but knowledge gained from your participation may benefit others.

143

(c) You may decide not to participate in the study or you may decide to stop participating in the study at any time without loss of any benefits to which you are entitled.

The purpose and nature of the study, possible benefits, risks, and discomforts, other options, your rights as a participant, and other information about the study are discussed below. Any new information discovered that might affect your decision to participate or remain in the study will be provided to you. You are urged to ask any questions you have about this study with members of the research team. You should take whatever time you need to discuss the study with your physician and family. The decision to participate or not to participate is yours. If you decide to participate, please sign and date where indicated at the end of this form.

The research is being sponsored by (*name of agency/company*). (*Name of agency/company*) is called the sponsor and the Medical Center is being paid by (*name of agency/company*), to conduct this study with (*name of investigator*) as the primary investigator.

WHY IS THE STUDY BEING DONE?

The purpose of this study is to: _____

(*Choose applicable text or customize your own:*)

Observational Studies: Learn about the natural history of (*name of disease*) and its causes and treatments.

Phase 1 Studies: Test the safety of (*drug/intervention*) and see what effects (*good and bad*) it has in your (*patient's condition*).

Or

Find the highest dose of (*drug*) that can be given without causing severe side effects.

Phase 2 Studies: Find out what effects (*good and bad*) (*drug/intervention*) has on you and your (*patient's condition*).

Phase 3 Studies: Compare the effect (*good and bad*) of the (*new drug/intervention*) with (*commonly used drugs/intervention*) on you and your (*patient's condition*) to see which is better.

This research is being done because _____.

[Explain in one or two sentences. Examples are: "Currently, there is no effective treatment for this type of condition," or "We do not know which of these commonly-used treatments is better."]

HOW MANY PEOPLE WILL TAKE PART IN THE STUDY?

Participants in the study are referred to as subjects.

About _____ subjects will take part in this study worldwide; _____ subjects will be recruited at this site.

WHAT IS INVOLVED IN THE STUDY?

[Provide simplified schema and/or calendar.]

[For randomized studies:]

You will be "randomized" into one of the study groups: (*describe the groups*). Randomization means that you are put into a group by chance. It is like flipping a coin. Neither you nor the researchers will choose what group you will be in. You will have an (*equal/one in three/etc.*) chance of being placed in any group. (*If blinded*) Neither you nor the investigator will know what group you are in but the study doctor can find out if medically necessary.

You will be given a study medication and it will either contain (*name of drug*) or placebo (*pills with no medicine*)

[For nonrandomized and randomized studies:]

If you take part in this study, you will have the following tests and procedures:

[List procedures and their frequency or use a simple table or chart. For randomized studies, list the study groups and under each describe categories of procedures. Include whether a patient will be at home, in the hospital, or in an outpatient setting. If objectives include a comparison of interventions, list all procedures, even those considered standard. You may use simple paragraphs or charts.]

[Describe study procedures that are part of regular care and may be done even if the subject does not join the study.]

[Describe standard procedures being done because you are in this study.]

[Describe procedures that are being tested in this study.]

Please advise the researchers of any medications you are taking. In addition, if you are taking any over-the-counter drugs or herbal supplements that you have obtained from the drug store, grocery store, etc., you should advise the researchers.

HOW LONG WILL I BE IN THE STUDY?

We think you will be in the study for (*months/weeks, until a certain event*).

[Where appropriate, state that the study will involve long-term follow-up.]

You can stop participating at any time. However, if you decide to stop participating in the study, we encourage you to talk to the researcher and your regular doctor first.

[Describe any serious consequences of sudden withdrawal from the study.]

Withdrawal by investigator, physician, or sponsor

The investigators, physicians, or sponsors may stop the study or take you out of the study at any time should they judge that it is in your best interest to do so, if you experience a study-related injury, if you need additional or different medication, or if you do not comply with the study plan. They may remove you from the study for various other administrative and medical reasons. They can do this without your consent.

WHAT ARE THE RISKS OF THE STUDY?

For trials of drugs or devices/procedures, there may be risks. These risks will be discussed with you by the research doctor and/or your regular doctor.

Risks and side effects related to the (*procedures, drugs, or devices*) we are studying include:

[List by regimen the physical and nonphysical risks of participating in the study in categories of "very likely" and "less likely but serious." You may choose instead to classify risks as "likely", "possible", or "rare." Nonphysical risks may include such things as the inability to work. Highlight or otherwise identify side effects that may be irreversible or long-term or life-threatening.]

[Observational studies—describe risks and discomfort of procedures and questionnaire.]

There may also be side effects, other than listed above that we cannot predict. Other drugs will be given to make side effects that occur less serious and less uncomfortable. Many side effects go away shortly after the (drug/intervention) is stopped, but in some cases side effects can be serious, long-lasting, or permanent.

For more information about risks and side effects, ask the researcher or contact _____.

[Reference and attach drug sheets, pharmaceutical information for the public, or other material on risks.]

ARE THERE ANY BENEFITS TO TAKING PART IN THE STUDY?

We cannot and do not guarantee that you will receive any benefits from this study. *[Add any appropriate language]*

WHAT OTHER OPTIONS ARE THERE?

Instead of being in this study, you have these options:

[List alternatives including commonly used therapy(ies)—disclose standard diagnostic procedures or treatment being withheld; option not to participate.]

WHAT ABOUT CONFIDENTIALITY?

Efforts will be made to protect your medical records and other personal information to the extent allowed by law. However, we cannot guarantee absolute confidentiality. Medical records of research study participants are stored and kept according to legal requirements. You will not be identified personally in any reports or publications resulting from this study. Organizations that may request to inspect and/or copy your research and medical records for quality assurance and data analysis include groups such as:

(The name of the sponsor), Food and Drug Administration, the Medical Center, the Institutional Review Board (IRB), *(name of Clinical Research Organization—CRO)*, federal research oversight agencies.

If information about your participation in this study is stored in a computer, we will take the following precautions to protect it from unauthorized disclosure, tampering, or damage:

[State here whether you are keeping data on a computer that will identify the subjects in the study. If you are, explain how you are protecting this information. Give details: for example, is the computer in a locked room, is it art of a network, is a password required for getting onto the system, who has access to these data, etc.]

CERTIFICATE OF CONFIDENTIALITY

(*NOTE: THIS IS ONLY AN INSTRUCTION FOR THE PI—DO NOT INCLUDE THIS SECTION IF IT DOES NOT APPLY TO YOUR STUDY*) A Certificate of Confidentiality has been granted by the Department of Health and Human Services (DHHS). This Certificate will protect the investigators (project staff) from being forced to release any research data in which the subject is identified even under a court order or subpoena. This protection is not absolute. For instance, it does not override any state requirement to report child abuse to the appropriate authorities.

WHAT ARE THE COSTS?

Study subjects will/will not have to pay for the study drug/treatment. You or your insurance company will have to pay for _____ .

Note to Researchers: Be as specific as possible about additional costs.

Taking part in this study may lead to added costs for you or your insurance company. Please ask about any expected added costs or potential insurance problems. You may wish to consult with your insurance company in advance about whether insurance will pay for these costs.

You or your insurance company will be charged for continuing medical care and/or hospitalization that are not a part of the study.

POLICY/PROCEDURES FOR RESEARCH RELATED INJURY

The Policy and Procedure for the Sponsor are as follows:

[Include the Sponsor's statement here—the sponsor, _(identify by name)__, will or will not pay for care necessitated by a research related injury]

The Policy and Procedure for New York Presbyterian Hospital-Weill Medical College of Cornell University ("the Medical Center") are as follows:

In accordance with Federal regulations, we are obligated to inform you about the Medical Center's policy in the event physical injury occurs. If, as a result of your participation, you experience physical injury from known or unknown risks of the research procedures as described, immediate medical care and treatment, including hospitalization, if necessary, will be available at the usual charge for such treatment. No monetary compensation is available from the Medical Center. Further information can be obtained by calling the Committee on Human Rights in Research at (212) 821-0577.

PAYMENT FOR PARTICIPATION

You *will/will not* receive payment for participating in this study. (*State payment schedule/amount*).

You should not expect anyone to pay you for pain, worry, lost income, or non-medical care costs that occur from taking part in this research study.

COMMERCIAL INTEREST (*if applicable*)

For your information, the (name of institution or individual investigator) holds a patent [or has applied for a patent or is an inventor (whatever applies)] for this device [or drug] and has a potential financial interest in the outcome of this study. [Note to investigator—insert the language that accurately and clearly describes the financial/commercial interest that is involved.] [See also samples of consent form language on the back of the RASP study specific financial disclosure form.]

[If applicable] Materials or data obtained from you in this research may be used for commercial purposes. It is the policy of the Medical Center [and the sponsor, if application] not to provide financial compensation to you should this occur.

WHAT ARE MY RIGHTS AS A PARTICIPANT?

Taking part in this study is voluntary. You may choose to not take part in the study or to leave the study at any time. If you choose to not participate in the study or to leave the study, your regular care will not be affected nor will your relations with the Medical Center, your physicians, or other personnel. In addition, you will not lose any of the benefits to which you are entitled.

We will tell you about new information that may affect your health, welfare, or participation in this study.

[Please include the following when a Data Safety and Monitoring Board exists:]

A Data Safety and Monitoring Board, an independent group of experts, will be reviewing the data from this research throughout the study. We will tell you about the new information from this or other studies that may affect your health, welfare, or willingness to stay in this study.

WHO DO I CALL IF I HAVE QUESTIONS OR PROBLEMS?

For questions about the study or a research-related injury, any problems, unexpected physical or psychological discomforts, or if you think that something unusual or unexpected is happening, call (*name*) at (*telephone number*) or the [*Department name, e.g., Neurology*] fellow on-call at (*telephone number*). Be sure to inform the physician of your participation in this study.

[Note to Researchers: Please note that this must be a 24-hour telephone number. The on-call number should be provided in addition to the PI number.]

If you have questions about your rights as a research participant, contact the Medical Center IRB Office. Direct your questions to:

Committee on Human Rights in Research at:

Address: 425 East 61st Street, Suite 301   Telephone: (212) 821-0577
            New York, New York 10021

RESEARCHER'S STATEMENT

I have fully explained this study to the subject. As a representative of this study, I have explained the purpose, the procedures, the benefits, and risks that are involved in this research study. Any questions that have been raised have been answered to the individual's satisfaction.

_____   _____   _____
Signature of person obtaining the consent   Print Name of Person   Date

SUBJECT'S STATEMENT

I, the undersigned, have been informed about this study's purpose, procedures, possible benefits, and risks, and I have received a copy of this consent. I have been given the opportunity to ask questions before I sign, and I have been told that I can ask other questions at any time. I voluntarily agree to participate in this study. I am free to withdraw from the study at any time without need to justify my decision. This withdrawal will not in any way affect my future treatment or medical management and I will not lose any benefits to which I otherwise am entitled. I agree to cooperate with (*name of principal investigator*) and the research staff and to inform them immediately if (*I/the patient name*) experience any unexpected or unusual symptoms.

_____   _____   _____
Signature of Subject   Print Name of Subject   Date

_____   _____   _____
Investigator (if not person obtaining consent)   Print Name of Investigator   Date

(NOTE: Signature lines should not stand alone on a page, without preceding text.)

In case needed, also add signature line for parent and/or include the following section:

_____   _____
Signature of Legally Authorized Representative   Date
And Relationship to Participant (When Appropriate)

ASSENT FORM FOR MINORS

If the subject enrolled in the study is a minor, please provide a separate assent form. It should be written in a language understandable to the subject and should contain the dialogue the investigator would use to present the study to the child.

Appendix 5.6

FINANCIAL DISCLOSURE FORM—WEILL MEDICAL COLLEGE OF CORNELL UNIVERSITY

Research and Sponsored Programs
Study Specific Financial Disclosure Form

Name of Investigator Submitting Disclosure: _____

Dept/Div: _____ Tel: _____ E-mail: _____

Project/Grant Title: _____

Project PI: _____ Dept./Div.: _____

Protocol #: _____ COEUS #: _____

Sponsor: _____ Agency/Sponsor Grant# (if known): _____

1. Do you or any member of your family have a Financial Interest in a business or outside entity, or an intellectual property interest, that relates to the project listed above? _____ Yes _____ No

If you checked YES to Question #1 above, complete Question #2 (A–E) below. If you checked NO to Question #1, sign and date this side of this form at the bottom. Return this completed form (with your submission) to the Office of Grants and Contracts, 425 East 61st Street, DV-223, and/or the Division of Research Compliance, 425 East 61st Street, DV-301, if needed.

2. Name and address of business or outside entity (indicate __ for profit or __ nonprofit), or description of intellectual property:

    _____

    _____

    A. You or your family's financial interest in the business or outside entity (check all applicable items):
        _____ 1. Consulting income equal to or greater than $10,000 annually.
        _____ 2. Stock, stock option, partnership share, or other ownership interest exceeding $10,000 in value or 5% of the capital stock of the company.

150

_____ 3. Service in an executive position for a business or compensation for service on boards.

_____ 4. Salary for other employee position.

_____ 5. Payments supported by commercial entities for commissioned papers, editing, lectures, or expert testimony.

_____ 6. Intellectual property such as royalties for inventions or publications, or pending patent applications.

_____ 7. Gifts, gratuities, favors, or anything of monetary value.

_____ 8. Other conduct requiring disclosure under the Conflicts Policy.

B. Your activities at WMC that might relate to the activities of the business or outside entity, or intellectual property interest:

_____ 1. Conduct research supported by or involving technology owned by the business.

_____ 2. Assign or supervise the work of students, fellows, or other faculty engaged in such research.

_____ 3. Make clinical referrals to the business.

_____ 4. Make or influence administrative or supervisory decisions regarding purchasing by, or contracting on behalf of, WMC; render professional advice to the Medical College or the University; or managerial, supervisory, or advisory functions related to the conduct of sponsored programs.

_____ 5. Service on an internal or external body with jurisdiction to award or distribute government funds (e.g., committees of NIH, FDA, or other governmental agencies, private professional, or regulatory body) where participation would reasonably appear to be influenced by the business interest or consulting relationship.

C. Indicate the aggregate fair market value of ownership interest by checking the appropriate box:

_____ Less than $10,000 _____ More than $10,000 but less than $25,000

_____ $25,000 or more _____ Not applicable

D. Indicate the aggregate annual amount of income/compensation by checking the appropriate box:

_____ Less than $10,000 _____ More than $10,000 but less than $25,000

_____ $25,000 or more _____ Not applicable

If a loan, amount $_____; security _____; interest _____% per annum.

E. Please provide explanations of A (1–8) and B (1–5) above on a separate page.

I have read the Cornell University Conflicts Policy for the Medical College and Graduate School of Medical Sciences, and the answers on this disclosure form are accurate to the best of my knowledge. If I am submitting a grant application for PHS (NIH) or NSF funding, I acknowledge that I have received a summary of the federal regulations relating to financial conflicts of interest applicable to PHS- and NSF-funded research, and I agree to abide by the disclosure responsibilities of "an investigator" as defined under these regulations. If Weill Medical College determines that a conflict of interest exists, I agree to comply with any condition imposed by the institution to manage, reduce, or eliminate the conflict, or I will withdraw as an investigator on this research. I will update this disclosure promptly if my circumstances change.

Name (printed): _____ Telephone: _____

Campus Address: _____

Signature: _____ Date: _____

See PHS/NSF definitions, and WMC guidance on reverse.

PHS (NIH) and NSF Grant Applications

Federal regulations require that all applicants for funding (grant, cooperative agreements, and contracts) from the Public Health Service (PHS/NIH) or from the National Science Foundation (NSF) must "disclose to an official(s) designated by the [applicant] institution a listing of Significant Financial Interests (and those of his/her spouse and dependent children) that would reasonably appear to be affected by research proposed for funding by the PHS [or NSF]. If the designated institutional official determines that a Significant Financial Interest may "directly and significantly affect the design, conduct, or reporting" of research funded by the PHS or NSF, then a conflict of interest exists and the institution is required to implement procedures to manage, reduce, or eliminate the conflict of interest prior to the institution's expenditure of any funds under the award.

Definitions (from 42 CFR 50.603)

1. "Investigator" means the principal investigator or any other person who is responsible for the design, conduct, or reporting of research . . . . [In considering financial interests,] "Investigator" includes the Investigator's spouse and dependent children.

2. "Significant Financial Interest" means anything of monetary value, including but not limited to salary or other payments for service (e.g., consulting fees or honoraria); equity interest (e.g., patents, copyrights, and royalties from such rights). The term [Significant Financial Interest] does not include:

    (a) salary, royalties, or other remuneration from [Cornell];
    (b) any ownership interest in the institution if the institution is an applicant under SBIR [Small Business Innovation Research] Program;
    (c) income from seminars, lectures, or teaching engagements sponsored by public or nonprofit entities;
    (d) income from service on advising committees or review panels for public or nonprofit entities;
    (e) an equity interest that when aggregated for the investigator and the investigator's spouse and dependent children, meets both of the following tests: does not exceed $10,000 in value as determined through reference to public prices or other reasonable measure of fair market value, and does not represent more than a five-percent ownership interest in any single entity; or
    (f) salary, royalties, or other payments that when aggregated for the investigator and the investigator's spouse and dependent children over the next twelve months are not expected to exceed $10,000.

Guidance for Conflicts Disclosure in Informed Consent

To facilitate appropriate disclosure of potential conflicts of interest in the informed consent document, the following suggested language is provided. It is not mandatory to use these specific provisions. Language should be modified to fit the specific facts and circumstances.

"This study is paid for by [*name of sponsor*] which [has no financial interest in its outcome] (or) [owns the {drug} (or) {device} being tested and thus has a financial interest in the outcome of the study]. Payments are made to Weill Medical College of Cornell University and the funds are used to cover the expenses of the study and related academic and research activities of the institution. [The investigators and the Weill Medical College do not have any financial interest in the out come of the study] (or) [*insert disclosure of potential conflict(s) of interest by investigator(s) and/or institution(s); using such statements as the following:*

1. The investigator, Dr. _____ (full name), owns equity (stock) of the company that is paying for this research.

2. The investigator, Dr. _____ (full name), personally receives consulting or other payments from the company that is paying for the study.

3. The Cornell Research Foundation, a fully owned subsidary of Cornell University, owns equity (stock) of the company that is paying for this study.

4. The investigator, Dr. _____, is an inventor of [the drug, compound, device, etc.,], for which a patent may be filed by the institution. If the patent is pursued, based on data from this and other research, royalties, and other compensation may be received by the institution and the investigator. Thus, WMC and the investigator have a financial interest in the outcome of this study.

"If you require further information regarding the financial arrangements described in this paragraph, you should discuss the matter with the investigator, Dr. _____, phone number _____; or you may contact the Associate Dean (Research Compliance) at 212-821-0612."

6

The Risk Management Professional and Medication Safety

Hedy Cohen
Nancy Tuohy

Before a health care culture can truly promote safety, there must first be an unquestioning acceptance, by everyone in the organization, of the premise that *all* practitioners make errors. There must be an appreciation by the entire staff that errors are never the result of any one isolated action or deed, but rather that they result from the interaction of practitioners functioning in poorly designed systems. When an organization's leaders understand and endorse these basic principles, that organization is able to move from the pointless disciplining of individual practitioners for unintentional mistakes—a tactic that has been shown in the literature to have little effect on error reduction, to a culture of safety that is focused on identifying and addressing multi-factor causes of errors. Organizations that further operationalize safety culture through strategies such as crew resource management (CRM), thereby empowering the lowest-ranking member of a team to question more senior personnel about practice concerns, and that use resources such as human factors science to facilitate safer interaction between humans and machines, are well on their way to becoming what is known as "high-reliability organizations." (Please see discussion of CRM and "high-reliability organization" theory in Chapter 1 of this text.)

When it comes to medication safety, health care organizations have proven to be highly unreliable. In the landmark report issued by the Institute of Medicine, *To Err is Human*, it was extrapolated that more than 7,000 hospitalized patients die each year due to preventable medication errors. Although the reason for this poor safety record is multi-faceted, it is historically grounded in a culture that has focused on addressing individual practitioner errors, rather than the more complex and significant role of the system in which that practitioner functions. Another critical influence is the ongoing demand by consumers that organizations provide more health care with less money.

This chapter will delineate key issues and suggest specific strategies to enhance medication safety. To achieve success, however, health care organizations and their practitioners must first acknowledge and commit to address the many situations in which front-line practitioners work with equipment and technology that is poorly designed, ambiguous policies and procedures, and inadequate communication between management and staff. The risk management professional's role as a facilitator of senior-level commitment, as a teacher of the importance of systems—rather than individual-focused issues analysis—and as a partner to clinicians who are seeking to implement new approaches, is essential and exciting.

··········
LATENT AND ACTIVE FAILURES

The Institute for Safe Medication Practices (ISMP), a non-profit organization dedicated to medication safety, recognizes that each unintentional medication error has its roots in multiple system failures. Although all errors are the result of active failures (which occur at the level of the front-line practitioner, with effects that are felt almost immediately), latent failures (weaknesses in the organization whose effects are usually delayed)[1] are often the most challenging causes of medical error. Active failures are sometimes characterized as "sharp-end," and latent failures denoted as "blunt-end." To illustrate the interaction of active and latent failures in the context of a medication error consider the following example (The eleven active failures are underlined and the thirteen latent failures appear in *italics*).

An infant was born to a mother with a prior history of syphilis. Despite having incomplete patient information about the mother's past treatment for syphilis and current medical status of both the mother and child, *a decision was made to treat the infant for congenital syphilis.* After consultation with infectious disease specialists and the health department, an order was written for one dose of "Benzathine Pen (penicillin) G 150,000U IM."

The physicians, nurses, and pharmacists, unfamiliar with the treatment of congenital syphilis, also had limited knowledge about this drug, which was not in their formulary. The pharmacist consulted both the infant's progress notes and Drug Facts and Comparisons[2] to determine the usual dose of penicillin G benzathine for an infant. However, she *misread the dose in both sources as 500,000 units/kg, a typical adult dose, instead of 50,000 units/kg.* Due to lack of a pharmacy procedure for independent double checking, *the error was not detected.* Because a unit dose system was not used in the nursery, the pharmacy *dispensed a tenfold overdose in a plastic bag containing two full syringes of Permapen 1.2 million units/2mL each,* with green stickers on the plungers reminding the provider to "*note dosage strength.*" A pharmacy label on the bag indicated that 2.5 mL of medication was to be administered IM, to equal a dose of 1,500,000 units.

After glancing at the medication, the infant's primary care nurse was concerned about the number of injections it would be necessary to give. (Because .5 ml is the maximum that providers are allowed to administer intramuscularly to an infant, a 1,500,000-unit dose would require five injections). Anxious to prevent any unnecessary pain to the infant, the nurse involved two advanced-level colleagues, a neonatal nurse practitioner and an advanced-level nursery nurse, who *decided to investigate the possibility of administering the medication IV instead of IM.*

NeoFax (1995 edition)[3] was consulted to determine if penicillin G benzathine could be administered IV. The NeoFax monograph on penicillin G did not specifically mention penicillin G benzathine: instead it described the treatment for congenital syphilis with aqueous crystalline penicillin G, IV slow push or penicillin G procaine IM. Nowhere in the two-page monograph was penicillin G benzathine mentioned, and no specific warnings that penicillin G procaine and penicillin G benzathine were to be given "IM only" were present.

Unfamiliar with the various forms of penicillin G, the nurse practitioner *believed that "benzathine" was a brand name for penicillin G.* This misconception was reinforced by the physician's method of writing the drug order, written *with benzathine capitalized and placed on a line above "penicillin G" rather than after it on the same line.* (See Figure 6.1.) It is noteworthy that many texts use ambiguous synonyms when referring to various forms of penicillin. For example, penicillin G benzathine is frequently mentioned near or directly associated with the terms "crystalline penicillin" and "aqueous suspension." *Believing that aqueous crystalline penicillin G, and penicillin G benzathine were the same drug, the nurse practitioner concluded that the drug could safely be administered IV.* While the nurse practitioner had been taught in school that only clear liquids could be injected IV, she had learned through practical experience that certain milky white substances, such as IV lipids and other lipid-based drug products, can indeed be given IV. *Therefore, she did not recognize the problem of giving penicillin G benzathine, a milky white substance, through an IV.*

Complicating matters further in this example, hospital policies and practices did not clearly define the prescriptive authority of non-physicians. Partially as a result of this lack of clarity, the neonatal nurse practitioner assumed that she was operating under a national protocol, which allowed neonatal nurse practitioners to plan, direct, implement, and change drug therapy. Consequently, the nurse practitioner *made a decision to administer the drug IV.* The primary care nurse, who was not certified to administer IV medication to infants, transferred care of the infant to the advanced level nursery RN and the nurse practitioner.

As they prepared for drug administration, *neither of these providers noticed the ten-fold overdose or that the syringe was labeled by the manufacturer "IM use only."* The manufacturer's warning was not prominently placed. The syringe needed to be rotated 180 degrees away from the name before the warning could be seen. The nurse *began to administer the first syringe of Permapen slow IV push.* After about 1.8 mL was administered, the infant became unresponsive, and resuscitation efforts were unsuccessful.

It is important that risk management professionals focus their energies on the role of latent failure to prevent other such heartbreaking outcomes from occurring. Because the medication administration process is, in reality, a complex system with parameters usually outside the control of the individual practitioner, most errors are rarely the fault of one individual. Thus, providing an optimal level of medication safety requires that

FIGURE 6.1   Chart Entry—Benzathine

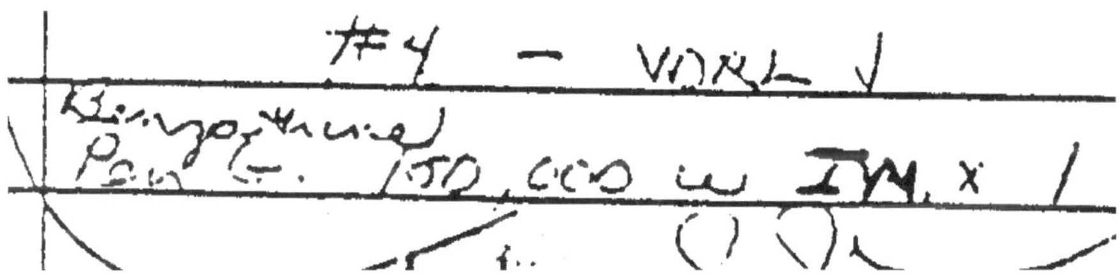

organizations proactively recognize and correct underlying system failures before injuries to patients occur. As noted earlier, this requires a shift in focus beyond "naming, blaming, shaming, and training" of individuals.

··········
SYSTEMS THINKING

Based on the foregoing discussion, in addition to committing to a culture of patient safety and aspiring to become "high-reliability operations," organizations addressing medication safety must also embrace "systems thinking." This approach assesses how individual processes interrelate. Most important, it helps us understand how individual flaws in a complex system like medication use can cause a serious error. As illustrated by Photo 6.1, we are vulnerable to system failures in our everyday life. In this example, we see how poor design may impede the process of entering a house. You want to open a door that has a pull handle. You pull the door toward you to open it, yet the door does not budge.

You pull again with no success. Then you realize that the door is to be opened by pushing, rather than pulling. Your expectation was that a door designed with a pull handle is supposed to be pulled, not pushed. This same type of misperception can occur when a nurse obtains a medication from an automated dispensing machine. When the medication bin is labeled with the name of a specific drug, the nurse assumes that the correct drug is in that bin. If, however, the wrong drug was inadvertently placed in the bin, an error can easily occur.

To facilitate understanding of the complex processes that interact to cause medication errors, ISMP identified ten safety-critical components of the medication use system and categorized numerous reported errors accordingly. The following discussion of

PHOTO 6.1   Door Pull-Handle

TABLE 6.1   Essential Patient Information

- Allergies
- Diagnosis and co-morbid conditions
- Renal and hepatic function
- Pregnancy and lactation status
- Age, weight (kg), height (cm)
- Full medication history (over-the-counter, herbals, cultural)
- Laboratory and other diagnostic results
- Clinical observations (vital signs, mentation)
- Demographics

issues associated with each component provides insight into medication use-related risk. Specific risk reduction strategies are also presented.

Patient Information

More than 18 percent of prescribing errors are due to inadequate patient information. Of particular concern are lack of information about allergies and co-morbidities such as hepatic function and pregnancy status.[4] A critical related issue is that key patient information (Table 6.1) is often unavailable to pharmacy and nursing staff prior to dispensing or administering drugs for new admissions.

When drugs are dispensed or administered without adequate patient information such as laboratory values or key patient co-morbidities, critical data that should be double-checked is omitted, and risk potentially increases. For example, warfarin, an anti-coagulant, is ordered on admission, but the provider ordering warfarin is unaware that the international normalized ratio (INR) is elevated. (The INR is a standardized measure of "clotting time.") In another hypothetical situation, a prescriber might order a standard dosage of aminoglycide, which is contraindicated, for an end-stage renal patient, because there is no available documentation of the patient's condition. Barring an emergency situation, drugs should never be dispensed unless specific clinical information has been reviewed during the ordering process. Clearly, health care practitioners must identify effective ways to facilitate the presence of key clinical information at this critical point in the patient's care.

A real-life example of an error due to lack of information about co-morbidities involved an 84-year old woman who was transferred from a nursing home to a hospital for a coronary artery bypass graft. After surgery, her platelet count dropped by 50 percent. A hematologist was consulted, who determined that the patient was suffering from heparin-induced thrombocytopenia. Although the physician documented this diagnosis in his consultation report, it was not written elsewhere in the patient's chart, and the pharmacy was not notified. As a result, two days later, when the patient was transferred to a surgical unit, nurses, unaware of the patient's co-morbid diagnosis of heparin-induced thrombocytopenia, flushed her IV lines with heparin. The patient suffered a stroke six hours later and died. Although her death was probably due to the surgery, the illicit heparin administration was likely a contributing factor.

Another error that resulted from inadequate patient information occurred when a double-strength concentration of a potentially dangerous or "high-alert" drug was ordered for a cardiac patient in the intensive care unit (ICU). A nurse called the pharmacy and inadvertently requested that an infusion of regular insulin be prepared, at twice normal strength. In carrying out this erroneous verbal order, the pharmacist failed to notice in the order entry system that diabetes mellitus was not documented as a patient diagnosis. Then, without seeing a copy of the written order, he prepared and delivered the insulin infusion. Subsequently, during ICU pharmacy rounds, he failed to obtain a copy of the physician's order or review the patient's chart to verify hyperglycemia. Without an independent double check, the nurse hung the double-strength regular insulin infusion. As a result, the patient suffered permanent central nervous system (CNS) impairment.

Information that is of obvious and closely related concern is the patient's identity. JCAHO requires that staff use two patient-specific identifiers before administering any medication. These are likely to include patient name and birth date. But accurate and complete validation of patient identification for purposes of medication administration cannot occur without *comparing* the patient identification to the medication administration record (MAR). Staff members should also encourage patients to state their name and show their identification bracelet before accepting any medications.

Further illustrating the importance of patient identification, medication errors also occur due to order sheets without a name. In one case, a potentially serious error occurred when an order for high-dose cytabarine, a chemotherapy agent, was written on a blank order sheet that contained no identifying patient identification. The order sheet was then accidentally stamped by the unit clerk with the wrong patient's name and faxed to the pharmacy. Luckily, the patient's diagnosis of hairy cell leukemia was in the pharmacy's computer system. The error was averted when an oncology pharmacy specialist, scanning patient demographics before entering the order, realized that the high-dose cytabarine was totally inappropriate for the patient.

To enhance the collection of key patient data, all medication forms, including prescriber order forms, the medication administration record (MAR) and the pharmacy profile should contain a designated area with pertinent prompts and sufficient space to document essential patient information. Such approaches should make it easy to capture issues such as weight fluctuation and new allergies. Health care organizations must educate all staff on the importance of obtaining accurate inpatient and outpatient information. Ideally, an electronic medical record (EMR) or other form of computer technology should integrate all collected data, including outpatient information.

As another safeguard, the organization should have policies and procedures in place that prevent medication orders from being profiled in the pharmacy without basic clinical and demographic information. It is also important that high-alert, non-profiled medications available from unit stock be independently double-checked before administration, except in emergency situations. An independent double-check is effective only if done in the following way: The first practitioner completes the task (calculation, pump programming, syringe verification, and so on) without sharing methods with the checking practitioner. The second checking practitioner completes the task again, without help or hints (for example, "Here's how I did this" or "This should be five units of insulin") from the first. The second practitioner then compares the results of both practitioners against the original order for accuracy.

Still other preventive strategies include the following. The pharmacy information system and Computerized Prescriber Order Entry (CPOE) should be kept up to date as drugs are added to the formulary. Additionally, all systems should contain alerts for allergies, cross sensitivities, weight and age restrictions, and drug duplications when new medications are added to a patient's profile.

Drug Information

In recent years there has been an explosion of new medications and innovative uses of older drugs. Keeping abreast of all this constantly evolving information is a daunting if not impossible task. It has been noted that most medication errors occur during the prescribing and administration stages because up-to-date drug information is not available at the point of care.[5] In addition, many health care organizations do not have pharmacists readily available to interact, face to face, with practitioners on patient care units.[6]

Because many medication errors occur due to lack of essential drug information, ongoing staff education regarding the appropriate uses, dosages, side effects, and interactions of drugs is critical. For example, the use of the cancer chemotherapeutic agent methotrexate is well established in the oncology setting. Recently providers have begun to prescribe this medication in low doses for rheumatoid arthritis, asthma, psoriasis, inflammatory bowel disease, myasthenia gravis, and inflammatory myositis. When used for these chronic diseases, such doses are administered weekly or sometimes twice a week. However, because relatively few medications are dosed on a weekly basis, practitioners who are unfamiliar with this new clinical approach make mistakes related to frequency of administration and to the novel dosage. In one reported case, a 79-year-old patient was to receive methotrexate for a non-oncology indication. The prescription was erroneously written and dispensed as methotrexate four times daily. This patient died after receiving nine doses of the medication over a 72-hour period.

Prescribers, pharmacists, and nurses must never order, dispense, or administer any medication with which they are not totally familiar. Although this might be challenging for organizations that face demands for efficiency, it is essential to provide practitioners with a workload that allows adequate time to learn about their patients' medications. In yet another example of an error, a cardiac patient was admitted from the ED as an "overflow" patient to a surgical ICU unit where the staff was unfamiliar with the administration of thrombolytics. The cardiologist mistakenly ordered a loading dose of epifibatide (used to inhibit platelet aggregation) as 180 mcg, not as 180 mcg/kg. The pharmacy was particularly busy and the pharmacist, who was unfamiliar with epifibatide dosing, did not read the package insert or verify the dose with the prescriber. The surgical ICU nurse, who had never administered this drug before, compounded the error when she misread the prescriber's order as "180 mg." She initiated the loading dose by giving 75 mg over one hour, planning to call the pharmacy for the remainder of the dose. As the infusion was ending, another pharmacist discovered the error and the infusion was discontinued. Fortunately, the patient suffered no permanent harm.

Strategies to make drug information available at the point of care include the use of rule-based computerized provider order entry (CPOE) systems that provide drug information, warnings, and alerts during order input. If CPOE is not available in the organization, the use of a sound, user-friendly computerized drug information system such as Micromedex[7] or up-to-date drug information books (most recent publication and year) can provide valuable current drug information. The pharmacy computer system should also give specific warnings for those drugs that have unusual dosing schedules, such as weekly or monthly, and alerts for cumulative drug dosing. Another effective strategy is to move the pharmacist, an expert in the clinical uses of medication, from the centralized pharmacy into satellite pharmacies within patient care areas. This allows the pharmacist to establish a close working relationship with the practitioners and patients, follow the patients' clinical courses, and consult regularly with the professional staff about appropriate drug selection, dosing, and administration. It has been shown that when the pharmacist is close to the point of care, patient outcomes are improved and errors and drug costs are significantly reduced.[8] If pharmacists are not already in place in patient care units, organizations can take a first step toward this model of care by having pharmacists make daily rounds of patient care units or enter medication orders directly at the computer terminals in patient care units. The next logical step in integrating pharmacists more closely with the care team should be to prioritize implementation of unit-based pharmacy support in key areas, such as the intensive care unit, the pediatrics or oncology units, the operating room, and the emergency department.

Communication of Information

Organizational barriers to communicating essential clinical patient and drug information effectively include drug information systems which do not interface with other vital patient information systems, such as the electronic medical record (EMR) and the laboratory system. Such disconnects clearly hamper the practitioner's access to information essential for safe administration, such as allergies and pertinent test results. Another closely related obstacle is the absence of computer order entry systems. Without such systems, there is increased risk of order-related error due to illegible handwriting, missing or ambiguous information, nonconventional abbreviations, and unclear documentation of dosage.

Another barrier is a provider's flawed communication style. Of particular concern is intimidation, which contributes to about 10 percent of the serious errors that occur during administration. In fact, ISMP receives many reports of lethal errors in which orders were questioned, but not changed. In a survey conducted by ISMP, almost half (49 percent) of all respondents related that their past experiences with intimidation had altered the way they handle order clarification or questions about medication orders. At least once during the previous year, about 40 percent of respondents did not act on concerns about a medication order or ask another professional to talk to the prescriber, rather than interact with a particularly intimidating prescriber. Three-quarters (75 percent) had asked colleagues to help them interpret an order or validate its safety so that they did not have to interact with an intimidating prescriber. Also, 34 percent reported that they had found the prescriber's stellar reputation intimidating and had not questioned an order about which they had concerns. When the prescriber had been questioned about the safety of an order and refused to change it, 31 percent of respondents suggested that the physician administer the drug, or simply allowed the physician to give the medication himself, and almost half (49 percent) felt pressured to accept the order, dispense a product, or administer a medication despite their concerns. As a result, 7 percent of respondents reported that they had been involved in a medication error during the previous year, in which intimidation clearly played a role.[9,10]

To address flawed communication style, many health care organizations are using established protocols, consistent with human resources protocols and medical staff bylaws, to follow up with providers who are perceived to be intimidating. Appropriate strategies in this regard may include the use of incident or event reports, objectively completed, to document clinically pertinent events. Of great assistance in improving communication house-wide is a crew resource management approach, in which a team member with minimal stature is empowered to question team leaders. Remember that effective implementation of such strategies cannot occur without senior administrative and clinical leadership endorsement.

Another key communication issue involves verbal orders. Such orders, whether spoken in person or over the telephone, are inherently problematic because they can easily be misheard or misinterpreted. For example, there have been error reports in which verbal orders for "Celebrex 100 mg PO" were misheard to be for "Cerebyx 100 mg PO." Drug names are not the only verbal information prone to misinterpretation. Numbers are also problematic. For example, an emergency room physician verbally ordered "morphine 2 mg IV," but the nurse heard "morphine 10 mg IV," and the patient subsequently received a 10-mg infusion that caused respiratory arrest. In another situation, a physician called in an order for "15 mg of hydralazine" to be given IV every two hours. The nurse, thinking that he had said "50 mg," administered an overdose to the patient, who developed tachycardia and had a significant drop in blood pressure.

To reduce the use of verbal orders, some organizations have instituted the use of fax machines to communicate orders. However, fax machines are connected to telephone lines, and significant line "noise" can result in the loss of important information, such as portions of a drug name or even the dose. For example, the order shown in Figure 6.2 was mistaken as Flagyl 250 mg instead of Flagyl 500 mg. A related problem occurs when prescribers write on the very edge of the order form, making it impossible for some fax machines and scanners to "read" the entire order. Thus an order for "Lomotil QID PRN" may appear as "Lomotil QID," as if the "PRN" were never written.

Verbal orders must be eliminated, except in emergency and sterile situations. Such orders are especially inappropriate when potentially lethal drugs, such as chemotherapy agents, are prescribed. To further decrease the risk of verbal order-related error, health care organizations should adopt yet another "crew resource management" principle. This particular strategy concerns the standardization of communication. Here are approaches that might help achieve standardization of verbal orders.

- When verbal orders are allowed, prescribers must enunciate the order clearly and the receiver should always repeat the order to the prescriber to avoid misinterpretation.

- As an extra check, either the prescriber or receiver should spell unfamiliar drug names, using "T as Tom," "C as Charley," and so forth. Pronounce each numerical digit separately, saying for example, "one six" instead of "sixteen" to avoid confusion with "sixty."

- The receiver must ensure that the verbal order makes sense when considered in conjunction with the patient's diagnosis.

FIGURE 6.2   Faxes Aren't the Problem

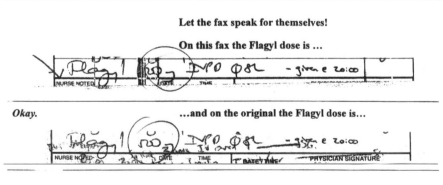

Let the fax speak for themselves!

On this fax the Flagyl dose is …

Okay.   **…and on the original the Flagyl dose is…**

- The verbal order must be immediately recorded on an order sheet in the patient's chart, whenever possible.

- For telephone orders, the recipient must obtain a telephone number in case it is necessary to call back with follow-up questions.

- Limit verbal orders to formulary drugs, as staff members are more likely to misunderstand drug names and dosages with which they are unfamiliar.

- Limit the number of personnel who routinely receive telephone orders, to reduce the potential for unauthorized orders.

Still another issue is poor communication of medical information at care transition points. According to the Institute for Healthcare Improvement (IHI), miscommunication when the patient moves from one care environment to another is responsible for about 50 percent of all medication errors and up to 20 percent of adverse drug events, in numerous health care organizations across the country.[11] One illustration of this type of error involved a patient who was transferred from one hospital to another and received a duplicate dose of insulin because the receiving nurse did not know that the medication had been given before transfer. In another case, enalapril 2.5 mg IV was administered to a patient after transfer from a critical care unit to a medical unit. The drug had been discontinued upon transfer, but the orders had not yet been transcribed. Yet another error occurred when, before discharge, the patient's Lexapro was increased to 10 mg daily, but the discharge instructions erroneously called for 5 mg daily. When the error was noticed, a pharmacist called the patient and learned that she had been cutting her newly prescribed 10 mg tablets in half.

JCAHO standards now require that health care organizations address medication reconciliation. Particularly helpful is documentation of this process, which assesses and addresses medication duplications and incompatibilities at vulnerable points of transition, such as admission, transfers between care settings, and at discharge. Refer to Chapter 10 on emergency department risk management in this volume for an approach specific to that clinical area.

Finally, to facilitate communication about medication orders, it is of great importance that written and computerized medication orders include the generic and brand names of the medication, without abbreviations. There are literally thousands of drug pair names that sound and look similar, so detailed information helps prevent these medications from being mistaken for one another. In addition, medication should never be prescribed by volume, number of vials, or ampules. When such orders are received, the staff should seek clarification immediately.

Labeling, Packaging, and Drug Nomenclature

Improper hospital drug labeling and failing to keep drugs in packaging until administering them contribute to medication errors. Additionally, the pharmaceutical industry has sometimes unwittingly undermined the safe use of medication by marketing drug names that look alike and sound alike, using confusing labeling, or providing drugs to health care organizations in non-distinct or ambiguously marked packages. In reports submitted to MEDMARX (a subscription-based reporting program sponsored by the United States Pharmacopaeia), nearly 32,000 medication errors over a 39-month period occurred among look-alike or sound-alike drugs due to packaging or labeling. Approximately 2.6 percent of these errors were classified as harmful.[12]

PHOTO 6.2   Capsule Quantity is Often Confused for the Product Strength

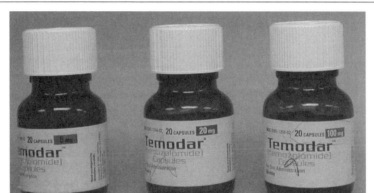

Labeling   Confusing labeling, sometimes associated with manufacturer's use of similar colors, font sizes and layout to achieve a product image, can result in errors.

For example, the drug Temodar (temozolomide) has reportedly been the subject of numerous dispensing and administration errors because labeling leads staff members to misinterpret capsule strength. This alkylating agent is available in 5, 20, 100, and 250 mg capsules. The strength is stated directly beside the quantity of capsules (Photo 6.2). One who reads the number of capsules right next to the strength might reasonably conclude that the total number of capsules in the bottle is equal to the strength, for example, 20 capsules = 100 mg, rather than 20 capsules, each containing 100 mg. Adding to the confusion is similarity between the strength of the dosage and the number of capsules in the bottle. Capsules in strengths of 5 mg and 20 mg are often dispensed in packages that contain either five or twenty capsules. The FDA pointed out that this confusing packaging and labeling can lead to serious, even fatal, errors.[13]

Just recently, an error was reported in which a prescription for oral Temodar 60 mg daily was written for a patient with a brain tumor. The pharmacist dispensed the dosage from a 100 mg bottle containing twenty capsules—and simply misread the label. The pharmacist was under the impression that twenty capsules were equal to 100 mg, so he concluded that each capsule contained 5 mg and dispensed twelve capsules to make up a 60 mg dose. Fortunately, the patient's mother caught the error when she was filling the patient's pillbox, before any of the medication was given.

To address these issues, the manufacturer has recently submitted a redesigned label to the FDA for approval.

To proactively address label confusion like this, organizations may affix "name and strength alert" stickers on products that have potentially confusing labels and highlight the differences with a pen or highlighter. The staff should also employ at least two independent checks in the dispensing and administration processes for these medications. Organizations also might consider implementation of point-of-care bar coding technology, which, for example, requires the provider to scan the patient's name band with the drug package before administering the drug. Other invaluable devices are "smart"

PHOTO 6.3   Top Group of 6 is Brethine, Bottom Group of 8 is Methergine

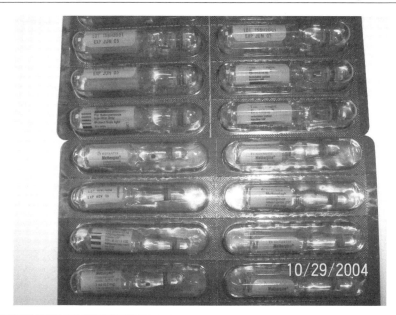

infusion pumps that contain drug libraries to further enhance safe administration of such drugs.

Packaging   Like confusing dose information, look-alike packaging is of great concern. Related errors generally involve assumptions by staff members that a medication that sounds similar to the one they are ordered to give is appropriate, or they pick up a wrong vial or other dispensing device because it looks like the medication they are ordered to give. In one example, a woman who was thirty-one weeks pregnant received Methergine (methylergonovine) instead of terbutaline (Brethine), which resulted in the emergency premature C-section delivery of her baby. Similar sounding names and similar-looking packaging contributed to the error (Photo 6.3). Fortunately, mother and child were unharmed.

Another look-alike medication issue involves respiratory therapy inhalation drugs, such as ipratropium (Atrovent) and levalbuterol (Xopenex), which are packaged in disposable, clear plastic containers with raised, embossed labels that are difficult to read. Compounding the risk, respiratory therapists often pocket several of each of these medications, to be more efficient. Of additional concern, other products, such as opthalmic solutions and preservative-free medications, like xylocaine, are also illegibly packaged in small plastic vials. See Photo 6.4.

To minimize confusion associated with look-alike packaging, health care organizations should, whenever possible, consider using equivalent products from different manufacturers. Organizations should also avoid storing look-alike products near one another in unit stock and automated dispensing cabinets.

Applying auxiliary labels might help distinguish similar-looking packages. Additionally, the use of "tall man" lettering might help to visually differentiate drug names on

PHOTO 6.4   Mix of Opthalmic and Respiratory Medications

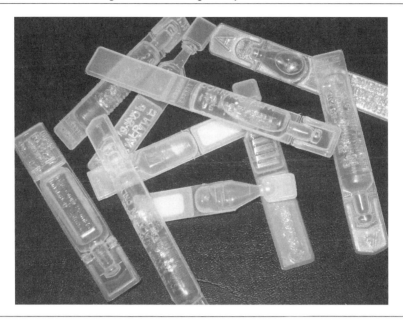

similar-looking packages. Tall man lettering uses capital letters within a drug name to highlight the letters of a name that differentiate two similar looking names. For instance, hydrALAZINE and hydrOXYzine. In 2001, the FDA's Office of Generic Drugs requested manufacturers of sixteen look-alike name pairs to voluntarily reformat the appearance of these drug names on their packaging, and "tall man lettering" was used extensively in this effort. The list can be viewed at: [www.fda.gov/cder/drug/MedErrors/nameDiff.htm]. This was a voluntary program, thus not all manufacturers complied. Facilities, however, may choose to employ tall man lettering on auxiliary labels, shelf and bin labels, or medication administration records.

Yet another packaging-related issue that contributes to errors involves the removal or discarding of packaging before the drug is administered. Although most drugs are packaged as unit doses, this does not assure that medications will remain labeled until they reach the patient's bedside. Often nurses prepare drugs at a central location, removing pharmacy or manufacturer drug packaging and labeling and placing the open medication in cups for administration. Thus, the chance for errors, especially administering a medication to the wrong patient, is greatly increased. Institutions should require that the drug remain labeled throughout the drug use process, up to the point of administration. Using bar code technology might make this easier. Until this technology is instituted nationwide, however, it might be valuable to convene staff focus groups to identify and address the reasons that providers remove drug packaging and labels before administering drugs.

Nomenclature   Errors in identifying medication sometimes occur when providers refer to medication by a shorter name. Other reasons for misidentification include confusion due to the indiscriminate use of brand and generic names, in combination and separately, in written and computerized orders. Sometimes confusion results from a "line extension," when the manufacturer substantively changes the drug, but changes only the suffix of the name, to better market the progeny of a successful pharmaceutical. To address such confusion, ISMP recommends that both brand and generic names be documented (if appropriate) in ordering and transcribing, with the indication for the medication.

One example of potential omission related to nomenclature was generated by a mix-up between the sound-alike medications, Cerebyx and Celebrex. In this case, Cerebyx (fosphenytoin) 100 mg IV TID, an anticonvulsant, was listed on a patient's medication administration record (MAR) from a transferring hospital. The admitting cardiologist at the receiving hospital was unfamiliar with Cerebyx and misread the drug as Celebrex (celecoxib), a pain medication, even though he knew it was not available in a parenteral form. He did not order the drug because the patient was not having pain. When a pharmacist reviewed the orders along with the old MAR and investigated, he was able to correct the order, thus preventing an omission error. Although often not considered as serious a potential threat to patient safety, patients can be harmed as much by the omission of a drug as from an erroneous dose.

In another issue related to nomenclature, Pamelor (nortriptyline), an antidepressant, was misheard as Tambocor (flecainide), an antiarrhythmic, and the prescription was dispensed as such. Although the patient took this erroneous medication for one month and experienced fatigue, he fortunately suffered no cardiovascular symptoms.

In yet another example, a pharmacist received an order for Gabitril (tiagabine), which is used for seizure disorders. He entered the order correctly but the patient still received the wrong drug because the pharmacy mistakenly dispensed Zanaflex (tizanidine), a drug used for muscle spasticity. Tiagabine and tizanidine were stored alphabetically by generic name in the pharmacy, separated by only one space on the shelves. Both drugs are also available in 2-mg and 4-mg strengths. The error occurred despite a bright-orange warning sticker stating "Name Alert" on the tizanidine supply. The potential for error was increased because the hospital had repackaged the drugs in unit doses using only the generic names. Fortunately, in this case, a nurse detected the difference before administering the drug.

Recent discussion of nomenclature-related safety issues has taken place at the United States Pharmacopeia (USP), resulting in adoption of a resolution to encourage the use of generic names alone for new single-active ingredient products marketed after January 1, 2006. However, a single drug name—generic or brand—would not prevent all such mix-ups. Examination of the drug pairs delineated in the new Joint Commission National Patient Safety Goal, requiring accredited entities to annually review a list of pertinent look- and sound-alike drugs, reveals that nine of ten problem pairs are similar generic names.[14]

Trademark extensions are another risk issue. There are no standard meanings for various suffixes such as "XL," "ER," and "SR" following drug names. The line of Wellbutrin (bupropion) products has been of particular concern in this regard. Twice in one week, a hospital psychiatrist ordered Wellbutrin XL 300 mg, but two tablets of Wellbutrin SR 150 mg were dispensed. The pharmacists filling the orders were unaware of the new XL formulation, and poor physician handwriting made it difficult to discern the XL portion of the drug name. In another reported case, a prescriber wrote Wellbutrin "XR" (instead of either XL or SR) 150 mg daily. The pharmacist could have looked at the once daily frequency and concluded that it must be the XL product. However, he reviewed the profile and found that the patient had, in fact, been taking Wellbutrin SR daily, so that is what he dispensed. Unfortunately, the physician actually meant to prescribe the XL formulation.

Different forms of a drug can also be confused. For example, significant harm can occur when liposomal and conventional products are mixed up. In one case, liposomal doxorubicin (Doxil) and conventional doxorubicin (brand names include Adriamycin and Rubex) both packaged in 20-mg vials, were stored together in the same drawer in a pharmacy refrigerator. Although both drugs are chemotherapeutic agents, their actions are very different. The patient involved received an IV push injection of 75 mg of Doxil, rather than the conventional doxorubicin that was intended. The patient's reaction was not serious, but other reports of similar incidents have resulted in severe side effects and even death.

To reduce drug mix-ups related to nomenclature, it is important that providers seek clarification if the drug being ordered does not seem to match the patient's condition. Additionally, institutions should require both the brand and generic names in all documentation, including orders, and on pharmacy labels.

Drug Storage, Stocking, and Standardization

The traditional floor stock model of medication storage and stocking has been phased out in most U.S. hospitals. Formerly, a nearly complete pharmacy was maintained on every unit in a hospital or nursing home, which increased the probability of errors. Acting alone, the nurse typically interpreted and transcribed a physician's order, chose the proper container from hundreds available on the shelves, prepared the correct amount, placed the dose in a syringe or cup, labeled it, took it to the patient, administered it, and verified that the dose had been administered. The obvious lack of check systems has led to the elimination of this medication administration model in most organizations.

Errors are still likely to occur, however, in organizations that employ a modified floor stock model on nursing units, even if there are just a few "stock bottles" for nurses to manage. The chance of error under these circumstances increases if drugs are stored by alphabetical name on units (or in the pharmacy) or the unit fails to sequester high-alert drugs (such as neuromuscular blockers).

Technologic solutions are helpful only to a point. For example, even when unit stock is placed in automated dispensing machines, problems still might occur if there are not enough machines, or if poor workspace planning results in nurses crowding the machines at times when many patients require medications simultaneously. Under such circumstances, staff members often try to circumvent an inefficient work environment by storing medications in their pockets. Also of concern is the partial implementation of technologic solutions—for example, the pertinent technology does not integrate with other documentation systems in-house or fails to encompass safety features such as patient profiling and on-screen alerts.

Indeed, if automated dispensing cabinets (ADCs) store a wide assortment of medications or excessive quantities of a single medication, yet do not interface with the pharmacy's computer-based profiling system, the risk of error actually increases. Pharmacy profiling allows a pharmacist to review each medication order and screen it for safety *before* the drug can be removed from the cabinet. Without this safeguard, nurses might not be alerted to unsafe doses, potential allergic reactions, duplicate therapy, contraindications, drug interactions, or other important information that could make the drug, dose, or route of administration unsafe. Additionally, medications in ADCs are not always limited to the dosage that is necessary for a patient. Also, manufacturer-generated unit dose medication is not often labeled with the individual patient's dose. These issues resulted in a serious error when a patient died after receiving 10 mg of colchicine IV. The physician had prescribed "colchicine 1.0 mg IV now," but the decimal point was hidden on the line of the order form, and the use of an unnecessary trailing zero led to misinterpretation. However, the error reached the patient primarily because there was an excessive quantity of colchicine in the ADC. Ten ampules of colchicine (1 mg each) were available in the ADC; thus the nurse had enough ampules to prepare the overdose.

Safety procedures for automated dispensing technology are essential error prevention tools. For example, without a protocol that addresses proper storage, drugs can erroneously be placed in compartments of a cabinet that has been labeled for other medications. Procedures should also require that no medication be routinely available for administering to patients without appropriate order screening by the pharmacist. This includes initial doses of medication. Particularly dangerous drugs should be dispensed directly only from the pharmacy.

Device Acquisition, Use, and Monitoring

Practitioners involved in the medication-use process often employ one or more drug-administration devices to administer a specific drug. Historically, many devices, such as infusion pumps, were designed without the benefit of human factors engineering. Human factors engineering and human factors ergonomics are the "scientific disciplines concerned with the understanding of interactions among humans and other elements of a system, and the profession that applies theory, principles, data, and other methods to design in order to optimize human well-being and overall system performance."[15] This definition was adopted by the International Ergonomics Association in August 2000. Failure to take human factors principles into consideration while designing medication delivery devices can contribute to patient harm.

For example, the misuse of infusion pumps and other parenteral device systems is the second-leading cause of serious errors during drug administration.[16] A classic human factors-related problem that involves infusion pumps is the free flow of medication into a patient due to the lack of free-flow protection on intravenous (IV) pumps. Before a Joint Commission standard that required free-flow protection on pumps, such errors occurred when practitioners forgot to slide the clamping mechanism closed when they removed the infusion tubing sets from pumps. As the issues associated with infusion pumps illustrate, reliance on human vigilance is inherently prone to error. All devices should be designed to compensate for normal error-causing human behavior, such as momentary lapses in attention and fatigue.

Even with more recent equipment, errors may still occur. For example, the design of infusion pump keypads makes it easy for tenfold dosing errors to occur. Specifically the close proximity of the "zero" and "decimal point" keys on some IV pumps, and multiple-function keys, such as an "up arrow" that also serves as an "enter" key, has led nurses to misprogram pumps with rates that can cause overdose. The newest pumps, called "smart" pumps, may include a computerized drug library of preset dose limits that alert nurses to programming errors, but many older pumps without such features remain in use.

Other problems involving IV infusion pumps include:

● Infusion pumps being turned off accidentally by users or when physically bumped against other objects

● Lack of visible or audible warning alarms when the syringe or cassette is not properly loaded, resulting in over- or under-dosing of medication

● Confusing tubings on pumps where multiple lines are used

- The inadvertent setting of a drug or solution at the primary IV rate instead of at the intended secondary rate

- Decimal point errors, such as keying in the infusion rate at ten times the intended rate (for example, 44.5 ml/h instead of 4.5 mL/h and 88 mL/h instead of 8 mL/h)

- Dosage calculation errors

- Keying in the volume of the drug to be infused as the infusion rate (for example, a volume of 500 mL heparin mistakenly entered as rate of 500 mL/h)

Special precautions are needed with patient-controlled analgesia (PCA) pumps. When used as intended, PCA reduces the risk of over-sedation by allowing patients to self-administer more frequent but smaller doses of analgesia through an infusion pump. However, because this therapeutic intervention combines inherently error-prone devices, and narcotics, serious unintended outcomes have frequently occurred.

Fortunately, by identifying specific issues, risks associated with this technology can be reduced. Table 6.2 summarizes some of the issues surrounding the use of PCA pumps and appropriate solutions.

TABLE 6.2   PCA Problems and Safety Recommendations

Problem	*Description*	*Safety Recommendation*
PCA by Proxy	When another person (health professional, family member) administers a dose of medication instead of the patient's dosing themselves. Can lead to oversedation, respiratory depression, and death. Patients are to control the PCA so that a sedated patient cannot press the button, thereby overdosing.	Warn patients, family members, and visitors about the dangers of PCA by proxy. Place warning labels on activation buttons that state "FOR PATIENT USE ONLY." Keep PCA flowsheets at the bedside to document PCA doses and patient monitoring.
Improper Patient Selection and Education	Only patients who have the mental alertness and sufficient cognitive, physical, and psychological ability should use a PCA. Can lead to inadequate pain control or oversedation. Teaching patients during the immediate postoperative period is ineffective if the patient is too groggy to understand. This has often led to poor pain control in the first 12 hours following surgery.	Check patient allergies, which should be visible on the MAR, before initiating PCA. Educate patients preoperatively about PCAs. Establish patient selection criteria. In general, infants, young children, and confused patients are not suitable candidates to use a PCA pump.
Inadequate Patient Monitoring	Patients using a PCA pump must be frequently and appropriately monitored. The level of consciousness achieved from physical stimulus is only a temporary way to monitor for toxicity. When the physical stimulus is removed, patients can quickly fall back into an oversedated state.	Ensure that nurses recognize the signs and symptoms of opiate toxicity. Have oxygen and naloxone readily available. Teach the need to assess using minimal verbal or tactile stimulation. Establish a standard pain assessment scale.

(Continued)

TABLE 6.2   PCA Problems and Safety Recommendations (*Continued*)

Problem	Description	Safety Recommendation
	Pulse oximetery alone can give a false sense of security since oxygen saturation is usually maintained even at low respiratory rates.	At minimum, evaluate pain, alertness, and vital signs, including rate and quality of respirations, every four hours. More frequent monitoring should be done in the first 24 hours and at night, when hypoventilation and nocturnal hypoxia may occur. Keep PCA flowsheets at the bedside to document PCA doses and patient monitoring. Monitor the use of naloxone to identify adverse events related to PCA.
Drug Product Mix-Ups	Many opiates used for PCA have similar names and packaging leading to selection errors. Morphine and meperidine have been packaged in similar boxes. Use of floor stock of opiates in PCAs has led to significant overdoses.	Require independent double checks for patient identification, drug and concentration, pump settings, and the line attachment. Establish one concentration for each opiate used for PCA. Separate the storage of hydromorphone from morphine. Affix prominent warning labels on non-standard concentrations. Use commercially prefilled syringes/bags/cassettes. Require pharmacy to review all PCA orders before initiation. Alert all clinicians to drug shortages and provide clear alternate dosing instructions.
Practice Related Problems	Misprogramming the PCA is the most frequently reported practice related issue. Other problems include: incorrect transcription of orders, miscalculation of dose or rate of infusion, and IV admixture errors.	Require independent double checks for patient identification, drug and concentration, pump settings, and the line attachment. Limit PCA pumps to a single model to promote proficiency. Provide laminated instructions attached to each pump. Program pumps to require a review of settings before infusing.
Device Design Flaws	Many PCAs are not intuitive in their design making programming problematic. Many PCAs have default programming for medication concentrations such as 0.1 mg/mL or 1 mg/mL but a higher concentration may be used in the device, leading to overdoses and deaths. Other drug delivery problems include lack of requiring review of programming before starting the infusion and free flow of medication as a result of syringe or cassette breakage.	Establish default settings of zero for all opiates. Connect PCA to a port close to the patient (to avoid dead space) and prominently label the infusion line to avoid mix-ups. Require pumps to be programmed in mg/mL and mcg/mL, not just mL. Program pumps to alert users and stop PCA if a syringe or bag is empty or damaged. Limit PCA pumps to a single model to promote proficiency.

(*Continued*)

TABLE 6.2   PCA Problems and Safety Recommendations (*Continued*)

Problem	Description	Safety Recommendation
	Patients may also confuse the PCA button with the nurse call button, resulting in overdosing and frustration.	Provide visual and auditory feedback to patients when the button is pressed.
Inadequate Staff Training	Nurses may not receive effective training or may not retain proficiency when PCA pumps are used infrequently or if multiple types of PCAs in use. Prescribers may not undergo verification of proficiency with this form of pain management, resulting in improper medications and dosing.	Ensure training is timely and comprehensive and that annual competency testing is required. Require independent double checks for patient identification, drug and concentration, pump settings, and the line attachment. Limit PCA pumps to a single model to promote proficiency. Provide laminated instructions attached to each pump.
Order Communication Errors	Mistakes are made in converting an oral opiate dose to the IV route. Most problematic is hydromorphone. Concurrent orders for other opiates while a PCA is in use have resulted in opiate toxicity.	Design standard order sets to guide drug selection, doses, and lockout periods; patient monitoring; and precautions such as avoiding concomitiant analgesics. Limit verbal orders to dose changes only. Require independent double checks for patient identification, drug and concentration, pump settings, and the line attachment. Use morphine as opiate of choice, use hydromorphone for patients needing very high doses, reserve meperidine for patients allergic to morphine and hydromorphone.

PCA Problems and Safety Recommendations

Nursing, biomedical engineers, and others should plan and monitor the effectiveness of infusion pump deployment. A first step is to provide nursing and other users with input into selection of all new pumps. All IV pumps should be tested for free-flow protection, and any that fail (medication flows freely from the tubing as the set is removed) should be removed from service. By limiting standard hospital IV pumps to a single model, and specialty pumps, such as syringe and PCA pumps, to clinical areas where the staff is fully competent in their use, the proficiency of all nurses using these devices can be maximized. Attaching laminated instructions and safety checklists to each pump raises awareness and reinforces key safety measures. Each provider who uses a pump should also be required to label all tubing and have a partner assist with independent double checks for patient identification, drug and concentration, pump settings, and line attachment.

Above all, an independent double check that verifies dose and rate settings is critical. This is because the settings on PCA pumps often default to a standard concentration, which requires the operator to change the settings if a non-standard concentration is used. Even when the staff has expertise in the proper use of these drug delivery devices, serious dosing errors have been associated with improper flow rate settings. Thus, PCA pump settings should be programmed by one individual and checked independently by another before administering. Settings at the time of administration should be documented, based on this independent check.

Other medication administration devices can also cause errors in a health care setting. For example, the wrong reservoir in implantable medication delivery devices has reportedly been filled with medication, causing patient death. Also, patients are often admitted to the hospital with implantable devices, such as insulin pumps, yet no instructions are available to assist nurses with the use of these devices.

Additional misuses of medication-related devices, with often serious outcomes, include the inadvertent connection of intravenous tubing to devices not intended for medication delivery. In one case, a nurse accidentally connected the blood pressure monitor tubing to a needleless IV port. Propofol, which is white and opaque, had been infusing through the patient's IV line. Thus, the IV tubing and its port looked very similar to the white length of tubing and connector on the BP cuff (Photo 6.5). In another similar case, an agitated patient died when he removed the tubing from his BP cuff and attached it to his IV line.

In another tubing-related event, a young child died when her oxygen tubing was mistakenly connected to her IV line. The child had been receiving medication via a nebulizer to treat asthma. While still attached to a wall outlet, the oxygen tubing became disconnected from the nebulizer fluid chamber (Photo 6.6).

The situation worsened when the staff member who discovered the disconnected oxygen tubing accidentally reconnected it to the injection port on a Baxter Clearlink Needleless Access System IV tubing Y-site. Although oxygen tubing does not have a Luer connector, the staff member managed to make the connection with Baxter's Clearlink valve work by applying considerable force (Photo 6.7). The oxygen tubing disconnected from the IV tubing in seconds, but not before the pressure of the compressed oxygen supply forced the needleless valve open and allowed air into the tubing. The child died instantly.

PHOTO 6.5   Tubing Lines

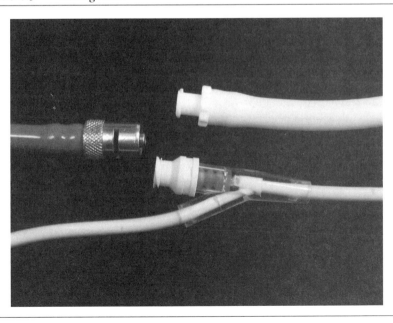

PHOTO 6.6   IV Tubing to Oxygen

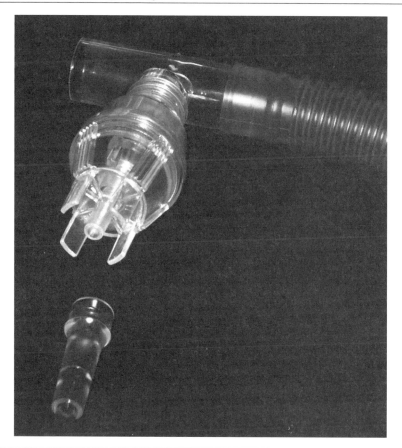

PHOTO 6.7   IV Misconnect

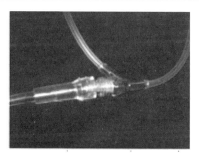

Other similar issues have occurred when medications have inadvertently been delivered into the balloon inflation ports of endotracheal tubes, gastrostomy tubes, and Foley catheters, instead of into the intended intravenous catheter. In each case, the balloon expanded when the medication was injected, causing harm to the patients.[17]

Health care organizations should review existing medical equipment used in their facilities to identify the potential for misconnection. Each practitioner who connects or reconnects tubing should be required by policy to completely trace the tube from the patient to the point of origin before they begin. Appropriately labeled IV lines help alert the staff that they may be about to access the incorrect line accidentally. Additionally, before introducing new tubes, catheters, and connectors, an interdisciplinary team should use failure mode and effect analysis (FMEA) to identify potential issues related to connectivity with other medical equipment.

As previously noted, medication safety is enhanced when health care organizations involve end users in the product selection process. Building on this principle by using a standardized evaluation process for devices and looking for areas of potential failure, before the device is acquired, might help the organization avoid future errors. A suggested approach for evaluating infusion pumps follows is identified in Table 6.3. The same process can be adapted for use with any new medical device.

Patient Monitoring

Connected to each medical device or piece of equipment is a patient. For therapeutic interventions to succeed, practitioners must continually assess their effectiveness by

---

TABLE 6.3   Using FMEA to Predict Failures with Infusion Pumps

I. Basic Functionality—How well does the pump perform the required task?
   a. Is this the correct pump to perform the desired task(s)?
   b. Can the pump deliver the volume/increments needed under the correct pressure?
   c. Are any features incompatible with the environment where it will be used (size, weight, number of channels)?
   d. Will the pump deliver medications in the concentrations most typically used?
   e. What tubing and other supplies are required for the pump to perform effectively and safely? Are they interchangeable with other pumps? Could interchangeable tubing be used for this pump, rendering it unsafe?
   f. Are users alerted to pump-setting errors? Wrong patient errors? Wrong channel errors? Wrong medication/solution errors? Mechanical failure?
   g. Does the pump have memory functions for settings and alarms with an easily retrievable log? If the pump is turned off, does it retain settings for a period of time?
II. User-Machine Interface—How easy and intuitive is it for people to use the pump?
   a. What functionalities do users expect the pump to have?
   b. Is the number of steps for programming minimal?
   c. Are the touch buttons used for programming clearly labeled, logically positioned, and the proper size?
   d. Are the screens readable with proper font size, lighting, contrast, and other cues to enhance performance?
   e. Do the units of medication delivery (e.g., mcg/kg, mcg/kg/min) match current practices?
   f. Do the medications, units of delivery, and strengths appear in a logical sequence for selection?
   g. Is there any information that defaults to a predetermined value? If yes, is it safe?
   h. Is it easy to install and prime administration sets and to remove air in the line?
   i. Are any special features such as drug/dose calculations and dose alerts helpful and easy to use?
   j. Are the screens free of abbreviations, trailing zeros (e.g., 1.0 mg), and naked decimal points (e.g., .1mg)?
   k. Do the alarms clearly guide staff to the problems? Is it possible to permanently disable audible alarms or set them too low to be heard?
   l. If the infusion rate is changed, but not confirmed, does the device continuously alert the user that the solution is infusing at the old rate?
   m. Could the administration sets be mispositioned during installation or accidentally dislodged, separated, or removed by patients?
   n. Does the administration set prevent gravity free-flow of the solution when it is removed from the pump?
   o. Is the device tamper resistant?
   p. Does the pump fit into the typical workflow?
   q. How does the pump compare to the pumps now in use?

monitoring the patient, based on predetermined parameters such as vital signs, including criteria for neurologic assessment, quality of respirations, and lab results. In addition to proactively defining key parameters as part of established protocols, order sets, and flow sheets, health care providers also might need to incorporate them in computerized monitoring systems.

Documentation of monitoring is critical, and all associated forms (for example, diabetic flow sheets, patient controlled analgesia flow sheets, and sedation flow sheets) should be used at the bedside, and the information should remain there for quick reference. This is the case whether documentation is entered on a paper graphic or into a computerized record. Appropriate antidotes and resuscitation equipment should also be readily available at the bedside, and their presence should be noted in the record. Subsequent chart audits should contrast documentation of patient monitoring with outcomes to identify patterns in untoward care results and opportunities for improvement.

Environmental Stressors

In an ideal health care setting, medications would be prescribed, transcribed, prepared, and administered in an environment free of distractions, with comfortable surroundings, adequate physical space, and lighting. Practitioners would come to work rested and could take rest and meal breaks to maintain focus and attention. In reality, hospital workers are constantly exposed to noise, interruptions, and non-stop activity. The process of order transcription is particularly vulnerable to distraction, as it usually occurs in an environment where unit secretaries, nurses, and pharmacy personnel are answering telephones and talking with other providers and patients. A study confirms that simple slips due to distractions are responsible for almost three-quarters of all transcription errors.[18] Some strategies that might minimize such distractions include overlapping of staffing coverage during peak activity times and encouraging fax or e-mail communications to the nursing station, instead of telephone calls.

Interruptions during any step in the medication-use process can have devastating consequences. In one example, an ED patient died after receiving a 10-mg dose of hydromorphone when morphine 10 mg was ordered. As the ED nurse was selecting the drug, she was temporarily distracted by another of her patients who was attempting to climb off the end of the stretcher. She quickly placed a vial of hydromorphone in her pocket while she attended to the second patient, interrupting her normal routine of checking the medication and documenting the signout on the narcotic record. After settling the agitated patient, she resumed medication administration to the first patient, inadvertently omitting the step of signing out the narcotic. After receiving 10 mg of hydromorphone, when 2 mg is the usual intramuscular dose, the patient was discharged. He subsequently suffered a respiratory arrest in the family car and could not be resuscitated.

Fatigue also can contribute to medication errors. Research conducted by the Anesthesia Patient Safety Foundation documented anesthesiologists' performance failures when fatigued.[19] One group of researchers observed the incidence of a phenomenon called micro-sleeps in a study of anesthesiologists. In videotapes of surgical procedures, the researchers identified behaviors indicative of micro-sleeps during 30 percent of a four-hour case.[20] Micro-sleeps are intermittent lapses in consciousness, lasting seconds to minutes. The person's eyes are open, yet, the person is not cognizant of surroundings, cannot process information, and, once fully conscious again, is unaware that the lapse has even occurred![21]

TABLE 6.4   Effects of Fatigue[24,25,26]

- Slowed reaction time
- Reduced accuracy
- Diminished ability to recognize significant but subtle changes in a patient's health
- Inability to deal with the unexpected
- Lapses of attention and inability to stay focused
- Omissions and neglect of non-essential activities
- Compromised problem-solving and decision-making
- Impaired communication skills
- Inability to recall
- Short-term memory lapses
- Reduced motivation
- Irritability or hostility
- Indifference and loss of empathy
- Intrusion of sleep into wakefulness
- Decreased energy for successful completion of required tasks
- Decreased learning of new activities
- Reduced hand-eye coordination

Research has also shown that the risk of nurses making medication-related errors is increased significantly when they work longer than twelve hours in a shift, when working overtime, or when working greater than forty hours in one week.[22] Performance of a fatigued health care worker has been shown to equal that of a person with a blood alcohol level of 0.1 percent—over the legal limit for driving in many states.[23] See Table 6.4 for a list of the effects of fatigue.

Addressing safety issues associated with fatigue requires that the institution must support a culture in which admission of fatigue is accepted and rewarded. To achieve this environment, the management and the staff must be educated about the risks associated with fatigue and research-based approaches to optimize performance in the face of fatigue, especially with regard to night shift workers. Based on organizational commitment to address this important problem, health care organizations should examine staffing patterns to ensure adequate rest and recovery opportunities for their employees. Contingency plans should be developed to manage staffing needs if personnel appear to be or consider themselves too fatigued to work safely. It is important to ensure that staff members can take fifteen- to thirty-minute rest breaks away from the work area and a meal break during each shift. Other interventions to consider are providing for short planned naps in the workplace and offering light therapy to reduce the effects of fatiguing schedules and disrupted circadian rhythms.[27]

To address all of these environmental impediments to medication safety, organizational leaders should aim to foster a "sterile cockpit" similar to the one used by the airline industry to promote safety. In a sterile cockpit environment, pilots and flight crew-members are specifically prohibited from participating in distracting activities while performing critical duties. The Federal Aviation Administration written policies (Sec. 121.542) state:

> (a) No certificate holder shall require, nor may any flight crewmember perform, any duties during a critical phase of flight except those duties required for the safe operation of the aircraft. Duties such as company required calls made for such nonsafety related purposes as ordering galley supplies and confirming passenger connections, announcements made to passengers promoting the air carrier or pointing out sights of interest, and filling out company payroll and related records are not required for the safe operation of the aircraft.

(b) No flight crewmember may engage in, nor may any pilot in command permit, any activity during a critical phase of flight which could distract any flight crewmember from the performance of his or her duties or which could interfere in any way with the proper conduct of those duties. Activities such as eating meals, engaging in nonessential conversations within the cockpit and nonessential communications between the cabin and cockpit crews, and reading publications not related to the proper conduct of the flight are not required for the safe operation of the aircraft.

(c) For the purposes of this section, critical phases of flight includes all ground operations involving taxi, takeoff and landing, and all other flight operations conducted below 10,000 feet, except cruise flight.[28]

Because a failure in any step of the complex medication use process could lead to a medication error and patient harm, every step equates to an aircraft's "critical phase of flight." Distractions, interruptions, and competing activities should be eliminated or minimized. Managers and staff members should focus on creating and supporting an environment that allows concentration on the critical task at hand.

Competency and Staff Education

Many practitioners have limited awareness of error-prone situations—even those that are well-documented in their own organization or published in professional literature. Without this information, these staff members are likely to make similar errors. With the information, staff members can help the organization identify ways to prevent such errors from occurring. Upon hire or joining the medical staff and regularly thereafter, staff members should be provided with current information about errors that have occurred within the organization, and those that occur elsewhere. Health care organizations should also develop a "medication safety" test for providers who will administer medications. Included should be questions that address problem-prone areas such as morphine and insulin dosing, and the use of cross-allergenic medications such as Toradol and aspirin.

Medication Competency Tests

Anecdotal evidence from ISMP shows that many medication competency tests currently in use are outdated. For example, the questions on such tests often contain, and thus legitimize, dangerous abbreviations and dose designations. They also test obsolete approaches such as conversion from apothecary units (formally eliminated in 2001 by the American Society of Health-System Pharmacists) to metric units.[29]

In addition to updating the content, it is critical that such tests go beyond mere calculation and memorization of drugs and doses to "critical thinking." Medication competency tests should incorporate questions about safety issues such as laboratory values associated with drug use, appropriate monitoring of patients, and correct patient identification procedures. They should address such issues as identifying high-alert medications and the special precautions that are essential to use with these drugs. It is, of course, important to have staff members explain the correct procedure for an independent double-check, and they should also be able to describe appropriate and inappropriate therapy for patients, based on medical history.

When administering a medication competency test, allow the practitioner who is unsure of an answer to use medication resources (books, Internet or intranet, other practitioners). With this approach, all questions should be answered correctly and any wrong response should be thoroughly followed up with the test taker.

While it is vitally important, staff education cannot be successful as a singular safety strategy—it must be provided in conjunction with other approaches. One case that illustrates the importance of this principle involved a nurse who successfully completed her medication competency test, but later administered a dose of pronestyl after checking the pronestyl level but not the NAPA level. (NAPA is a metabolite of pronestyl that has the same pharmaceutical effect as pronestyl.) The NAPA level was elevated. Therefore the medication should have been held and the prescriber contacted. The nurse was unaware of the need to check the NAPA level before administration of this drug.

Simply drafting a policy or including a question on a competency exam about NAPA levels and pronestyl administration is likely to be ineffective in addressing this situation, without the accompanying use of such resources as auxiliary warnings printed on MARs to check NAPA levels, warnings, and hard stops. A hard stop prevents the practitioner from proceeding with an order unless a current lab value or other patient data (weight, allergy status, and so on) is entered. In this case, a hard stop would probably take the form of a note which appears on the provider order entry screen, requiring the user to check—or enter—the NAPA lab result before administration. A hard stop requiring lab value entry could also be implemented in bedside bar code drug administration software. Tools like these compensate for natural lapses in human concentration and memory, in ways that education alone cannot.

Patient Education

An alert and knowledgeable patient can serve as the last line of defense in preventing medication errors. For example, patients who have been educated about the need for proper identification prior to procedures or medication can alert staff members when their armband has not been checked. Also, when patients are aware of the usual times for drug administration, they can remind staff members that their medication is due, to prevent drug omission errors. To fulfill this role in preventing errors, patients must receive ongoing education by physicians, pharmacists, and nurses about drug brand and generic names, indications, usual and actual doses, expected and possible adverse effects, drug or food interactions, and how to protect themselves from errors. Although this education takes additional staff time, it can pay significant dividends in patient safety.

Even patients who have merely been encouraged to ask questions and seek satisfactory answers can play a vital role in preventing medication errors. A tragic example of a case in which a staff member did not heed the patient's questions involved an informed patient at the Dana Farber Cancer Institute who told her health care practitioners that she felt that something was wrong after two days of cancer chemotherapy. Numerous times, both the patient and her husband requested that the staff check her chemotherapy orders for accuracy because she was experiencing different side effects from her previous courses of therapy. Without a thorough investigation of their concerns, the patient's practitioners reassured the patient and her husband that the medication she was receiving was correct. Unfortunately, she received an entire course of chemotherapy every day for four days. It is impossible to say whether the patient would have survived if the error had been detected earlier, but there is no doubt that those four days of chemotherapy were the direct cause of her death.

The way in which patients are educated about their medication is also critical. Simply handing a drug information sheet to a patient is often not sufficient, as patients might misunderstand or be frightened by the information concerning the risk of taking the medication. Also, one study claims that nearly 50 percent of the population has either low or limited literary skills. This represents approximately 90 million adults.[30] Thus, practitioners need to assess whether patients fully understands their medications by asking what they are taking and verifying that patients understand why these medications are being given. For patients receiving multiple drugs and those who are receiving medications with a narrow therapeutic index, the health care organization should consider involving a pharmacist in patient education during the admission process and at discharge.

············

RISK MANAGEMENT—A PRIORITIZING APPROACH

To help the organization address risk and improve safety of medication use, it is critical that the risk management professional be aware of strategies for prioritizing issues and interventions.

Some medication safety strategies are more effective, or have more leverage, than others. Actions that produce an output more powerful than the input are considered to possess high leverage, and thus are more effective in producing change. Leverage is considered to be highest when it meets ISMP's first principle of error reduction: reducing or eliminating the possibility of errors. The second principle of error reduction, possessing moderate leverage, is to make errors visible. The third is to minimize the consequences of errors after their occurrence. These principles provide a framework for developing error reduction strategies. The error reduction strategies in Figure 6.3 are presented in rank order of leverage, highest to lowest.

An example of a constraint is purchasing epidural tubing without any ports that might allow accidental injection of intravenous drugs. Forcing functions are strategies that do not allow an action to occur unless certain conditions are met, potentially preventing an error. (The terms "forcing function" and "hard stop" are often used interchangeably.) Computerized or automated devices can act as forcing functions—for example, the provider might be prevented from entering a drug order unless patient weight is entered, or might be unable to access an automated dispensing drawer unless the drug in that drawer is in the patient's pharmacy profile.

Automated devices may also alert the user in the event of a negative outcome, thereby making an error visible (for example, alarms on infusion pumps, patient monitors). Although the result might be after the fact and therefore is lower in leverage, automated alerts can also prompt drug orders for antidotes and reversal agents,

FIGURE 6.3   Rank Order of Error Reduction Strategies

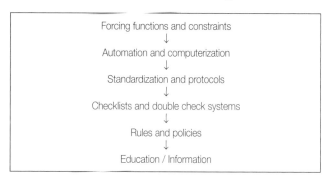

Forcing functions and constraints
↓
Automation and computerization
↓
Standardization and protocols
↓
Checklists and double check systems
↓
Rules and policies
↓
Education / Information

thereby minimizing the consequences of an error. Rules, policies, and education are important components of error reduction strategies but they have very limited leverage in creating real change.

Another important prioritizing strategy is to categorize certain medications and patient populations as "high-alert" or "high-risk." Those medications considered high-alert are those that pose the greatest risk of causing significant harm when misused. Refer to Table 6.5 for High-Alert Medications by Class or Category and Table 6.6 for High-Alert Medications by Specific Medications. High-risk patients are those at risk of suffering significant harm if they experience a medication error (Table 6.7). High-alert and high-risk does not mean that errors occur more frequently with these medications or to these patients; it simply means that the resulting harm is more difficult to ameliorate. Such categories help the health care organization properly prioritize error reduction efforts.

TABLE 6.5   High-Alert Medications by Class or Category

• adrenergic agonists, IV	• hypoglycemics, oral and insulin
• adrenergic antagonists, IV	• inotropic medications, IV
• anesthetic agents, general, inhaled, and IV	• liposomal forms of drugs
• cardioplegic solutions	• moderate sedation agents
• chemotherapeutic agents	• narcotics/opiates, IV and oral
• dextrose, hypertonic	• neuromuscular blocking agents
• dialysis solutions	• radiocontrast agents, IV
• epidural or intrathecal medications	• thrombolytics/fibrinolytics
• glycoprotein IIb/IIIa inhibitors	• total parenteral nutrition

TABLE 6.6   High-Alert Specific Medications

• amiodarone, IV	• methotrexate, oral, non-oncologic use
• colchicine injection	• nesiritide
• heparin, low molecular weight, injection	• nitroprusside, sodium, for injection
• heparin, unfractionated, IV	• potassium chloride for injection concentrate
• insulin, subcutaneous and IV	• potassium phosphates injection
• lidocaine, IV	• sodium chloride injection, hypertonic
• magnesium sulfate injection	• warfarin

TABLE 6.7   High-Risk Patient Populations

• Patients with renal/liver impairment
• Pregnant/breast-feeding patients
• Neonates
• Elderly/chronically ill patients
• Patients on multiple medications
• Oncology patients

TABLE 6.8   Error-Prone Processes

- Patient-controlled analgesia; epidural analgesia
- Use of automated dispensing equipment
- Preparation of complex products in the pharmacy with automated compounders
- Administration of enteral feedings in patients with IV catheters in place
- Obtaining accurate allergy information

Because risk reduction efforts must begin at the highest leverage point, where the most effectiveness can be gained from minimal actions, prioritization is critical to maximize the organization's resources, including staff time.

Additionally, certain sub-processes within the medication-use process may be considered more error-prone than others (Table 6.8). These processes should be examined in detail, with attention to various ways that things could go wrong at each step and the potential for patient harm that might result from a failure at each process step. A more formalized examination entails a failure mode and effects analysis (FMEA). ISMP offers a sample FMEA on the error-prone process of patient-controlled analgesia on its Web site at: [ismp.org/d/FMEAofPCA.pdf].

Yet another high priority activity that often involves the risk management professional is due diligence regarding a new clinical activity. In some settings, competition with other organizations is resulting in rapidly expanding services. Neonatal intensive care, organ transplants, open-heart surgery, home care infusion, and oncology units are but a few examples of the areas currently experiencing growth. Often, in such situations, there has been little time to properly prepare for the new activity by reorganizing workflow and providing staff education.

It is critical that appropriate planning take place and that medication use issues receive a high priority. In one unfortunate situation, soon after a hospital established a new pediatric emergency service, a pharmacist was called to supply the unit with ketamine injection to sedate children during procedures in the ED. Ketamine is available in vials with concentrations of 10 mg/mL, 50 mg/mL, and 100 mg/mL. The pharmacy sent five vials of 100 mg/mL vials to the unit. Before long, a four-year-old patient came to the ED for suturing of a wound. A physician who was accustomed to using vials of ketamine 10 mg/mL did not notice the 100 mg/mL concentration and inadvertently administered the total contents of the 500 mg vial instead of the 50 mg pediatric dose. The child suffered a respiratory arrest but was successfully resuscitated. During the review of the error, the pharmacy staff readily admitted that they were not well informed about the use of ketamine for ambulatory sedation in pediatric patients, and therefore were unsure about which concentration to supply. It was also determined that no one in the pharmacy department had prior pediatric care experience.

When a new service or expansion of an existing department is contemplated, senior management must ensure that all staff members are provided with timely communication. A failure mode and effect analysis (FMEA) should take place to discover potential areas of weakness and explore steps that are needed to promote safety. Staff orientation and proper education for new services must be planned as early as possible, but close enough to the start of the new service to maintain an appropriate skill level. In addition, consideration must be given to staffing levels, which might need to be increased (even if temporarily) in proportion to the new workload. The risk management professional can play an invaluable role in facilitating senior administrative support of necessary planning.

Error Reporting and Follow-up

Each individual practitioner must firmly believe that errors may be reported without disciplinary action and that the organization will use the incident report to evaluate the medication delivery system. In one case, a nurse was afraid to report a serious medication error to her manager because of her concern that this would blemish her record. She feared that the next time she committed an error she might be suspended or even fired. The nurse contacted ISMP because she was afraid to ask anyone at work if her patient, who was scheduled for an invasive procedure later that day, could be adversely affected from an inadvertent overdose of heparin. Although it seemed unlikely that the increased amount of heparin would have an effect several hours later, ISMP encouraged her to report the error because the physician might choose to postpone the procedure as a precaution. It was later learned that, because of her fears, she did not inform anyone of the incident. Therefore, any opportunity for preventing patient harm or addressing the system issues that caused this error was lost.

Although no one would condone this nurse's decision, it is easy to understand the mindset behind it. If practitioners do not see any benefit associated with reporting, there is no incentive to report. If they perceive a danger to themselves, they will be discouraged—and may discourage others—from reporting.

Patient safety cannot be promoted in any organization without open communication about errors. Risk management professionals have the opportunity to encourage such openness and maximize the value of reporting. Practitioners can be motivated to report if they are clear that the purpose of reporting is proactively aimed at protecting their patients from future harm.

············

CONCLUSION

It is fundamental that risk management professionals and the multidisciplinary team they are part of accept ownership of the medication-use process and enthusiastically embrace the opportunity to improve patient safety. While they may celebrate a "safety week" or "safety month," organizational leaders must also demonstrate around-the-clock commitment to medication safety. Risk management professionals can facilitate senior management support of the financial commitment and time required to train staff members in communication skills and implement a physical environment that promotes safe and effective medication use processes. Critical to achievement of this goal is a thorough understanding of exactly how each component of these processes interacts, taking into account the varied perspectives of practitioners and the complexity of their patients.

Endnotes

1. Reason, J. *Managing the risks of organization accidents.* Aldershot, United Kingdom, Ashgate, 1–19. 1990.

2. Drug Facts and Comparisons. St. Louis, Mo.: Facts and Comparisons.

3. NeoFax. Raleigh, N.C.: Acorn Publishing.

4. Leape, L. L., D. W. Bates, D. J. Cullen et al. "Systems analysis of adverse drug events." *JAMA* 1995; 274:35–43.

5. *Ibid.*

6. Institute for Safe Medication Practices. 2004 ISMP Medication Safety Self Assessment for Hospitals (workbook). Huntingdon Valley, PA: Institute for Safe Medication Practices; 2004.

7. Thompson Micromedex (database online). Available at: [www.micromedex.com/]. Accessed October 31, 2005.

8. Leape, L. L., D. J. Cullen, M. Clapp et al. "Pharmacist participation on physician rounds and adverse drug events in the intensive care unit." *JAMA*. 1999; 282:267–70.

9. Institute for Safe Medication Practices. "Intimidation: Practitioners speak up about this unresolved problem (Part I)." *ISMP Medication Safety Alert!* 2004; 9(5). Results available at: [www.ismp.org/S/Survey0311.asp]. Accessed October 31, 2005.

10. Institute for Safe Medication Practices. "Intimidation: Mapping a plan for cultural change in healthcare (Part II)." *ISMP Medication Safety Alert!* 2004; 9(6).

11. Institute for Healthcare Improvement. Reconcile Medications at All Transition Points. Available at: [www.ihi.org/IHI/Topics/PatientSafety/MedicationSystems/Changes/Reconcile+Medications+at+All+Transition+Points.htm]. Accessed October 31, 2005.

12. "Look-alike/sound-alike drug products affect cognition." *USP CAPSLink* [serial online]. May 2004; 1-5. Available at: [www.usp.org/pdf/EN/patientSafety/capsLink2004-05-01.pdf]. Accessed November 3, 2005.

13. Holquist C., J. Phillips. FDA Safety Page: Fatal medication errors associated with Temodar. *Drug Topics*. 2003;7:42.

14. Joint Commission on Accreditation of Healthcare Organizations. Most problematic look-alike and sound-alike drug names for specific health care settings. Available at: [www.jcaho.org/accredited+organizations/patient+safety/05+npsg/lasa.pdf]. Accessed October 31, 2005.

15. International Ergonomics Association. The discipline of ergonomics. Available at: [www.iea.cc/ergonomics/]. Accessed October 31, 2005.

16. *Ibid.*, Leape, Bates, Cullen et al., *op.cit.*

17. Institute for Safe Medication Practices Canada. "Devices with inflation ports–Risk for medication error-induced injuries." *ISMP Canada Safety Bulletin*. May 2004;4(5).

18. *Ibid.*, Leape, Bates, Cullen et al, *op.cit.*

19. *Anesthesia Patient Safety Foundation Newsletter*. Spring 2005; 20(1):1–24.

20. Howard, S. K., D. M. Gaba, B. E.; Smith, et al. "Simulation study of rested versus sleep-deprived anesthesiologists." *Anesthesiology*. 2003; 98:1345–55; discussion A.

21. Rosekind, M. R., P. H. Gander, L. J. Connell, et al. "Crew factors in flight operations X: Alertness management in flight operations." NASA Technical Memorandum #1999-208780. Moffett Field, CA: NASA; 1999.

22. Rogers, A. E., W- T Hwang, L. D. Scott, L. H. Aiken, and D. F. Dinges. "Hospital staff nurse work and patient safety." *Health Affairs*. 2004; 23: 1–11.

23. Dawson, D., K. Reid. "Fatigue, alcohol and performance impairment." *Nature*. 1997; 388:235.

24. Gillberg, M., G. Kecklund, T. Akerstedt. "Relations between performance and subjective ratings of sleepiness during a night awake." *Sleep*.1994;17(3):236–241.

25. Linde, L, M. Bergstrom. "The effect of one night without sleep on problem-solving and immediate recall." *Psychological Research*.1992; 54(2):127–136.

26. Howard, S. "Fatigue and the practice of medicine." *Anesthesia Patient Safety Foundation Newsletter*. Spring 2005; 20(1):1–4.

27. *Ibid.*

28. Code of Federal Regulations. 14CFR121.542. Title 14: Aeronautics and Space, Chapter I: Federal Aviation Administration, Department of Transportation, Part 121: Operating requirements: Domestic, flag, and supplemental operations, Subpart T: Flight Operations, Section 121.542: Flight crewmember duties. Doc. No. 20661, 46 FR 5502, Jan. 19, 1981, Revised as of January 1, 2003. U.S. Government Printing Office. Available

at [a257.g.akamaitech.net/7/257/2422/14mar20010800/edocket.access.gpo.gov/cfr_2003/14cfr121.542.htm]. Accessed October 28, 2005.

29. American Society of Health-System Pharmacists. AHSP Position number 8613. Policy Positions, Statements and Guidelines. Available at: [www.ashp.org/bestpractices/pharmaceutical.cfm]. Accessed October 31, 2005.

30. Kirsch, I. S., A. Jungeblut, L. Jenkins, A. Kolstad. Executive summary of adult literacy in America: A first look at the results of the national adult literacy survey. National Center for Education Statistics, U.S. Department of Education, 1993. Available at: [nces.ed.gov/naal/resources/execsumm.asp]. Accessed October 28, 2005.

7

The Risk Management Professional and Biomedical Technology

Sally T. Trombly

B iomedical technology should be part of an enterprise risk management (ERM) program in every health care organization, and the risk management professional should play an active role. Key biomedical technology-related issues for which the risk management professional can provide expertise include patient safety, staff education requirements, and resource implications. Equally important is the risk management professional's input on the potential effects of decisions on biomedical technology in relation to existing patient care needs, new services planned or desired, and the effect of each of these on the system or facility's overall strategic plan, financial resources, and its work force.

STRATEGIC CONSIDERATIONS

The risk management professional can help an individual facility or a health care system make correct decisions about the acquisition and use of biomedical technology.

Simply because a piece of medical equipment or new type of biomedical technology carries risk is no reason to forgo purchase; likewise, just because something is new is no reason to obtain it. An apparent increase in resource utilization (such as training time or changes in allocation of staffing) can ultimately result in increases in overall efficiency, benefits to patient care outcomes, and increased satisfaction for both staff and patients.

To effectively input risk benefit analyses, the risk management professional must participate in the strategic planning and evaluation process from the onset, not just after decisions have been made, equipment has been acquired, or problems have occurred.

....

RISK MANAGEMENT INPUT

The ultimate choices when pursuing new ventures that involve biomedical technology are likely to be senior management and governing body decisions. Risk management input at the beginning of the process can contribute to more effective decision-making. It also gives the risk management professional early notice of areas that might require additional risk management attention if the potential venture becomes a reality. For biomedical technology-related needs of existing services, the risk management professional can offer useful insights from past patient care situations and previous experiences with vendors. The risk management professional also might have current information on devices with enhancements that facilitate patient safety, for example, "smart" pumps (intravenous pumps that help prevent medication dosage and rate errors). Progressive institutions are beginning to recognize the value that risk management can bring to strategic planning and decision-making processes. As this trend grows, the ability of the risk management professional to effectively operationalize the institution's biomedical technology decisions and reduce the potential for risk exposure related to biomedical technology should become more widely recognized. (See Volume I, Chapter I on Basic Health Care Enterprise Risk Management and Volume III, Chapter 3 on Enterprise Risk Management in this series.)

....

FINANCIAL CONSIDERATIONS

As part of the biomedical technology due diligence process, the risk management professional should be involved in assessing the available options and fiscal effect of decisions concerning whether to buy, lease, or enter into a consignment arrangement for medical devices. Each of these options for obtaining such devices has ramifications for subsequent operational responsibilities. These extend far beyond the fiscal concerns of capital costs, the budgeting process, and ongoing funding and allocation of biomedical technology costs. For example, there might be varying regulatory mandates depending on which party actually owns the piece of biomedical technology at a specific time. Adverse events and equipment recalls made by the manufacturer or the federal government trigger reporting requirements by specific areas. Without risk management coordination, there might be unnecessary confusion within the institution over the division of mandated responsibilities. Considering these factors during the decision-making process can help identify the potential effects of short or long-term fiscal options. It can also provide useful background information for those involved in the subsequent contract negotiations relating to biomedical technology equipment.

....

BIOMEDICAL TECHNOLOGY CONTRACTS WITH VENDORS

In addition to the traditional elements of health care contracts (see Volume I, Chapter 12 in this series on contract review), contracts concerning biotechnology-related equipment should also clearly delineate:

- Responsibilities of each party regarding preventative and ongoing maintenance of the particular type of biomedical technology or medical equipment.
- For biomedical equipment critical to patient care, a guarantee of equipment "uptime" or prompt provision of a substitute acceptable to the health care organization (and identification of any associated costs).

- Circumstances under which a piece of biomedical equipment may be deemed "unsatisfactory" by the institution and remedies available, such as a full or partial replacement by the vendor or return for credit, and identification of the associated responsibilities of each party in this situation (comparable to a "lemon law" process for automobiles).

- Conditions under which credits towards future updates or trade-in are available.

- Provisions for an annual assessment of the vendor's service and support by the institution, with the ability to make recommendations for vendor improvements as necessary.

- Procedures for the vendor to notify the institution regarding product hazards identified or recalls instituted and the follow-up responsibilities assigned to each party.

- Allocation of mandated reporting responsibilities for biotechnology used on a consignment basis.

- Any institutional requirements or restrictions on representatives of the vendor who visit staff or departments in facilities (such as sign-in processes, identification badges, limitations on access to certain areas, and so on).

- Responsibilities of each party under the federal privacy and security regulations under HIPAA (See Volume III, Chapter 18 in this series). These may arise in several areas. First, if the biotechnology equipment (or its associated software) uses individually identifiable health information, a written "business associate" agreement (as defined by the HIPAA regulations and meeting the requirements of 45 C.F.R. 164.504 (e) (1)) must be incorporated into the contract or executed as a separate agreement or addendum between the parties. Second, the Food and Drug Administration's (FDA) regulations involving reporting, tracking, and recall policies for biomedical technology may require disclosure of individually identifiable health information subject to the disclosure requirements of HIPAA (see 45 C.F.R. 164.512(b) (1) (iii)). Finally, safeguarding the security of individually identifiable health information collected by a biomedical device's software and system components from reasonably anticipated threats or vulnerabilities is required under the security portion of the HIPAA regulations (see 45 C.F.R. 164.306). This presents challenges for a variety of health care devices, such as imaging systems that obtain, archive, and communicate across an institutional network, various types of patient monitoring systems, and laboratory information systems connected to clinical laboratory analyzers. Although manufacturers have significant responsibilities in this area, health care organizations need to be a knowledgeable partner to make the process successful and help avoid problems.

············

BULK PURCHASING ARRANGEMENTS AND BIOMEDICAL TECHNOLOGY

Purchasing arrangements among health care organizations have become much more common in recent years. The ability to aggregate several smaller requests into larger volume purchases can offer significant benefits in terms of efficiency, and potential cost savings due to greater bargaining power among the participants in these programs. When applied to biomedical technology-related equipment purchases, such arrangements can also enhance organizational efforts towards equipment standardization where applicable, much as health care entities have done with implementation of drug formularies. From a risk management perspective, the key considerations in purchasing arrangements should be the selection of biomedical technology items suited to the medical care needs of patients, and the safe and efficient use of such items by clinicians and staff. The health care organization can enjoy significant benefit when these objectives are achieved, in combination with the cost savings realized through group purchasing organizations.

············

STAFF TRAINING

Staff training is crucial to the successful management of risk exposures that can result from the interaction of humans and biomedical technology. The need for staff training in general and cross training to meet particular needs is not limited to permanent personnel of the facility. The increased use of clinical staff from per diem pools and commercial companies that provide individuals for short- or longterm assignments raise significant orientation and training challenges for health care facilities. However, the public expects that all staff authorized by a health care facility to use a piece of biomedical technology are competent to do so, regardless of the individual's employment status.

The institution must be prepared to meet the full spectrum of biomedical technology training needs, from initial training in the use and support of a new piece of equipment, to ongoing in-service training, to individualized remedial training when indicated. Depending on the complexity of the biomedical technology in use at a particular site, staff and the facility's clinical providers may require education about the equipment. For example, others whose job duties relate to maintenance or calibration, such as biomedical engineering personnel and those responsible for routine cleaning, disinfecting, or sterilization of certain medical devices also need appropriate ongoing training.

············

"TRAINING" PATIENTS, FAMILIES, AND NON-MEDICAL PERSONNEL

Consider the need for "awareness training" about biomedical technology for patients, families, and non-medical personnel. This need is not limited to hospital-based sites. It also applies to leased settings in which health care organization employees provide ambulatory health care services, but the building owner furnishes the janitorial staff. The public is increasingly aware of biomedical devices, such as automatic external defibrillators (AED) in airports and businesses, and television series that feature scenarios using such biomedical technology have become popular. This can encourage a cavalier attitude among lay people about the significant realities involved in biomedical technology. For example, in at least one reported case, a death occurred when a worker in a janitorial service "playing with a defibrillator" placed the paddles on a coworker's chest.[1] Similarly, harm to workers may occur if housekeeping staff are not trained in MRI precautions.

Situations that involve unauthorized access to, or handling of, biomedical devices by non-institutional personnel are not new. When protective containers for used needles and other sharps came into widespread use there were instances of children trying to access units that were within reach. The red plastic brick-shaped "sharps containers" resembled a popular building block for children. Children have also been involved in potentially serious incidents with electric beds during upward or downward movement of the bed.

Inadvertent unplugging of an intravenous pump by untrained staff can result in shut-off due to battery depletion, which sometimes goes unrecognized, with potentially serious patient care ramifications.

Recommendations made by ECRI, a nonprofit health services research agency dedicated to safe and effective patient and resident care, in "Playing with Medical Devices Can Be a Deadly Game"[2] include:

- Educating the facility's non-medical personnel and the clinical staff about the dangers of misusing medical devices, and the range of problems that could arise from improper use by any person

- Reminding the staff to remain alert for any evidence of tampering when setting up a medical device

- Reviewing the location of medical devices in the facility and, to the extent possible, storing them in an area accessible only to appropriate medical personnel

- Considering the availability of safeguards against tampering when selecting new medical devices

············

OPERATIONAL FACTORS

A systematic biomedical technology management process helps ensure that an institution uses its resources to benefit its patient base, meets applicable regulatory edicts, and reduces the likelihood of adverse outcomes and potential liability exposure. Management processes may vary with the type and complexity of both the biomedical technology and the care setting, but should include adequate risk management systems and structures to identify and resolve actual or potential problems generated by the biomedical technology in use. The core business practices that relate to biomedical technology must address applicable federal and state mandates or reporting requirements imposed by these governmental entities or relevant accrediting bodies. The risk management processes and supporting materials also need to recognize and respond to the realities of implementation, such as:

- Reporting of adverse events or "near-misses"
- Follow-up on reports of problems or concerns raised by the staff
- Preventive maintenance or repair of biomedical equipment
- Recalls instituted by a manufacturer or the FDA
- Inventory control and tracking of biomedical-related equipment
- Institutional decisions regarding reuse or reprocessing
- Disposal of biomedical equipment that is no longer needed by the facility

············

REALITIES OF IMPLEMENTATION

As discussed in Volume 1, Chapter 4 of this series, the timely identification and analysis of potential risk exposures is a key component in a risk management program, no matter where the care is being rendered. Although the mandatory reporting requirements of the Safe Medical Device Act (SMDA) (refer to Volume III, Chapter 16 for more information on statutes, standards, and regulations) might not apply in certain types of health care settings, the risk management professional still needs to be aware of issues and concerns about biomedical technology. Even if these issues might not need the same type of formal review and reporting as those in an SMDA-mandated setting, the requirements provide guidance in setting up appropriate internal review systems. Patient care is increasingly moving to non-hospital-based settings, and the scope of services in physicians' offices and the other limited number of locations where SMDA compliance is not mandatory is continually expanding. Inconsistencies in practice and processes across multiple affiliated locations that are promoted to the public as a "coordinated delivery system for health care" create potential risk exposures. Reducing variation among such locations presents an ongoing challenge for the risk management professional.

············

REPORTING AND FOLLOW-UP OF ADVERSE EVENTS AND NEAR-MISSES

The advent of the SMDA, effective in 1991, and its refinements in 1997 placed new emphasis on the responsibility of health care facilities to report medical device-related incidents to the device manufacturer and to the FDA and to track various types of biomedical technology, particularly certain devices implanted in patients. Although much of the SMDAs focus is on mandatory requirements, voluntary reporting still exists, and it plays an important role in timely identification of product design concerns that could lead to user errors and potential patient care problems.

Health care facilities need a systematic internal process to document, analyze, and follow up on incidents that may be related to biomedical technology. This is critical to achieving basic goals of the risk management program, such as promoting safe patient care, avoiding injury to the staff using biomedical technology, and reducing the likelihood of potential liability exposure from an adverse event that involves the biomedical technology. Developing a flow chart specific to the institutional structure can help clarify the process and serve as a training tool for the staff. For example, Exhibit 7.1 provides a road map for the risk management professional to document the review and decision process required to determine whether external reporting is indicated. Additional resources and information about the medical device reporting requirements are available online from the FDA [www.fda/gov/cdrh/mdr/].

When a medical device is potentially involved in an unanticipated outcome for a patient, it adds additional dimensions to the risk management follow-up. It is important to have institutional processes in place so that, no matter what the day or time, identification and preservation of what may be potential evidence can take place. A health care facility might not always have available on-site or on-call risk management and biomedical or clinical engineering staff, so there should be a plan in place to handle these circumstances. Areas that the institution's processes should address include:

- What institutional personnel to contact and how to reach them (or a designated alternate) during off-shift hours and on regular workdays.

- Protocols to identify, preserve, and impound the medical device, associated components and packaging. The medical device itself must be clearly labeled or tagged as out of service, not to be used, and placed in a secured area. The protocols should also include directives not to change any existing control settings, turn off or unplug the device, remove a battery, or otherwise do anything that might hinder retrieval by biomedical or clinical engineering of error codes that might be stored in the device's memory. Clearly identify circumstances when cleaning or processing the medical device should be delayed, because it might have an adverse effect on subsequent investigation.

- Maintaining and documenting a complete chain of custody for the medical device and any associated components or packaging. A paper trail should track the "who, what, and where" of the items originally impounded and the subsequent transfer(s) of

EXHIBIT 7.1   ECRI's Medical Device Reporting Decision Pathway

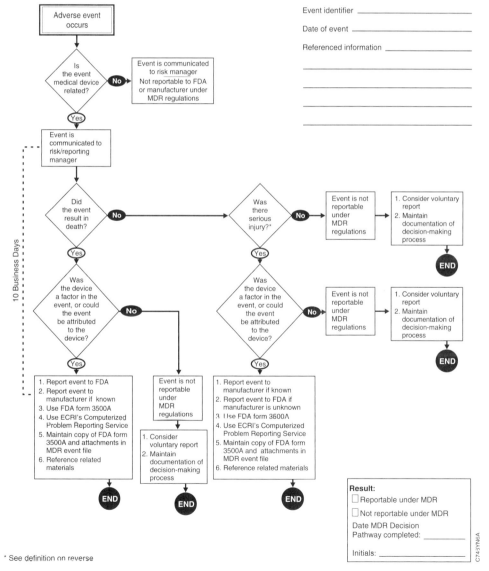

* See definition on reverse

C743YN6A

(Continued)

EXHIBIT 7.1   ECRI's Medical Device Reporting Decision Pathway *(Continued)*

Instructions for Using ECRI's MDR Decision Pathway

The ECRI MDR Decision Pathway should be used to document your deliberations when deciding whether an adverse event is reportable under the MDR regulations. The Pathway may be duplicated as often as you wish. Maintain MDR Decision Pathways for a minimum of two years from the date of the event. You may also wish to include a copy of the Pathway and these instructions in your MDR policies and procedures.

Complete the Pathway as follows:

1. Fill in the Event Identifier as prescribed by policies and procedures. **Do not** use the patient's name, clinician's name, or any social security number as an identifier.
2. Fill in the date of the event.
3. List other referenced materials related to the adverse event (e.g., engineering reports, medical records, incident reports, patient files).
4. Highlight the path followed to reach your conclusion of whether or not the event is reportable under the MDR regulations.
5. Check off the appropriate box indicating whether or not the event is reportable under MDR regulations.
6. Submit voluntary reports as desired to ECRI's Problem Reporting Program, 5200 Butler Pike, Plymouth Meeting, PA 19462-1298, phone: (610) 825-6000, fax: (610) 834-1275; the manufacturer; and/or to FDA on MedWatch Form 3500 (the voluntary reporting form).
7. Fill in the date the MDR Decision Pathway was completed.
8. Fill in the initials of the person completing the Pathway.

Serious Injury Considerations for MDR Deliberations

1. Was the injury or illness life-threatening?   ❏ yes ❏ no
2. Did the injury or illness result in permanent* impairment of a body function or permanent damage to a body structure?   ❏ yes ❏ no
3. Did the injury or illness necessitate medical or surgical intervention to preclude permanent* impairment of a body function or permanent damage to a body structure?   ❏ yes ❏ no

    **Permanent* means irreversible impairment or damage, excluding trivial impairment or damage.

"Decision Tree for Evaluating Single-Use Devices for Reuse" from pages 44-45 of ECRI's Special Report, "Reuse of Single-use Medical Devices: Making Informed Decisions," copyright ECRI 1997. www.ecri.org

control and custody of any or all of these items (whether internal or external) that might occur. The degree of thoroughness in handling and documenting these steps can be a significant factor if litigation ensues.

- Interactions with the manufacturer of the medical device. In most situations, the health care facility is the owner of the medical device involved, and it has a duty to protect its own interests. When a potentially significant problem or adverse patient care outcome is reported to a manufacturer, the company's first response is likely to be an attempt to regain possession of the medical device, ostensibly for "testing purposes." A health care facility may be offered a refund, exchange, or comparable new product in return. However, because the health care facility and the manufacturer might ultimately become defendants with differing interests if litigation results, the decision to send the manufacturer the medical device involved should not be made lightly. This is particularly true where death or serious injury resulted and the health care facility might ultimately need to have an outside evaluation of that medical device for potential liability purposes. In cases where injury is minimal and litigation seems less likely, completion and documentation of the facility's own investigation and testing, and any independent evaluation of the medical device should be done before deciding about sending the medical device to the manufacturer for its own testing. Expectations for return of the device should be explicitly documented in correspondence with the manufacturer. Complete documentation of all aspects of the process and transfer must be maintained, including chain of custody tracking.

TRACKING BIOMEDICAL TECHNOLOGY-RELATED DEVICES

The FDA has authority to require manufacturers to track certain classes of medical devices from manufacture down to the level of a specific patient. The FDA's goal with this requirement is to ensure that manufacturers remove potentially dangerous or defective medical devices from the market, or notify individual patients of significant medical device problems in a timely manner. This authority is in addition to the FDA's ability to order mandatory recalls and require manufacturers to notify health care professionals and patients regarding situations where the FDA determines that there is an unreasonable risk of substantial harm associated with a particular medical device.

The FDA also has the authority to change the list of devices that it requires manufacturers to track, and it has done so periodically. The current list is available at [www.fda.gov/cdrh/devadvice/353.html]. Items tracked include several medical devices that are implanted in patients, and another group of biomedical technology equipment that is tracked when used outside a health care facility. The responsibility for developing a written standard operating procedure to track a device rests with the manufacturer, but the health care facility and individual practitioners are involved in implementing the process, complying with documentation requirements, and maintaining the appropriate records. Health care facilities need to be aware that, for implants on the FDA's list, the manufacturer is responsible to track the implant to the patient and to update the patient's address as necessary. Because the manufacturer should specify in its operating procedure how that updating is to occur, health care facilities should make sure they know about (and agree with) any responsibilities the manufacturer may place on them to furnish information in the future.

RECALLS INVOLVING BIOMEDICAL TECHNOLOGY

Health care facilities need effective policies and procedures for handling reports of hazardous conditions or recalls that involve biomedical technology-related devices. For hospitals accredited by the Joint Commission on Accreditation of Healthcare Organizations (JCAHO), this requirement is specified in the commission's standards. Recalls may be instituted by the manufacturer (voluntary recall) or by the FDA (mandatory recall) under authority granted to the agency by the SMDA.

Manufacturers initiate most of the recalls involving medical devices, but the FDA plays an active role in the process. By law, the manufacturer must notify the FDA that it is recalling a medical device, and then make progress reports to the FDA. The initial report must be made to the FDA within ten working days for recalls that involve defective products that could cause serious health problems (for example, a defective artificial heart valve). The FDA reviews the manufacturer's proposed recall plan to determine whether it is adequate, and may recommend changes. If the FDA recommends modifications to the recall plan and the manufacturer declines the advice, the FDA can issue its own recall order.

Ordering a recall is only the first step in what can be a tedious and perhaps complicated process in health care institutions. Recall notices from a manufacturer can go unnoticed if they are sent to an incorrect address or labeled with the wrong department. Thus hospitals that frequently use various addresses for different areas on the facility's campus should develop a reliable internal notification system. Beyond issuing recall notices to facilities using the device, manufacturers are not required to publicize that they are recalling a medical device and may choose not to do so.

It is easy to see why medical device recall notices can fail to reach the individuals who need to know about them. Risk management professionals should take steps that improve the odds that the information will get to the right place in a timely manner. Those actions include the following:

- Designate a central collection point for recall notifications and instruct staff about their responsibility to immediately forward information that might come to them.

- Require faxing of all recall notifications to that central collection point as part of vendor contracts and purchase orders.

- Determine available options for tracking the type and location of medical devices in the institution and for maintaining an accurate inventory of medical and surgical supplies.

- Designate an ad hoc group that includes clinical, biomedical, risk management, patient safety, and administrative representatives that can be quickly convened to consider options, alternatives, and ramifications for patient care, and recommend a course of action when removal of a medical device from service is necessary.

- Identify an individual or group to coordinate the recall process and related activities, such as ongoing monitoring of FDA and industry information and selected Web sites relative to biomedical technology.

············

REPROCESSING OF MEDICAL DEVICES
LABELED AS SINGLE-USE

Whether or not to reprocess medical devices labeled as "single-use" by the manufacturer has been an ongoing issue in the health care environment. These medical devices can be very expensive to purchase. In some cases the packaging on the device might have been opened during a procedure without the device itself having been used on a patient. Many health care institutions have stopped doing their own reprocessing altogether in light of the many requirements now placed on this practice by the FDA; however, the debate surrounding "open but unused" single-use devices continues. The FDA offers a CD-ROM, "An Overview of the Regulatory Requirements for Reprocessing of Single-Use Devices by Hospitals," which may be obtained by any hospital by filling out a request form on the FDA Web site [www.fda.gov/cdrh/reuse/reuse-messages.html]. Other current information and guidance is available at [www.fda.gov/cdrh/reuse/index.html].

············

DISPOSAL OF BIOMEDICAL TECHNOLOGY-RELATED EQUIPMENT

What factors help determine that a piece of biomedical technology is becoming obsolete and replacement, retirement, or disposal should be considered? Guidelines from the American Society of Anesthesiologists[3] regarding anesthesia machines offer some broad categories that an institution can use as a starting point. These include:

- Lack of essential safety features
- Presence of unacceptable features (for example, multiple controls for the same function)
- Maintenance problems that potentially affect patient safety, such as adequate maintenance no longer available (for example, replacement parts)
- Increased potential for human error compared with newer technology

When health care institutions upgrade or otherwise replace items of biomedical technology, they may be faced with a decision about what to do with the prior piece of biomedical equipment. In some cases, eventual disposal might have been addressed as part of the prior purchase. In other situations, there might be trade-in options associated with the contract for the new biomedical technology being purchased.

Disposal concerns, in general, fall into two categories: (1) divestiture, including the sale or donation of a health care facility's equipment to another entity, group, or individual, or abandonment or destruction of the equipment and (2) an acquisition of a piece of biomedical equipment that is being disposed of by another facility. It might seem altruistic to recycle and pass on unneeded or outmoded equipment to others or to preserve institutional resources by acquiring a used piece of biotechnology. However, the potential for allegations that an adverse outcome is linked to the newly divested or acquired piece of equipment make it essential that the health care organization evaluate related risk as part of the decision-making process. There are many potential exposures, including:

- The selling or donating entity could find itself being considered part of the distribution chain, with a potential for product liability exposure.
- Compliance with FDA-mandated medical device tracking and documentation requirements may be associated with the disposal.
- Issues involving the existing condition of the biomedical equipment, its remaining useful life, and warranty concerns may arise for parties on both sides of the transaction.
- Whether the pertinent device was donated or sold could become a factor in how the biomedical equipment recycling or transfer to another entity is viewed, if something adverse subsequently occurs.
- If biomedical equipment is to be scrapped, it should be rendered unusable, and computer-related or potentially hazardous components and materials should be removed and disposed of properly.

There are national and international organizations that are willing to help facilitate the recycling, donation, and independent transfer of medical equipment. Recycling and appropriate sharing of biomedical equipment technology and resources should not be prohibited; however, consideration of the pros and cons in the particular situation should definitely address risk management issues.

••••••••••••

PATIENT SAFETY AND BIOMEDICAL TECHNOLOGY IN THE FUTURE

Patient safety will continue to affect biomedical technology. The movement of biomedical technology from the hospital setting, to the ambulatory setting, to the community at large will change the way the public views the risks and benefits of medical equipment and biomedical technology as a whole. This movement is already being seen in the widespread movement of defibrillators from hospitals, to ambulances, to businesses and organizations, and even to individuals as defibrillation becomes increasingly automated.

Risk management professionals have many issues to consider as the role of biomedical technology within the community continues to expand:

• Does your institution provide preventative maintenance services (either at no cost or for a fee) to community services such as local fire department or community ambulance services that have the regular type of cardiac defibrillators, or businesses and non-profit agencies that have the automatic (AEDs) on-site?

• If so, what formal agreements do you have with the participants, and does your professional liability insurance carrier need to be aware of this activity?

• Do you have physicians or other health care providers who provide "medical oversight" to such programs?

• If so, are they covered under the present institutional or their own individual professional liability insurance programs? Are there state statutes regarding such activities (and do they provide any immunity from litigation or damages for these activities)?

Risk management professionals will continue to need ways to keep abreast of new developments in the biomedical technology arena. One way to help with that task is to sign up for selective e-mail notifications from the FDA [www.fda.gov/emaillist.html] about particular areas of interest or relevance to the facility. The agency also provides Web broadcasts for health care personnel that include information on new medical devices, safety notifications, and recalls. To be notified when new programs are added to the series, go to [www.fda.gov/cdrh/subscribe.html].

Endnotes

1. "Playing with Medical Devices Can Be a Deadly Game." *Health Devices*, 31, (7), July 2002, 269–270.

2. *Ibid.*

3. "Guidelines for Determining Anesthesia Machine Obsolescence." *American Society of Anesthesiologists*, June 2004. [www.ASAhq.org]. Last visited June 2005.

Suggested Readings

Feigel, D., S. Gardner, and M. McClellan. "Ensuring Safe and Effective Medical Devices." *New England Journal of Medicine,* 348, (3), January 2003, 191–192.

Healthcare Information and Management Systems Society (HIMSS), "Medical Device Security Workgroup," [www.himss.org]. Last visited June 2005.

Porto, G., "Safety by Design: Ten Lessons from Human Factors Research." *Journal of Healthcare Risk Management,* 21(3), Fall 2001, 43–50.

U.S. Food and Drug Administration, Center for Devices and Radiological Health. "Device Advice (Self-service site for medical device information)," June 2005. [www.fda.gov/cdrh/devadvice/]. Last visited June 2005.

U.S. Food and Drug Administration, Center for Devices and Radiological Health. "Guidance for Industry and FDA Staff: Medical Device Tracking," May 2003. [www.fda.gov/cdrh/devadvice/353.html]. Last Visited June 2005.

U.S. Food and Drug Administration, Center for Devices and Radiological Health. "Identifying and Understanding Use Errors." March 2003. [www.fda.gov/cdrh/humanfactors/resource-users.html]. Last visited June 2005.

U.S. Food and Drug Administration, Center for Devices and Radiological Health. "Incorporating Human Factors Engineering into Risk Management," July 2000. [www.fda.gov/cdrh/humanfactors/index.html and www.fda.gov/cdrh/humfactors/1497.html]. Last visited June 2005.

U.S. Food and Drug Administration, Center for Devices and Radiological Health. "Information for Healthcare Organizations about FDA's 'Guidance for Industry: Cybersecurity for Networked Medical Devices Containing Off-The-Shelf (OTS) Software'," February 2005. [www.fda.gov/cdrh/osb/1553faq.html]. Last visited June 2005.

U.S. Food and Drug Administration, Center for Devices and Radiological Health. "Medical Device Reporting (MDR)—General Information" and "Medical Device Reporting (MDR)," September 2000 and January 2001. [www.fda.gov/cdrh/mdr/mdr-general.html and www.fda.gov/cdrh/devadvice/351.html]. Last visited June 2005.

U.S. Food and Drug Administration, Center for Devices and Radiological Health. "Reuse of Single-Use Devices," November 2004. [www.fda.gov/ccdrh/reuse/index.html and www/fda.gov/cdrh/reuse/reuse-messages.html]. Last visited June 2005.

8

Managing Primary Care Risk in the Ambulatory Environment

Robert F. Bunting, Jr.
Joyce H. Benton

Primary care focuses on proactive medicine. It is based on the belief that patients can be managed better and more effectively on an outpatient, or ambulatory, basis before diseases reach the point that acute inpatient care is warranted.

As inpatient care increasingly shifts to the ambulatory setting, it is important to be aware that there are several aspects that make up this environment. However, their definitions change frequently, as the health care delivery system evolves to meet the needs of patients, providers, and payers.

Table 8.1 provides a glimpse of the settings that provide ambulatory care.[1,2] They range from the traditional physician's office to newer environments such as infusion therapy and laser centers. Each offers new benefits and risks.

In addition to the variety of settings that characterize the ambulatory environment, innovative treatment modalities are also important vehicles for primary care. Alternative medicine certainly is not a new concept. Some of its affiliate practices have been in existence for centuries. Yet it is a growing field with several important implications for the risk management professional.

Traditionally, the study of quality, and of the risks associated with health care delivery, has focused on the acute-care setting. In 1999, the Institute of Medicine's Report estimated that between 44,000 to 98,000 hospital patients die annually from avoidable medical error. Regardless of the accuracy of this estimate, it fails to take into account the number of patients treated at ambulatory facilities each year.[3,4]

This chapter will explore the risks associated with delivering care in an ambulatory setting. Whenever possible, appropriate quality improvement activities will be discussed. This chapter is designed to understand and appreciate the more salient points of many topics that, though often considered only in the context of acute care, also apply to the vast array of ambulatory settings.

TABLE 8.1   Ambulatory Care Facilities

• Ambulatory Surgery Centers	• Office-Based Surgery Offices
• Birthing Centers	• Ophthalmology Practices
• Cardiac Catheterization Centers	• Oral and Maxillofacial Surgery Centers
• Dental Clinics	• Pain Management Centers
• Dialysis Centers	• Physician Offices
• Endoscopy Centers	• Plastic Surgery Centers
• Group Medical Practices	• Podiatric Clinics
• Home Health Agencies	• Prison Health Centers
• Imaging Centers	• Public Health Centers
• Indian Health Clinics	• Radiation/Oncology Clinics
• Infusion Therapy Services	• Rehabilitation Centers
• Laser Centers	• Sleep Centers
• Lithotripsy Services	• Sports Medicine Clinics
• MRI Centers	• Student Health Services
• Mental Health Centers	• Unconventional Medicine Centers
• Military Clinics	• Urgent/Emergent Care Centers
• Mobile Health Care Services	• Women's Health Centers
• Multispecialty Group Practices	• Wound Care Centers
• Occupational Health Centers	

···········

COMMON CONCEPTS

Though each of the ambulatory care facilities listed in Table 8.1 has its own specialized risk areas, they collectively share many aspects of risk. The following topics are presented in a general manner because they apply to various types of health care practices in the ambulatory environment.

Professional Liability

Medical services traditionally provided in an acute-care setting are now performed in an ambulatory care setting. This transition brings with it an increase in the severity and frequency of professional liability claims in the ambulatory care setting.

The Physicians' Insurers Association of America's (PIAA) Data Sharing Project, which contains medical professional liability claims information on twenty-eight specialties, revealed that obstetric and gynecologic surgeons, internists, and general and family practitioners were the three top specialties in the number of medical professional liability claims reported from 1985 to 2004. The top ten medical misadventures most likely to generate medical professional liability claims during this nineteen-year period included improper performance, no medical misadventure (situation where there is an absence of an allegation of any improper medical conduct on the part of this insured), errors in diagnosis, failure to supervise or monitor care, medication errors, failure to recognize a complication of treatment, performed when not indicated or contraindicated, not performed, delay in performance, and failure to instruct or communicate with the patient.

The list has changed little in the fifteen years since PIAA, a trade association of physician-owned and -operated professional liability carriers, first identified improper performance, diagnostic error, failure to monitor the care, performing a procedure not indicated, and medication errors as the most prominent medical mishaps for all specialties combined. The average indemnity award has steadily increased from 1994 through 2004.

From 1994 until 2004, the average indemnity paid on behalf of all practitioners increased 41.9 percent and rose 22.2 percent from 1999–2004.[5]

In a six-year study (1994–2000) of closed ambulatory care claims by CNA Insurance Companies, the three specialties reporting the highest number of medical professional liability claims for ambulatory care included internal medicine, family practice, and obstetricians and gynecologists. The top allegations included failure to diagnose, failure to perform surgery or improper surgery, improper performance of tests or procedures, delay in diagnosis, improper management of course of treatment, and failure to communicate or lack of informed consent. In this study, the average indemnity payment rose 47 percent.[6]

The incidence of and relationship among adverse events, negligence, and medical professional liability lawsuits have been debated for years, and studies have yielded some interesting findings. Levinson and her colleagues were the first to identify specific communication behaviors associated with physicians' risk for medical professional liability claims.[7] Some of the behaviors that were inversely related to the degree of risk included the length of time spent with the patient, orienting the patient about the care delivery process, facilitating conversations with the patient, and conversing in a warm, friendly manner.

Physicians continue to have malpractice-related issues related to key aspects of primary care. Of the thousands of claims against physicians in the PIAA Data Sharing Project, more than 40,000 had their origin in a diagnostic interview, evaluation, or consultation, and 17,000 more involved prescription medications.[8]

Communication

Poor communication is not listed by PIAA as an official cause of medical professional liability claims, but it underlies almost every medical professional liability action. Insurance claims administrators and medical professional liability defense attorneys estimate that communication failure is a contributing factor in 80 percent of all professional claims or lawsuits. In 20 percent of the cases, it is the reason for the filing of the lawsuit.[9]

Good communication skills often have been viewed as a personality trait that some people have and others do not. In fact, good communication skills can be learned and improved through systematic practice. The communication approach most commonly used by clinicians is the interview.

A typical clinician conducts more than 100,000 interviews during a professional career. It is possible for physicians to alter their communication behaviors in ways that both increase patient satisfaction and decrease risk. The history of the healing arts has emphasized the role of the physician as an identifier of disease and as an agent of healing. The traditional role of the clinician has been to find the problem and fix it. However, a new model of disease and healing has emerged that also accounts for psychological, sociological, and ever-present behavioral forces. This expanded context has focused attention on the medical interview, and the transactions that occur during the interview, as an area for change.[10]

The following model for physician-patient communication presents specific communication strategies to be used in the interview. Because the four elements of the model begin with the letter "E," the model is called the E4 component of clinical care. These include engaging, empathizing, educating, and enlisting the patient.[11]

Engagement is a connection between the clinician and patient that continues throughout the encounter. These simple techniques can help build rapport with patients in any practice setting.

- Greet the patient by name and shake hands. It is especially important to greet new patients when they are fully clothed.

- Build rapport by being as curious about the person as you are about your own medical condition.

- Elicit the patient's agenda, which should include their goals for the encounter and all complaints. Patients asked to explain their concerns by a physician were most often interrupted after the first voiced concern and after an average time of only eighteen seconds.[12]

Empathy is an active concern for the emotions, values, and experience of another. The first step in empathy is validating patients' expressed fears, concerns, symptoms, and pain. This step can create a positive atmosphere in the clinician-patient encounter. The second step in empathic communication is to accept the feelings and values of the patient. Third, empathy should convey an impression that the physician is present and with the patient. Physicians should sit down, maintain eye contact, and remove physical barriers between them and patients. The simple act of sitting while speaking with patients improves their perception of how much time they have spent with the physician. Open and relaxed body language should be displayed.

A major component of the physician-patient encounter is to *educate* patients about the encounter itself, medical diagnosis, etiology of the disease, treatment options, and follow-up requirements. Education occurs when the cognitive, behavioral, and affective needs are addressed. This process should start at the beginning of the encounter and continue through the patient visit. The following guidelines reduce the chance of misunderstanding.

- Assess the patient's current knowledge.

- Assume that there will be questions. Reassure patients that time will be available for them to ask questions.

- Ensure that patients understand the information provided by asking them to restate points that were presented.

Finally, *enlistment* is an invitation by the clinician to the patient to collaborate in decision-making involving the problem and the treatment plan. This final step involves two processes, decision-making and encouraging compliance. Most patients make a self-diagnosis. If the clinicians' diagnosis differs from the patients' diagnosis, the patient will act based upon their own diagnosis. Therefore, it is crucial that the clinician understand and discuss the patient's diagnosis. The following guidelines might improve patient compliance.

- Explain to the patient the specific details for the treatment plan, the expected benefits that will result, and the potential adverse results of patient non-compliance.

- Identify any concerns, fears, resistance, or real-life reasons why the patient might not comply with the proposed treatment.

- Make necessary referrals to assist the patient in obtaining appropriate physical, financial, social, and community support.

Clinicians and patients sometimes bring two totally different perspectives to a visit. These different perspectives can result in a breakdown of communication and leave the clinician and patient frustrated. A patient may be seen as difficult with one clinician but not difficult with another. Therefore, the word "difficult" does not refer to a specific type of patient, but to a clinician's experience.

"Difficult" is defined as "a function of the relationship" and is based on the interactions of two people. Difficulties occur in physician-patient relationships because of three core problems. These are frustrations for the clinician or patient, inflexibility, and misaligned expectations.[13]

Clinicians and staff often have to confront two types of difficult patients in their practices. These are the angry patients and the non-compliant patients.

Even when patients are angry or frustrated with the physician, office staff, their course of treatment, or their response to treatment, there are ways to improve the quality of physician-patient communication.

- Be aware that anger, dissatisfaction, and frustration can be expressed both verbally and nonverbally.

- Acknowledge patients' anger or dissatisfaction, as this is the first step in letting patients know that their concerns are being heard. Establish that the goal is to assist them in expressing and resolving their concerns in the best possible manner.

- Allow patients to express their anger in a private area, away from other patients.

- Demonstrate empathy by listening and maintaining eye contact. Maintain a nonjudgmental facial expression, a neutral tone of voice, and open body language.

- Focus on the content rather than the delivery of the patient's message, and ask for clarification as needed. Remain calm and respond to, rather than react against, the patient's concerns.

- Use self-disclosure, cautiously and only when appropriate, to indicate that one has had similar experiences and understands the patient's response.

- After the patient has vented anger, respond to the content of the message. Identify those issues that can be readily resolved.

- Enlist the patient in the problem-solving process, and ask for patient input before determining a plan of action.[14]

A friendly, mutually satisfying relationship with patients is a desirable goal; however, some patients fail to comply with agreed-upon treatment plans. A non-compliant patient can increase the likelihood of a negative outcome. (Refer to Exhibit 8.1 for a sample non-compliant letter.)

Whenever the physician accepts a patient or renders care to a patient, a physician-patient relationship is created that continues for as long as the patient's condition requires attention. The physician-patient relationship can be dissolved properly only by the mutual consent of the parties or by reasonable notice of the termination. If a physician withdraws services without providing reasonable notice to the patient, or when medical attention is still needed, the patient may sue on grounds of abandonment.

A physician may decide to terminate the relationship for reasons such as failure to comply with the recommended medical treatment, disruptive behavior, or other indications that the patient will not benefit from the physician's care. The reasons for terminating the relationship should be documented carefully in the medical record, as should conversations with the patient leading to the termination. Terminate the relationship by sending a certified letter requesting return receipt. A copy of the letter should also be sent via regular mail, in the event that the patient does not accept the certified letter. Keep a copy of the letter and mail receipt in the patient's medical record. Document in the record that the letter was sent and note any subsequent conversations with the patient. (Refer to Exhibit 8.2, Sample Termination Letter.)

EXHIBIT 8.1   Sample Non-Compliant Letter

<Date>

<Patient's Name>
<Address>
<City>, <State> <Zip Code>

Dear <Patient's Name>:

The purpose of this letter is to advise you that a recent review of the <Name of the Organization>'s records has determined that you are out of compliance with your physician's recommended treatment plan.

As you are aware, your primary care physician, Dr. <Primary Physician's Name> referred you to <Consulting Physician's Name> for <Treatment/Procedure>. Dr. <Consulting Physician's Name> has recommended that you undergo <Treatment/Procedure>. It is our understanding that at the present time you are opposed to the recommended procedure or treatment.

<Name of the Organization>'s primary concern is to accommodate your medical needs and deliver quality health care services. Due to your non-compliance with the recommended treatment plan, our ability to assess your health care needs in a complete and professional manner is affected significantly. <Name of Patient's Health Plan> has been notified of our concern as this may affect your health, as well as your health care coverage.

Should you dispute the content of this letter, you have the right to initiate a grievance. Please address in writing any contrary information you may have to:

> <Appropriate Company>
> <Address>
> <City>, <State> <Zip Code>

<Name of the Organization> looks forward to your cooperation in this matter.

Sincerely,

<Physician's Name>

cc: Health Plan
        Medical Record

Adapted from Benton and Taylor, *Ambulatory Healthcare: Stay a Step Ahead of Diagnostic-Related Claims,* Session Materials from ASHRM Annual Conference, November, 2000.

When a patient terminates the relationship, the physician should document the patient's decision in the medical record and advise the patient in writing of any incomplete treatment plans. The patient should be advised of any recommendation to continue any unfinished treatment. The physician should offer to forward a copy of the patient's records to the subsequent physician upon receipt of a signed authorization.[15] For a more in-depth discussion of Communication refer to Volume I, Chapter 8 in this series.

Medical Records Management

The medical record can be a health care provider's best friend or most formidable enemy. Management of the medical record, therefore, is critical. The primary purpose of the medical record is to document the course of a patient's illness and the treatment that the patient receives. It is the main communication medium for planning, coordinating, and orchestrating patient care. Although not always practical, it is best to document everything and omit nothing.

EXHIBIT 8.2   Sample Termination Letter

<Date>

<Patient's Name>
<Address>
<City>, <State> <Zip Code>

Dear <Patient's Name>:

I am writing to inform you that I will no longer be available to provide you with medical care for the following reasons.

> <Insert reasons for withdrawing medical services. Indicate the patient's current health status and include any recommendations you have for medical care.>

This notice will become effective on <Specify Date> or 30 days after you receive this letter, whichever is later.

I advise you to seek medical care from another physician. You might wish to contact the Member Relations Department of your Health Plan or Physician Referral Network <provide telephone numbers if available> for your referral. My office will forward a copy of your medical records to your new physician after I receive your written authorization on the enclosed release of information form.

If during this 30-day period you should require urgent care, please do not hesitate to contact my office or proceed to your nearest emergency department.

Please feel free to contact my office if you have any questions regarding this notice.

Sincerely,

<Physician's Name>

Enclosure: Release of Information Form

cc: Health Plan
         Medical Record

Adapted from Benton and Taylor, *Ambulatory Healthcare: Stay a Step Ahead of Diagnostic-Related Claims,* Session Materials from ASHRM Annual Conference, November, 2000.

Because the medical record can serve as objective evidence that the standard of care was met during the patient's treatment, complete, accurate, and legible documentation is a crucial risk management skill. It has been found that in medical professional liability suits in which documentation and recordkeeping were judged inadequate, damages were paid in two-thirds of the cases. When documentation and recordkeeping were judged adequate, damages were paid in only one-third of the cases. If a patient's file contains good documentation, the likelihood of a suit even being filed is generally reduced because the plaintiff's attorney knows that a settlement or a favorable verdict in court would be difficult.[16]

All staff should be trained in proper documentation practices, and a policy delineating how to document patient care should be developed and implemented. Refer to Volume I, Chapter 10 on Documentation and Medical Records in this series for more information.

The information included in the medical record is important to both the physician and the patient. The physician owns the original record and is responsible for safeguarding the information in the medical record against loss, defacement, tampering, and unauthorized access.[17] Because of the confidential nature of the information contained in the record, copies of the record usually cannot be released to any other person without appropriate authorization from the patient, the patient's legal guardian, or legal process.

Generally, patients have access to the information contained in their medical records. However, if a patient asks to see his medical record, the physician's staff should involve the physician because the physician is the best person to explain the information to the patient. Only rarely should a physician use therapeutic privilege to prevent releasing information to the patient, because it is intended to protect only patients who would be harmed by reviewing their records.

There is both a legal and an ethical basis for the confidentiality of medical information. The legal basis for confidentiality is derived from the physician-patient privilege, which is set forth by state statutes and court decisions. The ethical principle of confidentiality originates from the belief that confidentiality encourages patients to seek needed medical care and to be candid with their physicians about their medical condition. Confidentiality also is necessary to protect the patient's inherent privacy interests.[18]

Ideally, medical records would be kept forever. Because that is not possible, the following issues should be considered when establishing a medical record retention policy:

- Seek counsel regarding state legal requirements, including the statute of limitations and any applicable federal laws relating to record retention.

- Consider the age of the patients, keeping in mind that claims relating to minors might emerge many years after treatment. Identify the patient care, research, and teaching needs of any organizations that might require access to the medical records.

- Weigh the cost of archiving and microfilming records against the potential risk of their destruction.

- Destroy records, if applicable, on a regular schedule governed by written policies and procedures.

- Institute a policy for permanently listing all records that have been destroyed.

Absent other legal authorization or requirements, physicians and their employees should not release privileged information about a patient's treatment or diagnosis without first obtaining a written authorization from the patient or, if a minor, from the parent or legal guardian. Release of information should be carried out in accordance with all applicable state and federal laws, and with accrediting and regulatory agency requirements and written practice policy.

A waiver of the confidentiality privilege may be made only by the patient or patient's legal representative. Exceptions to the waiver requirements exist, however, in the context of active litigation where most medical records must be provided in response to a valid subpoena or request for production of medical records in accordance with state law.

Following the September 11, 2001, terrorist attacks that resulted in commercial airliner crashes in New York City, Pennsylvania, and Washington, DC, and the loss of thousands of lives, the United States Congress enacted the Patriot Act in 2001 and the Homeland Security Act in 2002.

In a separate action, the Health Insurance Portability and Accountability Act (HIPAA) privacy rule was enacted in 2003. These acts created confusion among health care providers and health information management professionals. Therefore, the American Health Information Management Association reviewed all three acts and drew the following conclusions.

- The United States government is permitted to access any and all protected health information (PHI) it deems necessary to protect the nation.

- PHI should be released to the requesting authority without delay after proper verification.

- Complete identification of the government official must be obtained and verified, including a copy of identification, office location, and the particular branch of government requesting the information.

- HIPAA regulations currently permit these disclosures.

- These disclosures must be recorded in the accounting of disclosures.

- A patient or legal guardian's authorization is not required when a request is responded to under either the Homeland Security or Patriot Acts.[19]

Policies and Procedures

A policy is a predetermined course of action established as a guide toward accepted business strategies and objectives. A procedure is a method by which a policy can be accomplished. It provides the instructions necessary to carry out a policy statement. Policies and procedures provide guidelines, limits or boundaries, alternatives, common understanding, definitions, roles and responsibilities, and internal controls. References for the policy development should be included on the policy.[20]

Policies and procedures are essential to any successful practice, whether it is primary care, an ambulatory surgery center, or other outpatient facility. Policies and procedures must be based on established, authoritative guidelines from nationally recognized entities such as the Occupational Safety and Health Administration (OSHA), the Centers for Disease Control and Prevention (CDC), or other professional organizations. Some commercial companies sell policies and procedures to assist organizations that lack the resources to develop them independently. However, any organization that implements a pre-established set of procedures must be sure that the procedures reflect its practice, and they should be individualized as appropriate.

Office practices should have a complete set of operational and clinical policies and procedures in place. All health care professionals should be knowledgeable about office protocols and committed to following them. Such protocols set the standard of care for a clinical practice and can be used as a guideline to identify negligence.

Sources for policies and procedures include national organizations, regulatory agencies, licensing agencies, experts, texts and journals, and standards in other health care entities.

General guidelines for policies and procedures include several elements.

- There is a need for consistency in policies within the clinical practice. A consistent format should be used throughout the organization. Policies should not conflict with each other or with national, state, or local standards of care. The policy should identify all affected areas. The format should include a section on authority. The policy should follow a pre-established approval process before it is finalized and implemented.

- Each policy should be dated at its inception. The policy manual itself should have a cover page that displays an annual review and approval date, and a table of contents for easy reference. The manual should be treated as an evolving document that is reviewed, added to, and modified whenever necessary. Policies and procedures should be archived when they are revised. This is important in a medical professional liability suit because the physician practice should be held to the standard of care contained in the policy in effect at the time of the incident, not currently.

- In lieu of a hard copy manual, many practices use an intranet to maintain the policy and procedure manual. Doing so ensures that the latest version is always readily available, and no one has to worry about whether the document is outdated.

- Policies must reflect reality or actual practice and should meet the national, state, or local standard of care.

- Policies and procedures must be analyzed on a regular basis for correctness and compliance.

- Education for all staff must be completed and documented before the policy is implemented.

Patient Rights

Since ancient times, physicians have recognized that they have a responsibility to ensure that the individual rights of patients are honored and that patient rights are restricted only as a last resort to protect the safety of the patient or others. Physicians realize that the health and well-being of patients are a joint effort between the physician and patient.

The American Medical Association developed a Patient Bill of Rights that includes the following:

- The right to considerate and respectful care.

- The right to obtain complete information concerning the diagnosis, treatment, and prognosis in terms that the patient can understand. When it is not medically advisable to give such information to the patient, the information should be made available to an appropriate person on the patient's behalf.

- The right to know by name the physician or other clinician responsible for coordinating the patient's care.

- The right to receive from the physician information necessary to give informed consent before the start of any procedure or treatment except in an emergency. The patient has the right to know the names of the persons responsible for the procedures or treatment.

- The right to refuse treatment to the extent permitted by law and to be informed of the medical consequences of such action.

- The right to every consideration of privacy concerning the patient's own medical care program.[21]

Informed Consent

Informed consent is a legal doctrine that encompasses a communication process, not simply executing a form or document.[22] A patient has the right to receive information about health care treatment from physicians and to discuss the benefits, risks, and costs of applicable treatment alternatives. Informed consent frequently is regarded legally as a memorialization of an understanding between the patient and the physician. The law of informed consent varies from state to state, and physicians should become familiar with the law in their state. Refer to Chapter 4 for a thorough discussion of informed consent.

Patient Complaints

Good technical skills and medical expertise are essential elements of the services an organization provides to the public. Today's health care consumers demand more. They want convenience, comfort, courtesy, and respect in addition to competent care. If one or more of these qualities is missing, the customer probably will complain. A satisfied patient tells four other people about care and service rendered. A dissatisfied patient tells twenty other people about the bad experience. The organization must satisfy five patients for every one patient it disappoints to maintain its positive reputation.[23] Every patient is essential to the well-being of an organization. When complaints are voiced, the organization has a second chance to correct and improve conditions for all customers of the practice.

There are many pitfalls to avoid when handling complaining customers. These include becoming defensive, citing organization policy, listening inattentively, giving the runaround, exhibiting negative non-verbal behaviors, overreacting, and siding against the organization. These actions are non-productive. They emphasize the notion that the organization is unresponsive, uncaring, and not a place of choice for receiving health care services. Patients want to be taken seriously, treated with respect, and listened to attentively. They may seek immediate action, compensation, and someone to be reprimanded. Patients desire to have the problem resolved so that it never happens again.

There are ten steps to handling complaints that are fairly simple and easy to practice. These include:

1. Listen without interruption.
2. Don't get defensive.
3. Use a "sad but glad" statement. For example, "I'm sad that you are upset, but I'm glad that you have come to me so I can address your concerns."
4. Express empathy.
5. Ask questions to clarify the problem.
6. Find out what the customer wants.
7. Explain what can and cannot be done.
8. Discuss the alternatives fully.
9. Take action.
10. Follow up to ensure customer satisfaction.[24]

Complaints must be documented and tracked so that the organization can identify repeated complaints and patterns that need attention, and preventive actions. A separate complaint form or the facility incident report can be used.

Professional Staff

Credentialing is the process of obtaining, verifying, and assessing the qualifications of a health care practitioner to provide patient care services. Evidence of licensure, education, training, and experience is necessary to determine whether a health care professional is competent. This information should be kept in a separate bound file for each professional staff member. Credentialing information is considered confidential. This information should not be disclosed to an outside party without a court order, statutory requirements, or an authorization from the individual.[25]

Office staffs today consist of a variety of professionals, including physicians, physicians' assistants, nurse midwives, nurse practitioners, registered nurses, licensed practical nurses, mental health counselors, surgical technicians, radiology technologists, medical laboratory technologists, and phlebotomists. Each of these professions has its own responsibilities and codes of ethics. Some require recertification or license renewal on a regular basis.

Thorough credentialing also requires well-defined job descriptions. Job descriptions should reflect the scope of practice defined by state professional practice acts, state licensing boards, and professional organizations. In some cases, employees may not be covered under the physician's medical professional liability insurance policy. It is important that everyone working under the physician's direction be insured appropriately. For more information on credentialing refer to Volume I, Chapter 9, Physician and Allied Health Professional Credentialing.

The United States Congress recognized that the health care system depends on the willingness of professionals to participate in reviewing quality of care issues, so it adopted the Healthcare Quality Improvement Act[26] in 1986. Under the act, immunity for participation in professional review actions by professional review committees is granted from federal and state law claims, except for civil rights violations, if the review actions meet the standards of the act. The act provides that a review activity meets the standards of the act for immunity purposes if it is performed in the reasonable belief that the action is in the furtherance of quality health care, a reasonable effort to obtain the facts is made, and notice and a hearing are afforded in the event that an action is warranted by the facts. Though protection afforded by the HCQIA is not absolute, protection can be maximized by performing peer review activities that follow a formal, objective plan.

The act established a national data bank for the collection of data on adverse actions against physicians and other health care providers.[27] To protect their immunity for peer review, entities that make malpractice payments or that take adverse professional actions as a result of formal peer review must report adverse professional review actions to the National Practitioner Data Bank (NPDB). Refer to Volume III, Chapter 16 on Statutes, Standards and Regulations for more information on the NPDB.

Hospitals and other entities that provide health care services and follow a formal peer review process to further quality health care are allowed to query the data bank. Hospitals must request certain information from the data bank before granting practice privileges to a new applicant. During the recredentialing process, which normally occurs every two years, a hospital must request information regarding physicians who are already on staff. Individual physicians, dentists, and other health care practitioners may query the data bank concerning themselves.

∙∙∙∙∙∙∙∙∙∙∙∙

CLINICAL AND SAFETY ISSUES

The clinical and safety issues inherent in the delivery of patient care range from safe medication administration and providing a safe physical environment, to ensuring that equipment is in good repair, to being prepared for a wide array of emergencies, both internal and external.

Medication Administration

Medication errors occur in every health care setting, including the physician's office. It is estimated that there are 218,000 medication-related deaths annually, with a total cost of approximately $177 billion.[28] Events related to medications are the third-leading cause of death in the United States, after heart disease and cancer.[29]

The chance for error is ever present in the prescribing, dispensing, and administering of medications. Common medication-related errors seen in physician office practices include incorrect prescribed dosage, incorrect medication for diagnosis or condition, multiple pharmacy prescriptions, medication incompatibility, inappropriate dispensing of sample medications, and illegible handwriting on prescriptions.

Proactive risk management practices can help prevent medication-related errors and theft of medications or controlled substances. In medication prescriptions and orders, use computer order entry or print in block lettering. The indication for the medication should be put on the order or prescription. The order should be complete, including strength and concentration of the product, and should include route and rate of administration. Abbreviations should be used sparingly if at all. Verbal orders should be used in emergencies only. Prescription pads should be locked or stored away from patient care and reception areas, and they should never be pre-signed or post-dated. Any lost or stolen prescription pads should be reported to local pharmacies, hospitals, and the Drug Enforcement Administration. An internal process to monitor, track, and correct medication errors should be established and reviewed on a regular basis.

There are also proactive risk management strategies for medication storage. The staff should be trained on the applicable state and federal regulatory standards for ordering, storing, and dispensing controlled substances and other medications. Only necessary pharmaceuticals should be stored in the office, and these should be stored away from patient or visitor access. Controlled substances should be double-locked, regularly counted, and have limited access. All administered and discarded doses should be accounted for in writing. Expiration dates should be monitored, and outdated supplies should be properly removed and disposed. Medication samples should be logged in and out, and manufacturer lot numbers should be tracked. The lot number of any samples given to patients should be recorded in the medical record. Medication containers with potentially lethal doses should be removed from patient care areas, and special controls for potentially dangerous drugs should be instituted.

Employees should be qualified by education or training to administer medications. A medication proficiency exam should be part of the employee skills list. Drug reference materials should be accessible. Patient allergies should be checked before administering any medication. Employees should triple-check the medication against the order, after dispensing, and before administration. The patient's identity should be checked before administering any medication. Staff should be educated to question any medication orders that are incomplete, ambiguous, or illegible. If there are questions about a medication or dose, the prescribing physician or a pharmacist should be consulted. The administered medication, route, and amount of medication should be recorded immediately in the medical record. Patients may remain in the office for a specified time after receiving certain medications such as conscious sedation, other drugs that may impair their abilities, or where the results might need monitoring for allergic reactions or efficacy.

A comprehensive medication education program for patients should be developed. This information should be documented in the medical record. The principles of informed consent should be considered whenever medications are ordered or changed in the ambulatory care setting.[30] At a minimum, the patient should be educated regarding the purpose of the medication, side effects, adverse effects, and key drug interactions, and this should be documented. Informed consent should be documented formally for medications that carry risk of severe complications or complications that occur frequently.

Adverse Patient Events

Accreditation manuals published by the Joint Commission on Accreditation of Healthcare Organizations (JCAHO) contain standards in the Leadership and Improving Organization Performance chapters that relate specifically to the management of sentinel events. Accredited ambulatory care organizations are responsible for reporting sentinel events to JCAHO.

According to JCAHO, a sentinel event is defined as "an unexpected occurrence involving death or serious physical or psychological injury or the risk thereof. Serious injury specifically includes loss of limb or function. The phrase 'or risk thereof' includes any process variation for which a recurrence would carry a significant chance of a serious adverse outcome. Such events are called sentinel because they signal the need for immediate investigation and response."[31] Sentinel events in the ambulatory care setting can include outcomes related to missed diagnosis, delayed treatment, failure to monitor care, and medication errors, among others.

Although it is sometimes difficult for the physician to determine if a patient's signs or symptoms are consistent with an adverse medication reaction, the physician should have a high degree of suspicion and should report any suspected adverse medication reaction via the appropriate mechanism to the pharmacy or drug company. The physician should investigate the patient's drug regimen and history to determine if the signs or symptoms are related to the medication. The reaction should be noted in the patient's medical record, and the patient should be educated about any drug allergies or precautions that are needed.

Disclosure

An important part of the diagnostic or treatment process is to provide the patient or authorized representative with outcome or results information. Sometimes diagnostic tests or treatment results are unplanned or unwelcome outcomes even if the treatment was appropriate. The critical issue is to disclose the results to the patient.

The issues surrounding disclosure of unanticipated outcomes have culminated in new accreditation requirements for hospitals. In 2001, the JCAHO Patient Safety Standards became effective for hospitals. One of these standards states: "Patients and, when appropriate their families, are informed about the outcomes of care, including unanticipated outcomes." The accompanying intent provision indicates "that the responsible licensed independent practitioner or his or her designee clearly explains the outcome of any treatments or procedures to the patient, and when appropriate the family, whenever those outcomes differ significantly from the anticipated outcomes."[32]

The JCAHO Disclosure Standard does not require health care professionals to make an admission of liability or error. The disclosure standard is directed at a communication process and is an important patient safety tool.

Safe Environment

An ambulatory care facility should attempt to ensure that the building and parking lot for patients and all staff are adequately lighted and free of potential hazards. Although many physicians do not own or control the building and land used for their office practices, they nonetheless should attempt to reduce the potential for serious physical injury to patients and visitors from accidents such as slips and falls. Often, a physician is named as a co-defendant in lawsuits involving these types of general liability accidents although the facilities are under the direct control and management of another entity, such as the landlord or building management company.

The risk exposures of the physician office facility should be addressed in the office policy manual. The manual should detail safety standards and outline specific inspection parameters and intervals. The policies should address general office safety, hazardous waste and materials, preventive maintenance for clinical and diagnostic equipment, security, personal safety issues, and injury prevention and reporting.

Medical Devices

Under the Safe Medical Devices Act (SMDA) of 1990, health care facilities must report serious device-related injuries to the manufacturer, or to the Food and Drug Administration (FDA) if the manufacturer is not known. A MedWatch medical device report by the FDA must be submitted. In addition, the SMDA requires that facilities submit to the FDA an annual summary of all device-related injury reports submitted during the preceding time period. This law currently applies to hospitals, ambulatory surgical facilities, nursing homes, and other facilities where health care is provided. The SMDA reporting requirements do not apply to the physician, dentist, chiropractor, optometrist, nurse practitioner, school nurse offices, and the freestanding care unit office. However, it is a prudent risk management strategy to establish and implement a safe medical device policy for the office to ensure patient safety and to reduce any potential liability that might arise from malfunctioning medical devices or equipment.[33]

MedWatch is the FDA's Safety Information and Adverse Event Reporting Program. This program is involved with several products, including but not limited to:

- Prescription medications
- Non-prescription (over-the-counter) medications
- Biologic
- Medical devices
- Radiation-emitting devices
- Special nutritional products[34]

One of the purposes of the program is to provide a consistent standardized process for monitoring product safety alerts, recalls, and important labeling changes. Reporting can be done via the Internet at [fda.gov/medwatch.htm], by telephone, or by submitting the MedWatch 3500 form by mail or fax.[35]

Physicians should carefully monitor the selection, inspection, and maintenance of medical office equipment and devices, as both physicians and manufacturers are often named in liability actions that arise out of patient injuries involving medical products and devices. To mitigate these types of allegations, a practice should establish, monitor, and document a procedure for purchasing, inspecting, and maintaining medical equipment and products. The American Medical Association suggests organizing medical device and product documentation using the "SERUM" formula:

- Selection of equipment (the rationale for purchasing the type of equipment in question)
- Education and training of equipment users
- Recognition of product hazards and limitations of equipment
- Use of equipment in a reasonable manner
- Maintenance and servicing of equipment[36]

When outside vendors are responsible for performing preventive maintenance inspections or repairs, make sure that contracts specify the interval at which the inspections are to be performed, and check to make sure that a current certificate of insurance is on file for the company responsible for inspection and maintenance. A policy that directs employees to sequester immediately any equipment involved in a patient injury should be in place. The company responsible for performing inspection and maintenance should not be allowed to examine the equipment until after an independent evaluation has been obtained.

Emergency Response

Health care providers need to know their responsibilities in medical and non-medical emergencies. The scope of medical emergency response activities can range from the provision of basic cardiac life support to more complex medical interventions depending on the patient populations being served. Regardless of the scope of medical emergency activities undertaken, each ambulatory care practice should establish a formal policy and procedure for the staff to follow in the event of a medical emergency.

Policies and procedures should address:

- Certification requirements for basic cardiac life support and annual requirements that certification be updated
- Inspection and repair record maintenance for all emergency equipment in the office
- Inspection requirements for an emergency crash cart if one is needed in the office
- Training and proficiency requirements for emergency equipment and medications maintained within the office
- Documentation of such training and proficiency in personnel files

If an automatic incoming telephone-call distribution system is used, it should include an option that allows patients to speak directly to office personnel in the event of a medical emergency, or referring them to 911.

Fire Safety

Fire safety management involves protecting patients, employees, visitors, and buildings from the threat of fire and smoke. Every building is required to be in compliance with the structure and fire protection rules set forth in the national fire protection association's life safety code. Contact the local fire marshal or other knowledgeable authority for information regarding fire safety standards. The practice should establish and maintain an office fire safety program, including emergency evacuation procedures for staff and patients.

These should be posted in a conspicuous place in the office. Emergency telephone numbers should be easily accessible to the staff. A fire safety orientation and related annual education program should be held for all employees. Fire drills should be conducted quarterly and results should be evaluated and documented. The building's fire alarm systems should be tested quarterly by a reputable testing service.[37]

Security

The goal of a health care organization's security program is to provide a safe environment for employees, physicians, patients, and visitors. A security risk assessment must be conducted as the basis for the development of a security risk exposure plan. Physicians and office staff in clinics and other ambulatory settings are exposed to potentially dangerous confrontation with patients, family members, and intruders. Prevention of violence in the workplace can be aided by the following:

- Do not argue with or provoke a hostile person. Avoid staring, which could be interpreted as confrontational.
- Be honest about situations; provide honest reasons for delays.
- Keep at least two or three arm lengths away from the hostile person.
- Use a firm tone of voice.
- Listen and acknowledge concern.
- Separate the hostile person from other patients, if possible.
- Develop an emergency code to alert other office staff that a violent person is on the premises.
- Summon help immediately if a patient or visitor:
  - ✓ Talks and complains loudly
  - ✓ Uses profanity or makes sexual comments
  - ✓ Demands unnecessary services
  - ✓ Hints at loss of control
  - ✓ Paces in the waiting room
  - ✓ Appears tense and angry
  - ✓ Appears intoxicated or under the influence of drugs
  - ✓ Has a history of violence
- Report serious threats of violence to law enforcement officials.[38]

Infection Control

All health care facilities run the risk of nosocomial infections (infections acquired in the facility) and of infections brought into the facility or setting. These infections may be endemic, defined as the habitual presence of an infection within a geographic area, which may also refer to the usual prevalence of a given disease within such an area. Infections may be epidemic, defined as an outbreak in a community or region of a group of infections of similar nature, clearly in excess of normal expectancy and derived from a common source. Infections may affect patients, health care workers, and others who come into contact with patients. The goal of surveillance, prevention, and control of infection is to identify and reduce the risks of acquiring and transmitting both endemic and epidemic infections among patients, employees, physicians, and visitors. Infection control is an organization-wide function.

Basic infection control practices should be implemented in all ambulatory care practices. Good personal hygiene and common sense are instrumental to developing an effective infection control program. Most infections are spread by direct contact with unwashed hands. Below are some basic infection control practices that are desirable for all ambulatory care offices to follow:

- Wash hands routinely. Hands should be washed immediately when hands are obviously soiled, after handling soiled equipment, after removing protective gloves, before eating, after using restroom facilities, and before leaving the health care facility.

- Employers shall provide handwashing facilities that are readily accessible to employees.

- Health care providers should not eat, drink, smoke, handle contact lenses, or apply cosmetics in work areas.

- Food and drink should not be kept in refrigerators or freezers, or on shelves, cabinets, countertops, or bench tops where blood or other potentially infectious materials are present.

- Mouth pipetting or suctioning of blood or other potentially infectious materials is prohibited.

- Use suitable personal protective devices such as gloves, face shields, masks, goggles, aprons, or impervious clothing when there is a likelihood of contact with potentially infectious materials. These protective devices should be readily accessible in all patient areas.

- Provide mouthpieces, resuscitation bags, or other ventilation devices in areas where the need for resuscitation is predictable.

- Change gloves after contact with each patient.

- Wear gloves when touching contaminated objects but do not touch items (doorknobs, telephones, test equipment, computer terminals, keyboards) with soiled gloved hands.

- Take precautions to prevent injuries while handling sharp instruments, disposing of used needles, or cleaning used instruments.

- Do not recap using a two-handed technique or purposely bend, break, or otherwise manipulate needles by hand.

- Sharps should be disposed of in containers that are closable, leak-proof, puncture resistant, and properly labeled or color-coded.

- Do not rub the eyes or other mucous membranes.

- Treat all body substances from all patients as potentially infectious, and place an adequate barrier between people and the body substance.

- Treat any device that is visibly soiled with patient material, even if dried, as contaminated. Even if a device appears to be clean, do not handle it in an unhygienic manner. Use gloves, a gown, and other personal protective equipment, if indicated.

- Place specimens of blood and other potentially infectious material in a container, seal tightly, and carry in an outer container.

- Disinfect surfaces contaminated with blood or other potentially infectious material with an Environmental Protection Agency (EPA)-approved tuberculocidal disinfectant.

- If a health care provider has lesions or weeping dermatitis, the provider should refrain from direct patient care and handling patient care equipment until the condition resolves.

- Personnel having direct patient contact should not use nail polish or artificial nails. Chipped nail polish and artificial nails have been the source of outbreaks of nosocomial infections in health care facilities.

- The employer shall establish and maintain an accurate medical record for each employee that is separate from the personnel file. The employer shall maintain the records required for at least the duration of employment plus thirty years.

The primary regulatory agency in the field of occupational safety and health is the Occupational Safety and Health Administration (OSHA), a federal agency in the U.S. Department of Labor. OSHA regulations are applicable to medical physicians' offices and other ambulatory care settings. OSHA has conducted numerous inspections of physicians' offices, many in response to complaints. Many infection control issues are of particular interest to OSHA. To protect workers from occupational exposures to blood and other potentially infectious materials, OSHA enacted the bloodborne pathogen standard in 1992.

Bloodborne pathogens include any microorganism that might be transmitted by contact with the blood or bodily fluids of an infected person. The pathogens of major concern are HIV, hepatitis B, and hepatitis C viruses. The United States Congress passed the Needlestick Safety and Prevention Act directing OSHA to revise the bloodborne pathogens standard to establish in greater detail requirements that employers identify and make use of effective and safer medical devices.

The act also mandated additional requirements for maintaining a sharps injury log and for the involvement of non-managerial health care workers in evaluating and choosing devices. This standard applies to all employers who have employees with reasonably anticipated occupational exposure to blood or other potentially infectious materials. Staff should be educated about precautions to prevent injuries while handling sharp instruments, disposing of used needles, or cleaning used instruments. An employee exposed to blood or other potentially infectious material is required to report the incident to a designated person within the facility. Evaluations should be available immediately by an accredited laboratory.[39]

Enforcement guidelines that OSHA promulgated for tuberculosis are based on the CDC's Guidelines for Preventing the Transmission of Tuberculosis in Health Care Settings. The agency's latest instructions are that these guidelines would be applied in physicians' offices for personnel present during the performance of high-hazard procedures on suspect or infectious tuberculosis (TB) patients. High-hazard procedures identified in CDC guidelines include sputum induction and administration of aerosolized pentamidine. These procedures should be performed on infectious TB patients only if absolutely necessary.[40]

············
HUMAN RESOURCES ISSUES

The management of human resources is an immensely complicated issue. In large organizations, the duties and responsibilities related to human resources are often assigned to a separate department that takes ownership of that function. In smaller organizations, risk management professionals might play a larger role in human resource issues than the consultative role they might otherwise play.

Employee Handbook

The employee handbook should serve as the official guideline for the office. It should contain work rules and policies pertaining to the personnel employed. At the beginning of the handbook, a bold disclaimer should be included informing the employee that the handbook is not intended to create an employment contract.[41] Its purpose is to clarify office operations and to prevent disputes and misunderstandings. All new employees should receive a copy or at least review the manual and sign a written statement attesting to the fact that they have received a copy and reviewed the information. Current employees should be required to review any additions or changes at least annually with written documentation of the review. The manual should include general information on the practice, wage and salary information, benefits, sick or absence leave, workers' compensation, and disability. Other information on work rules such as hours, dress, confidentiality, smoking, phone calls, and disciplinary procedures including probation, suspension, and dismissal should also be included.

Employee Proficiency

Medical personnel need to be qualified to perform their duties so that quality care is provided in a safe manner. A competency and proficiency monitoring process should be an integral part of the practice's quality improvement program.

The employee proficiency process includes:

- Implementation of a formalized orientation program for all employees that includes mentoring of new employees.

- Development of criteria-based, written position descriptions for all staff.

- Development and implementation of required skills checklists that reflect the responsibilities and duties of the position.

- Development of employee-prepared performance goals that have been agreed upon with the supervisor.

- Performance of periodic evaluation of employees' competence. This process should include input from the employee and the employee's supervisors and should be based on direct observation of the employee's work. Rewards or promotions should be awarded for high proficiency levels. Evaluation documents should be dated and signed by the employee and reviewer and retained in the employee file.

- Development of ongoing education programs for health care providers can promote competency, productivity, and efficiency; communicate recommended and consistent behaviors to support quality care, help staff identify actual problems or potential problems, generate ideas and problem-solving methods, and increase staff morale.

Confidentiality   The office practice should adopt a zero-tolerance policy for any staff member who knowingly violates patient confidentiality. This problem is so serious that many practices have made a breach of confidentiality grounds for immediate termination. A confidentiality statement should be signed upon employment and annually thereafter.

Confidentiality extends to more than just inappropriate access and distribution of patient chart data. Breaches of confidentiality can occur over the phone, at the reception area, and interdepartmentally. To avoid serious lapses in confidentiality:

- Give patient information only to the patient directly. Do not assume that family members are aware of the patient's condition.

- Never leave detailed answering machine messages.

- Phone triage should be done in a private area, not in the middle of the office or at a nurses' station.

- Receptionists or other employees who happen to become privy to a patient's health condition should never inquire about the status of it when speaking with the patient.[42]

············

PERFORMANCE IMPROVEMENT

Performance improvement has had many names throughout the years: quality assurance, quality improvement, quality management, and so forth. Regardless of the name, the goal remains the same: "Improve patient care and outcome." What originated in industrial settings has much applicability to the health care arena.

Outcome Measures

The provision of quality services to patients delivered in the outpatient setting can be measured. One important concept in measuring quality is to realize that patients come to health care providers with their own expectations for services. Typically, patients do not evaluate the physician and the office staff on their competence in technology and sophisticated medical procedures. Patients evaluate health care practices and expertise based on how they are treated and on what they have come to expect in terms of service.[43] The patients' quality measures are often very different from the outcome measurements that the health care providers traditionally have used to measure performance improvement.

Outcome is one type of performance improvement measure commonly used by health care organizations. Outcomes may be clinical or they may be service-focused. Indicators are the specific measures or indices that are collected to quantify the selected quality outcomes. For a performance improvement program to be effective and comprehensive, the indicators must be measurable, clinical, and customer-focused.

Health care is a service industry similar to many other service segments of the marketplace. In fact, many health care organizations use other industries as benchmarks for driving the changes and improvements in their systems. The hotel and hospitality industry may be used as a model to compare the health care patient registration process. Environmental engineering companies can be used to compare the decor, lighting, and traffic flows for patient care areas. Every aspect of the health care setting should be evaluated for its customer-friendliness and its ability to effectively meet customers' needs.

The clinical care delivered by hands-on caregivers should be monitored for quality. The staff that is providing the care accomplishes this monitoring best. The clinical care portion of the quality equation is monitored and evaluated by reviewing the clinical documentation in the medical record.

Specific indicators should be established for the monitoring of care. Many of the national professional organizations have promulgated guidelines, and external regulatory and licensing bodies also may be queried for information. High-risk, high-volume, and problem-prone areas are good places to start the selection process for clinical quality indicators. The areas for monitoring will differ by the kind of clinical practice delivered in that setting. The monitoring and evaluation process must be carefully documented.

There are some indicators that reflect basic quality monitoring strategies regardless of the patients' diagnoses or problems. Some generic indicators of quality can be included in the assessment of the clinical record. Some examples of meaningful measures that are generic in nature might include:

- Adequacy of documentation of medication refills ordered via telephone
- Adequacy of documentation of after-hours telephone calls
- Entries in the clinical record dated and timed by each practitioner who makes an entry
- Legible documentation from all staff and practitioners
- All documents in the record permanently secured in the record binder
- Adequacy of documentation of consultations and referrals, notations regarding review of the consultant's findings, and subsequent modifications, if indicated, in the plan of care
- All diagnostic testing results in the record and initialed by the ordering physician
- Information of abnormal test results or required changes in plan of care provided to the patient, and the plan of care modified appropriately

A complete, legible, and accessible clinical record is the best tool to demonstrate the adequacy, timeliness, and quality of service that is provided by the organization. To anyone outside the organization who might ever have reason to review the record, it will most likely appear that, "If it is not documented, it was not done." Such perceptions hold true regardless of what was actually done or what protocols, policies, and procedures indicate would have been done.

The old quality assurance paradigm identified the "bad apple" and focused intervention with that individual. The new performance improvement model looks at the system rather than the individual. Some studies have suggested that 85 to 95 percent of health care quality issues are system-driven and have minimal correlation with the competence or skills of the individual clinician. Professional liability claims are often the result of system failures in medical offices.[44]

Many companies provide outcomes benchmarking data. Participating with external sources is one way of meeting certain standards, such as those promulgated by JCAHO. Such analysis can identify areas or issues that should be addressed from either a risk management or performance perspective.

Patient Satisfaction Surveys

Customer satisfaction is a primary goal of any service organization. The practice must survey patients to identify expectations, indicators, variables, or factors that patients feel are important and that they will be using to judge and measure the practice's services. A practice cannot measure whether it is meeting its customer's needs if it is not cognizant of those needs. Patients should be asked about their satisfaction with the services provided at each episode of care. It might be necessary to collect this information confidentially or without patients disclosing their identity.

There should be a formal, systematic process for the collection and analysis of patient satisfaction data with subsequent improvement activity implemented based on this patient input. This information should be monitored on an ongoing basis to assure that the changes have improved patients' perceptions of the services being provided.

Some measures of patient satisfaction that might be used include waiting time; friendliness and helpfulness of the staff; a clean, efficient, organized facility; confidentiality of their medical information; and reasonable costs and fees.

Incident Reporting

Reporting of unusual occurrences or incidents is essential to the organization's risk identification program and is important to improving patient care. An incident is any happening that is not consistent with the routine care of a particular patient or a described operation of the facility. Incidents are early warning signs of potential problematic areas of patient care. The organization should establish a written policy and procedure that specifies all the situations when an incident or occurrence report should be completed and by whom. All incidents or occurrences that fit the established criteria are documented on a specified form and are investigated or followed up by designated individuals. A statement in the policy and on the form should designate the process and form as confidential.

The policy and procedure identifies issues for formal reporting. It is difficult to develop an all-inclusive list, but certain occurrences should qualify automatically. Some issues that always should be reported, documented, and investigated include:

- Patients who fall or sustain an injury on-site
- Patients who experience cardiopulmonary arrest at the office
- All patients who require "emergency measures" at the office
- Patients who must be transferred by ambulance from the office to an acute-care setting
- Medication errors
- Medication adverse or allergic reactions
- Patients who are injured due to an equipment failure or user error while at the facility
- Patients stating they are pursuing legal action because of their displeasure with an outcome of care rendered by the practice
- Patients who leave the office without being seen
- Patients whose adverse outcome was unexpected[45]
- Patients who experience a near-miss even if there is no injury

Incident report forms are most effective when completed by the person who first becomes aware of or witnesses the event. Once completed, the form should be reviewed and signed off by a manager.

Medical record documentation of the event is important. The occurrence should be documented in the medical record, along with any medical steps that were taken to minimize adverse effects. Incident reports should never be filed or alluded to in the medical record. If the event is a potential compensable event, the insurance company should be notified either directly or through an agent or broker. If a claim is made, the insurance company will be prepared to take appropriate claims management steps to protect the practice.

Incident reports must interface with the quality improvement program to maximize protection of information and ensure that significant safety issues are addressed in a comprehensive and timely manner. Another approach to providing protection is under the attorney-client privilege, which is also referred to as work product protection.

············

ACCREDITATION, LICENSURE, AND REGULATORY ISSUES

Health care remains one of the most regulated industries. From the local, state, and national level to the voluntary organizations that offer a wide variety of services, one can be overwhelmed by the vast array and immense volume of material related to the provision of health care.

JCAHO

The Joint Commission on Accreditation of Healthcare Organizations (JCAHO) [www.jcaho.org/accredited+organizations/ambulatory+care/index.htm] established the Ambulatory Health Care accreditation program in 1975 to encourage quality patient care in all types of freestanding ambulatory care facilities. The JCAHO standards apply to the full range of ambulatory care providers. A growing number of ambulatory care organizations seek JCAHO accreditation because its standards represent a national consensus on quality patient care. The Joint Commission's Office-Based Surgery Accreditation Program focuses on customer service, improving care and improving health, patient care, patient safety, qualified and competent staff, and responsible leadership.[46]

One surveyor typically conducts on-site surveys for two days. If the volume of the organization is more than 10,000 visits annually, two surveyors will be assigned for two days. The survey includes many activities, some of which are an opening conference, observation of the administrative and clinical activity, assessment of the physical facilities and patient care equipment, and a leadership exit conference.[47]

JCAHO updates its goals frequently, and the following indicates the breadth of its 2006 National Patient Safety Goals across the continuum of care:

- Ambulatory care and office-based surgery
- Assisted living
- Behavioral health care
- Critical access hospital and hospital
- Disease-specific care
- Home care
- Laboratory
- Long-term care
- Networks[48]

The Accreditation Association for Ambulatory Health Care

The Accreditation Association for Ambulatory Health Care (AAAHC) [www.aaahc.org], incorporated in 1979, is a non-profit corporation that serves as an advocate for the provision and documentation of quality health services in ambulatory health care organizations. AAAHC accreditation is a voluntary process that involves several steps. The first step in accreditation is for the organization to conduct a self-assessment using published AAAHC guidelines. The next step is to participate in an on-site survey conducted by trained AAAHC surveyors. Following the survey, the accreditation team makes recommendations that are reviewed by the AAAHC Accreditation Committee. This committee makes the final accreditation decision. Accreditation may be awarded for six months, one year, or three years, depending on the level of compliance with the published standards.[49]

The AAAHC strives to improve the quality of patient care. According to the association, its members benefit in the following ways:

- Find innovative ways to improve patient care and services.
- Increase efficiency and reduce costs.
- Improve risk management programs.
- Decrease insurance premiums.
- Motivate staff by instilling pride and loyalty.
- Strengthen public perception.
- Recruit and retain qualified professional staff.
- Develop alliances with other provider groups.[50]

The Institute for Medical Quality

The Institute for Medical Quality [www.imq.org/imqdoc.cfm/2], much like other accreditation agencies, offers several educational, consultation, accreditation, and certification programs. It also offers a program dedicated to ambulatory care.[51]

The American Society of Anesthesiologists

Founded in 1905, the American Society of Anesthesiologists (ASA) [www.asahq.org] serves as an advocate for patients who receive anesthesia. ASA offers many opportunities for improving and monitoring the quality of care provided to patients. The Anesthesia Consultation Program enables experienced consultants to evaluate the care delivered on-site, then issue a written report detailing its findings and recommendations.[52]

The Association of Perioperative Registered Nurses

The Association of Perioperative Registered Nurses (AORN) [www.aorn.org] is a professional association dedicated to nurses who provide nursing care related to operative patient care. It publishes position statements on topics such as correct site surgery, bloodborne diseases, and numerous personnel issues.[53]

Governmental Accreditation

Voluminous local, state, and federal rules and regulations are enforced by innumerable agencies. Perhaps the best recognized are state inspections of nursing homes. Though the details and impact of these legal issues are beyond the scope of this chapter, they are nonetheless important. Risk managers should explore other appropriate subject-focused resources for more information.

Managed Care

The health care delivery system has undergone significant change since the advent of managed care during the latter part of the twentieth century. What used to be a private matter between patient and physician has become a multifaceted collaboration involving patient, physician, other providers, and purchasers of health care. Managed care is a discipline with its own standards and guidelines, but it also has its own risks related to health care delivery.

Accreditation

Managed care accreditation is a phenomenon that originated during the early 1990s. The two primary accrediting agencies are the Utilization review Accreditation Commission (URAC) at [www.urac.org] and the National Committee for Quality Assurance (NCQA) at [www.ncqa.org].

URAC is a charitable foundation that was founded in 1990. It is a standards-based organization that promotes health care performance improvement. The commission has many purposes, but the one that pertains most to the field of risk management is accreditation. Organizations that successfully meet all URAC requirements are awarded a full two-year accreditation. Conditional accreditation may be awarded to organizations that have the necessary documentation but lack some policies and procedures.

The NCQA began accrediting managed care organizations in 1991. It has five different accreditation statuses: excellent, commendable, accredited, provisional, and denied.

NCQA uses a triangular approach to evaluating the delivery of health care. There is an accreditation process, a member satisfaction survey process, and a measurement process that uses the Health Plan Employer Data and Information Set (HEDIS®). Although the NCQA processes are voluntary, a majority of health maintenance organizations (HMOs) participate. In addition, approximately 90 percent of health plans use HEDIS to measure their performance.[54]

In the latter part of 2002, NCQA reported that there had been "substantial quality improvements, on average, for Americans enrolled in accountable commercial health plans." The improvements were believed to be attributed to "effective and accurate systems for tracking care, quality incentives, and partnerships between health plans and physicians."[55]

HEDIS's effectiveness of care measures are ever-growing, but some of them are listed below:[56]

- Adolescent immunization status
- Antidepressant medication management
- Beta blocker treatment after a heart attack
- Breast cancer screening
- Cervical cancer screening
- Childhood immunization status
- Chlamydia screening
- Cholesterol management after a heart attack
- Colorectal cancer screening
- Comprehensive diabetes care
- Controlling high blood pressure
- Follow-up after hospitalization for mental illness
- Prenatal and post-partum care
- Use of appropriate medications for people with asthma

Effective risk management programs incorporate, or at least collaborate with, performance improvement programs. It could be argued that participating in the above activities would improve patient outcome, improve patient satisfaction, and decrease medical professional liability. These activities certainly allow for benchmarking patient care activities with standardized, well-recognized national norms.

············

RISK MANAGEMENT ISSUES

One often hears how managed care organizations (MCOs) or health insurance companies "refused care for a patient." It must be remembered that such entities are not in the business of providing health care but rather paying for services rendered.

Physicians and other providers should, whenever possible, ensure that the patient receives whatever care is medically necessary. Although there is little debate about whether the current system contains excessive bureaucratic paperwork and steps, the ultimate goal is to deliver quality patient care. If the physician or provider disagrees with the managed care organization's decision, the physician should make every effort to ensure that the MCO has sufficient quality clinical information to make an informed decision. Likewise, if a denial of benefits is issued by the MCO, the physician or provider should appeal the decision vigorously if it is believed that the decision is flawed and the patient's outcome will be jeopardized.

Contract Management

Health care organizations and providers are faced with exposures that arise from contracts they enter into with other parties. Three of the most common contracts that can create risk for the medical practitioner are those with pharmaceutical companies or research organizations to conduct clinical trials on new products, with facilities to assume medical director duties, and with managed care organizations for the provision of patient care.

To ensure that all contracts are reviewed properly, the ambulatory care facility or practitioner should develop a contract management system, which should be integrated into the organization's policies. The policies should designate who is authorized to execute different types of contracts, define the review process, establish protocols governing outside contract review, and document compliance with contractual obligations. The policy should cover safety and security issues. These include storing all original contracts in a secure, fireproof location in the administrative office and establishing a back-up storage area; forwarding only copies of signed contracts to authorized individuals; and creating security procedures to ensure that only authorized individuals have access to original contracts. There should be a system in place to identify contracts nearing the expiration date and to ensure that all contracts undergo an annual review at least ninety days before termination.

The best way to ensure the practice or practitioner is not assuming unknown or uncovered liability through a contract is to read all contracts thoroughly before signing them. It is a good practice to have all contracts reviewed by an attorney. In most cases, signing a contract indicates agreement with and acceptance of all the terms and conditions of the contract.[57] For more complete information refer to Volume I, Chapter 12, on Contract Review.

Physicians' Offices and Ambulatory Care Facilities

Operating a physician's office presents several risk management issues. Though some of these concepts apply in one way or another to other types of ambulatory care settings, they have more relevance to physicians' offices. Therefore, modification of these examples may be needed before they can be applied to other settings.

············

CLINICAL ISSUES

The following clinical issues include some functions that might, at first glance, appear to be primarily clerical. However, considering the dynamics within a physician's office, even functions that may be considered as routine clerical tasks can have a profound effect on patient outcome and, therefore, risk exposure.

Patient Scheduling

Patient scheduling practices should be guided by written office protocols. By adhering to protocols, the office staff plays an important role in minimizing the risk of operational system failures and promoting continuity of care and patient safety. Such protocols should include educating new patients about office procedures before initial visits and arranging follow-up appointments. The office schedule should include time to treat unscheduled patients or walk-in visits. Clear guidelines should be developed for triage of emergency and urgent visits. A physician should evaluate all patients who arrive at the medical office for emergency conditions.

Missed appointments should be brought to the attention of the treating physician and documented in the medical record. If hard copy appointment books are used, entries should be made in pencil and appointment changes crossed out instead of erased. Included in the medical record should be accurate, objective notation of all attempts made to contact the patient, including telephone calls. Appointment books should be kept as long as clinical records are kept. If computerized logs are used, daily printouts can be saved in chronological order.

Patient Tracking and Diagnostic Follow-up

Diagnostic-related incidents are associated with the highest frequency and severity of claims. Many of these claims result from a detrimental delay in following a condition.[58] Often the physician is unaware that the patient failed to return as requested, so months elapse and the condition worsens.

Written office policies for diagnostic follow-up procedures should be developed and adhered to consistently. The importance of a log to track returning lab and other pertinent test results cannot be overemphasized.

All follow-up activities should be documented in the medical record. Notify patients of all test results, not only abnormal results. Office policy should state that it is the office's responsibility to relay test results to patients, not the patient's responsibility to request them. Messages regarding test results should not be left on answering machines, as this might breach confidentiality of patient medical information.

Many computer programs have excellent recall and follow-up capabilities. If the office is not computerized, a manual system using a 3″ × 5″ card system with monthly dividers will suffice. Place on the card the patient's name, patient file number, telephone numbers, address, the reason the patient needs to return and the month and year the follow-up is due. Generally, follow-up attempts include one phone call and, if that is not successful, a postcard or letter should be mailed. These attempts should be documented in the chart. If the condition is serious, such as cancer, the physician might want to send a certified letter with return receipt requested. This receipt is then filed in the chart with a copy of the letter.[59]

Primary Care Screening

More care is now delivered in the ambulatory care setting, and more attention is paid to preventive care. The physician's recommendations for screening and preventive care should be based on the patient's medical needs, professional guidelines, and medical judgment. When screening and preventive care are part of the patient care plan, office staff can develop and maintain a tickler system that tracks due dates for recommended preventive care, screening test dates, monitoring results, and physician review and discussion of the results with the patient. Physicians should document the informed refusal of patients who choose not to proceed with recommended preventive care for any reason.

Medication Summary Sheet

A medication summary sheet should be developed for all patients to assist in tracking medications. This sheet should include the date, name of medication ordered, dosage, quantity, number of refills, physician's initials, staff member's initials, and adverse reactions. Allergy information should be included prominently at the top of the sheet.

Referrals and Consultations

When the professional opinion of another party is needed, steps should be taken to prevent miscommunication and lack of coordination between providers and staff. The referring physician should document the formal request for consultation, and a copy of the request should become a part of the patient record. The request should indicate who is primarily responsible for patient care and the duties of each party. Discussions between the physicians, acceptance of the referral by the consulting physician, and timeframes for consultation should be documented. The referring office should be instructed to make the appointment for the patient. A copy of pertinent records should be forwarded to the consulting physician; the original records must be retained in the referring physician's office. Consulting reports, including the patient's relevant medical history or physician's summary, should be written, signed, and sent to the referring physician in a timely manner. All patient communication, including the patient's role in the referral process and the patient's understanding and acceptance or refusal of the recommendations, should be documented. Develop a procedure to monitor the receipt of consultation reports. The physician should review and initial the reports before they are added to the medical record. Document the plan and actual patient follow-up in the clinical record.

Patient Education

In the ambulatory care setting, written post-treatment and continuing care instructions are necessary because patients' interaction with health care professionals and office staff may be brief and infrequent. The following guidelines for education can assist staff and patients in this process:

- Review all materials for accuracy before adopting them.
- Design instructions for readability and provide reasonable accommodation to ensure patient comprehension.
- Maintain a master file of all patient education materials.
- Have patients confirm their understanding of instructions and perform a return demonstration if the activity is task-based.
- Ask patients and provider to sign off on the instructions, indicating the patient's understanding.
- Maintain a signed copy of the patient education and instructions in the medical record.[60]

Advance Directives

All states now recognize various types of advance directives, the most prevalent of which are living wills and health care powers of attorney. The latter allows a patient to name an agent to make health care decisions when the patient lacks the capacity to do so. Advance directives regarding end-of-life decisions and agents who may make health care decisions in the absence of a competent patient generally are matters of state statutory law.[61]

There are various state and federal definitions of competence and various statutory definitions of what is meant by "life support," that is, whether hydration and nutrition are included or excluded. Also, state laws differ as to the form of execution of such advance directives, with some states requiring only attestation by witnesses in the presence of the declarant of a living will or health care power of attorney and other states requiring notarization. Each physician should consult applicable state law concerning the matter.

In the transient society in which we live, it is possible for an individual to come to a medical practitioner with advance directive documents that were executed in another state. Although such documents might have been valid in the state in which they were executed, they may be either valid or invalid in the state where the physician is practicing medicine. If possible, new advance directives should be executed in accordance with the laws of the state where treatment occurs. It is recommended that the physician or someone on the physician's staff have a working knowledge of the requirements of the advance directive laws in the state where the physician is practicing and, if possible, maintain generally accepted statutorily prescribed forms for use by their patients.

············

AMBULATORY CARE SYSTEMS AND PROCEDURES

Numerous recent studies have shown that most adverse events can be attributed to issues related to systems rather than to individuals. This demonstrates the importance of developing effective systems and workflow procedures, and training the staff to ensure that the systems are used correctly on a consistent basis.

Information Flow

Office systems should be established to ensure efficient and appropriate processing and follow-up of clinical information. Office follow-up systems should be able to track and perform required follow-up when patients miss or cancel appointments, or fail to schedule or keep recommended appointments for diagnostic testing or specialty consultations. The consulting physician should notify the requesting physician of adverse reports that require immediate attention.

Billing and Collection

The objective of a billing and collection program is to assist the practice with meeting its cash flow needs. Written policies and procedures should be developed regarding the practice's billing and collection process. These should be evaluated on an annual basis and revised as necessary. If handled improperly, billing practices can hinder the early stages of the relationship between the patient and the practice and can set up a negative climate that can lead to litigation.

All fees should be disclosed before services are rendered. Threats of litigation often develop when a patient receives an unexpected bill. It is best to discuss and agree on the fees before providing the service to avoid creating an environment of distrust. A written fee schedule should be available on request.

Respond immediately to patient calls or letters regarding billing errors. All delinquent accounts and serious complaints regarding billing should be directed immediately to the physician and office manager or risk manager before being turned over to a collection agency. This will allow the physician the opportunity to evaluate the care that was rendered and the validity of the complaint. Other factors such as adverse outcome, which might influence pursuit of payment or collection proceedings, can be taken into consideration. Complaint reviews can also serve as an early warning of legal action and provide the practice with an opportunity to appease the patient. All written and oral communication should be documented in the patient's individual billing file, which should be separate from the patient's medical record.

An attorney should review the collection procedures to ensure that they comply with applicable federal and state laws and regulations. Send warning letters drafted by an attorney before involving collection agencies. Evaluate collection agencies on a regular basis.

Practice Coverage

All physicians in practice should have primary and secondary practice coverage arrangements for those times when they are not available. Covering physicians should be of the same medical specialty and have the same hospital privileges as the treating physician, if possible. When the treating physician has contractual agreements with managed care plans that entail specific payment methods, or referral guidelines or restrictions, arrangements should be made so that the covering physician's actions comply with the managed care plan requirements. Ascertain that the covering physician has adequate professional liability insurance. The treating physician should provide information to the covering physician regarding patients' course of treatment and anticipated problems. This should be documented in the medical record. Hospitalized patients should be informed of the coverage arrangement and, if possible, introduced to the covering physician. The physician on call should document all interactions with the patient. The treating physician should notify the hospital and answering service of the names and telephone numbers of the covering physician(s).[62]

Locum Tenens Providers and Agency Nurses

Physicians and other providers who deliver health care on a locum tenens (temporary replacement) basis create a unique set of risk management issues. Many providers who serve in this capacity are well trained and well respected, but these traits cannot be assumed to exist in all such providers.

Credentialing locum tenens providers is of utmost importance. Though the circumstances that necessitate the need for services of a locum tenens provider often are urgent, the process of using only qualified individuals should not be undertaken with less vigilance. Likewise, one must make sure that the care rendered by locum tenens personnel will be covered by an adequate amount of medical professional liability insurance purchased preferably by the company that provides the locum tenens personnel.

Another issue that arises when using a locum tenens provider or agency nurse is orientation and training. In theory, everyone who delivers care within a specific organizational setting should have similar orientation and training. Unfortunately, this is not the case in many situations. Each organization should develop at least an abbreviated orientation and training program for providers who are new to the organization and will be used only for a short period of time.

Telephone Protocols

Proper telephone protocols should be developed and implemented to promote consistent, accurate, and complete quality care over a wide variety of conditions. Such protocols will be scrutinized in medical professional liability lawsuits and must demonstrate that consistent advice is given for similar patient symptoms. They become the standard of care for that medical facility and, as such, must be developed with great care and must provide care within recognized, acceptable standards. Protocols should be developed under physician supervision and signed off before implementation. They are often prepared in checklist format and organized by symptom or patient complaint. Protocols should be reviewed regularly and modified as necessary to reflect changing practice standards.

Policies and procedures addressing the use of telephone triage should be developed and implemented to support written protocols. These policies should also establish telephone hours and the call-back procedure. Protocols, policies, and procedures should always err on the side of caution by making an appointment for the patient, or by referring emergent conditions promptly to an urgent care center or emergency room. Patients who request an examination by a physician should be given an appointment. An advisory physician should be available for consultation during triage.

The substance of all telephone calls related to patient care should be documented contemporaneously throughout the call. Special pre-printed telephone logs can be used, and the policy should require that no blank spaces be allowed. Information that should be documented includes at least the date and time of the call, identification of the caller, identification of the staff member taking the call, the subject of the call, the specific protocol used, and the exact advice given.

Protocol data collection, at a minimum, should identify the patient's symptoms and associated complaints; symptom characteristics and course; history of symptom(s); onset; location; aggravating factors; and relieving factors. Information that also needs to be identified during the data collection is the caller's pregnancy status or breast feeding status (if applicable), allergy history, current and recent medication use, previous medical and psychosocial history, and any history of recent injury, infection, or illness.

A quality improvement program is essential in promoting quality telephone triage. Job descriptions for all employees who perform telephone triage should be stated in accordance with all state practice acts, and physician supervision should be acknowledged. Employees who perform telephone triage should be formally trained under physician supervision, observed, evaluated, and regularly monitored. Receptionists and other clerks can handle administrative calls but, generally, nurses are assigned to handle calls that involve patients with symptoms. Calls involving symptoms that need to be addressed immediately by a physician should be routed expeditiously to the physician as specified in the written policy. Successful triage is also dependent on the communication skills of the staff member taking the call. Formalized telephone triage education is important and can be obtained through medical facilities' and colleges' or universities' education departments.[63]

Closing or Leaving a Practice

When a physician decides to leave a practice permanently, there are a number of steps that need to be followed. To avoid patient claims of abandonment, the physician should notify all patients treated within the past year of the intent to withdraw from practice. Such notification should be in writing and at least sixty days before the date of leaving or closing the practice. A copy of this letter should be placed in the patient's medical record. The termination letter should advise patients of the importance of continued care, the telephone number of the county medical society's referral service, the termination date, and a method and authorization form that enables patients to obtain copies of their medical records. Notices should be placed in the local newspaper.

Requests for release of records can come from many sources. Under most state laws, medical records must be released upon receipt of a valid written authorization, signed, and dated by the patient or the patient's authorized representative.

If a physician is withdrawing from practice, patients' records must be retained. The length of time that medical records should be retained depends on the statute of limitations in each state and any regulations issued by state regulatory or legislative bodies. If the physician is aware of a possible claim, the record should be kept in its original form as a hard copy until the incident or claim is resolved.

The physician's medical professional liability insurance company should be notified, and insurance coverage should be evaluated carefully so that the physician has adequate insurance to cover any event that is reported in the future, especially if the coverage is written on a claims-made basis. In all cases, the physician should consult with an attorney to ensure that all regulations have been complied with before leaving practice.[64]

············
PUBLIC HEALTH DEPARTMENTS AND AGENCIES

The mission of public health departments and agencies is to provide comprehensive public health services that protect, promote, and preserve the health of their citizens and to provide services to all people in their city, county, or district. The structure of the health department can vary from state to state but generally consists of a health director that reports to a board of health. Public health departments are usually under a state's Department of Environment, Health, and Natural Resources.

Risks Identified

Health departments traditionally have been considered low risk with few claims. Nevertheless, such departments often lack organized risk management, safety, and performance improvement programs. A claims analysis of a state program was performed over a ten-year period. Most of the 100 counties in the state were under the same insurance program. The loss ratio for this program was under 2.5 percent.[65] The low risk has been attributed to good community relations, low-risk procedures except for obstetrics, and the delivery of care regardless of payment.

Operational risks identified in public health departments often include polices and procedures that are not reviewed, revised, or kept current on a regular basis. Credentialing of physicians and other allied health professionals is often non-existent, and peer review is rarely performed. Risk management, performance improvement, safety, and infection control programs and plans are generally not formalized. Usually, there is no designated risk manager. Incident reporting systems may be part of the county- or city-wide incident reporting system and are not specific to health-related risks. Clinical skills checklists and annual evaluations may not be performed on an annual basis. Clinical risks include obstetrical issues such as home deliveries and high-risk obstetrical clinics. Medical emergency policies may not be developed and if they are, the staff often lacks the expertise to follow established policies.

Risk Management Steps

The risk management steps for public and county health departments and other private sector ambulatory care centers are basically the same. The common concepts and risk management strategies covered earlier in this chapter are applicable to local health departments and should be implemented.

....

AMBULATORY SURGERY CENTERS

As illustrated previously in Table 8.1, there are different types of ambulatory care facilities. Changes to the types of facilities and the services offered occur frequently.

Ambulatory surgery, also known as outpatient surgery and same-day surgery, refers to surgery performed on patients who are discharged home the day of the procedure.[66] It is estimated that in 2003 there were 3,700 ambulatory surgery centers in the United States.[67] Ambulatory surgeries accounted for 15 percent of all surgeries performed in the United States in 1980. By 2000, 70 percent of all surgical procedures were done in outpatient facilities. The number of surgeries performed in 2000 was 6.7 million, almost a 200 percent increase in just ten years.[68] According to the Centers for Disease Control and Prevention/National Center for Health Statistics, the number of ambulatory surgical procedures continues to increase because of the continuing need for cost containment, advances in medical technology including improvements in anesthesia, which allows patients to regain consciousness quicker and with fewer side effects, better relief of pain through improved analgesics, and the use in minimally invasive and non-invasive procedures. Most surgeons prefer ambulatory care centers to hospital-based facilities because they can perform two to three times the number of surgeries.[69] According to the American Medical Association, the top five reasons physicians decide to build ambulatory surgery centers are:

1. Increased efficiency
2. More control over operations

3. Better access to physical plant, for both physicians and patients

4. Decreased cost to patients

5. Additional revenue resource[70]

Anti-Kickback Issues

Most physicians tout the efficiency of ambulatory surgery centers, from both the perspective of the physician and the patient. Almost universally, it is less expensive to have a procedure performed in such a facility than in a hospital-based facility. Because costs and profit often are major issues pertaining to ambulatory surgery care, the referral of a patient to a facility must be made with some measure of caution because of the potential for allegations of illegal kickbacks, payments, or other improper financial incentives for referrals.

The safe harbor provisions in federal and state law and regulations pertaining to ambulatory surgery centers are divided into four categories:

1. Surgeon-owned

2. Single-specialty

3. Multi-specialty

4. Hospital or physician-owned[71]

Each type of ambulatory surgery center has its own specific requirements that must be met to be afforded the safe harbor protections. It is recommended that legal advice be obtained to ensure compliance, as the financial penalties and damage to public perception can be great.

Anesthesia Care

As in the acute-care setting, anesthesia care is a vital component of ambulatory surgery care. Each facility should be equipped to provide all types of anesthesia, including general, regional, spinal, and conscious sedation. All standards of care must be met regardless of the location or setting.

The anesthesia staff should be well-trained and credentialed to perform the services offered. The staffing and workload ratios must meet recognized standards, with appropriate supervision of personnel, such as certified registered nurse anesthetists.

Adequate plans should be in place if a surgical procedure must be aborted emergently. There should be an acute facility nearby in case a patient must be admitted for inpatient services.

Clinical Issues

A preoperative evaluation should be performed on each patient before surgery is performed. Standardized forms should be used and should explore subjects such as prior medical and surgical history, anesthesia history, current medications, and allergies.

Intraoperative monitoring is of paramount importance. Sufficient documentation by the nurse and the anesthesia personnel must be recorded in the patient's medical record. A suitable operative note must be either handwritten or dictated and signed by the surgeon.

Qualified staff must perform post-anesthesia care for an adequate period of time. The recovery time might vary based on factors such as the patient's medical history and the type of anesthesia used. Discharge criteria should be used to evaluate the patient before the patient is allowed to leave the facility. Suitable discharge instructions should be given to the adult who accompanies the patient home.

In 2002, the United States Department of Veterans' Affairs published a study it conducted beginning in 1994.[72] This study revealed that enhanced rapport with patients can be achieved by more personalized service before, during, and after surgery. Providing beepers for family members of surgery patients allows them the freedom to roam yet remain accessible to the medical team, if necessary. Follow-up telephone calls the day after surgery allows the medical staff to assess the patient's outcome while allowing for valuable feedback and maintaining a close relationship with the patient.

Following these guidelines will allow a facility to minimize its risk exposure while optimizing the quality of care provided to patients. One of the keys to operating a successful ambulatory surgery facility is patient selection. Therefore, it is crucial that facilities have appropriate relationships with physicians who understand the importance of performing procedures at an acute-care setting if the circumstances warrant doing so.

....
ALTERNATIVE MEDICINE[73]

Traditional medicine refers to the provision of health care services before the advent of conventional medicine. Traditional medicine, by its nature, was passed from one generation to another and was designed to meet the needs of the local community.

Conventional medicine, as practiced in many countries including the United States, involves care delivered by practitioners schooled at an accredited university and trained via accredited residency programs. Their discipline is based on scientific, peer-reviewed studies. These practitioners employ a variety of treatment techniques, including but not limited to medications, physical and occupational therapy, and surgery. During the past two decades, these practitioners began focusing more on preventive medicine and wellness programs.

Complementary and alternative medicine (CAM) may either augment or replace conventional medicine. According to the National Center for Complementary and Alternative Medicine (NCCAM), complementary medicine is used together with conventional medicine, and alternative medicine is used in lieu of conventional medicine. Integrative medicine combines conventional medicine with CAM therapies that have been proven safe and effective using the same scientific study techniques conventional practitioners use.[74]

NCCAM classifies complementary and alternative therapies into five categories:

1. Alternative medical systems (homeopathic and naturopathic medicine)

2. Mind-body interventions (meditation, mental healing, and so on)

3. Biologically based therapies (dietary supplements, herbal products, and so on)

4. Manipulative and body-based therapies (chiropractic manipulation, massage, and so on)

5. Energy therapies (biofield therapy and bioelectromagnetic-based therapies)[75]

Use of CAM

According to an article published by the American Medical Association, in 1997, there were 629 million visits to providers who practice CAM. It was estimated that 44 percent of the people living in the United States used at least one therapy, and "52 percent had seen at least one CAM provider in the last year."[76] In 1998, patients received approximately $4 billion of chiropractic care.[77]

Medical Insurance Coverage

Forty-two states mandate coverage for chiropractic care, and seven states mandate coverage for acupuncture.[78] Many insurance companies now offer coverage for some forms of alternative or complementary medicine.

Organizations and Literature

There are many sources of information on CAM. The September 11, 1998, issue of the *Journal of the American Medical Association* was devoted to alternative medicine. Editorial boards that have an appropriate mix of physicians and non-physicians publish *Integrative Medicine* and the *Journal of Alternative & Complementary Medicine*. There also is a wealth of information available on the Internet but as with any online material, caution should be exercised until the validity of the content is verified. Unlike conventional medical literature, there is little data from properly designed and conducted clinical studies.[79]

Legal Cases

Professional liability suits filed against providers of alternative or complementary medicine providers account for only a small percent of all medical professional liability claims. A comprehensive study published in the *Journal of the American Medical Association* revealed that in the early- to mid-1990s, primary care physicians experienced approximately 6.4 claims per 100 policyholders. During the same period, chiropractors experienced a rate of 2.7. The average indemnity payment per claim averaged $147,853 for primary care physicians and $49,873 for chiropractors. The percentage of claims that resulted in indemnity payments was approximately 31.4 percent for primary care physicians and 49.1 percent for chiropractors.[80]

Generally, medical physicians do not have additional liability exposure simply because they refer patients to other physicians. However, if the referral is made to a practitioner who provides alternative or complementary medicine, liability might be asserted on a basis of negligent referral, negligent supervision, or other similar theories.[81]

It is evident from the medical professional liability claims history that providers of alternative medicine must meet certain standards of care and take measures to provide quality care. However, it is also evident that physicians must be cautious about referring patients to providers of alternative medicine lest they be named in cases alleging patient damages related to the referral.

············

CONCLUSION

Risk management in the fields of ambulatory care, and complementary or alternative medicine is an important yet often overlooked component of a successful practice. The changes sweeping across the health care industry in recent years have affected ambulatory practices. As discussed in this chapter, many of the same principles and practices that originated in the acute setting are applicable to non-acute settings. Many of the references cited in this chapter can serve as valuable resources to risk management professionals who practice in these settings. As risk management evolves into a more enterprise-related discipline instead of a setting-focused one, the concepts and tools used by risk management professionals will become more universal with applicability to the myriad of settings experienced by today's risk management professionals.

Suggested Reading

The American Society for Healthcare Risk Management has produced an excellent resource titled "Physician Office Risk Management Tool Kit." Practicing risk managers developed this product and though it was designed specifically for physicians' offices, much of the advice pertains to other ambulatory settings. The tool kit is available through ASHRM's Web site [www.ashrm.org].

Endnotes

1. "Ambulatory Care Accreditation." Joint Commission on Accreditation of Healthcare Organizations. [www.jcaho.org/accredited+organizations/ambulatory+care/index.htm]. Accessed June, 2005.

2. "Conference Synthesis: Research Agenda for Ambulatory Patient Safety." The Agency for Healthcare Research and Quality (AHRQ). [www.ahcpr.gov/about/cpcr/ptsafety/ambpts2.htm]. Accessed June, 2005.

3. Kohn, L. T., J. M. Corrigan, and M. S. Donaldson (eds). *To Err is Human: Building a Safer Health System.* Institute of Medicine, Committee on Quality of Health Care in America. Washington, D.C.: National Academy Press, 1999.

4. "Conference Synthesis," *op. cit.*

5. "PIAA Risk Management Review: Combined Specialties." Rockville, Md.: Physician Insurers Association of America (PIAA), May 2005.

6. *Professional Liability in the Ambulatory Care Setting: A Comparison of Claims Data from CNA.* Chicago, Ill.: CNA Financial Corporation, 2001, 1–13.

7. Levinson, W., et al. "Patient-Physician Communication: The Relationship With Malpractice Claims Among Primary Care Physicians and Surgeons." *Journal of the American Medical Association,* 277(7), 1997, 553–559.

8. PIAA, *op. cit.*

9. Kelsay, E., et al. *Risk Management: Safeguarding Your Career.* St. Louis, Mo.: TIV, Inc., 1997, p. 11.

10. Keller, V., and J. Carroll. "A New Model for Physician-Patient Communication." *Patient Education and Counseling,* 23, 1994, 131–140.

11. Clinician-Patient Communication To Enhance Health Outcomes. West Haven, Conn.: Bayer Institute for Health Care Communication, Inc., 1995. For more information on communication workshops, visit [www.bayerinstitute.org].

12. Marvel, M., R. Epstein, K. Flowers, and H. Beckman. "Soliciting the Patient's Agenda: Have We Improved?" *Journal of the American Medical Association,* 281(3), 1999, 283–287.

13. White, M. K., and V. F. Keller. "Difficult Clinician-Patient Relationships." *Journal of Clinical Outcomes Management,* 5(5), 1998, 32–36.

14. Risk Management Strategies for the Physician Office. Chicago, Ill.: Continental Casualty Company, 2001, pp. 14.1–14.4.

15. *Ibid.,* pp. 15.1–15.2.

16. Kelsay, *op. cit.,* p. 49.

17. "Recordkeeping." Diagnosis and Treatment of a Medical Malpractice Suit: A Loss Control Workshop for Physicians. Chicago, Ill.: CNA HealthPro, 1993.

18. Davis, K., and J. McConnell. "Data Management." In Carroll, R. (ed.), *Risk Management Handbook for Health Care Organizations* (3rd ed.). Chicago, Ill.: Jossey-Bass, 2001, p. 120.

19. "Homeland Security Act of 2002." *Public Law* 107-296, November 25, 2002. [www.dhs.gov/interweb/assetlibrary/hr_5005_enr.pdf]. Accessed June, 2005.

20. Page, S. *Establishing a System of Policies and Procedures.* Mansfield, Ohio: BookMasters, Inc., 1998, p. 2.

21. Patient's Rights: Issues in Risk Management. New Haven, Conn.: Yale New Haven Medical Center, 1997. [info.med.yale.edu/caim/risk/patient_rights/patient_rights_7. html]. Accessed June, 2005.

22. Rozovsky, F. *Consent to Treatment: A Practical Guide* (2nd ed.). Gaithersburg, Md.: Aspen Publishers, Inc., 1990, p. 3.

23. Leebov, W. *Effective Complaint Handling in Health Care.* Chicago, Ill.: American Hospital Publishing Inc., 1990, pp. 1–3.

24. *Ibid.,* pp. 14–23.

25. Risk Management Strategies for the Physician Office, *op. cit.,* pp. 11.1–11.2.

26. 42 U.S.C. §311101.

27. Title IV of Public Law 99-660, Health Care Quality Improvement Act of 1986, as amended.

28. Eland, I. A., et al. "Attitudinal Survey of Voluntary Reporting of Adverse Drug Reactions." *British Journal of Clinical Pharmacology,* 48(4), 1999, 623–627.

29. Aspinall, M. B., et al. "Improving Adverse-Drug-Reaction Reporting in Ambulatory Care Clinics at a Veterans Affairs Hospital." *American Journal of Health-System Pharmacy,* 59(9), 2002, 841–845. [www.medscape.com/viewarticle/433319_5]. Accessed June, 2005.

30. Risk Management Strategies for the Physician Office, *op. cit.,* pp. 8.1–8.3.

31. Ambulatory Care: Sentinel Event Policy and Procedures. Joint Commission on Accreditation of Healthcare Organizations. [www.jcaho.org/accredited+organizations/ ambulatory+care]. Accessed June, 2005.

32. Rozovsky, F. "Perspective on Disclosure of Unanticipated Outcome Information." Chicago, Ill.: *American Society for Healthcare Risk Management,* April 2001, pp. 6, 10.

33. Cohen, M. "Statutes, Standards, and Regulations." In Carroll, R. (ed.), *Risk Management Handbook for Health Care Organizations* (3rd ed.). Chicago, Ill.: Jossey-Bass, 2001, p. 82.

34. "What is MedWatch?" Food and Drug Administration. [www.fda.gov/medwatch/what.htm]. Accessed June, 2005.

35. *Ibid.*

36. Risk Management Principles and Commentaries for the Medical Office (2nd ed.). Chicago, Ill.: American Medical Association, 1995, p. 35.

37. Risk Management Strategies for the Physician Office, *op. cit.,* pp. 9.2–9.3.

38. *Ibid.*

39. "Frequently Asked Questions." Occupational and Safety Health Administration. [www.osha.gov/needlesticks/needlefaq.html]. Accessed June, 2005.

40. U.S. Department of Health and Human Services, Centers for Disease Control. Guidelines for Preventing the Transmission of Mycobacterium Tuberculosis in Healthcare Facilities. Atlanta, Ga.: Center for Infectious Disease, October 1994.

41. Warnick, M. "Human Resources Issues." In Carroll, R. (ed.), *Risk Management Handbook for Health Care Organizations* (3rd ed.). Chicago, Ill.: Jossey-Bass, 2001, p. 724.

42. *Risk Management Handbook for Medical Personnel: A Collection of Readings.* Chicago, Ill.: Continental Casualty Company, 1995, pp. 38–39.

43. Scott, L. *It's A Dog's World: Leader's Guide.* Carlsbad, Calif.: CRM Films, 1993, pp. 1–2.

44. Risk Management Handbook for Medical Personnel: A Collection of Readings, *op. cit.*, p. 15.

45. *Ibid.*, p. 12.

46. "Office-Based Surgery Accreditation." Joint Commission on Accreditation of Healthcare Organizations. [www.jcaho.org/accredited+organizations/office+based+surgery/index.htm]. Accessed June, 2005.

47. "Ambulatory Care Accreditation." Joint Commission on Accreditation of Healthcare Organizations. [www.jcaho.org/accredited+organizations/ambulatory+care/index.htm]. Accessed June, 2005.

48. "2006 Joint Commission National Patient Safety Goals" 2005 Joint Commission International Center for Patient Safety [www.jcipatientsafety.org/show.asp?durki=10289&site=164&return=9335]. Accessed June, 2005.

49. "About AAAHC." Accreditation Association for Ambulatory Health Care. [www.aaahc.org]. Accessed June, 2005.

50. "About AAAHC," *op. cit.*

51. The Institute for Medical Quality. [www.imq.org]. Accessed June, 2005.

52. "What is the ASA?" American Society of Anesthesiologists.

53. "AORN Position Statements." The Association of Perioperative Registered Nurses. [www.aorn.org/about/positions/default.htm]. Accessed June, 2005.

54. National Committee for Quality Assurance. [www.ncqa.org]. Accessed June, 2005.

55. The State of Health Care Quality 2002: Industry Trends and Analysis. Washington, D.C.: The National Committee for Quality Assurance, 2002, p. 7.

56. HEDIS® 2005 Summary Table of Measures and Product Lines. National Committee for Quality Assurance [www.ncqa.org/programs/hedis/hedis%202005%20info.htm]. Accessed June, 2005.

57. McDonald, J. "Protect Yourself Against Common Contractual Risks." Vantage Point for the Medical Practitioner. Chicago, Ill.: *CNA HealthPro*, 1(2), Fall 1998.

58. Weiss, *op. cit.*, pp. 83–84.

59. *Ibid.*

60. Risk Management Strategies for the Physician Office, *op. cit.*, pp. 18.1–18.4.

61. U.S. Supreme Court, in *Cruzan v. Missouri Department of Health* (497 U.S. 261; 110 S.Ct. 2841; 111 L. Ed.2d 224 (1990).

62. Risk Management Principles and Commentaries for the Medical Office, op. cit., pp. 14–15.

63. Risk Management Handbook for Medical Personnel: A Collection of Readings, *op. cit.*, pp. 34–35.

64. McRae, J. "On 'Signing Off': When a Physician Leaves a Practice." *Risk Management Sourcebook.* Napa, Calif.: The Doctors' Company, June 1998, pp. 1–2.

65. CNA Claims Analysis, 1992–2002.

66. Peng, L. "Ambulatory Surgery." Emedicine. [www.emedicine.com/aaem/topic13.htm]. Accessed June, 2005.

67. "Ambulatory Surgery Centers" Encyclopedia of Surgery, ED. Anthony J. Senagore. Thomson Gale 2004. enotes.com. 222006. [health.enotes.com/surgery/encyclopedia/ambulatory-surgery-centers] Accessed May 17, 2006.

68. Derived in part from Jackson, C. "Cutting Into the Market: Rise of Ambulatory Surgery Centers," Amednews.com, American Medical Association. [www.ama-assn.org/amednews/2002/04/15/bisa0415.htm]. Accessed June, 2005; AHRQ, *op. cit.*

69. *Ibid.*

70. *Ibid.*

71. Harris, S. "Safe Harbor Rules for Ambulatory Surgery Centers Protect Investment." Amednews.com, American Medical Association. [www.ama-assn.org/amednews/2001/05/07/bica0507.htm]. Accessed June, 2005.

72. United States Department of Veterans' Affairs. "Addressing the Concerns of Ambulatory Care Patients." [www.va.gov/medical/ambulatorycare.htm]. Accessed June, 2005.

73. For a detailed review of the issues related to the integration of conventional and alternative medicine, see Washington State Office of the Insurance Commissioner's report Issues in Coverage for Complementary and Alternative Medicine Services: Report of the Clinician Workgroup on the Integration of Complementary and Alternative Medicine, January 2000.

74. "What is Complementary and Alternative Medicine (CAM)?" National Center for Complementary and Alternative Medicine. [nccam.nih.gov/health/whatiscam]. Accessed June, 2005.

75. *Ibid.*

76. Wolsko, P., et al. "Insurance Coverage, Medical Conditions, and Visits to Alternative Medicine Providers." *Archives of Internal Medicine,* 162(3), 2002, 281–287. [archinte.ama-assn.org/cgi/content/abstract/162/3/281]. Accessed June, 2005.

77. "Holistic Pediatrics = Good Medicine." *Pediatrics,* 105(1), 2000, 214–218. [www.pediatrics.org/cgi/content/full/105/1/S2/214]. Accessed June, 2005.

78. Dalzell, M. D. "HMOs and Alternative Medicine." *Managed Care.* [www.managedcaremag.com/archives/9904/9904.alternative.html]. Accessed June, 2005.

79. Fontanarosa, P. B., and G. D. Lundberg. "Alternative Medicine Meets Science." *Journal of the American Medical Association,* 280(18), 1998, 1618–1619.

80. Studdert, D. M., et al. "Medical Malpractice Implications of Alternative Medicine." *Journal of the American Medical Association,* 280(18), 1998, 1611.

81. *Ibid.,* 1612.

9

Pre-Hospital Emergency Medical Services

Alice L. Epstein
Gary H. Harding

The National Association of State EMS Directors (NASEMSD) and the National Association of EMS Physicians (NAEMSP) define a medical emergency as a sudden or unanticipated medical event that requires immediate assistance; emergency medical services (EMS) as the provision of services to patients with medical emergencies; and an emergency medical services system (EMS) as a comprehensive, coordinated arrangement of resources and functions that are organized to respond in a timely, staged manner to targeted medical emergencies, regardless of their cause or the patient's ability to pay, to minimize their physical and emotional impact.

An emergency arises, lives are at stake, and time is of the essence. Who should respond, how will they know where to go, and what can they do to save the life of the injured person? Depending on where you live and work, the answer can be quite different. Lives can be saved and the number of severe injuries reduced if emergency service personnel can recognize and act upon their responsibilities in a prompt, efficient, and clinically appropriate manner. This chapter presents the organization of emergency medical services (EMS), how they vary from locale to locale, and the inherent risks in the delivery of pre-hospital emergency services. Discussion of the clinical aspects of EMS (for example, how to assess and treat cardiac pain) are beyond the scope of this chapter, except as they relate to liability and risk management. Also excluded are disaster planning and response, and exposure to hazardous materials, as they are addressed elsewhere in this series.

Emergency medical services, systems, and the personnel who work in them, with a specific emphasis on risk management, are discussed. This discussion does not purport to be exhaustive in nature about the operations of the systems. It is intended to provide sufficient background and information to familiarize risk management professionals with risk exposures associated with pre-hospital emergency medical services and systems, and with proactive tactics designed to minimize the risk associated with the practice of pre-hospital emergency services system professionals.

· · · · · · · · · · · ·

LEGAL DUTIES

Duties of pre-hospital emergency services personnel and emergency medical service systems include the obligation to ensure that personnel are trained to a standard that is consistent and has been accepted by the community. The system must be sure that it is capable of expeditious, safe response, with suitable equipment and personnel. There is no duty to provide every technology available or the highest-level of training for every crew. Instead, the standard of care that would be applicable in any related negligence case is whether or not the emergency medical provider acted as another reasonably prudent peer would have done under same or similar circumstances. This duty of "reasonable prudence" is owed to any patient that the system undertakes to treat.

Very few professional liability claims studies have been performed for EMS services. Two published studies during the 1970s and 1980s indicate very similar rates of claims filed per number of patient encounters. During the decade 1972 to 1982, Dade County Fire Rescue handled 265,060 patient encounters; sixteen claims were filed with the Risk Management Division of Dade County. The claims were produced by eleven patient encounters, which yields a rate of one per 24,096 patient encounters. The two greatest causal factors identified were inadequate recordkeeping and "gray zone" patients who do not fit any particular protocol.[1]

A retrospective review of all claims brought against a large metropolitan emergency medical services system, that focused on paramedic-patient encounters during a twelve-year period (1976–1987), revealed a similar incidence of malpractice claims. During this period, EMS units responded to approximately two million calls and transported more than one million patients. During a ten-year period (1976–1985), sixty claims occurred. The overall litigation rate was one lawsuit per 27,371 patient encounters and one lawsuit per 17,995 patient transports.[2]

In a third, more recent study, all claims made against an urban 911 ambulance service, whether or not a lawsuit resulted, were analyzed for the ten-year period ending in 1993. Eighty-two claims resulting in eleven lawsuits were filed. Motor vehicle accidents involving an ambulance produced the overwhelming majority (72 percent) of claims and 53 percent of the dollars paid out. Medical negligence claims were few, but were the next-largest cause of dollars lost (35 percent).[3]

Professional liability issues that EMS providers face include failure to obtain consent, failure to diagnose, misdiagnosis, and unnecessary delay in transport or treatment. Additional examples of successful negligence allegations include:

- Patient transportation to a medical facility without specialty care, including trauma level support, needed by the specific patient
- Failure to properly maintain equipment, supplies, or vehicles
- Driving negligently or recklessly

  Liability may also be based on theories other than negligence, including:

- Abandonment—Improper termination of medical care or turning care over to less qualified personnel, resulting in injury to the patient.

- Assault or Battery—Physical contact with a person without the person's consent or against their wishes.

- False imprisonment—Intentional detention of an individual against their wishes.

- Breach of confidentiality—Sharing medical information with those who do not have a "need to know." In this regard, it should be noted that EMS providers do have a legal responsibility to report certain medical and other personal information to government agencies. For example, cases that are usually reportable under state law include neglect or abuse of children and the elderly, rape, gunshot wounds, stab wounds, animal bites, and certain communicable diseases.

Government immunity may protect state, county, local, and other governmental entities from litigation for negligent acts of their employees. However, many states have discarded this doctrine or have limited the extent to which it applies. Good Samaritan legislation exists in some form in all fifty states. It is intended to encourage people to help other people in an emergency without fear of litigation. These laws do not generally protect health care professionals from acts of:

- Gross negligence

- Reckless disregard

- Willful or wanton misconduct

There are several theories under which liability actions can be brought against EMS providers. The risk management professional's starting point for addressing risk should be helping providers deliver care that is timely, adequate, and safe. The following sections provide more insight into EMS operations, related risk management issues, and suggested risk reduction strategies.

············

BRIEF HISTORY OF EMS SYSTEMS

Emergency medical services and systems claim their roots in military medicine. It was recognized that early intervention in wartime injury could reduce deaths and improve "soldier outcome," thereby increasing the number of troops available for war. As one of the first efforts to improve the timeliness of medical intervention, some military operations brought medical specialists to the battlefield. More recent advances include dedicated vehicular emergency medical transport, rotary- and fixed-wing air evacuation, and mobile hospitals.

The evolution of the public emergency medical service system lagged behind the military system, because of the financial and political implications, and because of the massive size of the undertaking. Before the mid-1960s, due to the lack of any national standards or motivation, emergency medical service could be excellent in one locale, while virtually non-existent in others. Structure and operations might be reasonable and logical in one, while poorly thought out and prone to failures in others. Pre-hospital emergency service providers could be highly trained professionals with dedicated equipment, or the first responder and transport to the medical facility might have been your neighbor because your neighbor's automobile was the fastest way to get a patient to the local hospital.

A 1966 National Academy of Science National Research Council publication, "Accidental Death and Disability: The Neglected Disease of Modern Society," identified the gross inadequacies in our emergency health care systems, citing diversity, lack of standards, and the lack of a systemized approach. Based on these findings and the efforts of many, including those within the emergency medical service profession, the Highway Safety Act of 1966 resulted in formation of the National Highway Traffic Safety Administration (NHTSA). NHTSA was charged with assisting others to develop their own local emergency services programs. The Emergency Medical Services Systems Act of 1973 further exposed the issue of discontinuity in EMS delivery, provided standards for planning and intervention, and allocated resources to state and local governments for the implementation of comprehensive EMS systems. This program was administered through the Health Resources and Services Administration (HRSA). The original goal emphasized improving response to adult emergencies. Pediatric emergencies received less attention. Thus when the first data were examined, adult outcomes had improved substantially, while pediatric outcomes lagged. In 1993, the Institute of Medicine (IOM) published a report entitled "Emergency Medical Services for Children" (EMSC) detailing these concerns. A flurry of Congressional activity resulted, including Public Law 98–555, as amended, which authorized the use of federal funds for EMSC. This legislation was the origin of two consecutive Five Year Plans aimed at improving emergency medical services to children.

Also in 1993, a multidisciplinary group acting on behalf of the National Highway Traffic Safety Administration (NHTSA) developed the National EMS Education and Practice Blueprint to better define the levels of training required for emergency services providers. The goals of the document were to delineate required education and experience, and scopes of practice for EMS providers across the country. The Blueprint also set out a framework for future curriculum development projects and a strategy to address reciprocity concerns.

Aside from periodic governmental studies, there has never been a centralized federal effort to promote comprehensive emergency medical system planning and development. Federal legislation has instead focused on issues specific to EMS systems, such as the use of automatic emergency defibrillators (AEDs). The growth and direction of emergency medical services has been left, for the most part, to individual states and health care providers' professional organizations.

....

EMS STRUCTURE AND ORGANIZATION

As there is no central coordinating authority that enjoys jurisdiction in all locales, one could rightly assume that there are countless numbers of EMS structures in place throughout the country. There are differing opinions among health care organizations, emergency services providers, and communities on several issues, including the most appropriate sponsor of pre-hospital services, for example, whether emergency services should function under the auspices of a medical facility, a fire service, or as a volunteer organization. Similarly there is no definitive response to the question of which personnel may work within and direct EMS, what equipment to use in EMS, and what protocols should guide EMS operations. There are even multiple clinical approaches for the same injury or illness.

Certain issues are agreed upon, however. One is that providing emergency medical services requires coordination among emergency medicine providers, public health and safety agencies, and medical facilities. Another is that, regardless of the structure of the system, the response must meet the need. One of several organizational approaches that might be in place is a statewide entity responsible for many local EMS systems, including dispatchers, pre-hospital emergency care providers (ground and perhaps air), and base station operations. Other approaches include systems manned by volunteer personnel and privately held EMS companies. A comprehensive organizational chart of the current EMS structure is a valuable tool for emergency services administrators, which can also assist the risk management professional to better understand accountability, and thus the potential exposure for various parties.

············

EMS RESPONSE

In general, public health needs, from the occurrence of the emergent injury or illness through treatment and final disposition, can be met if the following stages of a comprehensive response system are in place.

Prevention

When possible, steps are taken to reduce the likelihood of emergent injury or illness from occurring. Examples may include public education emphasizing electrical safety in the home, poison and drug childproofing, the importance of routine physical exams, and so on.

Detection

Most emergent injuries and illnesses that require pre-hospital emergency medical services are detected by lay persons at or near the scene of occurrence.

Notification

Once detected, many locations, although not all, now have access to a local 911 service. In some locales, there is still the need to notify the law enforcement department dispatcher who, in turn, notifies the ambulance crew. A majority of calls are from lay people, perhaps the individual detecting the injury or illness, or a bystander, who is directed to: "Get an ambulance! Get help! Call 911!"

Dispatch

Although some emergency calls are found later not to be emergencies that require hospital services, reasonable prudence dictates that EMS dispatch a team to assess, treat, and transport the patient, if necessary. Recognize that the dispatcher may call for a ground or air response, or both.

Pre-arrival

It always takes time for the emergency team to arrive on the scene. Hence, the dispatcher has a secondary responsibility to provide immediate assistance to the caller and, if applicable, the first responder and any willing bystanders, concerning the actions they can take to respond to the injury or illness. These steps include support for the patient, and emotional and crisis control support for the bystander volunteers.

On-Scene

Once the pre-hospital emergency response team arrives, they assess and provide treatment to stabilize the patient, if possible, in consultation with more experienced and higher trained medical professionals who might be available on the scene or via communication systems. The initial assessment is an opportunity to validate which facility the patient should be taken to, and might result in a decision to take the patient to a more acute setting.

Transport and Facility Notification

Primary responsibilities during transport are to maintain patient stabilization, respond to new emergent problems, and as rapidly as practicable get the patient to a higher level of treatment capability. The team might or might not be in contact with the receiving facility during transport, depending upon the locale and situation. The team might have contacted the receiving hospital earlier, while they were enroute to the scene. Or, the responsibility for contacting the receiving caregivers might have been assumed by other members of the EMS team, such as the dispatcher or medical control representative.

Emergency Department

Once the transport vehicle arrives at the receiving facility, treatment is most often initiated within the ED, although prior communication should have alerted the facility to the need for immediate surgery or other treatment (for example, hyperbaric therapy for a dive injury) not typically available in the ED.

Interfacility Transport, Critical Care, Inpatient Care, Rehabilitation and Discharge, and Follow-Up

With admission to the ED, and documentation by EMS representatives who participated in the care of the patient, the role of EMS comes to an end, with two exceptions. If the patient requires interfacility transfer, the providers who brought in the patient might well be the ones to make the transfer. Also, EMS follow-up to determine the effectiveness of care, through quality improvement monitoring, may entail review of the patient's course during hospital care, rehabilitation, discharge, and follow-up.

The remaining sections of this chapter will deal primarily with the risks inherent in EMS processes from notification through transport. Also addressed will be risk-prone aspects of EMS care, such as consent, management of medical equipment, and staffing.

············

FEDERAL GUIDELINES

As previously noted, there is no centralized federal authority that dictates all aspects of emergency medical service systems. However, the following federal agencies do provide important resources or might affect EMS in other ways.

- Centers for Disease Control and Prevention (CDC)—The CDC is responsible for addressing, among other issues, communicable diseases and their treatment. The CDC often provides information and guidance about emerging infectious diseases, nosocomial infections, and blood-borne pathogens, such as hepatitis A, B, and C).[4]

- Food and Drug Administration (FDA)—The FDA has several subsidiaries that may affect the EMS. Through its Center for Devices and Radiological Health (CDRH), the FDA regulates medical devices, their manufacturers, and users. These devices range in complexity from very simple items such as bandages and gloves to defibrillators, transport incubators, and even ambulances. Further, CDRH has the authority to require manufacturers and users alike to report medical device-related incidents to the FDA under the Safe Medical Device Act (SMDA) through the MedWatch FDA Safety Information and Adverse Event Reporting Program.[5] Health care professionals can research the MedWatch database for information about a particular medical device manufacturer, type of device, or even a specific type of event.[6]

- Occupational Safety and Health Administration (OSHA)—OSHA has primary responsibility for regulating the employer's responsibility for safety of the workplace. OSHA often operates under its general duty clause, which requires the employer to provide a safe workplace. This allows OSHA representatives broad leeway to determine what practices are unsafe, making it possible for them to perform on-site, unannounced audits of the workplace. Specific areas overseen by OSHA and relating to EMS may include bloodborne pathogens,[7] ergonomic practices,[8] and emergency response in the workplace.[9] Note that the regulations of state organizations, which are the equivalent of OSHA, such as CalOSHA, and may be proscriptive, may take precedence over federal guidelines.

- Health Resources and Services Administration (HRSA)—HRSA has responsibility for key programs such as HIV/AIDS Services, Ryan White CARE Act, Primary Health Care, Health Professions, Special Programs, and Rural Health Policy. Guidance documents provided by this agency, such as "Integrating EMS Into Rural Health Systems,"[10] provide valuable resources[11] for EMS providers.

- National Institutes of Health (NIH)—The NIH is the steward of medical and behavioral research for the nation. NIH publications such as "Research on Emergency Medical Services for Children,"[12] and the extensive information available under NIH auspices through the National Library of Medicine, online, are invaluable to all health care professionals, including EMS providers.[13]

- Federal Emergency Management Agency (FEMA)—FEMA is an independent agency that reports to the president. The charge of FEMA is to plan for, respond to, and assist in recovery from disaster. Most often FEMA is responsible for mitigating the impact of catastrophes like the series of hurricanes experienced by the United States in 2005. An example of the proactive role of FEMA is the requirement that state and local off-site response organizations demonstrate their ability to address potentially injured members of the public, who might have been contaminated, through annual drills. The authority under which such exercises are carried out is found in FEMA regulations at NUREG-0654/FEMA-REP-1, Rev 1.[14]

- Department of Transportation (DOT)—This agency participates in the development of the curricula by which the EMT is certified and recertified.

- Health and Human Services (HHS), Centers for Medicare and Medicaid Services (CMS)— One particular matter under CMS purview, which recently received attention, is the responsibility to alert the public to the potential for fraud by ambulance companies. In a fraud flyer intended to help beneficiaries recognize fraudulent practices in the Medicare program, CMS advised beneficiaries to be suspicious of ambulance companies that bill for trips that are not emergency in nature. CMS subsequently recognized that the statement was misleading and published the following revised statement: "Non-emergency ambulance services are covered by the Medicare program when reasonable and necessary."[15]

Other federal government agencies, such as the Environmental Protection Agency (EPA) and the National Institute of Occupational Safety and Health (NIOSH), are responsible for resources relevant to EMS. For example, NIOSH is responsible for the requirement that all health care organizations have available Material Safety Data Sheets (MSDS) to make employees aware of how to safely handle hazardous materials. NIOSH also provides guidance on selection of sharps waste disposal units.

State Requirements

The definition of basic emergency medical services, and associated requirements, varies among the states. Also variable are state approaches to clinical issues such as the use of automatic external defibrillators (AEDs).[16] This chapter will not explore the various state regulations.

What does Mich. have?

············

ACCREDITATION

Although many EMS organizations have not sought voluntary accreditation of services available from private organizations, they should consider the standards of such organizations as the basis for their own audit. Such self-evaluation can be extremely helpful to risk reduction and can enhance quality improvement efforts.

are ours accredited?

An example of an acceptable accreditation process, which can assist EMS systems in assessing practice, is found in the standards of The Commission on Accreditation of Ambulance Services (CAAS), an organization which was originally developed by the American Ambulance Association. The accreditation process includes a comprehensive self-assessment and an independent outside review of the EMS organization. CAAS standards address risk issues such as vehicle maintenance, management of employees, disposition of the patient's personal property, key aspects of clinical care, incident reporting, and loss control. The process emphasizes the importance of coordination among public safety agencies and local EMS providers as a key factor in providing high-quality health care. For example, standards evaluate the effectiveness of operation among agencies during a disaster. Important principles addressed in this regard are conflict resolution and interagency dialogue.

Human resource practices recognized by CAAS to be critical to success of EMS organizations include credentialing, discipline or corrective action, problem resolution, training, and performance evaluations.

The Commission on Accreditation of Medical Transport Systems (CAMTS) was founded by a group of air medical professionals, to promote high-quality medical air transport. The commission offers air ambulance providers the opportunity to have their program assessed by a private outside organization, to determine compliance with nationally accepted accreditation standards. Several states, including Michigan, Arizona, and New Mexico, accept CAMTS accreditation in lieu of state licensing of the air ambulance operation.

············

STAFFING

Staffing volume, training requirements, and infrastructure vary dramatically, in keeping with the many forms of EMS structure discussed earlier. However, there are several key positions found in most EMS operations, including the medical director, emergency medical response professionals, dispatch team, and base station staff.

Medical Director Responsibilities

Organization and provision of emergency medical services requires the participation of physicians, although EMS systems do not routinely use physicians on ambulance staffs to provide pre-hospital emergency medical care. Every pre-hospital service provider should designate a physician medical director. The primary responsibility of this position is to ensure quality of patient care by directing the design, operation, evaluation, and any necessary modification of system processes such as notification, dispatch, pre-hospital care, and transport to the emergency department.

The medical director should oversee all clinical features of the EMS. To accomplish this, the medical director must have a defined position within the EMS system, which encompasses the responsibility to oversee development of medical policies and procedures. The position description should also articulate the medical director's responsibility and authority to address any deviation from established clinical standards of care, or compliance with required training standards of those under the medical director's supervision.

On a day-to-day basis, medical direction of pre-hospital emergency care involves developing and overseeing prospective and retrospective approaches that meet accepted standards, in addition to support of pre-hospital providers at the scene or by voice communication or on-line support. Key prospective approaches that should be overseen by the medical director include training, testing, and certification of providers, and development of protocols, policies, and procedures. Day-to-day support of these efforts can be provided by the medical director or by others, such as emergency department physicians or nurses, under the direction of the medical director. Examples of important retrospective approaches include medical audit and review of care, direction of remedial education, and changes in clinical procedures to address any negative clinical outcomes. Various aspects of these approaches can be handled by committees functioning under the medical director, with representation from applicable medical and EMS personnel.

Medical directors should have a license to practice medicine or osteopathy and experience in emergency medicine or pre-hospital emergency care of the acutely ill or injured patient. Board certification in emergency medicine is optimal. They should be familiar with the design and operation of pre-hospital EMS systems. Other advantageous experience includes training in medical direction of pre-hospital emergency units. It is essential to have experience or training in the instruction of pre-hospital personnel and in the EMS quality improvement process; knowledge of EMS-related laws and regulations; dispatch and communications, and local mass casualty and disaster plans. Also important is experience or training in labor relations, management, and fiscal oversight of health care organizations.

The National Association of EMS Physicians (NAEMSP) indicates that the medical director should oversee dispatch training and protocols, including:

- The level of medical training of call-takers and dispatchers
- Caller inquiry protocols
- Pre-arrival patient care instructions
- Ranking of call priority and triage according to potential medical significance of the patient complaint
- Criteria for dispatch of first responders, basic life support (BLS), and advanced life support (ALS) personnel

- Criteria for emergency and non-emergency response
- Criteria for implementation of the disaster or multiple casualty plan
- Procedures for reviewing and updating dispatch protocols
- Qualified direct (online) medical direction and implementation and evaluation of related protocols
- Development and implementation of a system for critical incident stress management

The medical director should also oversee field clinical practice, including medical training and credentialing of out-of-hospital personnel and periodic testing to verify skill proficiency. Protocols should be developed for transport and non-transport personnel. They should include criteria to help determine destination and transport methods. Such protocols should also address patient-initiated refusals and patient safety.

The medical director should oversee the development of medical standards that promote higher levels of patient care quality. This is the reason the oversight responsibility must include authority to limit the medical activities of patient care providers who deviate from established clinical standards of practice or do not meet training standards. In addition, the medical director should oversee staff education, including requirements for initial training and continuing education. Also important are medical competency evaluations for pre-hospital providers, to ensure that an adequate knowledge base and skill proficiencies are maintained.

The medical director should demonstrate leadership, by establishing standards for on-line medical direction including requirements for field experience on the part of the physicians who provide online support, and training of others to whom the authority for medical direction may be delegated, such as RNs and other dependent allied health personnel. Also important is the education of all base station personnel concerning their specific responsibilities to support online medical direction.

Although all of the above parameters are important and desirable, note that there is no specialty certification by the American Board of Medical Specialties for EMS medical directors. Moreover, not all EMS systems even have a medical director.

Pre-Hospital Emergency Medical Care Personnel

The ambulance staff is responsible for delivery of all emergency care from the time they first see the victim through transportation and transfer to the care of a physician. These positions may be staffed by employees or volunteers. In Public Law 105–19, the Volunteer Protection Act of 1997, certain protections were established for volunteers, nonprofit organizations, and governmental entities from lawsuits based on the activities of volunteers. For example, protection is provided from litigation relating to harm caused by an act or omission of volunteers, if the volunteers were acting within the scope of their responsibilities, and were properly licensed, certified, or authorized to practice in the state in which the harm occurred. To qualify for this protection, it is also essential that harm must not have occurred as the result of willful or criminal misconduct, gross negligence, reckless misconduct, or a conscious, flagrant indifference to the rights or safety of the individual. In addition to becoming knowledgeable about this act, risk management professionals should refer to state-specific Good Samaritan laws.

The skills needed by pre-hospital emergency personnel vary widely. Recognize that the need which requires emergency response can range from an uncomplicated fall by an elderly person to mass and severe casualties from a large catastrophe. Pre-hospital personnel must be able to appraise the extent of the injury and carry out whatever additional measures will make it safe to move the victim and minimize morbidity and mortality. They must operate the emergency transport vehicle safely and efficiently, and maintain communication among personnel at the scene of the emergency, dispatch, and the ED. They must render additional emergency care enroute while transmitting additional information to the physician. In some situations, the role of the pre-hospital provider is filled by a first responder (someone with forty hours of training) who is capable of handling certain minor needs. However, other pre-hospital medical emergencies are handled on-scene by highly trained, highly specialized nurses and physicians. Discussion of the clinical training for physicians, except for the medical director and online medical control, is beyond the scope of this chapter. However, the following provides additional information about the role and training of typical pre-hospital emergency medical providers.

The job titles, training, and experience of pre-hospital emergency providers vary from state to state. Typical titles and certifications include First Responder, Emergency Medical Technician—Basic, Emergency Medical Technician—Intermediate, and Emergency Medical Technician—Paramedic. Additional certifications available from the American Heart Association include Basic Life Support (BLS), Pediatric Advanced Life Support (PALS), Advanced Cardiac Life Support (ACLS), and others. This list of designations represents progressively higher levels of training in CPR and advanced life support. Although there is a National Registry of Emergency Medical Technicians, there is no national requirement that personnel on the pre-hospital emergency medical provider team have one or more of these designations. Yet most states do require one or a combination of them.[17] The National Fire Protection Agency (NFPA) has developed two voluntary standards—NFPA 1710—Standards for the Organization and Deployment of Fire Suppression Operations, Emergency Medical Operations, and Special Operations to the Public by Career Fire Departments and 1720—Standard for the Organization and Deployment of Fire Suppression Operations, Emergency Medical Operations and Special Operations to the Public by Volunteer Fire Departments. The NFPA does not have regulatory authority, but many communities use NFPA standards as the basis for building code and other public safety standards. Municipalities may also mandate compliance with NFPA codes related to response times and staffing, which may influence a jury's determination of whether the standard of care was met in a related negligence case. Key NFPA provisions require two EMT–Basics courses for providers responding to BLS incidents and two EMT–Paramedics for ALS incidents. NFPA 1710 requires a response time of four minutes (240 seconds) for first responder arrival and eight minutes (480 seconds) for ALS unit arrival. Departments are to achieve this with 90-percent reliability. Departments must evaluate compliance with the standard annually and address geography within the jurisdiction as they consider how to meet the objective. A quality management program is required, which must include review of response times and other clinical care issues.

There are state-specific requirements for certification of each level of provider. Certification requires successful completion of a state-approved training program in addition to passing a written and practical examination.[18] Many states require recertification, which may include an examination or evidence of continuing medical education. Often, states do not have reciprocal agreements for paramedic certification. For example, a paramedic certified in Florida does not have reciprocity in Arizona. The paramedic must take an Arizona refresher course before receiving an Arizona certification.

Basic recommendations for the development of training programs for pre-hospital emergency response team members include the following: State requirements are of course a starting point. Didactic training, combined with development of skills, based on actual clinical performance, is a highly effective way to achieve regulatory compliance. Didactic training should be considered for clinical aspects of care such as anatomy and physiology; trauma types, systems, and mechanism of injury; hemorrhage and shock; burns; clinical specialty issues (such as pulmonary, cardiology, obstetrics); airway management and ventilation; environmental conditions; infectious and communicable diseases; and behavioral and psychiatric disorders. Also important to include in a training program is education that addresses such topics as illness and injury prevention, medical and legal issues, therapeutic communication, history-taking, techniques of physical examination, patient assessment, clinical decision making, communication, documentation, ambulance operations, medical incident command, rescue awareness and operations, hazardous materials incidents, and crime scene awareness.

Practical skills training should include skills important to the provision of pre-hospital emergency care, such as ventilatory support, CPR, peripheral venous cannulation, cardiac monitoring, bleeding management, bandaging, defibrillation and cardioversion, spinal immobilization, patient extrication devices, splinting and traction, and medication administration. Clinical training in the hospital and the field is recommended. The aim is to develop entry-level competence in psychomotor skills and enable the trainee to apply skills and knowledge to actual patient situations. Trainees should log adequate patient contact experience to serve as a basis for future clinical decision making, and should demonstrate to educators their ability to perform key procedures, including safe medication administration and effective physical assessments, on several types of patients.

A special issue for pre-hospital emergency providers is the need to be aware of what action they should take, if a medical device might have contributed to a patient injury or death. To the extent practicable, equipment should not be touched. It may be removed from the patient if it continues to present a hazard (such as an electrical shock), but it should not be turned off and settings should not be changed unless it is necessary to do so. EMS pre-hospital providers should be cautioned that they are not experts on device performance and malfunction, and that they should avoid any use or handling of the equipment that might destroy evidence. The best approach is to sequester the equipment, that is, set it aside in a secure place, until it can be assessed by biomedical professionals and tag the equipment or device so that it is not inadvertently reused. If it is necessary to turn the device off, the operator should document observations such as all settings, measurements on displays, condition, and so on.

Emergency Medical Dispatch[19]

Efficient emergency medical dispatching is critical to the proper operation of the pre-hospital emergency medical system. The first communication of an emergent situation from a lay person at, or close to, the location of the incident typically is routed to an emergency medical dispatch center. The emergency medical dispatcher (EMD) who takes the call has the daunting task of obtaining key information about the emergency from a potentially hysterical lay person untrained in medicine, determining personnel and vehicular resources to dedicate to the emergency, and providing instructions to the caller concerning treatment and life support that can be provided before the arrival of the EMS professionals. The dispatcher must be able to:

- Identify the true nature and the urgency of the emergency in a manner that facilitates selection of the best response
- Understand the philosophy and psychology of interview techniques and telephone interventions, and use lay terminology to acquire a favorable response

Such abilities help preserve lives and prevent further injury. Without these skills, too few resources might be dispatched for major problems, or excessive resources might be mobilized for minor problems, potentially depriving others in need. Training, certification, and recertification of personnel in dispatch life support (DLS) should be required.

Emergency medical dispatch tools include use of predetermined questions, pre-arrival telephone instructions, and pre-assigned response levels and modes, all of which should be approved by the medical director. With these tools, the EMD obtains a telephone history and dictates emergency medical care, including instructions to lay persons on the scene. The EMD can also eliminate gaps that might otherwise occur between the time of the call and initiation of treatment upon EMS team arrival. Telephone instructions based on pre-approved medical protocols, provided by the EMD to the caller, can help protect the patient from further harm and initiate life-saving treatment.

Dispatch prioritization must reflect the appropriate level of response including personnel (First Responder, BLS, ALS), transport resources (number, type of vehicles), and mode of response (lights, siren). Poor dispatch decisions place patients at unnecessary risk and can result in significant liability. However, through use of standard protocols, the EMD can reduce exposure.

All medical care policies and procedures used by the medical dispatch center must be developed in conjunction with, and be reviewed and approved by, the medical director of the system. Routine medical review of dispatch center operations should be performed. Dispatch review committees should provide quality assurance oversight and, ideally, include pre-hospital EMS physicians, medical control, dispatch supervision and management personnel, dispatchers, and EMTs. Liability for dispatch centers commonly results from lack of essential skills, such as ability to operate and troubleshoot complex communication equipment, and to effectively use basic radio and telephone communication techniques.

Base Station Operations—Medical Control Resource

Emergency medical systems base station operations typically are housed within a hospital, often in the ED. The base station role in the emergency medical system is to provide medical control, consultation, and oversight to field personnel. When the emergency field personnel are non-physician health care professionals, direction of their assessment and treatment efforts must be provided by a physician. Ultimate responsibility for medical control rests with the medical director, who may delegate authority to surrogates (physicians, nurses, or others) on duty in the emergency department. The medical director may be online, which can mean either on the scene or available by voice communication (such as radio, telephone). However, it is common for the medical director to be offline (because of other duties or merely because there are twenty-four working hours in the day), that it is usual practice to identify an "online medical physician," who might not be the medical director.

Protocols should address the potential for other parties (such as the patient's personal physician or a physician bystander) to be present at the scene. Whereas reasonable prudence dictates that control of medical care at the scene be the responsibility of the individual who is most knowledgeable about pre-hospital emergency stabilization and transport, the patient's personal physician may assume responsibility, as long as that physician's orders do not conflict with established EMS protocols. If there is a conflict, the personal physician should be placed in direct contact with the online medical physician. Pre-hospital emergency providers do not have authority to displace the personal physician. If the online medical physician and the personal physician cannot agree on treatment, the personal physician has the option of assuming responsibility, and accompanying the patient to the hospital. The personal physician may also defer care to the online medical physician.

If there is an intervener (bystander) physician on the scene and willing to assume responsibility and document acceptable care, and the online medical physician is not available, the pre-hospital emergency provider should defer to the intervener physician even if the intervener's care differs from the local protocol. If the online medical physician is available, the online physician has the option of managing the case entirely. Policies must address the respective responsibilities for EMS personnel and bystander physicians, concerning transport arrangements, for example, ground or air emergency service transfer, interfacility transfer, and so on. A coordinated effort is clearly essential to patient welfare, and disagreements about appropriate disposition of the patient can result in liability for all parties, including the medical director(s).

Under the guidance of the medical director, the base station provides centralized control of EMS medical resources. The director and base station personnel have an ongoing responsibility to ensure adequate staffing by skilled competent personnel. For example, all authorities recognize that online medical control must be immediately available twenty-four hours a day. To achieve this goal, organizations may designate physicians, specially trained nurses, or physician's assistants with special training to be responsible for online medical control. It is important to consult state requirements and professional organization requirements in determining which personnel may take on this important role. The online professional is responsible for reviewing and approving all care delivered and for signing the medical record generated for the specific patient.

Other requirements for base station personnel include completion of adequate medical and procedural training, including field experience, which should be routinely refreshed and knowledge of the scope of practice for different types of pre-hospital emergency services providers. Base station performance reviews should be documented on an annual basis and personnel should participate in routine reviews of ambulance runs. Criteria for such reviews should include timeliness of response, effectiveness of transport, and outcome of response.

It does not follow that, because a base station is located in a particular hospital, patients should be transported to that facility. Patient welfare or logistical issues may result in conveyance to another medical facility. Also recognize that the structure, services, and authorities in one base station's operation might differ significantly from another's. For example, one base station might use only physicians in the online role, while another might use other professionals. Or, one base station might offer services such as real-time telemetry monitoring while others might offer a lower level of technical support. Still other operational differences include the way in which quality improvement activities are conducted: One base station might house all such review activities, while another might use a system-wide approach.

Base station-related liability issues range from clinical decision making to staffing to consent issues to inability to maintain communications. If voice or telemetry communication cannot be initiated or maintained due to equipment performance or shortcomings of architectural design, and these failures could have been prevented, the potential for liability is high.

AMBULANCE DIVERSION

There might be occasions when an ambulance must be diverted from what is ostensibly the nearest, most suitable medical facility to a facility that is farther away. This might occur when there is a specific patient or physician request, or when triage directs a patient with special needs to a facility that provides a specialized or higher level of care. Another important circumstance that results in redirection of patients is when a hospital goes on "diversion" because the emergency department cannot handle current patient volume.

ED diversion due to temporary inability to handle the needs of new patients has increased in frequency.[20] Typically, diversion occurs in large urban areas, but it can occur in rural areas due to a lack of available, adequately trained staff. The negative effects of diversion are many. They include an unacceptably prolonged transport time, necessitating out-of-hospital care when hospital resources are clearly needed, and seriously diminished availability of ambulances in the community. Another concern is that EMS personnel, under such circumstances, might feel forced to take on procedures they are not properly trained for.

Other factors that increase the frequency of diversion include overcrowded emergency departments due to increased use of the ED for other than emergency care, hospital bed shortages, staff shortages, increasing in-patient severity, hospital closures, and the difficulty of placing patients in nursing homes and skilled nursing facilities. Diversion also occurs because of temporary or long-term lack of available medical specialists, space, technology, or critical care beds. Managed care programs have in the past designated specific hospitals for emergency care. However, the Emergency Medical Treatment and Labor Act (EMTALA) dictates that, in an emergent situation, the patient should be taken to the nearest hospital with appropriate services for the emergency.

With the 2003 revisions to the EMTALA final rule, it is important to note that "an individual has come to the emergency department if that individual is in a ground or air ambulance owned and operated by the hospital, even if that ambulance is not on hospital property" or "if they are in an air or ground ambulance on hospital property, even if the ambulance is not owned by the hospital." However, the revised rule further notes that if "an ambulance that is not owned by the hospital is off hospital property and contacts the hospital stating that they want to bring the individual in for emergency treatment, the hospital is allowed to direct the ambulance to another facility if it is in diversionary status."[21]

According to the American College of Emergency Physicians (ACEP), each EMS system, including all of its component agencies, must develop a cooperative diversion policy designed to:

- Identify situations in which a hospital's resources are not available and temporary ambulance diversion is required.

- Notify the EMS system and hospital personnel of such occurrences. This notification must be communicated to the lead EMS agency or a designated communications coordination center.

- Regularly review and update the hospital's diversion status.

- Provide for the safe, appropriate, and timely care of patients who continue to enter the EMS system during periods of diversion.

- Notify EMS system personnel and affected hospitals promptly when the situation that caused diversion has been resolved.

- Explore solutions to address the causes of diversion and implement policies that minimize the need for diversions.

- Continuously review policies and guidelines governing diversion.

ACEP also requires that diversion policies require all hospitals and EMS agencies in the EMS system to have working agreements among themselves. Diversion criteria must be based on the defined capacities or services of the individual hospital. When the entire health care system is overloaded, all hospitals must open. Diversion should occur only after the hospital has exhausted all internal mechanisms to avert a diversion, and this includes calling in overtime staff. Hospital diversions should not be based on financial decisions. Hospitals should not go on diversion status to save beds for either elective admissions or potential deterioration of hospitalized patients.[22]

The decision to go on diversion should be made by the emergency physician in the ED, in consultation with the hospital's administration, including nursing managers. Appropriate EMS representatives should be notified as soon as possible of the diversion status. All personnel with diversion decision power must be identified and titles prospectively communicated to the EMS system's lead agency.

When on diversion, hospitals must make every attempt to maximize bed space, screen elective admissions, and use all available personnel and facility resources to minimize the length of time on diversion. A record of the diversion should be maintained by the hospital concerning disposition of each affected patient. This log should record the type of diversion, and the reason for it, and should include the appropriate approval. Also documented must be the time that the diversion was initiated and terminated. All patient-specific diversions must undergo concurrent physician review for clinical appropriateness.

············
DESTINATION PROTOCOLS

Destination protocols should be developed to assist EMS providers in the triage of all prehospital emergency patients. These protocols should provide direction to EMS personnel on the following issues: proper use of triage checklists; instructions, including usual dosage, frequency, route, and contraindications for medication administration; circumstances mandating online medical direction; and how to resolve any conflict between the patients' hospital preferences, physician relationships, and the proposed destination facility.

All community and regional EMS agencies should be integrally involved in destination protocol development and review. Due to the varied approaches among EMS services nationally, a single protocol is not suitable for all communities and regions. However, every community and regional protocol should reflect current ability of the receiving facilities to deliver routine and specialty care, and information on the hours that these services are available. The National Heart Attack Alert Program (NHAAP)[23] recommends that receiving facilities be categorized in a fashion similar to that used for trauma patient destination decisions. For example, receiving facilities should be classified into one of three levels of care, for example, tertiary, secondary, and primary, and by medical specialty, such as cardiac, trauma, or burn.

In those regions where timely transport to secondary or tertiary care facilities is not available, the highest level of care should be sought and specifics formalized in regional protocols. Acceptable EMS diversion practices should also be strictly defined in regional protocols. As previously mentioned, such protocols should also address issues associated with patient preference.

············

AIR AMBULANCE SERVICES

Transportation of critical patients can be a formidable task. Problems that affect patient outcome negatively include long transport times, distances to facilities, or transport of patients from inaccessible areas. Often the clinical situation, or the logistics associated with location, dictate consideration of air medical services. The National Association of EMS Pilots (NAEMSP) has identified both clinical and operational situations in which air medical services may provide the fastest, most direct transport to an appropriate regional trauma center. Examples of clinical situations in which air transport may be desirable include: a trauma score[24] less than twelve, a Glasgow coma score[25] less than ten, spinal cord injury or paralysis of an extremity, major burns, two or more long bone fractures, near drowning, serious trauma to a patient less than twelve or more than fifty-five years of age, and so on.[26] More recently these guidelines have been broadened to include non-trauma and certain pediatric conditions. Three operational situations identified include mechanism of injury (for example, a vehicle striking a pedestrian at greater than ten miles per hour), difficult access situations (such as wilderness rescue), and time and distance factors (for example, transport time to local hospital by ground greater than transport time to trauma center by helicopter).

FAA data shows that the majority of accidents involving air medical transport occur in mountainous regions and are commonly associated with air rescue operations. One professional association provides the following four categories of air rescue accidents:

- Aircraft accidents
- Operator error (including "rescue fever")
- Equipment failure
- Mother Nature[27]

However, guidelines cannot anticipate all of the clinical or operational circumstances under which air medical dispatch might be useful. The local emergency dispatch team members are likely to be in the best position to determine need because they are familiar with the incident and available regional resources. EMS providers and dispatchers should be specifically trained on the operations and respective value of ground and air transport services in their locale, so that a timely decision can be made about which to use in a particular situation. For example, stable patients who are ground accessible are probably best transported by ground emergency medical vehicles, whereas patients with injuries and unstable vital signs require the fastest, most direct route to a regional trauma center.

Emergency medical services directors, and other physicians and administrators should participate in the development of local criteria to facilitate the use of air medical transport resources. Pre-hospital emergency personnel, law enforcement, fire and rescue personnel, and agencies of jurisdiction over public-use lands should use these criteria to help them determine quickly whether to contact their local emergency medical dispatch team or an air medical service in a specific situation.

As of January 1, 2005, Medicare formalized guidelines for CMS surveyors to help them determine the appropriateness of rural air ambulance services. The determination of appropriateness includes whether the decision to transport was "reasonably made and whether the transport was made pursuant to an approved protocol, or whether the transport was inconsistent with an approved protocol." The "reasonable and necessary requirement" for rural air transport is met when such services are requested by a physician or other qualified medical personnel, based on a reasonable determination that the patient's condition would be compromised if the time to transport by land poses a threat to the patient's survival or endangers health. Other resources to facilitate determination about the reasonableness of transport include any already existing state or regional emergency medical services agency protocols.[28]

Specific equipment that has been identified as essential to air medical transport includes: oxygen (liquid, internal, external); a monitor, defibrillator, and pacer; an end-tidal CO_2 monitor; pulse oximeter; automated blood pressure monitors or doppler; ventilators; intravenous (IV) pumps; neonatal isolettes; and balloon pumps. Special considerations include the effect of altitude on hypoxia, liquid and gas interfaces, temperature and humidity on medical equipment, noise and vibration, and acceleration or deceleration forces.

Governmental regulations that apply to air transport include the following. The Federal Aviation Administration (FAA) 135 Air Carrier Certificate is issued for air ambulance operations. It outlines the specific operation standards that an aircraft owner must meet. It is not a federal requirement, however, and many air ambulance operators do not hold this certificate. Some states, such as Florida, issue a state air ambulance license after the provider has completed an on-site inspection. This demonstrates the provider's ability to meet local air medical standards.

Important resources on effective air transport from pertinent professional organizations include the following. The Association of Air Medical Services (AAMS) has developed standards related to basic, advanced, and instructor-level air medical crew training, and the National Flight Paramedics Association (NFPA) offers a national certification for flight paramedics. The Air and Surface Transport Nurses Association (ASTNA) also provides more detailed guidance on the role of the ground and flight nurse in pre-hospital transport, and this organization hosts an incident and accident reporting database for air medical services. Other air transport-related resource organizations can be found in the suggested Web sites at the end of this chapter.

Special Issues Applicable to Air and Ground Transport

Both ground and air transport of pediatric patients has received special attention in professional organization statements. The American Academy of Pediatrics Section on Transport Medicine recently published the second edition of *Guidelines for Air and Ground Transport of Neonatal and Pediatric Patients*. A pediatric transport newsletter entitled "Transport Dispatch" is published three to four times per year for the section members.

Legal and ethical issues that might need to be addressed by policy and procedure for both ground and air transport include: a) refusal to transport, b) termination of resuscitation during transport, c) licensure when crossing state lines, d) medical direction at the scene, and e) flight prioritization of air ambulance runs.

············

RISK OF VEHICULAR EMERGENCY RESPONSE

The vehicle operator has the responsibility to safely and rapidly deliver the pre-hospital emergency team to the scene and the patient and team to the receiving facility. At the same time, the operator must not jeopardize other drivers or pedestrians. Historically, there has been a high correlation between poor driving records and accident occurrence.

Hence, motor vehicle reports (MVRs) should be reviewed prior to employment and, preferably, on all drivers annually. Some organizations may require timely reporting by employees of moving violations, and so on, that are incurred while driving a personal vehicle. Driving-specific reference checks and a "hands-on" demonstration of skills behind the wheel may also be helpful. Pre-employment physicals and drug testing may also yield driving exposure-related insight.

Lights and sirens have been used to alert other vehicles and pedestrians of an emergency vehicle response for more than fifty years. Unfortunately, medical emergency response vehicles, using lights and sirens, have often been involved in collisions that resulted in serious injury and even death. Financial risk of emergency medical vehicle collisions include costs associated with damage to property, for example, involved vehicles and structures, in addition to settlements and awards for personal injury. Of course such expenditures trigger concomitant increases in insurance premiums. Collisions are the largest source of negligence-related losses.[29] Currently, there is no centralized, systematic collection of EMS collision information. For this reason, the extent of the problem may be under-appreciated.

The relationship between patient outcomes and the use of lights and sirens has not been examined. However, it is likely that emergency providers' urgency to reach a patient who may be seriously ill—and whom they know little about—plays a major role in the decision to use lights and sirens.

The National Association of EMS Physicians and the National Association of EMS Directors have stated that use of lights and sirens should be based on standard protocols, which address the acuity of the patient's situation, and on other issues such as traffic-related factors. Clinical situations in which lights and sirens are generally considered acceptable include cardiac or respiratory distress, severe airway issues, drowning, breech childbirth, electrocution, or critical trauma. It is important that the use of lights and sirens be monitored. Their improper use, such as during routine return to stations, should be identified and steps should be taken to minimize the likelihood of recurrence. The medical director should direct efforts to collect information about light and siren use, evaluate the frequency of use in the field, and take steps to reduce this practice wherever possible. By evaluating the way that dispatch currently prioritizes the need for lights and sirens, against the clinical circumstances being responded to, it might be possible to set up specific criteria for use of this approach. ASTM's Standard F1258—Standard Practice for Emergency Medical Dispatch,[30] cautions emergency medical dispatch personnel against using previous personal experience to determine the severity of a current situation, and notes that red lights and sirens are not always necessary. Of course, responses to non-emergent situations or emergent situations that are already stabilized at the scene do not require lights and sirens. Potential operators should be screened to ensure that they have adequate training in this area and no record of improper use of lights and sirens.

Remember that the operator of an EMS vehicle is not generally relieved of the responsibility to operate it with due care for the general public, including others on the highway. Vehicular manslaughter charges and convictions can and do occur, as have related civil cases. One proactive loss prevention strategy is to have vehicle operators attend an emergency vehicle operators course (EVOC), which educates drivers based on standardized, nationally accepted content.[31] These courses include classroom work and experience on a driving course and on-the-job performance recommendations. ASTM also provides guidance for ambulance operators including operators, in its F 1517–94 Standard Guide for Scope of Performance of Emergency Medical Services Ambulance Operations.

··········

GROUND AMBULANCE OPERATION

Several areas of ground ambulance operation have implications for risk management. They include vehicle safety, issues regarding patient equipment and supplies, and user training and problem reporting for ambulance personnel who use medical devices.

Vehicle Safety

The General Services Administration publishes requirements for ambulance operation in its Federal Specification for KKK-A-1822E Ambulances.[32] For EMS services to be effective, vehicles must be prepared and able to respond when the system is notified of an emergency and when the dispatcher decides the level and magnitude of the response. If the notification and dispatch aspects of the system function properly and the vehicle fails to "roll," poor patient outcome may result and the system may be subject to liability.

Periodic "critical item" inspections may help the organization maintain safe vehicles. Such inspections focus on the issues most often identified as causing or contributing to accidents, and may include brakes, the steering and suspension system, tires and wheels, lights, windshield and windows, windshield wipers, mirrors, and horn. Frequency of the inspection should be based on vehicle use. If it is in use twenty-four hours a day, inspections should be more frequent. Other items that affect vehicle operation, such as batteries, fluid levels, and heat source for the ambulance compartment should also be routinely assessed. Drivers should maintain vehicle inspection report copies and current documentation of the need for repairs and the completion of those repairs.

Vehicle maintenance is typically defined to include preventive maintenance, demand maintenance, and crisis (breakdown) maintenance. Although the majority of these tasks are the responsibility of the operator, base operations should also maintain related documentation, to make sure that an adequate number of properly functioning vehicles remain available. Preventive maintenance and repair records should be meticulously maintained and reviewed on a periodic basis to make sure that the vehicle remains reliable, and to help determine when it needs to be replaced. Mechanical breakdowns, and inability to respond due to weather or road conditions, should be reported to base control and documented there. Although adherence to the Federal Motor Carrier Safety Regulations (FMCSR) is not mandatory, it is prudent to log vehicle and performance information for each trip to ensure that the resolution of any problems is documented.

Patient Equipment and Supplies

For the vehicle to be capable of rolling once proper personnel are in place, adequate patient equipment and supplies must be on board. Requirements for specific equipment and supplies to be carried by emergency vehicles vary by state, and response mode, for example, ground versus aeromedical burn transport.[33]

It is common practice for home base hospitals or receiving hospitals to restock ambulances with drugs and supplies used during the transport, so that the ambulance is ready for the next call. Items typically provided in this process include appropriate medications and supplies, such as intravenous tubing and catheters. Hospitals should collaborate to ensure compatibility of equipment used in local emergency rooms. Of particular importance for risk management professionals, the HHS/OIG published a final rule at the end of 2001 establishing safe harbor protection for ambulance restocking arrangements.

Numerous requirements apply to these Safe Harbor provisions, and risk management professionals should ask legal counsel to provide guidance on developing adjunct policies and procedures.[34]

Most ambulances carry basic communication devices, such as a two-way radio for medical communication, a disaster communication device, and a cellular telephone. Consumable supplies such as gloves, bandages, and thermal blankets are usually available. When requisitioning supplies, remember the need for latex-free alternatives, safety products, such as safety needles and syringes, and other protective devices, including masks, eye protection, and a sharps container. Basic level provider equipment such as ventilation and airway equipment, monitoring and defibrillation, and immobilization devices is usually on hand. It is generally important to be sure that equipment and supplies onboard ground ambulances are adequate for the range of patients likely to be encountered—for example, adequate equipment and supplies must be available for pediatric patients, even newborns.

Advanced level provider supplies and equipment, such as vascular access devices and solutions, specialized airway and ventilation equipment, cardiac equipment, and monitoring devices like pulse oximeters, may also be required. Some ambulances may also carry advanced equipment such as antishock garments, extraction devices, and specialized equipment and supplies. Medications which must be available for advanced level support are specified by the American Heart Association's Emergency Cardiac Care Committee, and providers receive information about these drugs in the Advanced Cardiac Life Support Course offered by AHA (The American Heart Association). Current information may also be obtained from the American College of Emergency Physicians (ACEP), the American College of Surgeons, and the National Association of EMS Physicians. All medications should be in unit dose packages, and injectables should be pre-loaded to reduce the risk of medication errors.

One very important technological advance is the development of the automatic external defibrillator (AED). This device includes a computer function that automatically detects and interprets the electrical activity of the patient's heart. If it detects ventricular fibrillation, it will prompt a decision about whether to defibrillate. If the user elects to defibrillate, the device will automatically determine when to provide the shock. As with other defibrillators, there is coincident risk of shock to operators and bystanders who are in physical contact with the patient when defibrillation takes place. Therefore, it is important to train providers about clinical and personnel safety implications of AED use, and to develop appropriate supportive protocols.

The AHA makes available AED-related education programs that promote the use of AEDs in public areas such as sports arenas, gated communities, office complexes, doctor's offices, shopping malls, and on airplanes. The Cardiac Arrest Survival Act (CASA) became law in November 2000. The law requires placement of AEDs in federal buildings and provides nationwide Good Samaritan liability protection for anyone who attempts to save someone's life with an AED. The AHA recommends that public and private organizations implementing AEDs notify the local EMS office, and have a licensed physician or medical authority oversee training and operations. This role is often fulfilled by the EMS medical director and EMS system personnel. AHA further suggests that lay persons be educated in cardiopulmonary resuscitation principles, and the use of AED equipment. Since 2003, AHA has supported the use of AEDs on persons as young as one year of age.

Also remember that the FDA requires purchasers of AEDs to present a physician's prescription.

Although the AHA notes that the perceived potential for a suit has in some cases been a deterrent for non-governmental organizations that consider establishing a public access defibrillation (PAD) program, they also observe that suits have not been filed to date against users of AEDs. On the other hand, suits have been filed against airlines and the proprietors of public entertainment settings, alleging that they were negligent in being unprepared to respond to a cardiac arrest. As long as the current AHA recommendations concerning AED programs are adhered to, users of AED should be able to defend care rendered, if a plaintiff overcame the previously discussed immunity provisions.

Medical Devices: User Training and Problem Reporting

As in the hospital setting, training for equipment users is essential. For example, current competence in the use of equipment like defibrillators is particularly critical.

Because EMS equipment is just as acute as hospital equipment, it is essential that EMS medical equipment maintenance checks and repairs be performed by trained biomedical engineers, functioning under the auspices of a comprehensive biomedical program. The remote locations in which EMS equipment is used make this a particularly urgent priority, because device failure in such settings leaves few care options. Biomedical services may be accessed through a hospital affiliate's biomedical engineering program, or by participating in a shared services arrangement with other EMS operations. Another alternative is an individual contract with a biomedical services preventive maintenance firm. Information, program and detailed device problem and evaluation reports may be found on the Web site of ECRI, an independent non-profit health care research operation, at [www.ecri.org].

EMS personnel should also identify and promptly address any malfunction. There should be a formal process for notifying personnel of defective devices that they may encounter in the field. For example, one manufacturer reportedly implanted defective pacemakers in numerous patients.[35] There should also be a formal recall process to respond to issues such as defective patient monitors that EMS may already have in service.[36]

....

COMMUNICATION SYSTEMS

Communication systems are essential to mobilizing and coordinating emergency medical services. These communication systems must address incoming reports of emergencies from members of the public, vehicle dispatch and coordination, medical direction and control, and interservice communications, which enable all public services to collaborate. The scope of EMS communication goes beyond the radios in the vehicle, base station, and receiving facility. Also part of EMS communication are repeater towers, and biomedical data fax stations, which are used to transmit 12-lead ECG results to the ED. Other telemetric devices used to transmit vital signs may also be considered aspects of EMS communications.

From a regulatory perspective, it is important that all telecommunication systems not under the auspices of the federal government are subject to rules established by the Federal Communications Commission (FCC). EMS communications personnel should be familiar with FCC regulations regarding technical aspects of communication devices, such as appropriate wavelengths, and qualifications for operators. This information can be found in FCC documentation and in the appendixes of the American Society for Testing and Materials (ASTM) Standard F-1220.

From a risk management perspective, there are several key points related to communication. EMS communication systems should meet recognized performance standards that address systems planning and design,[37] EMS communications should be compatible with, and not interfere with, other communication systems, including EMS operations, within the originating community or neighboring communities. An interesting and important related issue that may be addressed by the state, federal government, or the international communications community in the near future is telemetry.

Allegations of negligence may arise if an emergency call comes in, and communications systems fail, or are unavailable due to improper use, for example, personal conversations among staff. Risk reduction strategies to lessen this exposure include documentation of adequate system maintenance, implementation of applicable backup communication resources, like cell phones, use of correct communications protocols, and staff education.

CONFIDENTIALITY

Numerous threats to patient confidentiality exist in pre-hospital care. EMS providers are routine recipients of sensitive information. Indiscriminate discussion or unauthorized release of such information presents both ethical and legal risks. All information that is encountered by pre-hospital personnel must be considered confidential. Information should be communicated only to those who are assuming direct care of the patient and on a need-to-know basis. The only information that should be discussed over the radio is that which is necessary to provide for optimal care of the patient.

The Health Insurance Portability and Accountability Act (HIPAA) and its associated procedural changes applies to EMS providers just as it does to any other health care provider. All EMS providers should be educated about the implications of this important federal privacy law. Please see Volume III, Chapter 18 of this series for more information on HIPAA.

It is also desirable, perhaps in the context of HIPAA education, to require that EMS personnel sign a confidentiality agreement. This approach raises their awareness of the importance of maintaining confidentiality.

DOCUMENTATION

The Pre-Hospital Care Report (Run Report) documents the objective data gathered at the scene, in addition to the subjective findings of the field personnel.

It is the only medical record of the care provided. As such, it may be used by insurance carriers, defendants, or plaintiffs in criminal or civil liability cases, or by law enforcement personnel when investigating child or elder abuse, rape, and death by questionable means.

It is essential that the record accurately and objectively reflect the patient's condition, and support the treatment provided. Poor medical record documentation can lead to costly damage awards and compliance issues associated with billing practices.

Important risk management documentation practices include the following:

- A pre-hospital care report form should be completed for every call, whether or not a patient is found, even if services are "not needed," or the trip is cancelled enroute. A report should be generated for every interfacility transfer.

- If services are cancelled at the scene, document the cancelling authority, time of cancellation, and the circumstance.
- Each patient must have a separate form.
- The form is initiated by the first EMS provider on the scene.
- The report should be completed at the scene whenever possible.
- Review the report and check for complete and accurate content.

    The documentation should include the following components:

- Relevant observations about the patient
- Treatment appropriate for the observed medical condition of the patient
- All care provided
- All information needed by others who rely on the record for ongoing patient care, for example, allergies
- Ability of the receiving facility to manage the patient's condition

    To see whether or not the report achieves its goals, EMS providers should periodically try to recreate the run, at a later date, with the information provided.

    The pre-hospital care report may help emergency department staff gather additional patient information after paramedics have left the hospital, or it may help a paramedic to recall a long-forgotten incident in a court of law. If the pre-hospital care report presents a comprehensive picture of the events surrounding the incident, it dramatically enhances the defensibility of any case with which the EMS personnel may be involved.

....

CONSENT AND REFUSAL TO ACCEPT SERVICES

Emergency medical service patients have a right to understand their injury or illness, the steps that may be taken to address the injury or illness, the risks of those steps, and the risks of refusing care. A cognizant patient may refuse all care or certain aspects of care.

    Unless there is a life-threatening emergency in which the patient is not cognizant or conscious, pre-hospital emergency care providers must have either explicit or implied consent before they can perform procedures. It is highly desirable to obtain explicit consent from the patient and the patient's signature on a consent form, if possible. The patient may be deemed to have implied consent to routine types of procedures, for example, blood pressure checks, if they allow these to be done without objection.

    Care must be used in applying the emergency exception which is intended to facilitate care of a patient who is in jeopardy and unconscious or otherwise incapacitated. It is not intended to pertain to all cases of intoxication, limited mental capacity, and psychiatric illness. In situations where EMS personnel are unsure about whether to proceed with treatment, the input of the medical director should be sought. The objective observations and interventions, in such situations, should also be carefully documented in the prehospital record. These include patient condition, results of pertinent assessment, and discussion with the medical control director. Refer to Chapter 4 on Informed Consent in this handbook.

    A mentally competent adult has the right to refuse care, even if refusal would result in death or permanent disability. Refusal may be based on religious beliefs, fear, or lack of understanding of medical procedures. If the injured party does not agree to treatment, the EMS provider should document the refusal and the condition of the patient in concise, objective language, based on discussion with the medical director. If patients refuse care, reassure them that they may call again for help, despite initial refusal.

Closely related to refusal of care, patients refuse hospital transportation in 5 percent to 25 percent of out-of-hospital calls.[38] In a study of seventeen advanced life support (ALS) ambulance agencies that serviced northeastern Illinois during July 1993 and February 1994, 30 percent of all runs resulted in refusal of transportation. Patients who most commonly refused transportation were asymptomatic, eleven to forty years old, and involved in a motor vehicle crash, with no past medical history, normal vital signs, and normal mental status. Patients generally signed for their own releases after evaluation.

A thoroughly objective and comprehensive record is the best defense in any related litigation. This is important, as pre-hospital refusals are often precipitators of malpractice cases.

If the call is of a non-emergent nature, the decision not to treat or transport can be a mutual agreement between the patient and provider. Otherwise, the provider should consult the online medical director for guidance.

The circumstances in which care is refused are often challenging because they require the pre-hospital provider to be the eyes and ears of an emergency medical director, assessing the patient's decision-making ability. Competencies that delineate specific assessment skills should be developed and maintained. EMS staff should routinely receive training to augment these skills.

⋯⋯⋯⋯
DO NOT RESUSCITATE (DNR) OR COMFORT CARE

Terminally ill patients (such as those with end-stage cancer or AIDS) are commonly encountered in pre-hospital emergency medical response because of the growing number of hospice programs and home health care systems. There are also an increasing number of persons without terminal illnesses who are executing do-not-resuscitate (DNR) wishes through living wills or advanced directives. However, as death draws near, family, friends, or even the patient may call emergency medical services (EMS) personnel to provide comfort care or to transport the dying patient.

In states without legislation that delineates DNR options, the EMS provider might need to initiate resuscitation, even when notified of the DNR request. EMS providers must be thoroughly familiar with pertinent state regulations and any DNR-related EMS protocol.

In addition to pertinent state regulations, several resources can be used to develop policies and procedures. For example, ACEP has developed "Guidelines for 'Do Not Resuscitate' Orders in the Prehospital Setting." A *Journal of the American Medical Association* article entitled, "Guidelines for Cardiopulmonary Resuscitation and Emergency Cardiac Care, Part VIII: Ethical Considerations for Resuscitation," Emergency Cardiac Care Committee of the American Heart Association, might also be helpful.[39] These guidelines address among other things, the difficult topic of discontinuing cardiopulmonary resuscitation (CPR) when there is a valid no-CPR order.

According to the National Guidelines for Statewide Implementation of EMS "Do Not Resuscitate" (DNR) Programs, DNR policies should:

- Recognize that life support may not be necessary or beneficial.
- Provide the basis for a prospective educational program for the public and the medical communities about appropriate use of the EMS system in treating terminal medical conditions.
- Emphasize presumption in favor of resuscitation when patient wishes are not known.

- Define conditions under which a DNR order should be implemented, taking into account patient competency and the role of acceptable surrogates in making an informed decision.

- Identify clinical procedures to be withheld, along with other medical therapies, including comfort care, that may be clinically indicated and should not be withheld.

- Define the manner in which the DNR order is to be carried out and the role of the EMS.

- Define response for the circumstance in which a patient decides to revoke a living will or other formal statement of their wishes.

- Identify information to be contained in a do not resuscitate order and the procedure for periodic review.[40]

Some states have implemented pre-hospital DNR forms. In these settings, it is recommended that EMS provide public information sessions concerning how they may be used. These forms typically require a statement by and the signature of the attending physician acknowledging that the condition is terminal or advanced, from which recovery is not expected; that the patient is capable of making or has made an informed decision; a statement by and signature of the patient that in the event of cardiac or respiratory arrest no resuscitation efforts be undertaken; and a date of issue and expiration. Forms in some locations may be filed with the EMS prospectively. Other methods whereby EMS personnel may be alerted to DNR status include wallet cards, bracelets, or necklaces. However, these are not substitutes for DNR orders. Any difficult situations require contact of the online EMS medical director.

Formal guidance on bereavement, to help EMS members assist grieving family members and friends, should be developed. Also formalized should be a policy for termination of resuscitation in the field.

....

DISCONTINUATION OF LIFE SUPPORT EFFORTS

On occasion, transport to an ED is delayed or prolonged for reasons beyond the control of the EMS personnel, and life support efforts must be discontinued. The Rural Affairs Committee, National Association of Emergency Medical Services Physicians, National Association of EMS Physicians, and EMS standards recommend that advanced life support (ALS) and basic life support (BLS) procedures, once initiated in the field, be discontinued only if: (1) the patient recovers; (2) the patient is pronounced dead by a physician; (3) the rescuers are exhausted; (4) procedures place providers at risk; or (5) there are significant delays in transport.

Most hospital emergency departments and some EMS agencies have adopted guidelines for the discontinuation of prolonged use of ALS or BLS procedures. Such guidelines may contribute to developing a reasonable basis for making informed decisions in the field, where circumstances might be complicated by the need to transport a patient to a receiving facility far from the emergency scene.

There are specific clinical principles for discontinuing life support efforts that all EMS providers should know:

1. Defibrillation—Generally, defibrillation is required to reverse cardiac arrest and restore functional cardiac activity. It can be effective when applied soon after the onset of cardiac arrest. Chest compressions do not produce enough effective circulatory function to sustain adequate tissue perfusion when continued for long periods.

2. Prolonged cardiac life support—Most medical authorities currently agree that if cardiac arrest is sustained for longer than thirty minutes without any return of a spontaneous pulse, there is no reasonable chance for functional recovery in patients with normal core temperatures, and further application of ALS or BLS procedures provides no significant benefit to the patient.

3. Prolonged ventilatory support—Functional recovery can and does occur after prolonged ventilatory support without chest compression when a patient has functional cardiac activity, but does not have adequate spontaneous ventilation.

Specific protocols to address transporting a patient who has suffered a cardiac or respiratory arrest and undergone prolonged resuscitative efforts, should not be rigid. They should, however, provide guidance to pre-hospital emergency providers in this difficult circumstance. Field protocols should be developed by EMS physicians, using available professional organization-generated and other related resources. Such protocols should routinely be reviewed to ensure that they incorporate current clinical standards of care.

When possible, the decision to discontinue life support efforts should be the responsibility of the online physician. A means should also be specified for pronouncement of death, disposition of the body, including desired organ donation procurement, and grief counseling.

DOA Policies

Dead on arrival (DOA) policies should guide medical directors and EMS personnel in determining which patients should not undergo resuscitation, because the effort would be futile. Like guidance for the decision to stop resuscitative efforts, such policies should not be rigid. For example, they should not state that resuscitative measures are "never" to be undertaken when specific conditions are present. However, objective criteria, such as the time that has elapsed since the patient became unresponsive, and so on, can diffuse bias that pre-hospital emergency care providers might harbor related to patient age, type of illness, or social standing.

· · · · · · · · · · · ·

BLOODBORNE PATHOGEN CONSIDERATIONS

Because of the potential for blood splashes in many pre-hospital emergencies, EMS personnel are particularly vulnerable to bloodborne pathogen exposures. It is important that all who might come into contact with bloodborne pathogens be educated about associated risks and the importance of adhering to the OSHA Bloodborne Pathogens standard (Occupational Exposure to Bloodborne Pathogens; Needlestick and Other Sharps Injuries; Final Rule [2001, January 18]. Federal Register # 66:5317–5325) and guidelines (Occupational Exposure to Bloodborne Pathogens: Precautions for Emergency Responders. OSHA 3130—Revised [1998]).[41] When educating providers, it is important to stress that bloodborne pathogen infections can be transmitted from a staff member to a patient just as easily as they can be passed from the patient to the staff member. EMS providers should also be aware of the numerous bloodborne pathogens that are of concern, including HIV, and hepatitis A, B, and C. For example, hepatitis B is transmitted annually to more than 8,000 health care workers in all settings, and more than 200 die each year. The cost in human suffering and financial risk is formidable.

Of many important procedures in the OSHA bloodborne pathogens standard, the one requiring use of personal protective equipment is particularly important to EMS workers, because they are likely to encounter infected persons. In addition to bodily fluids that they may be exposed to as they treat injured persons at an accident or conduct CPR, pre-hospital providers may also be called to a scene where they might inadvertently handle drug paraphernalia, including intravenous devices. Resources on strategies to enhance the effectiveness of personal protective equipment are available from ECRI (formerly the Emergency Care Research Institute), the Service Employees International Union (SEIU), International Health Care Worker Safety Center (IHCWSC), and the International Sharps Injury Prevention Society (ISIPS).

Also important for EMS workers to be aware of are key implications of the Needle-stick Safety Prevention Act (which became Public Law 106–430 on November 6, 2000). This act went far to enhance the safety of the EMS provider and other health care personnel by encouraging approaches like the use of needleless devices. Although clinicians sometimes perceive that safety syringes are less effective than retractable devices, this perception is unproven. Thus, wherever possible, EMS systems should implement needleless systems. Current ambulance supplies should be reviewed and immediate steps taken to replace any conventional syringes with safety products.

The act also requires identification, reporting, and trending of accidental needlestick injuries, including those which might occur in the provision of emergency medical services. The act mandates participation of "frontline workers," such as pre-hospital emergency care providers, in the selection of safety products.

Other measures that can help reduce bloodborne pathogen exposures include offering pre-hospital workers hepatitis B vaccinations. Even though the worker may defer the vaccination, making it available will protect some workers and will raise awareness of the issue for all.

A detailed protocol for seeking treatment in the event of accidental needlestick should be developed for pre-hospital emergency care providers. Emphasized in the policy should be immediate steps that the affected employee should take and applicable timeframes. A formal counseling program is a valuable adjunct to such a protocol.

All EMS managers and personnel must be educated about the importance of maintaining confidentiality of patient and employee information related to accidental needlesticks and other potential bloodborne pathogen exposures.

············

RISK AND RESPONSIBILITY OF RESPONDING TO VIOLENT SCENES

Pre-hospital emergency providers are routinely confronted with emotionally distraught, intoxicated, and unruly patients and other parties. They need to understand how to protect the patients and themselves should circumstances warrant such protection.

EMS providers must understand is that there is no duty to place themselves at risk when they encounter danger. If there are no law enforcement officials on the scene, no effort should be made to capture or physically restrain a violent patient until after such officials arrive. EMS providers should be trained to quickly assess potentially dangerous situations, and proactively enlist the support of law enforcement personnel.

Training is essential to enhance the judgment that EMS providers must apply in such circumstances. If, for example, law enforcement personnel are enroute and the patient is not already demonstrating violent behavior, providers should begin verbal deescalation.

Physical or chemical restraint might be necessary, based on established protocols and with the support of the medical director. Any restraint is a potential violation of patient rights. To maintain patient safety and avoid liability, providers should use the least restrictive approach available, in accordance with applicable JCAHO and other related standards. The pre-hospital environment is prone to a lack of clinical information, and this might make one restraining strategy preferable to another. For example, if EMS providers do not know what medications the patient takes, whether prescribed or illicit, and have no allergy information, physical restraints might be a safer course than chemical restraints. Once physical restraints are in place or sedative medication has been administered, EMS providers must monitor the patient to assure the patient's well being.

In any later defense of related litigation, objective and comprehensive documentation of the EMS providers' observations and interventions will be essential. For example, the record should include documentation of specific observations that led the providers to conclude that the patient was potentially a danger to himself or others and efforts to deescalate the situation verbally. If physical or chemical restraint is used, the provider should document cardiovascular and airway status after initiation of the restraint and periodically thereafter.

As EMS providers are often called to the scene of domestic violence, it is important they be aware of the unique issues inherent in these situations. For example, if the dispatcher indicates that domestic violence might have precipitated the call, law enforcement should be summoned and EMS personnel should not enter the scene until it has been "secured." If the EMS providers do not suspect domestic violence until after they are on the scene, the victim should be removed as quickly as possible.

Domestic violence is a crime. Therefore, the scene must be treated as a crime scene, and standard precautions regarding preservation of evidence should be exercised. Initial and continuing education programs for EMS personnel must incorporate information about domestic violence, including identification of victims, preservation of evidence, ways to maintain safety at the scene, and documentation requirements.

....

LIABILITY INSURANCE

All organizations and professionals that offer medical and health care services to the public face the potential of a lawsuit. Recommended insurance coverages include automobile, equipment, comprehensive general liability including products and completed operations, and professional liability. Currently, primary policy limits vary. Typical coverage limits are $1 or $2 million for each type of coverage, and premium is based on the number of patient encounters. Many services carry excess policies in addition to the underlying policy.

Many states have specific insurance coverage requirements for ambulance services, as contrasted with regular automobile and public transport coverage. Risk management professionals should be familiar with additional requirements. For example, Missouri requires ambulance service owners to carry coverage for the injury or death of an individual due to the owner's negligence in employing a person who negligently administers emergency care (Section 190.120, RSMo).

In applying for insurance coverage, the liability underwriter is likely to ask for information on the following topics:

1. Vehicle and equipment exposure—Number of owned and leased vehicles by type, year, make, description, insurance value, vehicle identification number, total stated value of all ambulance units and equipment

2. Employee exposures—Full-time equivalents and number of employees by position and responsibility

3. Volunteers—Number of volunteers and hours by position and responsibility

4. Medical Director—Qualification and hours worked

5. Revenue and expenditures

6. Other exposures—Known or anticipated

7. Additional activities—Sponsor or co-sponsor of events (such as health fairs, carnivals, rodeos, demolition derby, haunted houses, and so on)

8. Number of patient encounters

9. Regions served—Urban, community, rural

10. Claims history

The organization may also be asked to submit copies of risk management-related programs including safety, quality improvement, training, operations manual, and clinical policies, procedures, and protocols.

CONTINUOUS RISK IMPROVEMENT (CRI)

Participants in CRI should include the medical director, dispatch representative, field clinical personnel, drivers, and hospital ED personnel. The CRI process must be integrated into the day-to-day operations, and data should be shared among the participating agencies. Evaluation of any deficiencies in patient care involves first reviewing any applicable protocol to ensure its appropriateness or need for revision. Second, the particular deficiency must be assessed through a root cause analysis to determine where system improvements can be made. Third, appropriate education should be instituted, and any interventions implemented should be monitored through the CRI program.

The medical director, with the input of all levels of providers, should:

- Establish measurable standards that reflect the goals and expectations of the EMS system and local community.

- Establish a mechanism for data collection that captures information reflecting standards.

- Establish and ensure compliance with written patient care protocols and standard operating procedures.

- Convey feedback and stimulate necessary changes in the educational process.

- Monitor the effectiveness of EMS interventions, treatments, and system design.

ACCIDENT ANALYSIS

Because many liability-related incidents in the EMS arena are related to vehicular and flight accidents, it is important to analyze transport-related accidents. An accident review board can be an effective risk improvement tool. To support the activity of the board, a central accident database encompassing the factors associated with the accidents, for example, number of hours worked by involved staff, should be developed.

Valuable data to support this effort can be collected through front seat or cockpit monitoring by pilots or drivers. It also might be valuable to profile programs that have not had an accident.

Emergency medical vehicle-related (EMV) collisions occurring during an emergency response or transport should be evaluated by EMS system managers and medical directors. Specific issues assessed should include whether the dispatch process was clinically appropriate, the patient's condition on arrival at the scene and when the transport began, and the patient's eventual outcome.

···········
BENCHMARKS

Risk-related benchmarks should be established for each aspect of emergency medical service, to facilitate prioritization of risk issues, and monitoring of intervention-related progress. Such measures may include the following parameters.

Staffing

- Qualifications and credentials of management and crew
- EMS crew satisfaction: job turnover rate, self-surveys

Equipment

- Quality and maintenance of equipment
- Radio communications ability

Patient or Clinical

- Patient satisfaction and complaints
- Scene triage: ability of BLS and ALS to prioritize emergency
- Scene care: Proper protocol implementation including minimizing scene time to critically ill and injured

Public

- Recognition of an emergency: public awareness
- EMS System Access: 911 awareness and availability
- Bystander interventions: bystander CPR, first aid

Dispatch

- Ability to determine severity of call
- Ability to make contact with the right EMS responders

Response

- Timeliness
- Capability to care for emergency
- Lights and sirens use

licensure stops at door

license is for pre-hospital care, not hospital care

Transport

- Delivery to suitable medical facility
- Use of aeromedical transport and ALS intercepts
- System Recovery: Turnaround time to restock and return to service availability

Disposition

- Admitted, discharged, transferred, or died at receiving medical facility
- Outcome measures: Condition on arrival at hospital, return to pre-morbid condition

....

PROACTIVE RISK MANAGEMENT

The most effective way to manage risks is to reduce or eliminate them before they occur through the following "pre-loss" risk management strategies.

- Protocols—Protocols are uniform responses to specific clinical situations that tend to produce the safest and most reliable outcome. They should be based on objective clinical research rather than anecdotal experience. In any related negligence case, protocols will be considered, with other information such as expert testimony, as evidence of the system's standard of care.

- Education—Continuing education is critical to reducing risk, as it reinforces system protocols and expands providers' knowledge of out-of-hospital medicine. Education should include regular testing to ensure that every person demonstrates proficiency in critical skills. Risk management concepts and customer service skills should be part of all CE programs.

- Documentation—The pre-hospital care report can and will be used in court to support or condemn the EMS provider's—and the agency's—actions.

- Claims Analysis—Identification of trends in the types of claims against EMS both on a local and national level will allow a system to proactively evaluate identified issues and modify protocols and training methods.

....

POTENTIAL CLAIM INVESTIGATION AND LOSS MITIGATION

EMS organizations can use several strategies to limit or contain their risk after an incident. The risk management program should provide supportive resources, and the risk management professional may elect to participate in any or all of these processes.

- Investigation—Getting information about an incident as soon as possible dramatically makes for much more reliable data on which to base subsequent actions. The investigation should examine the pre-hospital care report, and incident reports and tape audits when available, and should be followed by crew interviews.

- Protocols—When an incident occurs, policies and procedures should be evaluated to see if they were in place and what effect EMS provider compliance or non-compliance had on the event. Determine if the related protocol exists. If it does, determine if it was followed, and if not, find out why.

- Remediation and evaluation—The crew members involved should be educated and tested on their skills competency (for example, intubation skills). Failure to correct clinical deficiencies may exacerbate later allegations of negligence.

··········

CONCLUSION

EMS is a critical aspect of health care. This arena exhibits constantly evolving clinical techniques, and a highly dynamic environment. Although provision of pre-hospital emergency services is an area with much potential for liability, the public perception that pre-hospital EMS providers "do good" reduces exposure.

It is essential that the risk management professional address exposures in this out-of-hospital environment in the same way that they are managed in the acute-care facility. Risk issues that should receive a high priority include biomedical equipment, vehicle safety, and bloodborne pathogen precautions.

Endnotes

1. Soler, J. M., et al. "The Ten-Year Malpractice Experience of a Large Urban EMS System," *Annals of Emergency Medicine,* 14(10), Oct. 1985, 982–5.

2. Goldberg, R. J., et al. "A Review of Prehospital Care Litigation in a Large Metropolitan EMS System." *Annals of Emergency Medicine*, 19(5), May 1990, 557–61.

3. Colwell, C. B., P. Pons, J. H. Blanchet, and C. Mangino. "Claims Against a Paramedic Ambulance Service: A Ten-Year Experience," *Journal of Emergency Medicine,* 17(6), Nov./Dec. 1999, 999–1002.

4. Available at [www.cdc.gov/ncidod/hip]. Last visited August 23, 2005.

5. Available at [www.fda.gov/medwatch/report/hcp.htm]. Last visited August 23, 2005.

6. Available at [www.accessdata.fda.gov/scripts/cdrh/cfdocs/cfMAUDE/search.CFM]. Last visited August 23, 2005.

7. Bloodborne Pathogens and Needlestick Prevention, U.S. Department of Labor, Occupational Safety & Health Administration. Available at [www.osha.gov/SLTC/bloodbornepathogens/index.html]. Last visited August 23, 2005.

8. Ergonomics, U.S. Department of Labor, Occupational Safety & Health Administration. Available at [www.osha.gov/ergonomics/guidelines.html]. Last visited August 23, 2005.

9. Emergency Preparedness and Response, U.S. Department of Labor, Occupational Safety & Health Administration. Available at [www.osha.gov/SLTC/emergencypreparedness/index.html]. Last visited August 23, 2005.

10. Fox, C. E., M. D., M.P.H. Remarks: Integrating EMS Into Rural Health Systems, U.S. Department of Health & Human Services, Health Resources and Services Administration,

December 13, 1999. Available at [newsroom.hrsa.gov/speeches/IntegratingEMS.htm]. Last visited August 23, 2005.

11. Bez, A., Emergency Medicine, in Telehealth Technology Guidelines. Two items available at [telehealth.hrsa.gov/pubs/tech/ems.htm] and [newsroom.hrsa.gov/NewsBriefs/2000/EMSC%20Resource%20Kit.htm]. Last visited August 23, 2005.

12. Research on Emergency Medical Services for Children, PA Number: PA-05-081, March 30, 2005, Department of Health and Human Services Available at [grants1.nih.gov/grants/guide/pa-files/pa-01-044.html] Last visited August 23, 2005.

13. Available at [www.nlm.nih.gov/medlineplus/]. Last visited August 23, 2005.

14. REP Program Strategic Review Implementation Products, Final FEMA Policy, Recommended Initiative 1.2—Reduce Frequency of Evaluation, EVALUATION OF EMERGENCY MEDICAL SERVICES DRILLS, October 23, 2004. Available at [www.fema.gov/rrr/rep/fnlp1-2.shtm]. Last visited August 23, 2005.

15. Medicare Fraud, Detection and Prevention Tips, Center for Medicare and Medicaid Services. Available at [www.medicare.gov/fraudabuse/tips.asp?PrinterFriendly=true]. Last visited August 23, 2005.

16. State Laws on Heart Attacks, Cardiac Arrest & Defibrillators, National Conference of State Legislatures. Available at [www.ncsl.org/programs/health/aed.htm]. Last visited August 23, 2005.

17. National Registry of Emergency Medical Technicians, State Office Information. Available at [www.nremt.org/EMTServices/emt_cand_state_offices.asp]. Last visited August 23, 2005.

18. National Highway Traffic Safety Administration, Department of Transportation, Emergency Medical Technician Paramedic: National Standard Curriculum (EMT-P). Available at [www.nhtsa.dot.gov/people/injury/ems/EMT-P/index.html]. Last visited August 23, 2005.

19. National Association of EMS Physicians (NAEMSP Position Paper for Emergency Medical Dispatching), 1989. Available at [www.naemsp.org/Position%20Papers/EmerMedDisptch.html]. Last visited August 23, 2005.

20. Hospital Capacity and Emergency Department Diversion: Four Community Case Studies, AHA Survey Results, April 2004. Available at [www.ahapolicyforum.org/ahapolicyforum/resources/content/EDDiversionSurvey040421.ppt]. Last visited August 23, 2005.

21. Federal Register: September 9, 2003 (Volume 68, Number 174). Section: Rules and Regulations, Agency: CENTERS FOR MEDICARE & MEDICAID SERVICES, Medicare Program; Clarifying Policies Related to the Responsibilities of Medicare-Participating Hospitals in Treating Individuals With Emergency Medical Conditions, Action: Final rule.

22. Emergency Medical Services Committee of the American College of Emergency Physicians, Policy Statement for Ambulance Diversion, October 1999. Available at [www.acep.org/webportal/PracticeResources/PolicyStatements/Diversion/AmbulanceDiversion.htm]. Last visited August 23, 2005.

23. National Heart Attack Alert Program, National Heart, Lung, and Blood Institute, National Institutes of Health, Available at [www.nhlbi.nih.gov/about/nhaap]. Last visited August 23, 2005.

24. The Revised Trauma Score is a physiological scoring system, with high inter-rater reliability and demonstrated accuracy in predicting death. It is scored from the first set of data obtained on the patient, and consists of Glasgow Coma Scale, Systolic Blood Pressure, and Respiratory Rate. Available at [www.trauma.org/scores/rts.html]. Last visited January 26, 2006.

25. The Glasgow Coma Scale is the most widely used scoring system used in quantifying level of consciousness following traumatic brain injury. It is used primarily because it is simple, has a relatively high degree of interobserver reliability, and because it correlates well with outcome following severe brain injury.

Glasgow Coma Score

Eye Opening (E)	*Verbal Response (V)*	*Motor Response (M)*
4 = Spontaneous	5 = Normal conversation	6 = Normal
3 = To voice	4 = Disoriented conversation	5 = Localizes to pain
2 = To pain	3 = Words, but not coherent	4 = Withdraws to pain
1 = None	2 = No words. . . . only sounds	3 = Decorticate posture
	1 = None	2 = Decerebrate
		1 = None
		Total = E+V+M

Available at [www.ssgfx.com/CP2020/medtech/glossary/glasgow.htm]. Last visited January 26, 2006.

26. For additional information regarding clinical indicators and scoring tools, please refer to [www.emedicine.com/splash/shared/etools/index.htm]. Last visited August 23, 2005.

27. Shimanski, C. Accidents in Mountain Rescue Operations, January 2002. Available at [www.amrg.org/accidentsin_rescue_Shimanski.pdf]. Last visited August 23, 2005.

28. Medical Review of Rural Air Ambulance Services, CMS Manual System Department of Health & Human Services (DHHS), Pub. 100-08 Medicare Program Integrity. Available at [www.cms.hhs.gov/manuals/pm_trans/r102pi.pdf]. Last visited August 23, 2005.

29. Colwell, et al. "Claims Against a Paramedic Ambulance Service: A Ten-Year Experience." *op. cit.*

30. American Society for Testing and Materials. Standard Practice for Emergency Medical Dispatch. Publication No. F1258-90. Philadelphia: American Society for Testing and Materials, 1990.

31. 1995 Emergency Vehicle Operators Course (Ambulance): National Standard Curriculum, National Highway Traffic Safety Administration, Department of Transportation. Available at [www.nhtsa.dot.gov/people/injury/ems/web%20site%20intro.htm]. Last visited August 23, 2005.

32. Federal Specification for the Star-of-Life Ambulance KKK-A-1822E, GENERAL SERVICES ADMINISTRATION, Federal Supply Service, June 1, 2002 GSA Automotive. Available at [www.gsa.gov/gsa/cm_attachments/GSA_DOCUMENT/ambulanc_1_R2FI5H_0Z5RDZ-i34K-pR.pdf]. Last visited August 25, 2005.

33. American College of Surgeons. "Essential Equipment for Ambulances," *Bulletin of the American College of Surgeons*, 79(9), 1994, 19–23; South Carolina. Ambulance Design and Equipment. Reg No. 61-7 (multiple parts applicable); California. Comprehensive emergency medical service equipment and supplies. Cal Code Regs tit. 22 § 70457.

34. DEPARTMENT OF HEALTH AND HUMAN SERVICES Office of Inspector General 42 CFR Part 1001 RIN 0991-AB05 Medicare and State Health Care Programs: Fraud and Abuse; Ambulance Replenishing Safe Harbor.

35. FDA Announces Guidant's Class I Pacemaker Recall, *FDA News*, P05-46, July 22, 2005 Available at [www.fda.gov/bbs/topics/NEWS/2005/NEW01210.html]. Last visited Augus 23, 2005.

36. Whistleblower Files Lawsuit Against HP, Agilent, Device Daily Bulletin, Feb. 28, 2005. Available at [www.fdanews.com/dailies/device/2_41/news/36468-1.html]. Last visited August 23, 2005.

37. National Advisory Commission on Criminal Justice Standards and Goals, Report on Law Enforcement, Wash DC, GPO, 1973 and Report on the Criminal Justice System, 1973.

38. Hipskind, J. E., J. M. Gren, and D. J. Barr. "Patients Who Refuse Transportation by Ambulance: A Case Series," *Prehospital and Disaster Medicine,* 12(4), 1994, 278–283.

39. American College of Emergency Physicians. "Guidelines for Do Not Resuscitate Orders in the Prehospital Setting." *Annals of Emergency Medicine,* 17, 1998, 1106–1108; Emergency Cardiac Care Committees and Subcommittees, American Heart Association. "Guidelines for Cardiopulmonary Resuscitation and Emergency Cardiac Care, VIII: Ethical Considerations in Resuscitation," *JAMA,* 268, 1992, 2282–2288; Adams, J.G.: "Prehospital Do-Not-Resuscitate Orders: A Survey of State Policies in the United States," *Prehospital and Disaster Medicine,* 8, 1993, 317–322.

40. National Association of Emergency Medical Services Directors and the National Association of Emergency Medical Services Physicians, National Guidelines for Statewide Implementation of EMS "Do Not Resuscitate" (DNR) Programs, April-June, 1994. Available at [www.naemsp.org/Position%20Papers/DNRPrograms.html]. Last visited August 23, 2005.

41. Available at [www.osha.gov/Publications/osha3130.pdf]. Last visited June 16, 2003.

Suggested Web Sites

There are many associations, organizations, and governmental agencies involved in setting EMS-related guidelines, policies, and standards. This list is not all-inclusive and listing of a particular organization does not imply endorsement.

Air Ambulance Service Companies Directory—[www.air-ambulance.net].

Air and Surface Transport Nurses Association (ASTNA)—[www.astna.org].

Air Medical Physicians Association (AMPA)—[www.ampa.org].

Air Medical Safety Advisory (AMSA) Council—[www.amsac.org].

American Academy of Orthopedic Surgeons (AAOS)—[www.aaos.org].

American Academy of Pediatrics (AAP)—[www.aap.org].

American Ambulance Association (AAA)—[www.the-aaa.org].

American Association of Critical-Care Nurses (AACN)—[www.aacn.org].

American Board of Emergency Medicine (ABEM)—[www.abem.org].

American College of Emergency Physicians (ACEP)—[www.acep.org].

American College of Prehospital Medicine (ACPM)—[www.acpm.org].

American Heart Association (AHA)—[www.americanheart.org].

American Red Cross (ARC)—[www.redcross.org].

American Society for Testing and Materials (ASTM)—[www.astm.org].

Association of Air Medical Services (AAMS)—[www.aams.org].

Association of Emergency Physicians (AEP)—[www.aep.org].

Basic Trauma Life Support (BTLS) International—[www.btls.org].

Centers for Disease Control and Prevention (CDC)—[www.cdc.gov].

Center for Medicare and Medicaid Services (CMS), Ambulance Services Information Resource for Medicare—[www.cms.hhs.gov/suppliers/ambulance].

Center for Pediatric Emergency Medicine (CPEM), PARAMEDIC TRIPP: Teaching Resource for Instructors in Prehospital Pediatrics—[www.cpem.org/html/trippals.html].

Commission on Accreditation of Allied Health Education Programs (CAAHEP)—[www.caahep.org].

Commission on Accreditation of Ambulance Services (CAAS)—[www.caas.org].

Commission on Accreditation of Medical Transport Systems (CAMTS)—[www.camts.org].

Committee on Accreditation of Educational Programs for the Department of Transportation (DOT)—[www.nhtsa.dot.gov/people/injury/ems/agenda/bridges2.html].

Emergency Medical Services Professions (CoAEMSP)—[www.coaemsp.org].

ECRI—[www.ecri.org].

Emergency Medical Services for Children (EMS-C)—[www.ems-c.org].

Emergency Medicine Foundation (EMF)—[www.acep.org/webportal/education/research/emergencymedicinefoundation/default.htm].

Emergency Medicine Residents Association (EMRA)—[www.emra.org].

Emergency Nurses Association (ENA)—[www.ena.org].

EMSresource.net—[emsresource.net].

EMTCity Online Community—[www.emtcity.com/phpBB2/portal.php].

Federal Emergency Management Agency (FEMA)—[www.fema.gov].

FlightWeb for Air Medical Professionals—[www.flightweb.com].

Food and Drug Administration (FDA)—[www.fda.gov].

Foundation for Air-Medical Research & Education—[www.aamsfoundation.org].

Health Resources and Services Administration (HRSA)—[www.hrsa.gov].

International Association of Dive Rescue Specialists (IADRS)—[www.iadrs.org].

International Association of Flight Paramedics (IAFP)—[www.flightparamedic.org].

International Critical Incident Stress Foundation, Inc. (ICISF)—[www.icisf.org].

International EMS—[www.international-ems.com].

International Health Care Worker Safety Center (IHCWSC), EpiNet—[www.healthsystem.virginia.edu/internet/epinet].

International Public Safety Resource Center—[www.ipsrc.com].

International Rescue and Emergency Care Association (IRECA)—[www.ireca.org].

International Sharps Injury Prevention Society (ISIPS)—[www.isips.org].

Joint Commission on Accreditation of Healthcare Organizations (JCAHO)—[www.jcaho.org].

Mountain Rescue Association (MRA)—[www.mra.org].

National Association for Search and Rescue (NASAR)—[www.nasar.org].

National Association of Air Medical Communication Specialists—[www.naacs.org].

National Association of Emergency Medical Services (EMS) Physicians—[www.naemsp.org].

National Association of Emergency Medical Technicians (NAEMT)—[www.naemt.org].

National Association of EMS Educators (NAEMSE)—[www.naemse.org].

National Association of State EMS Directors (NASEMSD)—[www.nasemsd.org].

National Collegiate EMS Foundation (NCEMSF)—[www.ncemsf.org].

National Emergency Medicine Association (NEMA)—[www.nemahealth.org].

National EMS Pilots Association (NEMSPA)—[www.nemspa.org].

National EMS Research Agenda—[www.researchagenda.org].

National Fire Protection Association (NFPA)—[www.nfpa.org].

National Flight Paramedics Association (NFPA)—[www.nfpa.rotor.com].

National Highway Traffic Safety Administration (NHTSA)—[www.nhtsa.dot.gov].

National Native American EMS Association (NNAEMSA)—[heds.org/nnaemsa.htm].

National Registry of Emergency Medical Technicians (NREMT)—[www.nremt.org].

National Ski Patrol System (NSP)—[www.nsp.org].

National Standard Curricula—[www.nhsta.gov/people/injury/ems/nsc.htm].

National Transportation Safety Board, Aviation Accident Database & Synopses—[www.ntsb.gov/ntsb/query.asp].

North American Ambulance Alliance—[www.n3A.org].

Occupational Safety and Health Administration (OSHA)—[www.OSHA.gov].

Office of Emergency Preparedness, National Disaster Medical System (NDMS)—[www.oep-ndms.dhhs.gov].

Prehospital Care Research Forum, UCLA Center for Prehospital Care—[www.pcrf.mednet.ucla.edu].

Radio Emergency Associated Communications Teams (REACT) International—[www.reactintl.org].

Service Employees International Union (SEIU)—[www.seiu.org].

Society for Academic Emergency Medicine (SAEM)—[www.saem.org].

Society of Critical Care Medicine (SCCM)—[www.sccm.org].

Society of Emergency Medicine Physician Assistants (SEMPA)—[www.sempa.org].

Society of Trauma Nurses (STN)—[www.traumanursesoc.org].

The AED Instructor Foundation—[www.aedinstructorfoundation.org].

The Journal of Prehospital Emergency Care—[www.peconline.org].

10

Emergency Department Risk Management: Promoting Quality and Safety in a Chaotic Environment

David Lickerman
Stephanie Lickerman

The Emergency Department (ED) is a rapidly changing and intense environment, one of the busiest and most chaotic in health care, yet it is also a place where the public has expectations of quality care. This dichotomy creates care issues and exacerbates malpractice risk.

A particularly concerning characteristic of the setting is the volatility of clinical circumstances and volume. Patients with widely differing severities of illness arrive in an uncontrolled manner, and the ED personnel must apply quick, yet thoughtful decision making and continual reassessment to ensure optimal health care for all who arrive at its doors. This activity has great significance to the entire health care organization, as 60 to 75 percent of hospital admissions arrive through the emergency department. For the most part, patients who come to the ED do so because they believe they have an emergency and require prompt attention, but other patients come because the ED allows them immediate access to medical care. Ambulance traffic adds to the influx, and unless patients are processed and discharged (or admitted) rapidly, in the in-patient units as in the ED, high volumes of emergency patients will create an ED logjam.

Typically, medical care in the ED is performed in a linear fashion, so if the patient's needs become too complex, if multiple seriously ill or injured patients arrive at once, or if processing by another hospital department is delayed, the process of ED care will be slowed, leading to overcrowded, potentially unsafe conditions and dissatisfied customers. ED overcrowding is a daily reality for many of the nation's hospitals. The CDC has reported that although the number of emergency departments has fallen by 12.3 percent, the number of visits has increased by 26 percent. EDs are seeing increased utilization rates for all age groups, especially among people over sixty-five years residing in an institutionalized setting, and for Medicaid patients who receive ED treatment at four times the rate of those privately insured.[1]

In addition to these issues, there are team and schedule discrepancies. Shift changes for all staff positions (physician, nurse, resident, technician) are unsynchronized and ED staff works all hours of the day, often several days in a row. Staffing of care teams is constantly changing, so ED workers must establish rapport and delineate leadership and must function as a team with a new mix of personnel daily. Further exacerbating this flux in personnel, rising malpractice rates and falling reimbursements have led some hospitals to contract with outside management groups to run emergency departments, and this can lead to revolving door ED physician staffing. Yet another major liability exposure is created because there are no established relationships between ED physicians and their patients. Because good relationships normally mitigate malpractice risk in private practice settings, caring and active communication are essential risk prevention behaviors for every member of the ED staff.

This multitude of patient safety and exposure-related issues point to the need for strong risk management approaches and ongoing monitoring of the effectiveness with which EDs function. By optimizing the safe handling of each patient, through carefully constructed approaches that recognize the role of the ED as a department, and an integral part of the health care organization, it is possible to enhance quality and reduce liability.

This chapter will expand on key issues and present practical solutions. The major focus is on emergency department care, as pre-hospital care is covered in another chapter of this book.

············

IN-HOSPITAL EMERGENCY MEDICINE (EM) CARE

The ED is the third most common site for significant medical errors, following only the operating room and the patient's hospital room. Considering the time spent by patients in each of these areas, the contribution of the ED is disproportionately large.[2] Because of high volumes, tight time constraints, and a need for ED physicians to act decisively even when hampered by incomplete data, errors are likely. However, some situations and conditions are more prone to error and generation of malpractice claims. As such, they fall into the hospital risk management professional's arena.

The Most Common Causes of ED Claims

The ED is an environment of controlled chaos and rapid decision making that is susceptible to error. An awareness of the changes in patient condition and teamwork can salvage many potentially poor outcomes, but not all ED patient visits end well. Adverse outcomes that lead to malpractice claims occur sporadically, often without pattern in individual institutions, but aggregate national data are available and instructive. Examination of these data yields both general and specific advice for risk management professionals and the clinicians who work in their institutions.

True emergency conditions are limited in number, but to prevent poor outcomes and later litigation, it is imperative that emergency physicians approach all patients as though they possess an emergent condition. Thus, each adult patient with chest pain must be regarded as a possible myocardial infarction; each headache must be suspected to be a cerebrovascular accident or meningitis; each abdominal pain must be seen as a potential intestinal obstruction, appendicitis, aortic aneurysm, ectopic pregnancy, testicular torsion, and so on. The problem, from a clinical standpoint, is that many of these conditions can present in an early stage or with unusual symptoms that make them difficult to recognize. This is particularly true of meningitis and appendicitis. However, the cases that are most costly to settle are those that present in a typical manner, yet are misdiagnosed or mismanaged. The physician must consider the risks and benefits of diagnostic testing to the patient and balance the necessity of a definitive diagnosis against its cost, the diversion of ED and hospital resources from other patients, and the perils of a missed diagnosis. Even with careful attention to detail, the variable course of human illness and the fallibility of rapid decision-making based on partial data have a strong tendency to deliver adverse outcomes that result in malpractice claims.

It is important for the risk management professional to understand both the nature of ED claims and the severity (cost) of the most common cases. National data for malpractice claims is fragmented because of the confidential nature of many settlements and because many institutions are self-insured with little policing for mandatory reporting as required by the National Practitioner Data Bank (NPDB). However, the Physician Insurers Association of America (PIAA) has conducted a large-scale longitudinal study (3,186 closed ED claims from 1985–2004) that can serve as a proxy for national data. These data are physician-specific rather than hospital-specific, but hospitals are frequently named as defendants in the same cases. As a specialty, Emergency Medicine (EM) ranks sixteenth among the twenty-eight major specialties in monies paid and seventeenth in the number of claims reported. Among all specialties, EM claims constituted 2.2 percent of the claims and 1.6 percent of the indemnity payouts. These have increased from 1.8 percent and 1 percent, respectively, over the past ten years. When medical misadventures (the most significant contributor to the medical error) are considered, errors in diagnosis were the largest category cited in a little over half of the claims. The second largest category was "no medical misadventure." This encompassed cases in which the EM physician was not negligent, but was named in the case. However, even in these cases, the EM physician participated in a payment 10 percent of the time. The most prevalent misadventures are illustrated in Figure 10.1.

FIGURE 10.1   **Ten Most Department Emergency Department Claims**

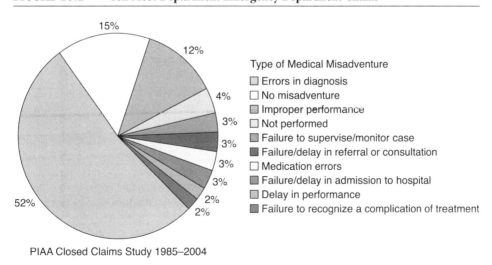

PIAA Closed Claims Study 1985–2004

TABLE 10.1.   Claims Categories

Failure to Diagnose	*Individual Payout Severity*	*Overall Payout Severity*
Appendicitis	Meningitis	Myocardial infarction
Myocardial infarction	Head & spinal injuries	Meningitis
Abdominal conditions	Septicemia	Chest pain
Chest pain	Pulmonary embolism	Abdominal conditions
Meningitis		Appendicitis

Note that medication errors accounted for only 3 percent of the total claims, yet addressing medication issues is one of the JCAHO/NQF goals for reducing errors in medical care. Although serious in their own right, they are targeted primarily because they are actionable and measurable items, and not because they are the most frequent, lethal, or costly types of error according to ED malpractice data.

In order of frequency, these are the clinical issues associated with the most common high-dollar failure to diagnose cases[3]:

1. Appendicitis (28%)

2. Myocardial infarction (26%)

3. Abdominal conditions (16%)

4. Chest pain—not further defined (15%)

5. Meningitis (14%)

Other insurers report head injury and cerebral condition, spinal injury and condition, obstetric-related, respiratory distress, and infection as categories with significant incidence and dollar losses.[4]

The diagnoses with the highest individual payout severity for the ED, in order, are meningitis, head and spinal injuries, septicemia, and pulmonary embolism. However, because these are not the most frequent, a different group of conditions has the highest overall payout. Myocardial infarction and meningitis lead this list, followed by chest pain, abdominal conditions, and appendicitis. See Table 10.1 for categories of claims. Among pediatric patients, failure to diagnose appendicitis and meningitis are the two most hazardous conditions for emergency room physicians.[5]

Although chest conditions other than myocardial infarction are not spelled out in this study, emergency conditions of the chest that result in malpractice claims include ruptured thoracic aortic aneurysm, pulmonary embolism, pneumonia, and cancer. Serious abdominal conditions other than appendicitis that can result in malpractice claims include ruptured abdominal aortic aneurysms, intestinal obstruction, bowel infarctions, abscesses, ectopic pregnancy, and cancers.

The following paragraphs will delineate clinical and risk management issues associated with or surrounding the highest severity conditions, accompanied by risk reduction strategies for risk management professionals.

Myocardial Infarction   Patients with chest pain, and in particular acute myocardial infarction (AMI), constitute the single most costly diagnostic group in emergency medicine, accounting for about one quarter of all EM malpractice dollar losses. In addition, chest pain is the most common symptom of patients who come to the emergency department. ED physicians and nurses must unerringly sort these patients into either minor (costochondral pain, heartburn) or emergent (myocardial infarction) categories, yet the variety of symptoms presented by this group of patients makes this difficult. Among all specialties, emergency medicine ranks third in claims frequency and severity for misdiagnosis or mistreatment of AMI. However, when considering ED cases only, misdiagnosis of AMI is the largest single category.

Misdiagnosis   The PIAA Acute Myocardial Infarction Study (May 1996) found that 77 percent of AMI patients whose care resulted in a malpractice claim died because of either diagnostic or treatment errors. Projected earnings losses and family hardships result in large awards especially when a relatively young patient experiences sudden death because of a missed diagnosis. These younger patients are also more likely to survive an AMI, and thus future medical care costs and non-economic damages increase indemnity costs. In fact, the age cohort with the highest average indemnity payout is the thirty-to-thirty-nine-year age group. However, this age cohort represents only about 12 percent of the total number of cases. Claimants in the forty-to-fifty-nine-year age group make up 58 percent of the total. The diagnosis of a typical AMI patient (male, older age, crushing chest pain, radiation down the left arm) is not often missed, though his care can still be mismanaged. Patients whose presentations are less typical are more frequently misdiagnosed and, in consequence, mismanaged.

Myocardial infarction patients who are misdiagnosed tend to be younger, female, and present with other than typical symptoms. According to this PIAA study, one quarter of these chest pain patients were given a gastrointestinal diagnosis, and another 20 percent were diagnosed as having rib cage pain. Other common features of these claims included an incomplete history or physical examination, an inexperienced ED physician, and, because AMI was not suspected in 21 percent of cases, no EKG was performed. Inexperienced physicians are also more likely to depend on enzyme tests—but enzyme levels do not become abnormal for several hours, and a clinical judgment based on early tests provides only false reassurance. Performance of a risk factor assessment has been promoted as a solution, but can be only partially effective. Among patients with AMI who sued for malpractice, the PIAA AMI Study found that nearly 70 percent of claimants had no prior history of coronary artery disease, and about half of males (and two-thirds of females) had no history of smoking or hypertension.

Women are more likely than men to have a missed diagnosis of myocardial infarction and are less likely to have been properly treated. This is, at least in part, because women delay coming to the hospital and their symptoms tend to be atypical. Almost half of heart attacks in women present with shortness of breath, nausea, indigestion, fatigue and shoulder pain, not chest pain.[6] It is clear from the preceding discussion that atypical symptoms should be considered as a typical presentation to most reliably diagnose AMI, especially in the female gender.

Delayed Treatment   Misdiagnosis is not the only issue in ED AMI malpractice claims. Delayed treatment is also increasingly important. As thrombolytic therapy ("clot-busting" drugs) and primary angioplasty (cardiac catheterization lab intervention) have become established as standard treatment, there has been an increase in the number of suits filed with claims of delayed diagnosis and delayed treatment of MI. An evolving trend is the allegation that failure to use or delay in the use of thrombolytics falls below the standard of care, and earlier use of these treatments would have preserved cardiac function or saved a life. The PIAA AMI Study found that 14.3 percent of all AMI cases that involved treatment errors originated in the ED, with the average payment being

44 percent higher for cases in which thrombolytic use was a factor. The current JCAHO performance measurement system, ORYX® criteria for acute myocardial infarction (AMI), evaluates an organization's success in using ED-delivered thrombolytic therapy for AMI in thirty minutes or less, or alternatively, angioplasty within 120 minutes. These outcome criteria appear deceptively simple, but achieving them requires a high degree of focus in the ED coupled with coordination between the ED and the department of cardiology. For the ED to administer thrombolytic therapy within thirty minutes, a series of events has to happen in rapid succession. First, there must be recognition by the health care staff that the patient's symptoms represent a possible AMI. Next, an EKG must be taken and assessed, then the physician ascertains the necessary treatment, the patient has intravenous access established, and finally, the clot-dissolving drug is administered. All of this should be performed and finished within thirty minutes.

How Can the Risk Management Professional Help?   Enhancing patient safety and reducing malpractice exposure are better achieved if certain resources are available to the emergency department to aid first in diagnosing and treating these conditions, and secondly to help move affected patients to a higher level of care promptly, either in the same hospital or by appropriate transfer to another facility. The risk management professional should advocate that the organization address the following points, which are key in meeting these very time-constrained targets:

- Make certain that there are enough EKG machines available in case of multiple simultaneous arrivals.
- Provide additional education that will make it easier for ED physicians when deciding to administer thrombolytics without first consulting a cardiologist.
- Make sure that the thrombolytic medications are stocked in the ED and available for immediate use.
- Make certain that there is a rapid retrieval system for obtaining prior EKGs for comparison.
- If direct intervention in the catheterization lab is chosen, there must be an established process for prompt identification of candidate patients and rapid mobilization of the responsible cardiologist and catheterization lab personnel.
- Make sure STAT[7] cardiac blood tests have both a rapid turnaround time and an established feedback route so the initial ordering physician receives the results in a timely fashion.

Some key strategies for risk management professionals apply to all high-risk conditions:

- Participate in construction of orientation materials for ED physicians. Make sure that clinical and risk management information concerning AMI diagnosis and treatment are part of the program. These should emphasize the high number of atypical presentations, the need to carefully evaluate complaints of chest pain, to correlate current and past cardiac diagnostic tests, to look for cardiac risk factors (family history, smoking, hypertension), and to coordinate diagnostic testing with primary care physicians and cardiology consultants. Above all, emergency physicians should be advised to maintain a high level of suspicion for coronary conditions and to admit patients if it is not possible to exclude a diagnosis of active cardiac disease in the ED.
- Participate in quality improvement committees and departmental staff meetings. Present clinical and risk management information to those present and disseminate information to those who are not able to attend the meetings.

- Speak at hospital grand rounds or arrange for a speaker to address risk management issues with clinical relevance such as communication, documentation, medical misadventures, and the need to immediately notify the risk management professional of any maloccurrences.

Meningitis

Meningitis is an infection of the covering of the brain that is difficult to diagnose, disastrous if not treated promptly, and costly to settle. The typical symptoms of meningitis include fever, headache, lethargy, vomiting, and neck stiffness. The difficulty is because these same symptoms are often seen in more common illnesses such as influenza or respiratory infections. The most severely affected patients are often children under the age of two, and they are even more difficult to diagnose due in part to communication problems. Meningitis can be caused by viruses, bacteria, or fungi. Patients with bacterial meningitis can die within hours to a few days, or be left with life-long disabilities that result in high medical care costs. Patients with fungal meningitis have a more drawn-out course, but no better clinical results.

Although not the most frequent of cases, meningitis is among the most costly to settle. The PIAA Data Sharing Project reported on 48,936 cases over ten years that were settled with indemnity payments. Of these, only seventy-three (0.8 percent) concerned meningitis, but indemnity costs for these cases averaged $308,303 while the average for all cases was only $163,711. Family practice and pediatric physicians were defendants in 66 percent of the cases and emergency physicians in less than 10 percent, but in 21 percent of the cases the critical incident occurred in the emergency department. Where the original point of contact for the patient was in the ED, indemnity averaged nearly $1.4 million and accounted for approximately half of the indemnity paid. The claims involving the worst outcomes and highest payouts were heavily weighted toward younger ages. Although the median age was two years and 60.3 percent of the patients died, the majority (82.6 percent) of deaths occurred in patients under one year of age. The highest indemnity costs were paid when patients survived the illness but were brain damaged, quadriplegic, or required lifelong care. For these cases, the average indemnity was $2,633,689, and although they made up only 17.8 percent of meningitis cases, they accounted for more than half of the total indemnity costs.

The most common error (70 percent) in these cases was a delay in or failure to diagnose meningitis. Meningitis is commonly misdiagnosed as a viral upper respiratory infection, ear infection, or migraine headache. Delay or failure to perform a diagnostic lumbar puncture was seen in 23.3 percent of cases. In these cases, there were multiple symptoms that should have prompted consideration of a lumbar puncture, but the procedure was not performed in a timely fashion to aid in diagnosis. Delay in admission to the hospital was also cited in 26 percent of cases. Data from the PIAA project also indicated that poor communication, telephone treatment, and inadequate documentation were common remediable causes for large settlements. Clinicians should be advised to maintain a high index of suspicion for meningitis and diligently record negative findings.

How Can the Risk Management Professional Help?   The risk management professional can assist the clinical staff by pointing out to key managers that lumbar puncture supplies should be readily available in the ED. In many institutions, radiologists perform lumbar punctures with the help of imaging equipment when emergency physicians encounter difficulties. This resource should be available on a round-the-clock basis. Quality improvement efforts should be focused on reducing delays in diagnosis and treatment, with coordination among emergency physicians, radiologists, and infectious disease specialists in the institution. Blood test results should be expedited and antibiotics stocked in the ED for ready access. Through orientation materials or risk management education initiatives, clinicians should be reminded of the following actions that can reduce losses and improve patient care:

- Maintain a high index of suspicion for meningitis when presented with a patient with a flu-like illness.
- Listen carefully to the history provided by the patient and especially to caregivers of infants.
- Document carefully, including positive findings, significant negative findings, and the treatment plan.
- Thoroughly evaluate patients with suspected meningitis, treat immediately, and admit if the diagnosis is not completed in the ED.
- Patients who are discharged should receive clear instructions (verbal and written) about symptoms that should prompt an immediate return.

Appendicitis

Cases involving a missed diagnosis of appendicitis were the most frequently cited error in diagnosis in the PIAA study and made up 28 percent of the missed diagnosis category. However, these were responsible for only 3 percent of the total indemnity. Whereas the average indemnity for all ED cases involving diagnostic errors was $266,661, the average for appendicitis cases was lower at $45,521. Appendicitis is a condition that develops over time and thus affords a greater opportunity to identify the problem at an earlier stage. When fully developed, a case of appendicitis with rupture is easily diagnosed, but treatment at that late stage can result in lasting complications or death. In the earliest stages, when diagnosis and treatment would prevent complications, it is often indistinguishable from common illnesses such as viral gastroenteritis and food poisoning. The "classic" triad of right lower quadrant abdominal pain, fever, and elevated white blood count occurs in only one third of cases, thus making the majority of cases more difficult to diagnose. The pediatric population poses a special problem for the ED physician, in part due to the inability to obtain a history from a child presenting with abdominal pain.

Unfortunately, there is no definitive appendicitis test. Currently, the best test is a computed tomography (CT) scan of the abdomen, which can be falsely negative, and is always costly and time-consuming. For these reasons, patients who will be scanned must be chosen carefully from among a larger group of patients who present to the emergency department with abdominal pain. Further, these scans are too complex to be interpreted by most emergency physicians and must be read by a radiologist. Even their interpretations are not infallible for reasons of anatomic variability, technical difficulty, and human judgment error. The well-known difficulties inherent in making an early diagnosis with any degree of reliability and the non-fatal outcomes in most cases of appendicitis contribute to the low average awards for misdiagnosis of this condition.

How Can the Risk Management Professional Help?   The most important action is to advocate for the round-the-clock availability of in-house abdominal CT scans followed by timely radiologic interpretation provided to the emergency department physician. Other actions include:

- Provide clinical education for ED physicians so that they recognize the subtlety of early presentations of appendicitis. A high degree of suspicion is essential.

- Encourage ED physicians to specify a short follow-up interval in the discharge instructions, when patients with "gastroenteritis" are sent home, and make certain that these instructions specifically name symptoms that should prompt an immediate return to the ED.

- Point out the critical importance of having a procedure in place to facilitate rapid ED to OR transfer to prevent rupture in diagnosed patients.

Head Injuries and Conditions

These conditions do not make up a substantial proportion of ED malpractice claims in large studies, but they are high-severity and high-cost conditions when death or disability is the outcome. This group includes acute subdural and epidural hematomas, and to a lesser degree slower-developing subdural hematomas. Headache is a common complaint among emergency department patients, and in some cases, there is little to distinguish between patients who are innocuously versus emergently affected. Whereas subdural and epidural hematomas are relatively easy to see on head CT scans, early subarachnoid bleeding is not easily visible. Subarachnoid bleeds require a lumbar puncture (LP) for diagnosis, and the decision to perform this somewhat invasive and time-consuming procedure can be a difficult clinical decision for the ED physician. Knowledge of the serious consequences (death, stroke) of missing a subarachnoid hemorrhage may push the ED physician to perform an LP. Any related malpractice cases may be costly because the conditions, if diagnosed early, can be treated with a high degree of success, whereas even brief delays can result in the death of the patient. These conditions have in common the need for a high index of suspicion on the part of the ED physician, ready accessibility of properly interpreted head CT scans, and rapid neurosurgical support.

How Can the Risk Management Professional Help?   Twenty-four-hour availability of head CT scanning and rapid interpretation by neuroradiologists are key to proper diagnosis and treatment for these patients. The risk management professional should investigate the availability of these services in the institution and facilitate their installation when necessary. Other actions might include:

- Rapid access to neurosurgical support means having a neurosurgeon on call or having pre-arranged transfer agreements with another institution when neurosurgeons are not available at your hospital.

- Performance of a lumbar puncture requires the full attention of a minimum of two staff, one to hold and position the patient, the other to perform the LP. Adequate staffing is necessary.

Spinal Injuries and Conditions

Spinal injuries are the result of accidents. They become risk management problems when there is either a failure to stabilize (support) the injured area during transport to the hospital, transfer from stretcher to bed, movement for imaging studies or during treatment, or a failure to recognize the significance of patient complaints of neck or back pain. In many cases, the crucial error was that a stabilizing cervical collar was removed for x-rays and not replaced, thus allowing too much freedom of movement of an unstable fracture or ligamentous injury. Injury to the spinal cord can result in permanent paralysis for the patient and the need for costly medical care for the rest of their lives. If such a preventable injury occurs during medical care, it will surely result in a costly malpractice claim. Failure to rapidly treat these injuries with high-dose methylprednisolone, though a controversial treatment, may also be the source of a malpractice claim.

Spinal conditions are caused by objects that take up space in the spinal canal, crowding and injuring the spinal cord. These may include herniated disks, vascular malformations, and malignant tumors. These can grow without notice until a critical size is reached, at which time they compress and may irreversibly damage the spinal cord. When a patient presents with symptoms of this type, they must be diagnosed and treated within a narrow window of a few hours. Failure to do so creates lasting disability for the patient and liability for the health care providers and institution.

How Can the Risk Management Professional Help? The risk management professional should advocate for the following:

- Development and adherence to protocols regarding safeguards for patients with back and neck injuries in the field, ED, and radiology department

- Development of specific protocols that delineate the process for "clearing" a cervical spine injury including under what circumstances a cervical collar can be removed, and by whom

- Education for ED physicians and staff about the importance of early diagnosis for spinal conditions

- Assuring availability of spinal CT and MRI for patients with potential spinal injuries and conditions

- Maintenance of an on-call list for neurosurgery to facilitate emergency surgical treatment

Medical Procedure Errors

Among medical procedures, errors in intubation are the most common (49 percent), followed by cardiac arrest management (13 percent), vascular line placement (13 percent), restraints (6 percent), and others (19 percent).[8] Errors in performance of skin procedures (primarily laceration repairs) are also important contributors. Excessive severity and high losses disproportionate to the injury are found in cases that involve intubation errors and vascular line placement. Missed foreign bodies in wounds continue to make up a frequent, and avoidable, cause of emergency medical malpractice claims.

Wounds are a common reason for patients to visit an emergency department, and they represent up to 24 percent of malpractice claim allegations in some studies. However, they are typically of low severity and therefore account for only about 3–4 percent of total indemnity.[9,10] Most malpractice allegations that involve the wound are concerned with failure to find and remove a foreign body, failure to diagnose nerve or tendon injuries, and failure to identify and treat infection-prone wounds.[11,12] These cases are remarkable because they are both numerous and easily avoidable. Discharging a patient with a retained foreign body in a wound is both embarrassing and difficult to defend, not to mention aggravating to the patient.

Most foreign bodies are visualized using the proper modality. Metallic foreign bodies (including aluminum) and glass foreign bodies that are 2 mm in size or greater can easily be seen on radiographs.[13] Wooden foreign bodies are often difficult to detect clinically but can be well visualized by ultrasound, CT, or MRI.[14] Plastic is particularly well visualized with MRI scanning. Finally, remember that undiagnosed tendon lacerations are an important problem, accounting for 8 percent of all ED diagnostic errors in one study.[15]

Patients are often sent home from the ED with a full foreign body or partial piece still present that will later be identified when imaging studies are read by a radiologist. Physician responsibility for radiograph interpretation and patient follow-up is frequently an issue in malpractice claims.[16] There must be coordinated action between the departments of emergency medicine and radiology. Potential misinterpretations in x-rays, which are often subtle and often read quickly, necessitate a reliable system for over-reading by radiologists. The same principle of cross-checking by specialists also is important to consider for EKGs and lab results. Patients with discrepant readings or new findings must be notified, and this notification must be documented. The ED's quality improvement program should review all ED discrepancy reports that offer guidance and support to physicians and staff for system and process redesign.

How Can the Risk Management Professional Help?   The risk management professional should educate the ED physicians so that they understand the necessity of x-raying or imaging wounds that potentially contain foreign bodies and the likelihood of success when these tests are performed. Other actions might include:

- Provide education about the frequency and cost of these claims.
- Establish protocols for the management of all x-ray, lab, and EKG discrepancies, including patient follow-up notification, documentation, and reporting to risk management when injury is sustained.

Deficiencies of the Diagnostic Interview and Physical Examination

The most basic elements of emergency medical practice (the diagnostic interview and physical exam) are sometimes either not performed or not documented well enough to serve the defense. When the different components of an ED visit are broken out as procedures, failure to perform a diagnostic interview (patient history) is the most common root cause of claims, with failure to perform a general physical examination listed as another of the most common omissions.[17] History and physical examination are the mainstays of proper physician diagnosis. They are essential in the process of elimination (ruling out what the patient does not have) and discovering the proper diagnosis (defining what the patient does have). However, many serious conditions can present in an early stage when symptoms might be minimal and physical signs subtle or non-existent. The role of the history and physical examination should not be underestimated, for this is where the majority of ED diagnoses are made. It is also where the majority of misdiagnoses occur.

Diagnostic testing is critical in sorting benign conditions from emergencies. Although the emergency physician's training and experience come into play in arriving at judicious test choices, ultimately, ordering the right diagnostic tests is based on what information is obtained during the history and physical exam. It is not possible, nor economically feasible, to perform diagnostic tests for every condition in every patient; therefore it is vital to take a complete and thorough history and physical exam (H&P). One of the most important things a doctor can do during the H&P is to listen to the patient and realize that most patients often list the real reason they came to the ED as an addendum, at the end of the history. Attention paid to an "oh, by the way, doc" can help both the physician and patient prevent many hours of clinical sleuthing. Additionally, a 1984 study found that doctors initiating a medical interview wait an average of only 18 seconds before interrupting a patient.[18] A 1999 follow-up study showed the average length of time given patients to itemize their concerns before the first redirection (interruption) was 23.1 seconds per interview or 28 percent longer than the original 18 seconds reported in 1994.[19] Patients who come to the ED often are injured and in pain. Interrupting their train of thought and verbal flow will not help the doctor decipher the patient's problem. The ED physician must use both technical diagnostic and active listening skills during the physical exam to achieve optimum results.

Importance of Discharge Plans

To reduce risk, discharge plans must be carefully constructed to direct patients to the next step in care, or prompt a return to the ED. Inevitably, some patients will be sent home without a definitive diagnosis, some will leave with the wrong diagnosis, and some will need follow-up care at a more specialized medical or surgical practice. Discharge plans must specify a physician or practice along with a definite time interval for an appointment when the patient can receive continuing care. It goes without saying that it is important to include family members in the discharge planning of pediatric patients, but this also needs to be done with geriatric patients because the prevalence of cognitive impairment among elderly patients in the ED is 16 percent.[20] Discharge instructions should provide information about the diagnosis and should include a delineation of symptoms for which the patient should seek immediate physician consultation or return to the ED. Patients retain this information better when they receive it verbally and in written form. Written information must be carefully evaluated to make certain that the reading level is calibrated for best comprehension by the widest patient audience: this is at about the sixth-grade level. Attaining this comprehension level is nearly impossible to achieve with handwritten instructions. Many EDs use written templates, which allow common conditions to be circled or checked, but computerized systems now on the market are more complete and condition-specific in their explanations and advice. Patients with limited reading skills also benefit from verbal descriptions and visual depictions of their conditions.

············

EMERGING TRENDS IN ED MALPRACTICE

The Emergency Medical Treatment and Labor Act (EMTALA) is a federal law intended to prevent "dumping" of uninsured emergency department patients from one hospital to another. The "dumping" referred to in the act was the rapid transfer of unstable patients from private to public hospitals without evaluation or provision of stabilizing treatment in an effort to avoid the financial loss associated with an uninsured (or under-insured) patient. Media attention to this practice and public outcry forced Congress to act, and the law was quickly passed in 1986. The act's basic principles have been sustained; however, its language has been subject to a series of judicial and administrative interpretations. Because it mandates initial ED medical screening examination (MSE) and stabilizing treatment, backed with the threat of fines or removal of a hospital from the

Medicare program, EMTALA has become the legislative equivalent of an unfunded national health insurance program.

The Department of Health and Human Services, CMS, issued the "Revised Emergency Medical Treatment and Labor Act (EMTALA) Interpretive Guidelines" on May 13, 2004. These guidelines define "hospitals with an emergency department" to mean a hospital with a "dedicated emergency department." These regulations further define "dedicated emergency department" as any department or facility of the hospital that either:

1. is licensed by the state as an emergency department;

2. is held out to the public as providing treatment for emergency medical conditions; or

3. where one-third of the visits to the department in the preceding calendar year actually provided treatment for emergency medical conditions on an urgent basis.[21]

The basic tenets that apply to emergency medicine are 1) that all dedicated EDs (free-standing or within hospitals) have to provide a medical screening exam (MSE) (a triage evaluation is not acceptable) calculated to determine the presence or absence of an emergency medical condition and, 2) that all emergency medical conditions are treated and stabilized within the organization's capabilities before discharge or transfer with two exceptions. Unstable patients may be transferred if they require a higher level of care than is available in the present ED or if they request a transfer in writing. Transferring physicians must send pertinent test results and all documentation (including the name and location of the receiving physician and hospital). The law applies to all patients, not just Medicare recipients, and includes any patients presenting within 250 yards of the main hospital buildings.[22] Please see Chapter 16 on Statutes, Standards and Regulations in Volume III of this series for a more in-depth discussion.

EMTALA has created many challenges for the ED. Appropriate patient stabilization may require the services of on-call medical staff. This has created a situation wherein physicians have resigned from hospital medical staffs to avoid their on-call obligation, usually because of concern about increased medical malpractice liability, lack of financial compensation, and the time commitment. In the most recent "final rule" publication by the Center for Medicare and Medicaid Services (2003), physicians are given latitude to be on call for more than one institution, schedule surgeries during on-call time periods, and limit calls when there are only a few physicians on staff to take a call for a specialty. This most recent interpretation has been helpful to hospitals (who are required to supply on-call physicians with no more leverage than medical staff bylaw provisions) in recruiting some physicians to take calls, while at the same time making it difficult to completely fill the call schedule, especially with specialists. Physician specialists, where they are few in number, are "off the hook" and free to limit their on-call obligations. This is undesirable from an emergency medicine and arguably, a liability standpoint, as the result in many hospitals has been to create gaps in physician specialist coverage, which make it necessary to transfer patients to hospitals with available physician specialists.

Additionally, the law does not state who (physician, nurse, physician extender) has to perform the medical screening exam (MSE), but compliance is generally ensured if it is done by a physician. Those EDs using non-physicians for MSEs must have a hospital board-approved plan and even with this plan, a ruling may be made that a physician should have completed the exam.[23]

Note that admission to the hospital (whether the patient is stable or unstable) or following treatment in the ED such that the patient is considered medically stable, ends the hospital's obligations under EMTALA. An ED physician's judgment that the patient has reached stability should be documented in the medical record prior to discharge. Risk management professionals can contribute to ED efforts to comply with the law by ensuring that the hospital has standing transfer agreements with neighboring hospitals that represent "higher levels" of care, whether that means possessing specialized care units or the services available in tertiary referral centers.

Psychiatric patients, who frequently require transfer to other institutions, present special problems. If acutely ill, they are often not competent to give consent for or refuse transfer. In addition, their psychiatric problems are not typically resolved within the course of ED treatment. Transfer, in the first case, requires documentation of the patient's condition and decision-making incompetence. In the second, the stabilization required by law has a different meaning than in medical cases—that the patient is rendered unable to harm himself or others prior to discharge or during transport. As detailed in the next section, the disposition of psychiatric patients is a complex issue, which includes EMTALA ramifications.

············

MANAGEMENT OF PSYCHIATRIC PATIENTS—A SPECIAL CHALLENGE

Safe handling of psychiatric patients in the ED represents a special challenge. These patients may present with psychiatric complaints or exhibit dangerous and aggressive behaviors, yet have underlying medical problems that require immediate attention.

The Assessment of the Psychiatric Patient

Although screening by psychiatric social workers is a boon to busy ED physicians, EMTALA and reasonable prudence make it desirable that an ED physician personally evaluate the patient. This is particularly true in two circumstances. The first arises if there is any sign of medical illness. Psychiatric patients admitted to the hospital with no sign of acute medical illness can receive more extensive assessment on an as-needed basis as inpatients. Patients who are being discharged from the ED require more careful scrutiny.

The second concerns patients who are depressed and have expressed suicidal thoughts. Under these circumstances, ED physicians must carefully consider the level of risk before deciding that discharge is safe. This is problematic in that it is not possible to be correct 100 percent of the time. Trained psychiatric specialists occasionally underestimate the suicidal potential of their patients. Psychiatric patients can also be a danger to others, which requires that the physician who is discharging such a person has a "duty to warn." When these patients make threats against named persons, the ED doctor has a duty to either detain the patient (admit) or warn the named parties so that they may take necessary action to protect themselves. Usually admission is the safest course, in which case an evaluation by the patient's psychiatrist can be made.

The Psychiatric Patient Awaiting Disposition

It is wise to establish ED procedures for handling psychiatric patients so that their care is well reasoned and consistent. It also goes without saying that medical record documentation, observation, and interventions concerning psychiatric patients are key to the defense of any subsequent medical malpractice action.

Aggressive, agitated psychiatric patients may require restraint or seclusion, making them a high-risk subset of the ED population. JCAHO requirements include careful assessment of patients in restraints so that the least restrictive measures are used, the indications are clear and criteria for release are set. Patients must be reevaluated at prescribed intervals. Initial face-to-face physician evaluation is required and must be repeated every four hours. This is true for the use of both physical and chemical restraints. Patients who are in seclusion should have one-on-one monitoring by an ED staff member. Video surveillance of such patients is not a substitute for direct observation, and videotaping without monitoring the patient merely documents neglect if patients harm themselves. All psychiatric patients should be searched for weapons on arrival, preferably by hospital security personnel. Medications and weapons might be concealed in clothing. To enhance the security of patients and staff, patients should therefore be asked to exchange their clothing for paper scrub suits.

Transfer or Discharge of Psychiatric Patients

When psychiatric patients are transferred, it must be done after reasonable measures have been undertaken to "stabilize" the patient. This may include physical or chemical restraints, and should be undertaken with the use of ambulance crews who have been trained to prevent either self-harm or elopement. As previously noted, EMTALA forms must be completed and medical record documentation should include clear, objective documentation of any lack of competency to consent.

If these patients are discharged, medical record documentation should reflect a well reasoned assessment indicating that the patient is medically clear and emotionally stable.

....

PROCESS ISSUES

The flow of patients in and out of emergency departments, and the EDs' ability to treat those patients successfully and process them correctly, carries significant implications for risk management professionals.

Patient Flow

ED patient flow is a significant patient safety issue and is the product of patient volume, illness severity, ED flow, and hospital throughput. National ED annual patient volume has increased steadily from 89.8 million in 1992 to 113.9 million in 2003. In 2004 alone, ED visits averaged 309,000 visits per day, 9.2 percent more than five years ago.[24] While not evenly distributed among EDs, this increase has been nearly universal, and EDs have been forced to deal with a higher volume of patients, many of whom are elderly, ill, or both. At the same time, in-patient bed availability has been adversely affected by financial pressures and a shortage of nursing staff. The end result has been that patients "stack up" in the ED, particularly during evening hours when incoming volume peaks and patients admitted during the day are still occupying ED beds. When the ED becomes overloaded, patients wait for inordinately long periods of time in the waiting room, ambulances are diverted away from the hospital, patients who need care leave against medical advice (AMA), or leave without being seen (LWBS), and the hospital suffers loss of revenue and reputation while patient care diminishes.

In 2003, 1.9 million potential patients (1.7 percent) walked out of U.S. EDs without being seen and another 1 percent left without completing their care.[25] This is a failure of the ED's function as a safety net for the community's health care. The importance of this function has been recognized in the JCAHO's 2005 focus on ED patient flow as a patient safety issue. This is also a legitimate concern of the risk management professional. As patient care is delayed, there is an increased potential for adverse events in the waiting room, in the crowded ED, and among those patients whose ambulance transport is prolonged. As an example, a University of Texas School of Public Health study found that severely injured patients are twice as likely to die when area Level I Trauma Centers are on diversion.[26]

Inefficiencies of the ED Process that Result in Errors

The ED is adversely affected by an inability to control patient inflow and outflow, by ED staff, by space limitations, and by the need to depend on other departments for rapid turnaround of diagnostic testing. Although all of these factors contribute to delays, the Government Accountability Office (GAO) found that the factor most commonly associated with crowding was the inability to transfer emergency patients to inpatient beds once a decision had been made to admit them as hospital patients rather than to treat and release them.[27]

As previously mentioned, ED patients are typically processed in a linear fashion. The patient enters at the triage desk, proceeds to registration, is placed in an ED bed, assessed by an ED nurse, and examined by the physician who then writes orders for patient diagnosis and treatment. Testing and treatment are completed and a disposition is made. Refer to Figure 10.2 for an annual plot of ED patient registration times for a community hospital.

This system is vulnerable to catastrophic failure during high-volume periods, and high-volume periods are encountered on a daily basis in most emergency departments.

FIGURE 10.2.   **Emergency Department Patient Registration Time (2004)**

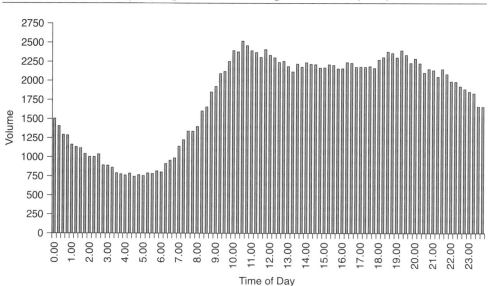

Several solutions have emerged in emergency departments across the country to counter these problems.

- Use of real-time information or tracking systems to monitor patient flow accompanied by proactive steps to reduce crowding. This is most efficiently accomplished by using computer tracking systems coupled with preplanned protocols for overload conditions.

- Use of a fast track system, which diverts patients with minor illnesses away from the main ED to a smaller area with a dedicated physician or mid-level provider and nursing staff. This can significantly reduce treatment time for these patients and unburden the ED of up to 40 percent of the normal volume.

- Flexible staffing of the ED and triage areas. For example, in overload conditions, on-duty staff may be asked to extend their shifts, on-call staff may be called in, a nurse or tech may float to the triage area to handle a large number of simultaneous arrivals, and physicians and nurses in administrative positions may assume temporary clinical roles at triage or in the main ED.

- Use of observation areas. Patients who require extended stays for administration of IV fluids, diagnosis of abdominal pain, evaluation of chest pain, or treatment of resistant asthma episodes can be observed and released from such units. This not only relieves pressure on the ED, but "saves" hospital beds for other ED patients who need them. Slightly more than 25 percent of U.S. metropolitan EDs are using observation areas to decrease inpatient admissions, lengths of stay, and costs.[28]

- Creative use of the triage area. Some EDs have used a physician during peak times to perform evaluation and treatment "up front" in the triage area, thus shortening door-to-doctor times and expediting treatment. Selected patients are not undressed or placed on a stretcher but rather are treated in rolling reclining chairs. A significant number of these patients can be treated and released without ever occupying space in the ED, effectively increasing the area available for treatment of sicker patients in the main department.

- Use of protocols that allow nursing staff in triage and the ED to assess patients, order initial tests, and initiate immediate treatment when necessary. These can be phased to increase nursing responsibility as the ED becomes progressively overloaded and physician arrival at the bedside is predictably delayed. Protocol-driven care is often used for patients with chest pain, respiratory distress (asthma, COPD, pneumonia), pain, extremity injuries, diabetes, and eye injuries. Protocols are critical for satisfying time-dependent goals such as the ORYX AMI reperfusion and pneumonia standards. They can also be used correctly to initiate testing for patients with stroke, abdominal pain, urinary tract infections, and others. If properly chosen tests are completed before the patient is seen by the physician, immediate disposition or discharge is possible at the time of physician evaluation with significant time-savings. Protocols must be approved at the departmental level by the ED physicians, and should be ordered under the name of the physician(s) on duty in the department at the time the patient is seen.

- Parallel processing of patients. Instead of following a linear sequence, patients can be placed in a room, seen simultaneously by a physician and nurse, and registered at the bedside. This significantly reduces treatment time in EDs where it is a routine practice.

- In-department testing is another important area where time efficiencies can be achieved. A radiology suite in the ED with a dedicated x-ray technologist, the use of a pharmacy technician for processing medication orders and completing a mediation reconciliation list, and point-of-care testing (fingerstick blood sugars, hemoccult testing for stool specimens and gastric aspirates, urine pregnancy testing, and rapid urine "dip" tests) can significantly affect patient flow. Some EDs take these ideas further, performing electrolytes, CBC, cardiac enzymes, and even treadmill stress tests in the department. Bedside testing carries an economic cost and duplicates laboratory services. Each institution must balance the needs of the ED and the benefits of rapid test turnaround times with redundant costs to the hospital.

A multidepartmental approach to address patient flow is essential.

The inability of patients to move smoothly through the emergency area is sometimes unfairly characterized as an ED problem, where in reality the ED is at the mercy of the efficiency (or inefficiency) of the hospital admission process. Improvements in the ED admission process require a reexamination of nearly every hospital function from admission to discharge, for example, housekeeping, nursing assignments and staffing procedures, and the intricacies of hospital discharge.

Formation of a multidisciplinary committee composed of all participants and stakeholders in the hospitalization process is required to delineate and then streamline the steps of a hospital admission and discharge. On a once- or twice-daily basis, representatives of the hospital's nursing units and ED nursing should meet to discuss patient needs and plan their movements. The ED can facilitate the movement of admitted patients by making admission decisions early in the visit, thus alerting the floors to the need to maintain or increase staffing for the next shift.

The Institute for Healthcare Improvement (IHI) has published a helpful document with a set of procedures for sorting through these issues. It conducts Web-facilitated programs to help hospitals redesign patient flow.[29] The JCAHO has also become involved in this issue and has added "Managing Patient Flow" to the Leadership chapter LD. 3.3.10.10, of the 2005 Hospital Accreditation Manual. It states, "The leaders develop and implement plans to identify and mitigate impediments to efficient patient flow throughout the hospital." This standard requires hospital leaders to assess patient movement through the hospital, patient care in temporary bed and overflow locations, shared accountability between the administration and medical staff for patient flow, use of specific performance indicators to measure components of the patient flow process, to monitor capacity, and to support service processes and the safety of hospital services and areas that receive patients. The standard also specifies that hospitals must improve inefficient or unsafe practices, and must develop criteria for ambulance diversion decisions. This is a sweeping mandate that could do much to alleviate the problems of national ED overcrowding and threats to patient safety.

············

POLICY & PROCEDURE ISSUES

JCAHO standards require written policies and procedures for high-volume or high-risk conditions. These must be approved by the department and hospital leadership. They should also be reviewed periodically to make certain that they conform to current medical treatment standards. In the case of an adverse outcome, a failure to follow the department policy will predictably become an issue in litigation. Similarly, an outdated policy that does not conform to the current standard of care is hard to defend. It implies that the hospital does not provide quality health care to the community. Inclusion of a policy review in staff orientation can prevent medical and risk management misadventures.

Evidence Based Medicine—ORYX Initiative (Emerging Standard of Care)

There is a trend in clinical medicine toward implementation of evidence-based care. Some of what has been taught regarding patient care in medical and nursing schools is the result of long experience in the medical profession rather than actual scientific data based on research. When these teachings have been approached in a scientific manner it has often been found that they have no basis in fact. For example, for many years patients who received a lumbar puncture (LP) have been instructed to lie down for a period of hours after the procedure and to drink fluids to avoid a post-LP headache. However, when tested scientifically, these measures do not prevent a post-LP headache, rather the type of needle (smaller, more narrow with a blunt tip) is the primary preventive measure.[30] Similar evidence has been used to formulate standards for care of patients with acute myocardial infarction (AMI), congestive heart failure (CHF), and community-acquired pneumonia (CAP). These standards have been adopted by the JCAHO as part of its ORYX initiative and are being implemented in hospitals across the country. As a result, they are becoming national standards of care. Hospital performance on these measures is reported publicly and will be used as a means of comparison. This has risk management implications, and risk management professionals are advised to become active in promoting their institution's compliance with these standards.

There have been some systematic attempts to make the use of x-ray studies, in particular, evidence-based. These include the Ottawa Rules for ankle injuries, and the NEXUS studies' rules for x-rays after neck injuries.[31,32] These provide recommendations for ordering (or not ordering) x-rays according to set criteria, resulting in a savings of both time and money from a reduction in the number of tests ordered. Reliance on the criteria has been shown to have near-perfect results, suggesting that their use would be quite defensible in the event of a (rare) adverse outcome.

Quality Improvement and Risk Management

Risk management and quality improvement (QI) are closely linked. Each should inform the other. Quality improvement is concerned with developing and monitoring processes used to deliver care to ensure that patients receive the maximum benefit and least harm from their visit to the ED. Risk management identifies potential risks and develops means to prevent or reduce their occurrence. QI efforts should enable ED staff to learn from their own errors and those of others to avoid repeating them. Because most errors can be traced back to systemic process failures that ensnare individuals, the ED's processes of care must be "tuned" to become more predictable for safe outcomes and efficient both in use of time and resources.

Ultimately, improvements in both department-specific and system-wide designs should be expected to improve the safety and effectiveness of patient care. Quality improvement leaders can monitor several parameters (time intervals, census, processes, and outcomes) to assess the efficacy of current processes and the later results of implemented improvements. Overall ED patient care can be judged against earlier measurements or benchmarked against other institutions' performance. The focus of QI activities should change over time—as current goals are reached, new ones should be chosen. The risk management professional can participate in this process by attending ED QI committee and hospital quality council meetings, helping facilitate data collection, and recommending actions to the hospital's administrative team. Use of an ED Risk Management Self-Assessment tool is also recommended to highlight areas for improvement.

TABLE 10.2.   Quality Improvement Assessment

Type of ED QI Assessment	*Example*
Time Intervals	Triage to room time Triage to physician contact ("door-to-doc" time) Triage to analgesic time Admission decision to in-patient bed time Total ED time ("door-to-door" time)
Census	By arrival time, day of the week, monthly Compared to the previous year Ambulatory vs. ambulance arrival Patients signing AMA or leaving before treatment

Process	Frequency of use of ED protocols
	Frequency of use of in-patient protocols
	Aspirin use for patients with chest pain
	Reperfusion within target for AMI
	Antibiotics within four hours for pneumonia
	Proper evaluation and treatment by physician
	    (disease-specific goals)
	Proper documentation (including repeat vital
	    signs, pain reassessment, etc.)

Outcome	Patient satisfaction Cardiopulmonary arrest survival Adverse events Patient, family, staff complaints

Table 10.2 depicts risk-oriented topics that might be helpful to include in the emergency department quality improvement program.

The risk management professional should also be concerned with intradepartmental ED issues. Specifically, how are patients in the waiting area supervised? How does the ED change staffing and processes to accommodate increased patient volume during peak times? Are there sufficient resources (ED space, lab, x-ray, and staff) at the appropriate times to meet the basic needs of acutely ill patients? Are patients being admitted and transferred out of the ED in a timely fashion?

Sentinel Events in the ED

Another function of the ED QI program is to analyze adverse events and seek solutions for process errors. As the discipline of quality improvement has matured, focus has shifted from identifying poor individual performance to identifying how poorly designed systems produce errors. Thus, adverse events are seen as a source of information that points to areas where redesign is needed. Sentinel events are adverse events of sufficient severity that they have caused or could have caused permanent loss of function or death.[33] Each institution is expected to carefully examine and learn from its own sentinel events. The JCAHO has mandated reporting of sentinel events and maintains a database with the intent of helping healthcare organizations learn from each other's mistakes. While it is assumed that there is widespread under-reporting, a pattern of these events has emerged.

The most common root causes of sentinel events are issues of communication, orientation and training, patient assessment, staffing, and availability of information.[34] Root cause analysis (RCA) is a special procedure in which all participants (or stakeholders) in a significant adverse event are asked to meet and contribute to a detailed reconstruction of the events that led to the adverse outcome. Each such panel should have a trained facilitator to make certain the process is organized, impartial, and non-punitive. A rigorous examination of all possible contributory factors is conducted with the intent of discovering the single proximate cause of the adverse event. This is termed the "root cause." It qualifies as such only if, in the opinion of the panel, elimination of this factor would have prevented the adverse outcome. In actuality, there can be several root causes for a single incident. It is expected that the panel's recommendations will be acted upon by the institution to eliminate the root cause(s) so that a similar incident does not occur again. Risk management professionals should participate in RCA sessions so that lessons learned can be applied elsewhere in the organization. The ED QI program's design should also encompass several methods by which the "lessons learned" are disseminated to the members of the department without compromising patient privacy. Case presentations at department meetings, morbidity and mortality conferences, and department newsletters (e-mail and print) are vehicles to improve the safety of the hospital's future patients.

·············
NATIONAL PATIENT SAFETY GOALS PERTINENT TO THE ED

In 2002, the JCAHO presented the first set of National Patient Safety Goals (NPSG). These goals were developed to promote specific improvements in patient safety. They are based primarily on information derived from the Joint Commission's Sentinel Event database. The goals focus on system-wide solutions by delineating problematic areas and formulating specific improvement standards for each safety issue. Those solutions and standards are then used by reviewers to determine compliance and to assign accreditation.[35] Each goal is subdivided into specific requirements and implementation expectations. The goals, which are revised and updated annually, can be found online at [www.jcaho.org]. At present, six of these goals (1, 2, and 3, and 7, 8, and 9) are pertinent to the Emergency Department.

Goal 1: Improve the Accuracy of Patient Identification

The purpose and requirement of this goal is to reliably identify the patient and then to match the care and treatment of that same person during the administration of medications, blood products, collection of blood or other specimens (which should be labeled with two identifiers in the patient's presence), or during the provision of treatments or procedures.

Identify the Patient   Identification is essential for ED patients, as they are frequently moved from room to room or to other departments (radiology, cardiac catheterization); patient turnover is rapid so health care personnel do not often get to know patients; patient movement may take place during a shift change; and the ED's staff must care for multiple patients simultaneously while being interrupted frequently. All of these factors increase the incidence of mislabeling of lab specimens and erroneously administered medications and treatments. Positive identification avoids errors in test and drug administration, or at worst, notification of death delivered to the wrong family. Reliable methods of identification require at least two different identifiers, but these do not have to be physically separated. A patient ID band with name and date of birth provides two identifiers on one source. Acceptable identifiers include: individual's name, an assigned identification number, telephone number, photograph or other person-specific identifier.[36] Room or bed number are not acceptable identifiers. Bar coding that includes two or more person-specific identifiers (not room number) will comply with this requirement. Scoring will be based on the above and how the identifiers are complied with in all phases of patient care, including admitting processes.[37]

Match Identity with Care   When matching the care with the patient, an active verification process that uses facial recognition and verbal affirmation is required before the start of any invasive procedure (percutaneous aspirations, biopsies, cardiac and vascular catheterizations). Placing an intravenous line, drawing blood, and inserting a nasogastric tube or a Foley catheter are not within the scope of this goal.[38] Challenges to ED patient identification include the unresponsive, confused, traumatized, mentally handicapped, or drug- or alcohol-intoxicated patient. These patients might be unable to state their names or might incorrectly respond affirmatively to the verbalization of another patient's name. Solutions include having a family member, police officer, or EMS personnel identify the patient or assign the patient a temporary name (John Doe) with an associated emergency department or medical record number.[39]

Goal 2: Improve the Effectiveness of Communication Among Caregivers

Ineffective communication is the most frequently cited category of root causes of sentinel events.[40] Lack of or ineffective communication results in more legal claims by patients than poor technical skills on the part of health care personnel. There are many reasons for communication errors: different communication techniques, language and cultural barriers, lack of teamwork, informal versus formal communication, miscommunications. Physicians and nurses are trained to communicate in different ways; doctors learn to diagnose and treat, nurses learn to describe and narrate, not diagnose.[41] Teamwork is not part of the curriculum taught in most medical schools where practitioners are instead instructed to function independently. Most communication occurs informally when clinicians make rounds or read charts. Often it is not structured.[42] Effective communication (timely, accurate, complete, structured) that is understood by all members of the health care team results in fewer lawsuits, increased patient safety, and happier staff. Task-specific communication is now being taught to health care providers with positive results for team morale and patient safety. The SBAR (Situation, Background, Assessment, and Recommendation) technique, developed by Michael Leonard, M.D., is one of these, and another is Crew Resource Management, first used for critical military aviation applications such as flight crew communication. These techniques teach problem-solving and team communication dynamics so that each member of the team can contribute to the success of the procedure and prevent errors.

SBAR Communication Technique   The elements of the SBAR Communication Technique are:

- Situation—identification of the speaker, patient, and location
- Background—a description of the patient's condition and current problem
- Assessment—the speaker's evaluation of the problem
- Recommendation—the speaker's solution to the problem

SBAR training emphasizes the use of briefings at the start of shifts to make sure all clinicians are starting from the same point, teaches the use of assertive language, and emphasizes sharing situational awareness to enhance planning and problem-solving.[43]

Crew Resource Management   The key areas in Crew Resource Management are:

- Managing fatigue
- Creating and managing a team
- Recognizing adverse situations
- Cross-checking and communication techniques
- Developing and applying shared mental models for decision making
- Giving and receiving performance feedback[44]

Because many aspects of communication are hard to quantify, currently this goal is separated into the measurable tasks of receiving orders and test results; implementing a "Do Not Use" list of abbreviations, acronyms, and symbols; establishing an acceptable turnaround time for reporting test results; and instituting a standardized approach for handing off communications.

Reporting Test Results   Verbal or telephone orders, or telephonic reporting of critical test results, should be verified by having the person read back the complete order or result after writing it down or entering it in a computer. Each organization will determine what test results are critical but these generally include "stat" tests and "panic values" reports.[45] Verbal orders are discouraged except in emergency situations such as a cardiac arrest, where they should be orally reiterated (repeated back). Surveyors will gauge compliance by evaluating performance based on your approach for tracking compliance. This may or may not include documentation.[46]

Do Not Use List   The Do Not Use list is a short catalogue of medical abbreviations, acronyms, and symbols that are easily miswritten or misread, thus leading to confusion and error. An analysis by MEDMARX of 19,457 error reports from 498 facilities from January 2000 to August 2004 found abbreviations to be a main source of medical errors. Physicians were the staff persons most often involved, in 67 percent of the cases, with nurses involved in 17 percent, and prescribing errors were the most frequently (73 percent) reported type of error.[47] Each organization is required to establish a list of abbreviations, acronyms, and symbols that are not to be used. In addition, this list must also include the official JCAHO "Do Not Use" list found online. The "Do Not Use" list applies to all orders and all medication-related documentation when handwritten, entered as free text into a computer, or on pre-printed forms. It does not currently apply to computer-generated forms or displays, but these should comply with the list wherever possible for consistency, and to reinforce staff behavior change.

Failure to eliminate the "Do Not Use" abbreviations in medication orders is one of the most frequent (27 percent) non-compliance findings during Joint Commission surveys.[48] The minimum expected level of compliance for handwritten documentation and free-text entry is 90 percent; for pre-printed forms it is 100 percent. Clarification of an order prior to implementation and after-the-fact correction of the order does not eliminate those occurrences from being counted. Three uses of "Do Not Use" Abbreviations equal a Requirement for Improvement.[49] The JCAHO also has an online list of implementation tips from various organizations for eliminating dangerous abbreviations.[50]

The ED is a rapid-paced environment where physicians and nurses are time-constrained, and the use of abbreviations and acronyms decreases the time required to input patient data. Use of pre-printed order forms or computer-generated templates that use accepted abbreviations, computer-provider order entry (CPOE), posting of the "Do Not Use" list in physician ordering areas, and in-services on this safety issue can reduce the risk of these occurrences.

Turnaround Times for Results   Turnaround time (TAT) is defined as the amount of time it takes from ordering to receiving a lab or test result. Numerous liability suits and patient safety issues relate to turnaround time for lab results. As the ED clinician is usually starting from scratch with an often complex patient and timely action is necessary to avoid adverse outcomes, availability of lab results is particularly critical in the ED environment.

TATs for relaying and receiving critical test results should be evaluated and implemented by the organization for timeliness. The organization must define the acceptable length of time between 1) ordering and reporting results, and 2) availability and receipt by the responsible licensed caregiver. JCAHO surveyors will be checking to see that TAT data has been assessed, needed changes to shorten the length of time have been made, and that these changes have been measured and evaluated.[51] Standardization of the chain of communication between caregivers (physician, nurse, ward secretary, and phlebotomists) and departments (lab, messengers, ED, radiology, and so on) and a consistent approach to the use of mechanical forms of relayed information (phone, fax, computer) must be established in protocols. If the ordering caregiver is not available when the test results return, a formal process to make sure that they receive the results should be established. One solution for improved TAT is a Service Guarantee written by diagnostic departments (laboratory, x-ray, others) that promises test results within a specified time interval. Another is Computerized Provider Order Entry (CPOE), a process where physicians input their orders and receive the results digitally. This method decreases the number of steps, people involved, errors, and turnaround times. Although CPOE is expensive to implement for an entire hospital, beginning implementation in the ED is a less costly solution in a critical environment.

Handoffs   Handoffs are defined as the transfer of patient care from one health care provider to another. In the ED, these take several forms: nursing shift changes; physicians transferring complete responsibility for a patient (sign-outs); physicians transferring on-call responsibility; temporary responsibility for staff leaving the ED for a short time; and nursing and physician handoffs from the emergency department to inpatient units, different hospitals, ambulances, nursing homes, and home health care. The JCAHO requires that a standardized approach for handoffs be implemented in all such situations, and that they should include the opportunity for personnel to ask and respond to questions. In a study done by the Getting at Patient Safety (GAPS) Center in Cincinnati, Ohio, on handoff solutions in high-risk settings, several strategies were observed that improved the effectiveness of the handoffs in the health care setting. One strategy was the use of an overlap period of time between the incoming and outgoing care givers that allowed both sides to ask questions, clarify issues, review patient historical data, update missed patient care that occurred during shift change for nurses, conclude patient care for ED physicians, and allow a face-to-face final turnover of care. Other strategies include the use of new technologies such as a computerized sign-out form (which caused the error rate to fall by a factor of three in one study), digital recorders, and automated records.[52] Many EDs have adopted the above strategies, especially the use of overlap time periods and computerized sign-out forms. Overlap periods in the ED also have the added benefit in that the original physicians and nurses can complete the care of specific patients rather than handing them off to new staff. This leads to greater patient and staff satisfaction because continuity of care is achieved.

JCAHO surveyors define an effective handoff as: interactive communication that allows questioning between the giver and receiver of patient information that includes up-to-date information regarding the patient's care, treatment and services, condition and any recent or anticipated changes; has limited interruptions; has a process for verification of the received information (repeat-back or read-back); and allows the receiver to review patient data (previous care, treatment, and services).[53]

Goal 3: Improve the Safety of Using Medications

This goal has two primary requirements, both important in the ED. The first is to standardize and limit the number of drug concentrations available and the second is to create a list of look-alike/sound-alike (LA/SA) medicines, accompanied by actions to prevent associated errors.

Standardize and Limit Drug Concentrations   The U.S. Pharmacopeia reported wrong dose and prescribing errors more often in the ED than in other areas.[54] Implementation expectations for drug concentrations include limiting the number of concentrations to the minimum necessary for patient care and standardizing concentrations. The JCAHO's mandate to limit the number of standard concentrations for medications by 2008 resulted in the elimination of the Rule of Six. The Rule of Six is a mathematical equation used to prepare and administer continuous infusions in the pediatric population. In 2003, the ISMP stated that the Rule of Six was not optimal for patient care. The JCAHO continues to support that position. The Rule of Six or the Broselow tape's[55] use for pre-calculated medication concentrations may be used until December 31, 2008, only in neonatal and pediatric acute care units if they have met the participation requirements for exceptions and are showing, as an organization, movement toward standardization of concentrations.[56] (Note that the Broselow tape has other beneficial features and is considered to be a useful tool for quickly determining the proper size of pediatric equipment and the correct dose of standardized concentrations.[57])

Because of the large difference between adult concentrations and dosages and pediatric formulations, emergency departments in pediatric hospitals are in a unique situation. Pediatric EDs treat infants and children whose medication concentrations and dosages are based on their weight-to-height ratios, which vary with age. Adult EDs use standardized concentrations and dosages based solely on patient weight. For this reason, pediatric EDs should request an exception to JCAHO standardization requirements. This type of exception will be allowed only during the transition period, until December 31, 2008. Requirements which must be addressed before the exception will be granted include the following: Emergent and non-emergent admixtures are to be prepared only by pharmacy staff in a sterile environment. Calculations of drug solution concentrations must be validated during preparation. Labeling of solution concentrations and drug per millimeter must be clear, and solution concentration (amount of drug per unit volume of solution) must be clearly indicated on the label. If the Rule of Six is used in a pediatric setting, but standardized drug concentrations are used in other parts of the hospital, guidance aids must be made available to caregivers who might not be familiar with one of these systems. If the organization has a neonatal intensive care unit, the pharmacy must be open twenty-four hours a day to support the admixture service. Smart pumps are to be used, and the organization must have received JCAHO approval of a Request for Review of an Alternative Approach to the NPSG.[58] Sample request forms can be found at: [www.jcaho.org/accredited+organizations/patient+safety/05+npsg/sample_rfr.htm].

Developing a national consensus on drug concentrations will increase safety and decrease error by ensuring that all organizations have standardized mixtures, encouraging pharmacies to manufacture more premixed infusions, and facilitating programming of drug libraries into smart infusion pumps.[59] Computerized software is available for developing the concentration standards used by each individual organization.

Look-Alike/Sound-Alike Drugs   Look-alike/sound-alike (LA/SA) drugs are medications that sound similar (Adderall/Inderal, vinblastine/vincristine), look the same either in the spelling of their name (Celebrex/Cerebyx, Lovenox/Lotronex) or the packaging of the product (Xylocaine-MPF/Shur-Clens, tuberculosis skin tests/influenza vaccines, Brethine/Methergine), or have similar names and similar actions (glipizide/glyburide). It has been reported that LA/SA medication errors account for 25 percent of all drug errors, with 12.5 percent of the mistakes due to medication names.[60] Various medical specialties such as medicine, orthopedics, oncology, and so on, use certain common medications on a routine basis. The ED is no different in this regard, but ED personnel must also care for patients whose medications might have been prescribed by practitioners from any of the other specialties. The difficulty of maintaining this knowledge is further complicated by the introduction of new drugs. The LA/SA requirement states that individual organizations must create and implement a list containing a minimum of ten LA/SA drug combinations from the three JCAHO tables (five from Table I for the ED and five from any of the three tables) available online [www.jcaho.org/accredited+organizations/patient+safety/npsg.htm]. JCAHO surveyors will be looking for the use and implementation of several strategies for each drug combination on every organization's list. (Refer to Chapter 6 in this volume for more information on Medication Safety including strategies for LA/SA drugs.)

Additional strategies to help avoid human error due to attention and memory failures include these: "Really" read the label. Avoid fatigue and distractions. Use checklists to avoid reliance on memory. Have a second person double-check your work. (Ninety percent of errors will be found by the second checker.) Take a time out when needed and, finally, enlist the patient's help.[61]

In reviewing the NPS goals, note that four out of six goals have to do with medication safety. In part, this is because medication protocols are readily defined and measurable, but their implementation can also produce meaningful results. With delineation of the main problem areas, patient drug safety can be affected positively. A five-year study of medication errors in the ED showed that:

- Performance deficit was the number one cause of error.

- Wrong administration technique was associated with the greatest percentage of harmful errors.

- Wrong dose and prescribing errors were the most common types of error.

- Distractions were the leading contributing factor in errors.

- Heparin was the most commonly involved drug, followed by insulin, ceftriaxone, morphine, and acetaminophen.[62]

Automated medication dispensing, unit-based pharmacists, electronic health records, bar coding, and computerized medication ordering will also help to change the way we handle the medication safety initiatives in the ED. The American Hospital Association (AHA), Health Research & Educational Trust (HRET), and the ISMP have created *Pathways for Medication Safety,* a ten-page assessment for organizational risk and medication safety practices that outlines specific questions for use by risk management professionals Refer to: [www.medpathways.info/medpathways/tools/tools.html].

Goal 7: Reduce the Risk of Health Care-Associated Infections

Hospital-acquired infections affect nearly two million patients with 90,000 deaths annually at a cost of $17 billion to $29 billion.[63] ED staff make personal contact with millions of patients each year. Each contact risks transfer of infection to that health care worker and then to the next patient. At the same time, health care worker (HCW) compliance with hand hygiene practices runs only an overall average of 40–48 percent.[64]

Hand Hygiene Statistics   Physicians are the least compliant, having a self-estimated handwashing rate of 73 percent with an actual rate of 8.6 percent before and 10.8 percent after patient contact.[65] Additionally, when the ranking group member (usually a physician) did not perform hand hygiene, compliance was worse for all health care personnel.[66] Not surprising, staff compliance increased to 95 percent if the HCW perceived a significant threat to self, such as when caring for an HIV patient.[67]

Whereas lack of time has been listed in several sources as the leading factor for handwashing non-compliance, note that the duration of handwashing times by health care staff averages only 6.6 to twenty-four seconds, with an overall average less than ten seconds.[68] Note also that good hand hygiene has been listed as the single most important preventative measure to avoid HCW-to-patient transmission of infection in several studies.[69] Goal 7 has clear risk management implications for the ED's fast-paced, rapid-turnover environment. Requirements for this goal include adherence to the Centers for Disease Control and Prevention's (CDC) hand hygiene guidelines and treating cases of unanticipated death or major permanent loss of function connected with a health care-associated infection as a sentinel event.

Handwashing Guidelines   The CDC's guidelines for handwashing can be found online at [www.cdc.gov/handhygiene/]. JCAHO surveyors will be looking for consistent handwashing techniques to be followed by all caregivers and judged by direct observation and staff interviews. Consistency is the key word as any *pattern of non-compliance,* more than a sporadic miss, will be scored as non-compliance.[70] Health care workers know to wash their hands and why, they "just need to do it." Even though electronic monitoring devices with voice prompts have been shown to affect a modest compliance increase in handwashing, the risk management professional can assist by initiating system-wide strategies aimed at changing culture that sanctions poor compliance behaviors of health care workers.[71]

Sentinel Event Infections   When root cause analysis of sentinel event infections is conducted, the ED is not the primary location for discovery of sentinel event infections (cases of unanticipated death or permanent loss of function), but it might be found to be the initial source. For example, when central lines are inserted, or when invasive procedures are done in an emergent manner (under less than optimal conditions) the patient may develop sepsis from the line insertion and die later in the course of hospitalization. The second requirement of Goal 7 mandates that these be considered sentinel events and that a root cause analysis be completed if the outcome was not the result of the natural course of illness or underlying condition at the time of admission. The analysis questions should include, but not be limited to: why did the patient become infected, suffer permanent loss of function, or die? JCAHO surveyors will be looking for improvements that lessen future infection risks due to these sentinel events. Examples of improvements include identification of system and process factors that can be redesigned to decrease negative patient outcomes.[72]

Goal 8: Accurately and Completely Reconcile Medications Across the Continuum of Care

The requirements of this goal include: 1) creating a standardized process for obtaining and documenting a complete list of all medications the patient is on and 2) ensuring that this list is transferred with the patient during transitions of care.

Create a Medication Reconciliation List   Reconciliation of medications is defined as the identification of a complete list of medicines each patient is currently taking. This inventory begins with the drugs they are taking at home, continues with the physician's writing of admission, transfer, and discharge orders and is kept current through all phases of medical care.[73] At a minimum, the list should include the patient's name, medication dose, when drug was last taken, and the route and frequency of administration. The function of "reconciling" medications from the ED, to hospital admission, to transfer to nursing home, outpatient care, a different service, another setting, or readmission, is fundamental to preventing medication errors, treatment mistakes, and malpractice claims (adverse drug events account for 6.3 percent of malpractice claims).[74] Transfers of care are critical points in the reconciliation process because chart reviews show that over half of all hospital medication errors occur at the interfaces of care.[75]

The three-part process of producing a reconciliation medication list first involves collecting the medication history, then ensuring that the medicines and dosages are appropriate, and finally, documenting changes in the medication orders.[76] Because the ED is most often the first contact point for a patient, it is critical for EDs to implement a medication reconciliation form that has been developed in concert with inpatient personnel, pharmacy, and the medical and nursing staffs. Implementing medication reconciliation has been shown to decrease the rate of medication errors by 70 percent, reduce adverse drug events by over 15 percent, decrease nursing admission time by over twenty minutes per patient, and reduce pharmacist discharge time by over forty minutes per patient.[77] The ideal vehicle would be a computerized list stored at a central location, accessible to all health care providers, and easy to update in outpatient offices, emergency departments, extended care facilities, and inpatient settings.

Reconciliation List with Each Transfer   Whatever form it takes, either written or computerized, the patient's medication list should be reconciled at admission and with each transfer of the patient. Completion of the form should include: patient and family involvement, a comparison of the initial patient list with what providers order, and consideration of the full range of medications as defined in the accreditation manual (prescription medications, sample medications, vitamins, nutriceuticals, over-the-counter drugs, vaccines, diagnostic and contrast agents, radioactive medications, respiratory therapy-related medications, parenteral nutrition, blood derivatives, intravenous solutions and any product designated by the FDA as a drug).[78] The use of medication cards carried by the patient is especially helpful in emergent situations where the patient is too ill, confused, or psychotic to divulge the necessary information. If the patient cannot supply the medication list, then family members should be queried. Some health care organizations have distributed "Vial of Life" kits—plastic tubes that contain medication lists that patients keep on the shelf of the door of their refrigerators, where paramedics are trained to look for them. This serves a community outreach function and a practical aid to emergency health care delivery. Direct access to the patient's electronic medical record supplements (or replaces) these, and is time-efficient and potentially life-saving. With implementation of this goal, electronic versions of the medication reconciliation form will become increasingly available, bringing tangible benefits for patient safety especially in the ED, one of the first portals of patient entry.

The JCAHO requirement states that the medication reconciliation form is to be used any time orders are rewritten, new orders are prescribed, or the patient changes service, setting, provider, or level of care. JCAHO surveyors will check for communication from provider to provider, whether inside or outside of the organization, and will review the organization's medication reconciliation list for accuracy.[79] Examples of forms in use by other organizations, a how-to guide for getting started in medication reconciliation, and tools for measuring unreconciled medication errors can be found online at the Institute for Healthcare Improvement [www.ihi.org].

Goal 9: Reduce the Risk of Patient Harm Resulting in Falls

The JCAHO requirement for this goal is to institute a fall reduction program in the context of the patient population the ED serves, and then evaluate its effectiveness. The program should include risk reduction strategies, in-services, department redesign, and the involvement of patients and families in education. The program should also include development and implementation of transfer protocols (for example, ambulance stretcher-to-bed) when relevant.[80] Falls are the most common cause of hospital admissions for trauma. They affect more than one-third of adults sixty-five years and older, cause the majority of elderly fractures, and are the leading cause of injury deaths in the aged population.[81]

Cause and Incidence of Falls Emergency departments in 2001 treated more than 1.6 million seniors for fall-related injuries and hospitalized nearly 388,000.[82] Although most falls occur in or around the home, a study from the National Center for Patient Safety showed that 20 percent of falls happened in nursing homes and 15 percent in acute care units. Another study showed that the average health care cost of a fall for patients aged seventy-two and above averaged $20,000.[83] Patient falls are among the most common occurrences reported they account for 10 percent of fatal falls in hospitals.[84]

The ED serves a large volume of patients who are treated on elevated beds, stretchers or gurneys, and rolling recliners. Additionally, patients may be placed in small, confined rooms where they are not easily seen by ED personnel who must care for multiple patients in different locations. ED personnel perform triage for patient severity, which often leaves the older potential fall victim low on the ladder of emergent crises. Patients may be placed in hallways when overcrowding occurs, at which time no staff member is available to "sit" with someone who needs constant watching. It is clearly essential that ED personnel recognize risk factors and possible solutions to prevent patient falls.

At-risk patients include:

- Those with impaired mental status (the most commonly identified factor)
- Those who have already experienced one fall during hospitalization
- Those with impaired mobility and those who need special toilets
- Those who have visual or hearing deficits
- Those who are taking certain medications (sedatives, tranquilizers, class 1A antiarrhythmics, digoxin, diuretics, psychotropics, anticoagulants)
- Those who must have assistance transferring from one location to another (usually a bed or chair)
- Those who are sixty-five years of age or older

Environmental risks for falls include:

- Poor lighting
- Loose carpeting
- Wet floors
- Bed siderails
- High bed height
- Unlocked wheels on wheelchairs, beds, stretchers
- Cluttered rooms
- Secluded patient spaces
- Use of assistive devices
- Inaccessible or distant nurse call light
- Having the toilet too far from the bed
- Slippery patient footwear and hard flooring[85]

Possible solutions include use of the Morse Fall Scale,[86] a rapid and simple scale to determine a patient likelihood of falling, upon admission. Those with a high score receive universal fall precautions and a colored bracelet that identifies them as a high-risk candidate. Putting all bed siderails in the up position is the approach most often used for the cogent patient. Development of a transferable checklist of potential fall information, including history of previous falls, impairment of vision, hearing, cognition, mobility, and other risk factors can also be helpful. Still other risk prevention strategies include bed alarms, having the family sit with the patient, placing the patient in a room close to the nursing station for easier monitoring; padding the patient's hips prophylactically, education of staff, patient, and families on fall prevention, and modifying environmental risks.[87]

Although the research on falls within hospitals is scant, and even less in the ED, the best programs have included the implementation of multiple interventions. The National Center for Patient Safety [www.patientsafety.gov] has a 139-page *Toolkit to Prevent Senior Falls*, and a fall rate calculator that is downloadable and free.

············

INTEGRATION OF ED AND HOSPITAL OPERATIONS

Remember that emergency departments do not function as independent units within the hospital. Because of the time-sensitive nature of their workflow, EDs rely heavily on the services of other departments. These services must be rendered in an efficient and timely manner, or the passage of patients through the ED will be impeded. Delays in testing and specialized care constitute a safety risk for both patients in the ED and those who will come to the department in the ensuing hours. ED operations are affected most by health information management systems (HIM), diagnostic services (principally radiology and laboratory services), ancillary departments (respiratory therapy, EKG), operating rooms, and cardiac catheterization labs, and in-patient units (general medical-surgical floors, telemetry, ICU, and specialized units). Each of these areas has time-critical functions.

Health Information Management Systems

HIM's main function is to provide past medical history, but for this information to be useful it must be complete and delivered rapidly. Even in the "information age," provision of care is often impeded by information gaps—previously collected information that is not available when care is rendered. One study found an information gap in the care of 32 percent of 1002 ED visits.[88] Past medical history and prior diagnostic test results allow the ED staff to understand the full depth of the patient's condition (often not divulged by the patient), avoid duplication in testing, and identify the patient's primary care providers and consultants. This information is difficult to transport and digest in paper form and, increasingly, hospitals are using electronic data repositories for this purpose. An effective use of technology, computer-automated HIM serves both clinical and patient safety functions. However, the utility of information is improved if ED physicians can access patients' medical records anywhere within the health care system. Many multi-hospital health care systems have accomplished this, but broader access to patient data remains more difficult. Information retrieval from outside (the hospital or system) is a cumbersome process that requires providers to do the legwork. Indeed, before any information can be shared, a consent form must be faxed to the information-holders for the patient to sign, so that data can eventually be sent back to those in an active caregiver role. Services that store patient information on the Internet so that they can be accessed selectively by health care providers with patient (or family) permission are in operation in other countries and are seeing their first use in the United States. Other solutions, such as Smart Card-based portable patient records, have been devised but not implemented widely. Ultimately, once the patient privacy issues are worked out, national access to electronic patient health care records would assure that the patient's health care providers have the necessary information immediately available.

Laboratory

Laboratory services are critical to the function of the ED, as nearly every patient processed in the main ED will require at least one laboratory test. Results of these tests can radically alter the course of the patient's care. Because of the time-sensitivity of these test results, some ED's use point-of-care testing for tests such as hemograms, electrolytes, cardiac enzymes, urinalysis, pregnancy testing and blood glucose measurements. Strict Clinical Laboratory Improvement Amendments (CLIA) quality-control measures and training requirements increase the difficulty of performing bedside testing and add to the job-complexity of ED nurses. The goal of the process is to deliver the results rapidly to those caring for the patient. Each facility finds its own balance point in this equation, with many relying entirely on services from the laboratory.

Radiology

X-rays or other "imaging" tests are commonly used for ED patients with an average of about 0.6 tests per visit.[89] Delays in the process of obtaining radiographs and learning the results of their interpretation significantly affect the duration of emergency department visits. For billing purposes, a reason for the examination is required for all studies, and for clinical purposes, radiologists should be supplied a history that helps them understand what to look for. In the most efficient systems, radiologists read films before the films are taken to the ED, and this service is available for the majority of the day, but is usually not available on evening or night shifts. As radiologists are more skilled in performing interpretations of these images, it is obvious from a risk management point of view that the services of a radiologist are desirable to have for as much of the 24-hour day as possible. Because radiologists need to sleep, and prefer to do so at night, hospitals have found many solutions to the problem of how to get films read at night. Some employ radiology residents for night and weekend readings, others use digital transmission of the images that allows reading at remote sites with the results faxed back to the requesting ED physician. The physicians who read the films can be medical staff members housed in a location in a different time zone, or the services can be contracted with outside companies who use physicians living in other parts of the globe, such as Israel or India. Refer to Volume III, Chapter 14 in this series for more information on Telemedicine.

Respiratory Therapy

Respiratory therapy services are needed by many ED patients and when required must be provided immediately. For this reason, ED nurses are often trained to administer initial respiratory updraft treatments, with subsequent treatments administered by respiratory therapists (RT). For staffing efficiencies, nurses and respiratory therapists are sometimes cross-trained for this function, and RTs may also be asked to perform other services such as EKG testing in the ED. In any case, it is essential that respiratory therapy treatments and EKG testing be provided on an immediate basis to those who need them.

Obtaining Rapid EKGs

There is a renewed emphasis on rapid acquisition of EKG data due to the ORYX requirement for rapid reperfusion therapy for patients with acute myocardial infarction (AMI). EDs must find successful strategies to identify these patients rapidly, and EKG data is essential for determining which patients will benefit from these therapies. This is not as simple as it may seem, as patients who are ultimately diagnosed with AMI arrive with a wide variety of complaints. Protocols that mandate EKGs for patients with weakness, dizziness, shortness of breath, and advanced age will capture a larger proportion of these patients. The ED should also have more than one EKG machine so that multiple simultaneous arrivals can be promptly evaluated.

Emergency Surgery or Cardiac Catheterization

Patients who require emergency surgery, or emergency cardiac catheterization, typically have a limited time in which these services must be provided. In some states, a response time is mandated by law for physicians (typically surgeons) and these requirements may place constraints for on-call physicians to live within a travel-time defined radius of the hospital. Trauma centers have the tightest timelines for availability of surgical staff and services, and in many cases physicians-in-training who remain on call in the hospital at night are used to satisfy these requirements. ORYX requirements for AMI specify a target time of 120 minutes to open the affected coronary artery in the cardiac catheterization laboratory, and this requires rapid response from the on-call cardiologist and cath lab team. Longer response times result in poor patient outcomes, and a lower rating for the hospital on publicly available health care report cards. CMS also plans to tie financial incentives to performance in the future.

INFORMATION SYSTEMS

Documenting the events of an emergency department visit is important for three primary reasons: clinical utility, billing, and legal purposes. To meet all three needs, the medical record must be legible, organized, complete, and retrievable. There are dozens of steps in the process of completing a single emergency department visit, and documentation of each step is the ideal. However, emergency physicians and nurses must deal with the chaos caused by multiple arrivals, numerous active patients, and disruptive emergency situations. In the midst of chaos, patient care is the highest priority, and documentation sometimes suffers. The plaintiff's attorney's oft-used assertion, "If it wasn't documented, it wasn't done," does not describe the realities of emergency care. However, it is certainly correct to say, "If it wasn't documented, it is difficult to prove it was done." Because of time pressures in the active emergency department, it is essential that documentation be easy and quick. As with medical record documentation in other parts of the hospital, the staff must be trained to use only approved abbreviations; to cross out errors with a single line; to date, time, and initial error corrections and addendums; and to complete charting in as reasonably close a time to the actual occurrence of events as possible.

There are many ED charting solutions in use across the country, and with respect to patient safety, the most complete systems are superior. A handwritten page is the lowest-tech solution. It is prone to illegibility and serious omissions. Dictation systems produce a supremely legible document, but are also vulnerable to omissions, transcription errors, and are often not available for editing on the same day as the patient's visit. Accuracy of the transcribed information thus suffers. Many EDs use templates (either paper or electronic) where positive and negative items in the history and physical can simply be checked off. Finally, there are a growing number of electronic systems for emergency department documentation. Although more costly than paper-based systems, fully implemented systems are superior for several reasons, which include:

- Work is streamlined by eliminating many communication and documentation steps.
- They enable the use of Computerized Physician (provider, practitioner) Order Entry (CPOE).
- They facilitate the retrieval of results from any linked computer.
- Safety is enhanced by prompts regarding required elements to assure completion.
- The organization of the medical record is consistent—and more easily understandable to clinicians reviewing it.
- Legibility is ensured.
- Multiple users can document in and read the chart simultaneously.
- Communication between members of the ED team in the system is enhanced.
- Automatic time-stamps identify all caregivers with entry times.

- Drug allergies are automatically checked, and duplications are identified, helping to avoid drug interactions and wrong doses, and helping to ensure that the right patient receives medication.

- It should be easier to export electronic documents to hospital systems and office-practice systems.

- Records of prior visits can be retrieved rapidly.

- Billing and coding are facilitated.

- Medical records cannot be lost in the traditional sense.

- Quality improvement analysis is automated.

- It is easier to identify addendums, and to properly initial, time, and date them.

As one of its three patient safety recommendations, the influential Leapfrog Group for Patient Safety has recommended that CPOE be used to enter medication orders and has set an initial goal of 75-percent compliance.[90] Emergency departments are arguably the place where hospitals could most readily implement this standard. Still, computerized order entry does not solve all problems associated with the medical record. The medical record is only as complete as it is made by health care providers—prompts and required entries cannot be reasonably used for every piece of information. Additionally, data entry might be more cumbersome than paper systems, and significant amounts of customization must be done by the facility. The ED system must interface with hospital billing systems, laboratory and x-ray computers, and HIM systems. Electronic systems require an on-site administrator who can rapidly make changes to fit the department's workflow, and the support of the IT department for hardware maintenance and periodic upgrades. Ease of learning the system is important as all staff must be trained to use the system. Some facilities are struggling with transition systems in which some elements are on paper (these must be scanned in, and can be lost) and there might be confusion about orders that pertain to other departments. Confusion results in delays, which can be costly, and at times, dangerous for the patient. A final consideration is the need for automated backups for the data, and a process that allows care to continue during planned or unplanned system downtime. A completely electronic health record that includes CPOE, automated medication reconciliation, cross-referencing error messages, and a full history of the patient's medical health, is the ideal.

············

TRAINING OF PERSONNEL

Orientation of new personnel in the emergency department is very important to assure the smooth function of the department. A disoriented staff member is of little use in emergency situations and is more likely to commit errors in patient care. The JCAHO reports that orientation and training failures were the second most common root cause of sentinel events in a survey that covered the years 1995–2004, and they were the most common staffing-related factor in root cause analyses completed in 2004.[91]

Orientation and Preceptorship

There are many aspects to proper orientation of new ED personnel. New staff need to be acquainted with the physical layout of the department and hospital; the location of patient rooms, work areas, and supply spaces; and the location of all supplies. Each staff member (tech, secretary, nurse, NP, PA, or physician) needs to be well-oriented to the required job functions and up to full speed before stepping into the rushing current of patient flow. In most emergency departments, this is accomplished by use of a department-specific orientation manual, some classroom work, a demonstration and return demonstration of clinical skills, and preceptorship with an experienced staff member. In preceptorship, new staff work alongside experienced team members at their positions, gradually assuming more responsibility for direct patient care.

Each emergency department is required by accrediting bodies (state and national) to have policies and procedures that spell out how things are done in the department. New staff should be acquainted with these, not only because many are part of the daily flow of patient care, but because deviation from them can result in adverse consequences for patients. If a lawsuit is filed that alleges substandard care, the fact that the hospital's own policies and procedures have not been followed will only substantiate the claim of negligence. At a minimum, each staff member's orientation should be documented with a checklist that is signed by the staff member and preceptor and kept on file. It is in the interest of the hospital's risk management professional to make certain that proper medical record documentation, policies and procedures, and legal obligations such as EMTALA requirements and HIPAA regulations are part of the formal orientation process. Finally, the most successful hospitals also require new staff to be oriented to the mission of the hospital and the service culture of the institution. It follows from the above discussion that an introduction to patient safety in the ED should be part of new-employee orientation (or periodic skills training). This introduction could be taught or written by the hospital's risk management professional.

In-Servicing New Equipment, Refresher Courses (ACLS, ATLS, PALS, BLS)

Other types of training should occur in every emergency department. Periodically, as new equipment is purchased, in-service training should be conducted in the proper use of the equipment. Disaster drills should be held on a regular basis to assure familiarity with procedures, and to maintain the readiness of the department. Formal courses in emergency procedures such as Basic Life Support (BLS), Advanced Cardiac Life Support (ACLS), Advanced Trauma Life Support (ATLS), and Pediatric Advanced Life Support (PALS) helps assure that every team member knows how to participate in emergency resuscitation events. In some cases, board certification encompasses these training programs, and the requirement may then be waived for ED physicians. However, state regulations may stipulate current certification in the programs for the department's medical director.

Non-EM-Trained versus EM-Trained Physicians

Presently, the nation's emergency medicine physician workforce is a hodgepodge of various medical educational backgrounds and different board certifications. ED physicians can be residency trained in emergency medicine and board certified in EM (38 percent), not emergency medicine residency trained or board certified (38 percent), residency trained in another specialty (usually internal medicine, family practice, pediatrics, or general surgery) and board certified in EM (20 percent), residency trained in emergency medicine and not board certified in EM (4 percent).[92] This correlates with a 2003 CDC study that found only 63.5 percent of EDs were staffed with board-certified ED physicians.[93] These numbers leave roughly 40 percent of the doctors working in the ED without ED-specific training or passage of a national certification exam that tests their ED proficiency and skills. It is no surprise that the current trend is to hire physicians who have either completed a residency in emergency medicine or those board certified in emergency medicine. Board certification, which requires that the ED physician demonstrate ongoing competency in a comprehensive and nationally consistent array of topics, is a logical precedent to safer practice. Of particular interest to the risk management professional is a recent analysis of ED malpractice cases showing that non-emergency medicine trained physicians and residents working in the ED are more likely to generate claims.[94]

Residents in the ED

When emergency medicine residents-in-training work in the EDs of teaching hospitals, proper supervision is essential. Lack of proper supervision is frequently cited as a factor in malpractice cases in hospitals where residents are trained. However, in the executive summary of the PIAA data-sharing study mentioned earlier in this chapter, failure to supervise or monitor the case was the primary cause in only 3 percent of the large series of malpractice claims. This might be because supervision is naturally assumed to occur and often is not documented whether it happens or not. Regardless, residents undoubtedly play a contributing role in a larger proportion of cases.

Researchers at Vanderbilt University School of Medicine cited supervision problems as a contributing cause in 31 percent of seventy-four cases.[95] In a recent ED closed-claims study in the Netherlands, residents were involved in 76 percent of the claims, and resident supervision by an attending physician was documented in only 15 percent of the medical records.[96] Supervising physicians must document their own contact with each patient, validate the findings of each resident or medical student, and sign off on each medical record. Serious errors in patient care due to the inexperience of residents can be avoided with proper on-site supervision. This means that attending physicians must work night and weekend shifts alongside their residents.

············

PRE-HOSPITAL CARE: EMS MEDICAL CONTROL

Emergency physicians frequently are asked to function as medical control officers for ambulance crews working in the field. This is a serious responsibility to undertake on behalf of patients who are not yet in the emergency department. However, the movement of these patients falls under both state regulations and federal EMTALA proscription. In both cases, these patients are considered to be under the care of the medical control hospital. However, in most cases, state law allows discretion on the part of the ambulance (EMS) personnel to take critically ill patients to the closest appropriate facility even if it is not the medical control hospital.

An instructive case is *Arrington v. Wong*, an EMTALA case originating in Hawaii in which the physician acting as medical control officer directed the ambulance crew to transport a patient with extreme shortness of breath to a hospital in which he had previously received care, but was farther away. The patient died shortly after arrival at the receiving hospital, and the Ninth Circuit Court of Appeals ruled that the decision to transport the patient to a more distant facility was a violation of EMTALA. This decision may not be upheld in other jurisdictions, but it reinforces that acting in the best interests of the patient is a highly defensible course of action. It should also be noted that "failure to transport" is the most common reason for EMS lawsuits. It is not permissible to transport an unwilling, yet competent, patient, as this is a medical form of kidnapping, but it is expected that the crew will attempt to persuade the patient to be transported and, if transport is refused, they should thoroughly document this refusal as part of the prehospital record. In cases where the patient is obviously ill and should be transported, physician intervention (asking to speak directly with the patient) should be undertaken.

Telephone Advice to Call-ins (not EMS)

Although poison control centers across the United States have an excellent record in fielding calls for cases of accidental or intentional poisoning, the same cannot be said for other medical providers. Studies have repeatedly shown that those attempting to treat patients by phone make improper decisions. This is largely the result of collecting incomplete and indirect data about the patient. The inability to physically assess the patient is another important factor in telephone misdiagnosis. Poison Control Centers are effective because they work in a narrowly focused area for which a specific set of information is collected about the patient, and these data serve as the basis for decision making. In addition, the Centers are vigilant about follow-up.

Examples of the dangers of telephone advice have been provided by the managed care industry, which uses "Ask a Nurse" advice lines to perform triage on patients, often away from "expensive" emergency departments, to their own network providers. Two recent medical-legal cases demonstrate the dangers of these systems. In *Adams v. Kaiser Foundation Health Plan of Georgia,* (*Adams v. Kaiser Foundation Health Plan of Georgia,* C.A.F.93VS79895 [1995]) the parents of an ill six-month-old infant were directed to an in-network facility forty-two miles away instead of to closer out-of-network emergency facilities. The infant subsequently died. A similar outcome resulted when a thirty-five-year-old man was instructed to use an antacid for apparent indigestion, then died as a result of myocardial infarction and dysrhythmia before arrival at a hospital. (*Cummins v. Kaiser Foundation Health Plan of Georgia,* unpublished decision.) These types of errors must be avoided by emergency departments, all of whom receive calls from the public asking for advice.

The problem of managing calls from the public to emergency departments asking for advice has been addressed by the American College of Emergency Physicians in a policy statement. This statement advises each ED to develop a procedure to identify the nature of incoming calls. Those who have a life- or limb-threatening emergency should be instructed to call the "911" or similar local emergency medical services system. Calls from patients recently discharged from the ED should be managed using prearranged protocols that include the circumstances in which the patient should return to the ED.[97] The Emergency Nurses Association (ENA) adds one further category, that of providing basic first aid advice. However, this advice should be monitored to ensure that it does not extend beyond the most basic level. The ENA also advises creating a log that includes the caller's name, telephone number, primary care provider, chief complaint, and brief history; advice provided; disposition, and, if possible, the caller's response. To ensure quality advice, the ED should require continuing medical education for those staff involved, and the ED should maintain a continuous quality improvement program for tracking calls.[98]

············

CONCLUSION

The Emergency Department is one of the most complex and dynamic environments in health care. The high volume of patients, wide variety of problems, and rapid pace of care lend themselves to error. Prevention of harm and reduction of risk in this arena can be accomplished only with a comprehensive approach, which requires the input, oversight, and active participation of the risk management professional.

Endnotes

1. McCaig, L. F., C. W. Burt. National Hospital Ambulatory Medical Care Survey: 2003 Emergency Department Summary Advance Data No. 358:1–37.

2. Leape, L. L., T. A. Brennan, N. Laird, et al. "The nature of adverse events in hospitalized patients: results of the Harvard Medical Practice Study II." *New England Journal of Medicine*. 1991; 324:377–84.

3. PIAA Executive Summary, 2005.

4. Premier Insurance Management Services, Inc., 2005.

5. American Academy of Pediatrics Committee on Medical Liability. "Test your knowledge of medical malpractice claims." *AAP News*; 2002. p. 240–1. November.

6. Patel, H. "Symptoms in acute coronary syndromes: Does sex make a difference?" *American Heart Journal*. 7/1/2004; 148(1): 27–33).

7. "Stat" in medical parlance is actually not an acronym; it is short for *statim,* the Latin word for *immediately*. Accessed on January 6, 2006 at [ask.yahoo.com].

8. Premier Insurance Management Services, Inc.

9. Karcz, A., R. Korn, M. C. Burke, et al. "Malpractice claims against emergency physicians in Massachusetts: 1975–1993." *American Journal of Emergency Medicine*. 1996:14:341–345.

10. Western Litigation Specialists. Closed claim data. 2001.

11. American College of Emergency Physicians. "Avoidable errors in wound management." *Foresight*. 2002:55:1–8.

12. Montano, J. B., M. T. Steele. "Foreign body retention in glass-caused wounds." *Annals of Emergency Medicine*. 1992 Nov; 21(11):1360–63).

13. Ellis, G. L. "Are aluminum foreign bodies detectable radiographically?" *American Journal of Emergency Medicine*. Jan 1993; 11:12–13.); Courter, B. J. "Radiographic screening for glass foreign bodies—What does a "negative" foreign body series really mean?" *Annals of Emergency Medicine*. 1990 Sep; 19(9):997–1000.

14. Sutton, D. *A Short Textbook of Clinical Imaging*. Springer-Verlag London 1990:400.

15. Sites, R. L. "Emergency department closed claims: Ohio." *Perspect Healthcare Risk Management*. Spring, 1990:1721.

16. George, J. E. "Legal issues in emergency radiology. Practical strategies to reduce risk." *Emergency Medicine Clinics of North America*. 1992. Feb; 10 (1):179–203.

17. PIAA Data Sharing Study.

18. Beckman, H. B., R. M. Frankel. "The effect of physician behavior on the collection of data." *Annals of Internal Medicine*. 1984; 101: 692–6.

19. Marvel, M. K., R. M. Epstein, K. Flowers, H. B. Beckman. "Soliciting the Patient's Agenda—Have We Improved?" *JAMA*. 1999: 281; 283–287.

20. Chiovenda, P., G. Vincentelli, F. Alegiani. "Cognitive impairment in elderly ED patients: Need for multidimensional assessment for better management after discharge." *American Journal of Emergency Medicine*. Volume 20, Number 4, July 2002.

21. CMS Memorandum May 13, 2004 Ref: S&C 04-34, Revised Emergency Medical Treatment and Labor Act (EMTALA) Interpretive Guidelines. State Operations Manual Appendix V. Available at: [www.aans.org/legislative/aans/EMTALA_Guidelines_5-13-04.pdf] Site accessed January 6, 2006.

22. CMS: EMTALA statute—42 USC 1395dd. Available at: [www.emtala.com/law/index.html]. Accessed 8/8/2005. Naradzay, J., J. Wood, et al. eMedicine Specialties: Legal aspects of emergency medicine: COBRA Laws. May 4, 2005. [www.emedicine.com/emerg/topic737.htm]. Accessed August 7, 2005.

23. Naradzay, Wood, et al., *op. cit.*

24. AHA Hospital Statistics—2006 edition released November 1, 2005. Available at [www.ahaonlinestore.com].

25. McCaig, L. F., C. W. Burt. National Hospital Ambulatory Medical Care Survey: 2003 Emergency Department Summary Advance Data No. 358:1–37.

26. The Connection, State Report (Dec, 2002) American College of Emergency Physicians. [www.acep.org].

27. United States General Accounting Office. Hospital emergency departments: crowded conditions vary among hospitals and communities. GAO Report GAO-03-460. March 14, 2003. Available at [www.gao.gov].

28. Ross, M., S. Compton, D. Richardson, R. Jones, T. Nittis, A. Wilson. "The use and effectiveness of an emergency department observation unit for elderly patients." *Annals of Emergency Medicine*. May 2003. Volume 41, Number 5.

29. Institute for Healthcare Improvement. Optimizing patient flow. 2003. Further information available at [www.ihi.org]. Accessed July 31, 2005.

30. Walling, A. "Atraumatic vs. standard needles for diagnostic lumbar puncture." *American Family Physician;* 5/1/2001. [www.aafp.org/afp/20010501/tips/6.html]. Accessed August 7, 2005.

    Serpell, M., G. Haldane, D. Jamieson, Carson. "Prevention of headache after lumbar puncture: questionnaire survey of neurologists and neurosurgeons in United Kingdom." *British Medical Journal*. 1998; 316:1709–1710. 6 June.

31. Stiell, I. G., G. H. Greenberg, R. D. McKnight, et al. "A study to develop clinical decision rules for the use of radiography in acute ankle injuries." *Annals of Emergency Medicine*. 1992; 21:384–90.

32. Hoffman, J. R. et al. "Validity of a set of clinical criteria to rule out injury to the cervical spine in patients with blunt trauma." National Emergency X-Radiography Utilization Study Group. *New England Journal of Medicine*. 13-JUL-2000; 343(2): 94–9

33. O'Leary, D. S. Reducing medical errors: a review of innovative strategies to improve patient safety. [www.jcaho.org/new+room/on+capitol+hill/oleary_test.htm]. Last accessed May 11, 2005.

34. [www.jcaho.org/accredited+organizations/ambulatory+care/sentinel+events/root+causes+of+sentinel+event.htm]. Last accessed July 30, 2005.

35. Joint Commission on Accreditation of Healthcare Organizations: Introduction to the National Patient Safety Goals. [www.jcaho.org/accredited+organizations/patient+safety/05+npsg/intro.htm]. Accessed June 23, 2005.

36. Improving the Accuracy of Patient Identification, an excerpt from *Patient Safety: Essentials for Health Care,* Third Edition, 2005. [www.jcipatientsafety.org/show.asp?durki=10221&site=171&return=10131].

37. Joint Commission on Accreditation of Healthcare Organizations: 2006 Implementation Expectations. [www.jcaho.org/accredited+organizations/patient+safety/06_npsg_ie.pdf]. Last accessed July 23, 2005.

38. Joint Commission on Accreditation of Healthcare Organizations: 2006 Implementation Expectations. [www.jcaho.org/accredited+organizations/patient+safety/06_npsg_ie.pdf]. Last accessed July 23, 2005.

39. Improving the Accuracy of Patient Identification, an excerpt from *Patient Safety: Essentials for Health Care*, Third Edition, 2005. [www.jcipatientsafety.org/show.asp?durki=10221&site=171&return=10131].

40. Joint Commission on Accreditation of Healthcare Organizations: Root Causes of Sentinel Events. [www.jcaho.org/accredited+organizations/ambulatory+care/sentinel+events/root+causes+of+sentinel+event.htm]. Last accessed July 7, 2005.

41. Joint Commission Resources: The SBAR technique: Improves communication, enhances patient safety. Joint Committee on Patient Safety 5(2): 1–2, 8, Feb. 2005.

42. Arford, Patricia H. "Nurse-physician communication: An organizational accountability." *Nursing Economics.* 2005; 23 (2): 72–77.

43. Leonard, M.: The Human Factor: Teamwork and Communication in Patient Safety. [www.mihealthandsafety.org/2004_conference/Leonardslides.ppt] Joint Commission Resources: The SBAR technique: Improves communication, enhances patient safety. Joint Committee on Patient Safety 5(2):1–2, 8, Feb. 2005.

44. Grogan, E. L., R. A. Stiles, D. J. France, et al. "The impact of aviation-based teamwork training on the attitudes of health-care professionals." *Journal of the American College of Surgeons.* Dec 2004; 199(6):843–848.) Moorman, D. W. "On the quest for six sigma." *American Journal of Surgery.* 2005; 189:253–258.

45. Joint Commission on Accreditation of Healthcare Organizations: 2006 Implementation Expectations. [www.jcaho.org/accredited+organizations/patient+safety/06_npsg_ie.pdf]. Accessed July 23, 2005.

46. Joint Commission on Accreditation of Healthcare Organizations: Questions about goal #2 (Communication) and the official "do not use" list. [www.jcaho.org/accredited+organizations/06_goal2_faqs.pdf]. Accessed July 8, 2005.

47. Santell, J. P. "Beware of abbreviations: A 'do not use list' can help avoid problems." *US Pharmacist.* 2004; 11: 58–63. Santell, J. P., S. Camp. "Confusing abbreviations can lead to drug errors." *RN.* November 2004. Vol. 67, No. 11.

48. Joint Commission on Accreditation of Healthcare Organizations: Facts about the do not use list. [www.jcaho.org/accredited+organizations/patient+safety/dnu_facts.htm]. Accessed July 7, 2005.

49. Joint Commission on Accreditation of Healthcare Organizations: Questions about goal #2 (Communication) and the official "do not use" list. [www.jcaho.org/accredited+organizations/06_goal2_faqs.pdf]. Accessed July 8, 2005. Furthermore, the Institute for Safe Medication Practices [www.ismp.org] has an extended online list of error-prone abbreviations that are beyond the minimum JCAHO requirement. Institute of Safe Medication Practices: ISMP list of error-prone abbreviations, symbols, and dose designations. [www.ismp.org/PDF/ErrorProne.pdf]. Accessed June 20, 2005.

50. Joint Commission on Accreditation of Healthcare Organizations: Implementation tips for eliminating dangerous abbreviations. [www.jcaho.org/accredited+organizations/patient+safety/05+npsg/tips.htm]. Accessed July 8, 2005.

51. Joint Commission on Accreditation of Healthcare Organizations: 2006 Implementation Expectations. [www.jcaho.org/accredited+organizations/patient+safety/06_npsg_ie.pdf]. Accessed July 23, 2005.

52. Patterson, E., E. Roth, D. Woods, R. Chow, J. Gomes "Handoff strategies in setting with high consequences for failure: lessons for health care operations." *International Journal for Quality in Health Care;* Volume 16, Number 2: pp.125–132.) Wachter, R., K. Shojania,. "From internal bleeding: Handoffs and fumbles." *MEDscape General Medicine* 6(2), 2004. Accessed 7/14/2005. Excerpted from: *Internal Bleeding: The Truth Behind America's Terrifying Epidemic of Medical Mistakes.* Rugged Land, LLC. Copyright 2004, 441 pages. ISBN: 1590710169.

53. Joint Commission on Accreditation of Healthcare Organizations: 2006 Implementation Expectations. [www.jcaho.org/accredited+organizations/patient+safety/06_npsg_ie.pdf]. Accessed July 23, 2005.

54. Hicks, R. and S. Camp. "Medication errors in emergency department settings." *US Pharmacopeia*, 2005. [www.usp.org/patientSafety/resources/posters/posterEmergency]. Accessed June 22, 2005.

55. . . . . . . the Broselow tape, (which) is used during pediatric emergencies to quickly estimate a child's weight, determine weight-based drug doses, and select the correct size emergency or resuscitation equipment., ISMP Medication Safety Alert, Broselow Tape: Measuring the Changes from 1998 to Today, February 26, 2004, Available at: [www.ismp.org/Newsletters/acutecare/articles/20040226.asp]. Site accessed January 7, 2006.

56. Joint Commission on Accreditation of Healthcare Organizations: 2006 Implementation Expectations. [www.jcaho.org/accredited+organizations/patient+safety/06_npsg_ ie.pdf]. Accessed July 23, 2005.

57. Questions about Goal #3 (Medication Safety) What is the Joint Commission's position with respect to the Broselow Tape, the Rule of Six, and the requirement under NPSG #3 for limiting and standardizing drug concentrations in health care organizations? Available at [www.jcaho.org/accredited+organizations/patient+safety/06_npsg_3_faq. pdf]. Site accessed January 7, 2006.

58. Joint Commission on Accreditation of Healthcare Organizations: 2006 Implementation Expectations. [www.jcaho.org/accredited+organizations/patient+safety/06_npsg_ ie.pdf]. Accessed July 23, 2005.

59. National Consensus on Standardized Concentrations. Why develop a national consensus? [www.icudrips.org/nationalconsensus.html]. Accessed July 18, 2005.

60. Lambert, B. L., S. J. Lin, K. Y. Chang, S. K. Gandhi. "Similarity as a risk factor in drug name confusion errors: The look-alike (orthographic) and sound-alike (phonetic) model." *Medical Care*. 1999 Dec 37 (12):1214–25. Phillips, J. Look-Alike/Sound-Alike (LA/SA) Health Product Names Consultative Workshop. October 20–21, 2003: Proprietary Name Evaluation at the FDA, Office of Drug Safety.

61. Feroli, B. Anatomy of a medication error. Lecture from the Maryland Patient Safety Council Conference, March 2005. Department of Pharmacy, Johns Hopkins Hospital. [www.marylandpatientsafety.org/html/edu_calendar_docs/033105/index.html]. Accessed June 20, 2005.

62. Santell, J., R. Hicks, D. Cousins. Center for the Advancement of Patient Safety. Medication errors in emergency department settings—Five year review (1998–2003). [www.usp.org/patientSafety/resources/posters/posterEmergency]. Accessed June 22, 2005.

63. Joint Commission on Accreditation of Healthcare Organizations: Sentinel Event Alert, Issue 28: January 22, 2003. [www.jcaho.org/about+us/news+letters/sentinel+ event+alert/sea_28.htm]. Accessed July 21, 2005. Kohn L., J. Corrigan, M. Donaldson. *To err is human: Building a safer health system*. Washington, DC: Institute of Medicine, National Academy Press, 1999.

64. Jarvis, W. R. "Handwashing—The Semmelweis lesson forgotten?" *The Lancet*. 1994; 344:1311–2. Katz, J. "Hand washing and hand disinfection: More than your mother taught you." *Anesthesiology Clinics of North America*., 22; 2004:457–471. Boyce J. M., D. Pittet. "Guideline for hand hygiene in health-care settings: Recommendations of the Healthcare Infection Control Practices Advisory Committee and HICPAC/SHEA/ APIC/IDSA Hand Hygiene Task Force." *MMWR Morbidity and Mortality Weekly Report*. 2002; 51: 1–44. [www.cdc.gov/mmwr/preview/mmwrhtml/rr5116a1.htm#tab8]. Accessed July 21, 2005.

65. Arroliga, A., M. Budev, S. Gordon. "Do as we say, not as we do: Healthcare workers and hand hygiene." *Critical Care Medicine*. Volume 32, Number 2, February 2004.

66. Lankford, M. G., T. R. Zembower, W. E. Trick, et al. "Influence of role models and hospital design on hand hygiene of health care workers." *Emerging Infectious Diseases Journal*. 2003; 9: 217–223.

67. Katz, J., *op. cit.*

68. Pittet, D., J. M. Boyce. "Revolutionizing hand hygiene in health-care settings: Guidelines revisited." *The Lancet*. Volume 3, May 2003. [infection.thelancet.com]. Accessed July 18, 2005. Katz, J., *op. cit.* Boyce, J. M., D. Pittet. "Guideline for hand hygiene in health-care settings," *op. cit.*

69. Katz, J., *op. cit.;* Pittet and Boyce, *op. cit.*

70. Joint Commission on Accreditation of Healthcare Organizations: 2006 Implementation Expectations. [www.jcaho.org/accredited+organizations/patient+safety/06_npsg_ie.pdf]. Accessed July 23, 2005.

71. Pittet and Boyce, *op. cit.*; McGuckin, M. "Hand hygiene accountability." *Results in Nursing Management*. 2003; 34 (Suppl 4): 2. Swoboda, S. M., K. Earsing, K. Strauss, et al. "Electronic monitoring and voice prompts improve hand hygiene and decrease nosocomial infections in intermediate care unit." *Critical Care Medicine.* 2004; 32: 358–363.)

72. Joint Commission on Accreditation of Healthcare Organizations: 2006 Implementation Expectations. [www.jcaho.org/accredited+organizations/patient+safety/06_npsg_ie.pdf]. Accessed July 23, 2005.

73. Institute for Healthcare Improvement: Medication reconciliation review, Luther Midelfort-Mayo Health System. [www.ihi.org/IHI/Topics/PatientSafety/MedicationSystems/Tools/Medication+Reconciliation+Review.htm]. Accessed July 25, 2005.

74. Minogue W. F., W. Krimsky. The Saving 100,000 Lives Campaign: Deploying a Rapid Response Team (RRT). [www.marylandpatientsafety.org/html/edu_calendar_docs/033105/index.html]. Accessed June 25, 2005.

75. Rozich, J. D., R. K. Resar. "Medication Safety: One organization's approach to the challenge." *JCOM.* 2001; 8(10):27–34.

76. Justesen, J. The Saving 100,000 Lives Campaign: Getting Started Kit: Prevent adverse drug events (medication reconciliation). Jan 2005–July 2006: 1–20. [www.ihi.org/IHI/Programs/Campaign/]. Accessed July 26, 2005.

77. Whittington J., H. Cohen. "OSF Healthcare's journey in patient safety." *Quality Management in Health Care*. 2004; 13(1):53–59. Rozich, J. D., R. K. Resar, et al. "Standardization as a mechanism to improve safety in health care: Impact of sliding scale insulin protocol and reconciliation of medications initiatives." *Joint Commission Journal on Quality and Safety*. 2004; 30(1):5–14.

78. Joint Commission on Accreditation of Healthcare Organizations: 2006 Implementation Expectations. [www.jcaho.org/accredited+organizations/patient+safety/06_npsg_ie.pdf]. Accessed July 23, 2005.

79. *Ibid.*

80. *Ibid.*

81. Centers for Disease Control. National Center for Injury Prevention and Control: A toolkit to prevent senior falls. [www.cdc.gov/ncipc/factsheets/fallcost.htm]. Accessed July 26, 2005.

82. *Ibid.*

83. VA National Center for Patient Safety: NCPS 2004 Falls Toolkit, Inside the Falls Toolkit Notebook: 1–139. [www.patientsafety.gov/SafetyTopics/fallstoolkit/notebook/index.html]. Accessed July 26, 2005. Rizzo, J. A., R. Friedkin, C. S. Williams, J. Nabors, D. Acampora, M. E. Tinetti. "Health care utilization and costs in a Medicare population by fall status." *Medical Care.,* 1998; 36(8):1174–88.

84. The Institute for Healthcare Improvement: Preventing Falls. [www.ihi.org/IHI/Topics/PatientSafety/PreventingFalls/]. Accessed July 18, 2005.

85. Centers for Disease Control. National Center for Injury Prevention and Control: A toolkit to prevent senior falls. *op. cit.,* The Joanna Briggs Institute. Best Practice: Falls in hospitals. [www.joannabriggs.edu.au/best_practice/bp4.php#anchor496639]. Accessed July 18, 2005. Agency for Healthcare Research and Quality: Morbidity and Mortality Rounds on the Web, Case and Commentary. Another fall. Commentary by Bogardus, S. April 2003. [www.webmm.ahrq.gov/case.aspx?caseID=6]. Accessed July 30, 2005.

86. Morse Fall Scale available at [www.nursing.upenn.edu/centers/hcgne/gero_tips/PDF_files/Morse_Fall_Scale.htm].

87. Institute for Healthcare Improvement: Patient fall prevention and management protocol with toileting program—VAMC Bay Pines. [www.ihi.org/IHI/Topics/PatientSafety/PreventingFalls/EmergingContent/PatientFallPreventionManagementProtocolwithToiletingProgramVAMCBayPines.htm]. Accessed July 26, 2005. Agency for Healthcare Research and Quality: Morbidity and Mortality Rounds on the Web, Case and Commentary. Another fall. Commentary by Bogardus S. April 2003. [www.webmm.ahrq.gov/case.aspx?caseID=6]. Accessed July 30, 2005.

88. Stiell, A., A. J. Forsters, I. G. Stiel, C. van Walraven. "Prevalence of information gaps in the emergency department and the effect on patient outcomes." *Canadian Medical Association Journal.* Nov 11, 2003; 169(10).

89. McCaig, L. F., C. W. Burt. National Hospital Ambulatory Medical Care Survey: 2003 Emergency Department Summary Advance Data No. 358:1–37.

90. Joint Commission Journal on Quality and Safety. The Leapfrog Group for Patient Safety: Rewarding higher standards. December 2003; 29(12):634–639.)

91. JCAHO. Sentinel event statistics at [www.jcaho.org].

92. Moorhead, J., M. Gallery, D. Hirshkorn, et al. "A study of the workforce in emergency medicine: 1999." *Annals of Emergency Medicine.* Volume 40, Number 1. July 2002.

93. McCaig and Burt , *op. cit.*

94. PIAA Research Notes. Emergency Departments. Summer 2001.

95. White, A. A., S. W. Wright, R. Blanco, et al. "Cause-and-effect analysis of risk management files to assess patient care in the emergency department." *Academic Emergency Medicine.* 2004; 11(10):1035–41.

96. Elshove-Bolk, J., M. Simons, J. Cremers, A. van Vugt, M. A. Burg. "Description of emergency department-related malpractice claims in The Netherlands: Closed claims study 1993–2001." *European Journal of Emergency Medicine.* 2004 Oct; 11(5): 247–50.

97. ACEP Policy Statement #400100, Approved by the ACEP Board of Directors, July 2000.

98. Emergency Nurses Association. Telephone advice (position statement). Approved September 1998. Available at: [www.ena.org/redircct.asp? PATII=/services/posistate/statements/telephoneadvice.htm]. Accessed May 22, 2002.

Suggested Readings

Series

Lancet "Uses of Error" series.

ACEP "Foresight" clinical risk management series.

Academic Emergency Medicine "Profiles in Patient Safety" series.

JCAHO. Healthcare at the crossroads: Strategies for improving the medical liability system and preventing patient injury. 2005.

Books

Berwick, D. *Escape Fire: Designs for the Future of Health Care*. ISBN: 0787972177. Publisher: Jossey-Bass (November 26, 2003).

Berwick D., A. B. Godfrey, J., Roessner. *Curing Health Care: New Strategies for Quality Improvement*. ISBN: 0787964522. Publisher: Jossey-Bass; 1st edition (October 15, 2002).

Corrigan J., L. Kohn, M. Donaldson. (Editors). *To Err Is Human: Building a Safer Health System*. ISBN: 0309068371. Publisher: National Academies Press; 1st edition (April 15, 2000).

Institute of Medicine (Editor). *Crossing the Quality Chasm: A New Health System for the 21st Century*. ISBN: 0309072808. Publisher: National Academies Press (June 1, 2001).

Wachter, R., K. Shojania. *Internal Bleeding, The Truth Behind America's Terrifying Epidemic of Medical Mistakes*. ISBN: 1590710738. Publisher: Rugged Land. Copyright February 3, 2004.

Resource Web Sites

www.abem.org/public (American Board of Emergency Medicine)

www.aha.org/aha/index.jsp (American Hospital Association)

www.ahrq.gov (Agency for Healthcare Research and Quality)

www.apic.org//AM/Template.cfm?Section=Home (Association for Professionals in Infection Control and Epidemiology)

www.cdc.gov (Centers for Disease Control)

www.cms.hhs.gov (The Centers for Medicare & Medicaid Services [CMS] is a federal agency within the U.S. Department of Health and Human Services)

www.fda.org (Food and Drug Administration)

www.hret.org/hret/about (Health, Research and Educational Trust)

www.ihi.org/ihi (Institute for Healthcare Improvement)

www.ismp.org (Institute for Safe Medication Practices)

www.jcaho.org (Joint Commission on Accreditation of Healthcare Organizations)

www.leapfroggroup.org (The Leapfrog Group)

www.marylandpatientsafety.org (Maryland Patient Safety Center)

www.medpathways.info/medpathways/index.jsp (Pathways for Medication Safety)

www.qualityforum.org (National Quality Forum)

www.shea-online.org (Society for Healthcare Epidemiology of America)

www.thepiaa.org (Physician Insurers Association of America)

www.usp.org (United States Pharmacopoeia)

11

Risk Management and Behavioral Health

Robin Burroughs
Bruce W. Dmytrow

The provision of behavioral health care services creates the potential for both traditional and emerging risk exposures. In this chapter, corresponding risk control techniques and activities are discussed. For purposes of this handbook, behavioral health includes diagnoses, behaviors, and symptoms related to disturbances in behavior, mental processes (excluding developmental delays), and those diagnoses, conditions, and behaviors previously referred to as psychiatric or mental illness. Also included are diagnoses, behaviors, or conditions related to addiction and substance abuse.

Although behavioral health care involves risks specific to the services provided, a root cause of patient injury and health care-related litigation continues to be the breakdown in written and verbal communication between providers and patients, as is often the case in other types of health care delivery. The behavioral health care risk control program must identify and implement opportunities to address and minimize these risks.

Behavioral health risk control programs must integrate with the organization's quality improvement and patient safety initiatives. When monitoring activities are indicated to assure quality care and treatment, the organization may delegate such monitoring to its quality improvement program. Similarly, when the risk identification process recognizes opportunities for improved patient care and safety, referrals to the appropriate committees, departments, and individuals should be among the risk control techniques applied.

This chapter focuses on risk management in the behavioral health care setting. It should be noted, however, that patients with behavioral health symptoms or diagnoses are encountered in all areas of health care delivery and by all health care and ancillary service providers. Therefore, all staff members should be trained to recognize behavioral health symptoms and to be aware of the behavioral health resources available to staff members and patients throughout their organization.

The specialized needs of behavioral health patients should be considered on an organization-wide basis when considering safety and security needs and during all safety, disaster, and evacuation drills and exercises.

············

HISTORICAL PERSPECTIVE

Over the past several decades, behavioral health care has changed dramatically from a long-term, inpatient-based model to one that is primarily outpatient-based. Many factors contributed to these changes. During the 1960s and 1970s, health care costs for all specialties began to escalate at alarming rates. Long-term, government-funded psychiatric hospitals had become increasingly expensive to run, and there was a growing public perception that the institutionalization of patients was inhumane. Additionally, health care reformers were advocating the need for defined patient rights.

Simultaneously, there were significant advances in the medications used in the treatment of behavioral health diagnoses. More effective anti-psychotic, anti-depressant, and anti-anxiety medications made patients better candidates for outpatient treatment and more receptive to psychotherapy.

Inpatient behavioral health care or treatment might always be necessary for certain diagnoses, behaviors, and symptoms. However, the ability to safely and effectively manage patients in outpatient settings has increased both the public's access to behavioral health care services and society's acceptance of people with behavioral illness.

············

LEGAL ISSUES

Emerging awareness of the potential for abuse of behavioral health patients has resulted in nationwide legislative activity that has codified specific patient rights.

Federal and State Legislation

In 1981, the federal government established the President's Commission on Mental Health and enacted a Bill of Rights for behavioral health care patients. Under this legislation, individual states are empowered to implement the patient Bill of Rights, perform ongoing review and revision of the Bill of Rights, and assess provider compliance affecting those rights on behalf of the patient community.

State Legislation   Every state has promulgated behavioral health care regulations and mental hygiene laws that govern the provision of behavioral health care. Proper risk technique can ensure that:

• All behavioral health care providers are conversant with the governing mental hygiene laws

• Facility or organization protocols, policies, and procedures comply with all applicable regulations and laws

Bill of Rights—Title 42, Chapter 102, Section 9501   Behavioral health patients are a vulnerable population, and health care professionals must take all necessary steps to protect their rights. In its Patient Bill of Rights (U.S.C.A, Title 42, Chapter 102,

Section 9501), Congress directed the states to ensure that mental health patients receive the protection and services they require. To preclude the possibility of litigation and control risk, the legal requirements set forth in the Bill of Rights must be fully implemented. Moreover, written protocols, policies, and procedures must ensure the provision of each right.

Appropriate Treatment and Related Services   Once patients have entered treatment, they have the right to receive timely, appropriate, individualized treatment and services according to pertinent diagnoses, behaviors, symptoms, and individual needs.

Individualized Written Treatment or Service Plans   Each behavioral health patient must have initial medical, psychosocial, and behavioral health assessments that are used to develop a specific plan of care that has measurable goals and achievable treatment objectives. The plan of care is adjusted, as necessary, based on the patient's response to treatment. Initial and periodic health assessments are performed to help evaluate complaints and symptoms.

Informed Consent   Informed consent requires a discussion between the patient and the physician that includes the risks, benefits, and alternatives to the proposed treatment, medication, or procedure, and of the ramifications that could flow from refusal to consent to a medical procedure or treatment protocol. The same elements of informed consent are required for behavioral health patients as for any other patient group. This discussion is the responsibility of the physician who proposes the treatment, procedure, or medication. It is not delegable to another. The discussion must be memorialized through the patient's signature on an informed consent form. The informed consent process should be implemented for any proposed treatment, procedure, or medication that involves a significant risk of patient injury or adverse effect.

Many behavioral health patients are competent to make their own health care decisions and to provide informed consent. However, if there are questions regarding the patient's capacity to fully understand all the required elements of the informed consent discussion, a competency evaluation should be performed by a licensed physician. The physician must document clearly any findings that relate to the patient's ability to provide informed consent for health care decisions. Remember that patients may have the capacity to make decisions regarding their health care even if they are not competent in other areas.

If the patient is deemed incompetent to provide informed consent, this should be clearly documented, and the informed consent discussion should be conducted with the patient's legal representative. In the absence of an authorized guardian or representative, the court may be asked to appoint a legal representative to act on the patient's behalf.

The age of consent varies according to state statute. Many health care professionals have begun to recognize the rights of mature or emancipated minors (those nearing the age of maturity or having a clear and in-depth understanding of their illness and diagnosis). This is particularly true of situations in which the parent(s) or guardian give consent for treatment in the presence of major objections on the part of the mature minor. Of particular concern are treatments or medications that have significant risk or potentially permanent side effects such as electroconvulsive therapy or anti-psychotics. When related conflict exists between the parent and the mature minor, proper risk control techniques should include involvement of the facility's health care counsel or obtaining a court order to ensure the mature minor's wishes are considered.

Refer to Chapter 4 of this volume for additional information related to the informed consent process.

Right of Refusal   Competent patients (those who are capable of understanding the risks of refusing proposed treatment) have the right to refuse treatment without fear of reprisal from the involved physician, facility, or other health care providers. Risk increases when the refusal of treatment has the potential for serious negative effects on the patient's health or even the risk of death. When the refusal of treatment has the potential for severe adverse effects on the patient's health, reassess the patient's competence and involve the facility's health care legal counsel.

For incompetent adult patients, the legal representative may refuse treatment in accordance with the patient's known wishes at the time that the patient was competent. However, legal counsel, and in some cases the courts, should be involved when refusal of treatment involves the following issues:

- Refusal will or could result in significant adverse effects to the patient
- Refusal will or could result in a danger to the patient or others
- A parent or guardian wants to refuse clinically indicated treatment for their minor child
- A parent or guardian wants to refuse clinically indicated treatment for the mature minor, and the mature minor wants to consent to treatment, or the mature minor wishes to refuse treatment to which the parent(s) have consented

As stated, the patient's right to refuse treatment must be without fear of reprisal by the care provider. However, in some cases when a patient refuses clinically indicated treatment, that individual may no longer be a suitable patient for the present practitioner or facility. In that situation, a revised plan of care must be discussed with the patient or the patient's representative. Referrals to alternate practitioners or facilities should be made and documented. Assistance with proper referrals should continue until the patient's transfer is successfully completed or the patient's non-compliance or refusal of referral is documented.

An additional possible consequence of refusal of treatment may be the cessation of health insurance benefits for the involved behavioral health diagnosis. Although patients have the right to refuse treatment, they should be informed that such refusal might have insurance benefit consequences that are outside the control of the health care provider. Patients who refuse treatment should be advised of this possibility, informed that they might be personally responsible for continued charges and fees, and encouraged to contact their insurance carrier. If necessary, the patient should be provided assistance with this process. Notice of possible loss of benefits and any subsequent assistance provided should be documented in the patient's clinical record.

Freedom from Restraint or Seclusion   Patients have a right to receive treatment in an environment free from restraint or seclusion. However, if patients are deemed to be an imminent threat to themselves or others, the practitioner may order physical or chemical restraint or seclusion.

Sound risk control technique requires that the least restrictive yet effective restraint be used. All behavioral health organizations must have specific policies and procedures that govern the ordering, application, release, and documentation of restraints. When chemical restraint is clinically indicated and ordered, the pharmacist must assess its appropriateness and make recommendations if alternative medications or equally effective medications with fewer side effects or adverse reactions are available.

Humane Treatment   Behavioral health care must be delivered by qualified practitioners in a safe, humane environment. Compassionate treatment helps promote a positive therapeutic experience and increases the opportunity for favorable treatment outcomes.

Confidentiality All patients have the right to confidentiality of their clinical, personal, and financial information. Except in the case of medical or clinical emergencies, health care providers and practitioners may not release any patient health information (verbal or written) in the absence of written patient consent or authorization. Even in such emergency situations, providers may only release that information necessary to ensure continuity of care for the acute event.

A general consent for the release of medical information typically used in other types of health care services is not sufficient when the patient has received treatment for a behavioral health or mental health diagnosis, or treatment for drug or alcohol abuse. Behavioral health patients have additional confidentiality protections. They must specify that they are consenting to the release of information that includes treatment related to drug or alcohol use or a behavioral health diagnosis.

Access to Behavioral Health Records Behavioral health patients have the right to review or obtain copies of their clinical records. On occasion, practitioners may have concerns regarding the potential for adverse effects on a patient if that patient reads the clinical record. If this determination is reached, practitioners should clearly document their rationale in the patient's clinical record, to support the decision and communicate this information to other involved providers. However, if the patient continues to request access to the clinical record, despite being informed that it could be therapeutically harmful, the practitioner should elicit assistance from risk management or legal counsel. Each behavioral health organization must establish and implement policies and procedures that govern these processes.

As previously discussed, access to behavioral health records by other individuals and organizations is specifically restricted. In most instances, such information may only be released with written permission of the patients or their legal representatives. There are exceptions when patients need immediate care or treatment, and their behavioral health records are clinically necessary to ensure safe and proper continuity of care. These exceptions should be clearly defined in the organization's policies and procedures.

Should records be released under emergent conditions, correct risk technique includes generating detailed documentation regarding the circumstances necessitating their release. Additionally, if the patient is later deemed able to give consent or has been stabilized with treatment, the releasing organization should subsequently attempt to obtain the patient's retroactive authorization for the release of that information. Retroactive authorization should be clearly documented, with reasons noted for its retroactive nature.

Grievance Process Patients have the right to object to any or all of the treatment as an infringement upon their rights. This is equally true for patients who have been formally committed or have voluntarily agreed to treatment. The organization must develop and implement procedures for providing patients with an impartial and timely fair-hearing process.

ACCESS TO BEHAVIORAL HEALTH SERVICES

As a result of improvements in the management and control of behavioral health illnesses and symptoms, the majority of behavioral health patients are successfully integrated into their communities. This development emanated from the creation of readily accessible local services. Even with these improvements, challenges that negatively affect access to care remain.

Commercial Insurance Coverage

Health care costs continue to rise, and the increased cost of commercial insurance with coverage for a narrowly defined scope of services creates additional burdens for those suffering from behavioral health conditions. Behavioral health care insurance benefits are often separate or are excluded from standard commercial health care insurance. Even when some level of coverage or benefit is included, one or more of the factors described here might cause patients to avoid or abandon treatment.

- Annual coverage restrictions: There are often specified benefit limits for inpatient and outpatient behavioral health care services within each policy year.

- Lifetime coverage limits: Many insurance policies limit the total benefit for a patient's lifetime behavioral health care services. Limits vary widely.

- Restricted medication coverage: Insurance policies may limit coverage benefits for medications to only those included in their approved formulary.

- Deductibles and co-payments: Deductibles and co-payments may apply for both medications and provider or practitioner payments.

- Complex patient reimbursement procedures: Many patients are required to pay directly for behavioral health care services and submit requests for reimbursement. Paperwork required for reimbursement may be complicated.

Risk Control Techniques   Because financial or reimbursement issues can negatively affect access to and patient compliance with care, these matters must be addressed in an organization's risk control program. The following risk control techniques are offered:

- Require comprehensive documentation of the clinical justification for prescribed treatment and medications to meet third-party payer requirements for benefits.

- Establish patient assistance programs to help patients apply for and understand their benefits, and submit documents for reimbursement.

- Help patients identify additional resources when primary third-party benefits are exhausted.

Managed Care

Managed care contracts may include the restrictions noted previously and also may include the following additional restrictions, which further limit access to services:

- Restricted to approved locations: Patients may be restricted to specific locations or facilities where the managed care organization is contracted to provide patient services.

- Restricted to approved providers or practitioners: Patients may be restricted to specific providers and practitioners with whom the managed care organization contracts.

- Restricted to approved medication formulary: Managed care organizations may cover only those medications that are included in their approved formulary.

Risk Control Techniques   In addition to risk control techniques addressed in the previous section, an organization's risk control program must also confront the specific risks involved with managed care-related restrictions. Some of those restrictions and risk control techniques include the following:

- When a patient needs to change providers, avoid allegations of patient abandonment by actively facilitating the referral to an approved provider within the managed care network. Document all assistance efforts in the patient's clinical record.

- While consideration should be given to assuring the most cost-effective, clinically indicated treatment or medication, the provider is responsible for assuring that the patient's plan of treatment is based on the patient's individual needs and is not governed by financial or benefit restrictions.

- When it is clinically contraindicated to restrict the patient's medication or treatment to those included in the managed care approved benefits, help the patient to apply for extended or out-of-formulary coverage benefits.

Greater Reliance on Ambulatory Care

Ambulatory care services are cost-effective, and patients often benefit from obtaining treatment while remaining in the community. However, the countervailing interest of patient or community safety might require a patient to receive care in an inpatient setting.

Ironically, the otherwise successful outpatient treatment model might actually create access issues for these patients. Because outpatient care addresses the clinical needs of the majority of behavioral health care patients, inpatient facilities may be less available, and third-party payers might resist providing inpatient benefits for what they deem can be provided on an outpatient basis.

Risk Control Techniques   The organization's risk control program must address inpatient access issues.

- Require comprehensive documentation of the clinical justification for inpatient treatment that specifies why the patient treatment cannot be safely delivered on an outpatient basis.

- The provider must be responsible for ensuring that the patient's plan of treatment is based on the patient's individual needs and is not governed by financial or benefit restrictions.

- Should the patient's inpatient benefits be denied by a third-party payer, the provider must assist the patient with the appeals, grievance, and fair-hearing processes required by the insurance company. These efforts should be documented in detail in the patient's clinical record.

SCOPE OF PRACTICE

The behavioral health staff is composed of both employed and independent practitioners and is further delineated by licensed, or certified and non-licensed staff.

Licensed Staff

Some aspects of behavioral health care can be provided only by licensed or certified professionals. Professionals must practice within the scope of their authority. This pertains to both independent practitioners and employed professionals.

Every state licenses professional health care practitioners and providers including, but not limited to, physicians, clinical psychologists, social workers, physician assistants, and nurses. Each professional state licensing board also defines the scope of practice for its licensees.

In addition, other levels of behavioral health staffs may be certified to practice in a particular state. Examples may include certified nurse assistants, mental health technicians, alcoholism and addiction counselors, and certified medication technicians.

Each state licensing and certification board defines the provider's scope of practice. The scope of practice also includes the level of supervision that is required.

Risk Control Techniques   Risk management professionals should consider these control procedures for purposes of behavioral health staffing:

- As part of the initial application or credentialing process, obtain references and criminal background checks for every professional prior to initial patient contact.

- Every independent practitioner and provider should carry professional liability insurance. In several jurisdictions, this is mandated by state law. Some states have imposed caps on losses so appropriate limits will vary. Generally, practitioners and providers should carry limits that respond adequately to the professional liability climate within the state or region.

- Health care organizations must develop and implement competency-based performance parameters for each professional category. The scope of competencies required should be in accordance with the state's scope of practice for each professional group.

- The health care organization must ensure adequate supervision of the clinical practice of each of its professionals. This process is frequently included in the organization's credentialing and peer review programs.

Professional Competence

Practitioners must be competent to provide their defined scope of services. They are required to demonstrate core competencies to attain licensure or certification. Behavioral health professionals are responsible for maintaining expertise and completing required continuing education credits defined by their professional licensing or certification board. Knowledge of current trends and innovations in the profession represents an added responsibility.

All health care practitioners should be trained to identify patients at risk for behavioral health illness. Additional behavioral health care training and educational programs for practitioners in other health care delivery sites are especially important where behavioral health patients are more likely to be encountered. These sites include the emergency department, intensive care service, and gerontology unit. Non-clinical staff, including security, transport, laboratory, and admissions personnel, should be trained to manage situations that might arise when interacting with, or in the presence of, a patient who has a behavioral health illness.

Risk Control Techniques

- At least annually, the organization must perform competency-based performance assessments for each professional.

- Any area of identified lack of competence must be addressed and the professional's performance monitored until acceptable competence is achieved.

- Professionals must annually submit evidence that they have completed the required number of continuing education credits.

Non-Licensed Staff

Behavioral health staff categories such as nurse's aide or assistant might not require licensure or certification. It is not uncommon for these behavioral health workers to obtain their experience and expertise through on-the-job training. Workers who interact with behavioral health patients, such as admissions clerks, security, laboratory, dietary, and housekeeping personnel, also typically receive on-the-job training. When this is the case, the organization that employs such workers is responsible to provide acceptable work-related training and ongoing staff education.

Risk Control Techniques   Non-licensed staff must be cleared as authorized members of the organization's workforce. This is achieved through the following risk control techniques:

Screening   Every employee, contract worker, and volunteer in a behavioral health setting, including support staff such as dietary and housekeeping, should be screened to ensure that they are suited to work with this potentially vulnerable population. References must be verified and criminal background checks performed. A list of crimes that would bar employment must be established and uniformly applied.

Some states require criminal background checks for certain health care personnel by statute. Irrespective of legal requirements, behavioral health care facilities should require such checks before an employee, contract worker, or volunteer begins work in the facility.

Skills Assessment   Define the skills or competencies required for a person to fulfill each position in the organization. Managers and supervisors should directly observe each staff member's skills and competency level on a regular basis. Skill deficits can be addressed through focused education and staff development programs. Following the implementation of the action plan, the staff member's skills should be reassessed until the competency standard is met, or it is determined that the individual lacks the requisite skills for the position.

Staff Development   Staff must continue to develop their skills and areas of competence as advances in behavioral health are developed and become standards of practice. All staff must be required to undergo orientation to the facility's protocols, policies, and procedures at the time of hire and at least annually thereafter. Additional in-service and staff development programs designed to address modifications in the standard of care in behavioral health should be provided regularly. Some areas of increased risk related to behavioral health care delivery include patient's rights, reporting of suspected abuse or neglect, physical and chemical restraint use, and confidentiality.

Supervision Requirements   Behavioral health facilities must ensure adequate supervision for each level of staff. Facility policies and procedures must define the type and frequency of supervision as part of each position description and as part of the staff member's performance evaluation. Staff should be routinely supervised through direct observation of their patient care practices and through competency testing on a regular basis.

Practice Environment—Facility-Based and Affiliated Organizations

Independent practitioners and allied health professionals (psychologists, physician assistants, and psychiatric nurse practitioners) are credentialed as members of the organization's medical staff.

Risk Control Techniques   Risk control techniques for independent practitioners and allied health professionals include:

Credentialing and Reappointment   Behavioral health care organizations are required to employ and contract with qualified clinical staff. They must formally credential and reappoint their professionals at least every two years. The credentialing and reappointment policies and procedures must be defined in the medical staff bylaws and rules and regulations. Credentialing criteria must be applied uniformly for each medical staff member.

Delineation of Privileges   Practitioners must request in writing specific clinical privileges based on their training, experience, and expertise. Procedures for approving, reducing, or denying privileges should be included in the medical staff bylaws, and rules and regulations. The bylaws must also include a process for medical staff members to appeal adverse credentialing and privilege decisions or reductions in requested privileges, through a defined fair-hearing process. Any such reductions or denials of privileges are reportable to the National Practitioner Data Bank and to the practitioner's state licensing board.

Competency Monitoring   Practitioner competency is best assessed through the ongoing monitoring and peer review of the quality of the services provided to patients. Non-physicians should undergo skills and competency evaluations as defined in their position descriptions.

Practice Environment—Freestanding Organizations

Freestanding behavioral health organizations, such as private clinics and supportive living environments, must define the required scope of practice for all employees and independent clinical practitioners. When assessing the risks associated with the delivery of care in such organizations, remember that in the event of litigation, they will be held to the same quality and patient safety standards as hospital-based facilities. Freestanding organizations are also subject to essentially the same state department of health and other accrediting agency standards.

Risk Control Techniques   Risk control techniques particular to freestanding organizations include:

Contractual Agreements   All independent practitioners should provide services to the organization in accordance with a formal written contract. Such contracts should be carefully developed by the organization's legal counsel to ensure sufficient mutual hold-harmless and indemnity provisions, and professional liability insurance requirements.

Professional Liability Insurance   Freestanding organizations must ensure that independent practitioners maintain professional liability insurance in amounts deemed acceptable by the organization and in accordance with any state requirements and the local litigation climate.

Some freestanding organizations require their independent practitioners to include the organization as a named insured on their professional liability insurance policies. This would provide additional protection for the organization in the case of alleged vicarious liability related to the negligence of one of its affiliated practitioners.

Safety and Security   Ensure adequate security and safety of patients and the staff, and provide staff with the ability to summon emergency assistance as needed through the use of alarms, panic buttons, cellular telephones, camera surveillance, and other technical systems.

Practice Environment—Independent Practices

Each state defines the scope of practice for each type of practitioner who is licensed to practice independently. Independent practitioners may elect to practice in solo, group practice, or contracted status. Many practitioners maintain private independent practices while they also practice in freestanding or hospital-based facilities. Most practitioners maintain privileges on a hospital medical staff if their private outpatients should require inpatient services at some point during their courses of treatments.

Risk Control Techniques   Several risk control techniques apply to independent practitioners, regardless of setting.

- All licensed practitioners are required to obtain and renew their licenses to practice in accordance with state laws and regulations.

- All licensed practitioners are required to maintain their professional skills and are responsible for attending continuing professional education programs in accordance with state continuing education requirements.

- Practitioners are required to present proof of such ongoing education when applying for renewal of their professional licenses.

- Practitioners must maintain professional liability insurance in adequate amounts and in accordance with state requirements and the local litigation climate.

....

CLINICAL RISKS

Risk management issues related to behavioral health risks need to be identified, controlled, and monitored just as in any other area of service.

Duration and Continuity of Care

Behavioral health professionals must develop and implement a specific plan of care for each patient. The course of treatment must be provided in a clinically suitable setting, maintained for the adequate length of time to meet treatment goals and objectives, and include the coordinated efforts of all involved providers.

Risk Control Techniques   Several risk control techniques apply to continued care and treatment of behavioral and mental health patients.

Development of Treatment Plan   Every patient must have a specific plan of care that includes goals and objectives of treatment, the acceptable setting for care, the projected length of treatment, and the support systems and services the patient will require.

The treatment plan must be continually evaluated and modified as the patient's condition changes or treatment approaches require revision. The organization's continuous quality improvement process may be the optimal mechanism to ensure ongoing assessment of the efficacy of treatment plans.

Each element of the patient's treatment plan and all subsequent modifications to that plan must be documented in the patient's clinical record.

Management of Missed Appointments   A missed appointment might be an indication of a patient at risk. The behavioral health provider has an obligation to address the issue of a missed appointment.

Patients must be initially educated to the requirement that they contact their provider if they are unable to keep a scheduled appointment. Patients who repeatedly cancel appointments might require a reassessment of their treatment plan.

Organizational protocols, policies, and procedures should define what steps will be taken to contact patients who miss appointments. Providers must consider the patient's illness when determining how aggressive and extensive contact efforts will be. All efforts to contact patients who have missed appointments must be fully documented in the patient's clinical record.

Community Support Service   The treatment plan should address and incorporate suitable community services that will support the patient throughout the course of treatment and post-discharge. Some examples might include:

- Transportation services to and from appointments
- Twelve-step programs for patients abstaining from an addiction
- Directly observed medication administration services
- Family counseling resources
- Medical health care resources
- Disability benefits
- Job training or retraining programs
- Employment support programs
- Financial aid

Discharge Planning   Each patient's behavioral health treatment plan must include discharge planning that will support a successful and safe termination from treatment.

It is essential to document each aspect of the discharge planning process to support the clinical decision-making process involved. In particular, such documentation is critical to defense of any subsequent allegation that the patient was wrongly discharged from treatment.

Monitoring Interventions for Effectiveness

Every patient's course of treatment should be regularly monitored to ensure that it is addressing the patient's specific needs, has been modified in accordance with the patient's progress, and adequately addresses the patient's response. As each aspect of the patient's treatment is monitored, the risks inherent in that aspect of treatment must also be addressed and managed.

Risk Control Techniques Several risk control techniques apply to monitoring the course of treatment for behavioral and mental health patients.

Proper Use of Medications and Treatment Modalities Even though improved psychoactive medications and treatment modalities have revolutionized behavioral health care, they also might carry significant side effects and potential for adverse patient reactions. These must be addressed. Consideration of specific risks, such as patient age, ability to adhere to the medication regimen, access to prescribed medication, and likelihood of compliance with monitoring and follow-up, are critical to the determination of appropriate medication and treatment plans. Obtain informed consent for all medications and treatment modalities and frequently assess the patient for their effectiveness or as any negative effects.

De-escalation Techniques Some behavioral health patients experience episodes of increased activity, agitation, behavioral outbursts, or aggressive behaviors that place them or others at risk for injury. Such symptoms must be managed to ensure the safety of the patient and others. The treatment plan must define the best techniques for the particular patient in the event of such symptoms. Some examples of these techniques include:

- Removal from stimulus or conflict-causing situation or person
- Therapeutic holding
- Non-stimulus environment including "time-outs" or isolation
- Therapeutic activity
- Physical or chemical restraint

    Risk control techniques related to de-escalation applications ensure that

- There is a written practitioner order for de-escalation applications.
- There is a completed and documented informed consent discussion. Such discussion may be carried out during the patient's quiet times or retroactively.
- Techniques are applied by trained personnel.
- Techniques are applied in the correct manner for prescribed periods of time.

    Documentation of de-escalation activities must include a detailed description of patient behaviors that necessitate the use of de-escalation techniques, the specific techniques applied, and the patient's response.

Participation in Treatment Plans Treatment plans are often more effective when the patient, the patient's representative, and significant others are included in the design and implementation of the patient's plan. Even patients thought to have cognitive impairments or who are minors should be included in the treatment planning process to the level of their ability.

As an additional risk control technique, some facilities and practitioners formally contract with patients for their compliance with treatment plans and goals and objectives. Although such "treatment contracts" are not legal documents, they serve as an affirmation of the practitioner's and patient's commitment to the agreed-upon plan of treatment.

Any and all patient, representative, or family participation in treatment plans should be fully documented in the patient's clinical record. Whenever applicable, it is desirable to obtain the patient's signature in agreement with the plan of care.

Documentation of Clinical Outcomes and Changes in Interventions   Documentation must reflect patients' specific responses to each treatment modality included in their treatment plans. Complete documentation must be provided whenever a patient's response or lack of response results in a change in treatment plan or other type of intervention. The documentation should include a description of the element of care, the analysis and assessment of the patient's response, the proposed change, intervention or modification, and the patient's awareness of and, if possible, consent to the change.

Documentation of Referrals for Additional Services   Behavioral health patients might have problems of living related to their behavioral health diagnosis and symptoms. Problems might include disruptions within the family or at school, difficulty managing finances, addictive behaviors, or difficulties with the legal system and law enforcement. Social services referrals, initiation of family support services, assistance with obtaining financial support, and referral to legal services may be essential to keeping the patient in treatment.

Referral for a physical assessment is essential for every behavioral health patient and should be included in a comprehensive treatment plan. All referrals must be documented in the patient's clinical record.

Suitability and Effectiveness of Discharge Plan   As previously stated, the patient's discharge needs must be assessed throughout the course of treatment. Failure to plan for discharge services creates significant risks to the patient for relapse or non-compliance with treatment.

As with the treatment plan, it is recommended that the patient's input be considered in the development and implementation of the discharge plan.

Follow-up on Post Discharge Compliance with Referrals and Continuing Care
Part of the discharge planning process includes follow-up of the patient's compliance with post-discharge activities and services. Documentation should accurately reflect the patient's compliance with post-discharge plans and an assessment of post-discharge status.

Suicide and Homicide Prevention

Behavioral health patients must be assessed for the risk of suicidal and or homicidal ideation or acts. Practitioners should use proper clinical interview techniques and the patient should be evaluated for these specific risks. All such evaluation(s) must be documented in the patient's clinical record. Each significant change in a patient's condition or in the response to treatment should be viewed in terms of the patient's risk for suicide or homicide.

Whenever a patient is assessed to be at significant risk for suicidal or homicidal behavior, all steps necessary to ensure the safety of the patient and the community must be taken. In some cases, this might require a breach in patient confidentiality to warn a potential victim of their homicidal ideation, or to inform a parent or guardian of the significant risk for suicide and the need for involuntary commitment. Should the behavioral health professional deem it necessary to warn a third party, it might be necessary to involve legal counsel. The courts have upheld exceptions to the duty of confidentiality in the landmark case of *Tarasoff v. Regents of University of California*, 131 Cal.Rptr.14, 551 P.2d 334 (Cal. 1976). In Tarasoff, a psychiatrist was held liable for failing to warn the victim of a mental patient's threat to kill a former girlfriend. The duty to warn of potential danger to others was held to outweigh the public policy that favored protection of confidential communications between a patient and a psychotherapist. Most state courts have adopted some variation of *Tarasoff* and many have expanded its meaning to include most behavioral health professionals. Each facility must address this risk with legal counsel and determine the steps to take when there is a potential need for a warning.

Risk Control Techniques   Several risk control techniques apply to suicide and homicide prevention for behavioral health patients.

Initial and Ongoing Clinical Risk Assessments   Every patient must be assessed for suicidal or homicidal ideation at the time of entry into treatment and regularly thereafter. The risk of suicide or homicidal behavior will be a major factor when selecting the optimal treatment facility and the safest, most effective level of care for the patient.

Reassessment for these risks should be performed on a routine basis and whenever there is a significant change in the patient's affect or behavior. Sometimes, a sudden peacefulness in a previously agitated and depressed patient might be a sign that the patient has resolved the issue internally and has a specific plan of action regarding suicidal or homicidal behavior.

Suicide Precautions and Treatment Plans   When there is an identified risk for suicide or homicide, the patient must be placed on specific clinical protocols for prevention of such actions and behaviors. Typically, this requires voluntary or involuntary admission to an inpatient facility, at least until the patient can be further assessed, and to implement necessary suicide or homicide prevention techniques.

The primary consideration must always be to assure patient and community safety. Necessary precautions and suicide- and homicide-prevention techniques must be implemented even if the patient objects and there is a risk of patient litigation. Some preventive actions include:

- Close Observation, or One-On-One (1:1): The patient is never left alone for any reason and is kept in total visual contact by a staff member at all times, including bathroom and grooming activities, sleep, meals, and at all other times. During a 1:1 assignment, the staff member may have no other assigned duties. Another staff member must cover for the 1:1 staff member for breaks, and so on.

- Contraband Controls: A suicidal or homicidal patient can be extremely creative and persistent in attempting to carry out the plan of action. Almost any object can be modified into a danger or weapon. Patients should be informed at the time of admission that their rooms and possessions will be initially and periodically searched and, if deemed necessary, they may be required to submit to a body search.

   a) Room Searches—When a patient is identified as being at risk for suicide or homicide, routine searches and additional focused searches of patient rooms, communal areas, dining rooms, activities areas, and so on are essential to ensure as safe an environment as possible.

b) Personal Effects Searches—Each patient's personal effects must be searched at the time of admission and periodically thereafter for any object or item that could be used to carry out a suicide or homicide plan. Identified contraband must be confiscated and stored in a safe place and returned only when the patient is discharged. Weapons or items that could be made into weapons must be permanently confiscated. Under certain circumstances, such as discovery of a concealed firearm, police involvement is required.

c) Body Searches—If a body search is necessary, it should only be carried out by a same-sex professional staff member and should be witnessed and documented by a same-sex staff member. Some organizations stipulate that only medical professionals (physician, nurse) perform body searches.

It might be necessary to carry out an even closer body search, such as a skin search or a body cavity search for patients at high risk for suicide or homicide. This type of search may be indicated if there is reasonable suspicion that the patient has an object, weapon, or medication, and so on, hidden somewhere on their person, that could be used to carry out the suicide or homicide plan.

A clinically indicated body search must be conducted by a same-sex professional staff member and witnessed by a same-sex staff member to ensure patient safety and to assist in the defense of the staff and organization if allegations of abuse or injury arise. Both staff members who participate in the search should document the details of the search independently in the patient's clinical record.

Medication Management   Behavioral health facilities must have stringent controls on medications and biologicals. Inpatients' personal medications should be confiscated and returned only at the time of discharge and only if they continue to be prescribed postdischarge.

Medications prescribed for patients during their inpatient course of treatment must be kept in locked storage. Patients should be required to report to the nursing station or medication room to obtain their medications. Mouth checks should be performed to ensure that patients have swallowed their medication.

Family members and other visitors must be prohibited from carrying any medications or drugs when they are visiting in a behavioral health setting. Even if the family member is not at risk for suicide or homicide, other patients in the setting might be at risk. In some cases, it may be necessary to perform voluntary searches of visitors or their personal items such as purses, backpacks, and so on, and to deny visiting privileges to those who decline to permit search procedures.

Physical Plant Controls   Some behavioral health inpatient units are designated as locked units to prevent patients from eloping or injuring themselves or others. Patients at high risk for suicide or homicide, incompetent or confused patients, minors, or other patients unable to protect themselves in the community should be protected from elopement or infliction of injury to themselves or others.

Locking or otherwise alarming doors, windows, elevators, and so on can assist in providing a safe environment for these patients. Windows must be locked, nonopening, or adapted to open only one to two inches. Doors that lead to lobbies, elevators, and stairways should be alarmed and locked so that the staff is alerted to any unauthorized exit attempts. Many behavioral health units use camera surveillance for entrances and exits so that out-of-sight-line areas can be visually monitored. Some facilities include the immediate grounds and parking lots in their camera surveillance capabilities.

Visitor Controls   Behavioral health facilities must establish specific policies and procedures to govern the management of visitors. Many behavioral health organizations require orientation for all visitors to ensure that they do not purposely or inadvertently bring potentially dangerous medications or contraband items into the patient care unit.

Some behavioral health organizations limit visitors for behavioral health patients. Others require visitors to pass through metal detectors and undergo voluntary searches.

When there is significant risk to the patient, the practitioner may order that visitors be completely prohibited for all or part of the patient's course of treatment. The practitioner may require that all or specific visitors only be allowed under the direct 1:1 observation of staff.

Clinical Monitoring Protocols   There must be ongoing monitoring of the effectiveness of the facility's policies and procedures to identify patients at risk for suicide or homicide. There must also be monitoring of each patient's treatment plan to ensure proper assessment and treatment for these risks.

The facility must monitor patient injuries, incidents, and accidents related to suicidal or homicidal behaviors to identify gaps in the patient safety program and physical plant controls. When an issue is identified it must be investigated and a plan of correction immediately developed and implemented. Continued monitoring should be maintained to assure the effectiveness of the plan of correction.

Reporting Attempted and Completed Suicide or Homicide   Attempted and completed suicide or homicide must be reported to the following:

- Facility risk management department
- Facility administration
- Facility legal department or attorney
- Any person identified by the patient as a potential violence or homicide victim, this is called Duty to Warn (see *Tarasoff v. Regents of the University of California*, cited earlier)
- Patient's physician
- Patient's family or representative
- Law enforcement, when applicable
- State Department of Mental Health
- State Department of Health
- Professional licensing board, if applicable
- Facility professional liability insurance broker and carrier

Requirements to report suicide or homicide attempts or completed actions are defined in each state's health or mental health laws and codes. All reporting activities should be documented in the patient's clinical record.

A confidential investigation and analysis of any such event should be carried out immediately. The investigation should include whether or not the organization's protocols, policies, and procedures regarding the identification of patients at risk for suicide or homicide were properly carried out. A detailed plan of correction must be developed and implemented to prevent any recurrence.

Elopement Prevention

For some behavioral health patients, remaining in the protected environment of an inpatient unit is essential to ensuring their safety or the safety of others. It might be necessary to prevent the patient from leaving the inpatient unit even if it requires involuntary or court-ordered commitment and is against the patient's wishes. As noted previously, some behavioral health care units are locked or otherwise secured to prevent patients from eloping.

Periodic elopement drills should be carried out to evaluate the effectiveness of the facility's elopement prevention program. Any gaps or deficiencies identified through the drill process must be addressed and the prevention program properly modified.

Risk Control Techniques   Several risk control techniques apply to prevention of patient elopement.

Initial and Ongoing Clinical Assessments   All behavioral health patients must be evaluated for the risk of elopement at the time of their admission to an inpatient treatment setting. Such assessments should be repeated periodically, as the patient's needs dictate.

Elopement Precautions and Treatment Plans   The patient's treatment plan should include any and all indicated elopement precautions. Some of the methods used to prevent elopement and potential injuries to patients at risk for elopement include:

- Close Observation (1:1): The loss control technique of close observation is the same as for suicidal and homicidal patients. Please see previous discussion in this chapter.

- Frequent Checks: Some patients might not require 1:1 observation, but do require frequent staff checks to ascertain that they remain in the unit and are not in a position to elope. In these instances, patients may be placed on face-to-face checks by staff on a schedule of every five, ten, or fifteen minutes. The staff must actually observe the patient and document the patient's location in the unit (patient's room, activities department, therapy room, and so on) and that the check was performed.

- Physical Plant Controls: As described previously, exit doors on some behavioral health care units are locked to ensure patient safety. All staff members must carry keys to exit doors to ensure that doors can be readily unlocked if a fire or other internal disaster necessitates rapid evacuation of patients.

- Visitor Controls: Because many behavioral health care inpatient units require patients to wear regular street clothes, there is a risk of patient elopement where visitors or staff enter or leave the treatment unit. Visitors should be required to show a pass to enter the unit and when exiting. When visitors are entering and exiting, staff should confirm that elevator doors have fully closed before unlocking the unit door.

- Clinical Monitoring Protocols—Patient treatment plans must be monitored for their effectiveness in preventing patient elopements.

Reporting Elopement In most states, elopements are reportable events. In addition to notifying the physician, family or responsible party, facility administration, and facility security, the following must be notified:

- Facility risk management department
- Facility legal department or attorney
- Local police department
- State Department of Mental Health
- State Department of Health

All elopements must be investigated, the method of elopement fully determined and assessed, and a detailed plan of correction developed to ensure that future similar elopements are prevented.

Additionally, an analysis of the patient's treatment plan and the facility's elopement precautions must be completed. Any factors that contributed to the elopement must be addressed to ensure that they do not recur. All efforts should be documented in the patient's clinical record.

Chemical and Physical Restraints

Restraints can be effective therapeutic tools, but they can also affect patient rights. Because of the critical nature of patient rights, every effort should be made to provide safe, effective treatment in a restraint-free environment. However, at times restraints are clinically required. Based on the particular patient's needs, the specific type of restraint must be ordered by the practitioner and must be implemented, monitored, and removed in accordance with the written order and the facility's protocols, policies, and procedures.

The facility must ensure that its protocols, policies, and procedures comply with the Special Conditions of Participation through the Centers for Medicare and Medicaid Services under HFS 124. This regulation requires that a licensed independent practitioner perform a face-to-face evaluation of each patient within one hour of initiating an episode of restraint. (Locked seclusion is also included in this regulation. See the portion of this chapter that discusses locked seclusion.) The evaluation must include an assessment of the appropriateness of the intervention, whether continuation of the intervention is justified, and the identification of any precursors that could prevent further episodes of restraint.

Physical restraints include individual patient equipment such as wrist restraints, and environmental techniques such as locked seclusion. Not all psychoactive medications constitute chemical restraint, including those that are prescribed over an extended period for chronic treatment of behavioral health symptoms. The same medications, however, may be considered a chemical restraint when used on a periodic or urgent basis (PRN), or in dosages used to significantly alter behavior on an immediate basis.

Risk Control Techniques At the onset of treatment, the practitioner should evaluate both the patient's behavioral and medical needs. The clinical indications and patient safety considerations related to the use of environmental, physical, or chemical restraints must be addressed as part of each patient's initial and ongoing clinical assessment.

Additional patient assessments should be performed whenever there is a significant change in the patient's behavior or medical condition, whenever the patient responds or fails to respond to prescribed treatment or medication, or whenever there is a change in the patient's plan of care.

Restraint Policy   The protocols, policies, and procedures for the use of chemical and physical restraints must be specifically defined and implemented. At a minimum, they must include:

- Specific clinical and patient safety indications for the use of environmental, physical, or chemical restraint
- Informed consent process
- Emergency restraint use
- Practitioner orders for restraint
- Specific restraint to be used
- Specific time limits for the restraint to be used
- Frequency and duration of periodic release of physical restraints
- Indications for discontinuance of the restraint
- Requirements for patient monitoring and observation during and after the application or use of restraint
- Documentation requirements for all aspects of restraint assessment, application, monitoring, efficacy, and removal

Restraint Reduction Protocols   Restraints may be used only in accordance with facility protocols, policies, and procedures, and practitioner's orders. When a patient's clinical condition requires that a restraint be used to protect the patient or others, the least restrictive restraint that produces the desired effect must be used. For example, the staff may recommend the use of the quiet room before implementing a more restrictive technique. Similarly, practitioners may prescribe relatively simple medications before using major tranquilizers. Efforts to reduce the level or degree of the restraint or to eliminate the need for the restraint altogether must be ongoing, focused, and clearly documented in the patient's clinical record.

Documenting and Complying with Restraint Protocols and Treatment Plans Elements that should be addressed as part of the organization's protocols, policies, and procedures for all restraints include the informed consent process.

Use of restraints requires informed consent, except in cases of emergency when patients are deemed to be a risk to themselves or others. Often the symptoms or behaviors that necessitate involuntary restraint are the same symptoms or behaviors that render patients, at least temporarily, unable to control their behaviors adequately to participate in the informed consent process. When a patient is deemed unable to provide consent due to behavioral symptoms, the family or legal representative should be notified and consent obtained through the proxy informed consent process under applicable state law, if possible. Patients may be able to provide retroactive consent after they have regained behavioral control.

Documentation relating to the informed consent process for involuntary restraint must indicate:

- The specific reasons or behaviors that rendered the patient unable to provide informed consent
- The steps taken to obtain consent from a parent or legal representative
- Subsequent (retroactive) patient consent if obtained
- A practitioner's order, required for the use of any restraint

Emergency Use   Restraints may be used without the patient's consent when it is determined that the patient is a danger to himself or others. Consent, physician orders, and notification to the family or legal representative must be carried out as soon as practicable.

Restraint Efficacy and Patient Safety   The efficacy and propriety of the restraint in meeting the patient's treatment needs must be documented. The patient's safety and well-being, and the safety of others, is a paramount consideration and any adverse patient response must be immediately addressed by the clinical staff or practitioner. Any patient injury resulting from restraint must be reported in accordance with regulatory requirements and facility policy.

Monitoring and Observations Protocols   Consistent, ongoing monitoring of the patient's behavior and physical condition immediately before, during, and after restraint must be carried out.

Seclusion

Seclusion, a form of therapeutic isolation, is generally characterized as a restraint. As such, it must be carefully monitored to protect patients' rights while their safety and well-being are ensured. Seclusion can be an effective therapeutic tool for some patients. Conversely, self-isolation may be a problem behavior. Therefore, each patient's practitioner must provide written orders regarding seclusion. Such orders should authorize staff to impose involuntary seclusion in situations when patients are a risk to themselves or others. The orders should also indicate whether patients may use voluntary seclusion or quiet rooms. In the case of patients for whom self-isolation is a clinical problem, the practitioner may require that they be prohibited from isolating themselves from the general patient community.

Once again, the facility must ensure that its protocols comply with the Special Conditions of Participation through the Centers for Medicare and Medicaid Services under HFS 124, which requires that a licensed independent practitioner perform a face-to-face evaluation of each patient within one hour of the initiation of an episode of locked seclusion. (Physical and chemical restraints are included in this regulation. See the portion of this chapter that discusses physical and chemical restraints.) The evaluation must include an assessment of the appropriateness of the intervention, the appropriateness of continuation of the intervention, and the identification of any precursors that could prevent further episodes of restraint.

Patients may be at greatest risk of injury when they have lost control of their behavior. Seclusion may be an effective technique in assisting the patient in regaining control and providing protection for both the patient and others. Informed consent for seclusion should be obtained whenever possible, even if it is obtained following the seclusion episode. The patient's family should be notified when involuntary seclusion is required.

Included in this section is a discussion of desirable characteristics of seclusion rooms that minimize risks. This discussion does not address regulatory or building code requirements. Specific state or federal codes related to behavioral health physical plants are defined by the appropriate regulatory agencies and must be consulted in formulating plans regarding seclusion rooms.

Risk Control Techniques   The facility must develop and implement protocols, policies, and procedures to govern the use of therapeutic seclusion. The type of seclusion to be used, seclusion duration, patient observation requirements, and patient monitoring requirements should be clearly defined, adhered to, and documented in the patient's clinical record. Levels of seclusion include:

Locked Seclusion—Most Restrictive   The patient is involuntarily placed in a locked seclusion room that is equipped with observation access (shatterproof, safety-glass windows, recessed cameras, and so on) and patient safety equipment such as a mat. Otherwise, the room should be free of all other objects.

There must be no electrical outlets, wires, vents, dropped ceilings, and so on. The room must be shaped so that the staff can visually observe the patient at all times. When less than ideal room characteristics are unavoidable, suitable alternatives such as multiple cameras or other adaptations must be implemented.

In cases of severe agitation, it might be necessary to remove the patient's clothing as protection from injury. At the very least, shoes, belts, jewelry, dentures, glasses, and pocket contents must be removed before the patient is placed in seclusion.

Other risks requiring observation and prevention include misuse of seemingly safe objects including plastic trash bags, plastic eating utensils, blankets, pillows, and so on.

Patients have been known to use virtually any item to injure themselves or to assist in an elopement from seclusion. For example, there have been elopements through air ducts, injuries from screws or nails that were used in the room construction, and injuries from sharpened plastic eating utensils used as weapons. Staff must consider any object in the seclusion room as a potential danger to the patient or staff.

Staff must enter seclusion only with backup, and all patient encounters involving seclusion should be witnessed by at least one other employee. Patients should be periodically removed from seclusion to evaluate whether or not they can be reintegrated into the patient population.

The patient's physical condition must be monitored during periods of seclusion. This may include checking the patient's blood pressure and pulse and closely monitoring the effects of any psychoactive medications that are given.

Seclusion may never be used as a threat or punishment for a patient's failure to behave in a manner desired by the staff or physician. Seclusion is a major curtailment of a patient's freedom and should be used only when other therapeutic techniques have failed to assist the patient in attaining adequate behavioral control.

Regardless of the reason for seclusion, and regardless of the type of seclusion used, all patient encounters, monitoring efforts, and patient assessments during periods of seclusion must be fully documented in the patient's clinical record. Staff also must document all steps taken to assist the patient in regaining control of behavior before using seclusion.

Claims related to seclusion are generally based upon allegations of false imprisonment or patient abuse. Therefore, all efforts to avoid seclusion and to remove the patient from seclusion must be documented to effectively defend against future allegations.

Open Door (Unlocked) Seclusion—Moderately Restrictive   Open door (unlocked) seclusion may be an acceptable environmental restraint for patients who have difficulty maintaining behavioral control but who are not a danger to themselves or others. Patients with these needs may voluntarily enter the seclusion room but the door, although it may be closed for privacy and decreased environmental stimulation, must remain unlocked.

Although patients with behavioral control issues may request open door seclusion, it is also acceptable for staff to offer open door seclusion whenever it becomes evident that the patient is having difficulty maintaining behavioral control.

The same patient safeguards must be employed for open door seclusion as for locked seclusion. This includes monitoring the patient's response to seclusion, monitoring vital signs as needed, periodically removing the patient from seclusion to assess the ability to return to the patient community, and ensuring the absence of any objects that could be a danger to the patient or staff.

The seclusion room should be kept locked when not in use. This ensures that staff must permit patient access, and it decreases the possibility of unsupervised seclusion.

As with locked seclusion, open door seclusion must be included in the patient's treatment plan. Documentation in the patient's clinical record should include the symptoms or behaviors that led to the seclusion, the results of patient monitoring during the episode, the patient's response to the seclusion, and the patient's response to re-entry into the general patient community. The time the patient entered seclusion, the duration of each aspect of the episode, and the time the patient exited should be included in the documentation.

Voluntary Quiet Room—Minimally Restrictive   Some behavioral health treatment units have a designated area where patients may be alone or away from any significant environmental stimulation. Some facilities allow patients to return to their bedrooms during the day if they need a quiet place. But others, in an effort to encourage patient participation in therapeutic activities, restrict patient access to any isolated area including their bedrooms. In such cases, there may be a designated quiet room. Patients must be instructed regarding the use of the quiet room, and all use must be documented in the patient's clinical record.

The patient's treatment plan should reflect how often the quiet room may be used, the duration of quiet time, and patient observation and monitoring requirements.

"Time-Outs" for Minors and Mature Minors—Minimally Restrictive   Time-outs are used for minors who have lost control of their behavior while interacting in the patient community. Time-outs generally involve removal from the major activities or source of stimulus in the group, but not from the group's presence. There is often a section of the perimeter of the patient treatment area or a particular chair in the room that is designated as a time-out area.

Often, the patient is encouraged to sit alone for a defined period of time. The duration of the time-out should be established when the minor is removed from the ongoing activities of the group. When the time-out has expired, the minor patient is asked to rejoin the group. If the time-out was not successful in helping the minor patient to regain behavioral control, other de-escalation techniques may be required.

As with all other types of seclusion, time-outs must be documented in the patient's clinical record.

Physical Environment Controls   Locking doors is the most common method for controlling the behavioral health care environment. In the behavioral health inpatient unit, doors may be locked to restrict patient access to certain areas and the unit's exit doors may be locked to prohibit unauthorized entrance or exit. Other environmental controls include alarms or keypad controls on doors and elevators and locked window covers.

Risk control techniques involving the use of environmental controls must include ensuring adequate protocols, policies, and procedures for timely evacuation of patients and staff from locked units or areas in the event of fire or other internal disaster.

Environmental controls seclude or restrict patients from accessing high-risk areas. Examples include:

- Entrances or exits to the unit or facility
- Elevators and stairways
- Windows
- Nursing stations, staff lounges, or locker room areas
- Seclusion room(s)
- Medication storage, preparation, and dispensing areas
- Examination and treatment areas
- Electroconvulsive therapy treatment and recovery areas
- Patient rooms except during hours of sleep or rest periods
- Bathing or shower rooms
- Activity or craft areas
- Exercise or gym facilities
- Individual or group therapy rooms
- Housekeeping supplies and equipment storage areas
- Dietary or kitchen facilities

Seclusion Policy   The following are elements that should be addressed and documented as part of the organization's protocols, policies, and procedures for all locked and unlocked seclusion and voluntary use of quiet rooms and time-outs:

Informed Consent Process   The use of seclusion requires informed consent except in cases of emergency when patients are deemed to be a risk to themselves or others. Often the symptoms or behaviors that necessitate involuntary seclusion are the same symptoms or behaviors that render patients, at least temporarily, unable to control their behaviors adequately to participate in the informed consent process. When a patient is deemed unable to consent because of behavioral symptoms, family members should be notified and consent obtained, if possible. Patients might be able to provide retroactive consent after they have regained behavioral control.

Documentation relating to the informed consent process for involuntary seclusion must indicate the specific reasons or behaviors that rendered the patient unable to provide informed consent, the steps taken to obtain consent from a parent or legal representative, and subsequent (retroactive) patient consent, if obtained.

Other components of a seclusion policy include:

Practitioner Orders   A practitioner's order is required for the use of any patient-specific environmental restraint including locked, voluntary, or open door (unlocked) seclusion, or the patient's voluntary use of a quiet room.

Emergency Use   As noted previously, involuntary controls may be used without the patient's consent in instances when it is determined that the patient presents a danger to himself, herself, or others. Consent, physician orders, and notification to the family or legal representative must be carried out as soon as it is practicable.

Seclusion Efficacy and Patient Safety   The efficacy and propriety of the seclusion in meeting the patient's treatment needs must be documented. The patient's safety and well-being (and the safety of others) are paramount considerations, and any adverse patient response must be immediately addressed by the clinical staff or practitioner. Moreover, any patient injury resulting from seclusion must be reported in accordance with regulatory requirements and facility policy.

Monitoring and Observations Protocols   Consistent, ongoing monitoring of the patient's behavior and physical condition immediately before, during, and after seclusion must occur.

Electroconvulsive Therapy

Electroconvulsive therapy (ECT) has been used for behavioral health patients for decades. Commonly called "shock therapy," it has been both praised and criticized by behavioral health professionals, patients' rights advocates, and society at large.

ECT and other "shock therapies," such as insulin shock, have been, at various times, both popular and controversial. They have sometimes been depicted as cruel and inhumane in the public media. Movies such as *The Snake Pit* from the 1950s, *One Flew Over the Cuckoo's Nest* during the 1970s, and *Girl, Interrupted* in 2000 have given the impression that psychiatric hospitalization and treatments such as ECT were used as a form of punishment or to control a patient's undesirable behavior. These negative depictions of psychiatric hospitals or ECT in the media might have been effective in focusing the general population's attention on the need to ensure behavioral health patients' rights and that all behavioral health patients receive humane, safe, and effective treatment.

Traditionally, ECT treatments are given in a series over a prescribed period. The number of treatments in the series will depend upon the practitioner's custom and practice, the patient's response to treatment, the presence or degree of adverse or side effects, and the patient's overall therapeutic response to the ECT treatments.

ECT patients receive sedation or anesthesia before receiving the controlled application of an electrical stimulus. The resulting convulsive response is controlled to minimize the risk of physical injury or post-treatment discomfort. The treatment is administered by a physician and can be provided in both inpatient and outpatient settings depending on the patient's needs. Patients are monitored during the treatment and until they have recovered sufficiently to leave the treatment area.

Risk Control Techniques   The following risk control techniques apply to electroconvulsive therapy issues:

Informed Consent   As with many medical treatments and procedures, results from ECT and the occurrence of adverse or side effects might vary. The physician must clearly discuss the risks, benefits, and alternatives to ECT with the patient to ensure that the informed consent process is fully implemented.

As noted previously, ECT is typically given through a series of treatments, and the informed consent should specify the number of treatments authorized by the patient.

Should additional treatments be needed beyond those included in the initial informed consent, additional consent should be obtained.

Documentation of each informed consent discussion and the patient's resulting decision is critical to the effective defense of any subsequent litigation that might arise. Because some patients who receive ECT complain of memory loss following treatment, it is recommended that whenever possible, a family member or patient legal representative be included in each informed consent discussion and that their witnessing of the patient's consent also be documented in the patient's clinical record.

Clinical Assessment   ECT patients should undergo an assessment that includes:

- A detailed description of the patient's clinical condition including diagnoses, symptoms, behaviors, and past and present treatments, that necessitates the proposed ECT treatment

- Identification of the patient's specific symptoms that are included in the organization's clinical indications for ECT

- Ongoing clinical evaluation of the patient's initial and continuing response to ECT treatment

Health History and Medical Clearance   Patients must have a complete medical history and physical examination to ensure that they are medically stable and medically suited for ECT. Pre-treatment anesthesia evaluations must be performed to assess the anesthesia risk and to determine the applicability of the specific type of anesthesia proposed.

Intra- and Post-Procedure Monitoring Criteria   The ECT clinical protocol must clearly define the type and extent of clinical monitoring of the patient's medical condition required during and following ECT.

Management of Medical Emergencies   The ECT clinical protocol must address the manner in which medical emergencies will be managed should they occur during or after an ECT treatment. During the treatment, a physician and an anesthesia or nursing professional are in attendance, and patients are medically monitored. Depending on the ECT unit location, it may be desirable for the unit to maintain an emergency cart that includes emergency equipment and medications. Regardless of the type of facility, there should be adequate emergency equipment available for the clinical personnel to establish an airway, provide CPR, administer oxygen, and obtain transportation to an acute medical care setting.

If the ECT is being administered in a behavioral health facility that is contained in a hospital or medical center, it might be clinically appropriate to have an arrangement with the hospital's CPR team to respond to emergencies in the ECT unit. It also might be proper for the ECT professional staff to begin emergency treatment, stabilize the patient's medical emergency, and then transport the patient directly to the hospital emergency department.

Documenting of and Complying with Electroconvulsive Therapy Treatment Plans   Clinical justification, informed consent discussion, results of monitoring, and the patient's response to treatment must comply with the treatment plan and be documented in the patient's clinical record.

Addiction or Substance Abuse Therapies

People who seek treatment for addiction, substance abuse, and some related uncontrollable repetitive behaviors are often recognized as having behavioral health diagnoses and thus may be appropriately treated in a behavioral health facility. This section of the chapter is not intended to be an in-depth discussion of addiction, substance abuse, or repetitive behaviors, nor does it discuss all their applicable medical and behavioral health treatments. The focus here is on identified risks and practicable risk control techniques.

The following is a partial list of substances, medications, and repetitive behaviors that may result in the patient's seeking treatment in a behavioral health facility:

● Alcohol

● Narcotics (includes legally prescribed narcotics, illegally obtained narcotics or "street drugs," or illicitly produced forms of narcotics)

● Hallucinogens

● Sedatives

● Hypnotics

● Amphetamines

● Anti-anxiety agents

● Caffeine

● Nicotine

● Gambling

● Sex and sex-related behaviors

● Eating

● Debting

● Cleaning

● Handwashing

Because some substances are illegal, patients might be involved in allegations or criminal charges within the legal system. Patients must be notified at the start of their course of treatment that entering treatment is not a substitute for their participation in legal or criminal proceedings that might ensue, nor is it in lieu of criminal charges or incarceration, unless so ordered by the courts.

Risk Control Techniques   The following risk control techniques are related to addiction or substance abuse therapies:

Initial and Ongoing Clinical and Behavioral Assessments   Patients who seek addiction therapies must have initial and periodic clinical and behavioral assessments. Additional clinical and behavioral assessments must also be performed whenever there are significant changes in a patient's symptoms or condition.

Medical Clearance for Detoxification   Patients who undergo detoxification might have co-existing acute or chronic medical conditions that require concomitant assessment and treatment. Withdrawal from a substance, even when managed under clinical protocol, can cause additional stress on the patient's health. It is necessary to establish the patient's underlying medical condition, identify any co-existing medical conditions, and treat them as needed.

Ongoing Medical Management   Some patients who undergo addiction therapy will require ongoing treatment of co-existing acute and chronic medical conditions or medical symptoms that result from the detoxification process. Concomitant treatment of co-existing or detox-related medical conditions or symptoms must be documented in the patient's clinical record.

Contraband Controls   Addiction therapy patients might suffer severe physical and emotional symptoms during detoxification and throughout the course of their treatment. Such symptoms might occur even with supportive therapy, medication, and stress management. The patient can experience strong cravings for the substance for which detoxification is indicated and could at increased risk for unauthorized use of that substance.

It is critical to the success of addiction therapy that the patient be completely removed from any access to the substance of choice. The behavioral health addiction therapy unit must employ strict contraband controls to ensure a safe, substance-free environment for patients.

Facility protocol must stipulate what steps will be taken to discard or otherwise destroy any contraband substances located during a search. Identification of an illegal substance in a patient's possession might require notification of law enforcement. Each facility should consult with its legal counsel to ascertain its legal and regulatory responsibilities related to illegal substances. Such legal advice should be incorporated into the facility's addiction therapy protocols, policies, and procedures.

Patients should be informed at the time of admission that their rooms and possessions will be initially and periodically searched and, if deemed necessary, they may be required to submit to a body search.

- Room Searches: When a patient is identified as being at risk, routine searches and additional focused searches of patient rooms, communal areas, dining rooms, and activity areas are essential to ensure a substance-free environment.

- Personal Effects Searches: Each patient's personal effects must be searched at the time of admission and periodically thereafter for any contraband. Identified contraband must be confiscated and discarded, or surrendered to law enforcement as necessary.

- Body Searches: If a body search is necessary, it should only be carried out by a same-sex professional staff member and should be witnessed and documented by a same-sex staff member. Some organizations stipulate that only medical professionals (physician, nurse) perform body searches.

It might be necessary to carry out an even closer body search such as a skin search or a body cavity search for patients at high risk for contraband. Such searches may be indicated if there is reasonable suspicion that a substance is hidden somewhere on the body.

It is important to reiterate that whenever any level of body search is clinically indicated, it must be respectfully carried out by a same-sex professional staff member and witnessed by a same-sex staff member. This will help defend the staff and organization against any allegations of abuse or injury during a search. Both staff members should independently document the details of the search in the patient's clinical record.

Medication Management   Behavioral health facilities must have stringent controls for managing all medications and biologicals. Any prescribed or unauthorized medications must be confiscated. Prescribed medication may be returned only at the time of discharge and only if it continues to be prescribed. It might be preferable to have the patients sign an acknowledgement of the facility's protocols, policies, and procedures related to the management of both prescribed medications and unauthorized drugs in the patient's possession at the time of admission into the treatment facility. The acknowledgement may contain information related to possession of illegal substances including the information that law enforcement may be notified.

Family members and other visitors must be oriented to the risks of carrying medications or drugs when they are visiting the patient in a behavioral health setting. Even if their family member is not at risk, other patients in the setting might be at risk. If necessary, at-risk patients should be prohibited from having visitors. In some cases, it might be necessary to perform voluntary searches of visitors or their personal items such as purses, backpacks, and so on, and to deny visiting privileges to those who are unwilling to submit to reasonable search procedures.

Physical Plant Controls   Some addiction therapy treatment facilities or units in a facility are designated as locked units to prevent the introduction of contraband and to protect patients from eloping. This may be true for addiction therapy patients who are also at high risk for suicide or homicide, are incompetent or confused, are minors, or have other high-risk factors.

See the section on elopement in this chapter for the physical plant controls recommended as risk control techniques.

Visitor Controls   Addiction therapy facilities must establish specific policies and procedures that govern the management of visitors. Many such facilities require orientation of all visitors before they meet with patients to ensure that they have not purposely or inadvertently brought a potentially dangerous medication or contraband item into the facility. Some facilities greatly limit the visitors for addiction therapy patients. Others require visitors to undergo contraband searches.

When there is significant risk to the patient, the practitioner may order that visitors be completely prohibited for all or part of the patient's course of treatment. The practitioner may require that all or specific visitors only be allowed under direct 1:1 observation by staff, or when they are participating in a patient care activity.

Clinical Monitoring Protocols   There must be ongoing monitoring of the effectiveness of facility protocols, policies, and procedures designed to ensure that the facility is providing quality care to addiction therapy patients in a safe environment that is free of contraband. There must also be ongoing monitoring of addiction therapy patients' treatment plans to ensure that they are properly assessed and treated.

The facility must monitor instances when contraband is identified, used, or seized, to identify gaps in their patient safety and physical plant contraband controls. When an issue is identified, it must be investigated and a plan of correction developed and implemented. Continued monitoring is maintained to ensure the effectiveness of the plan of correction.

Discharge Planning and Referral for Ongoing Supportive Care   Each addiction therapy patient must receive a comprehensive discharge plan that includes necessary referrals for ongoing supportive care. This is especially important when patients have been admitted for substance detoxification. Such admissions are usually of a limited nature and are confined to the initial withdrawal of the substance. Addiction therapy patients might have a long history of symptoms and also might have lost their housing, employment, and social support systems.

The patient should be referred for follow-up therapy and medical care as needed. A partial list of applicable referrals includes:

- Emergency or long-term housing assistance
- Financial assistance for living expenses
- Financial or insurance coverage for ongoing behavioral and medical health care
- Individual or group behavioral health and addiction therapy
- Suitable twelve-step and other community-based support program(s)
- Medical care provider
- Social agencies for assistance with meals, clothing, and so on

Documentation of Compliance with Addiction Therapy Treatment Plans   The patient's level of compliance with the addiction therapy treatment plan, including abstinence from substance(s), must be documented in the patient's clinical record. Documentation of patient compliance with the treatment plan also must indicate which support systems and services have been provided to help the addiction therapy patient maintain abstinence and follow the prescribed treatment plan.

Experimental Treatments

The behavioral health research community is continually developing and implementing research protocols, especially in the area of medications. Research directed at developing more effective psychoactive medications and improving behavioral health care treatments is regulated by the Food and Drug Administration (FDA). Behavioral health patients may meet criteria for inclusion in one or more ongoing research clinical trials.

There are very specific guidelines and regulations that control research involving human subjects. This section is not to be considered a comprehensive discussion of clinical research or of the FDA guidelines. Rather, it is a brief discussion of some risks involved in clinical research, and suggests several risk control techniques that might reduce patient injury or investigator and facility liability. For more information regarding this topic refer to the FDA Web site at [www.fda.gov].

Risk Control Techniques   Risk control techniques associated with experimental treatments include the following:

Institutional Review Board Approval of Investigational Protocols   Every clinical trial must meet the FDA requirements for research that involves human subjects. Every health care organization that participates in clinical trials must have an institutional review board (IRB) that reviews and approves investigational protocols. IRBs are composed of clinicians, administrators, ethics professionals, clergy, and at least one lay person from the immediate community. Additional information about Clinical Research and Institutional Review Boards can be found in Chapter 5 of this volume.

Investigational Protocol   Every FDA- and IRB-approved protocol must be permanently maintained by the IRB. The patient's participation in the investigational protocol must be documented in that patient's clinical record.

Use of Additional, Protocol-Specific, FDA-Approved Consent for Participation in Investigational Protocol   Every FDA clinical trial includes a protocol-specific consent document. The informed consent process must include a review of the FDA-approved consent information that provides the risks, benefits, and alternatives to the proposed experimental medication or biomedical equipment. Additionally, the consent discussion must expressly inform the patient that the treatment is experimental in nature, that there may be no benefit derived from it, and that adverse or side effects may result from the treatment.

Initial and Ongoing Assessment of Clinical Appropriateness for Investigational Protocol   A comprehensive patient assessment is required initially and periodically, as defined in the protocol, to ensure that the patient meets the clinical criteria for inclusion. An additional assessment must be performed whenever there is a significant change in the patient's condition.

Initial Medical Clearance and Ongoing Medical Management   Patients who participate in investigational behavioral health protocols must have medical clearance to ensure that their medical condition is suited for them to participate and to ascertain their baseline health status. It is then possible to more accurately evaluate their response to the protocol or the development of adverse or side effects of the experimental treatment.

Use of concomitant or subsequently approved Treatment Participation in an investigational protocol may include the patient's agreement to forgo initiating other known or experimental therapies or treatments pending completion of the protocol.

The informed consent process is essential to ensuring that the patient makes an informed decision regarding participation in the investigational protocol. As previously noted, the informed consent discussion must include not only the risks and benefits of the proposed protocol, but also the information regarding any other alternatives to that treatment.

FDA and State Department of Health Reporting of Patient Adverse Effect or Injury   Any adverse effect or patient injury resulting from participation in an investigational protocol must be reported to the FDA and the Department of Health for the state in which the patient is being treated.

Documentation of Patient's Response to Protocol   The patient's response to the investigational protocol must be documented in that patient's clinical record.

Referral for Ongoing Approved or Investigational Treatment   Upon completion of the investigational protocol, the behavioral health patient may require referral for other investigational treatments or for standard, approved therapies. All efforts made to refer the patient for additional treatment or therapy must be documented in the patient's clinical record.

Proper referrals and documentation of those efforts and the patient's subsequent compliance may be especially critical for behavioral health patients at high risk for suicidal or homicidal ideation, addiction, or with a history of non-compliance with their treatment plan.

············

ABUSE RISKS

Many behavioral health patients may be at high risk for abuse or for exhibiting abusive or aggressive behavior themselves. There is also a heightened risk for allegations of abuse when the patient population is composed of vulnerable groups including children, adolescents, developmentally delayed, physically handicapped, and geriatric patients. All behavioral health patients must be assessed for the risk of abusive behavior. Additionally, a careful history must be obtained that includes queries regarding episodes of abuse in the patient's life.

Each organization should build its foundation on a zero-tolerance philosophy regarding abuse. To maintain a safe patient environment, prevention efforts must be comprehensive and ongoing. However, once abuse has occurred, risk control techniques must be implemented in a timely fashion.

Because the behavioral health population is composed of known vulnerable groups, there is a potential risk for attracting unsuitable workers. Therefore, all employees, contract personnel, and volunteers must be fully screened to eliminate potential abusers. Once they are approved to be part of the organizational workforce, they must undergo training in the recognition and prevention of abuse.

Alleged Abuser

Abusers of patients can be other patients, staff, family, or visitors.

Patient-Patient Abuse   Trained staff must supervise all patient-to-patient contact, including therapeutic and social encounters. To minimize the risk of patient-to-patient abuse, staff should consider that any unsupervised encounter might result in actual or alleged abuse.

Staff-Patient Abuse   Staff must be aware that behavioral health patients might have an altered or heightened sense of vulnerability and might experience even justifiable staff contact as abusive. It is important that all staff be made aware of patients with a history of abuse or of having been abused, so that the staff can behave accordingly.

When patients act out against staff, there must be emergency procedures and mechanisms to enable staff members to protect themselves from abusive patients.

Visitor-Patient Abuse   Patient-visitor encounters should be limited to staff-supervised areas. Family and other visitors who have a history of abusing the patient or being abused by the patient may properly be barred from visiting.

Alleged Abuse

The facility must have formal protocols, policies, and procedures relating to abuse. Such policies and procedures must include the guidelines for preventing, investigating, correcting, and reporting instances of abuse.

Any allegations of abuse or complaints of abuse must be fully reported, investigated, and, when substantiated, corrective measures must be taken. In addition to reporting such allegations or instances of abuse internally, most states require that abuse be reported to the state department of health or department of mental health.

The facility must provide clinical and administrative guidelines for managing abusive patients (see the discussions of the use of de-escalation techniques, seclusion, and restraint).

Any staff found to have been abusive must be removed immediately from the patient treatment area. Facility procedure should require that once allegations of abuse have been verified, the employee should be terminated from employment, reported to any relevant licensing, certifying or professional monitoring authorities, and, when appropriate, reported to law enforcement.

Abuse might be of sufficient degree to be considered a criminal act and require notification of law enforcement. The criminal codes in each state provide legal definitions of the various forms of abuse. Additional legal definitions may be included in child or senior welfare agency regulations. Each organization's legal counsel should be consulted whenever a question of criminal acts may arise.

Physical Abuse   Any unwarranted or unauthorized physical contact that did or could have caused an injury or that was experienced as abuse by the patient should be treated or investigated as abuse.

Sexual Abuse   For purposes of this document, sexual abuse will include any verbal or physical contact of a sexual or improperly intimate nature that involves a minor or incompetent adult, and any unwarranted or unauthorized contact of a sexual or improperly intimate nature between adults when one adult has not consented.

Emotional Abuse   Emotional abuse is perhaps more difficult to define. For purposes of this discussion and establishing a threshold for implementing risk control techniques, it should include any verbal or written event or perceived personal slight, or neglect of a patient's needs or requests that results in patient distress or emotional pain and suffering. Clearly, this definition is articulated from the patient's perspective, but the patient's perception of abuse will lead to allegations and potential litigation.

Reporting Abuse

Any allegation or confirmed instance of abuse must be reported internally as a patient incident. The patient's physician, family, or legal representative should be notified of the alleged abuse and informed of the patient's immediate condition. Treat any physical injuries or sexual or emotional abuse and note the treatment in the reports. All allegations of abuse should be additionally reported to the applicable state agencies pending the results of the facility's or law enforcement's investigative findings. The investigation's findings that deem the allegation to be either substantiated or unsubstantiated also should be reported to the involved parties and agencies. Following the investigation, develop and implement a plan of correction and report this to the proper parties and agencies.

Although reporting requirements may vary from state to state, reports to the following are typically required:

- State Department of Mental Health
- State Department of Health
- Internal or organization-specific requirements, including family, legal representative, and physician
- Law enforcement

Investigation and Documentation of Abuse Allegations

All allegations of abuse must be diligently investigated and the findings reported. Develop and implement a plan to ensure that no further abuse can occur. Any treatment provided to the patient related to alleged or confirmed abuse must be documented in the patient's clinical record.

Abuse Prevention Techniques

The organization must have protocols, policies, and procedures that ensure a safe treatment environment without the threat of abuse. Prevention requires learning from past episodes when abuse occurred despite the organization's best prevention efforts. Prevention of future occurrences will require a plan of correction that specifically addresses the contributing factors identified during the investigative process.

Abuse prevention includes ensuring that patients are receiving behavioral health care in the proper setting. This might require improving an organization's admission or acceptance criteria to more adequately screen patients at risk for abusive behavior and assign them to units where such behaviors can be controlled.

Mandatory screening for employees, contract personnel, and volunteers is required. Professional guidelines, organizational manuals, and in-service programs define and explain proper behavior among staff and behavioral health patients. Such programs also reiterate that termination or criminal consequences will result when allegations of abuse are substantiated.

Documentation Practices and Requirements

All actions undertaken to investigate abuse allegations, all investigative findings, and any corrective actions taken must be fully documented in the incident and investigational reports. Patient injuries and resulting treatments should be documented in the patient's clinical record.

••••••••••••

ENVIRONMENTAL RISKS

Every aspect of the patient's environment must be assessed for the risk of patient injury. Although patient's rights include the right to privacy, it is essential that staff can visualize patients in every area. All resident property should be carefully checked for potentially dangerous items and contraband at the time of admission. Unscheduled room checks further protect residents.

- Door Locks: Door locks must be designed so that patients cannot lock or unlock any unit door. Conversely, every staff member must have access to keys that lock and unlock every door in the unit.

- Patient Rooms: Patient rooms are ideally square in shape and do not have any "blind" areas where staff cannot immediately visualize the location of the patient. Patient's closets should be equipped with "breakaway" hanging rods that support only minimal weight.

- Bathrooms: All unit bathrooms must be equipped with "breakaway" shower rods and showerheads and shatterproof mirrors. Plumbing should be fully enclosed with no exposed pipes.

- Windows: Windows should be made of shatterproof, breakproof materials. If windows can open, they should be modified to allow one to two inches in opening. Some facilities use locked window covers made of wire mesh that allow windows to be safely opened for ventilation purposes.

- Seclusion or Quiet Rooms: There should be no materials in the room except for a mat or mattress. There should be no patient-accessible electrical outlets, vents, screw-on plates, or guards that could be removed. Dropped ceilings should not be used in these areas. The room should be square in shape to allow for complete visualization of the patient. If a camera is used, it must be out of reach and may not be covered by any material that can be unscrewed, loosened, or dislodged.

- Medication Storage Areas and Administration Areas or Carts: Medication storage and administration areas should be centrally located and patients should go to that area to receive medications. Require a mouth check after every medication is administered. If medication carts are used, they should not be left unattended for even a moment and must be kept locked at all times. Ideally, carts should be kept in a locked medication preparation or administration room. Medication rooms often have "Dutch" doors in which the lower portion can remain closed and locked while the upper portion is opened for the staff to provide the patient's ordered medications.

- Housekeeping, Maintenance Chemicals, and Equipment: Housekeeping equipment must be kept under direct observation at all times. Toxic cleaning agents must be kept locked away from patient access. Plastic trashcan liners or other plastic bags for waste disposal should be prohibited.

- Razor or Sharps Management: Any object that could be used directly, or modified to be used as a cutting tool or weapon for self-injury or to injure someone else, must be carefully monitored and should be considered a sharp. All personal effects must be searched at the time of admission and all sharps or potentially dangerous items removed. All sharps must be maintained under locked staff control and should be counted and accounted for at each change of shift. Any missing sharps should constitute an incident and must initiate a total unit search until the missing sharp is located.

Although battery-powered razors are recommended, even they can become a sharp if disassembled. Sharps may not be provided to patients at risk for suicidal or homicidal behavior. If sharps are provided to patients, they must be logged in and out and used by patients under the staff's visual supervision to ensure that high-risk patients do not obtain access to a sharp signed out for use by another patient. A time limit should be imposed for each sharp released to a patient; if it is not accounted for within the time limit, it should be considered missing. Once again, a missing sharp constitutes an incident, and a total unit search must be conducted until it is located.

Examples of sharps include:

- Razors
- Scissors
- Nail clippers, cuticle clippers, or scissors
- Nail files
- Any form of knife, including butter knives and cooking knives
- Eating utensils

....

CONCLUSION

Behavioral health care services have evolved significantly during the past several decades, with the primary shift being the provision of more outpatient behavioral health care services. Risk control in the behavioral health care arena also has evolved to address changing risks. A successful behavioral health care risk control program addresses proper hiring, training, and supervision of staff; well-planned and managed physical facilities; thorough patient evaluations and treatment plans; comprehensive informed consent process; and many other components discussed in this chapter.

Like all risk control programs, the behavioral health risk program should be constantly evaluated and adapted to meet changing needs and circumstances. Any incidents should be investigated, analyzed, and used as learning experiences, with sufficient risk control techniques implemented to prevent future similar incidents. Risk control is always a process and not just a program. Success can be measured in part by a facility's ability to learn from its own mistakes, from the mistakes of others, and to proactively adjust the risk control program in response to those lessons learned.

Suggested Reading

Health Intelligence Network re: Hospital and Health Systems Management "JCAHO Revises Behavioral Restraint and Seclusion Standards." [www.hin.com/sw/hospital_Hsmanagement.shtml].

LII – Legal Information Institute re: Title 42 Chapter 102, Sec.9501 US Code Collection [www4.law.cornell.edu/uscode/42/9501.html].

Lehmann, C. "AACP Issues Guidelines on Seclusion, Restraint Use." *Psychiatric News, American Psychiatric Association*, 37 (7), 2002, p. 12. [pn.psychiatryonline.org/cgi/citmgr?gcq=psychnews].

Tarasoff v. Regents of University of California, 131 Cal.Rptr.14, 551 P.2d 334 (Cal. 1976).

12

Managing Risks and Improving Safety in the Intensive Care Unit

Kathleen Shostek
Peter J. Pronovost

Intensive care units (ICUs) account for 10 percent of all inpatient acute care beds in the United States, collectively making up one of the largest and most costly components of the nation's health care system.[1] ICUs provide care to over 5 million acutely ill patients per year at an annual cost of $180 billion.[2] In addition to being high volume and high cost, ICUs are also very high risk. Mortality in ICUs approximates 10 percent, and some studies suggest that medical errors and adverse events affect nearly all ICU patients.[3] Equally alarming are the numbers of ICU patients who are harmed by errors of omission—therapies that ought to be administered but are not—resulting in significant and preventable morbidity, mortality, and cost of care.[4] These attributes make ICUs high risk for poor patient outcomes, exposing health care organizations to potentially high medical malpractice losses and to operational and other losses.

The U.S. is not alone in facing quality and risk challenges in intensive care. A recent study in the United Kingdom revealed that 25 percent of all patients admitted to ICUs there during one month in 2003 died, and nearly half of those patients received care judged to be suboptimal.[5]

Contributing to the high mortality and suboptimal care were delays in having an intensivist see ICU admissions and less-experienced physician house officers being overtaxed by the high number of acutely ill patients.[6] Similarly, a U.S. hospital study concluded that delays in having physicians see new ICU admissions were associated with increased mortality.[7]

Modern error theory suggests that ICUs are error prone due to the complexity of the environment, the presence of multiple caregivers, and the high number of interactions among them. Contributing to the intricate nature of the ICU is the high acuity of patient illnesses, the use of complex medical technologies, the performance of invasive procedures, and the need to continuously monitor patients who are medically unstable In addition, the devices and technology used to perform procedures or monitor patients require specific sequential procedures, interventions, and occurrences for optimal outcomes.[8]

Principles of human factors[9] analysis also indicate that the high stress, high complexity, and staff diversity typically found in ICU environments make them fertile ground for distractions, miscommunications, and fatigue that lead to mistakes, errors, and adverse events. Time pressures, space limitations, and budgetary constraints also affect patient safety in ICUs by restricting the availability of direct care providers at the bedside, limiting the ability of family members to remain with (and advocate for) patients, and reducing staff access to critical equipment and supplies.

Common occurrences that contribute to adverse events and poor outcomes, which lead to increased lengths of stay and potential liability claims in ICUs, include medication and intravenous (IV) errors, events during physical transport outside the ICU or transfer of responsibility for care ("hand-offs"), injuries associated with airways or ventilator use, central catheter-related complications, infections such as catheter-related blood stream infections (BSI) and ventilator-associated pneumonias (VAP), and failures to rescue or intervene in a timely or appropriate manner when a patient's condition worsens. Studies of human errors in ICUs indicate that communication breakdowns and the failure to transfer important information from one caregiver to another contribute significantly to these types of occurrences.[10] This is consistent with the finding that communication issues are the most frequent root cause of all categories of sentinel events reported to the Joint Commission on Accreditation of Healthcare Organizations (JCAHO).[11]

The aging of the nursing workforce and a shortage of critical care-trained nurses also affects the ability of ICUs to provide high-quality bedside care. Provision of medical care to ICU patients by resident physicians in various levels of training is common in ICUs where teaching programs exist. The quality of supervision provided by senior physicians who oversee critical care in teaching facilities varies, as does compliance with limitations on residents' work hours—and inexperience and fatigue inevitably have a major effect on patient safety. Also, the use of intensivists in ICUs—physicians with specialized training in critical care medicine—is low, even though evidence suggests that the use of intensivists in ICUs improves patient outcomes, reducing hospital mortality by 30 percent.[12]

The quality of hospital support services also affects ICU care. Hospital information systems vary in their ability to support clinicians in communicating the information necessary for critical decision-making. Pharmacy, laboratory, and imaging services may or may not provide an optimal level of therapeutic and diagnostic support for the care of critical patients.

Risk management professionals and patient safety officers can address these and other challenges by collaborating with senior leaders, physicians, ICU managers, and the critical care staff to transform ICUs into safer, more patient-friendly units with lower liability risk exposure. They can also help the hospital and community capitalize on the value of critical care services. With proper support and commitment, ICUs can become high-reliability organizations (HROs)—organizations that perform extremely well with few errors or adverse events over the long term even though they face high intrinsic hazards and risks.[13] In this chapter, current approaches to improving quality, enhancing safety, and managing risks in ICUs are reviewed and examples of advances and successes in ICU safety are highlighted.

············

CULTURE AND PATIENT SAFETY IN THE ICU

An integral part of improving safety is creating a culture of safety across the health care organization. Patient safety initiatives focused on the ICU have a much greater chance of success if they are preceded by such a culture.[14] In fact, safety culture can be thought of as the lubrication that allows system redesign. Without it, work cannot be reorganized or safety practices implemented because the individuals who are expected to implement the safety initiatives don't yet know how best to work together or communicate effectively. Characteristics of a culture of safety in ICU include comfort in asking questions, and in challenging behaviors and processes of care that have the potential to compromise safety. Also, when system defects are identified, the organization with a culture of safety can make changes to eliminate or minimize the defects. The degree to which communication and teamwork failures contribute to JCAHO's sentinel events highlights the impact of safety culture on patients. Indeed, currently, JCAHO's proposed leadership standards for 2007 include requirements for a culture of safety and a systems approach to quality improvement with a focus on responsibilities and accountabilities of leadership.

Crucial to the embodiment of a safety culture is enduring support from key leadership of the organization's administration and medical staff. Hospital administrative support is vital to obtaining the financial, human, and moral support necessary for organizational change and care unit improvement. Physician champions are vital to ICU patient safety programs, in particular, as they facilitate the support of other clinicians and promote motivation of the front line staff.

We now have evidence that safety culture is both measurable and improvable. The Safety Attitudes Questionnaire (SAQ) provides a valid and reliable means to measure safety.[15] A comprehensive unit-based safety program (CUSP), has been implemented and validated as successful for improving safety culture and other safety outcomes in the surgical intensive care units (SICUs) at Johns Hopkins Hospital (JHH), Baltimore, Maryland. CUSP incorporates the SAQ as part of the program. CUSP is based on the following six steps:[16]

1. **Assess the culture of safety:** A starting point for the achievement of an improved culture of safety is an assessment of the current culture (or climate) to determine whether and how that culture affects the provision of safe patient care. Several safety culture survey instruments which evaluate communication, teamwork, management support, and other aspects of a safety culture are available, including the previously referred to SAQ, and the Hospital Survey on Patient Safety Culture by the Agency for Healthcare Research and Quality (AHRQ), available at [www.ahrq.gov/qual/hospculture/].

2. **Provide sciences of safety education**: Physicians and staff need to understand safety concepts to apply them to patient care processes. Resources for developing safety science education programs are provided at the end of this chapter. A free audio presentation of the science of safety is available at [www.jhsph.edu/CPHP/Training/Online%20Training/patient_safety.html].

3. **Identify safety concerns**: Safety teams seek to identify safety concerns. There are multiple ways to accomplish this, including walking rounds by leadership, patient safety reporting systems, morbidity and mortality conferences, review of the facts underlying liability claims, and perhaps most important, asking staff how they think they might harm the next patient and what they could do to prevent it.

EXHIBIT 12.1   Daily Goals

Room Number _____   Date ____/____/____

		AM shift (7am)	PM shift (7pm) **Note Changes from AM**
Safety	What needs to be done for patient to be discharged from the ICU?		
	• Patient's greatest safety risk? • How can we decrease risk?		
	What events or deviations need to be reported? ICUSRS issues?		
Patient Care	Pain Mgt / Sedation (held to follow commands?)	Pain goal ____/10 w/	
	Cardiac Review EKGs	HR Goal_____ ☐ at goal ☐ ⇧ ☐ ⇩ β Block_____	
	Volume status Net goal for midnight	☐ Net even ☐ Net positive ☐ Net neg:____ w/_____ ☐ Pt determined	
	• Pulmonary: • Ventilator: (vent bundle: HOB elevated), **RTW/Weaning)**	☐ OOB ☐ pulm toilet ☐ Ambulation ☐ Maintain current support ☐ Wean as tol ☐ Mechanics q am FIO2 <_____ PEEP____ ☐ PS/Trach trial___h	

	SIRS/Infection/Sepsis Evaluationo
	
	 SIRS Criteria
	 ☐ Temp > 38° C or ☐ < 36 ° C
	 ☐ HR > 90 BPM
	 ☐ RR > 20 b/min or
	   ☐ PaCO2 < 32 torr
	 ☐ WBC > 12K ☐ < 4K or
	   ☐ > 10% bands
		☐ no current SIRS/Sepsis issues
		 ☐ Known infection:
		   ☐ PAN Cx ☐ Bld x2 ☐ Urine ☐ Sputum
		   ☐ Other
		
		 ☐ ABx changes; D/C ☐ AG Levels:
		 ☐ Sepsis Bundle	

	Can catheters/tubes be removed?	☐ Y ☐ N	
	GI / Nutrition / Bowel regimen (TPN line, NDT, PEG needed?)	☐ TPN ☐ TF ☐ NPO	

	Is this patient receiving DVT/PUD prophylaxis?	DVT: ☐ Hep q8 / q12 / gtt PUD: ☐ PPI
		      ☐ TEDS/SCDs ☐ H₂B
		      ☐ LMWH	

	Anticipated LOS > 2 days: **TGC** 3 days: **fluconazole** PO, **KCl SS**	☐ TGC ☐ Fluc ☐ KCl ☐ N/A	
	Can any meds be discontinued, converted to PO, adjusted?	☐ N/A ☐ D/C: ☐ PO: ☐ Renal: ☐ Liver:	
To Do:	Tests / Procedures today	☐ N/A	
	Scheduled labs	☐ N/A	
	AM lab needed CXR?	☐ CMP ☐ BMP ☐ H8 ☐Coags ☐ABG ☐ Lactate ☐ Core 4 ☐ CXR Wed: ☐ Transferrin ☐ Iron ☐ Prealb ☐ 24h urine	
	Consultations	☐ Y ☐ N	
Disposition	Is the primary service up-to-date?	☐ Y ☐ N	
	• Has the family been updated? • Social issues addressed (LT care, palliative care)	☐ Y ☐ N ☐ Y ☐ N ☐ N/A	

Protocols available if bolded
For WICU only: ICU status   IMC status: vitals q___ Fellow/Attg Initials: _____

Reprinted with permission: Johns Hopkins Hospital.

4. **Senior leader partnerships with units**: Successful safety programs assign responsibility to senior executives for specific care units and make them accountable to follow through on safety improvement initiatives. With this approach, senior leaders become part of the unit-based teams, meeting with them monthly and seeking to mitigate safety concerns.

5. **Learn from one defect per month**: Staff are asked to learn from one defect (safety concern) per month. Patient safety issues are prioritized and improvements are implemented. It is important that staff learn from all reported episodes of health care, including those in which harm occurred. To achieve a better understanding, employees are provided with a structured tool to learn from defects. Specific questions include: what happened, why did it happen (that is, what contributed to it), what did you do to reduce the probability that it will happen again? Results are summarized as a one-page document for sharing in the organization. Employees are also asked to implement one teamwork tool per quarter. These tools include, among others, a daily goals sheet, shadowing another caregiver, observing rounds, briefings and debriefings, assertive communication, and disclosing mistakes. Refer to Exhibit 12.1.

6. **Remeasure culture**: After one year, the successful organization remeasures culture. While, at the inception of this program, culture was remeasured unit by unit, it is now measured annually throughout the entire organization. Units in which 80 percent of employees report positive safety and teamwork culture are considered good.

The success of CUSP at JHH has been demonstrated in several ways, including lower rates of infections, reduced SICU (surgical intensive care unit) patient lengths of stay, and decreased nurse turnover rates.[17] Based on the success of the CUSP program at JHH, ASHRM entered into a co-marketing arrangement with the Patient Safety Group, a Massachusetts-based patient organization whose mission is to promote a safety culture in health care, by providing the electronic version of the comprehensive unit-based safety program (*e*CUSP) to health care organizations. *e*CUSP greatly aids in project management by keeping a database of safety concerns and active and completed projects. It also summarizes what was learned into a "shared story" that can be broadly disseminated. For example, one shared story describes a project that aims at improving physician-nurse communications through the use of two-way text pagers. The new technology reduces the number of times nurses have to leave the bedside for phone calls, and promotes quicker physician responses to the nurses' calls. Information about *e*CUSP and the shared stories are available online at [www.patientsafetygroup.org].[18]

···········

COMMUNICATION AND TEAMWORK

To effectively manage the complex work involved in providing care to critically ill patients, caregivers need a clear understanding of what tasks and treatments are to be performed and when, what observations and interventions need to be made, and how to prevent, detect, and manage complications and pain. But, most important, the entire care team must know what the goals of treatment are—what needs to be done today to help a patient progress to the next level of care. The use of an ICU Daily Goals Checklist has been shown to improve communication between physicians and nurses by clarifying work goals, setting forth written reminders, and identifying the greatest patient safety concerns.[19] This process involves the completion by the care team of a daily goals sheet, for each ICU patient during daily rounds. The goals sheet referenced in Exhibit 12.1

captures the patient's needs for the day and is used as a communication tool for caregivers and the patient and family.

Recognizing the importance to patient safety of communication during transitions in care, JCAHO requires specific approaches for complying with its National Patient Safety Goal to improve the effectiveness of communication among caregivers. Effective 2006, health care organizations are required to implement a standard approach to "handoff" communications, including an opportunity to ask and respond to questions.[20] Accredited hospitals must address communication during handoffs in ICUs where there are multiple types of transitions in care. Examples of ICU handoff situations include nursing shift changes, physician transfer in or out of units, or to-or-from on-call responsibility, and patient transfers into and out of the critical care unit. It is clear that a taped change of shift report that does not allow for real-time interaction between caregivers is no longer acceptable. At JHH, a "morning briefing" tool was implemented in the cardiac-surgical ICUs, to communicate important patient information, relay the occurrence of any adverse events that need investigation, establish priorities, and relay concerns about potential problems for the day to the oncoming team.[21] The morning briefing does not replace the shift-to-shift report, but rather focuses on clinical safety and integrates a safety perspective into the routine of the ICU.

An innovative means of verbal communication that is now being used to enhance exchanges of information among caregivers and can be applied in the ICU follows the acronym "SBAR", which stands for:[22]

- Situation (define the problem)
- Background (keep information brief, related, and to the point)
- Assessment (summarize what you found or think)
- Recommendation (describe what you want)

When all members of the care team understand how to communicate in a consistent way, such as by using SBAR, authority gradient issues are reduced, differences in communication styles are less problematic, and patient safety is enhanced. This has huge implications for the ICU setting, where the quality of collaborative communication is a key factor in patient outcomes.[23]

One health care organization, Kaiser Permanente, adopted a combined approach to improving patient safety through improving teamwork, using human factors applications designed to improve patient safety and strategies to enhance interpersonal relationships and common understanding of how best to communicate important patient information. In implementing this approach, Kaiser used many tools and techniques to educate physicians and staff in human factors science and to empower them to practice safely. Assertiveness training, briefings and debriefings, and situational awareness are among the communication and teamwork training programs that Kaiser continues to provide today.[24] Assertiveness empowers staff to speak up and "stop the line" if necessary when they have a safety concern. Briefings are communications between team members that allow concerns to be raised, the plan of care to be clarified, and important information to be relayed either before a procedure begins or information that is reviewed after an event occurs. Situation awareness is just that—being aware of what is going on around you—to decrease the risk of errors. In addition, because it is important for teams to practice their skills and rehearse the handling of high-risk or emergency situations, life-like simulators are used at Kaiser in conjunction with human factors education and communication training to enhance teamwork. Simulation allows the team to develop critical thinking skills while rehearsing the procedures to be implemented when certain situations arise. It also allows team members to learn how to work together.

Improving quality and creating a culture of safety in ICU necessarily involves training in patient safety and risk management. All levels of medical, nursing, and ICU support staff should receive education in safety science and be oriented to institutional and unit-specific risk and safety procedures. Ideally, a staff that works as a team should train as a team. As part of implementing CUSP at JHH, educational sessions are provided to all ICU staff including physicians, nurses, pharmacists, respiratory therapists, aides, and clerks. The objectives of these sessions are to provide the staff with an understanding of the following:[25]

- Patient safety is a significant problem.

- Efforts to improve safety should focus on improving systems rather than blaming caregivers.

- When harm occurs, it is preceded by a cascade of system breakdowns.

- Interpersonal skills, such as speaking up when you have a concern, listening when others do, and acknowledging personal and organizational vulnerabilities, play a critical role in patient safety.

- Blame-free does not mean responsibility-free—we all need to accept responsibility for the systems in which we work.

ICU staff should also be trained in how to report events, errors, and near-misses through easily accessible reporting systems, and receive regular feedback on causes and trends identified through reported events and on actions taken to prevent or reduce them. See the section, "Event, Error, and Near-Miss Reporting in the ICU" for additional information on this topic.

············

ICU STRUCTURE, STAFFING, AND TRAINING

The makeup of the medical, nursing, and support staffs varies greatly in ICUs, as do their organizational structures. The "open" ICU model allows for patient care and management by a diverse medical staff (not all of whom have specific training in critical care medicine), with no single physician responsible for overall management of the ICU. It is estimated that 80 percent of ICUs in the United States use the open model.

There is strong evidence that staffing ICUs with physicians who are specifically trained in critical care medicine improves patient outcomes. Studies of ICU attending-physician staffing strategies, and outcomes of hospital and ICU mortality and length of stay have shown that hospitals that used specially trained intensivists in their ICUs had lower hospital and ICU mortality rates and lower hospital lengths of stay.[26] The Society for Critical Care Medicine (SCCM) has advocated for an intensivist-led, multi-professional ICU team as a model for ICU staffing. Indeed, support for the use of ICU-certified physicians to staff ICUs has been echoed by AHRQ and included in its *30 Safe Practices for Better Health Care,* based on evidence that, through the use of intensivists, adverse events and errors in ICUs can be reduced or prevented. Likewise, the Leapfrog Group, a coalition of employers and other purchasers of health care services, has adopted use of intensivists as one of the standards it uses for rating patient safety in health care organizations.

Estimates of the use of intensivists by U.S. hospitals range from 10–20 percent. Of the 914 hospitals with ICUs that responded to the Leapfrog Group Hospital Quality and Safety Survey in 2004, 19 percent said they had physicians who are intensive care specialists (intensivists) on their ICU staff, and another 13 percent indicated that they planned to implement the use of intensivists by 2006.[27] This still contrasts sharply with Europe and Australia, where "closed" ICUs are the norm and the majority of care (80 percent) is initiated by intensivists. The reasons for the underuse of intensivists in the U.S. are varied and may include the *perceived* costs of implementing intensivist-staffed ICUs, a shortage of critical care-certified physicians, and resistance to a major change in how critical care is provided. (See discussion which follows on the cost-benefit analysis that supports use of intensivists in the ICU.)

Although it is desirable that ICUs have physicians with subspecialty training or equivalent qualifications in critical care medicine, it is not always possible because of a shortage of physicians with this type of training. Therefore, physicians that provide care to patients in the ICU should continuously seek to improve and maintain skills in the management of the critically ill. SCCM recommends that non-ICU specialists improve their skills by taking critical care courses and continuing education programs geared toward the management of critically ill or injured patients in the first 24 hours and in the handling of the sudden deterioration of a patient.[28]

Proper credentialing of critical care physicians and midlevel providers is fundamental to managing provider-related risks, and the granting of privileges according to validated training and skill level is crucial to patient safety. Guidelines for granting privileges for the performance of high-risk, high-volume, and problem-prone procedures such as central venous catheterization, pulmonary artery catheterization, airway intubation, mechanical ventilation, and cardioversion and defibrillation have been published by the American College of Critical Care Medicine. Nevertheless, there is wide variation in training, supervision, and certification for these procedures, and failures in these areas commonly contribute to patient harm. It is also important for the ICU staff to have ready access to information about who can perform what procedures and under what degree of supervision, especially in teaching facilities.

A sufficient number of properly trained critical care nurses is also essential for safe and effective ICU care. Studies of patient outcomes following abdominal aortic surgery showed that having fewer ICU nurses per patient was associated with increased risk of respiratory complications.[29] Validation of critical care competencies for ICU nurses is recommended annually. It is especially important to evaluate and document the skills of agency or temporary nursing staff before the start of their shift. Certification in critical care nursing can enhance ICU nurse competencies and provide a specialty credential.

As previously noted, an intensivist-led ICU multidisciplinary team model has been advocated to optimize the delivery of critical care. In addition to physicians and nurses, pharmacists, respiratory therapists, and other ICU support staff play important roles in promoting optimal outcomes and preventing errors and adverse events. For example, the effectiveness of respiratory therapists in weaning patients from mechanical ventilation, and in performing other support procedures using protocol guidance in the ICU, has been demonstrated.[30] Team staffing plans for ICUs should identify all members of the team and delineate their roles and responsibilities on the team.[31] In addition, adequate staff training and orientation is crucial to the prevention of adverse events in the ICU. For example, JCAHO published recommendations for preventing ventilator-related deaths and injuries in a Sentinel Event Alert on the topic in 2002. ECRI, a health service research agency in Plymouth Meeting, Pennsylvania, echoed and expanded on these recommendations as follows:[32]

- Include job-specific ventilator safety content in staff competency assessments.

- Ensure effective staffing for ventilator patients at all times.

- Implement regular preventive maintenance and testing of alarm systems, and ensure that alarms are sufficiently audible.

- Provide interdisciplinary training for staff who care for ventilator patients.

- Recognize that alarms do not replace direct observation of ventilator dependent patients.

- Confirm that the respiratory care group follows an accepted and documented method for calculating ventilator alarm settings.

- Require staff to confirm, during regular ventilator checks, that all alarms are active and that the alarm volume is loud enough to be heard outside the room.

- Identify staff authorized to operate ventilators, and do not allow other staff to make changes to settings.

············

AN INTEGRATED SYSTEMS APPROACH

ICUs operate as subparts of larger health care facilities—subsystems within larger systems—namely hospitals. When transforming ICU care, it is important that the rest of the hospital organization recognize and support the efforts of the ICU. Indeed, all local efforts to improve patient safety and reduce risk must be supported by the organization as a whole to be successful. This is due to the interdependency between the ICU and various other hospital departments, personnel, and processes. For example, as part of an initiative to reduce catheter-related bloodstream infections (BSIs) in surgical ICUs (a major contributor to ICU morbidity and mortality) central catheter insertion kits were redesigned to improve skin disinfection and provide a larger sterile field during central catheter insertion. This redesign required not only the input of the ICU staffs, but also the commitment and cooperation of personnel and departments outside the ICUs.[33] Individuals representing administration, materials management, central sterile supply, and other departments had to understand and agree with the product and process changes before it was possible to alter the contents of central line insertion kits. Specifically, it was necessary to change the skin preparation product in the kits to a 2-percent chlorhexidine-based solution and replace the kit's small sterile drapes with large ones—two evidence-based interventions for reducing the risk of catheter-related BSIs. Although these steps sound easy to accomplish, in many organizations they constitute major purchasing adjustments that require product changes, renegotiation of applicable contracts, solicitation of alternate supply distributors, and reevaluation of inventories. Therefore, the subsystem (the ICU) is dependent upon the larger system (the hospital) having an administrative system capable of minimizing system defects.[34] As illustrated in this case, the potential defect is an inability to make changes in products and supplies deemed necessary for improved patient safety.

············

ENTERPRISE RISK AND THE BUSINESS CASE FOR IMPROVED ICU SAFETY

As discussed in Volume I, Chapter 1 in this series, the risks identified through enterprise risk management (ERM) go far beyond the traditional focus of clinical error that causes professional liability or environmental safety issues that create general liability or property exposures. ERM stresses the value of managing and capitalizing on the broad range of risks faced by the health care organization rather than focusing on risk avoidance alone. The quality and safety of ICU care affects many of the risk domains of ERM, including operational, human, and strategic. In fact, applying this approach in the ICU reinforces the ERM principle that risks can be managed for positive gain. Strategies aimed at reducing the complications of ICU care (central line infections, ventilator injuries, errors of omission, and so on), improving patient outcomes, and reducing lengths of stay clearly create opportunities for operational gain. In addition to the cost reductions associated with fewer complications, the benefits of improved patient and family satisfaction, increased availability and turnover of ICU beds, reduced lengths of stay, and probable achievement of better "scores" on patient safety indicators and quality/outcome data reports can help the hospital realize gains in reputation, improved ICU utilization, and increased patient volume. Once thought of merely as "risks" to be managed, the activities associated with ICU operations (providing medical care to high-risk, acutely ill patients) can instead be considered sources of "capital," to help the hospital gain advantage in the health care marketplace.

Although patient safety proponents dispute the need to quantify return on investment to take actions aimed at transforming ICU care, efforts have been made to justify patient safety efforts from a business perspective. Recently, a financial model was developed that reflected the costs and savings achieved over one year as certain hospitals implemented the Leapfrog Group's ICU intensivist physician staffing standard. By demonstrating significant reductions in patient morbidity and mortality rates when a dedicated intensivist was present in the ICU during daylight hours, the model provided objective evidence of cost savings ranging from $510,000 to $3.3 million for non-rural hospitals.[35]

Cost savings through reduced staff turnover have also been demonstrated in ICUs and other hospital departments following implementation of comprehensive patient safety programs that include positive culture change. Nurse turnover decreased by from 8–9 percent to 2 percent in the SICUs at JHH following implementation of CUSP.

Similarly, Kaiser Permanente has been able to show that human factors education, simulation, and teamwork training as part of an overall patient safety program have contributed to a significant cost savings in the recruitment and training of nursing staff. For example, a 19-percent nurse turnover rate was not uncommon two years before human factors training and other safety culture interventions were implemented in the perioperative areas at Kaiser. After implementing measures to improve teamwork, better communication, and increased collaboration between team members, the perioperative nurse turnover disappeared. At an estimated cost of $100,000 for the recruitment and training of one surgical nurse, this organization's "investment" in patient safety, which included providing human factors training and improving culture, paid off.[36]

EVENT, ERROR, AND NEAR-MISS REPORTING IN THE ICU

Event reports (often called incident reports) were originally designed to serve as risk identification tools for the risk management professional and notices of potential claims for liability insurance companies. The patient safety movement—stimulated by the Institute of Medicine's 1999 report, *To Err is Human,* increased the importance and expanded the purpose of event reports. The value of reporting events, to learn what factors contribute to their occurrence, and to take actions to reduce or eliminate those factors is now recognized as key to improving patient safety. However, protection of event reports under peer review and other quality improvement statutes is largely a state-specific and jurisdictional matter with wide variation among states.

Because of the high incidence of errors and adverse events in ICUs, the internal reporting and collection of ICU events for analysis and trending promotes the identification of system problems that contribute to the events.[37] Therefore, an easily accessible, low-burden system for reporting will enhance the staff's willingness and ability to report errors, events, and near-misses. To be successful, however, the culture of the ICU (and the hospital) must be a non-punitive one in which event reporting is supported and the staff does not fear reprisal for reporting. Also, to encourage continued compliance with event reporting, the staff needs meaningful feedback on how the information in the reports was used and whether any changes were made as a result.

In spite of some limitations, the value of external event reporting in identifying trends and common causes of adverse events has been demonstrated through national and state event reporting programs, and by JCAHO's sentinel event database.[38,39,40] One state-mandated adverse event and near-miss reporting program is the Pennsylvania Patient Safety Reporting System (PA-PSRS). In the first year of reporting (June 2004 to June 2005), PA-PSRS received nearly 12,000 reports of adverse events and near-misses from ICUs, representing 8.5 percent of all hospital reports received. Reports of medication errors, adverse drug reactions, and complications of procedures, treatments, and tests involving the ICU were more likely to be categorized as serious events than reports not involving the ICU (10.1 percent of all serious event reports from hospitals involved the ICU.) Refer to Figure 12.1.

Analysis of data from a European event-reporting database reveals similar findings. In a multi-center study on adverse event and near-miss reporting to the National Health Service in

FIGURE 12.1   ICU Events Reported to PA-PSRS

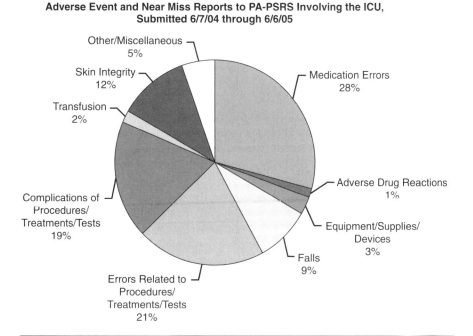

Adverse Event and Near Miss Reports to PA-PSRS Involving the ICU, Submitted 6/7/04 through 6/6/05

Other/Miscellaneous 5%
Skin Integrity 12%
Transfusion 2%
Complications of Procedures/ Treatments/Tests 19%
Errors Related to Procedures/ Treatments/Tests 21%
Falls 9%
Equipment/Supplies/ Devices 3%
Adverse Drug Reactions 1%
Medication Errors 28%

Source: Pennsylvania Patient Safety Reporting System (PA-PSRS) Conversation between William Marella and Kathleen Shostek. 2005 Jul 21.

England and Wales, nearly 30,000 reports were received from September 2001 to June 2002.[41] Of these, 4 percent of the events arose from intensive care, high-dependency units, and neonatal intensive care units combined. Further analysis revealed that of the events that had a major or catastrophic outcome, almost 10 percent arose from these same critical care areas.[42]

A recent study of the incidence and nature of adverse events in intensive care at an academic, tertiary-care urban hospital in the U.S. revealed additional insights into the risk of iatrogenic injury for critically ill patients.[43] The AHRQ-sponsored critical care safety study was conducted from July 2002 to June 2003 in two critical care units using direct continuous observation, review of incident reports, information from a computerized adverse drug event detection system, and chart extraction. Among the systems factors associated with the serious medical errors identified in the study, treatment and procedure errors, including those involving medications, accounted for nearly 75 percent of the errors. Sterility hazards occurred in over half of central intravascular catheter insertion procedures when interns failed to wash their hands. Also, a significant number of errors in reporting or communicating clinical information were the result of system failures. Other study findings with important patient safety and risk management implications for ICUs include the following:[44]

- More than 20 percent of patients admitted to the ICUs experienced an adverse event.

- Almost half (45 percent) of the ICU events were preventable.

- More than 90 percent of incidents occurred during routine care, not at admission or during an emergency.

A short time ago, an external ICU-specific event reporting system was implemented to detect systemic patient safety issues common to many ICUs and to improve the identification of errors and events that occur too infrequently for individual ICUs to easily trend based solely on their own data.[45] Funded by AHRQ, the ICU Safety Reporting System (ICUSRS) is a voluntary Web-based reporting system that collects reports of adverse events and near misses. It involves twenty-three participating ICUs. Originally, thirty ICUs were selected to participate, but seven withdrew due to concerns about their potential exposure to undue risk of claims from participation in the project. As previously discussed, discoverability concerns prevail in states with high levels of malpractice claim activity. Although ICUSRS was designed with two levels of protection from discoverability; the first as a research project with protection of the data under peer review from the principal investigator's institutional review board, and the second as a project funded by AHRQ, these protections have not been tested thus far in a court system.[46]

Preliminary reports from ICUSRS show promise in that a large number of reports to the system have been on near misses, where most of the reporting ICUs did not previously report or collect data on near misses.[47]

Analysis of specific types of ICUSRS events will help identify system factors that contribute to their occurrence. For example, as of June 30, 2003, 54 percent of the events reported to ICUSRS listed training and education as a contributing system factor and 31 percent of the events identified team factors as system factors contributing to the events.[48] Analysis of airway events reported to ICUSRS during a twelve-month period that ended June 30, 2003, revealed the following:[49]

- Airway events constituted 10 percent of all events reported during the period studied.

- More than half of airway events were considered preventable.

- One patient death was attributed to an airway event.

- Physical injury, increased hospital length of stay, and family dissatisfaction occurred in at least 20 percent of airway events.
- Factors mitigating the impact of airway events included adequate ICU staffing and use of skilled assistants.

Analysis of line, tube, and drain incidents reported to ICUSRS during the same twelve-month period (ending June 2003) showed that more than 60 percent of these incidents were preventable and 56 percent of patients who experienced line, tube, and drain incidents sustained physical injury.[50] This type of aggregate ICU event data is most useful in prioritizing efforts to prevent and reduce occurrences that affect patient safety.

·········

INTRAHOSPITAL TRANSPORT OF ICU PATIENTS

Critically ill patients who must be transported outside the ICU are vulnerable to unexpected events during transport because of the difficulties posed by the instability of their conditions and the need for continued monitoring. In a study of neurosurgical ICU patients, 40 percent experienced technical mishaps during transfer, with monitor power failure and electrocardiogram and ventilator disconnections being most common.[51] Policies and procedures for transferring ICU patients should be based on *Guidelines for the Transfer of Critically Ill Patients,* developed by the American Association of Critical Care Nurses in conjunction with SCCM. Unless it is absolutely necessary for an ICU patient to have diagnostic testing or other procedures performed outside of the unit, testing and procedures should be delayed until the patient is stable. Testing and procedures should be performed at the bedside whenever feasible. One facility approached the development of policies on intrahospital transport by establishing criteria based on patient acuity that, when met, requires accompaniment by nursing personnel and specifies monitoring and documentation throughout. Called "Patient Transportation Hallpass," the policies and forms were designed to promote safe transport of patients with varying acuity levels and equipment.[52]

·········

MEDICATION ERRORS AND INTRAVENOUS INFUSION ERRORS IN THE ICU

Medication errors, including errors that involve IV infusions, are common in health care organizations and the problem is of major concern in the ICU setting, where many high-alert medications are administered. In one study of medical errors in an intensive care unit, medication errors accounted for slightly more than 20 percent of all reported events.[53] A Jury Verdict Research® (JVR®) analysis of medical negligence plaintiff awards from 1996 to 2002 found that the jury award median for medication errors was $1 million.[54] To reduce medication errors, a health care organization might evaluate its strengths and weaknesses in medication-use safety by completing a medication self-analysis. Assessment tools are available from organizations such as the Institute for Safe Medication Practices [ISMP] [www.ismp.org], Huntington Valley, Pennsylvania, and ECRI [www.ecri.org].

Intravenous infusions in critical care areas are most often delivered via IV pumps to more carefully regulate the flow of infusate. However, because of the dangers associated with IV pump free-flow, (an unregulated flow of infusate into a patient through an intravascular line), the frequency with which such hazards occur when unprotected sets are used, and the availability of set-based mechanisms that effectively prevent this condition, facilities should no longer be using IV pumps with unprotected administration sets. Citing the experience of ECRI[55] in evaluating infusion pumps and advocating free-flow protection, JCAHO requires that facilities follow ECRI's recommendations and use only infusion pumps that offer set-based free-flow protection.

Medication event and error reporting is crucial to identifying factors and systems that contribute to their occurrence. The previously discussed ICUSRS includes reports of medication events, errors, and near misses. It collects this type of data based in part on the U.S. Pharmacopoeia (USP) adverse drug event reporting system, MedMARx (SM), which uses a pre-established classification scheme for medication errors. Although reports from ICUSRS, MedMARx(SM), and other external medication error databases can be extremely useful for collecting and analyzing aggregate data, they are also limited because they are not well suited to support real-time event reporting for internal, ICU-specific purposes, including follow-up and root cause analysis. This is particularly the case when an event involves other areas of the hospital, as many do. Note that many ICUs participating in ICUSRS use the same reports internally to avoid the burden of duplicate reporting. But in general, a reporting system should meet the needs of the organization as a whole. Therefore, ICUs should have hospital-specific internal medication error reporting processes in place. How to make the best use of resources like ICUSRS may be a suitable topic for discussion by ICU unit leaders in conjunction with risk management and quality improvement representatives.

In addition to medication error reporting systems, automated pharmacy or medical record-based triggers have been useful in monitoring adverse drug events caused by many high-alert drugs used in the ICU. One example includes triggers that indicate when a patient received a medication used to reverse the effect of a medication, such as when naloxone is given for opiate overdose, prompting an investigation of the reason for the use of the reversal agent.

Medication safety experts have expounded on the value of pharmacists on the patient care team and recommended that they be available on patient care units, particularly when medication orders are written. One study found that the availability of pharmacists in one hospital's ICUs helped identify potential errors with medication orders.[56] Also, according to ISMP, medication errors are reduced by two-thirds when a senior pharmacist accompanies physicians on rounds in an intensive care unit.

············

HIGH-ALERT MEDICATIONS AND SMART TECHNOLOGY IN THE ICU

The Institute for Safe Medication Practices (ISMP) defines high-alert medications as drugs that bear a heightened risk of causing significant harm when they are used in error.[57] This does not imply that errors with these medications occur more frequently, but rather that the consequences of errors involving their use can be devastating. According to ISMP, common high-alert medications include insulin, opiates and narcotics, injectable potassium chloride (or phosphate) concentrate, anticoagulants, thrombolytics, and chemotherapeutic agents—many of which are commonly administered in ICUs. Special precautions must be taken when prescribing, dispensing, and administering high-alert medications. These precautions are especially applicable to the ICU. They include the following:[58]

- Eliminating high-alert drugs from floor stock wherever feasible
- Requiring independent checks (a doublecheck by a second clinician) of doses and preparations of high-alert medications
- Using premixed infusion products and removing vials of high-alert drugs from stock

- Having a pharmacist review all high-alert medication orders
- Using safety checklists that prompt clinicians to review important safety considerations for high-alert medications and delivery systems

Compounding the risk of administering high-alert medications in the ICU, the parenteral routes of administration (that is, intravenous [IV], intramuscular, subcutaneous, and epidural) are frequently used to administer ICU medications. These routes provide a more direct means of delivering medication for faster and more effective results and are beneficial to patient care. However, high-alert drugs administered rapidly by direct routes can also be dangerous if given erroneously, because there is little time to reverse their immediate effects. Furthermore, when a high-alert drug is administered with an infusion device capable of rapid IV delivery, a mistake in dosing or rate programming can have grave consequences. Because these potent IV drugs have a narrow margin of safety, technologically "smart" IV infusion systems, programmable pumps with real-time decision support feedback on drug doses and delivery rates, have been employed to detect and prevent serious medication errors. In a study that used smart IV infusion pumps in the cardiac surgical ICUs at Brigham and Women's Hospital, Boston, Massachusetts, many drug errors were detected.[59] However, because there was no difference in the number of serious drug errors detected when the smart pumps were used and when they were not, enhancements had to be made to expand the pump's drug library, make the library the default system, make it more difficult for nurses to override system-generated drug alerts, and improve bolus dosing. The key to using any new technology to improve patient safety is to educate physicians and staff in its use.

Independent checks are recommended to help prevent errors that involve high-alert medications. In practice, however, the checks are often not independent and as such, the preventive effects are abnegated. For example, nurses commonly check insulin and narcotics together, potentially encoding each others errors, rather than independently checking them. Physicians often co-sign chemotherapy orders rather than independently calculating the required dose. These misuses of the concept suggest that broad education about the meaning and benefits of independent checks might be helpful to the ICU staff.

As noted previously, ICU care involves multiple "hand-offs" and transitions in care—transitions that present opportunities for medication errors and adverse events to occur. JCAHO includes the improvement of medication safety in its National Patient Safety Goals, with reconciliation of medications across the continuum of care being one specific goal. To decrease medication errors that occur during transfer from a surgical ICU at JHH, a computerized tool was developed to reconcile patient medications. ICU nurses use the tool to record all preoperative and ICU-ordered medications. Before transfer out of the surgical ICU, a nurse reviews the form for any discrepancies in orders or medication allergies. The tool was effective in detecting medication errors in transfer orders in the surgical ICU and prevented potentially harmful errors in 21 percent of patients.[60] Based on an earlier paper version, the success of the electronic tool has been attributed to making medication reconciliation a system process, rather than leaving it solely to the discretion of individual physicians and nurses.[61]

············

INFECTIONS IN THE ICU

The incidence of health care-acquired infections—a major health issue and a serious patient safety concern—has become a focus for the Centers for Disease Control and Prevention (CDC) and for JCAHO. Of particular concern for ICUs are central catheter

FIGURE 12.2   Nosocomial Infections in ICU Patients, 1998–2002

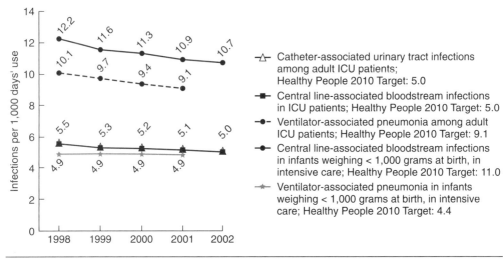

Source: Centers for Disease Control and Prevention, National Nosocomial Infection Surveillance (NNIS) System.
Note: The lines for catheter-associated urinary tract infections and central-line bloodstream infections in ICU patients overlap. Both ventilator-associated pneumonia measures were redefined in 2002; thus data for these two measures for 2002 are not presented in the chart.

Reprinted from: Agency for Healthcare Research and Quality. National Healthcare Quality Report 2004 Dec; AHRQ Publication No. 05-0013. Available at [www.qualitytools.ahrq.gov/qualityreport/browse/browse.aspx].

(or central line) associated bloodstream infections, infections related to indwelling urinary catheters, and ventilator-associated pneumonia.

In its 2004 National Healthcare Quality Report, AHRQ specifically reported on nosocomial infections in ICU patients using data from CDC's National Nosocomial Infection Surveillance System. Refer to Figure 12.2. On a positive note, a gradual overall decline in some types of ICU infections was noted during the reporting period.

CDC has issued several guidelines to help health care facilities reduce infection. They include guidelines for hand hygiene, for prevention of health care-associated pneumonia, and for prevention of intravascular catheter-related infections. JCAHO's focus on reducing the risk of health care-associated infections includes National Patient Safety Goals centered on compliance with CDC's hand hygiene guidelines, and a requirement that identified cases of unanticipated death or major permanent loss of function that are associated with a health care-associated infection be managed as sentinel events.

Recently, a renewed interest in bringing lawsuits against health care facilities, alleging acquisition of infections in hospitals due to substandard care and negligence, could prove a harbinger of additional, future litigation. A $31-million settlement in 2004 by a hospital corporation on behalf of a Florida facility to close 106 lawsuits that alleged postsurgical infections is an example of this potential trend. And in 2005, fifty-two plaintiffs alleging hospital-acquired infections filed separate lawsuits against a Kentucky hospital seeking a total of $500 million.[62] A short time ago, Pennsylvania published statewide infection rates that ignited much publicity and discussion. Public reporting of infections is likely to continue; the impact on litigation is unknown. Previously, because of the difficulty in proving the causes and sources of infection, liability cases involving infections centered mainly on prompt diagnosis and treatment, and not on whether or not they were hospital-acquired.

The potential for operational losses due to increased lengths of stay for ICU patients experiencing infection complications is high. When this is coupled with the previously discussed threat of liability losses from infection-related suits, it becomes clear that risk management and patient safety efforts should concentrate on prevention and reduction of infections in the ICU. Some specific strategies aimed at preventing infections are discussed next.

··············
CLINICAL CARE "BUNDLES"

"Bundling" is the grouping of evidence-based interventions to improve patient safety. One bundling initiative, which originated in the ICU, focuses on reducing catheter-related (central line) BSIs. This initiative is known as the "central line bundle," and it includes the following five components:[63]

1. Hand hygiene: compliance with strict hand hygiene practices before insertion and use of central lines

2. Maximal barrier precautions: use of sterile gloves, gown, mask, and large enough drapes to prevent contamination of the catheter on insertion

3. Chlorhexidine skin antisepsis: use of faster-drying disinfectant to reduce remaining bacteria on the skin

4. Proper catheter site and post-placement care: insertion site individualized to patient's needs and standardized, meticulous care of the line once placed

5. Daily review of line necessity with prompt removal of unnecessary lines: ongoing assessment of need for central lines, removal as soon as possible

Organizations that have successfully implemented the central line bundle have reduced their rates of central line infections (and death rates) significantly.[64]

Using a systems approach, JHH nearly eliminated catheter-related BSIs through multifaceted interventions in one of its surgical ICUs.[65] This systems approach consisted of the following five interventions:[66]

1. Educating providers to ensure competency while still providing adequate supervision

2. Creation of a catheter line insertion cart containing all necessary supplies to avoid staff skipping essential steps due to lack of equipment

3. Asking providers during daily rounds whether catheters could be removed to reduce exposure to central lines

4. Implementing a checklist to be completed by the bedside ICU nurse to ensure adherence to evidence-based guidelines for preventing catheter-related BSIs

5. Empowering nurses to stop the catheter insertion procedure if a violation of the guidelines was observed, and notify the attending physician if a violation was not corrected

The fourth and fifth interventions required significant support by the clinical leaders of the SICU and a focus on the creation of a culture of safety in the unit whereby interpersonal communications and teamwork prevailed. Tools developed to promote the use of this systems approach include the sample central line insertion checklist. Refer to Exhibit 12.2.

Another set of evidence-based interventions originating in the ICU, the "ventilator bundle," is being used to prevent and reduce the incidence of ventilator-associated pneumonia (VAP)—the leading cause of death among hospital-acquired infections—a condition that carries a mortality rate of 46 percent. VAP is also associated with longer

EXHIBIT 12.2   JHH Central Line Insertion

Care Team Checklist

➤ If any item on the checklist is **not** adhered to or there are any concerns, contact the ICU attending

---

Purpose: To work as a team to decrease patient harm from catheter-related blood stream infections
When: During **all** central venous or **central** arterial line insertions or re-wires
By whom: Bedside nurse

If there is an observed violation of infection control practices, line placement should stop immediately and the violation should be corrected. If a correction is required, mark yes to question #6 *and explain violation at the bottom of the page and what corrections were made*

Patient's name or Room Number_____

1. Today's date   ____ / ____ / _____

2. Is the procedure: ☐ Elective   ☐ Emergent

3. Procedure: ☐ New line   ☐ Rewire

4 Site Rite Used: ☐ Yes   ☐ No   ☐ Internal Jugular   ☐ Subclavian   ☐ Femoral
   If equipment is available, ultrasound guidance should be used for all non-emergent internal
   jugular line placements. (Optional for subclavian and femoral line placement.)

	Yes	Yes After correction	Don't Know
5. Before the procedure, did the house staff:			
Perform a **"time-out"**	☐	☐	
Wash hands (chlorhexidine or soap) immediately prior	☐	☐	(ask if needed)
Was hand washing directly observed?	☐	☐	
Place pt in trendelenburg position (< 0 degrees)	☐	☐	to prevent air embolism
Sterilize procedure site (chorhexidine)	☐	☐	☐
Drape entire patient in a sterile fashion	☐	☐	☐
During the procedure, did the house staff:			
Use hat, mask, sterile gown and gloves	☐	☐	☐
Maintain a sterile field	☐	☐	☐
Did all personnel assisting follow the above precautions	☐	☐	☐
Ensure line aspirates blood to prevent hemothorax	☐	☐	
Transduce CVP or estimate CVP by fluid column	☐	☐	
After the procedure:			
Was a sterile dressing applied to the site	☐	☐	☐

6. **Was a correction required to ensure compliance with**   Yes   No
   Safety & Infection control practices? Explain.

Please return completed form to the designated location in your area

---

time spent on a ventilator, an increased length of stay, and an increase in hospital costs estimated at $40,000.[67] The ventilator bundle has four key components:

1. Elevation of the head of the bed to between thirty and forty-five degrees

2. Daily "sedation vacation" and daily assessment of readiness to extubate

3. Peptic ulcer disease (PUD) prophylaxis

4. Deep venous thrombosis (DVT) prophylaxis (unless contraindicated)

An ICU collaborative improvement project using the VAP bundle by the Institute for Healthcare Improvement (IHI), a Boston-based patient safety and health care quality improvement group, documented an average 45-percent reduction in the incidence of VAP.[68]

A third care bundle focuses on sepsis—an infectious process frequently encountered in, but not limited to the ICU, that is life-threatening if treatment is delayed. With mortality rates of up to 50 percent for septic shock, the most severe form of sepsis, sepsis treatment has gained worldwide attention. SCCM, in partnership with IHI and other international groups, formed a coalition to improve sepsis care through adoption of evidence-based guidelines for the care of critically ill patients with sepsis. Additional information about the "Surviving Sepsis Campaign," including a Web-based suite of information and tools for hospitals and caregivers to use in implementing sepsis care bundles, is available online at [www.ihi.org].

While not an official "care bundle," another intervention aimed at reducing mortality in the ICU is to maintain blood glucose levels at or below 110mg/dl. Based on the premise that critically ill patients experience hyperglycemia due to the release of certain hormones under stress even in the absence of a history of diabetes, implementation of intensive insulin therapy resulted in significant reductions in morbidities and mortality rates in a surgical ICU.[69] This intervention is being replicated at JHH using a "Tight Glucose Control" protocol, monitored by an ICU nurse manager.

Another intervention aimed at reducing possible exposure to microorganisms that cause urinary tract infections (UTIs) from indwelling urinary catheters is a simple reminder system for physicians to evaluate the need for patients to continue having the indwelling catheters after 48 hours. Researchers at the University of Michigan Health System found that the use of a "urinary catheter reminder" can reduce the incidence of indwelling urethral catheterizations and thereby decrease the number of hospitalized patients who develop a nosocomial UTIs.[70]

A risk management issue that arises with the use of care bundles is that of compliance. The question of whether instances of non-compliance with care bundles can result in liability claims alleging deviations from the standard of care has not been directly answered, although it can be reasonably assumed that if care bundles become standard of care, then non-compliance with the care bundle can be considered substandard when a patient is injured and causation is linked to the non-compliance. Indeed, components of the ventilator bundle have been included in national quality measures. However, whether the delivery of medical care is thought of in terms of "standards" or "care bundles," the overriding precedence should be to do the right things right, in the interest of improving quality and safety, while seeking protection of compliance monitoring data under whatever peer review and quality improvement protective statutes are available. Documentation in committee minutes of clinical rationale supporting the choice or modification of care bundles can help the organization track progress and prove that a reasonable approach was used if "protected" minutes are ever successfully subpoenaed.

....

TECHNOLOGY AND PATIENT SAFETY IN THE ICU

Two promising technology solutions for medical errors are bar-coding systems (used to match patient identification for testing and specimen collection and to ensure drugs are dispensed and administered to the correct patient) and computerized systems to help prescribers order medications, treatments, and tests more safely.

A bar-coded medication administration (BCMA) system verifies that administered medications match provider orders at the point of care: A clinician scans a bar-coded label on the patient's identification wristband and one on the medication packaging; the system then confirms that the patient has been prescribed that particular medication.

The information from each label is pulled from (and, in some cases, relayed back to) the hospital information system, pharmacy information system, and the patient's medication administration record.

One Veterans Administration Hospital successfully implemented a BCMA system in its acute- and long-term care sections; however, implementation proved problematic in the combined medical surgical ICU.[71] Reasons cited for the ICU's decision to stop using BCMA include software problems that limited the ability to document IV fluid administration and delays in processing and documenting urgently needed one-time medications. Following root cause analysis of the BCMA process failures, significant restructuring and software enhancements were made, and the BCMA system was reintroduced in the ICU.[72] Lessons learned? Although new technologies can help reduce human errors, unanticipated side effects of the new technologies can open up new pathways to potential errors.

Computerized provider order-entry (CPOE) systems are networked computer systems used to electronically document the full range of orders found in a paper-based environment, including patient-specific diagnostic orders—such as laboratory tests and radiology exams—and medication orders. Characteristics that may make CPOE systems safer than paper-based systems include the fact that orders are input electronically with no handwriting to be misread and no dictated orders to be misheard. Most notably, CPOE systems offer safety alerts and clinical decision support to help guide caregivers. For example, orders entered in the system are automatically analyzed for appropriateness, and improper orders (such as for a contraindicated treatment or a test that has already been performed) will cause the system to display an alert. Additionally, the system might be able to perform drug dose calculations based on a patient's condition or physical characteristics.[73]

CPOE systems were originally developed for general areas of the hospital and not the complex environment of the ICU. Therefore, computerized systems must be adapted to meet the needs of a critical care environment. In an observational study of the health care team following implementation of CPOE in an ICU, it was noted that policies designed to increase safety instead increased coordination load on the staff, creating additional sources of potential errors. It was suggested that workflow studies would assist in optimizing CPOE in the critical care setting.[74] Some studies of CPOE use in pediatric and neonatal ICUs had more positive findings, including reduced medication errors, and reduced response times for ancillary services,[75] in addition to near elimination of medication prescribing errors.[76]

SCCM has set forth essential elements required for a CPOE to be functional in the ICU in its *CPOF (Computerized Provider Order Fulfillment) System Requirements for Intensive Care Use* available online at: [www.sccm.org/corporate_resources/coalition_for_critical_care_excellence/Documents/cpoe.pdf].

ICU IMPROVEMENT SUCCESS STORIES

Perhaps some of the most dramatic successes in patient safety and quality improvement in critical care have arisen from an ICU improvement program called Transformation of the Intensive Care Unit (TICU). TICU began when a group of hospitals belonging to VHA, Inc., came together to participate in a program first piloted with IHI. Launched in 2002, TICU has helped decrease mortality rates by 20 percent, average length of stay by 11 percent, and ventilator-associated pneumonia (VAP) by 41 percent in participating

ICUs by increasing teamwork, redesigning basic processes, and changing the organization to a safety culture.[77,78] Clinical interventions targeted in the ICU improvement programs include better control of blood glucose levels, aggressive treatment of sepsis, prevention of bloodstream infections, and prevention of VAP. Modeled in a similar fashion, several statewide ICU improvement programs that include both culture change and clinical interventions have since been initiated. They include projects in Michigan, New Jersey, Rhode Island, and Ontario. One hallmark of these efforts is the requirement for rigorous data collection to answer the question, "How do we know we are safer?"

STATEWIDE ICU IMPROVEMENT PROJECTS

Keystone ICU, a partnership between the Michigan Health & Hospital Association, Keystone Center for Patient Safety & Quality and Johns Hopkins University, is one successful statewide ICU improvement project. Focused on implementing best practices in the ICU to reduce medical errors and enhance patient protections, Keystone ICU involves the participation of about 80 hospitals taking a five-step approach to achieving safer ICU care. The five steps are as follows:[79]

1. Develop a comprehensive unit-based patient safety program that uses a Web-based error-reporting system.

2. Use ICU specialists to coordinate care and implement a daily rounds checklist to improve communication among ICU staff.

3. Target catheter-related bloodstream infections for reduction.

4. Ensure that patients on ventilators receive evidence-based interventions to prevent ventilator-associated pneumonia.

5. Ensure that patients with sepsis receive evidence-based interventions.

Early reports of the effectiveness of the Keystone ICU initiative have been impressive. Examples to date include a 50-percent reduction in ICU length of stay and a reduction to zero of catheter-related bloodstream infections for a six-month period by nearly a third of participating ICUs. Of equal importance, occurrences of VAP markedly decreased.[80]

Another statewide project—the ICU Collaborative—sponsored by the New Jersey Hospital Association (NJHA) Quality Institute—is also designed to improve patient safety and quality of care in critical care units. The goals of the NJHA ICU Collaborative include the following:[81]

1. Eliminate bloodstream infections and ventilator-associated pneumonia.

2. Reduce ICU and hospital length of stay by one day.

3. Reduce ICU and hospital mortality rate by 30 percent.

4. Improve culture by 50 percent.

5. Learn from one defect per month.

Similar to the results in Michigan, the twenty-five plus participating hospitals in the NJHA ICU Collaborative saw the incidence of VAPs go down 36 percent after just seven months of implementing specific interventions in their ICUs.[82] In addition, catheter-related BSIs were reduced by 45 percent and several hospitals cut their ICU length of stay by a half day or more.[83]

············

TELEMEDICINE AND ICU SAFETY

The electronic ICU (eICU) is steadily gaining acceptance as a viable means of providing intensivist care, demonstrating enhanced patient outcomes, in spite of a shortage of physicians trained in critical care medicine. Having a centralized medical intensivist monitor critically ill patients in multiple ICUs by way of a complex system of cameras, monitors, and communication links powered by specialized software provides an extra set of eyes on each patient in each ICU. On-site physicians and nurses still conduct regular rounds for each patient in the ICUs; however, a real-time video of each patient, vital signs data, x-ray and laboratory data, and medical records are also transmitted to a centralized ICU command center that monitors the patients remotely.[84]

Sentara Norfolk General Hospital, Norfolk, Virginia, was the nation's first hospital to test and set up this technology, which was developed by VISICU, Inc. (Baltimore, Maryland), and powered by its eVantage™ software.[85] Sentara's eICU system serves a command center staffed by physicians and nurses who can detect and notify ICU staff of any changes in a patient's condition. Through microphones in the patient's room, the nurse can communicate with on-site ICU staff. Since the eICU technology has been implemented at Sentara facilities, the mortality rate for ICU patients has decreased by more than 20 percent in some of the units. In addition, average length of stay for patients has decreased by 17 percent.[86]

············

TRANSPARENCY, DISCLOSURE, AND THE PATIENT-CENTERED ICU

In *Crossing the Quality Chasm,* the Institute of Medicine called for transparency as one of the six aims in improving health care. Steps have been taken towards this aim in the hospital quality reporting for full reimbursement initiatives sponsored by the Centers for Medicare and Medicaid Services (CMS), which makes the quality data reported to them available to consumers and purchasers alike. Similarly, JCAHO has posted quality reports on accredited organizations at its Web site, and several other quality and safety organizations and coalitions are publishing reports on performance of health care providers and organizations. ICUs have a vested interest in continuously striving to improve and maintain positive patient outcomes, because much of the care provided to patients whose outcomes are monitored for quality and safety reporting is provided in the ICU. The ICU safety and quality programs and projects described in this chapter and in the literature present opportunities for critical care providers and ICUs to move forward in achieving improvements which will reflect positively when viewed by patients and payers alike.

In keeping with honest and open communication among physicians, administrators, and health care staffs as a means of promoting patient safety, open communication with patients and their families is also considered characteristic of a culture of safety. Numerous regulatory, accrediting, and professional organizations, including JCAHO, ASHRM, and the National Patient Safety Foundation, (NPSF) have published standards and guidelines in support of informing patients and families about outcomes of care, including unanticipated outcomes, errors, and adverse events. Also, several state-mandated laws on disclosure and reporting of serious or "sentinel" events have been enacted. Concerns initially expressed about increased liability claims resulting from the disclosure of medical errors persist today, but to a lesser degree. In fact, some studies suggest that although the frequency of health care liability claims may increase (with disclosure) the severity (costs of monetary payments) of those claims will not.[87,88]

Taking this concept further, apologizing when an error occurs and has been determined to cause injury, and offering to compensate the patient up front might eventually become standard practice. Disclosure with apology is increasingly common because it is being accepted as the right thing to do and because it is a viable liability claim avoidance strategy. ICU leaders, physicians, and staffs should understand and promote the communication and disclosure policies of their institutions and strive to incorporate improved patient and family involvement in care, treatment, and decision-making. This might require training, education, and skill building.

The concept of patient-centered care is not new. However the patient safety movement has increased its visibility and importance to health care organizations. In addition to open communication and active involvement in care, environmental modifications and non-traditional interventions are being embraced by organizations desiring to become patient-centered. There is a growing belief that patient and family involvement improves outcomes and decreases the incidence of errors and mishaps, and nowhere is this exemplified more readily than in the ICU, where great strides have been already been made in actively involving patients (and families) in their care as patient safety and quality improvement strategies. Some patient-centered components that are increasingly applied in ICU settings include the following:[89]

- Flexible, or open, visiting hours
- Redesigned patient units that consider the comfort and participation of family members
- Active participation of patients and family members during rounds and in care planning
- Implementation of JCAHO's Speak Up safety initiative
- Including patient representatives on quality and safety work groups and committees
- Availability of alternative techniques such as a spiritual component, massage therapy, and music and art therapy

CONCLUSION

The high risks inherent in the ICU can be managed so that patients, caregivers, and health care institutions benefit from safer environments, better clinical outcomes, and improved reputations in the communities served. Critical care units and the hospitals they operate in must begin by creating a culture of safety whereby caregivers work in teams that communicate effectively and understand the goals of medical treatment. A culture of safety in the ICU is characterized by people and processes aimed at identifying and correcting system defects that affect patient safety and quality of care. All levels of critical care providers, managers, and staff should receive education in the science of safety. Medical error reporting must be supported and rewarded through continuous feedback on how learning takes place through the analysis of individual errors and aggregate event data. Because the potential for human and financial loss is arguably the highest when medication errors occur and infections result, these should be a priority for prevention and reduction in the ICU. System and process improvements must be measured to determine the effectiveness of strategies and interventions undertaken to enhance safety and improve outcomes. Technology should be employed to improve safety and decrease errors whenever possible, but with the understanding that new equipment and devices present their own potential for failure which can be exacerbated by human factors and work flow issues.

With the support of risk management professionals and patient safety officers and the commitment of leaders, physicians, and staff, the execution of a clear plan of action and the verification of effectiveness through measurement of improvements, ICUs can be units where caregivers work as teams to implement best practices, prevent complications, identify errors, potential, errors and adverse events, and strive to reduce and prevent them.[90]

Endnotes

1. Wu, A. W., P. Pronovost, L. Morlock. "ICU incident reporting systems." *Journal of Critical Care* 2002; 17(2): 86–94.

2. Halpern, N. A., L. Bettes, R. Greenstein. "Federal and nation-wide intensive care units and healthcare costs: 1986–1992." *Critical Care Medicine.* 1994; 22:2001–7.

3. Donchin, Y., D. Gopher, M. Olin, et al. "A look into the nature and causes of human errors in the intensive care unit." *Critical Care Medicine.* 1995; 23:294–300.

4. Pronovost, P. J., S. M. Berenholtz, K. Ngo et al. "Developing and pilot testing quality indicators in the intensive care unit." *Journal of Critical Care.* 2003 Sep; 18(3):145–55.

5. An acute problem? A report of the national confidential enquiry into patient outcome and death 2005 May (cited June 6, 2005). Available at [www.ncepod.org.uk].

6. *Ibid.*

7. Engoren, M. "The effect of prompt physician visits on intensive care unit mortality and cost." *Critical Care Medicine.* 2005; 33(4):727–32.

8. Wu, A. W., supra note 1.

9. Human factors is the study of the interrelationships between humans, the tools they use, the environment in which they live and work, and interpersonal relations. It applies them to the complex systems and processes for delivering health care. Source: National Patient Safety Definitions (cited June 8, 2005) Available at [www.npsf.org/html/definitions.html].

10. Donchin, Y., supra note 3.

11. Joint Commission on Accreditation of Healthcare Organizations. Sentinel event statistics. Sep 20, 2004 (online). December 31, 2004. [cited July 10, 2005] Available at [www.jcaho.org/accredited+organizations/ambulatory+care/sentinel+events/root+causes+of+sentinel+event.htm].

12. Pronovost, P. J., D. C. Angus, T. Dorman et al, "Physician staffing patterns and clinical outcomes in critically ill patients. A systematic review." *JAMA.* 2003 Nov 6;288(17):2151–62.

13. ECRI. Healthcare embracing concept of the high-reliability organization. *Risk Management Representative.* 2005 Feb: 24(1):8.

14. Perspectives on Safety. In conversation with . . . Peter Pronovost, MD, Ph.D. Morbidity & Mortality Rounds on the Web 2005 Jun (online) cited June 10, 2005. Available at [webmm.ahrq.gov/].

15. Sexton, J. B., E. J. Thomas, R. L. Helmreich, et al. Frontline assessments of healthcare culture: Safety Attitudes Questionnaire norms and psychometric properties. Technical Report 04-01. University of Texas Center of Excellence for Patient Safety Research and Practice AHRQ Grant # 1PO1HS1154401. Available at [www.utpatientsafety.org].

16. Pronovost, P., B. Weast, B. Rosenstein et al., "Implementing and validating a comprehensive unit-based safety program." *Journal of Patient Safety.* 2005 Mar 1/1(1):33–40.

17. Improving patient safety: from rhetoric to reality. 2003 May 28, Symposium at Johns Hopkins University, Baltimore, MD.

18. Peter Pronovost, MD, is a principal in The Patient Safety Group, a Massachusetts LLC whose operating charter states that all net proceeds will be used to further advance safety and quality efforts in health care.

19. Pronovost, P., S. M. Berenholtz, T. Dorman et al. "Improving communication in the ICU using daily goals." *Journal of Critical Care*. 2003 Jun; 18(2): 71–5.

20. Croteau, R., "The 2006 National Patient Safety Goals: Are you ready?" Joint Commission on Accreditation of Healthcare Organizations. Audio conference. June 8, 2005.

21. Thompson, D., C. Holzmueller, D. Hunt et al., "A morning briefing: Setting the stage for a clinically and operationally good day." *Joint Commission Journal on Quality and Patient Safety*. 2005 Aug; 31(8):476–9.ECRI. "Teamwork takes hold to improve patient safety." *Risk Management Reporter*. 2005 Feb; 24(1):4.

22. ECRI. "Teamwork takes hold," supra note 20.

23. Baggs, J. G., M. H. Schmitt, A. I. Mushlin et al., "Association between nurse-physician collaboration and patient outcomes in three intensive care units." *Critical Care Medicine*. 1999; 27(9):1991–8.

24. ECRI. "Teamwork takes hold." supra note 20. Pronovost et al., supra note 15.

25. Pronovost et al., supra note 15.

26. Pronovost, Angus, supra note 11.

27. The Leapfrog Group. Leapfrog 2004 Survey Results Released: Consumers urged to use data to make hospital choices. Leapfrog News 2004 Nov. (cited 7/6/2005). Available at [www.leapfroggroup.org/media/file/Leapfrog-Survey_Release-11-16-04.pdf].

28. Improving your ICU. Tips for better care. Society of Critical Care Medicine 2004 Available at [www.sccm.org].

29. Pronovost, P. J., D. Dang, T. Dorman. "Intensive care unit nurse staffing and the risk for complications after abdominal aortic surgery." *Effective Clinical Practice*. 2001;4(5): 199–206. Stoller, J. K. Are respiratory therapists effective? Assessing the evidence. Donald F Eagen Scientific Lecture. Presented at: International Respiratory Congress 2000 (cited July 7, 2005). Available at [www.rcjournal.com/contents/01.01/01.01.0056.asp].

30. Stoller J. K. Are respiratory therapists effective? Supra note 29. Brilli, R. J, A. Spevetz, R.D. Branson et al. "Critical care delivery in the intensive care unit: defining clinical roles and the best practice model." *Critical Care Medicine*. 2001; 29(10):2007–19.

31. Brilli et al., supra note 30. ECRI, "JCAHO, ECRI offer advice to prevent ventilator-related deaths, injuries." *Risk Management Representative*. 2002 Jun; 21(3):9–10.

32. ECRI, "JCAHO, ECRI offer advice," supra note 31.

33. Berenholtz, S. M., P. J. Pronovost, P. A. Lipsett et al., "Eliminating catheter-related blood-stream infections in the intensive care unit." *Critical Care Medicine*. 2004; 32(10):2014–20. Pronovost, P., C. Goeschel. "Improving ICU care: it takes a team." *Healthcare Executive*. 2005 Mar/Apr: 14–22.

34. Pronovost, Goeschel. "Improving ICU care," supra note 33.

35. Pronovost, P. J., D. M. Needham, H. Waters et al., "Intensive care unit physician staffing: financial modeling of the Leapfrog standard." *Critical Care Medicine*. 2004; 32(6):1247–53.ECRI. Teamwork takes hold to improve patient safety, supra note 20.

36. ECRI. Teamwork takes hold to improve patient safety, supra note 20.

37. Rothschild, J. M., C. P. Landrigan, J. W. Cronin et al., "The critical care safety study: the incidence and nature of adverse events and serious medical errors in intensive care." *Critical Care Medicine*. 2005 Aug; 33(8):1694–1700.

38. National Nosocomial Infection System (NNIS). Centers for Disease Control and Prevention Division of Healthcare Quality Promotion. Available at [www.cdc.gov/NCIDOD/hip/SURVEILL/About_NNIS.HTM].

39. Pennsylvania Patient Safety Reporting System (PA-PSRS). Patient Safety Authority, Independent Agency of the Commonwealth of Pennsylvania. Available at [www.psa.state.pa.us/psa/site/default.asp].

40. Joint Commission on Accreditation of Healthcare Organizations, Preventing ventilator-related deaths and injuries. Sentinel Event Alert Issue 25 2002 Feb 26. Available at [www.jcaho.org/about+us/news+letters/sentinel+event+alert/sea_25.htm].

41. Shaw, R., F. Drever, H. Hughes et al., "Adverse events and near miss reporting in the NHS." *Quality and Safety in Health Care*. 2005;14:279–83.

42. *Ibid.*

43. Rothschild, J. M., supra note 36.

44. *Ibid.*

45. Wu, A. W., C. G. Holzmueller, L. H. Lubonski et al., "Development of the ICU safety reporting system." *Journal of Patient Safety*. 2005 Mar; 1(1):23–32.

46. Holzmueller, C. G., P. J. Pronovost, F. Dickman et al., "Creating the Web-based intensive care unit safety reporting system." *Journal of the American Medical Informatics Association*. 2005 Mar/Apr;12(2):130–9.

47. *Ibid.*

48. Holzmueller, C. G., supra note 45.

49. Needham, D. M., D. A. Thompson, C. G. Holzmueller et al., "A system factors analysis of airway events from the Intensive Care Unit Safety Reporting System (ICUSRS)." *Critical Care Medicine*. 2004; 32(11):2227–33.

50. Needham, D. M., D. J. Sinopoli, D. A. Thompson et al., "A system factors analysis of 'line, tube, and drain' incidents in the intensive care unit." *Critical Care Medicine*. 2005; 33(8):1701–7.

51. Pope. B. B., "Provide safe passage for patients." *Nursing Management*. 2003 Sep; 34(9):41–6.

52. SSM Healthcare/DePaul Health Center. Patient Transportation Hallpass. Personal email communication from E. Summy, ASHRM August 9, 2005.

53. Osmon, S., C. B. Harris, W.C. Dunagan. "Reporting of medical errors: an intensive care unit experience." *Critical Care Medicine*. 2004; 32(3):727–33.

54. Jury Verdict Research. Current awards in personal injury—43rd edition. Jury Verdict Research releases verdict study (press release) 1.20.10. Horsham [PA]: LRP Publications; 2004 Apr 1.

55. ECRI is an independent nonprofit health services research agency, collaborating center of the World Health Organization, and a designated evidence-based practice center by the U.S. Agency for Healthcare Research and Quality located in Plymouth Meeting, PA. [www.ecri.org]. Institute for Safe Medication Practices. Survey on high-alert medications. Differences between nursing and pharmacy perspectives revealed. ISMP Medical Safety Alert 2003 Oct 16; 8(21):1–2.

56. Leape, L. L., D. J. Cullen, M. D. Clapp et al. "Pharmacist participation on physician rounds and adverse drug events in the intensive care unit." *JAMA*. 1999 Jul; 282(3):267–70. ECRI, High-Alert Medications. Healthcare Risk Control 2004 Mar; 4 Pharmacy and Medications 1.4.

57. Institute for Safe Medication Practices. Survey on high-alert medications. Supra note 55.

58. ECRI, High-Alert Medications. Supra note 56. Pronovost, P., D. B. Hobson, K. Earsing et al., "A practical tool to reduce medication errors during patient transfer from an intensive care unit." *Journal of Clinical Outcomes Management*. 2004 Jan; 11(1):26–33.

59. Rothschild, J. M., C. A. Keohane, E. F. Cook et al., "A controlled trial of smart infusion pumps to improve medication safety in critically ill patients." *Critical Care Medicine*. 2005 Mar; 33(3):533–40.

60. Pronovost et al., A practical tool to reduce medication errors. Supra note 58. Tooher, N. L., "Plaintiffs' lawyers cautiously eye hospital-infection suits." *Virginia Medical Law Report*. 2005 Mar: 8, 16.

61. *Ibid.*

62. *Ibid.*

63. Institute for Healthcare Improvement. Putting safety on the (central) line. (cited 4/20/2005). Available at [www.ihi.org/IHI/Topics/ImprovementMethods/Literature/PuttingSafetyontheCentralLine.htm].

64. *Ibid.*

65. Berenholtz et al., Eliminating catheter-related bloodstream infections. Supra note 33.

66. *Ibid.*

67. Institute for Healthcare Improvement. 100k lives campaign; getting started kit: prevent ventilator-associated pneumonia. (cited 7/7/2005). Available at [www.ihi.org/NR/rdonlyres/A448DDB1-E2A4-4D13-8F02-16417EC52990/0/VAPHowtoGuideFINAL.pdf].

68. *Ibid.*

    Saint, S., S. R. Kaufman, M. Thompson et al., A reminder reduces urinary catheterization in hospitalized patients." *Joint Commission Journal on Quality and Patient Safety*. 2005 Aug;31(8):455–62.

69. Van Den Berghe, G., P. Wouters, F. Weekers et al., "Intensive insulin therapy in critically ill patients." *New England Journal of Medicine*. 2001 Nov 8; 345(19):1359–67.

70. Saint, et al., A reminder reduces urinary catheterization. Supra note 68.

71. Wideman, M. V., M. E. Whittler, T. M. Anderson. Barcode medication administration: lessons learned from an intensive care unit implementation. Advances in Patent Safety. Volume 3. Agency for Research and Quality. (cited 7/12/2005). Available at [www.ahcpr.gov/downloads/pub/advances/vol3/Wideman.pdf]. ECRI. Computerized Provider Order-Entry Systems. Healthcare Risk Control 2002 May; Supp A. Pharmacy and Medications 6.

72. *Ibid.*

73. ECRI. Computerized Provider Order-Entry Systems. Healthcare Risk Control 2002 May; Supp A. Pharmacy and Medications 6.

74. Cheng, C. H., M. K. Goldstein, E. Geller et al., The effects of CPOE on ICU workflow: an observational study. Proceedings of the American Medical Informatics Association's fall 2003 symposium. (cited 7/12/2005). Available at [www.smi.stanford.edu/pubs/SMI_Reports/SMI-2003-0976.pdf].

75. Cordero, L., L. Kuehn, R. R. Kumar et al., "Impact of computerized physician order entry on clinical practice in a newborn intensive care unit." *Journal of Perinatology*. 2004 Feb; 24(2):88-93.

76. Potts, A. L., F. E. Barr, D. F. Gregory et al., "Computerized physician order entry and medication errors in a pediatric critical care unit." *Pediatrics*. 2004 Jan; 113(1):59–63.

    Landro, L. "Hospitals push to improve intensive care." *Wall Street Journal*. 2003 Sep 25.

77. Schilling, L., S. Berenholtz, K. Smithson. Improving the Effectiveness and Safety of ICU Care: Transformation of the Intensive Care Unit: A National Collaborative. Presented at: National Patient Safety Congress; 2005 May 4–6; Orlando, Fl.

78. Landro, Hospitals push to improve intensive care. Supra note 76.

79. Pronovost Goeschel, supra note 32.

80. *Ibid.*

81. Brook, K. "ICU collaborative takes off." *Healthcare New Jersey*. 2004 May/Jun; 14(3):3-4. (cited 6/28/2005). Available at [www.njha.com/qualityinstitute/files/69200590700AM54.pdf].

82. Holmes, Aline M. (Director, New Jersey Hospital Association Quality Institute). Conversation with K. Shostek 6/6/2005.

83. New Jersey Hospital Association. Initiative to improve ICU quality yields impressive early results. Leading Opinion 2005 Apr; 14(1):1. [cited 2005 Jun 28] Available at [www.njha.com/qualityinstitute/files/421200534559PM73.pdf].

84. Imaging the ICU of the future. In Care in the ICU Teaming Up to Improve Quality. Accelerating Change Today (ACT); National Coalition on Heath Care and Institute for Healthcare Improvement. 2002 Sep. Popp, P., "How will disclosure affect future litigation?" *Journal of Healthcare Risk Management*. 2003 Winter. 23(1):5–9.

85. Dr. Peter Pronovost owns a fraction of 1% of the currently issued shares of VISICU, Inc.

86. ECRI. "A culture of safety that sticks: Sentara Norfolk." *Risk Management Representative*. 2005 Aug; 24(4):1. 3–8. Kramann, S. S., G. Hamm. "Risk management: extreme honesty may be the best policy." *Annals of Internal Medicine*. 1999; 131:963–7. (cited 6/8/2005). Available at [www.annals.org/cgi/reprint/131/12/963.pdf].

87. Popp P., How will disclosure affect future litigation? Supra note 84.

88. Kramann et al. Risk management: extreme honesty may be the best policy. Supra note 86. ECRI. "JCAHO proposal for patient-centered care brings concept to mainstream healthcare settings." *Risk Management Representative*. 2005 Jun; 24(3):1, 3–7.

89. *Ibid.*

90. Perspectives on Safety. In conversation with . . . Peter Pronovost, MD, PhD. Morbidity & Mortality Rounds on the Web 2005 Jun (cited 6/10/2005). Available at [webmm. ahrq.gov/].

ICU Risk and Safety Resource List

In addition to the references listed in the endnotes to the chapter, the following resources* are provided to assist with risk management and patient safety efforts in critical care.

American Association of Critical Care Nurses
[www.aacn.org]
Education, Certification, Publications

Society of Hospital Medicine
[www.hospitalmedicine.org]
Online Education: Core Competencies and CME Courses:
* Preventing Health Care Acquired Infections
* Recognizing and Treating Ventilator-Associated Pneumonia in the ICU
* Educational Module for Central Venous Catheter Insertion (Vanderbilt University)

Society of Critical Care Medicine
[www.sccm.org]

Professional Resources, Online Guidelines
* Sepsis Information
* CPOE System Requirements for Intensive Care Use
* Improving Your ICU: Tips for Better Care
* Guidelines for the inter- and intrahospital transport of critically ill patients
* Critical Care Delivery: Defining Clinical Roles and the Best Practice Model
* Guidelines for Granting Privileges for the Performance of Procedures in Critically Ill Patients

Institute for Healthcare Improvement
[www.ihi.org]
Topics: Critical Care—Measures
* Intensive Care: Ventilator Bundle, Central Line Bundle, Rapid Response Teams, Glycemic Control
* Sepsis: Sepsis Resuscitation Bundle, Sepsis Management Bundle
  Programs: 100k Lives Campaign—How-to Guides:
* Adverse Drug Event (ADE) Prevention, Central Line Infections, Ventilator-Associated Pneumonia

Intensive Care Unit Safety Reporting System
[www.icusrs.org]
Publications, Projects, Safety Information, Safety Talks and Presentations

Johns Hopkins Center for Public Health Preparedness (JHCPHP)
[www.jhsph.edu/preparedness/training/online/patient_safety.html]
* Patient Safety: The Quality Imperative (Three-part online training module)

Johns Hopkins Center for Innovation in Quality Patient Care
[www.hopkinsquality.com/CFI/]
* Patient Safety Information
* Teamwork and Communication Video
* Quality Grand Rounds

Michigan Health and Safety Coalition
ICU Toolkit:
[www.mihealthandsafety.org/ICU/]
* A Toolkit for Intensive Care Units to Improve the Safety and Quality of Patient Care

Credentialing Resource Center
Clinical Privilege White Papers:
[www.online-crc.com/wpaper/indexm.cfm]
* Critical Care Medicine
* Mechanical Ventilation
* Pulmonary Artery Catheterization

ECRI
[www.ecri.org]
* Patient Safety Center
* ViewPoint: Breathe Easy: Commonsense Guidance on Current Ventilator Concepts
* Health Devices System: [www.ecri.org/Products_and_Services/Membership_Programs/
  Health_ Devices_System/Default.aspx]—Ventilators, Intensive Care; Physiologic Monitoring
  Systems
* Healthcare Risk Control System: [www.ecri.org/hrc]—Risk Analyses: Critical Alarms, Physio-
  logic Monitoring Systems, Ventilator Disconnections, Invasive Lines Self-Assessment Question-
  naires: Patient Safety, Medication Safety, Neonatal ICU
* Medical Device Safety Reports [www.mdsr.ecri.org]
* Patient Safety Videos

Agency for Healthcare Research and Quality
[www.ahrq.gov]

* Hospital Survey on Patient Safety Culture [www.ahrq.gov/qual/hospculture/]
* Medical Errors and Patient Safety [www.ahrq.gov/qual/errorsix.htm]
* Patient Safety Network [www.psnet.ahrq.gov/]
* Web M&M Morbidity and mortality rounds [www.webmm.ahrq.gov/]
* Making Health Care Safer: A Critical Analysis of Patient Safety Practices; Evidence Report/Technology Assessment, No. 43. Chapter 38. "Closed" Intensive Care Units and Other Models of Care for Critically Ill Patients, Jeffrey M. Rothschild, M.D., M.P.H. [www.ahrq.gov/clinic/ptsafety/chap38.htm]

Patient Safety Group
[www.patientsafetygroup.org]
* eCUSP: Electronic Comprehensive Unit-based Safety Program
* Safety Program information, links, video demo

Institute for Safe Medication Practices
[www.ismp.org]
*ISMP Medication Safety Alert! newsletter
*Medication self assessment tool

* Resource listings are representative of information and tools available at selected Web sites.

13

Management of Risk: Promoting Perinatal Patient Safety

G. Eric Knox, MD
Kathleen Rice Simpson

············

SCOPE OF PROBLEM

The personal, professional, and financial cost of perinatal liability remains high. For more than twenty years, obstetrics has led or been close to the top of severity statistics for professional liability claims.[1] According to the latest survey of physician fellows of the American College of Obstetricians and Gynecologists,[2] during a sixteen-year career, the average obstetrician can expect 2.64 professional liability claims, whereas 41.5 percent of ACOG fellows surveyed reported three or more claims. The primary clinical issue in an obstetric claim was a neurologically impaired baby (34.3 percent) followed by stillbirth or neonatal death (15.3 percent). Hospital-based treatment such as fetal monitoring (47.7 percent neurologically impaired baby; 21.9 percent stillbirth or neonatal death) and oxytocin administration (43.4 percent neurologically impaired baby; 14.7 percent stillbirth or neonatal death) were significant factors in both types of claims.[3] The mean length of time from filing of an obstetric claim involving neonatal harm to resolution is four years, with 13.4 percent requiring seven years or longer to resolve.

Many obstetricians reported changes in practice as a result of professional liability affordability and availability; 25.2 percent have decreased the amount of high-risk obstetric care they undertake, 12.2 percent have decreased the number of births they manage, and 9.2 percent have stopped practicing obstetrics altogether. The American College of Obstetricians and Gynecologists[4] has identified twenty-three "red alert" states with a medical liability insurance crisis. Factors that contribute to designation as a "red alert" state are a lack of available professional liability coverage for obstetricians because only a few carriers are currently writing policies in the state; the number of carriers leaving the medical liability insurance market; and the cost and rate of increase of annual premiums based on reports from industry monitors.

Of course, similar liability concerns have an impact on health care organizations. The average settlement for a claim against a hospital is just over $1.5 million, and the average jury verdict exceeds $7 million.[5]

The devastation of families when labor and birth results in a brain-damaged baby is enormous and long-standing, particularly when the adverse outcome is determined to have been preventable. The effect on the health care providers who are involved cannot be minimized. They often suffer from related stress and guilt, sometimes giving up their clinical practice entirely.[6]

As a result of an increase in the number of related obstetric suits and severity of associated losses, some health care systems have implemented obstetrical patient safety initiatives with the goals of decreasing the financial loss associated with claims and promoting safer care for mothers and babies during labor and birth.[7,8] Key components of these initiatives include:

- Measuring the safety culture in each labor and delivery unit
- Changing the culture to be more patient safety-oriented
- Implementing team training programs
- Standardizing key clinical protocols and physician orders based on professional standards, guidelines, and the latest evidence
- Promoting a common understanding of fetal monitoring and expectations for interventions when the fetal heart rate (FHR) patterns are nonreassuring through interdisciplinary education and certification
- Establishing professional standards for accountability and appropriate follow-up

This chapter will discuss the evolution of loss prevention practices, which has culminated in these advanced strategies, and will suggest implementation approaches.

············

HISTORICAL ATTEMPTS/FAILURES AT MANAGING OBSTETRICAL RISK

Until recently, the following traditional approaches to managing obstetrical risk have been employed by health care organizations:

- Blaming and training
- Documentation
- Technology
- Credentialing
- Outcome screening
- Causation defenses

However, none of these techniques, either alone or in combination, have been able to stop the increasing dollar amounts of plaintiff settlements, jury awards, or the percentage of cases decided against hospitals or physicians.[9] In these discouraging overall trends, there exists an important dichotomy not readily explained by legal jurisdiction; that is, some perinatal units have encountered a disproportionate number of obstetrical claims, while others have had very few or only minor nuisance-type liability claims brought against them.[10] This dichotomy mirrors that of the physician professional liability experience; that is, a minority of physicians account for a majority of claims filed and dollars paid.[11,12] If a systematic and successful approach to managing obstetric risk is to be found, then understanding the differences between high liability and lower risk units is crucial.

Units at High Risk for Patient Injury and Harm

Perinatal units that experience an unacceptably high amount of patient harm or professional liability have the following organizational features:[13]

- Patient safety is not explicitly stated as a primary and important goal or value.
- Production and financial considerations have a higher priority than patient safety in operational decision-making.
- Clinical practice is not based on evidence and professional standards. Instead, clinical action and decision-making are determined by "the way we've always done it." Wide variation in clinical practice persists in spite of existing clearly articulated professional standards and guidelines. Autonomy routinely trumps standardization.
- Nurses and physicians cannot articulate or agree to the mission, vision, or goals of the clinical team.
- Provider convenience takes precedence over patient safety.
- Effective peer review and interdisciplinary case analysis are non-existent.
- Reporting of near misses or good catches is not done or valued.
- Systems or unit operations are not evaluated as potential sources of error. Rather, individuals are blamed when errors occur.
- Accidents are often attributed to "circumstances beyond our control."
- Physician-patient relationships are patriarchal with little effective patient-centered decision-making.
- Women are not fully informed of risks and benefits of procedures prospectively, as applicable.
- Labor and birth are routinely viewed as medical procedures to be managed and controlled rather than a natural, predominantly low-risk phenomenon made riskier by unnecessary iatrogenic (induced inadvertently by a physician or surgeon or by medical treatment or diagnostic procedures)[14] intervention.
- Hierarchical deference in nurse-physician relationships is the expected behavioral norm.
- Nurse-physician relationships are characterized by ongoing conflict, overt or covert. Professionals uneasily co-exist or barely tolerate one another's presence.
- Hostility and inappropriate workplace behavior are tolerated or taken for granted.
- A formal "chain of command" is frequently used to modify behavior instead of informal group norms and open direct communication.
- Conflict is downplayed or avoided rather than used as an opportunity for learning.

In sum, organizational and individual behavior in high-liability, high-risk perinatal units is dysfunctional at best and destructive at worst.[15] The atmosphere is one of hierarchy, blame, and retribution, with professionals in constant conflict. Clearly, this is the antithesis of teamwork, high reliability, and patient safety as defined in other high-risk domains.[16]

Low-Risk Units are Different

In contrast to obstetrical units at high risk for professional liability, low-risk units, regardless of size or level of care, are markedly different, in the authors' experience. For example, administrative leadership, while recognizing the importance of fiscal stewardship, ultimately believes that the "mission of preventing fetal and neonatal injury creates the margin" and makes "safety first" a day-to-day reality. The tension between production and safety is balanced rather than shifted in a hazardous way toward production. The resulting environment fosters a much more objective and transparent appreciation of risk for all stakeholders. Low-risk units have invested in an administrative medical director of obstetrics who works in tandem and in partnership with the nursing leader of perinatal services to ensure high reliability and quality. Adequate educational support is provided. The unit is routinely staffed according to American Academy of Pediatrics[17] and Association of Women's Health, Obstetric and Neonatal Nurses (AWHONN)[18] recommendations. Administrators recognize that their organization holds the majority of perinatal risk and are willing to hold providers accountable for standards-based practice and, most important, professional workplace behavior.

Complementing the administrative infrastructure, low-risk units also feature a supportive clinical infrastructure. There is a commitment to creating and sustaining a "culture of safety"[19] for mothers, babies, and health care professionals. Strong interdisciplinary clinical leadership and an interdisciplinary perinatal practice committee[20] define unit policy and hold all providers accountable for standards-based practice.[21] The interdisciplinary practice committee must have a standing agenda item each month to review the most recently published science, standards, and guidelines from professional organizations such as AWHONN, ACOG, AAP, and the Joint Commission on Accreditation of Healthcare Organizations (JCAHO). When new standards and guidelines are published, the discussion should focus on how and when (rather than, if) such professional guidance will be incorporated into unit operations and daily practice. Obstetric department membership requires a commitment to clinical practice based on good science, the latest evidence, and published national professional standards of care. Standardization and simplification of clinical protocols and unit operations is accepted and routine. In rare cases, where there might be a need to practice outside of unit policy, interdisciplinary discussion occurs, medical record documentation objectively details clinical rationale, and the case is evaluated through the quality review process.[22]

Professional attitude and unit culture are recognized as major determinants of degree of perinatal risk. Collegial professional relationships and superb communication predominate, rather than a more traditional hierarchical way of doing business. There is the expectation that all professionals will act professionally all of the time. There is meaningful follow-up when behavior is inappropriate. Teamwork is promoted and practiced. For example, the "different but equal" contribution of nurses to patient care and clinical outcomes is recognized, acknowledged, and valued by physicians and administrators. Constant communication by everyone is encouraged. Briefing and debriefing communication mechanisms are used extensively. Creating and maintaining a "safety net" is part of unit mindset. The "one thing that could go wrong" and "what ifs?" are routinely and openly discussed; change of shift reports emphasize "what if?" and "are we prepared?"

Emergencies are rehearsed.[23] Refer to Chapter 3 in this Handbook for information on clinical crisis management. As specified by unit policy, physicians come to the unit and personally evaluate a patient at any time they are requested by a nurse to do so. In sum, there is universal agreement to use professional standards, and professional behavior as the basis for clinical practice, all within the context of a culture of safety.

· · · · · · · · · · · ·

STEPWISE STRATEGY FOR MANAGING PERINATAL RISK

Creating a safe clinical environment during labor and birth requires effective leadership, a clearly articulated, shared philosophy, professional workplace behavior, and excellence in key clinical practices. Without effective administrative and clinical leaders, staff members are challenged to implement essential criteria for safe care. Leaders must be fully committed and must have the will to do the right thing for mothers and babies, caregivers, and the institution, even as they are faced with the very real pressures of economics, production, and perceived provider convenience.[24]

Several organizations have enhanced the safety of their perinatal environments by employing a basic set of strategies, albeit with slightly different emphases and approaches to managing perinatal risk, based on their history, organizational structure, and administrative strengths:

- MCIC Vermont, composed of university teaching hospitals representing academic leadership

- Providence Health System and Catholic Healthcare Partners, community faith-based institutions with system-wide collaboration

- HCA, a for-profit hospital company that is data- and protocol-driven

- Kaiser Permanente, an integrated health system with an emphasis on culture and team building

Although the methodological emphasis or tactics differ slightly, there is an emerging consensus among these organizations that executive leadership is absolute in its support of the perinatal safety initiative and that the following seven steps are critical to decreasing perinatal harm and liability:[25]

Policy and protocol development

Organizations that have enhanced obstetric safety apply national and professional standards to all unit policies. They give priority to induction and augmentation of labor; timely, accurate fetal assessment and response to nonreassuring fetal status; and second-stage labor management. Refer to discussion of specific clinical issues later in this chapter.

The following are steps by which organizations can achieve this objective:

- Use an interdisciplinary perinatal practice committee to review and revise policies and procedures to be consistent with current national standards of all pertinent professional organizations.

- Develop a uniform set of standing orders that reflect unit policy based on national professional standards. With the exception of rare clinical situations, variation of practice which is outside of good science (the latest evidence and national professional standards) should be prohibited.

- Educate all providers together as an interdisciplinary team on national professional standards and standing orders.
- Review perinatal practice for compliance with national professional standards through direct observation and medical record audits.
- Identify, update, and implement practice as new standards are published.

Conduct a Baseline Perinatal Safety Attitude Survey Using the Safety Attitude Questionnaire (SAQ)[26]

The previously mentioned organizations have found it helpful to anticipate perinatal safety enhancement by measuring effectiveness of unit teamwork, patient safety, and provider attitude; that is, the sum and substance of a perinatal "culture of safety."

- The perinatal SAQ provides information on teamwork climate, safety climate, job satisfaction, perceptions of management, working conditions, and individual stress recognition.
- Professional attitude and organizational culture help explain other forms of health care performance data such as absenteeism, turnover, case delays, length of stay, and readmission rates, in addition to safety performance in other high-risk domains.
- The SAQ is designed to be a pre- and post-intervention measurement tool and should be initiated with this capability in mind.

Initiate Teamwork and Patient Safety Education

Once the SAQ is completed, effective perinatal organizations address issues of dysfunctional communication, collaboration, and teamwork that have been identified. They also encourage the value of including principles of human factors and the role of systems in creating harm[27,28] in all unit orientation and ongoing work.

The following are related insights and suggested approaches:

- Poor teamwork and communication (miscommunication or lack of communication) are often significant factors in mishaps that occur in non-medical high-risk domains, medical accidents, and perinatal malpractice claims.[29]
- Initial education should emphasize assertive communication, situational awareness, and conflict management.
- It is important to routinely conduct drills for common high-risk clinical situations such as shoulder dystocia, emergent Cesarean birth, and postpartum hemorrhage.[30]
- Use role-playing to simulate clinical situations with potential for conflict between team members.
- Routinely observe handoffs and use opportunities for improvement that are identified to improve the handoff process.[31]

Begin Daily Interdisciplinary Unit Review and Debriefings of Select Medical Records

This method can help improve team performance and educate all care providers to the system issues involved when a near miss or harm occurs. The following points are to be considered:

- Standardize and select patient safety indicators specific to risk or potential liability for medical record review every twenty-four hours (for example, unanticipated maternal return to the OR, admission to ICU, intrapartum fetal death, and neonatal pH of less than 7.20).

- Focus on *process of care rather than adverse outcomes*—Such adverse outcomes occur rarely and are difficult to assess with statistically stable data, even in large samples. For example, a "failure to rescue" indicator can be a useful way to measure fetal safety because it captures gaps and limitations in unit processes.[32]

- Monitor medical records for adherence to unit policies and protocols (care processes).

- Include fetal monitor strips with the medical record as part of each case review.

- Transmit lessons learned to all unit providers.

Use Defined Neonatal Injuries as Part of Credentialing and Peer Review

Include and emphasize such information as an integral component of obstetrical peer-review, credentialing, and privileging activities.

- Conduct peer review of the maternal medical records leading to the neonatal injuries (for example, intrapartum fetal death, neonatal asphyxia, brachial plexus injury, meconium aspiration, forceps or vacuum extraction injury).

- Include fetal monitoring strips with the medical record as part of each case review. Process and outcome should be assessed and emphasized.

Institute Interdisciplinary Education and Certification in Electronic Fetal Monitoring (EFM) as a Condition of Privilege and Practice

Successful perinatal programs emphasize the importance of interdisciplinary education to increase team communication and proficiency through adoption of a common EFM language and demonstration of competence. This initiative should be both individual and team-based.

Physicians and nurses in these settings should obtain certification in electronic fetal monitoring from a nationally recognized certifying organization that provides examinations that are psychometrically valid and reliable. Privileging and credentialing should require documentation of such certification. It is important to continue EFM team review and learning through regular interdisciplinary forums.

Create the Position of Perinatal Patient Safety Nurse[33]

The perinatal patient safety nurse can work in collaboration with perinatal physicians and nursing leaders. The role is designed to:

- Actively advocate "safety first," ask the tough questions, and "stop the line" when re-evaluation of risk is indicated.

- Be a clinical link to and support organizational risk management professionals

- Ensure that all care providers in the unit and unit practices adhere to national professional standards and the principles and practice of a culture of safety.

- Coordinate safety culture survey process and team training.

- Coordinate analysis of medical records to objectively measure process and improvement.
- Coordinate electronic fetal monitoring certification.
- Provide interdisciplinary education in the principles of patient safety.
- Serve as a constant reminder of the organization's commitment to safe care for mothers and babies.

....

KEY CLINICAL PRACTICES KNOWN TO INCREASE RISK OF PERINATAL INJURY AND HARM[34]

The following discussion of solutions for specific obstetric issues may provide additional insight.

Fetal Assessment

As previously discussed, safety during fetal assessment is based on a common language for fetal heart rate (FHR) patterns, common knowledge and understanding of fetal physiology, and common expectations for interventions when the FHR pattern suggests fetal compromise. The terminology to describe FHR patterns recommended by the National Institute of Child Health and Human Development[35,36,37] is used in all professional communication concerning fetal assessment. The written and electronic medical records provide cues to the appropriate terminology. There is ongoing interdisciplinary fetal monitoring education. Knowledge and skills in fetal assessment are not assumed to be discipline-specific. All members of the team participate in case reviews and offer suggestions for future care improvement. Communication among team members about nonreassuring FHR patterns should include baseline rate, variability, presence or absence of accelerations and decelerations, the clinical context and pattern evolution.[38]

Intrauterine Resuscitation

There should be common expectations for intrauterine resuscitation including:

- Maternal repositioning
- An intravenous fluid bolus of at least 500 mL of lactated Ringer's solution
- Oxygen administration at ten liters per minute via nonrebreather facemask
- Reduction of uterine activity
- Correction of maternal hypotension[39,40]
- Agreement among team members concerning which type of FHR patterns require bedside evaluation by the primary care provider and within an identified timeframe[41]
- Timely and appropriate interventions for nonreassuring fetal status, including emergent Cesarean birth
- Neonatal resuscitation based on the Neonatal Resuscitation Program (NRP)[42]
- Completion of the NRP course by all team members

Labor Induction

Labor induction should be carried out on suitable candidates, with proper timing, pharmacologic agents, dosing protocols, and recognition and treatment of complications as recommended by ACOG[43,44] and AWHONN.[45] There are standard unit policies and corresponding order sets for each pharmacologic agent. There is an expectation that all providers will practice based on these established unit policies. A physiologic dosing regime for oxytocin is used (start at 1 milliunit per minute and increase by 1–2 milliunits per minute no more frequently than every thirty minutes until adequate progress of labor, as long as there is reassuring fetal status and the absence of uterine hyperstimulation). Nurses must not be pressured by physician colleagues to "push the pit" or "pit to distress."

Routine elective induction should not be allowed before thirty-nine completed weeks of gestation. Labor induction should be initiated only when there are enough qualified nurses to safely monitor the mother and fetus. The definition of uterine hyperstimulation (a series of single contractions lasting two minutes or more, a contraction frequency of six or more in ten minutes, or contractions of normal duration occurring within one minute of each other) is known by all members of the team.[46,47,48] Interventions for hyperstimulation must be initiated before the FHR becomes nonreassuring.

Second-Stage Labor Care

It is recognized that the second stage of labor is a period of stress for the fetus and efforts are made to minimize that stress by shortening the active pushing phase and using applicable pushing techniques. There should be common expectations among team members concerning when to begin pushing and how to encourage women to push. Women with epidural anesthesia who do not feel the urge to push at ten centimeters cervical dilation should be allowed to rest until the fetus has descended enough to stimulate the urge to push. (up to two hours for nulliparous women and up to one hour for multiparous women).[49] When the urge to push is noted, women are encouraged to bear down as long as they can at the peak of the contraction, no more than three times per contraction.[50] Women are told not to take a deep breath and hold it while the nurse or physician counts to ten.[51] Breath-holding longer than six to eight seconds per pushing effort is discouraged.[52]

Women are assisted to suitable positions for pushing such as upright, semi-Fowlers, lateral, and squatting.[53] The supine lithotomy position and stirrups are not used during pushing efforts. The woman's knees are not forcibly pushed back against her abdomen in positions that stretch the perineum or risk joint or nerve injury; rather, she is allowed to position herself for comfort or keep her feet flat on the bed as desired.[54] Repetitive pushing efforts are not encouraged if the FHR is nonreassuring. Instead, women are coached to push with every other or every third contraction to maintain a stable baseline FHR and allow the fetus to recover between pushes. Uterine hyperstimulation is avoided during the second stage and the same intrauterine resuscitation techniques used during first-stage labor are used during the second stage.

Vaginal Birth After Caesarean Section

In the early 1990s, organizations like ACOG and the National Institutes of Health (NIH) endorsed trials of labor by post-Caesarean mothers who met specific criteria to reduce a national Caesarean rate of approximately 25 percent.[55] Subsequently, whereas many mothers successfully attempted vaginal birth after Caesarean (VBAC), a small number—just under 1 percent—experienced uterine rupture that occurred with little or no warning. In 1999, ACOG issued a Practice Bulletin which cautioned that, although trial of labor is "appropriate for most women who have had a previous low transverse Caesarean delivery, increased experience with VBAC indicates that there are potential problems."[56]

In July 2004, ACOG reiterated that selection criteria for VBAC included: "One previous low transverse Caesarean; Clinically adequate pelvis; No other uterine scars or previous rupture; *Physician immediately available throughout active labor capable of monitoring labor and performing an emergency caesarean delivery; Availability of anesthesia and personnel for emergency caesarean section."* In addition, the July 2004 ACOG Practice Bulletin on VBAC went further, discouraging physicians from using prostaglandins for these patients.[57]

The 2004 ACOG statement has been interpreted by many organizations to require in-house support, immediately capable of performing a Caesarean section. In the case of VBAC, the earlier ACOG position requiring that the team take no longer than thirty minutes from decision to perform an emergent Caesarean procedure, is arguably inapplicable.[58] Many hospitals have ceased to offer VBAC opportunities to mothers, because they cannot provide the requisite support.

Clinicians and organizations providing VBACs should provide a thorough informed-consent process for the woman who elects VBAC over a Caesarean section. The practitioner must also remember that maternal consent to try VBAC can mean VBAC consent can be withdrawn at any time. Refer to Volume 2, Chapter 4 for more information on informed consent.

Another important risk management strategy for VBAC or other high-risk patients and the general population, is the importance of making certain that the maternal medical records are transferred from the practitioner's office to the hospital setting at least a month before the expected date of confinement (EDC).

Shoulder Dystocia

Shoulder dystocia is a condition that creates delivery difficulty because of the mother's inability to deliver vaginally after the head is born due to the size and position of the shoulders. In essence, the upper body of the infant becomes wedged behind the maternal pubic bone, the umbilical cord becomes compressed, reducing the amount of oxygen to the baby, and delivery is impeded. More than 30,000[59] babies are born in the United States each year with shoulder dystocia, making it another source of litigation. Allegations include the failure to predict the adverse outcome and the lack of communicating risk. Once shoulder dystocia becomes evident, the physician is faced with limited options, all of which are risky at best and can lead to further damage to the brachial plexus due to stretching or injury. Erb palsy is injury to the upper part of the brachial plexus, and injury to the lower part of the brachial plexus is called Klumpke Palsy. Both can have lifelong devastating effects upon the baby, mother, and family.

Most babies born with a diagnosis of shoulder dystocia and brachial plexus injury will recover in time, with no long-lasting injury. However, for those who do not fully recover, injuries can be severe. They include fractured clavicle and injury to the brachial plexus, both leading to and contributing to long-term disability. If the physician's efforts to deliver the baby are not successful and timely, the resulting damages can also include brain damage and death. Avoidance is facilitated to some degree by screening patients with the potential for the condition—for example, diabetic mothers who are prone to have infants with large upper bodies and heads. However, most shoulder dystocia events have not been predictable, and if the circumstance arises suddenly, emergency management is required. Strategies to address shoulder dystocia include McRoberts' Maneuver, which involves sharply flexing the legs above the mother's abdomen, and suprapubic pressure, in which an attendant makes a fist and pushes the infant's shoulder to the right or left.[60] A well-researched and clear resource on shoulder dystocia can be found at the Web site of Dr. Henry Lerner, clinical instructor in obstetrics and gynecology at Harvard Medical School, at [www.shoulderdystociainfo.com].

One issue that historically has been problematic in defending shoulder dystocia-related malpractice suits is the substitution by staff of fundal pressure for suprapubic pressure. Fundal pressure is applied much higher than suprapubic pressure, and can result in a ruptured uterus. Nursing staff and others who might assist in addressing shoulder dystocia in the delivery room must be educated regarding the difference between these two approaches. It is also critical that all interventions be objectively documented.

Shoulder dystocia is an excellent example of a clinical situation that arises infrequently, yet requires rapid and correct execution of a team approach. Steps to manage shoulder dystocia should be formalized in a protocol, and staff members should then participate in shoulder dystocia drills, as often as necessary to maintain their proficiency. An excellent resource for planning and critiquing shoulder dystocia drills is an ACOG video on this topic, which can be obtained at [www.acog.com].

With the proliferation of advances in medical technology, the risk inherent in conditions such as shoulder dystocia may be reduced by the application of advanced technology. The evolution of computer-generated predictive modeling will expand the treatment options for practitioners, allowing them to evaluate the potential for should dystocia prior to delivery and to facilitate a planned strategy with full disclosure to and informed consent from the mother.[61] For further discussion on the use of advanced technology, see *Hope for the Future* on Dr. Henry Lerner's Web site mentioned previously.

Drills for Obstetric Emergencies

Safety is enhanced when all team members know what to do during other common obstetric emergencies such as nonreassuring fetal heart rate patterns, emergent Caesarean birth, postpartum hemorrhage, and neonatal resuscitation. Routine drills for these emergent clinical situations have been recommended by JCAHO.[62] Although there are no specific recommendations for how to conduct drills, these basic suggestions may be useful:

- Develop pocket cue cards with clinical algorithms for intrauterine resuscitation, shoulder dystocia, emergent Caesarean birth, and postpartum hemorrhage.
- Use the clinical algorithm for neonatal resuscitation as outlined.[63]
- Use a scribe or video to record during each drill so that team member roles and organization can be reviewed retrospectively as a basis for planning for improvement.
- Debrief after actual emergencies, comparing care provided with the clinical algorithms.
- Pay particular attention to team communication and timely response.
- Develop a list of everything that went well and things that could have been done better.
- Use the list as a basis for interdisciplinary discussion concerning what the perinatal team needs to do should a similar clinical situation occur in the future.

··········

CONCLUSION

The risk manager is encouraged to facilitate implementation of principles that will enhance perinatal safety. The specific approaches discussed in this chapter can both improve safety and reduce liability for obstetric providers and organizations.

Endnotes

1. Jury Verdict Research, (2004). Current awards trends in personal injury. Horsham, PA: Author.

2. American College of Obstetricians and Gynecologists, (2004). 2003 ACOG survey of professional liability. Washington, DC: Author.

3. *Ibid.*

4. *Ibid.*

5. Jury Verdict Research. *op. cit.,* (2004). Current awards.

6. Wu, A. W. (2000). "Medical error: The second victim." *British Medical Journal,* 320(7237), 726–727.

7. Knox, G. E., K. R. Simpson, and K. E. Townsend. "High reliability perinatal units: Further observations and a suggested plan for action." *Journal of Healthcare Risk Management,* 2003 23(4), 17–21.

8. McFerran, S., J. Nunes, D. Pucci, and A. Zuniga. "Perinatal patient safety project: A multicenter approach to improve performance reliability at Kaiser Permanente." *Journal of Perinatal & Neonatal Nursing.* 2005. 19(1):37–45.

9. Jury Verdict Research *op. cit.,*. (2004). Current awards.

10. Knox, G. E. and K. R. Simpson. "Teamwork: The fundamental building block of high reliability organizations and patient safety." In B. Youngberg & M. J. Hatlie (Eds.). *The patient safety handbook.* Chicago, IL: American Hospital Association, 2003.

11. Rolph, J. E. "Merit rating for physicians malpractice premiums: Only a modest deterrent." *A Rand Note* (N-3426-MT/RWJ/RC). Rand Corporation, Santa Monica, CA, 1991. Sexton, B. Safety Attitude Questionnaire (SAQ). 2001. Available at: [www.qualityhealthcare.org].

12. Sloan, F. A., P. M. Mergenhagen, W. B. Burfield, R. R. Bovbjerg, and M. Hassan. "Medical malpractice experience of physicians." *Journal of the American Medical Association,* 1989. 262(23), 3291–3297.

13. Knox, Simpson. Teamwork, *op. cit.*

14. Merriam-Webster Online Dictionary, accessed January 26, 2006.

15. Knox, Simpson. Teamwork, *op. cit.*

16. Knox, G. E., K. R. Simpson, and T. J. Garite. "High reliability perinatal units: An approach to the prevention of patient injury and medical malpractice claims." *Journal of Healthcare Risk Management,* 1999. 19(2), 24–32.

17. American Academy of Pediatrics & American College of Obstetricians and Gynecologists. (2002). *Guidelines for perinatal care* (5th ed.). Elk Grove Village, IL: Author.

18. Schofield, L. M. "Perinatal staffing and the nursing shortage: Challenges and principles-based strategies." (Practice Monograph.). 2003, Washington, DC: Association of Women's Health, Obstetric and Neonatal Nurses.

19. Reason, J. T. "Understanding adverse events: The human factor." In C. Vincent (Ed.). *Clinical risk management.* London, UK: BMJ Books, 2001.

20. Simpson, K. R. & G. E. Knox. "Strategies for developing an evidence-based approach to perinatal care.) *MCN The American Journal of Maternal Child Nursing*, 1999. 24(3), 122–132.

21. Simpson, K. R., and G. E. Knox. "Common areas of litigation related to care during labor and birth: Recommendations to promote patient safety and decrease risk exposure." *Journal of Perinatal and Neonatal Nursing*, 2003, 17(1), 94–109.

22. Simpson, K. R., and G. E. Knox. "Essential criteria to promote safe care during labor and birth." *AWHONN Lifelines*. 2005, 9(6).

23. Joint Commission on Accreditation of Healthcare Organizations. Preventing infant death and injury during delivery. 2004. (Sentinel Event Alert No. 30.). Oak Brook, IL: Author.

24. Simpson, Knox. Essential criteria to promote safe care, *op. cit.*

25. Knox, et al. High reliability perinatal units, *op. cit.*

26. Sexton, J. B., E. J. Thomas, R. L. Helmreich, T. B. Neilands, K. Rowan, K. Vella, J. Boyden, and P. R. Roberts. Frontline assessments of healthcare culture: Safety Attitudes Questionnaire norms and psychometric properties. Technical Report 04-01. 2001, The University of Texas Center of Excellence for Patient Safety Research and Practice AHRQ Grant # 1PO1HS1154401.

27. Reason. Understanding adverse events, *op. cit.*

28. *Ibid.*

29. JCAHO. Preventing infant death, *op. cit.*

30. *Ibid.*

31. Simpson, K. R. "Handling handoffs safely." *MCN The American Journal of Maternal Child Nursing*. 2005. 30(2), 152.

32. Simpson, K. R. "Failure to rescue: Implications for evaluating quality of care during labor and birth." *Journal of Perinatal & Neonatal Nursing*. 2005. 19(1), 23–33.

33. Will, S. B. K. Hennicke, L. Jacobs, L., O'Neill, and C. Raab. (in press). "The perinatal patient safety nurse: A new role to promote safe care for mothers and babies." *Journal of Obstetric, Neonatal and Gynecologic Nursing*. 35(3).

34. Simpson, K. Essential criteria to promote safe care, *op. cit.*

35. National Institute of Child Health and Human Development Research Planning Workshop: Electronic fetal heart rate monitoring: Research guidelines for interpretation (1997). *American Journal of Obstetrics and Gynecology*, 177(6), 1385–1390 and (1997). *Journal of Obstetric, Gynecologic and Neonatal Nursing*, 26(6) 635–640.

36. American College of Obstetricians and Gynecologists. (2005). Intrapartum fetal heart rate monitoring. (Practice Bulletin No. 62). Washington, DC: Author.

37. Association of Women's Health, Obstetric and Neonatal Nurses. (2005). Fetal heart monitoring principles and practices. Washington, DC: Author.

38. Fox, M., S. Kilpatrick, T. King, and J. T. Parer. "Fetal heart rate monitoring: Interpretation and collaborative management." *Journal of Midwifery and Women's Health*. 2000. 45(6), 498–507.

39. ACOG, Intrapartum fetal heart rate monitoring, *op. cit.*

40. Simpson, K. R. and D. C. James. "Effects of immediate versus delayed pushing during second-stage labor on fetal well-being: A randomized clinical trial." *Nursing Research*. 2005. 54(3), 149–157.

41. Fox. Fetal heart rate monitoring, *op. cit.*

42. American Academy of Pediatrics & American Heart Association. (2002). Textbook of neonatal resuscitation. Chicago, IL: Author.

43. American College of Obstetricians and Gynecologists (1999). Induction of labor. (Practice Bulletin No. 10). Washington, DC: Author.

44. American College of Obstetricians and Gynecologists. (2003). Dystocia and augmentation of labor. (Practice Bulletin No. 49).Washington, DC: Author.

45. Simpson, K. R. Cervical ripening and induction and augmentation of labor. (Practice Monograph). 2002. Washington, DC: Association of Women's Health, Obstetric and Neonatal Nurses.

46. *Ibid.*

47. *Ibid.*

48. *Ibid.*

49. Hansen, S. L., S. L. Clark, and J. C. Foster. "Active pushing versus passive fetal descent in the second stage of labor: A randomized controlled trial." *Obstetrics and Gynecology*, 2002. 99(1), 29–34.

50. Roberts, J. E. "The 'push' for evidence: Management of the second stage." *Journal of Midwifery and Women's Health*. 2002. 47(1), 2–15.

51. Simpson, K. R. and D. C. James. "Efficacy of intrauterine resuscitation techniques in improving fetal oxygen status during labor." *Obstetrics and Gynecology*. 2005. 105(6), 1362–1368.

52. Roberts, "The 'push' for evidence," *op. cit.*

53. Association of Women's Health, Obstetric and Neonatal Nurses. Nursing management of the second stage of labor. (Evidence based clinical practice guideline). Washington, DC, 2000.

54. *Ibid.*

55. ACOG Practice Bulletin No. 54, July 2004.

56. ACOG Practice Bulletin No. 5, July 1999.

57. ACOG Bulletin No. 54, July 2004, *op. cit.*

58. American Academy of Pediatrics, American College of Obstetricians and Gynecologists, Guidelines for Perinatal Care, Fourth Edition, 1997, p. 112.

59. LMS Medical Systems, Inc. Press release, LMS Announces Clinical Breakthrough in Predicting Key Obstetrical Challenge, June 21, 2005, Montreal, Quebec Available at:[www.lmsmedical.com/4105/pdf/PR_June%2021_Dystocia.pdf] or [www.lmsmedical.com].

60. Lerner, Henry, MD, of Harvard Medical School "Shoulder Dystocia Information" [at www.shoulderdystociainfo.com/index.htm].

61. LMS Medical Systems, Inc. Press release, *op. cit.*

62. *Ibid.*

63. Simpson & James, Efficacy of intrauterine resuscitation, *op. cit.*

14

Pediatric Risk Management

David Stallings
Jeff Sconyers

P
ediatric patients are one of the most vulnerable populations cared for by the health care professional. This chapter will identify and analyze key risks that pertain to this "at risk" class of patients, and will examine strategies to enhance safety and reduce liability.

CLINICAL ISSUES

Although pediatric patients are often small people, they are not also little adults. There is significant risk associated with inappropriate modification of adult treatment approaches for pediatric patients. Also, providers must have age-specific training in their specialties.

Age and Size-Specific Clinical Needs

Highly skilled adult cardiologists usually know very little about congenital malformations of the heart seen in infants or children. Even within the ranks of pediatric specialists, there may be a range of expertise. Some are highly skilled in conditions affecting the neonate, while others specialize in adolescent medicine, and so on.

The awarding of medical staff pediatric privileges must provide for a process that ensures that the provider's skill level is suited to the care that they deliver. Any need for supplemental training and practice should be identified and addressed immediately. The same principle applies to nurses and other allied health care professionals who care for children.

It might also be desirable, in pediatrics more than any other specialty, to delineate circumstances under which consultation is required for specific diagnoses and procedures. Similarly, if a facility lacks practitioners skilled in managing the particular condition of a given patient, it might be wise to transfer the patient to a pediatric facility that can manage that condition (referral center) rather than attempt care without needed expertise. The common sense exception is emergency care, which is necessary to save the patient's life. However, once a complex critical pediatric patient in a non-tertiary setting is stabilized, transfer should be considered.

One of the most obvious differences between adult and pediatric patients is simple: it is size. Health care providers and organizations entrusted to care for children must ensure that they have on hand and use the right supplies and equipment to provide needed care. Beds, ventilators, endotracheal tubes, thermometers, surgical instruments, infusion pumps, and casting supplies are just some of the many products that must be sized to the patient receiving care. And of course, within the pediatric population, there also is great variation, from the 500-gram neonate to the 200-pound adolescent. The special size issues associated with pediatric care make it more complicated to protect the patient from equipment-related injury. However, this issue must be addressed to promote safety and avoid medical malpractice cases with the potential for substantial damages.

Communication with Pediatric Patients

"Age-specific competencies" of providers are required by JCAHO and other regulators. Arguably, pediatric communication skills should be considered an age-specific competency. The ability to communicate with pediatric patients, and to facilitate their participation in their own care, is an important therapeutic measure that also reduces risk. Effective communication enhances the quality and substance of the pediatric provider's physical assessment. It also enables the practitioner to present information in a way that helps children understand what to expect and prepare themselves for their treatment.

The amount of information that can be shared, and the timeframe required, varies according to age level. For example, techniques involving storytelling and playtime provide the best possible comfort level for some young patients, while still imparting significant information. Simply developing rapport with children can help make them more amenable to the things that need to be done to treat their illness.

Particular challenges are presented by infants and toddlers, two groups with limited ability to communicate. Providers must find ways to elicit the information they need. Infants might exhibit auditory and visual clues when they are experiencing painful stimuli; however, the clues may be non-specific. For toddlers who have not yet developed significant language skills or are hard to understand, providers must rely on parents to help them assess what a child may be trying to express. This puts pediatric practitioners at a significant disadvantage, when compared with other providers who deal with adolescent and adult patients.

The child's parents can provide important assistance to the provider trying to assess the patient's communication, and they can provide additional information about particular behaviors and vocalizations. However, cases often arise in which the parents are not sure what is wrong and cannot provide more information. In situations with limited information, the provider must rely on a thorough clinical assessment, and age-specific skills in this regard become invaluable. Particularly important are skills that facilitate assessment of pain, and correct interventions to address the pain of pediatric patients. In general, many facilities are finding that the assistance of child life specialists who routinely see pediatric patients can also help in assessing communication.

Communication with Parents, Guardians, and Families

Pediatric facilities often employ the concept of family-centered care, which recognizes that the family is an integral part of the patient's life, and a critical factor in helping the patient manage illness. Parents or guardians who are present should be woven into the ongoing activities that surround the patient's care, once providers determine how involved these individuals want to be. Most parents are anxious when their child is hospitalized. Informing and assisting them to participate in a satisfactory level of care can be helpful from several perspectives. For example, helping parents or guardians understand treatment plans and giving them an opportunity to ask questions promotes dialogue that can enhance the quality of care. Knowledgeable parents might, for example, detect deviations from the expected course of recovery, or the care plan, and raise good questions. Keeping the parents informed on an ongoing basis also naturally keeps expectations realistic and reduces the chance of misunderstanding about the course of treatment. Finally, teaching the parent or guardian about treatments the child might require at home is an important step in effective discharge planning.

Of particular importance, the parent or guardian who is with the patient all the time can play a significant role in patient safety. Here are some ways that properly informed parents or guardians can help maintain a safe environment of care:

- Keep crib or bed rails up when they are not actively interacting with the patient.
- Notify the assigned nurse when they will be leaving the patient unattended.
- Know the importance of hand hygiene and avoid visiting when they are sick.
- Know and follow whatever isolation restrictions are in effect, and make sure that care providers do the same, and as noted previously.
- Speak up and ask questions when a care provider is doing something that differs from the discussed plan, or when something just doesn't seem right.

It is particularly important that staff members let parents and guardians know that they are expected to speak up and to overcome any hesitation they might have about questioning providers.

Several additional points pertaining to security and accountability that are necessary for staff to explain to parents:

- Parents must wear facility-approved or -sponsored identification tags and abide by the facility's security policies.
- Parents are expected to respect the needs of other patients and families, and therefore must respect quiet hours and avoid disruptive behavior.
- Parents must not bring in weapons, liquor, or illicit drugs.
- Parents must support facility policies designed to protect patients and staff.
- Parents who stay overnight must be aware that the nursing staff is responsible for checking on the patient at all hours.

It might help to develop an outline of these principles as a basis for teaching the parents.

One challenge associated with involving parents in care, may be maintaining the necessary privacy for the patient. Pediatric patients often have many family members and friends visiting, so providers need to be cognizant of the effect of large groups on the child's well-being and on the expectations of parents or guardians regarding privacy.

Privacy can also be challenging when there are two (or more) patients to a room. Providers must work through such issues on a case-by-case basis. Keeping the parents informed of their efforts may ease any tension about a semi-private room.

Sleeping Position[1]

The sleeping position of an infant is a very important safety factor. It is general public knowledge that infants sleeping prone, or on their stomachs, are at risk for sudden infant death syndrome (SIDS). In 1992, the American Academy of Pediatrics (AAP) recommended that infants sleep in the supine position to reduce of the risk of SIDS. Since that time, epidemiological evidence and infant mortality statistics show that the United States' SIDS rate has fallen markedly. The possible cause of SIDS has to do with the fact that prone patients may rebreathe exhaled air, a phenomenon has been shown to cause ventilatory compromise and death. Sleeping in the prone position has also been linked to changes in cardiovascular and arousal responses in infants. Another unrelated potential cause of SIDS is hyperthermia due to excess bedclothes or room temperature.

The supine position should be used during sleep until the infant is developmentally able to independently roll out of supine. At that point, the infant should go to sleep in the supine position and be allowed to assume a preferred sleep position. Although the supine position is the recommended position for healthy infants, there are certain exceptions to this rule, including:

- Any preterm infant with signs of respiratory distress such as increased work of breathing, apnea, or tacypnea may be benefited by the prone position.
- Prone positioning provides a respiratory and developmental advantage for asymptomatic very low birth weight preterm infants (less than 1250 grams).
- Infants with known or suspected airway obstruction may benefit from prone positioning.
- Infants on assisted ventilation may benefit from prone positioning.
- Children with birth defects in which supine sleep would be contraindicated, such as neural tube defects and Robine Malformation Sequence, clearly benefit from sleeping prone.
- Infants receiving phototherapy also benefit from being in the prone position.
- Infants with severe gastroesophageal reflux may also respond positively to prone positioning.

Parents of infants fitting any of the above categories need training to understand the rationale behind the exceptional positioning recommendations.

Also, whereas the supine position may be generally recommended for sleeping, prone and side-lying positioning for infants during supervised awake periods helps to promote development of symmetrical head control and age-appropriate motor skills. It may also reduce the risk of skull deformity (positional brachycephaly or plagiocephaly).

In addition to the sleeping position of the infant, suitable bedding materials are another important safety factor. Infants should be dressed warmly while avoiding overheating. Blankets or other bedding materials might provide warmth, but they should not cover the infant above the chest or shoulders. This prevents any accidental pulling of the covers over an infant's face during movement, which is dangerous because the covers might trap air that the infant will be forced to rebreathe.

Use of Restraints

As is required by JCAHO and other regulatory bodies, an important goal of any facility is to minimize the use of restraints and to maximize the patient's health and safety when restraints must be used. Restraints should be used only in behavioral emergencies when there is an imminent risk of physical harm to the patient or others (including staff members). They may also be judiciously used to protect a patient from injury. Any use of restraints requires clear indications, considered in the light of reasonable alternatives, and accompanied by safe application, and routine monitoring and reassessment.

Medication Administration

Pediatric medication errors can be devastating in outcome, because harm to patients can affect them for many years afterward. Certain factors also make pediatric patients more susceptible to medication errors. It is critical that drugs be prescribed based on the patient's age, weight, and body surface area. Weight of a child, especially a small child, can change rapidly, so it is essential that medication dosage be based on a recent weight, and that the patient's weight is routinely assessed and documented. A single system of measurement should be used to assess pediatric weight, preferably metric. Grave errors can occur when English units are confused with metric or vice versa. In addition, other factors such as the child's ability to absorb or excrete medication can have a significant effect. A child that is premature might have different functioning levels than does a normal newborn. This could alter the effect of the drug and therefore its dosage.

The calculation of a pediatric dose is another critical factor. As information on pediatric indications, dosage, and required monitoring is limited, the pediatric practitioner who prescribes a traditionally adult medication might be forced to calculate dosage based on physiologic factors, without any supporting research or literature. Another concern is that such drugs are often manufactured in a dose or form that is unsuitable for pediatric patients, making it necessary to cut tablets in half, or crush pills so that pediatric patients can ingest them.

Certain pediatric illnesses occur rarely in comparison to the incidence affecting the adult population, therefore there is a smaller market for manufacturers to serve. Thus, it is expected that drug development will continue to focus on the adult, rather than on the pediatric patient. Pediatric providers must continually seek ways to reduce prescribing and administration errors. One technological resource which can be extremely helpful, if implemented correctly, is a computer physician-provider order entry (CPOE) system. (Please see Chapter 6 in this volume for more information on CPOE and medication error management.)

Patient Role in Medication Administration

Two issues related to medication administration may affect the pediatric facility. The first is that patients or parents may request that medications from home be administered. Some facilities allow such use when the medication is not on their formulary and an alternative cannot be arranged in a timely manner. Other facilities prohibit it.

If such medications are to be allowed, then the organization should have a protocol requiring that the pharmacist inspect the medication and approve its use during an inpatient stay. Such use should be supported by a current written physician order. Under all scenarios, medication reconciliations should be done at admission and discharge.

Generally, the following criteria must be met before home medication use should be allowed: Only medications that can be positively identified by the pharmacist are permitted. This means that tablets and capsules with an imprint code and manufacturer's name or emblem must be identifiable. Liquid medications must be contained in a properly sealed original manufacturer's container. The pharmacist will inspect the prescription label and the container. The medication will not be used if there is any concern about cleanliness, storage, or contents of the medications.

Once a product is identified, it should be labeled by the hospital pharmacist as approved. There are some exceptions that should be considered. The facility may allow research patients on investigational drugs to supply their own medications, because investigational drugs might not have identifying imprints and thus might not be identifiable to a pharmacist. The research drug may be used if, in a pharmacist's judgment, it meets requirements for cleanliness, storage, and content. Another potential exception may apply to drugs available in other countries, but not in the United States. Both exceptions require that a medical practitioner provider writes an authorizing order.

Another issue involving the patient or family member's role is that they may ask to self-administer medications while the child is an inpatient, rather than relying on the hospital staff. The clinical care team should determine whether the request is acceptable. If so, the nurse or pharmacist should instruct the patient or non-staff caregiver about the indication for the medication, dosage form, administration route, frequency, side effects, and objective ways to monitor the effectiveness of the medication. This instruction should be documented in the medical record. The caregiver's technique should also be assessed through observation. When the non-staff member administers the medication, they should advise the nursing staff, who will document that the medication was administered by this individual.

Psychiatric Patients

Facilities that serve pediatric psychiatric patients and hospital emergency rooms that potentially manage such patients must evaluate their physical and clinical environment(s) and implement any interventions needed to reasonably ensure safe care while protecting other patients, staffs, and property. Depending on age and specific diagnosis, pediatric psychiatric patients can be both strong and volatile. Emotional outbursts can therefore result in harm to other patients, the patients themselves, or staff members. Property is also at risk, as these patients might be capable of damaging walls, furnishings, and equipment.

Additional clinical staffing might be needed to manage this population. Some facilities use a sitter who is trained to work with psychiatric patients to keep the patient safe and free other clinical personnel to care for other patients. Some emergency settings that see an influx of acute pediatric psychiatric patients have also implemented seclusion areas for these patients. Although seclusion might benefit the patient therapeutically, it does not reduce the need for monitoring. Also, any seclusion area must allow such monitoring and be routinely screened for risk such as projections from the ceiling that patients might use to hang themselves, and so on.

In general, all patient care areas that see pediatric psychiatric patients must be made as safe as possible by eliminating objects that the patients might use to harm themselves and by using materials that are hard to destroy.

....

ENVIRONMENTAL SAFETY

Obstetric and neonatal facility personnel work hard to establish precautions that will prevent infant abduction. Pediatric facilities face a broader range of potential scenarios, because pediatric patients are vulnerable to abduction at any age. In general, abductors are more likely be non-custodial parents or other family members known to the staff than a stranger. Therefore protection of pediatric patients is complicated by the need to be alert to potentially deceptive intent on the part of the child's family.

Infant and Child Abduction and Patient Elopement

The possibility of abduction varies with the type of facility. To some degree, the level of risk depends on whether the facility is a dedicated pediatric operation or simply a health care setting with a maternity ward and newborn nursery or small pediatric unit.

Risk management professionals must work with safety and security and the clinical staff to determine where their vulnerabilities are and how to minimize or alleviate them. Basic issues that should be examined include: 1) access to and from the facility; 2) methods to control and secure entrances such as proximity card readers; 3) video surveillance; 4) staff, parent, and visitor identification; 5) patient identification band products that alert the staff if the patient leaves a designated area.

In addition, facilities may require infants and toddlers to be transported only in transport devices rather than by carrying them. If such an approach is implemented, staff members and family must be educated accordingly. Routine mock abduction drills for pediatric staff are important to help them maintain ability to manage this frightening situation. It is also very important that the staff knows what to do if a patient is actually taken. Mock drills related to abduction follow-up are also worthy of consideration.

Another potential risk that is more likely to pertain to the older pediatric patients is patient elopement, for example, leaving the facility without parental supervision or against medical advice. Adolescents are particularly vulnerable, because they might long to get a "break" from treatment. Younger children may run or simply get separated from their parents in clinic areas, lobbies, elevators, cafeterias, and other public areas. Facilities need mechanisms to alert staff to a lost child situation and to mobilize a timely search for the child. The same response mechanism should be used consistently for all events, because it is not often immediately clear whether the child has run away, gotten lost, or been abducted. In the worst case scenario, a child or abductor can leave the facility grounds quickly, necessitating an immediate and satisfactory response.

Patients and Parents Who are Sexual Offenders

In a facility that works with a large pediatric population, it is possible that the risk management professional and staff may occasionally see a pediatric patient who is a registered sex offender. Some of these patients may be identified at the outset because they are being admitted from a juvenile detention facility, and the detention facility should clearly share such information with the health care organization to ensure that pertinent safety issues are addressed. However, for those patients admitted from home, it is unlikely that the health care setting will receive any warning about the patient's status. Because it is important to know about sex offender status, and any other propensity that the patient has for violence, it is important for clinicians who perform the admitting assessment to ask the patient and parent or guardian whether there are any security issues that might create safety or security issues for the patients themselves or anyone else at the facility. Documentation that this question has been raised may later help to refute any allegation that the facility did not exercise due diligence concerning protection of other patients or staff.

Once a patient is confirmed to be a registered sex offender, reasonable precautions may include placing the patient in a private room. While it is possible to use a bracelet monitoring device that tracks the patients when they leave their rooms, this does not prevent undesirable behavior. The use of a trained sitter may more effectively assure that other patients and staff are not affected by the patient's presence.

A related situation arises when a patient's parent or relative is a sexual offender. Information about the status of these individuals usually comes from one of the parents through the admission or psycho-social assessment. These situations are sometimes addressed preemptively because the offender may be judicially limited by restraining orders, probation-related provisions, and so on, from being near children. In this case, security must be notified of the identity of such individuals, and they should be barred from the institution. Where the parent is a sexual offender, but whose presence might be therapeutically valuable to the child, clinicians, the security staff and the risk management professional may devise an approach that allows supervised visitation. Clinical providers should be trained about how to identify and manage such situations, and they should understand how to access resources who can help determine a rational approach that is beneficial and safe for patients and the organization.

Another issue of concerns for the safety of the pediatric patient is the admitted adult patient who is a sexual offender or sexual pedophile. Every precaution must be taken to ensure that these patients have no access to the pediatric population of patients. The use of private rooms, monitoring devices, sitters, and limited access to pediatric areas are all ways to minimize the potential for contact. The staff needs to be made aware of the admission of such people and their potential whereabouts. They should be accompanied when off their assigned floor for any reason and not be left to wander or have free access to the hospital.

Infection Control

Infection control is both important and challenging for the pediatric staff. Special considerations include the need to educate parents who are sometimes with their children continually, and visitors who might want to hold or feed a child, about infection control. In particular, staff should educate all family and visitors about the importance of handwashing, and the frequency and technique with which hands should be cleaned. Parents also need to be informed about the risks of transmitting infectious disease to the patient, if they are ill. Staff should be alert to the potential of infection from sick family members or visitors, and should be prepared to ask them not to visit the child if they may be contagious. Finally, the staff should educate parents as to what to do if they come in contact with the child's infectious waste.

Balloons, Flowers, and Plants

Friends and family often want to bring flowers, plants, and particularly balloons to cheer a child. Flowers and plants might help infection spread, and so many facilities limit their presence. They are typically not allowed in intensive care units, hematology or oncology units or clinics, or in any room occupied by an immunocompromised patient. Parents and other visitors should be advised to check with the staff before they purchase flowers or plants.

Latex balloons in particular can create several problems for the pediatric patient. Latex balloons affect those who have latex allergies, and they also present a potential choking hazard for children when deflated or popped. Children who chew or suck on deflated balloons can aspirate them, choke, and even die. Balloons and other soft objects that potentially conform to the shape of a child's airway are especially dangerous because they cannot be removed by the Heimlich maneuver. Children therefore should not be allowed to continue playing with a balloon that has popped or deflated.

According to the American College of Allergy, Asthma and Immunology,[2] at least 1 percent of the American population is allergic to latex. About 10–15 percent of health care workers may be allergic to latex, from their frequent exposure to latex gloves. Because latex balloons pose risk of exposure through touch, or by releasing rubber particles into the air, many health care facilities have banned them.

Mylar balloons are a safer alternative to latex balloons, because they eliminate both the risk of latex allergy and aspiration. Many hospitals have chosen to stock only mylar balloons in their gift shops. The staff must still be vigilant, however, to the possibility that latex balloons will be brought into the facility by visitors or family members. The security staff and others based at the entrance should be trained to intercept anyone who brings latex balloons into the facility, and explain the policy to them. Facilities can also proactively contact local flower and balloon vendors with information about their policy. However, this approach can be difficult because of the large number of potential vendors, so the most important strategy is for the staff to be vigilant about such items.

Pets in the Hospital

Many facilities have policies that allow visits from service animals (an animal that is trained to do work or perform tasks for the benefit of a person with a disability) and animal-assisted activities such as pet therapy. All such policies must address infection control issues such as the need for hand hygiene, and so on. Reasonable expectations and limitations must be established and monitored. Facility environmental services should also be prepared to manage animal urination, defecation, and vomiting.

In addition to hygiene requirements, it is essential that the behavior of a service or pet therapy animal be the responsibility of the owner or handler. The animal must be trained and controlled to permit the staff to care for the patient and work in the room. The facility should establish reasonable limits on where the animal can go within the premises, for example, pet therapy animals may visit only certain units. If the animal is disruptive or presents a risk to other patients, hospital staff, or property, the animal should be removed immediately.

It is generally a good practice to obtain the consent of the physician and the bedside nurse before a pet therapy animal's visit, to make sure that the child's condition will allow them to participate, to validate that the child is not afraid of the animal, to ensure the child is not allergic to pet dander, and so on. In addition, the hospital staff should accompany the handler to make sure that the visit goes as planned, and that each patient or family member performs hand hygiene at the end of the visit.

If the family asks to bring the patient's pet in for a visit, the same criteria should apply as to service animals and pet therapy animals. Additional points to consider include common sense issues such as size, consideration of other patients, and so on.

Allowable Toys and Cleaning Toys[3]

The toys that parents, relatives, and friends may bring to the child in a pediatric setting introduce additional risk issues. For example, some toys create a choking or digestive hazard for small children. Toys not suitable for children under three include small cars and planes, mini-animals, wind-up toys, bubbles, and games with small pieces. Such items might create a choking hazard for children in this age range, who often put things in their mouths. If plush or stuffed toys have buttons or eyes that can be chewed off, they might create similar problems. Most plush toys are marked by the manufacturer as to age appropriateness. Staff must be vigilant about the type of toys brought in to cheer the child up, and educate family members and visitors as necessary about pertinent safety concerns.

Another toy-related concern involves devices with portable radio transmitters (for example, radio- or remote-controlled toys) that can cause electromagnetic interference. Such interference might cause biomedical equipment malfunction, and restrictions similar to those that pertain to cell phones should apply.

Yet another toy-related issue is infection control. Playrooms in hospital waiting areas, in pediatric units, and in physicians' offices are particularly high risk environments in this regard. To make these services safe for patients, facilities need to have adequate procedures for checking the serviceability of all toys, proper storage for unused toys, and cleaning and maintenance of all clean toys.

With regard to infection control, it is important that toys that contain fabric or cloth (material) such as chenille, velvet, and fur are not shared between patients, and that they should be discarded after the patient leaves the facility, or if suitable, given to the patient to take home. Shared toys should be made of materials that are easy to clean, such as hard plastic, vinyl, metal, finished wood, and so on.

Before buying toys, games, and so on, facilities should work with their infection control practitioners to determine whether the materials they are made of can be cleaned, once they have been contaminated with moist body substances such as saliva, respiratory secretions, urine, stool, blood, and so on. If they can be cleaned, it is also, of course, important to know what cleaning agent and method should be used. Procedures should be developed and distributed to the areas controlling the toys. Any items being evaluated for purchase should also be checked to see that they do not represent a choking or digestive risk, as noted previously regarding concerns about toys for small children.

Crib Tops, Canopy Beds, and Side Rails

Parents of toddlers know that sometimes it can be hard to keep their children in the bed. When a child is in the hospital, adequate sleeping arrangements need to be made to keep the child safe. One solution is to use crib tops or canopy beds that will not allow the child to get out of bed unassisted. These beds help protect the patient from falls and also prevent wandering, and thus help the staff avoid using restraints.

If a facility does not have beds to prevent falling and wandering, it might be necessary to engage a sitter to protect the patient. If a family member who is staying with the patient around the clock is to prevent them from falling or getting out of bed unassisted, the staff must communicate this expectation, and document the discussion with the parent, including their agreement. Parents or guardians in such circumstances should be specifically instructed to alert the facility staff whenever they will be leaving the child alone, even for a short period of time.

Side rails are important safety features for both the younger and older pediatric patient. Side rails can help prevent patients from falling or rolling out of bed. It is critical that side rails be kept up. Leaving them down, even for a short time, can lead to a fall. The hospital staff, including volunteers who may interact and play with the patient, must be aware that it is their responsibility to put the rail back up anytime they are not with the child. In addition, the staff should advise the parent or guardian about maintaining this safety feature when they are interacting with the child. All such instructions to the parent must be documented in the medical record.

Other Environmental Hazards

Just as in the child's home, a pediatric facility needs to be "childproofed" to protect the patient, and others, from any negative effects that might result from their natural curiosity. Items that are important to include in such a childproofing inventory include the following.

Electrical Outlets   Children are fascinated with electrical outlets. Some think that this is because outlets are near their eye level, drawing the child's attention to them. Although the chance of electrocution is very small, such a result clearly would be devastating. Any related litigation would be indefensible, because there are simple ways to make outlets safe. The facility's bioengineering resources should be knowledgeable about, and facilitate, implementation of child tamper-resistant outlets. It might also be possible simply to reposition the outlets out of reach.

Plastic Bags   As noted on dry cleaning and other plastic bags, they create risk that a child might suffocate if the bag adheres to the patient's nose and mouth. This hazard has been so well publicized that parents should be familiar with it. However, the staff should still be alert to those who might not recognize the risk of bringing toys or clothing for the patient into the facility in a plastic bag, and then leaving it in the patient's room. Staff should remind such individuals about the hazard, and direct them to place any such bags out of reach for the child. They should also be told to remove the bag when they leave. If they do not, the staff should dispose of it.

Needle Boxes, Sharps Containers, and Hazardous Waste   Needles and other sharps used in medical care must be disposed of properly, using an approved disposal container. Pediatric patients create a particular safety issue regarding sharps receptacles, because these containers provide a tempting target if they are within reach of young hands. Sharps containers must thus be mounted at a proper height, and providers in the pediatric setting must be especially cautious to avoid overfilling them. Other hazardous waste should also be placed in suitable containers for pickup and proper disposal. Such containers should be placed in areas that are not accessible to curious children or their parents.

Doors and Stairs   Doors and stairs might also be tempting to a child. Some pediatric facilities place door handles and other opening mechanisms higher than usual to keep them out of reach of young hands. Others increase staffing to provide for close monitoring of external exits. Doors that lead to stairs are associated with particular risk, because stairs are a potential fall hazard for young children. Stairs also might allow patients access to other parts of the facility and even allow them to leave the building. Facilities that work with older children and teens who might want to investigate the floor below or brain-injured or psychiatric patients who might not understand that they are exiting the building may consider installing tracking devices, like the identification bands used to keep elderly patients from wandering in nursing homes.

Medication Storage   There are many potential locations for medication storage besides the pharmacy. These locations include medication rooms, medication carts, treatment room medication cabinets, code carts, and transport boxes, among others. The pharmacy should be responsible for maintaining a list of sanctioned medication storage locations, and items for which drug storage outside the pharmacy is allowed. Medication may also be stored in a patient room either by use of an in-room medication cabinet or within a childproof bedside box. The nursing staff should be responsible for documenting the medications given on the medication administration record. When the patient is discharged, the box should be cleared of the medications, and the medications should be credited to the patient or labeled and sent home as required.

....

PERSONNEL ISSUES

The pediatric provider must undergo annual competency review, like other health care providers, to ensure that providers have the knowledge and skills to provide competent, safe care to patients. Competency requirements should be assessed at least annually for any necessary revisions related to changes in the diagnoses cared for, procedures performed, and ages cared for.

Competency Assessment

There are seven pediatric age ranges that may be appropriate for specific competency delineation, including newborns, infants, toddlers, preschoolers, school age, adolescents, and adults, because many pediatric facilities continue to see patients through the age of twenty-one or beyond for certain conditions.

Lifting Patients   As mentioned earlier, pediatric patients come in all shapes, sizes, and weights. Although the infant or small toddler is easy to lift, staff may also be faced with a six-foot, 250-pound high school football player, or a bariatric patient struggling with obesity issues. Staff risk injury to themselves if they take on the task of moving such patients alone.

The staff should be trained in lifting techniques and related procedures that are in place to minimize injury, and should follow them. Particularly important are the following:

- Staff must be trained to assess the task, determine the resources needed, and request them.

- Two or more staff members should be used when transporting patients in full-size beds or beds that are difficult to maneuver. Use of additional personnel should also be considered when moving or positioning with the following risk factors: limited cognitive abilities and difficulty following verbal directions; history of violence and unpredictable behavior, and recent sedation, including those awakening from anesthesia.

- Facilities should consider obtaining assistive devices such as slider boards and ceiling lift systems.

- Staff should apply ergonomic principles when moving patients, for example, adjusting the bed or other surface to waist height when working with patients who are lying down.

Background Checks   Health care organizations owe patients a duty to assure them that they have adequately screened the individuals staffing their facilities. To protect the pediatric population, in particular, the organization must avoid having staff with criminal backgrounds caring for patients, especially if the charges against them involve violence or abuse of a child. During the pre-employment process, the facility should perform a criminal background check on all applicants. In addition to checking the local database, the facility should also use a background check service that identifies charges and convictions from other jurisdictions.

To reduce the risk of liability due to inadequately conducted hiring processes, the employment application form must clearly identify those items that prospective employees must disclose to be considered for employment. Applicants who fail to disclose requested background information should automatically be ineligible for hire. Note that convictions do not necessarily bar an applicant from employment. The facility should consider the relationship between the conviction and the duties of the job for which the applicant is applying.

Professional Relationships with Patients and Families   Staff who work with pediatric patients often encounter very compelling and emotional stories. To ensure proper therapeutic relationships, organizations must have policies or guidelines in place to help the staff identify acceptable professional boundaries, and set proper limits on relationships with patients and families. Some guiding principles include the following:

- Provide care only within the scope of one's practice.
- Provide care only within regularly scheduled work hours.
- Provide care and support to patients and families consistently, without preferential treatment.
- Refrain from accepting gifts of significant monetary value from patients and families.
- Do not offer gifts of money or significant financial value to patients or family.
- Refrain from sharing personal information with patients or families, including home phone numbers, addresses, e-mail, and fax.
- Do not engage in romantic, sexual, or intimate physical relationships with any patient, any members of a current patient's family, or any former patients under the age of 18.
- Do not provide foster care or initiate adoption proceedings for patients that you encounter in their role as employees.
- Never transport patients or patients' family members in your personal vehicles.

Staff should understand that some of these actions might result in liability for them and for the organization. Supportive supervisors should help them identify resources that can help patient and family, once the limits of their professional relationship have been reached.

....
SPECIAL ISSUES

Risk management professionals in pediatric health care face the same range of issues, and responses to those issues, as do risk management professionals in adult health care. But these issues deserve special mention regarding their application in the pediatric context.

Informed Consent

Informed consent, although important for patients of all ages, is an extremely important and potentially complex process for a practitioner providing pediatric care. In most adult cases, practitioners can obtain consent directly from the patient. The reverse is true for pediatric patient situations, where, with a few exceptions, such as those that apply to emancipated or mature minors, the provider is usually obtaining consent from a third party. Clearly, practitioners must be diligent in identifying and involving the correct authorized parent or guardian. (Refer to Volume 2, Chapter 4, on Informed Consent.)

Obtaining Consent in a Variety of Family and Social Situations

The pediatric practitioner works with many family situations in which it is challenging to determine the individual who is authorized to give an informed consent. These situations include, but are not limited to: 1) parents who disagree on treatment options; 2) divorced parents; 3) putative fathers; 4) court-appointed custodians or guardians; 5) patients undergoing adoption, and 6) parents who are no more than adolescents themselves. In addition, practitioners might be faced with family members who are caring for the child in the parents' absence, and therefore believe that they have the authority to make health care decisions. Laws regarding who may consent for a child can vary from state to state, so it is essential that practitioners be familiar with the regulations in their jurisdictions.

Such challenging scenarios also make it necessary for the practitioner, office, or hospital staff to address the topic of legal custody when the patient enters the practice or is admitted to the hospital. A copy of any pertinent legal documents should be placed in the medical record.

Emancipated and Mature Minors

Many states allow an adolescent to pursue full legal rights, including the right to make care decisions, when they can show that they are emancipated from their parents or guardians. Minors can demonstrate in several ways that they live, or can live, independent of a parent or guardian. Rules on emancipation vary state by state. For example, depending on the state, a minor can make a case for emancipation through circumstances such as being married, being the parent of a child, serving in the military, or living independently. To obtain an official determination of emancipation, the minor must go through the legal system and receive that determination from the court. Therefore, when patients identify themselves as emancipated minors, the facility staff should request a copy of the court documents to confirm the status. A copy should also be placed in the medical record so the process will not have to be repeated in the future. If no determination exists, the practitioner should consult the risk management professional or hospital counsel to determine whether the minor can be treated as emancipated.

"Mature minor" is a designation that physicians in some states can bestow upon a minor if it is determined that the patient has a level of judgment and reasoning that is sufficient for medical decision-making. The courts in many states have elevated the rights of minors by ruling that minors who are age fourteen and older can consent to certain types of health care treatments. These include drug and alcohol abuse, pregnancy, sexually transmitted diseases, and mental health. Given this legal precedent, it might be desirable to allow minors to consent to other care, if they can show the required maturity level. Practitioners should make sure that they are familiar with the regulations of their particular jurisdiction. If mature minor statutes exist, the clinician should be diligent in assessing minors' ability to understand the treatment options and assessing their decision-making abilities. This should be followed up with explicit documentation regarding what the practitioner relied upon to determine maturity.

In general, the right to obtain treatment goes with the right to have the organization maintain confidentiality of the medical record. Practitioners should be careful to maintain the confidentiality of records of mature minors and should not disclose them to others, including parents, without the minor's consent, or as otherwise permitted or required by law.

Preparing Patients for Approaching Adulthood and Decision-Making

Pediatric practitioners can greatly benefit their adolescent patients by involving them in decision-making with their parents or guardians. Their involvement will build confidence and prepare them for adult decision-making. Without preparation, patients are generally no more ready to make decisions on their eighteenth birthday than they are the day before, when still a minor. Also, as adolescent patients with chronic conditions often continue to be seen in a pediatric system between the ages of eighteen and twenty-one, preparing such patients to make their own decisions assists the entire care team. Involving adolescents in decision-making discussions also helps the parents or guardians, and the patients, better understand each other's points of view. This leads to more collaborative decision-making and increases the accountability of the adolescent patient.

End of Life Decision-Making

End-of-life care creates special issues with pediatric patients. State law will determine whether a minor, of any age, can execute a valid directive to physicians. Such a directive is also known as a living will or durable power of attorney. There is certainly a trend toward allowing older minors to express their wishes about withholding or withdrawing life-sustaining treatment when they are in a terminal condition. Whether the provider can, should, or must follow these wishes varies by state. In addition, it is a matter of state law whether the parents may make their own decision to withhold or withdraw care when a child is in a terminal condition or permanent vegetative state. Some states allow the parents or guardians, acting with the care team, to reach and implement this decision, whereas others require a court hearing, sometimes including appointment of a guardian ad litem. In addition to learning the laws of their state, practitioners might want to consult with their institutional ethics committee for advice in these very difficult situations.

Pediatric Clinical Research and Consent

Pediatric patients and their families have benefited from research over the years. Research led to development of vaccines to combat measles, polio, and other deadly or debilitating diseases that used to strike children. Continued clinical research and development of equipment and pharmaceuticals has led to a marked decrease in pediatric morbidity and mortality.

Despite the significant advances in pediatric care that have come from research, children have not benefited as much as they might have, for several reasons. One is that the numbers of studies involving children have decreased. Another is the difficulty in conducting research on rare diseases, which by definition have few patients to participate. In some cases, clinicians must treat pediatric patients with drugs that were developed through adult studies, without specific and substantive information about pediatric dosages or effects. Community awareness of this lack of pediatric research-based information has recently led to increased funding, as academic medical centers focus more on this patient population.

Because pediatric patients cannot consent to medical care until they are teenagers, and then only in limited circumstances, informed consent for pediatric research raises important ethical questions. It is of interest that federal regulations governing research create an exception to the common law's general requirement that individuals must achieve the age of majority before they can consent. Specifically, these regulations require "assent" from children involved in research to the extent that they are capable of understanding and providing it.

Assent is considered to be a child's agreement to participate in research. Assent is a nebulous concept, and the age at which a child can give assent is also vague, as federal regulations do not specify a particular age at which assent should be obtained. Researchers should consider a child's age, maturity, and psychological state. Children six years of age can give assent to participate in research. For children, then, agreement to participate in research is a two-step process. First, the child's parents or guardians must consent to have their child involved in research. Only if this occurs can researchers then discuss the research protocol with the child to determine if the child also wants—"assents"—to participate. Although this process is more cumbersome than informed consent issues associated with other research, it provides a framework for making sure that researchers deal with children ethically. (Refer to Volume 2, Chapter 5, on Clinical Research and Institutional Review Boards for more information.)

Protected Health Information—Pediatric Implications of HIPAA

The Health Insurance Portability and Accountability Act (HIPAA), and its related regulations, established federal privacy standards for individually identifiable health information. HIPAA affects all patients, including pediatric patients. Disclosing a child's health information might be necessary for multiple reasons, including the request of a parent or guardian, qualification for services from community resources, program assistance from educational institutions, and so on. Requests for information on pediatric patients should be evaluated to see whether the request is for a purpose for which HIPAA permits disclosure, and whether state privacy and medical record confidentiality regulations apply. When a request for information requires an authorization, the provider, in consultation with the risk management professional or counsel, must determine who may provide a valid authorization for the pediatric patient.

Often, the pediatric patient's parent or guardian will be the proper individual to authorize release of information. However, depending on state laws and regulations, situations might arise in which the patient must provide authorization. Emancipated or mature minors are likely to be included in this group, as it is a general rule that a minor may consent to the release of information pertaining to care that the minor authorized. Such situations might include treatment related to mental health, HIV, sexually transmitted diseases, and so on. Relevant state laws and regulations must be reviewed to clarify the scope of information that may be authorized for release by the minor patient.

Immunizations and the National Childhood Vaccine Injury Act (NCVIA)

Immunizing children is an important part of childhood disease prevention. Diseases such as smallpox, measles, and polio have been greatly reduced or eliminated through vaccine development and administration. The degree to which immunization has become a part of our culture is illustrated by general requirements that children must be immunized before they can attend school. Allegations that adverse outcomes resulted from vaccine administration, however, have created liability-related concerns.

In the 1970s and 1980s, in particular, patients and families were concerned about adverse effects of vaccines while practitioners and manufacturers were concerned about being sued for the adverse events. In some cases, companies ceased to manufacture the vaccines, and shortages resulted. In 1986, Congress, spurred on by these events, enacted the NCVIA (U.S. Code 42 U.S.C. 300), which established the National Vaccine Injury Compensation Program (VICP).

Any patient, parent, or guardian can file a VICP claim if they have experienced particular adverse events, related to several commonly administered vaccines, in a specified timeframe. A claimant must file a claim under this program before suing a manufacturer or practitioner. If the claimant accepts a settlement from the VICP, then a secondary claim against a manufacturer or practitioner cannot be filed. Risk management professionals and practitioners should be aware of this program, to direct patients to applicable resources. Practitioners must also understand their obligations under the program, such as recording certain information in the medical record when a patient receives a vaccine (manufacturer, vaccine, lot number, practitioner who administered the vaccine, and date of administration). In addition, practitioners need to know what adverse events they need to report to the program. The program is a reasonable approach that protects practitioners from lawsuits, and ensures that patients get the immunizations they need.

············

CHILD ABUSE AND NEGLECT

Child abuse and neglect reporting laws have been enacted in every state in the U.S. to deal with the large number of children that are physically, emotionally, and sexually abused each year. Health care providers are mandatory reporters of child abuse, or suspected child abuse, under these laws.

Abuse Reporting

Authorities to whom such reports must be made may include, depending on the state and the circumstances, a child protective services or law enforcement agency, or both. Many professionals are specifically designated as "mandated reporters," for example: audiologists, counselors, coaches, dentists, nurses, pharmacists, phlebotomists, physician assistants, physicians, podiatrists, psychiatrists, psychologists, occupational or physical therapists, optometrists, respiratory therapists, social workers, speech therapists, and so on. Thus, the risk management professional and clinical managers in a health care facility or private practice must be aware of local law and which providers must report. All pertinent staff must then be educated as to their responsibilities.

Health care providers are generally immune from civil or criminal liability when they report or provide testimony in good faith. If they do not report, however, there might be serious professional consequences, including litigation for failure to act and potential loss of licensure. Although it is less likely, failure to report child abuse could also lead to criminal charges against a provider.

Abuse Identification

Pediatric patients who present with abuse or neglect-related injuries might have been admitted for other conditions as seen by the provider or health care facility. It is important for the provider to have a clear set of screening criteria to help determine when additional medical care or review is needed, and when a potential case of child abuse or neglect should be reported. A provider should consider assessing for child abuse or neglect when any of the following conditions are present. Circumstantial criteria include:

- An attending physician or other medical consultant has determined that an injury is not due to an accident.
- The case has been recently referred to child protective services by another community agent, such as another medical center, paramedics, or the police department.
- A parent or caregiver(s) admits to abuse or neglect.
- A witness reports abuse or neglect of the child.
- The child has been exposed to violence of any kind in a living situation.
- There has been delay in seeking medical treatment.
- The pattern of family interaction or involvement does not seem consistent with child's needs.
- The history related to the injury or condition is dubious.

    Clinical criteria include:

- An infant who fails to thrive
- Fracture(s) in patients under the age of two, without sufficient explanation of injury
- Unexplainable bruises, cuts, burns, and so on
- Intracranial or intra-abdominal injury(ies) without sufficient history of accident
- Rectal or vaginal injury with no clear accidental causes
- Drug or toxic injections (prescription drugs, illegal drugs, gasoline) and so on

As these examples illustrate, abuse, neglect, or sexual abuse can look like another condition entirely. The Children's Protection Program at Children's Hospital and Regional Medical Center in Seattle, Washington, has developed a specific list of indicators that identify when an abuse evaluation is warranted. These indicators also specify patient-specific characteristics, and parental or caretaker characteristics, that might raise questions about the presenting problem, and trigger a more in-depth assessment by the provider. (Refer to Tables 14.1–13 for indications for further investigation.)

TABLE 14.1   Physical Abuse ~ General Indicators

Factors, individual or in combination, which suggest that an injury/situation may be the result of abuse:

- **Child's level of development:** It takes a certain stage of development to injure oneself. Judgment should be based on child's own developmental abilities, e.g., any traumatic injury or poisoning of pre-toddlers is considered suspicious.
- **Shape of injury:** Assaults may be inflicted by identifiable objects, e.g., shape of some immersion burns may suggest intentional dunking.
- **Location of injury:** Injuries to thighs, upper arms, genital and rectal areas, buttocks, and back of legs or torso are frequently inflicted.
- **Force to produce injury:** It takes substantial force to cause a bruise that remains visible for more than a few hours. Even more force is needed to break a bone.
- **Type of injury:** It is almost impossible for some injuries to be self-inflicted. Metaphyseal fractures or choke marks on a child's neck are two examples.
- **Number of old and new injuries:** Multiple injuries on various parts of body unlikely to occur in accidents and/or multiple injuries in various stages of healing are indicative of a continuing pattern of assaults. Severe injuries that are untreated or signs of delay in seeking treatment are very concerning.

Reprinted with the Permission of Children's Hospital & Regional Medical Center. Seattle, WA.

TABLE 14.2   Specific Indicators that Warrant an Abuse Evaluation

Specific Indicators that Warrant an Abuse Evaluation	*Medical**	*Psycho Social*	*SCAN Attending*
		SCAN ASSESSMENTS √ = recommended	
Intracranial Bleeding (especially SDH and SAH) in absence of major documented trauma (such as MVAs) or preexisting bleeding disorders in children *3 years old & under*	√	√	√
Altered consciousness plus retinal hemorrhages in children *3 years old & under*	√	√	√
All skull fractures in children *3 years old & under not explained by significant trauma*	√	√	√
Fractures in *preambulatory and preverbal children not explained by significant trauma*	√	√	√
Intraabdominal trauma (bowel perforations, injuries to liver, pancreas or intestines) in absence of documented major trauma such as MVAs in children *of all ages*	√	√	√
Burn injuries Distinctly shaped burns suggesting an object was used to inflict them; cigarette burns; immersion burns suggesting intentional dipping in hot water in children *of all ages*	√	√	√
Rib fractures in children *3 years old & under* (without abnormal bones or documented major trauma)	√	√	√
Bruises Any bruise on a child under *9 months or not cruising,* without documented bleeding disorder	√	√	√
Any bruise with a recognizable pattern; adult bite marks; unusual location; clustered injuries; multiple, apparently inflicted injuries in different stages of healing; injuries on several different body planes in children *of all ages*	√	√	√
Munchausen Syndrome by Proxy Any concern for fictitious illness in a child of *any age* requires a consultation with CA/N Attending and Children's Protection Team	√	√	Required
Any disclosure by child and/or caretaker; statements by witnesses indicating child maltreatment has occurred.	√	√	
Tying, binding and other forms of tortuous confinement	√	√	

*Consider differential diagnosis

Reprinted with the Permission of Children's Hospital & Regional Medical Center. Seattle, WA.

TABLE 14.3   Characteristics of Abuse ~ Child

The following conditions may have any one of a number of organic or environmental causes besides maltreatment and should be evaluated within the context of a comprehensive assessment, which includes the developmental level of the child and parent's response to the child's problems.

| | SCAN ASSESSMENTS $\sqrt{}$ = recommended | | |
Child Characteristics	*Medical**	*Psycho Social*	*SCAN Attending*
Developmental lags (physical, mental or emotional)	$\sqrt{}$	$\sqrt{}$	
Extremes of behavior (excessive compliance and passivity or overly aggressive, demanding, negative, hyperactive)		$\sqrt{}$	
Wary of physical contact with parents or other adults; fears going home Displays hypervigilence		$\sqrt{}$ $\sqrt{}$	
Is clingy and indiscriminate in her/his attachments		$\sqrt{}$	
Overly adaptive behavior (inappropriately adult or inappropriately infantile)		$\sqrt{}$	
Shows no expectation of being comforted; extreme sense of hopelessness		$\sqrt{}$	
Children who have complications with prenatal exposure to **drugs** may be at higher risk for maltreatment because of their physical and neurological impairments		$\sqrt{}$	
Children with chronic illnesses and/or disabilities, particularly those that lead to difficult child behavior, may be at higher risk for maltreatment.		$\sqrt{}$	

*Consider differential diagnosis

Reprinted with the Permission of Children's Hospital & Regional Medical Center. Seattle, WA.

TABLE 14.4   Characteristics of Abuse ~ Parental or Caretaker

| | SCAN ASSESSMENTS $\sqrt{}$ = recommended | | |
Parental or Caretaker Characteristics	*Medical**	*Psycho Social*	*SCAN Attending*
Inappropriate response to seriousness of child's condition	$\sqrt{}$	$\sqrt{}$	$\sqrt{}$
No explanation for injury	$\sqrt{}$	$\sqrt{}$	$\sqrt{}$
Explanations which are at variance with clinical findings	$\sqrt{}$	$\sqrt{}$	$\sqrt{}$
Changing explanations/histories	$\sqrt{}$	$\sqrt{}$	
Concealment of past injuries	$\sqrt{}$	$\sqrt{}$	
Delay in seeking medical help; continuing or gross parental inattentiveness to child's need for safety; indifference to repeated accidents	$\sqrt{}$	$\sqrt{}$	
Hospital and/or physician shopping	$\sqrt{}$	$\sqrt{}$	
Parental limitations (lack of basic parenting and problem solving skills); inappropriate discipline; inflexible and controlling behaviors; frequent crises/chaotic lifestyles, homelessness; lack of consistency to family members and peers; cognitive, developmental or physical limitations	$\sqrt{}$	$\sqrt{}$	
Domestic violence	$\sqrt{}$	$\sqrt{}$	
Substance abuse	$\sqrt{}$	$\sqrt{}$	
Severe mental health problems (major depression, psychosis)	$\sqrt{}$	$\sqrt{}$	
An extended family history of abuse or neglect	$\sqrt{}$	$\sqrt{}$	
Open Child Protective Services case	$\sqrt{}$	$\sqrt{}$	

*Consider differential diagnosis

Reprinted with the Permission of Children's Hospital & Regional Medical Center. Seattle, WA.

TABLE 14.5   Neglect ~ Specific Indicators

Factors, individual or in combination, which suggest that an injury/situation is suspicious

	SCAN ASSESSMENTS √ = recommended		
Specific Indicators that Warrant an Evaluation for Neglect	*Medical**	*Psycho Social*	*SCAN Attending*
Ingestions	√	√	
Near Drownings	√	√	
Failure to Thrive—in absence of causative major medical problems or if family support issues complicate major illnesses	√	√	
Medical Neglect—parent's failure to provide medical, dental or psychiatric care needed to prevent or treat serious physical or psychological injuries or illnesses. It includes failure to provide, consent to, or follow through with: preventative care, such as immunizations, diagnostic care, such as medical exams and hospitalizations, remedial care, such as surgery or regular medication, or prosthetic care, such as eye glasses or an artificial limb. Apparently untreated injuries, illnesses or impairments that suggest medical neglect and failure to make court ordered appointments require medical and psychosocial CA/N assessments. Other missed appointments, treatments, inappropriate medication applications are dependent on acuteness of situation. For some children, a single missed treatment could be fatal.	Assess with social worker. Determine seriousness of consequences for health/safety of child		
Burn injuries of children *3 years old & under*. Medical provider consults with social work regarding child's development and history of injury to decide if SCAN psychosocial interview should take place.	Consult with social worker	Consult with PMD	
Any disclosure by child and/or caretaker; statements by witnesses indicating child **maltreatment** has occurred.	√	√	
Abandonment of child or child left in physically dangerous situation (consider child's age and maturity as well as actual conditions)	√	√	

*Consider differential diagnosis

Reprinted with the Permission of Children's Hospital & Regional Medical Center. Seattle, WA.

TABLE 14.6   Characteristics for Neglect ~ Child

The following conditions may have any one of a number of organic or environmental causes besides neglect and should be evaluated within the context of a comprehensive assessment, which includes the developmental level of the child and parent's response to the child's problems.

	SCAN ASSESSMENTS √ = recommended		
Child Characteristics	*Medical**	*Psycho Social*	*SCAN Attending*
Developmental lags (physical, mental or emotional)	√	√	
Failure to thrive or less severe deficits in growth or development	√	√	
Sudden and severe drops in child's school performance, emotional appearance or general functioning		√	
Delinquency (e.g. thefts)		√	
Exploitation—excessive responsibilities placed on child to care for home and other younger children		√	

*Consider differential diagnosis

Reprinted with the Permission of Children's Hospital & Regional Medical Center. Seattle, WA.

TABLE 14.7   Characteristics for Neglect ~ Parental or Caretaker

The following conditions may have any one of a number of organic or environmental causes besides neglect and should be evaluated within the context of a comprehensive assessment, which includes the developmental level of the child and parent's response to the child's problems.

		SCAN ASSESSMENTS √ = recommended	
Parental or Caretaker Characteristics	*Medical**	*Psycho Social*	*SCAN Attending*
Delay in seeking medical help; continuing or gross parental inattentiveness to child's need for safety; indifference to repeated accidents		√	
Hospital and/or physician shopping		√	
Parental limitations (lack of basic parenting and problem solving skills); inappropriate discipline; inflexible and controlling behaviors;frequent crises/ chaotic lifestyles, homelessness; lack of consistency to family members and peers; cognitive, developmental or physical limitations		√	
Domestic violence		√	
Substance abuse		√	
Severe mental health problems (major depression, psychosis)		√	
An extended family history of abuse or neglect		√	
Open Child Protective Services case		√	

*Consider differential diagnosis

Reprinted with the Permission of Children's Hospital & Regional Medical Center. Seattle, WA.

When in doubt about whether a situation warrants reporting to the local child protective agency, a provider should consider consulting with the particular agency, which should have staff members designated to assist them on such issues. Remember that agency personnel are not obligated to share information, as their first obligation is to solicit potential abuse reporting. However, agency representatives should be able to respond to any of the following questions:

- Whether or not to make a referral to child protective services or law enforcement
- Whether or not a family has a child protective services history
- Whether or not there are differences of opinion regarding the handling of a case
- The protocol for making complaints to an agency
- General questions regarding the policy or philosophy of child protective services
- Where to turn for more specific answers
- Cases from other child protective services offices outside of the local area

This external resource can help the health care team determine how to proceed when they are unsure whether the patient situation involves reportable abuse or neglect. By documenting the attempt at and result of consultation, the provider also minimizes potential liability, because turning to the authorities on questions of reportability is a reasonable approach.

Factitious Disorder, or Munchausen Syndrome by Proxy

According to the *Diagnostic and Statistical Manual of Mental Disorders*—Fourth Edition (DSM-IV),[4] "factitious disorders are characterized by physical or psychological symptoms that are intentionally produced or feigned in order to assume the sick role." It

TABLE 14.8   Characteristics for Emotional Maltreatment—Child

Factors, individual or in combination, which suggest that an injury/situation may be the result of abuse

The following conditions may have any one of a number of organic or environmental causes besides emotional maltreatment and should be evaluated within the context of a comprehensive assessment, which includes the developmental level of the child and parent's response to the child's problems.

| | | *SCAN ASSESSMENTS* | |
| | | √ = recommended | |
Child Characteristics	*Medical**	*Psycho Social*	*SCAN Attending*
Developmental lags (physical, mental or emotional)	√	√	
Failure to thrive or less severe deficits in growth or development	√	√	
Enuresis and/or encopresis	√	√	
Habit disorders (head banging, sucking, rocking, biting)	√	√	
Conduct disorders (antisocial or destructive behaviors)	√	√	
Neurotic traits (sleep disorders, speech disorders, and inhibition of play)	√	√	
Psychoneurotic reactions (hysteria, obsession, compulsion, phobias, hypochondria)		√	
Extremes of behavior (excessive compliance and passivity or overly aggressive, demanding, negative, hyperactive)		√	
Wary of physical contact with parents or other adults; fears going home		√	
Displays hypervigilence		√	
Is clingy and indiscriminate in her/his attachments		√	
Overly adaptive behavior (inappropriately adult or inappropriately infantile)		√	
Sudden and severe drops in child's school performance, emotional appearance or general functioning		√	
Attempted suicide	√	√	
Any disclosure by child and/or caretaker; statements by witnesses indicating child maltreatment has occurred.	√	√	
Abandonment of child or child left in physically dangerous situation (consider child's age and maturity as well as actua conditions)	√	√	

*Consider differential diagnosis

Reprinted with the Permission of Children's Hospital & Regional Medical Center. Seattle, WA.

is hard to believe that someone would feign illness, but affected individuals apparently have such a great need to gain attention, that they subject themselves to unnecessary medical care. Although the condition is more commonly seen in adults than in children or adolescents, and even then affects only a small percentage of the population, practitioners should be aware of the potential that they could have a pediatric patient with factitious disorder.

Factitious disorders are difficult to diagnose. When patients are confronted regarding factitious disorders, they often cease seeing that practitioner and find another practitioner who will provide the attention that they seek. Practitioners may help some of the patients afflicted with this condition if they are able to honestly, but empathically confront the patient.

Another form of factitious disorder exists where an adult, usually a parent, exaggerates or feigns illness of a child, or deliberately causes or exacerbates actual medical problems that the patient is experiencing. This disorder is called factitious syndrome by proxy (sometimes called Munchausen Syndrome by proxy).[5] Sometimes the effects of the feigned illness are minor, but some cases can have tragic outcomes. One example is a

TABLE 14.9   Characteristics for Emotional Maltreatment ~ Parental or Caretaker

	SCAN ASSESSMENTS √ = recommended		
Parental or Caretaker Characteristics	*Medical**	*Psycho Social*	*SCAN Attending*
Inappropriate response to seriousness of child's condition	√	√	
No explanation for injury	√	√	
Explanations which are at variance with clinical findings	√	√	
Changing explanations/histories	√	√	
Concealment of past injuries	√	√	
Delay in seeking medical help; continuing or gross parental inattentiveness to child's need for safety; indifference to repeated accidents	√	√	
Hospital and/or physician shopping		√	
Parental limitations (lack of basic parenting and problem solving skills); inappropriate discipline; inflexible and controlling behaviors; frequent crises/ chaotic lifestyles, homelessness; lack of consistency to family members and peers; cognitive, developmental or physical limitations		√	
Domestic violence		√	
Substance abuse/drug dealing		√	
Severe mental health problems (major depression, psychosis)		√	
Caretaker exhibits psychically destructive behaviors towards child, e.g. extreme rejection, isolation, terrorizing, ignoring o corrupting		√	
Open Child Protective Services case		√	

*Consider differential diagnosis

Reprinted with the Permission of Children's Hospital & Regional Medical Center. Seattle, WA.

TABLE 14.10   Sexual Abuse ~ General Indicators

Factors, individual or in combination which suggest that an injury/situation is suspicious

Signs of sexual activity cannot be automatically interpreted as signs of sexual abuse, but should be further assessed. Even without a disclosure a report to CPS may be necessary. (Refer to Recommended Guidelines for Sexual Assault Emergency Medical Evaluation, Child 12 years and under; Recommended Guidelines for Sexual Assault Emergency Medical Evaluation, Adult and Adolescent)

	SCAN ASSESSMENTS √ = recommended		
General Indicators	*Medical**	*Psycho Social*	*SCAN Attending*
Exam indicative of acute penetrating injury: vaginal bleeding, genital trauma, anal injury	√	√	√
STD—Including GC, CT HPV, herpes, syphilis, HIV, which are recognized beyond the normal age for appearance of perinatally acquired disease; other in non-sexually active patient. When STDs are found in the consensually sexually active patient, consider age and power difference between the two partners to determine whether consent is legitimate.	√	√	√
Exam concerning for sexual abuse e.g. trauma to breast, lower abdomen, thighs, genital/ rectal areas	√	√	√
Presence of semen	√	√	√
Pregnancy	√	√	√
History of sexual assault/abuse and/or any disclosure by child and/or caretaker; statements by witnesses indicating child maltreatment has occurred.	√	√	

*Consider differential diagnosis

Reprinted with the Permission of Children's Hospital & Regional Medical Center. Seattle, WA.

TABLE 14.11   Characteristics of Sexual Abuse ~ Child

The following conditions may have any one of a number of organic or environmental causes besides sexual abuse and should be evaluated within the context of a comprehensive assessment, which includes the developmental level of the child and parent's response to the child's problems.

| *Child Characteristics* | *Medical** | SCAN ASSESSMENTS √ = recommended | |
		Psycho Social	*SCAN Attending*
Insecurity; lack of trust; behavioral problems; denial of painful feelings or perceptions; excessive fears; overwhelming desire to please others; shame; compulsive or obsessive behavior problems; regressive or aggressive behaviors		√	
Sexualized behavior towards adults, other children; promiscuity or prostitution; expressed unusual curiosity towards sexual parts of the body; has specific knowledge of sex beyond developmental age; inappropriately exposed genitals to others or extreme discomfort with own body		√	
Nonspecific behavior changes e.g. fear of being alone with any male, or particular person; sudden refusal to sleep in regular bed; poor peer relationships; unusual ownership of money or gifts		√	

*Consider differential diagnosis

Reprinted with the Permission of Children's Hospital & Regional Medical Center. Seattle, WA.

TABLE 14.12   Characteristics of Sexual Abuse ~ Parental or Caretaker

The following conditions may have any one of a number of organic or environmental causes besides sexual abuse and should be evaluated within the context of a comprehensive assessment, which includes the developmental level of the child and parent's response to the child's problems.

| *Parental or Caretaker Characteristics* | *Medical** | SCAN ASSESSMENTS √ = recommended | |
		Psycho Social	*SCAN Attending*
Domestic violence		√	
Substance abuse		√	
Parental limitations (lack of basic parenting and problem solving skills); inappropriate discipline; inflexible and controlling behaviors; frequent crises/chaotic lifestyles, homelessness; lack of consistency to family members and peers; cognitive , developmental or physical limitations		√	
Severe mental health problems (major depression, psychosis)		√	
Parental concern for sexual abuse: refer to PMD or GYN Specialty Clinic	√	√	
An extended family history of abuse or neglect		√	
Open Child Protective Services case		√	

*Consider differential diagnosis

Reprinted with the Permission of Children's Hospital & Regional Medical Center. Seattle, WA.

TABLE 14.13   Non-Specific Physical Complaints

The great majority of sexual abuse cases do not involve violent or forced physical assaults. In these nonviolent cases, physical evidence is often ambiguous or nonexistent.

Anorexia (if anorexia nervosa)	If physiological causes are
Abdominal Pain	evaluated by a physician and
Enuresis and/or encopresis	found to be non-contributory to
Dysuria	the symptoms, a psychosocial
Genital or rectal pain, itching, discharge, bleeding, bruising	assessment should occur.
Urethral discharge	
Painful defecation	

Reprinted with the Permission of Children's Hospital & Regional Medical Center. Seattle, WA.

parent who smothers a child to the point that the child stops breathing, in an effort to pretend that the child has an apnea problem.

Factitious disorder by proxy can be very difficult to prove, unless the provider actually observes the perpetrator in the act. Determining the causes of suspicious results or behaviors is a time-consuming and stressful process. It can be particularly difficult in cases where the child actually does have a physical or medical problem, and the perpetrator is simply exacerbating the condition. Practitioners and facilities treating children should have resources available to investigate suspected child abuse with this etiology. The use of video surveillance may be helpful in some cases, though the most helpful tool may be a multidisciplinary team that can help assess whether the factitious disorder by proxy exists. A multidisciplinary assessment can validate that a single practitioner is not over- or under-reading a situation. It can also promote defensibility of the provider if litigation ensues.

Understandably, parents who are reported for child abuse due to factitious syndrome by proxy may be very upset. They may be even more upset if child protection services subsequently determines that the report is unfounded. Further, if the child is returned to the parent after removal, the parent may feel vindicated. In either circumstance, there is high potential for a volatile malpractice suit. It is therefore essential that practitioners be diligent in their investigation of possible abuse. In addition, it is extremely important that they accurately document their assessment, actions, and rationale, so that it can subsequently be established that any report was made in good faith.

• • • • • • • • • • • •

CONCLUSION

By helping pediatric clinicians manage the complex and thorny regulatory, ethical, and safety-related issues that are unique to their fragile population, the risk management professional can address significant liability concerns, minimize risk, and contribute to an enhanced quality of care. Particularly valuable strategies include development of tools and mechanisms that facilitate partnership with patients and their families.

Endnotes

1. Children's Hospital & Regional Medical Center. Seattle, WA. "Infant Sleep Position and Bedding Recommendations" policy. March, 2005.

2. American College of Allergy, Asthma & Immunology, 85 West Algonquin Road, Suite 550, Arlington Heights, IL. 60005 (telephone 847-427-1200).

3. Children's Hospital & Regional Medical Center. Seattle, WA. "Toy Cleaning and Disinfection" policy—Infection Control Policies and Procedures. September 2004.

4. The American Psychiatric Association, *Diagnostic and Statistical Manual of Mental Disorders* (4th ed.). (DSM-IV) p. 513.

5. Terminology in this area is in some flux. Generally speaking, the term "Munchausen syndrome by proxy" is a diagnosis of the adult fabricating the illness. The term "factitious disorder" describes a condition caused by deliberate acts, and is sometimes used as a diagnosis of the perpetrator and sometimes (when speaking of factitious disorder by proxy) of the victim. The term "pediatric falsification," though not yet in wide use, can be expected to become the preferred term for diagnosing the child victim of a falsification disorder, because it merely identifies the child as suffering from a falsified condition without attempting a psychiatric diagnosis of the adult perpetrator.

15

Patient Safety and Risk Management in the Operating Room

David Earle, MD
Mary Lynn Curran

For many years, the operating room (OR) has been a significant source of malpractice liability. Plaintiff attorneys have been quick to exploit the vulnerability of an anesthetized patient, harmed by a medical error that lay persons have no difficulty understanding, like surgery on the wrong limb. The irony of the analysis which has been so effective in the courtroom is that the function of the OR is anything but simple. This chapter will discuss risk associated with specific characteristics of the OR setting, and present risk reduction strategies that will also enhance patient safety.

RISK REDUCTION IN THE PHYSICAL ENVIRONMENT

The OR is an alien environment to all except the health care professionals who practice there. The physical layout often comprises a "holding area" where surgical patients go through final preparation for their procedures, for example, chart checks to be certain that all lab work has returned and is satisfactory. It also usually includes large rooms in which procedures that require many personnel and much equipment, for example, open heart operations, can be performed and smaller rooms for less complex procedures, such as appendectomy. Outside each room are large sinks where personnel can scrub before they conduct procedures. Much space in the OR is usually dedicated to storage of equipment and supplies. Adjacent to the procedure rooms is a recovery room, where patients can be monitored closely during their emergence from anesthesia.

Many health care organizations have dedicated rooms adjacent to the "main OR," or in other locations in the hospital to accommodate specialty operations which are usually lower in acuity, and which sometimes generate significant income. For example, the endoscopy suite is often separate from the OR, and staff in the labor and delivery area often perform their own Caesarean sections. Even farther removed from the central operating room are off-site surgical centers, in which a broad array of increasingly acute procedures are performed.

The OR is isolated in many ways from the rest of the health care organization. This is necessary in part to facilitate infection control and security of equipment. Historically, it was also important to protect the rest of the hospital from the operating room. As surgical areas once housed highly flammable and explosive anesthesia agents, traditionally they were located at the outer edge of the building or on top of the hospital. Although the risk associated with explosive anesthetic agents has dissipated, other risks associated with the physical environment have continued to evolve.

Infection Control

News media coverage regarding hospital-acquired infection has often focused on the surgical environment. Although health care organizations seek to reduce the risk of surgical infection by physically separating the OR from other areas of the hospital with special doors and other spatial dividers, and requiring masks and protective gowns during procedures, these are only superficial aspects of an effective OR infection control program. Other specific strategies include the following:

- Involvement of the infection control professional in evaluation of risk associated with construction. Many health care organizations are expanding their surgical environments to manage a greater volume and variety of procedures. Every project must be preceded by an Infection Control Risk Assessment (ICRA), including appropriate interventions and modifications, many of which must be implemented before construction begins. Please see the Premier, Inc., Web site for a comprehensive overview of the standards and best practices that relate to Infection Control Risk Assessment.[1]

- Inclusion of the infection control professional on the team which inspects the operating room. Routine walk-through inspections are essential to identify infection control issues (and safety issues, such as outdated biomedical equipment). It is particularly important that the team enter each operating room to ascertain if the physical environment is impaired from an infection control perspective; for example, cracks in the wall or floor. This level of surveillance does not always occur, due to time constraints for the inspection team and the level of activity in OR procedure rooms. In some settings it might be necessary to inspect rooms in off hours, or on a rotating basis as approved by the infection control practitioner.

- Suitable geographic layout, including well-separated "clean" and "dirty" equipment areas.

- Limited use of "flash sterilization." Most ORs have equipment that can quickly sterilize certain types of equipment for immediate reuse, rather than sending them to be cleaned by the department usually known as "central processing." As noted by Mangram, et al., in the 1999 CDC publication, *Guideline for Prevention of Surgical Site Infection*:

  The Association for the Advancement of Medical Instrumentation defines flash sterilization as "the process designated for the steam sterilization of patient care items for immediate use." During any operation, the need for emergency sterilization of equipment may arise (for example, to reprocess an inadvertently dropped instrument). However, flash sterilization is not intended to be used for either reasons of convenience or as an alternative to purchasing additional instrument sets or to save time. Also, flash sterilization is not recommended for implantable devices because of the potential for serious infections. . . . Flash sterilization is not recommended as a routine sterilization method because of the lack of timely biologic indicators to monitor performance, absence of protective packaging following sterilization, possibility for contamination of processed items during transportation to operating rooms, and use of minimal sterilization cycle parameters (time, temperature, pressure). . . . To address some of these concerns, many hospitals have placed equipment for flash sterilization in close proximity to operating rooms and new biologic indicators that provide results in one to three hours are now available for flash-sterilized items. Nevertheless, flash sterilization should be restricted to its intended purpose until studies are performed that can demonstrate comparability with conventional sterilization methods regarding risk of SSI.[2]

Even if adequate protocols are in place, overuse of flash sterilization may increase risk, and may also be a sign of inefficiency in the central sterilizing process. The volume of flash sterilization might thus be a desirable quality improvement indicator for the operating room.

As disinfection and sterilization strategies continue to evolve, infection control practitioners and OR managers should routinely consult the Centers for Disease Control and Prevention (CDC) Web site.[3]

Physical Infrastructure to Support Technology

The OR has unique requirements for physical infrastructure, analogous to the intensive care area, to make certain that procedures run safely. Inadequate support increases risk. Strategies to consider include the following.

- Dedicated elevators and contingency plans. Wherever critical patients must be transported to the OR via elevator, it is essential that advance planning address any malfunction of, or competition for, the elevator. For example, some health care organizations transport emergent caesarean section cases from the labor and delivery area to an OR on another floor. It is critical that the transport team know what they would do if the elevator stalls, or is simply not available due to demands of other units.

- Dedicated power sources and inlaid piping for oxygen and nitrous oxide, and vacuum for suctioning. A traditional concern that remains important to address is how to eliminate waste anesthetic gases. This issue is addressed comprehensively on the OSHA Web site. OR managers and risk management professionals should routinely check this site to remain current.[4] To promote safety, the OR department should also be designed with its own air flow system to provide frequent changes or exchanges of ambient air per hour, and exhaust should be vented to the outside or into a special filter system.

As any power source can be incapacitated, all staff members should drill on how they would proceed without electricity. A protocol should specify where emergency supplies, such as batteries and flashlights, are located.

Fire Management in the Operating Room

In addition to general health care organization policies and procedures, it is critical to have explicit policies and procedures for the oxygen-rich, isolated operating room suite. OR-specific fire policies should address all areas of the surgical theater: holding areas, preanesthesia areas, all operating rooms, storage areas, materials management areas, post anesthesia care unit(s), and clinician lounges. Specific considerations include:

- The immediate responsibility of the person who discovers the fire should include pulling the alarm box and calling for help. The charge person also should be notified at this time.

- The role of the charge person in managing such emergencies should be familiar to each staff member, and all staff should know who the charge person is. Protocols should designate this person as responsible for delegation of specific responsibilities, including directing fire fighters, media, and so on. As emergency responders are unlikely to be familiar with the OR, generic information to be shared with them should be formalized ahead of time. The charge person should also assign another individual to evaluate and address the status of patients. It might be logical for this person to be an anesthesia professional, as a key issue will be whether oxygen and anesthetic gasses can or should be turned off.

- All personnel should know the location of fire alarm boxes, fire extinguishers, and oxygen shutoff locations. Maps should be posted, illustrating the locations of smoke barriers, oxygen shutoff locations, fire pull locations, fire extinguisher locations, and evacuation paths. This information should be logically delineated in as many separate maps as necessary, to be certain that each individual map is legible.

- Steps to take to manage an OR fire, where a patient is present, must be spelled out. Consider least three possible scenarios, including management of a patient who is not anesthetized, a patient who has been anesthetized, but is not yet undergoing surgery, and management of patient who is anesthetized and undergoing surgery.

- Oxygen and other anesthetic gases should be shut off after consultation with the anesthesia professional working with the charge nurse, or in charge of the case, as specified by protocol.

Routine drills for fire management when a patient is undergoing surgery should be conducted with the input of the risk management professional and safety officer. It might help to videotape responses so that they can be critiqued later. Particularly important in this regard are "airway fires" that might arise during laser surgery. The Association of Perioperative Registered Nurses (AORN) 2005 "Guidance on Fire Safety" contains detailed guidance on fire management, including laser safety.[5]

External Disaster Plan

An external disaster can test OR operations in unexpected ways. OR-specific approaches should be delineated in the house-wide disaster plan, to guide OR team members as they respond to incoming casualties. Specific points to address include the following:

- All approaches should take into account the number of staff and physical space likely to be available.

- The plan should specify a method for triage, including the role of the individual who would be responsible for this activity, for example, surgeon or anesthesia professional in charge.

- It should provide guidance on how to manage scheduled cases, such as cancellation.

- Also detailed should be methods of communicating with the emergency department and EMS field personnel.

- Disaster simulations that include the OR are a critical aspect of preparation. Such simulations should routinely include scenarios that assume that the operating room has no power, or is reliant on emergency generators.

Security

It is possible to conclude that the OR is safer because it is separate from the rest of the organization. The volatility of patients' families who have received word of an unexpected bad outcome and the sheer volume of masked staff in many settings make this a fallacious assumption. Associated strategies are as follows:

- The OR staff should be oriented as to how to contact the security staff, and the security staff should be oriented to the OR.

- The OR desk should maintain a current photo roster of medical staff members and their privileges, to help the staff become familiar with these individuals.

- Security of the surgical center environment should be assessed in particular, as the public is likely to be aware that it houses narcotics and anesthetic agents. Many of these settings are located at a significant distance from the hospital, yet they often lack arrangements for security twenty-four hours a day.

Reduction of Staff-Related Risk

The operating room staff is composed of many highly specialized professionals who bring unique skill sets to the care of increasingly acute patients. Key risk management principles to enhance safe practice include the following:

- Medical staff privileges and employed staff job descriptions must specifically support the procedures undertaken in the environment. Because technology is changing so fast, the medical staff credentials committee, clinical area managers, and the human resources department should constantly be alert to changes in training requirements and new skill sets. Medical staff privileges should be maintained at the OR desk, or online in a computer database that is accessible to all nursing and other authorized staff. By protocol, the scheduler should always validate the privileges for a new member of the medical staff or a medical staff member performing a new procedure.

- As the OR sometimes reports to an organizational area other than nursing, special effort might be necessary to obtain nursing peer input for OR practitioners. This is important to promote consistency of practice in the setting.

- Similarly, the clinical manager of the OR should have input on the training and evaluation of medical staff-employed nurses and other allied health medical staff members with hospital-employed peers.

- The OR's clinical manager and the risk management professional should be aware of clinically pertinent responsibilities specified in agreements with independently contracted personnel, such as perfusionists. For example, there should be a provision in such agreements that requires independent contractors to support the performance improvement activities of the health care organization. (Refer to Volume 1, Chapter 12 in this series for more on the risk management implications of contract review.)

- To avoid violating infection control policies and to promote safety, it is essential that all persons who enter the environment receive basic orientation to OR-specific precautions. New clinicians including physicians and nurses should also be oriented to pertinent infection control and safety resources, for example, the location of the crash carts.

- Many surgical area medical malpractice claims and related safety issues are due to communication breakdown. See the discussion in Chapter 1, Patient Safety, and Chapter 3, on Clinical Crisis Management, of this volume on specific strategies to enhance communication skills and Volume 1, Chapter 8, on Patient Communication.

- The supervision of residents in teaching programs presents a special challenge for the operating room staff and attending physicians. Strategies include clear delineation of attending physicians' responsibilities to attest to the abilities of the individuals whom they supervise, and their availability to directly supervise resident care provided during a procedure.[6]

- Vendor-employed equipment representatives are yet another group of professionals often present in the surgical environment. It is imperative that they demonstrate their qualification to advise a surgeon on use of a new piece of equipment. They should also provide evidence of required insurance coverage, and their presence should be noted in the medical record, in accordance with AORN's pertinent 2005 statement. Among other principles that this statement endorses is the need for the patient to consent to the presence of such individuals.[7]

············
MANAGING RISK ASSOCIATED WITH THE CONTINUUM OF CARE

Continuum of care issues that risk management professionals must deal with include informed consent, preoperative preparation, operative procedure, wrong-site surgery, immediate postoperative care, and many specific risk situations associated with these broader areas.

Informed Consent

Informed consent should be obtained by the surgeon or provider performing the procedure. The ideal setting for an informed consent discussion is the surgeon's office. Generally, the hospital confirms that consent was obtained by having a nurse witness the patient's signature on an "informed consent" form, after validating that the patient has no further questions regarding the procedure.

The procedure specified on this form should be based on a written order, not the operating room schedule or any other source. Any discrepancies or questions should be directed to the surgeon, and addressed before the procedure. The surgeon and charge nurse should be informed immediately if the patient has received potentially judgment-altering medication before having signed the consent.

Once documentation of consent is completed properly, the staff can check it against other documentation to validate that the planned procedure is the one the patient anticipates having. This is just one of many double checks that need to occur before the procedure actually takes place. (See related checklists elsewhere in this chapter.) The anesthesia provider should obtain consent for the anesthetic procedure and document it separately. (Please see Chapter 4 in this volume for more on informed consent principles.)

Preoperative Preparation

The preoperative preparation process sets the stage for successful completion of an operation. We've all heard the carpenter's adage "measure twice, cut once." It means that acting without planning can be expensive, and because of the potential cost of poorly thought-out actions, we should not only plan, but plan twice.[8] This old adage has never rung more true than in the OR setting. Checks must include the patient's participation. Yet it is critical to remember that patients are psychologically vulnerable immediately before the surgical procedure. For example, as patients might simply agree with any suggested response, it is extremely dangerous for staff to inquire if the patient is indeed Mrs. Jones. A much safer approach is to ask patients to identify themselves and the procedure they understand they will have.

The special needs of pediatric and elderly patients, patients who are disabled by a hearing impairment or psychiatric disorder, and those who speak a foreign language, call for formalizing specific strategies in advance, such as availability of a language bank. Sensitivity and common sense should also be applied in working with those who are undergoing a controversial or cosmetic procedure, and patients who have security needs, such as trauma patients who are gang members or VIPs.

Other specific strategies that are important in preparing for surgery include:

- Staff must positively identify the patient at every stage of the process, for example, during paperwork preparation, consent signature, and surgical site marking, which should be done by the surgeon.

- Logistical support for the procedure must be in place before conclusion of preoperative preparation. Issues that might need to be resolved include:
  - Specific equipment needs, such as long instruments for a bariatric case
  - Availability of a radiology technician and equipment
  - Availability of previously taken X-ray films, and validation that they are indeed those of the patient scheduled for the procedure
  - Notification of pathology that interpretation of a biopsy specimen will be needed
  - Availability of a specific type of preparation in which to place a pathology specimen

Logistical support can be facilitated by checklists, which may be tailored to fit specific procedures. Checklists and other documentation that demonstrate that the surgical patient was processed properly should be signed, dated, and made part of the medical record. Refer to Exhibit 15.1 for a sample checklist for the preoperative period.

EXHIBIT 15.1   Preoperative Checklist

☐ Identify patient
☐ Check orders for consent language, medications, availability of blood, etc.
☐ Make sure preoperative antibiotics are administered within 60 minutes of procedure
☐ Perioperative beta blockers for cardiac patients, unless there are contraindications
☐ Consent signed (identify patient)
☐ Surgical site marked by surgeon (identify patient)
☐ Check with room staff to make sure all necessary equipment is available
☐ Confirm room number with room staff

Operative Procedure

When the patient arrives in the operating room, the pre-operative process continues, although responsibility for the process shifts from holding area personnel to the surgical team (circulating nurse, scrub technician or nurse, anesthesia personnel, first assistant, and surgeon). The transfer of care from the staff in the holding area to the staff in the operating room should be based on a formal protocol, and documented.

Checklists are essential to completing the final steps before the procedure begins, as the circulating nurse frequently has many tasks to perform simultaneously. Once the procedure begins, each unchecked item may represent time away from the patient. For example, if the electrocautery unit has not been checked off, and is unavailable, the staff might need to leave the room to get it. This unanticipated interruption prolongs the time the patient spends under anesthesia and also constitutes a distraction that increases risk of error. (Refer to Exhibits 15.2 and 15.3 for examples of OR pre-arrival and arrival checklists.)

EXHIBIT 15.2   Pre-Arrival of Patient—Room Set-Up

❏ Read surgeon's preference card and any related protocols
❏ Obtain all necessary equipment and instrumentation
❏ Place equipment in proper position (energy sources, foot controls, video equipment, etc.)
❏ Place necessary foot controls in proper position (prior to use)
❏ Keep expensive, disposable items ready for use, but do not open until confirmation of need.
  Remember to have items such as sutures and closing paraphernalia ready.
❏ Energy source available and functioning
❏ Video equipment available and functioning
❏ Communicate with holding area staff regarding room number to bring patient to
❏ RN validates need for radiologic studies during the procedure
❏ Radiologic support available
❏ Previous radiology studies available and identify validated
❏ Lab contacted re anticipated need to interpret specimen
❏ Appropriate medium and container available for pathology specimen
❏ Positioning paraphernalia available (foam, tape, stirrups, split leg table, bed extensions, foot boards, etc.)
❏ Anesthesia supplies in place or to be checked separately by their personnel

---

EXHIBIT 15.3   Patient Arrival in the Operating Room Checklist

---

❏ RN meets patient, reviews chart, assures patient of individual treatment
❏ RN reviews history and physical, operative plan, etc.
❏ Identify patient
❏ Appropriate preoperative medications given
  • antibiotics
  • beta blockers
  • others
❏ Identify and communicate medical allergies (drugs, latex, iodine, etc.)
❏ Utilize all appropriate positioning aids (pillows, foam padding, etc.) Remember to always fit the equipment
  to the patient, rather than the patient to the equipment.
❏ Go over operative plan (and contingency plan) with surgeon and anesthesia staff after anesthesia has
  been administered, and prior to prepping the operative site.
❏ Time out to
  • Identify patient
  • Identify procedure
  • Identify surgical site by the surgeon's mark
❏ Place equipment in proper position (energy sources, foot controls, video equipment, etc)
❏ Place necessary foot controls in proper position (prior to use)
❏ Have supplies for beginning of case ready prior to preparing supplies that will be needed late in case
  (this list would be individualized for a given institution)

Checklists are particularly critical to help the OR team prepare for a procedure which is performed infrequently, in off hours, or as an emergency. They are also important to promote continuity of care during change of shift. The content and protocols that support checklists should be reviewed and updated as necessary to reflect current practice.

Transfer of Care or Hand-Off in the Operating Room

Transfer of care or "hand-off" from one provider to another is a particularly high risk process in the OR. Hand-offs may occur multiple times during a particular procedure because the OR schedule is not aligned with any particular work shift. Further complicating transfer of care is that different providers are essential to the procedure. For example, nurses and anesthesia providers often work shifts that begin at different times. Many moderate-sized and larger hospitals schedule staffing for two shifts and a swing shift to accommodate a fluctuating and unpredictable OR schedule.

By documenting issues raised during a team briefing, conducted by the surgeon before the procedure starts, original team members create a record of key points for those to whom care is transferred later on. It is logical for this briefing to immediately precede the "time out," which allows the team to verify the identity of the surgical site, and so on. (Please see Chapter 3 in this text for more on team briefings.) The documentation of briefings and related follow-up can be very helpful to the performance improvement program of the organization. Accordingly, briefings forms should specify that they are intended as quality improvement tools, to promote protection under any available peer review protection statutes.

As anesthesia personnel typically have their own schedule of assignments, it is critical that they be included in the team briefing or apprised of the notes made during that process. Information that incoming anesthesia providers must be aware of includes the resolution of any issue associated with equipment, the count on instruments, sponges, and sharps, and current status on blood loss and blood availability, in addition to the patient's history.

Hand-off drills are particularly important to assuring safe transfer of care in a teaching environment, or any setting with multiple hand-offs. Retrospective review of charts should focus on completion of medical record documentation concerning hand-offs.

Wrong-Site Surgery

Wrong-site surgery is a broad term that encompasses all surgical procedures performed on the wrong patient, wrong body part, wrong procedure, wrong side of the body, or at the wrong level of the correctly identified anatomic site. The Joint Commission on Accreditation of Healthcare Organizations (JCAHO) considers all wrong-site surgeries, regardless of the extent of the procedure, to be sentinel events.[9] As such, they are subject to review under the JCAHO sentinel event procedure. This procedure calls for a root cause analysis of each sentinel event. Review of several root cause analyses by the JCAHO Accreditation Committee of the Board of Commissioners found wrong site surgery most commonly occurs during orthopedic procedures, followed by urologic and neurosurgical procedures.

Another review of surgical errors identified that patients with unusual physical characteristics, those undergoing multiple procedures, those with multiple surgeons, or those with time pressures to initiate the surgical procedure, are at greater risk for surgical error. Other factors that contribute to surgical errors include:[10]

- Unusual equipment or setup in the surgical suite
- Staffing problems
- Distractions

- Lack of access to pertinent information
- Failure to require adherence to verification processes
- Failure to verify and mark the operative site
- Failure to require a patient assessment
- Human factors, such as communication breakdowns, novice providers, and lack of teamwork

The Physician Insurers Association of America (PIAA) has documented 1,000 closed claims related to wrong site surgery across more than eighteen specialties in a database of 155,000 claims.[11] In Florida alone, for the year ending July 1, 2005, thirty-eight physicians, up from thirty-six the year before, were fined by the Florida Board of Medicine for wrong-site errors. In 2001, the Board raised the penalties for wrong-site errors. Responsible physicians are now fined $10,000–$20,000, ordered to perform 50–100 hours of community service, undergo remedial training, and publish reports of their mistakes.[12]

The American Academy of Orthopedic Surgeons (AAOS) has stated that the responsibility to properly identify and mark the correct site lies with the surgeon.[13] Recognizing that specialties other than orthopedics are also affected by this problem, the JCAHO and other organizations now require that each surgical procedure be preceded by a *time out* for all team members to confirm the surgical site, and other elements of procedure preparation. Checking x-ray films, x-ray reports, medical records, and written consent forms during this process is recommended.

The AORN agrees with AAOS and the JCAHO regarding the importance of avoiding wrong site surgery, and suggests the following strategies for developing facility procedures and protocols for identifying the correct surgical site.

- Involve the patient or family members or significant others in identifying the correct site.
- Use a specified, clear, unambiguous, indelible, hypoallergenic, latex-free method for marking only the correct surgical site.
- Specify in individual facility policy and procedure how, when, and by whom the surgical site is to be marked.
- Use a verification checklist immediately before surgery that includes the following:
  - Verbal communication with the patient or family members or significant others
  - Medical record review, including the face sheet, history and physical, and preoperative assessment
  - Review of the informed consent; review of all available imaging studies
  - Direct observation of the marked surgical site; verbal verification of the correct site with each member of the surgical team
  - A "timeout" by the surgical team immediately before the incision or start of the procedure for final confirmation of the surgical site
  - Quality control initiatives to monitor compliance with protocol

AORN also advises establishing a process to address and clearly resolve any discrepancies noted during the verification process before beginning the procedure.[14]

Unusual Emergencies

Planning and simulated drills can help address the following situations that occur infrequently, yet might cause severe harm.

Malignant Hyperthermia   Malignant hyperthermia, although rare, is life threatening. As it can be treated if recognized early, it is essential that staff be trained regarding clinical signs, and that adequate policies and procedures be in place. These should include:

- Methods used to identify patients at high risk.

- Avoidance of succinylcholine and halogenated anesthesia agents in high-risk patients.

- Training of OR and PACU nurses regarding the signs of malignant hyperthermia to facilitate early identification and notification of the anesthesia professional and surgeon.

- Availability of necessary equipment and medications. Many institutions have on hand a malignant hyperthermia kit or cart, equipped with pertinent equipment, drugs, and a current copy of the organization's malignant hyperthermia protocol.

Missing Equipment or Instruments   Every OR should have a policy that requires that all sponges, sharps, and instruments be accounted for, in all procedures. The count protocol should detail the frequency with which case counts are to be performed during a procedure, and what to what to do if there is a miscount, For example, inform the surgeon and the anesthesiologist; call for assistance in searching for the item (Rapid Response Team); call x-ray personnel to be available to take an x-ray during the procedure. Examples of situations in which it might apply to suspend the policy on counting should be included; for example, a patient's condition indicates that prolonged anesthesia could increase the patient's risk. However, it must be clear that the policy on counting should be suspended only under exceptional circumstances.

Risk of Sharps-Related Injuries to OR Providers   It is important from an employee safety perspective to prevent the injury of OR providers by sharps. A comprehensive overview of this issue is provided by "Sharps Injury in the OR—A New Focus for OSHA," an article published by ECRI in December 2004.[15]

Positioning   Positioning the patient to avoid pressure-induced skin breakdown, nerve injury, or aspiration is a critical preventive step in every procedure. The longer the procedure, the more frail or obese the patient, the greater the risk associated with positioning.

It is essential that a protocol delineate the respective responsibilities of team members for positioning the patient. The specific approach taken, in addition to adequate condition checks, should also be thoroughly documented in the medical record.

Unexpected Change in Patient Status and Rapid Response Teams
Rapid response teams (RRTs) provide expert staff members to help patients who are becoming unstable avoid cardiopulmonary arrest on a medical surgical unit. Such teams can also be deployed in the operating suite to enhance safety, for example, when there is emergent need to convert from laparoscopic to open surgery, or when extensive bleeding occurs. These teams may also relieve staff members during stressful periods when emergencies arise that might otherwise require OR providers to leave cases that they are working on. The concept not only supports patient safety, it should improve staff morale. It also potentially provides an opportunity for feedback to established staff members and training of new OR team members.

From a risk management standpoint, the OR should have a policy and procedure describing the responsibilities and function of an OR RRT. (Please see Chapter 3 of this volume for more on rapid response teams.)

Equipment Failure or Malfunction   The OR staff should also have a policy and procedure to follow when equipment fails or malfunctions. In addition to specifying how to obtain necessary backup, the policy should require that equipment which malfunctioned be tagged for repair by the biomedical area, so that it is not reused. If equipment malfunction might have harmed the patient, the OR staff should complete a report, consistent with the hospital's Safe Medical Device Act (SMDA) reporting requirements, and the risk management professional should be consulted immediately. Of particular importance is to ensure that equipment that might have caused injury is never returned to the manufacturer for repair without the input of the risk management professional. (Please See Chapter 7 in this volume for additional information on malfunctioning equipment, including preserving equipment as potential evidence if there has been a related patient injury.)

The risk management professional should also review OR policies to make sure that they account for complete reporting of implant-related issues under the SMDA. Although the SMDA has been modified to shift some related reporting responsibilities to the manufacturer, the health care organization is well served to maintain its own records. Of particular note, the 2003 guidance on implant reporting published on the FDA site notes that "While the hospital has no legal responsibility to inform the manufacturer (of an explant) the hospital should notify the manufacturer identified on the device. . . . If the manufacturer cannot be identified by the device . . . the institution should make a good faith effort to find out who the manufacturer is and report the explantation. . . . If the hospital cannot . . . then a record of the explantation and attempt to identify the manufacturer should be maintained in the hospital's tracking files. . . "[16]

Electrical Safety   Although the electrical safety of the OR has been enhanced by reduction in use of flammable anesthetics, patients and staff are at risk of burns and other injuries due to use of electrocautery and other devices. Of particular concern is the use of electrical equipment which is monopolar, and more likely to disperse an electrical current, than is bipolar equipment. A comprehensive list of interventions to reduce electrosurgical unit risk can be accessed on the AORN site.[17]

Lasers represent an important subset of electrical safety issues. As previously noted, staff should be aware of and implement strategies to reduce the risk of airway fire. Other important laser-related safety measures include designation of a "laser officer" who is responsible for coordinating staff education on how to safely use new laser technology, how to oversee biomedical equipment servicing agreements, and so on.[18]

Immediate Post-Operative Care

Immediate post-operative care can be viewed in three phases—1) while the patient is still in the operating room, 2) when the patient is transferred from the OR to the post-anesthesia recovery unit (PACU) or critical care unit, and 3) when the patient is transferred from the PACU to the floor. Each phase has risks, making adequate monitoring of the patient as important as it was during the procedure itself.

Once the operation is over, a sterile field must be maintained until the necessary dressings have been applied, to decrease the risk of post-operative wound infection. Then care needs to be taken when removing the drapes, not to dislodge any drains or tubes. When the drapes have been removed, the drains and tubes must be secured so they won't inadvertently be pulled during transfer.

The anesthesia professional's careful attention to the patient is as important during emergence from anesthesia as it was during induction. The operating room must be quiet and the vital signs must be closely monitored. Once extubated and stable, the patient is ready for transfer to the recovery environment, for example, post-acute care unit or intensive care unit. Formal transfer of the care of the patient starts in the operating room when the circulating nurse calls the nurse who will be assuming care to report on the procedure and status of the patient. Whether being transferred to the post anesthesia care unit or the intensive care unit, the patient must be escorted by an anesthesia professional, whose role is to guard the airway, and a member of the surgical team to report on the procedure and transfer care to the PACU or ICU nurse. All team members must know where to locate the surgeon, in the event of an emergency.

If patients are routinely recovered on the intensive care unit, it is important to ensure that the ICU staff receives adequate training to support this activity. By protocol, the availability of the anesthesia personnel and the surgeon should be required, as necessary, to support the post-operative patient.

When the patient is transferred from the PACU to a surgical unit, it is important that the patient meet all discharge criteria defined by anesthesia professionals. The nurse should accompany the patient to the floor and report to the staff member there who will assume care for the patient. In the case of a minor procedure, the staff nurse should call the floor and communicate about the patient's status, and should validate that a bed and the staff are ready to receive the patient. A protocol and supporting form can help assure consistency in this transition of care.

If the PACU staff sets up a morphine pump for the patient, it is particularly critical that the PACU staff and floor nurse communicate directly about this intervention. If the patient has received preoperative teaching about how to use the pump, that should have been asked about during the preoperative phase, and the PACU nurse should validate that there is documentation that reflects this training. (Refer to Chapter 6 in this volume for more information on morphine pump management.)

If the patient is to be discharged home after an outpatient surgical procedure, all clinical criteria established by anesthesia professionals must be met. Discharge instructions must be conveyed to the patient and a home care giver, and should be thoroughly documented in the medical record.

Team Debriefing

After the procedure is complete, team members may use the notes from the original briefing as the starting point for evaluating how the procedure went. During this process, team members should be encouraged to contribute any ideas for improving future similar procedures, or general approaches in the OR. As previously discussed, briefing and debriefing are effective performance improvement activities, and their documentation should be made part of the OR performance improvement program.

RISK MANAGEMENT AND QUALITY IMPROVEMENT

In this complex environment, it is essential that OR team members feel comfortable raising safety issues, whether through the team briefings previously discussed, by completing an occurrence report to document an unusual occurrence which may be part of a trend, or by seeking the guidance of the OR manager or risk management professional.

Analyzing trends in the clinical issues in pertinent malpractice cases, sentinel events, and occurrence reports can provide helpful information for performance improvement activity.

Examples of OR events that may be desirable to report include the following:

- Unexpected death in the operating room, or immediately post-surgery
- Injury due to a fall from the table or gurney
- Departure from the planned surgery that results in injury or death
- Equipment or device mishap that results in injury or death
- Impaired member of the surgical or anesthesia team
- Surgeon's illness requires another surgeon to step in
- Unauthorized person in the OR, such as a manufacturer's representative who has not complied with pertinent organizational policies
- Evidence of questionable sterility of instrumentation or implanted devices
- Wrong-site surgery
- Cardiac or respiratory arrest in the PACU or holding area
- Foreign body discovered on x-ray postsurgery following an unresolved instrument, needle, or sponge count. (Refer to Chapter 1 on Patient Safety in this volume for a comprehensive list the sentinel events that JCAHO requires health care organizations to report and perform root cause analyses on.)

The variety of disciplines that interface in complex ways in the OR environment make a collaborative multidisciplinary forum essential to identifying and addressing issues. This group may also have a rotating position for a non-OR member, because many high-risk OR activities involve interface with other areas of the hospital (for example, report by the PACU nurse to the floor nurse, and transfer of a specimen to the pathology area). In addition to reviewing informational trends, as noted previously, this group also can benefit from review of key processes, such as the "time out." Senior management of the organization should also support OR-related patient safety efforts by conducting safety rounds in the OR. (Refer to Chapter 3 in this volume for more information on safety rounds.)

....

CONCLUSION

The operating room is a mysterious environment to many health care professionals. It is critical that the risk management professional have a strong familiarity with the many risks in this important setting, and with loss prevention strategies that can help OR providers promote patient safety.

Endnotes

1. [www.premierinc.com/all/safety/resources/construction/].

2. Mangram, Alicia MD; Teresa C. Horan, MPH, CIC; Michele L. Pearson, MD; Leah Christine Silver, BS; and William R. Jarvis, MD; Members of The Hospital Infection Control Practices Advisory Committee for the Hospital Infections Program National Center for Infectious Diseases, the Centers for Disease Control, "Guideline For Prevention Of Surgical Site Infection," January 1999.

3. [www.cdc.gov/ncidod/eid/vol7no2/rutala.htm]. Accessed January 3, 2006.

4. [www.osha.gov/SLTC/wasteanestheticgases/solutions.html]. Accessed January 3, 2006.

5. [www.aorn.org/about/positions/pdf/SECTI-2e-firesafety.pdf]. Accessed January 3, 2006.

6. Driver, Jeffrey, presentation on "Resident Supervision: Issues and Practical Approaches," during the Web conference, "Addressing Patient Safety and Managing Risk in The OR: It Takes a Team," presented by Premier Insurance Management Services, September 21, 2005.

7. [www.aorn.org/about/positions/industryrep.htm]. Accessed January 3, 2006.

8. Hart, G. J. "Measure twice, cut once." *Computerworld Canada*, 2000. Nov. 17/2000:21. Available at: [www.techwrl.com/techwhirl/magazine/usersadvocate/usersadvocate_ measuretwice.html]. Accessed January 4, 2006.

9. Joint Commission on Accreditation of Healthcare Organizations, "Lessons learned: Wrong site surgery." *Sentinel Event Alert*, No. 6, [www.jcaho.org/%20edu_pub/sealert/sea6.html]. Accessed January 3, 2006.

10. Strickland, S. Preventing Medical Errors: Wrong Site Surgery, DCMS Legal & Legislative Available for FPIC at [www.dcmsonline.org/FPIC4.htm]. Accessed January 4, 2005.

11. White, S., Hints on Preventing Surgery on the Wrong Site. Florida Health Care Risk Management Basics; Florida Society for Healthcare Risk Management. Revised 2004–2005, p. 56.

12. "Florida to Crack Down on Wrong Site Surgery," *Outpatient Surgery Magazine.* Posted 7/25/2005. Available at [www.medlaw.com/healthlaw/Professional_rights/florida-to-crack-down-on.shtml].

13. American Academy of Orthopedic Surgeons, Advisory Statement on Wrong Site Surgery, October 2003. [www.aaos.org/wordhtml/papers/advistmt/1015.htm].

14. AORN Position Statement on Correct Site Surgery, April 2005, [www.aorn.org/about/positions]. Accessed January 3, 2006.

15. "Sharps Injury in the OR—A New Focus for OSHA." *Operating Room Risk Management,* December 2004.

16. "Medical Device Tracking Guidance for Industry and FDA Staff." Published May 5, 2003, p. 14.

17. "An example of a Perioperative Nursing Data Set outcome and interventions: Electrical Injury" at [www.aorn.org/research/examples.htm]. Accessed January 3, 2006.

18. [www.laserinstitute.org/]. Accessed January 3, 2006.

16

Risk Management in the Laboratory

Christine Clark
Laurence Sherman

isk management in the laboratory requires an understanding of the structure and background of a highly regulated, information-generating, multi-process operation. The majority of clinical diagnoses and therapeutic decisions are based, at least partly, on laboratory data. Each information-producing process, whether a blood count, a pap smear, or a throat culture, is subject to error at each of three stages:

(1) Pre-analytic—This phase includes ordering the correct test, which is then obtained in the correct manner and time, from the correct patient, then labeled and transported appropriately to a testing facility.

(2) Analytic—This phase occurs in a laboratory and includes specimen identification, order entry, proper specimen processing, reliable test performance, result entry, and specimen retention.

(3) Post-analytic—This phase includes the transmission of accurate results to the authorized caregiver.

For each of these phases there are multiple layers of private standards and governmental regulations. Failure to comply with regulations can jeopardize care, subject the health care site and workers to possible fines and closure, and potentially weaken any professional liability defense. Also, formal guidance such as FDA opinions, guidelines, recommendations from professional organizations, and state requirements weigh heavily in determining the standard of care.

Each phase is also fraught with liability issues associated with the potential for error.

Paradoxically, although the analytic phase has the most complex regulatory structure, the other two phases can be more challenging to risk management professionals, because the pre- and post-analytic phases involve many more hospital staff members, in addition to medical staffers and their private employees. There are also several interfaces and "handoffs" between departments, often with separate lines of reporting. The result is substantial complexity and, thus, increased risk.

This chapter will point out key regulatory issues of which the risk manager should be aware. It will also expand on specific risks associated with each of the three phases described previously, and offer strategies to reduce exposure.

FEDERAL REGULATIONS

The primary source of regulations pertaining to the laboratory is the federal legislation known as the Clinical Laboratory Improvement Amendments (CLIA), originally passed in 1967 and updated in 1988. A set of final regulations was issued in 1992, although refinements are routinely published in the Federal Register. The purpose of the law is to "ensure the accuracy, reliability, and timeliness of patient test results regardless of where the test was performed."[1] Under CLIA, laboratories are required to be licensed, and they must renew licensure every two years.

The Impact of Other Regulations

Before considering specific CLIA mandates, it is important to note that these regulations often intertwine with those of other organizations, whose requirements sometimes exceed CLIA's. From a risk management perspective, it is key that the standards of these private organizations may establish the standard of care in a related case. For example, many organizations apply for a Certificate of Accreditation (COA) under CLIA.[2] This certificate is awarded when they pass an inspection by a private organization with standards equal to or higher than those set out in the law, such as the College of American Pathologists (CAP)[3] or JCAHO. As long as the organization holds a COA, it is not subject to routine inspections by employees of the Centers for Medicare and Medicaid Services (CMS), which is the agency responsible for enforcing CLIA. Similarly, facilities that pass an inspection in states whose programs are "CLIA exempt," such as New York, are not routinely subject to CMS inspection.[4]

Although compliance with more stringent standards might raise comfort levels about ability to pass a CMS inspection, it is important that accreditation, and "exempt" status conferred by state program compliance, do not entirely free a laboratory from the specter of federal oversight. The federal government performs random, follow-up inspections to ensure that private and state agencies are conducting inspections equivalent to the federal government's. Also, when there has been a credible complaint or apparent violation of pertinent regulations, federal, state, or nongovernmental inspectors may appear unannounced. Obviously, the recent trend by JCAHO to have routine unannounced surveys, and the potential of such activity by other agencies, reinforces the concept that compliance is a twenty-four hour-a-day, 365 day-a-year endeavor.

CLIA Is Facility Specific

Risk management professionals should be aware that CLIA defines a laboratory as "any facility which performs laboratory testing on specimens derived from humans for the purpose of providing information for the diagnosis, prevention, treatment of disease, or impairment of, or assessment of health."[5] This facility-based approach means that CLIA is generally site-specific, and there may be several licenses within one health care organization. For example, if respiratory therapists perform blood gas analysis in their department in a large teaching hospital, they may have a separate CLIA license. Remote physicians' offices with labs may have their own licenses. A medical school may perform genetic analysis or drug monitoring in the context of research. Another important factor that may play a role in licensure is the reporting relationship of the lab. For example, "satellite labs" or special labs that report to the central hospital laboratory will usually be inspected under the hospital laboratory's license, even though they are geographically separate.

The risk management professional should understand the status of laboratory licensure in various settings throughout the organization. One resource may be the laboratory manager of the main lab in a large facility, who is likely to be knowledgeable about licenses in other departments or may be able to collect such information. It is also possible to ask CMS for a list of the laboratories with your hospital or health care organization's name. Laboratory managers should update the risk management professional about upcoming inspections by any organization, and about any negative findings, including follow-up.

Testing Complexity

The final CLIA regulations, published February 28, 1992, are based on the complexity of the test method. The more complicated the test, the more stringent the requirements. Three categories of tests have been established: waived complexity, moderate complexity, and high complexity. Some of the factors considered in determining complexity include (1) degree of knowledge needed to perform the test; (2) training and experience required; (3) complexity of reagent and materials preparation; (4) characteristics of operational steps; (5) characteristics and availability of calibration, quality control, and proficiency testing materials; (6) troubleshooting and maintenance required; and (7) degree of interpretation and judgment required in the testing process.[6] For moderate- and high-complexity tests, CLIA specifies quality standards for proficiency testing (PT, in which the lab tests samples sent by independent third parties to see if their results are the same as peers who have tested the same material[7]), patient test management, quality control, personnel qualifications, and quality assurance for laboratories that perform moderate- or high-complexity tests.[8]

The criteria that define "waived testing" are set out under Sec. 493.15 (b) as follows.

(b) *Criteria.* Test systems are simple laboratory examinations and procedures which

- Are cleared by FDA for home use
- Employ methodologies that are so simple and accurate as to render the likelihood of erroneous results negligible
- Pose no reasonable risk of harm to the patient if the test is performed incorrectly

Although the processes pertaining to "waived tests" are not subject to routine CMS inspection, in those facilities that have achieved a "waived testing" certificate, the laboratory must follow manufacturer specifications for the testing. "Waived test" processes are also subject to inspection by surveyors of JCAHO and CAP, whose standards are more stringent.

Also note that waived tests may generate liability exposure if they are incorrectly performed. For example, HIV antibody tests are "waived tests."

The second category of testing complexity under CLIA encompasses "moderate" complexity tests, which include provider-performed microscopic interpretation (PPMI). The third category, high-complexity tests, includes surgical pathology specimens.

State Regulations and Staff Training Requirements

State-based regulation of laboratory procedures varies widely. As previously noted, states such as New York have achieved "CLIA exempt" status because they have comprehensive licensure and inspection programs. At the other extreme, some states require federal CLIA licensure and compliance.

Staff training requirements in individual state programs are particularly variable. For example, some require that medical technologists have state licenses to work in a laboratory, analogous to licensure for registered nurses. This is a step beyond the usual requirement that medical technologists earn a bachelor's degree and be tested, certified, and registered by the American Society for Clinical Pathology (ASCP).

Also acceptable in some locales are training programs that require less stringent prerequisites for certification, for example, two years of post-high school education or training. Because there are many approaches, human resources departments should be familiar with the requirements of each type of certification presented by job applicants. The high level of variation in state requirements also makes it critical that each laboratory be familiar with the state requirements, and communicate changes to risk management on an ongoing basis. Position descriptions should be based on state and CLIA requirements, and independent verification of licensure, educational degrees, and special certifications should be carried out routinely, similar to the approach taken with registered nurses.

State requirements also vary as to who can order laboratory tests, for example, whether ordering tests is exclusively the responsibility of physicians, or whether other health care providers, such as nurse practitioners, may also order tests. There are active legislative endeavors by non-physician health professionals to gain this prerogative. Risk managers should be aware of local requirements, and whether third-party payers will reimburse for laboratory tests ordered by non-physicians.

Unless state requirements are more stringent, federal CLIA guidance concerning laboratory personnel must be adhered to. Current information can be found on the CLIA Web site at [www.cms.hhs.gov/clia]. Pertinent specific information about training will be provided later in this chapter.

Medical Staff and Outside Laboratories

Pathologists should go through the same credentialing process as the rest of the organization's medical staff, whether they are independently contracted or not. It is also important to know whether pathologists will function exclusively onsite or occasionally perform testing in an outside independent laboratory.

When such an outside laboratory is used, it is the duty of the hospital to verify the "bona fides" of that laboratory, including licensure. The same criteria should apply to referral laboratories. Formal contracts with all such laboratories should specify that the outside laboratory is responsible for taking steps to ensure reliable testing. The outside lab should also be required to notify the hospital of any change in licensure status or pending investigations that might result in a negative determination about the quality of patient testing.

The Safety of Laboratory Conditions

OSHA regulations, and private organizations, such as JCAHO, address the safety of conditions under which testing is performed. All specimens are potentially infectious, and information on biosafety issues particular to the laboratory is available at [www.cdc.gov/od/ohs/biosfty/bmbl4/bmbl4s2.htm]. Certain reagents and controls also might be infectious or might contain hazardous materials. Information about chemical safety in the laboratory is available at the OSHA Web site [www.osha.gov/SLTC/laboratories]. Laboratory personnel should be familiar with all pertinent OSHA, JCAHO, and state-specific requirements that pertain to laboratory safety and should document compliance.

Federal Oversight of Blood Transfusion and Laboratory Instruments

Blood products are licensed pharmaceuticals and thus are subject to Food and Drug Administration (FDA) oversight.[9] Hospital transfusion services that perform only minimal processing of blood products are only required to register with the FDA, but are not under the same level of scrutiny as hospitals performing more complex processing. Blood centers and other facilities that collect blood from donors must be registered[10] and must have periodic unscheduled inspections by the FDA. Unlike CMS, which has delegated certain inspection responsibilities to CAP and JCAHO, the FDA retains responsibility for blood services and conducts all inspections.

Therefore, an FDA-licensed hospital transfusion service commonly will be inspected when CAP and JCAHO inspect the laboratory and when the American Association of Blood Banks (AABB) performs an accreditation survey. However, no determination of compliance by another organization exempts the transfusion service from unannounced inspections by the FDA. The FDA also has jurisdiction over all laboratory instruments and tests in any way related to blood collection or testing. A representative list of equipment affected can be found on the FDA Web site under the Center for Biologics Evaluation and Research (CBER).[11]

Although, in general, the requirements of inspecting organizations are similar, differences do occur. When there is conflict, it is prudent to follow the most stringent set of rules and always to be in compliance with the regulations, recommendations, or advisory publications of the FDA.

············

POLICIES AND PROCEDURES

All laboratory processes should follow written procedures. Formalization of the laboratory's interactions with other areas of the hospital is particularly important and challenging. Risk increases exponentially when areas such as the operating room or emergency department have their own individual procedures for processes such as patient identification, obtaining and labeling blood and tissue specimens, and blood administration. Therefore it is essential that representatives from each area participate in development of common procedures. Once created, there should be no changes to such multidisciplinary procedures, without the input of the risk management professional and approval of the laboratory manager.

Procedures should be reviewed routinely by representatives from applicable clinical areas, and updates must be distributed to all affected staff. All new employees should be oriented to pertinent procedures. This orientation should include the rationale for procedures. For example, phlebotomists and the nursing staff must understand why certain specimens must be collected at a certain time, and they should be educated as to the causes of hemolysis and contamination. Phlebotomists and the nursing staff should also be taught to describe any difficulty in obtaining specimens to other clinical staff, such as the ordering physician. Orientation to laboratory procedures should be documented.

People who develop procedures for the laboratory should seek guidance from applicable accreditation and licensure requirements. They must also remember that equipment and lab test-related procedures should be consistent with the applicable instrument manufacturer's recommendations. Many sample procedures are available from the Clinical and Laboratory Standards Institute. Contact information for the institute is provided at the conclusion of this chapter.[12]

Laboratory Information System and Data Management

Information systems can facilitate many aspects of the laboratory's work, from ordering tests to printing tube labels with bar codes identifying the patient and the test that has been ordered. Certain systems now also generate bar coded wristbands, which help the phlebotomist identify the patient before drawing blood. Still others assist in performing the test and conducting quality control checks. Some systems also report results, and some facilitate billing. The extent to which these features are in use varies among systems and from site to site. The laboratory information system (LIS) may be separate from the hospital information system (HIS) and connected by an interface for reporting and billing, or the LIS may be part of an integrated system offered by the HIS vendor. Additionally, many individual instruments have complex computer systems that may perform some of these functions on a stand-alone basis. For example, chemistry instrument systems may document specimen identification and processing. Other IT resources, located within instruments, perform and document preventive maintenance tests. All this information can then be directly transmitted to the LIS or an HIS.

We will touch on the practical and regulatory issues associated with information system selection only briefly here. One major issue involves security of information in the system. Preceding implementation, there must be rigorous analysis as to what information is needed by each health care provider with access. For example, a phlebotomist needs to know the types of blood tests to be drawn on a given patient, but often does not need to know the results. In contrast, a nurse drawing a finger-stick glucose for an immediate blood sugar test must know the result to administer insulin per the attending physician's orders. Attending physicians need access only to the clinical information of patients that they are seeing on a primary or consultative basis—not the information of all patients in the hospital. HIPAA (Health Insurance Portability and Accountability Act)[13] and local state laws should be consulted regarding such access issues.

Where management of test results is concerned, information systems should be programmed to meet the standards of various regulatory agencies and laboratory specific-requirements. The system must be screened routinely to be certain that it is compliant, and data must be "backed up," with electronic copies maintained off-site.

Depending on the lab test, automated access to prior results (delta checks) can help prevent errors. For example, routine comparison of blood type results with those previously obtained on a patient is a requirement of many private accrediting organizations.

Important steps to take before implementing an LIS include the following:

- The hospital should contact other health care organizations to get feedback on the systems under consideration.

- The hospital must also determine how well the candidate system can handle the volume of tests that is generated by the laboratory.

- If the LIS is to be separate from the main HIS, the question of how the systems interface must be addressed early on.

- As health care givers should only need to consult one source for all patient information, one objective of the interface should be automatic transfer of laboratory reports into the HIS's patient record. Another objective is efficient movement of information into the billing database.

- If possible, the interface should be tested before the system is purchased. High-volume validating test runs are an important part of pre-testing, and the staff must plan for potential system malfunctions, or "crashes," during this process.

- Yet another important consideration is training for all staff who will use the system.

- This comprehensive orientation should be documented.

Design of Data Reports

The laboratory data report, whether electronic or manual, should be formatted with the input from the medical staff. Formatting should make it easy to identify abnormal results, and to report such results in keeping with the health care organization's critical value reporting system. Reports should facilitate communication of critical results and those results that are "non-critical," but still outside normal parameters. Abnormal results that are not timely reported should be monitored through the quality improvement program, and followed up as required. The communication of critical and abnormal values on out-patients is particularly important, because the patients are remote, and physicians might not be as attuned to the potential for aberrant values.

············
RISK REDUCTION STRATEGIES IN THE PRE-ANALYTICAL PHASE

Specific written procedures on specimen collection should be available to all providers in the facility who collect specimens. These procedures should address test ordering, patient identification, specimen collection, labeling, and transporting. Procedures should also detail preparation, type and amount of specimen to be collected, special timing of collection if applicable, type of container to use, special handling requirements (such as refrigeration), proper labeling, and test requisition completion. Access to current procedures can be facilitated through use of a properly programmed HIS.

Other issues that should be procedurally addressed include the need for all specimen collection processes to be supported by a specific requisition, and access to the original order. For a telephone STAT, or a telephone-added test, it is important to document the telephone order and the identity of the person who orders it. As will be detailed in the post-analytic section that follows, it is now a JCAHO requirement that orders be "read back" and verification documented.[14] Any telephone order should also be documented in the medical record and then signed by the ordering practitioner within twenty-four hours of ordering.

Certain accepted practices, which are reimbursable, allow laboratory personnel to add tests at their discretion. For example, the use of special stains on surgical specimens in anatomic pathology does not require a specific order. Additional discretionary tests are less common in clinical pathology. An example is performing a definitive HIV test after a positive screening test. To ensure consistent performance of such discretionary tests, it is desirable to have specific algorithms reviewed and approved by a medical staff committee.

The highest risk step in obtaining patient samples is identification of the patient. Most laboratories print specimen labels, within the laboratory, based on test orders, and then distribute them to phlebotomists. It is incumbent upon the phlebotomist to properly identify the patient and label the specimen at the time of collection. JCAHO standards now require the use of two unique identifiers, such as name and medical record number (MRN). Use of the latter assumes that there is a wristband, as patients are unlikely to know the MRN. Date of birth (DOB) is sometimes used instead of MRN. Although some cultures de-emphasize the significance of the DOB, it is a useful alternative when the MRN is not available. Use of inpatient room numbers as a second identifier is unwise and also unacceptable to JCAHO.[15]

Some facilities that use bar coding are capable of producing bar coded labels, which can be matched to the bar code on the patient's identification bracelet at the point of collection. Wristband bar coding can reduce error, but it is not error-proof. It must be supplemented by other common-sense measures, such as communicating effectively with the patient. Conscious and alert patients should be asked to state their name, rather than being asked if they are "Mrs. Jones." The latter approach is fraught with error, particularly when hearing or language barriers are present. When anatomic pathology specimens are obtained, the patient is frequently unconscious. In these situations, the patient's identity should be confirmed by wristband. It is also critical that the specimen be labeled before the provider who has collected the specimen leaves the procedure area. Similarly, clinical pathology specimens should be labeled at the bedside. Specimen tubes for multiple patients should not be labeled in advance. Some institutions generate multiple specimen labels for a single patient undergoing a long procedure, or when several tubes are needed. However, to avoid specimen misidentification, it is essential to destroy any unused labels immediately after the procedure or collection process. This issue is of particular concern in areas such as operating rooms and invasive radiology suites, where several patients go through an individual room in a day.

In general, many erroneous laboratory tests result from mislabeling of tubes or drawing the specimen from the wrong patient. Even if it does not cause delayed or wrong care, misidentification can have a serious impact on the hospital's reputation. For example, many prestigious hospitals are now best known for transfusion or transplant-related patient and specimen identification errors. When collecting specimens related to transfusion and tissue transplant, it is therefore important to implement as many safeguards as are practical. For example, once the phlebotomist has collected and labeled a blood bank specimen, a second person might verify that the patient identification and specimen labels match.

Another common source of specimen collection error is using the wrong container. For example, the stronger anticoagulants designed to preserve a blood gas specimen, in a green top tube, or a blood count specimen, in a purple top tube, may significantly skew the results of a prothrombin test, which measures clotting time and should be collected in a blue top tube. Most such errors are recognized in the laboratory, after the sample has been improperly collected. It then is usually necessary to draw another sample from the patient, which results in delayed communication of test results to the treating provider, not to mention patient inconvenience. Depending on the circumstances, such delay may have negative effect on outcome. On the other hand, if the specimen collection error is not recognized, an incorrect test result can bring dire consequences. For example, when a heparinized syringe is used to draw a blood gas sample from a patient in the operating room, and the remaining blood in the syringe is injected into a blue top tube for coagulation tests, the coagulation test results will be quite abnormal. The surgeon may conclude that STAT plasma transfusions are needed, even though the patient is not bleeding excessively.

When the wrong type of container is used for a surgical biopsy, it might not be possible to obtain a second specimen. Operating room and other authorized staff should be trained to consult the laboratory, whenever feasible, as to the container and preservative they will need before they collect unusual specimens, or specimens for tests which with they are unfamiliar. The operating room staff—and staff in other areas where specimens are collected—should also routinely check the availability of suitable collection containers, before any procedure begins.

All specimens must be accompanied by a complete and accurate requisition which documents date and time collected, the name of the person who collected the specimen, the type and source of the specimen, test(s) requested, and, as relevant, clinical history and differential diagnosis. It is also essential that the source and type of specimen be specific and accurate, because these factors often determine how testing will be carried out. For example, in microbiology, growth culture material (media) is selected, based on the site of collection and type of specimen. This is partly due to differences in pH among specimen sources. For example, urine has a very different pH from spinal or thoracentesis fluid and must be cultured in a different medium. Even in simple home tests for the presence of blood in body fluids, the test kit used to assess the presence of blood in gastric contents is different from the one used to check for blood in stool.

Similarly, the history and potential diagnoses are critical to the laboratory's management of tissue specimens for surgical pathology, hematopathology, and cytopathology. This information must be specifically documented by the individual collecting the specimen, and the laboratory should also correlate the test order with the differential diagnosis.

Sample storage and transport might require specific approaches depending on the test, particularly if a sample is sent to a distant central or reference laboratory. Also, before using a pneumatic tube system for specimen or blood product transport, the laboratory should validate that use of the tube system does not adversely affect the sample or blood product.

RISK MANAGEMENT STRATEGIES IN THE ANALYTIC PHASE

To maintain specimen identity, it is essential for laboratory personnel who receive the specimen to check specimens and labels against requisitions for discrepancies. Specimens should be submitted in sufficient quantity in the proper container with the required preservative, and they should arrive in the laboratory undamaged. If the specimen is unacceptable, the collection location should be notified as soon as possible and another specimen requested.

Written criteria should guide rejection of specimens, and under certain circumstances, the lab could be forced to test a specimen that otherwise would be rejected. For example, the laboratory might accept difficult-to-replace specimens that are mislabeled, such as timed blood draws, biopsies, or cerebrospinal fluid. In these cases, the laboratory can require clinical staff to label the specimen again, or sign a voucher, affidavit, or confirmation attesting to the identity of the patient from whom the specimen was collected. Refer to Exhibit 16.1.

EXHIBIT 16.1   Confirmation of Specimen Identification

SuperDuper Hospital
Anywhere, USA

Irreplaceable Specimen

** THIS ENTIRE FORM MUST BE COMPLETED.

Name on Specimen Label _____

Name on Requisition _____

Collection/Patient Location _____

Provider/Physician Notified _____

Notification Date/Time/By _____

Physician's Statement

Use of Confirmation of Specimen Identification Form

This form is completed to verify the accuracy of information for irreplaceable specimens. This form will only be used for the following limited purposes (please check one or more of the following):
___ The test is critical and delay for a new specimen could compromise care
___ Clinical reasons for not obtaining a second specimen exist—explain:
_____
___ The patient is unavailable for a second collection.
___ Other—explain:
_____

Correct Specimen Information: _____

I affirm the accuracy of the corrected information provided and request that the specimen be analyzed. The process of obtaining a new specimen could have a negative impact on the condition of the patient, and is not possible at this time.

Print Physician's Name: _____ Date: _____ Time: _____

Physician's Signature: _____

Collector's Statement (if not the Physician above)

I affirm the accuracy of the corrected information provided.

Print Collector's Name: _____ Date: _____ Time: _____

Collector's Signature: _____

Laboratory Medical Director

Print Name: _____ Date: _____ Time: _____

Medical Director Signature: _____

The policy for acceptance of mislabeled specimens should be written with the input of the risk management professional or legal counsel. It should include safeguards such as the following. The specimen should be reasonably identifiable. The person signing the voucher should also receive authorization from the facility's chief medical officer, chief nursing officer, or the medical director of quality or patient safety. A laboratory representative should document objectively on the test report regarding the original error, such as, "This specimen was relabeled prior to testing—see voucher on file." The voucher should then be retained by the laboratory. Some laboratories have resorted to DNA testing, at the expense of the health care organization, to match irreplaceable specimens to patients.

When irreplaceable specimens must be relabeled, or their labels must be modified, the laboratory should complete an occurrence report. Mislabeled specimens should be monitored through the health care organization's quality improvement program. Failure Mode and Effects Analysis (FMEA) can be also be used to reduce labeling and collection errors. Refer to Chapter 3 of this volume for further discussion of FMEA.

One general safeguard against the loss of specimen integrity is that during the analytical phase, a part, or aliquot, of a sample is commonly transferred to another container before the actual testing. All aliquots and dilutions must be readily identifiable, and the identity and integrity of samples must be maintained throughout the entire testing phase.

············

RISK MANAGEMENT STRATEGIES IN THE POST-ANALYTIC PHASE

A "critical value" is defined as a laboratory result that indicates that adequate and timely intervention is needed to correct a potentially life-threatening condition. Critical values, formerly known as "panic values," are those that fall outside high and low limits defined by the laboratory. CLIA and CAP require that each laboratory establish a list of critical values, which may be individualized to reflect the facility's patient population.

Reporting Critical Values

When a test result falls outside the parameters on the critical value list, a caregiver must be notified immediately. To accomplish this, laboratory personnel usually place a telephone call to the clinical staff who are caring for the patient. However, common pitfalls in this process include failure of the laboratory staff to make the telephone call, the failure of the clinical staff, such as nurses on the floor, to communicate the result to the physician or other ordering health care provider, and the provider's failure to act on the results in a timely manner. Such communication gaps often lead to allegations of delay in diagnosis or delay in treatment in a related malpractice suit.

To ensure that the process is effective, the critical values selected should be logical and meaningful, and the list of critical values that potentially can be reported should be short and manageable. Critical values should be developed in consultation with health care providers. Patient variables such as age, weight, and co-morbidities play a role in determining the criticality of a test result. For example, a renal specialist does not want to be continually bothered about a creatinine result of 6.2, which is abnormal for most patients, but normal for an end stage renal disease patient. One concept that might be helpful, in consultation with the treating physician, is a "first time alert." In this approach, the first time the patient has a creatinine above 4.0, the physician is immediately notified. After that, delta check values (significant changes from shift to shift or day to day or week to week) may be more useful to the physician. Guidance in developing critical values is provided by CAP. Another resource is the Massachusetts Coalition for the Prevention of Medical Errors, which has developed a comprehensive "starter set" of critical values for laboratories. This resource, which includes implementation and monitoring guidance can be found at [www.macoaltion.org/initiatives.shtml].

Computer alert systems have also proved invaluable in reducing erroneous or omitted reporting of critical values. Several laboratory computer systems detect critical values and notify the laboratory staff through the use of pop-up or colored notice screens. Technologists are not permitted to proceed further in the computer system without acknowledging the result. Laboratory technologists then initiate the critical value reporting process. Some computer systems even page the physician automatically with critical value results, thus reducing delays in necessary treatment.

Reporting timeframes are an essential part of critical value reporting and should be established in collaboration with the medical staff. Risk managers can assist the laboratory through education on key points to document in the reporting process, and in implementing the chain of command, if laboratory personnel find that the caregiver is unavailable or unresponsive.

The chain of command policy should be consistent with other such approaches in the facility. It should be triggered by written criteria and contain no more than three steps. For example, the chain may be initiated if the laboratory pages the ordering physician three times within forty-five minutes with no response. The next step may be to notify applicable house staff, the hospitalist, or the applicable department chairman with the critical test results, to ensure that the patient receives the necessary timely treatment. When the chain of command or back-up system is implemented, the laboratory should subsequently work with the medical staff to learn what can be done to improve the process.

Critical value reporting documentation should include the name of the person reporting the test result, the name and title of the person receiving the results, the test name, the value and interpretation, and the date and time. It is also essential, in keeping with JCAHO's new requirement, that there be documentation that the recipient confirmed their understanding of the results by reading them back to laboratory personnel. Read-backs can be encouraged by using simple dialogue such as, "I want to be sure that you have the correct information, could you please repeat the patient's name, test, and result that I just gave you?" Several facilities have the nursing staff document receipt of critical values results on a special label, which is then placed on the patient's chart. The label also documents action taken, such as implementation of orders received.

The laboratory manager and the risk management professional should educate all health care providers regarding the importance of the critical value test reporting process. For example, ordering physicians should be educated as to their responsibility for tracking the test results of their patients. The laboratory can facilitate this process by providing checklists or other tools to help physicians remember key points in critical value reporting. Physicians should also understand the importance of ensuring their availability, or a covering provider's availability, for receipt of critical test values on a twenty-four-hour basis. For settings such as outpatient, long-term care, and home health, a list of personnel who are to be contacted with critical values results should be provided to the laboratory.

Laboratory personnel must also be educated that communication of critical values does not necessarily stop with the first provider that the information is conveyed to. For example, if the laboratory calls the nurse caring for the patient, the nurse might assume that the physician already knows about the critical test result. Many organizations such as the Massachusetts Coalition for the Prevention of Medical Errors strongly recommend that critical test values be communicated directly by the lab to the physician.

As critical values reporting is an excellent example of a multidisciplinary process, variances should be monitored through the facility-wide quality improvement program. Laboratory managers should also monitor the frequency and effectiveness of the process' use, on a daily basis. The risk management professional can be a valuable resource to assist in resolving any issues.

Specimen Retention

State and private accrediting organizations require that specimens be retained for specific periods of time. For example, CAP has established a set of minimum standards in this regard which can be accessed at [www.cap.org/apps/docs/laboratory_accreditation/retention_1101.pdf].

Specimen retention protocols should reflect compliance with retention requirements, and with any specific requirements concerning storage of particular specimens, for example, refrigeration.

....

RISK MANAGEMENT STRATEGIES IN SPECIFIC LAB SPECIALTIES

Risk management in the laboratory must consider specific testing practices, each of which carries its own implications for risk assessment and avoidance. These include, but are not limited to, clinical pathology, anatomic pathology, cytopathology, and issues involving blood transfusions.

Clinical Pathology

Clinical pathology includes clinical chemistry, microbiology, virology, urinalysis, blood banking, and parts of hematology. Each of these disciplines performs manual or automated tests on various kinds of blood, body fluids, and tissue samples from patients. Choice of a particular test method can be difficult. For example, counting the number of blood platelets in a sample can be done manually, although more often it is accomplished by one of several indirect methods that uses hematology instruments. Recently, a flow cytometry technique has been advocated as more accurate. Approaches vary from laboratory to laboratory. In all cases, procedures should be written clearly and should be kept up to date. All reagents and instruments should be federally licensed, although for some testing, licensed reagents are not available. Flow cytometery is one example of a test for which there are no licensed reagents. Test reports should clearly indicate when unlicensed reagents are used. These results should be considered less credible than results of tests performed with licensed regents. Instrument manufacturers should approve the source of the reagents used in their products. Attempts to cut costs by using reagents that might not work with the organization's instrumentation can result in testing delays, erroneous results, and more costs later.

Proficiency testing is an important CLIA regulatory requirement for many tests. This generally involves the laboratory's receipt of five samples for tests such as blood glucose, hemoglobin, microbiological culture, and so on, from a third party that is also licensed under CLIA. Usually the laboratory performs the test and submits the results on sets of samples three times per year. The laboratory's results are then compared to the correct answers and to those of peer settings. Unsatisfactory results on two of three successive sets can result in loss of the ability to do such testing. For most tests it is possible to "fail" on one sample of the five, and still pass overall (80 percent pass rate). For blood typing, a 100 percent passing rate is required. All failed individual samples should be reviewed when they occur, and a written corrective action plan should be followed.

Blood Transfusion Services

As previously noted, blood transfusion services have additional unique regulatory requirements, because blood products are FDA-licensed pharmaceuticals. They also have unique handling requirements because blood products are biologicals with strict temperature and expiration-related requirements. The reagents used for testing are in large part also biologicals with similar restrictions. Unlike most other pharmaceuticals, each bag of red cells or plasma is from an individual source (donor) and is considered an individual lot, only for patients with that particular blood type. A permanent record must be retained concerning the source of the blood, the testing (including retesting of ABO & Rh of the blood), reagent lot numbers, storage, transfusion process, and name of the recipient.

There are many reasons for the increased focus on the handling of blood products. Blood is a pharmaceutical with potential immediate lethal risk if given to the wrong patient or incorrectly tested. As compared with other drugs, blood has stricter storage needs and a shorter shelf life. It is also important that the complications of a transfusion might not manifest themselves for decades after the transfusion. All staff involved in any aspect of blood transfusion, including collecting recipient blood specimens, and prescribing, crossmatching, administering, and monitoring the transfusion, must realize that they are responsible for creating a record which verifies that each step in a high-risk process was followed.

Logically, adverse reactions to transfusions should be reported immediately to the supplier of blood products, so any related concerns may be identified and addressed. FDA reporting requirements change frequently, and so laboratory personnel should routinely update themselves regarding events and standards deviations that are reportable. Transfusion-related deaths must be reported to the FDA,[16] as must any deviation from transfusion-related standards that results in patient injury—or with the potential for patient injury.[17] For example, a transfusion reaction involving hemolysis of the red blood cell bag warrants reporting, even without severe patient injury, whereas a mild febrile reaction without injury, where there is no evidence of improper processing, storage, testing, or transfusion of the blood, may not be reported. The febrile reaction would, however, be noted in the medical record, as an observation made in the course of a customary transfusion reaction workup.

Requirements for blood bank record retention have steadily increased. In some cases transfusion services have been asked to identify recipients of transfusions more than ten years previous. One reason for this involves an important regulatory aspect of transfusion known as "Lookback." This term defines the mandatory process that ensues when a blood donor tests positive for HIV or hepatitis C. Briefly, the blood collection organization must identify prior previous donations from the particular donor that tested negative and were transfused. The recipient patients are identified, contacted, and retested. There are specific federal requirements concerning how far back to review records, time limits for completing the process, and so on.

It is important for laboratory staff and risk managers to stay current with newsletters from CAP, AABB, JCAHO, FDA, and state agencies for changes in record retention requirements and other regulatory or accreditation changes that pertain to blood transfusion.

Anatomic Pathology

The number of autopsies has steadily decreased over the last forty years. However, a significant number of "missed diagnoses" continue to be identified during autopsies, and sometimes the unsuspected diagnosis was important in the patient's demise. Some physicians avoid requesting autopsies, for fear of such findings and potential related lawsuits. Others seek autopsy results to help them avoid the same problem in a subsequent patient. The hospital and the pathologist might be concerned that there will be no reimbursement for an autopsy. There is no clear resolution to this multifaceted dispute. However, discouraging the family's request for an autopsy can create suspicion of the physician and the hospital. When an autopsy is performed, it should be done with sufficient care, and attention to the presumed cause of death. When implants such as pacemakers or replaced joints are present, they should be examined for defects. They should be carefully removed and preserved, and pertinent Safe Medical Device Act reporting requirements should be complied with if they might have contributed to morbidity and mortality.

Cytopathology

Cytopathology has risk management ramifications in all its aspects, including but not limited to training and proficiency testing and practice requirements, and in the special area of cervicovaginal cytology.

Training and Proficiency Testing Requirements   CLIA and private accrediting organization requirements vary for training of laboratory staff who perform cytology testing. The laboratory director of a cytology lab can be a pathologist, other MD, or DO with experience and training, or a Ph.D. with required experience and training. The technical supervisor must be an MD or DO, certified in anatomic pathology. The cytology general supervisor may be qualified as a technical supervisor in cytology or a cytotechnologist with three years of full-time experience as a cytotechnologist in the preceding ten years.

Of particular note, CLIA 1988 discussed the importance of proficiency testing for any individual who examines gynecologic preparations. After many years of internal debate, CMS finally approved two national gynecologic cytology proficiency testing programs in December 2004. CAP and others have raised concerns that the programs are based on outdated standards and have recommended their suspension until they can be updated to reflect technological advances. The CAP position articulated in June 2005 can be reviewed on the CAP Web site at [www.cap.org/apps/docs/advocacy/advocacy_issues/cytology_proficiency_testing.htm]. Risk management professionals should follow this issue carefully. However, compliance dates were set for 2005, and until the regulatory dust settles, laboratories must ensure that individuals who examine gynecological preparations are enrolled in one of these programs. All such professionals had to be tested at least once before April 2006 and had to achieve a passing score. If the laboratory fails to ensure that individuals are tested, or fails to take remedial action when an individual fails gynecologic cytology proficiency testing, sanctions will be imposed. More information on resources to assist providers in achieving compliance can be found on the CAP Web site at [www.cap.org/apps/docs/news_service/0503/0503_Resources.html].

Practice Requirements for Cytopathology   The laboratory must ensure that diagnostic interpretations are not based on unsatisfactory smears and that all cytology slide preparations are evaluated on the premises or referred to a laboratory certified to conduct testing in cytology. All gynecologic smears are to be stained using a Papanicolaou or modified Papanicolaou method. Workload limitations are also imposed by CLIA '88. Each individual who evaluates cytology preparations by non-automated microscopic technique must examine no more than 100 slides (gynecologic and non-gynecologic or both) in a twenty-four-hour period. The total number of slides examined by each individual during each such period must be documented. The maximum workload of 100 slides can be completed in no less than an eight-hour workday, and it includes all slides that an individual reads during employment in another setting.[18] The hospital should consider requiring that those who are employed elsewhere report the total number of slides read daily, for the protection of the laboratory, the individual technologists, and the patients whose results are being interpreted.

Overreading requirements for slides are based on criteria that prioritize certain pathologic conditions. All gynecologic smears interpreted to show reactive or reparative changes, atypical squamous or glandular cells of undetermined significance, or to be premalignant or in a malignant category are to be confirmed by a technical supervisor in cytology. A technical supervisor in cytology must review all non-gynecologic preparations.

The laboratory must establish and follow a program designed to detect errors in the performance of cytologic examinations and the reporting of results. A 10-percent rescreen of negatives must occur, from random patients and from "high-risk" patients, based on available patient information. The review must be completed before reporting patient results on those selected cases. The laboratory must compare all malignant and pre-malignant gynecologic reports with the histopathology report, if available in the laboratory, and determine the causes of any discrepancies. For each patient determined to have an intraepithelial lesion of high grade, or exceeding a high grade, the laboratory must review all normal or negative gynecologic specimens available within the previous five years. If significant discrepancies are found that would affect patient care, the laboratory must notify the patient's physician and must issue an amended report.

Reports and records are required by many of the CLIA regulations. The laboratory must, for example, document an annual statistical evaluation of the number of cytology cases examined, reporting the volume of patients by diagnosis, number of discrepancies found, and so on. The laboratory must also document an assessment that contrasts the results of case reviews of each individual who examines slides against the laboratory's overall statistical values. Any discrepancies, including reasons for deviation and corrective action taken, must be documented. The laboratory report must clearly distinguish specimens or smears that are unsatisfactory for diagnostic interpretation. The report must contain narrative descriptive nomenclature for all results, and must indicate the basis for correction on any corrected laboratory report issued. The laboratory must retain all slides for five years from the date of examination. Slides may be loaned to proficiency testing programs if the laboratory obtains written documentation of the receipt of the slides by the recipient program and if the slides are retrievable upon request.

Because of the unique requirements of cervicovaginal cytology, this area is discussed separately.

Cervicovaginal Cytology

Cervicovaginal cytology is, to a certain extent, a victim of its own success, as the public perceives it to be 100-percent foolproof. However, this screening procedure is useful in the reduction of cervical cancer only to the degree to which it is properly collected, handled, and interpreted. This section addresses the overlap of quality improvement concepts and risk management principles as they apply to cervicovaginal cytology, and discusses the responsibilities of women, health care providers, and laboratory personnel.

The Pap smear is a safe, non-invasive, cost-effective screening procedure. A health care provider (obstetrician or gynecologist, family practitioner, internist, nurse clinician, and so on) collects (scrapes) the specimen, composed of cellular material, from the cervix and places it on a glass slide. The specimen is then specially preserved and processed for microscopic evaluation.

Cervicovaginal Cytology Screens for Cervical Cancer, Precancerous Lesions, and Infectious Conditions   The individuals usually responsible for the initial evaluation and interpretation of the cervicovaginal cytology specimen are cytotechnologists. In some laboratories, a pathologist may perform the initial screening and interpretation, and the ultimate diagnosis of the cellular sample. Cytotechnologists are highly skilled individuals. Since 1988, a baccalaureate degree has been required as a prerequisite to the certification examination in cytotechnology. The certification examination is a rigorous national examination administered by the American Society for Clinical Pathology (ASCP). The cytotechnologist evaluates whether or not the sample is adequate and satisfactory and determines if the cellular sample is within normal limits or negative. A report is then issued to the health care provider. If the cytotechnologist detects an abnormality or determines the cellular sample to be positive, the slide is reviewed by a pathologist who renders a final diagnosis. High-risk patients may have all of their samples routinely examined by the pathologist.

Despite the successes of cervicovaginal cytology, it is important to understand its limitations. False negatives may occur as false positives do. A false negative may occur when a patient has a cervical lesion, however, the abnormal cells are not present on the slide. This could be because the lesion is small and was not sampled when the Pap smear was taken. False negatives also occur when abnormal cells are present on the slide, but the cells are either missed or misinterpreted or misdiagnosed. Even in a high-quality laboratory that follows all the CLIA '88 requirements and other published standards, abnormal cells will occasionally be missed. Two-thirds of false negatives are attributed to sampling and specimen collection errors. This emphasizes the role of the primary caregiver who performs the pelvic examination and obtains the specimen.

All laboratories that perform cervicovaginal cytology should use a widely accepted reporting nomenclature called the Bethesda System. Using the Bethesda System reduces the chance a clinician will not fully understand the patient's condition, resulting in delayed, inadequate, or omitted treatment.

The health care provider is generally responsible for recommending that Pap smears be performed. It is imperative that the health care provider instruct female patients as to the optimal time for performing a Pap smear, for example, not during menses. Patients should not use vaginal creams, contraceptive foams or jellies, douche, or tampons twenty-four to twenty-eight hours prior to a Pap smear. Having intercourse in that timeframe or a current vaginal infection can hinder accuracy due to associated creams, blood, douches, and so on. All of these variants can remove or contaminate the cells necessary for proper evaluation. The task of collecting an adequate sample and ensuring that it is properly labeled and preserved belongs to the provider who collects the specimen. This professional is also responsible for providing the laboratory with a pertinent clinical history that includes symptoms and other risk factors. Omitting the clinical history on the requisition for a patient with a history of abnormal Pap smears could lead to delayed or missed diagnoses. The laboratory should provide a sample requisition that encourages providers to routinely include the clinical history. The health care providers should complete the requisition themselves and not leave it to the office staff.

Ensuring open, high-quality communication between the laboratory and the referring clinician is essential. The laboratory's findings should be correlated with the observations of the clinician who submits patient specimens. The laboratory should report all cytologic findings using concise, descriptive, unambiguous terminology. Finally, the clinician should review all cytology reports and communicate the information to the patient. The circle of open, direct communication is then complete, facilitating prompt patient treatment if issues are identified. If the laboratory recommends repeat testing, it is the physician's responsibility to notify the patient verbally and in writing. The physician's office should maintain a log of patients notified of abnormal Pap results that require repeat testing or other follow-up. Dates of notification and follow-up appointment or referrals should be logged. The log should be used as a "tickler file" so that patients can be contacted to remind them of needed follow-up. Any other specific details should also be documented in each patient's medical record. Table 16.1 details the responsibilities of each of the parties involved.

TABLE 16.1   Breakdown of Responsibilities

Physician Responsibilities

1. Educate female patients over the age of 18, particularly those at risk, to have annual PAP smears.
2. Keep up-to-date on current testing guidelines promulgated by professional organizations such as the American College of Obstetricians & Gynecologists.
3. Advise patients as to the best time to obtain a PAP smear, e.g. just before ovulation.
4. Learn to properly collect the cervicovaginal cytology specimen.
5. Send specimens to an accredited laboratory.
6. Provide the laboratory with a pertinent clinical history and information including symptomology and risk factors.
7. Correlate laboratory findings with clinical observations.
8. Recommend appropriate follow-up promptly; send reminders.

Patient Responsibilities

1. Schedule an appointment for an annual Pap smear with someone who is skilled in taking Pap Smears such as a gynecologist.
2. Properly prepare for the Pap smear.
3. Call her practitioner if she doesn't receive results within a reasonable period of time.
4. Follow the health care practitioner's recommendations for follow up such as biopsies.

If she changes health care providers she should notify her new physician of her gynecologic history.

Laboratory Responsibilities

1. Provide qualified personnel to direct and staff the cytology laboratory.
2. Ensure that all appropriate personnel (cytotechnologists) participate in proficiency testing.
3. Monitor cytotechnologist workload.
4. Ensure that slide interpretations are not reported on unsatisfactory smears.
5. Use a uniform grading system and terminology for reporting.
6. Establish and utilize a complete quality management program from cervical cytology.
7. Maintain all cervical cytology slides and records in accordance with state and federal law.
8. State results in a standardized manner, and clearly indicating when repeat or follow up testing is needed.

The CLIA 88 section on cervical cytology outlines the many responsibilities of the laboratory. The following risk indicators are suggested for inclusions in a cytopathology laboratory performance improvement program.

- Specimen procurement, including proper identification, clinical information and fixation
- Specimens lost and not received
- Specimen adequacy
- Proper preparation and staining of slides
- Comparison of cytotechnologist interpretation to cytopathologist diagnosis
- Upon review, new or additional cellular findings that are significantly different from the initial report
- Significant discrepancy between cytopathology diagnosis and histopathology diagnosis

Additionally, it might be helpful to set up a system to recognize when clinicians submit multiple patient specimens in a short period of time. Rescreens of some of these slides may be called for.

New technologies include computerized screening of cervicovaginal pathology specimens. Whereas the FDA has approved only certain specific computerized devices to rescreen negative smears, and identify any issues missed by the initial screener, it will only be a matter of time before manufacturers apply and receive approval from the FDA for all initial screening. New methods for collecting and preparing cervicovaginal cytology specimens have also been developed. For example, liquid-based Pap tests, commonly known as "thin prep," are said to produce specimens with less blood and thick clumping of cells, which makes it easier to identify abnormalities.[19] One concern is that such new technologies might drive up the cost of Pap smears, possibly limiting access to Pap smears by lower-income women. Before implementing automated screens, laboratories should conduct a thorough cost-benefit analysis.

Surgical and Hematopathology Responsibilities

There is a tendency in some laboratories to regard these areas as removed from the usual laboratory requirements concerning written procedures, proper reagent use and storage, and so on. In fact, the same principles apply, and the pre-analytic and post-analytic aspects of these areas are of particular concern, from a risk management standpoint.

In the pre-analytic stage, it is important to note that the specimen is much more likely to be unique than is the case with clinical pathology. When a clinical pathology specimen is lost or mislabeled, it is frequently possible to obtain a new sample of blood or urine from the patient. Repeating a surgical biopsy because of mislabeling obviously poses many more concerns. (Refer to the previous discussion of specimen collection earlier in this chapter.)

The analytic phase of surgical and bone marrow pathology involves microscopic examination of tissue after processing and staining. The processing and staining procedures should be detailed in writing, and are subject to CLIA inspection. The examination and diagnostic interpretation is performed by a CLIA-qualified physician, generally a pathologist. Diagnostic interpretation is performed in a manner which is similar to a radiologist's interpretation of an x-ray. And two pathologists may differ in their interpretation of a specimen, just as two radiologists may arrive at different diagnoses based on the same set of x-rays. In some instances the differences are matters of nomenclature and classification, without clinical import for the patient involved. Others involve diagnostic differences that are of clinical significance.

In pathology, the need for immediate readings by means of "frozen sections" further complicates issues of diagnostic variance. In this technique, part of a tissue specimen is rapidly frozen with liquid nitrogen, which allows immediate sectioning and limited staining. Thus it is possible to have a microscopically readable slice in minutes, while a patient is still in the operating room, and the surgeon is deciding what to do next. The technical drawbacks of the technique include less microscopic detail, and the perspective provided by ancillary stains is not available. Also, the size and quality of the pre-analytic sample is critical because less tissue is available for examination than can later be evaluated in the "permanent sections." Thus a diagnostic "mistake" might occur because the lesion was not present in the limited frozen section sample, or the collection technique itself prevented an accurate reading. Estimates of the variance between frozen and final diagnoses are around 2–3 percent. The frozen section diagnosis should always be compared with the final report, and the bases for differences evaluated. The ordering clinician should always be promptly notified when such discrepancies occur. Indeed, a discrepancy should be treated as a "critical value" and accorded an equivalent response. (Refer to the section on critical value reporting.)

Even with conventionally processed and stained permanent microscopic sections, there can be interpretive differences between pathologists. In many cases, the interpretive differences are not of clinical significance and involve matters such as differences in classification systems, and so on. In a multi-institutional study, specimens were reread by at least one pathologist in several formats, and it was determined that 1 percent of the subject specimens had a second reading that was different from the first and which involved a difference of clinical import. Thus in a small hospital, with perhaps two pathologists and 5,000 surgical pathology specimens a year, fifty specimens, or roughly one per week, might be read differently.

Given the above data, it is recommended that pathologists engage in some type of rereading system as part of the laboratory's quality improvement program. This can be by random allocation of a certain percentage of specimens, similar to cytopathology, or through concentration on known areas of interpretive difficulty, such as breast, prostate, and skin. Alternative approaches can also be developed. Preferably, whatever approach is used, the lab should track the results by individual pathologist. Specimens can be sent for outside consultation, which can result in additional input for quality assessment. This input is, of course, particularly valuable when the outside expert states that a diagnosis is materially different than the one determined locally. In considering variances in pathologists' interpretations, it is important to distinguish two major categories of disagreement. In the first, the original pathologist has doubts about the diagnosis, and has requested another opinion from a local partner or colleague. Here, a discrepancy is due to professional prudence by the original pathologist, rather than error. The second category involves cases where the first pathologist had no doubts about the diagnosis, but a second evaluation occurred randomly, or because the patient or the patient's primary physician requested outside review. In these latter instances, disagreement may indicate error, and third opinions should be sought, if necessary. Such discrepancies should be a regular part of the quality improvement data reported by the laboratory to the facility's quality improvement department. Other submitted data should include the previously noted correlation rate between frozen and final diagnoses. Most pathologists do have such reread systems and monitor their own performances.

Whatever the system used, it is important that the selected rereads cover all types of specimens that reach a given pathologist. For a general pathologist, this would mean all types of specimens. In larger departments, a given pathologist might only examine cytology specimens, or bone marrows, and so on. The pathology department should have objective benchmarks, based on the literature or on standards set by national professional organizations. As is the case with other laboratory physician positions, the anatomic pathologist(s) must meet CLIA requirements, and be properly licensed and credentialed.

Tissue and Organ Donor Services

These areas are not often based in the pathology department, but will be covered briefly here.

The hospital is obligated to ensure that tissue or organs are donated under the auspices of a licensed tissue bank and organ procurement organization (OPO). There should be formal agreements, and all hospitals are obligated to refer possible organ donors. A new JCAHO standard requires hospitals to monitor the conversion (success) rate on their eligible patients.[20] Hospitals that perform organ transplants should have standard protocols that address a wide range of topics, including consent, delineation of roles within the OPO, safety checks on organ suitability, cadaver and live donor procedures, IRBs, and so on. Based on the authors' experiences, such programs should include input from the ethics committee and risk management area. A more detailed discussion is beyond the scope of this chapter.

The FDA has jurisdiction over tissue storage and transplant.[21] Tissue should be obtained only from a licensed, accredited facility. Storage of tissue should be per supplier's instructions, with continuous temperature monitoring in alarmed refrigerators or freezers. Many institutions find that storage in a freezer in the blood bank, using the same alarm system, is a practical approach. The tissue receipt is placed in a log, and the expiration date is documented. For each tissue fragment, a permanent record is kept of receipt, source, type, lot number, date of transplant or other disposition. A note of this information is also made in the patient's chart. The hospital must be able to trace the tissue back to the supplier, in case of a patient reaction. Conversely, the hospital should be able to locate the recipient, if the supplying tissue bank later finds a defect in the particular lot.

Unless a hospital can fulfill all of the regulatory and licensure requirements, it is unwise for it to maintain a tissue retrieval or storage bank, even for autologous tissues. Success and complication rates for tissue and organ transplants should be the subject of routing quality improvement reporting for the departments involved.

Bone marrow progenitor cell transplants (bone marrow or peripheral blood stem cell) programs require systems similar to those that support tissue transplantation, and extensive processing and storage protocols that are similar to those of tissue and blood banks, including alarm-monitored storage areas.

••••••••••••
CRITICAL VALUES

Critical values are as important in anatomic pathology as they are in clinical pathology. In the present environment of increased outpatient biopsies and surgeries, mailed reports may go astray or be missed in a busy practitioner's office. Whether by mail, computer interface, or manual messenger, all steps associated with transfer of information have risks of failure. A summary of concepts (and associated tips) regarding laboratory testing appears in Table 16.2. The following list of circumstances that require direct communication with the ordering physician is not intended to be all-inclusive, but rather to stimulate institutions to reexamine their systems:

- Cases with significant variance between frozen section and final diagnoses
- Amended reports based on special stains or testing
- New or substantively changed diagnoses by an outside consultant
- Reports of malignant or possibly malignant tissue
- Recommendations for follow-up or repeat examinations, or repeated screening at more frequent intervals
- Placentas submitted for examination that are suspected of being incomplete
- Unsatisfactory specimens

The pathologist should document the direct follow-up in some manner. Some pathologists do this as an addendum to the diagnostic report itself.

TABLE 16.2   Summary of Concepts and Tips for the Risk Management Professional

---

1. Laboratories are highly regulated by multiple entities
   TIP—Overall JCAHO Hospital accreditation is NOT sufficient for laboratory accreditation.
2. Even in a low volume setting, if laboratory testing is performed for clinical purposes, then CLIA certification is required
   TIP—Pay attention to medical center newsletter articles on exciting new testing in a clinical area separate from the main laboratory. Check to see if there are clinical purposes and/or research implications (See Chapter 5 on Clinical on Research.) Also, find out if the patient is billed. (See Chapter 19 in Volume III on Corporate Compliance). In a large tertiary institution, risk managers may not always be told about small laboratories in departments other than pathology.
   TIP—Contact CMS for a list of laboratories identified with your institution's name and/or address.
3. Regulations and standards frequently change, and can be difficult to follow.
   TIP—Always have and follow a current copy of the CAP Inspection Checklists, or the JCAHO Accreditation Manual for Laboratories. If you have a transfusion service, then a current copy of the AABB Standards should be in the laboratory. Regulatory changes can also be followed in monthly newsletters, such as JCAHO Perspectives, and CAP Today.
4. Blood transfusion services and banks receive more regulatory oversight when they do more processing, and if they draw blood from donors. If blood is drawn from donors, the provider must perform complex tests for HIV and hepatitis.
   TIP—If donors are drawn, consider "contracting out" these complicated expensive tests for viruses. Contracting services can also shift liability to another organization.
6. Progenitor cells may be kept frozen for many years, for potential needs of the intended recipients.
   TIP—Have protocols from the outset defining who "owns" the cells if years later, they are not needed by the intended recipient.
5. Laboratory activities involve ongoing interfaces with nursing staff.
   TIP—Ongoing committee, task force, coffee chats, etc., are essential to establishing effective relationships among nursing and laboratory staff.
6. Transport of specimens has many associated risks.
   TIP—The most common causes of prolonged turnaround in obtaining test results are not intralaboratory (analytic). This issue usually results from delay in receipt of samples (pre-analytic), delay in receipt of result by the physician, or delay in the physician taking action on the result (post-analytic). In each of these areas, a root cause analysis aids in defining underlying systems issues and areas (e.g. lab, nursing, physician, transport) as well as identifying simple effective solutions.

....

CONCLUSION

Laboratory testing poses a wide variety of risks to the patient, laboratory, and hospital staff. Significant among these is the risk of violating the regulations of government agencies and private accrediting organizations. Given the rapid evolution of technology and regulations controlling technology, laboratories and risk management professionals should monitor publications and other informational resources for changes in requirements and best practices that can help alleviate risk.

Endnotes

1. "Types of CLIA Certificate" accessed through CMS site on December 11, 2005, at [www.cms.hhs.gov/clia/certypes.asp].

2. *Ibid.*

3. Notice: Medicare, Medicaid, and CLIA Programs; Continuance of the Approval of the College of American Pathologists as a CLIA Accreditation Organization Federal Register: September 12, 2001 (Volume 66, Number 177), Page 47493–47497. From the Federal Register Online via GPO Access [wais.access.gpo.gov], accessed through [www.phppo.cdc.gov/clia/docs/fr12se01n.htm] December 11, 2005.

4. "List of CLIA Exempt States" accessed on CMS Web site on December 11, 2005 at [www.cms.hhs.gov/clia/exemstat.asp].

5. "CLIA General Program Description" accessed on the CMS Web site, December 11, 2005, at [www.cms.hhs.gov/clia/progdesc.asp].

6. *Ibid.*

7. "List of CLIA Approved PT Proficiency Testing Programs 2005" accessed on the CMS Web site December 11, 2005, at [www.cms.hhs.gov/clia/ptlist.pdf].

8. "CLIA Program General Description," *op.cit.*

9. U.S. Food and Drug Administration Center for Biologics Evaluation and Research, "Blood," accessed on December 11, 2005, at: [www.fda.gov/cber/blood.htm].

10. U.S. Food and Drug Administration Center for Biologics Evaluation and Research, "Blood Establishment Registration and Product Listing (BER)," accessed on December 11, 2005, at [www.fda.gov/cber/blood/bldreg.htm].

11. U.S. Food and Drug Administration Center for Biologics Evaluation and Research, "Devices Regulated by CBER," accessed on December 11, 2005, at: [www.fda.gov/cber/dap/devlst.htm].

12. Clinical and Laboratory Standards Institute (CLSI) (formerly known as National Committee for Clinical Laboratory Standards—NCCLS) 940 West Valley Rd., Ste. 1400, Wayne, Pa. 19087-1898, (610) 688–0100, [www.clsi.org].

13. [www.hipaa.org].

14. Patient Safety Goals, accessed through JCAHO Web site on December 10, 2005 at [www. jcaho.org/accredited+organizations/patient+safety/05+npsg/05_npsg_hap.htm].

15. *Ibid.*

16. Guidance on Reporting Fatality Related to Transfusion to the FDA at [64.233.161.104/search?q=cache:ydowQ4gPvioJ:www.fda.gov/cber/gdlns/bldfatal.pdf +FDA+and+requirements+for+transfusion-related+death&hl=en].

17. Wise, Robert P., FDA and CBER "FDA's Safety Surveillance for Blood and Blood Products" for presentation to the Advisory Committee on Blood Safety and Availability, May 16, 2005, accessed at [www.hhs.gov/bloodsafety/presentations/Wise.pdf].

18. CLIA Final Rule published February 28, 1992, at 42 CFR 493.1257(b)(1) and (b)(3)(i).

19. "Screening For Cervical Cancer, Guideline Synthesis on the National Guideline Clearinghouse web page of the AHRQ site, accessed December 12, 2005 at [www.guideline.gov/Compare/comparison.aspx?file=CvCSCREEN1.inc].

20. JCAHO Online, accessed December 10, 2005 at [www.jcaho.org/about+us/news+letters/jcahonline/jo_01_05.htm].

21. Wells, Martha, MPH, CBER "Implementation of 21 CFR 1251" accessed at [www.fda. gov/cber/summaries/aatb092005mw.pdf], December 10, 2005.

Resources

American Association of Blood Banks (AABB), 8101 Glenbrook Rd., Bethesda, MD 20814–2749, (301) 215–6499. [www.aabb.org].

American Society for Clinical Chemistry, 2101 L Street, NW, Ste. 202, Washington, DC 20037-1558, (800) 892–1400. [www.aacc.org].

American Society for Clinical Laboratory Science (ASCLS), 6701 Democracy Blvd., Ste. 300, Bethesda, MD 20817, (301) 657–2768. [www.ascls.org].

American Society for Clinical Pathology (ASCP), 2100 West Harrison Street, Chicago, IL 60012-3798, (312) 738-1336. [www.ascp.org].

American Society for Hematology (ASH), 1900 M Street, Ste. 200, Washington, DC 20036, (202) 776-0544. [www.hematology.org].

American Society for Microbiology (ASM), 1752 N Street, NW, Washington, DC 20036, (202) 737–3600. [www.asm.org].

Centers for Disease Control & Prevention (CDC), 1600 Clifton Road, Atlanta, GA 30333, (404) 639-3311. [www.cdc.gov].

Centers for Medicare & Medicaid Services (CMS). CLIA Program: Clinical Laboratory Improvement Amendments [Web site]. [Cited 2004 Feb 17]. Washington (DC): CMS. [www.cms.hhs.gov/clia].

Clinical and Laboratory Standards Institute (CLSI) (formerly known as National Committee for Clinical Laboratory Standards—NCCLS) 940 West Valley Rd., Ste. 1400, Wayne, PA 19087-1898, (610) 688–0100. [www.clsi.org].

College of American Pathologists (CAP), 325 Waukegan Road, Northfield, IL 60093, (847) 446-8800. [www.cap.org].

ECRI, 5200 Butler Pike, Plymouth Meeting, PA 19462-1298, (610) 825–6000. [www.ecri.org].

FDA [www.fda.gov].

Joint Commission on the Accreditation of Healthcare Organizations (JCAHO), Laboratory Accreditation, One Renaissance Blvd, Oakbrook Terrace, IL (630) 792-5000. [www.jcaho.org].

Massachusetts Coalition for the Prevention of Medical Errors, (located in the Massachusetts Hospital Association), 5 New England Executive Park, Burlington, MA 01803, (781) 272–8000. [www.macoaltion.org/initiatives.shtml].

National Accrediting Agency for Clinical Laboratory Sciences (NAACLS), 8410 W. Bryn Mawr Ave., Ste. 670, Chicago, IL 60631, (773) 714–8880. [www.naacls.org].

National Library of Medicine (NLM), 8600 Rockville Pike, Bethesda, MD 20894. [www.nlm.org].

17

Enhancing Patient Safety in Radiology

Sylvia M. Brown

S ince Wilhelm Conrad Roentgen discovered x-rays in 1895, professionals associated with the field of radiology have continued to refine a provider's ability to envision the body's inner workings without breaking the skin.[1] For example, the interventional radiology setting combines characteristics of the operating room and the radiology suite, housing sophisticated technology that helps physicians diagnose complex patients in the least invasive manner possible. At the same time, advanced telemetric communication systems enhance the capability and efficiency of health care organizations by allowing radiologists to interpret and overread films and studies from the other side of the world. Another important advance is the digitalization of radiology films, which saves storage space and has the potential to interface the film or study directly with the medical record.

Each advance made by radiology is associated with patient safety concerns, and the potential for liability. Of particular note, alleged failure to properly interpret films and diagnostic studies, or to communicate findings, has caused dramatic increases in the severity of malpractice awards against radiologists.[2] This chapter will suggest approaches to help the risk management professional work with clinicians to mitigate key risks associated with increased technology and to interface with other clinical environments.

TECHNOLOGY

The technology associated with radiology has never been without risk. Following are examples of technology-associated safety issues, which have resulted in liability over the years, and key strategies with which to alleviate them. As technology is evolving at a feverish pace, it is hoped that the general approaches suggested here might also be helpful when the risk manager must address equipment or procedures not yet in existence.

Radiation Exposure

The wonder of x-rays was quickly tempered by fear when many suffered burns as a result of radiant energy. Thomas Edison's own experiments with x-rays came to an abrupt halt when his friend and assistant, Clarence Dally, suffered serious burns which ultimately led to his death in 1904. Dally is widely reported to have been the first x-ray related fatality in the United States.[3]

Although modifications have long since reduced the risk, radiation burns are still a source of safety and liability concerns. Following are key approaches:

Radiation Safety Committee   An effective radiation safety committee that has the input of a physicist is a critical mechanism for the health care facility. The guiding principle of radiation safety is ALARA, or "as low as reasonably achievable."[4] With this central goal in mind, routine review of quality objectives by this group is an excellent way to promote radiation safety.

Safety Protocols   Pertinent safety protocols that protect patients and staff will address topics such as adequate shielding, use of lead aprons, and so on. It is important that there are multiple federal and state agencies that speak to radiation safety. For example, OSHA standards address worker safety.

New Equipment Standards   The U.S. Center for Devices and Radiological Health under the Food and Drug Administration sets standards for new equipment that produces radiation, and the Nuclear Regulatory Commission (NRC) governs the safety of individuals who are exposed to all material produced by nuclear reactors. Of particular note are the NRC standards intended to prevent misadministration of nuclear isotopes. These parallel the traditional medication safety approaches by requiring patient identification, and a physician's written order specifying type, dosage, and duration of each pharmaceutical to be administered, accompanied by a written dosage and directive explaining how to calculate dosage.[5]

Precautionary Standards   The American College of Radiology (ACR), an important source of information on the standard of care in radiology, also has published statements on radiation safety. For example, the ACR Standard for Diagnostic Procedures Using Radiopharmaceuticals states that imaging facilities should "reasonably attempt" to identify pregnant patients before performing any diagnostic examination that involves ionizing radiation. The standard also states "There shall be posting of radiation precaution signs in areas where radioactive agents are used or stored (and posting of) warnings to patients to inform the staff if they are or could be pregnant." Regardless of whether ionizing radiation is to be used, it is reasonably prudent to post signs that instruct patients to inform the receptionist or technologist if there is any possibility that they might be pregnant before undergoing a diagnostic radiology study.

Biomedical Preventive Maintenance   A biomedical program that provides for preventive maintenance and repair by technicians who document current equipment-specific training is another important risk management strategy to bolster radiation safety.

CT Scan

Developed in 1972, CT scans enable the provider to view multiple "slices" of an organ, enhancing the traditional single dimension view produced by x-rays[6]. Although risk of cancer is thought to increase with full body CT scans performed on a regular basis[7] (an approach not recommended by the American College of Radiology), the major liability and safety issues pertaining to CT scans concern failure to perform them, or misinterpretation. General principles to assist in preventing misinterpretation, which apply to all diagnostic studies, include the following:[8]

- Other pertinent reports should be available to the clinician.

- Any limitations in the study should be noted by the clinician, addressed as necessary, and documented in the record.[9]

- The clinician should be alert to lesions outside the area of interest (for example, lung-based mass on a kidney-ureter-bladder film).

- Current training in interpreting the study is critical.

- It is important for the clinician to recommend any other studies that may be helpful.

MRI

Of technologic advances in the last twenty years, magnetic resonance imagery (MRI) has been associated with the most dramatic risk. Although the use of magnetic imaging reduces risk associated with traditional radiology exposure, and provides valuable diagnostic perspective for the clinician, the force of the magnet has resulted in numerous patient injuries—and liability suits. The American College of Radiology has published detailed white papers[10] on magnetic resonance safety, which include helpful checklists and practical tips. Risk management professionals and clinicians should access the ACR Web site for updates as necessary. Basic safety principles include the following:

- Orientation to MRI safety should be provided for *everyone* who may practice in the environment, from the chief of surgery to the housekeeping personnel.

- Screening of patients for metallic objects must be routine and thorough. Items that the patient might not regard as problematic should be asked about specifically, for example, the foil associated with drug patches used to administer some medications. Specific checklists to facilitate screening are available on the ACR site.[11]

- Care devices such as intravenous poles, which appear metallic but have been specially treated to be safe in the MRI, should be color-coded. The staff must be instructed that these are the only such devices to be allowed in the environment.

- Emergency protocols must include a provision which requires the security staff and staff in the MR suite to inform firefighters, and other emergency providers, of the risk associated with bringing metal equipment into the environment, if the magnet is operational.

- Mock codes should be run routinely. The relative infrequency of cardiac arrest in the MRI suite make this a particularly important strategy, to help the staff maintain current competency regarding the complex process of extricating a patient who requires resuscitation. Another important factor is the considerable distance that the MRI is often located from code teams and other resources, due to the immense size of many units. The white papers referred to above address MRI code practice specifically.[12]

- Quench procedure. In some older units, a malfunction of the MRI can release helium gas, which displaces oxygen, creating risk of asphyxia, and necessitating immediate removal of all staff and patients from the area. Dependent on the equipment involved, mock drills for this eventuality are also a prudent risk management measure.

Contrast Media

Several risk management issues are associated with contrast media. The first is the role of technologists in injecting any form of contrast media. The following are important principles to consider.

- Technologists who inject contrast media must be certified to do so by a physician, who observes their technique for a specific number of times. They should also be educated on principles of injection, and competencies in both the basic principles and their injection technique should be evaluated annually. When the technologist is injecting, a physician should be near, and available to assist.

- A second major issue associated with contrast media is the importance of screening the patient, and taking other prudent measures to avoid reactions. Key points include:

  – Any patient who is allergic to shellfish or iodine might also be allergic to contrast media. All patients should be asked about allergies, their responses should be documented, and the physician should follow up on any such issues prior to injection.

  – In general, the higher the degree of osmolarity and the higher the dose of contrast media, the greater the chance of a reaction. Ionic media are high in osmolarity and radiologists should be consulted about the clinical risk associated with purchasing an ionic contrast medium product. Commercially available non-ionic contrast media are available but at an increased price. The risk management professional, in conjunction with the radiology staff, should evaluate the risks and benefits of carrying both media or only non-ionic contrast media.

Anesthesia

As surgery is now performed in the magnetic resonance imaging suite in very sophisticated operations, and radiologists are routinely performing "moderate sedation," management of anesthesia is an important factor in addressing the risk of the radiology area. Of note, the American Society of Anesthesiologists issued new credentialing guidelines in October 2005, which specify training and performance improvement activities important for any non-anesthetic provider who administers moderate sedation.[13] Other important guidance with regard to anesthetic administration in radiology is an ASA paper on anesthetics in the MRI suite. This document discusses the importance of screening the patient, providing an MRI compatible anesthesia machine, and addressing logistical concerns such as being able to access other providers for backup.[14]

Of great significance in any discussion of "moderate sedation" is the use of Versed, also know as Midazolam, which was first heralded as the "stingless Valium" many years ago, and is still frequently used to sedate radiology patients for CT or MRI. Versed first became a source of concern when patients became unresponsive and could not be revived. Since that time, pressure from liability carriers and JCAHO has resulted in several important principles that must be adhered to in the radiology area, as in other clinical settings.

- All providers who administer "moderate" sedation must meet credentialing requirements established with input of the anesthesiologists.

- To address the risk of having moderate sedation become deep sedation, the physician must be immediately available and the necessary reversal agents must be on hand. Subsequent evaluation through performance improvement, of any cases in which moderate sedation became deep sedation, might be a useful way to evaluate effectiveness of the management of these cases. All such quality improvement information should be evaluated by the authorized peer review committee to maximize available protection under any applicable law.

Another sedation agent that providers in the radiology area and risk management professionals should be aware of is propofol. Although this drug produces few aftereffects, a lack of effective reversal agents make it critical that staff who are capable of rescuing the patient be immediately available, if the level of sedation becomes too deep. Whereas nurse practice acts vary regarding whether nurses may administer the drug at all, the American Society of Anesthesiology has issued a statement[15] that emphasizes the physician's responsibility to remain immediately available during administration and recovery.[16] The administration of propofol is particularly important for the risk management professional to be aware of, because it is often used in pediatric sedation.

Telemedicine

This broad topic is covered comprehensively in Volume 3, Chapter 14 in this series on Evolving Risk in Telemedicine; nevertheless, one new practice approach is particularly important regarding radiology. "Nighthawking" entails the electronic transmission of films to be overread in other locations. The latest trend in this area involves physicians on the other side of the world. Issues to be addressed in such arrangements include compliance with HIPAA, and the legal amenability of a foreign physician to being joined in a lawsuit if one were brought. The largest concern, which has recently caught the strong interest of Congress, is difficulty in ascertaining the quality of the training that such providers have been through and assuring quality of interpretation.[17]

Of particular note, JCAHO, which has recently begun to promulgate telemedicine-related standards, has asked the American College of Radiology to help develop requirements for teleradiology providers. An advisory committee was scheduled to meet in early 2006.[18]

INTERFACE WITH OTHER CLINICAL AREAS

The high volume of patient flow in many radiology areas and the acuity of the patients makes effective interaction with other clinical areas an essential risk management strategy. There are several important issues and approaches.

The patient who comes to the radiology area from the intensive care environment and is clinically fragile should be accompanied by a registered nurse. The radiology department and key nursing managers should evaluate proactively any logistical issues associated with maintaining the level of care that such patients require.

In addition to evaluating the scheduled procedure for a patient, nursing managers, radiology professionals, medical records personnel, and others involved should evaluate the way in which clinical issues such as "fall risk" and "do not resuscitate" are communicated.

There are at least three issues underlying this premise. First, although the medical record should always accompany the patient to radiology, this does not always happen. Second, when the record is there, these key points must be easy for the staff to locate in the record. This, too, is sometimes an issue, either because the radiology staff are not trained as to where they need to look, or there are not designated places for this information. Third, some situations require a telephone discussion.

Where there are multiple physicians caring for a patient, and anesthesia or other medication may be required while the patient is in the radiology area, it must be clear which physician is to write that medication order. This can be a particularly problematic issue in the pediatric area. Should the pediatrician, the anesthetist, or the radiologist control the decision about which medication is best to sedate a young child?

There should be a predetermined approach for managing an intravenous line while the patient is in the radiology area. Many patients suffer needlessly and clinical risk is increased when intravenous lines must be restarted because the solution ran out or the pump battery died.

Radiologists should overread emergency department films within twenty-four hours on weekdays and both days of the weekend. There also should be a formalized way to track the overread interpretation and to follow up. Please see Chapter 10 in this volume on Risk Management in Emergency Services, for a suggested approach.

As interventional cardiologists and radiologists begin to perform the same types of procedures, it is important that a consistent credentialing process be maintained for both.

As the acuity of patients grows, it is essential that the referring physicians work with radiologists to make sure that patients are not too fragile to undergo procedures. Depending on the population of patients, development and monitoring of relevant criteria may be necessary.

....
TRADITIONAL RISK MANAGEMENT PRINCIPLES

Credentialing, informed consent, medical record documentation, and performance improvement are risk management issues in radiology, as they are in other areas of any health care facility.

Credentialing

It is important for the credentials committee of the organization to review radiology-related medical staff privileges on a frequent basis, as they might need to be updated to encompass new technology and procedures. For example, percutaneous transluminal coronary angioplasty (PTCA) may now be performed in an interventional radiology lab, followed by a minimum twelve-hour observational stay. A "credentialing statement" published on the Web site of the Society for Interventional Radiology details the recommendations of a team of interventional radiologists and cardiovascular surgeons concerning training requirements for practitioners.[19]

Another important question for the credentials committee of the organization is whether the obstetric practitioners who read ultrasounds on the labor and delivery unit should document training to do so and be overread by radiology professionals who are trained in ultrasound.

Informed Consent

As radiology and the surgical suite come closer together, the complexity and risk of the procedures performed increases. All patients should be given adequate information to provide informed consent for invasive procedures, according to American College of Radiology standards.[20] (Please see Chapter 4 in this volume for more information on the general principles of informed consent.)

Medical Record Documentation

Risk management professional must be aware of two major areas in regard to medical records. The first is the rapid pace with which picture archiving and communication systems (PACS)[21] are digitalizing films, and eliminating "original" images. When considering PACS, points to consider from a risk management perspective include:

- What is the view of the courts in your locale regarding the credibility of electronic imaging?
- How will the PACS system manage documentation associated with the film? Will clinicians be able to access other providers' interpretations? Will they be able to view the order—and rationale—for a procedure?
- In general, how will the PACS interface with your existing documentation system?

Risk managers with traditional film libraries should be sure, as much as possible, that original films are not released. Once they are gone, they might not be seen again until discovery in a lawsuit. Exceptions to this general rule sometimes include release of films to physicians' offices. There should be a tracking system if such release is allowed, and the risk manager must recognize that getting a film back from a co-defendant physician might be difficult. The other exception is supported by the federal government. It requires the release of original mammograms, rather than copies, because copies are too difficult to interpret.

The second major area for risk management professionals to be aware of is the important role of radiology technologists in documentation. Many radiation technologists do not document in the medical record, beyond the fact that they administered contrast medium, and yet they often observe critical changes in patients while they are with them. For example, when asked if they document about a fall in the radiology department, many technologists will respond that they make out an adverse occurrence form. Although this is an important and proper approach, it does not take the place of concurrent documentation in the medical record when a case must be defended. Calling the floor nurse and describing what happened is an alternative approach, but it does not have the credibility of documentation by the person who was there. Also, if a patient experienced dizziness before a fall, the physician will not know about that if the information is only on the incident report. The floor nurse is likely document it, but there is still increased likelihood that the information will fall between the cracks.

Performance Improvement

Because radiology interfaces with so many other areas of the organization, it is important that the radiology staff participates in facility-wide performance improvement initiatives. For example, the representative of the radiation safety committee discussed earlier might be part of the organization's performance improvement committee or the patient safety committee.

At a minimum, quality indicators reviewed should include monitors shared with other clinical areas, such as nursing units, regarding information received about MRSA patient status before patients are transported to the radiology area. The basis for indicators to be reviewed may also be drawn from standards and statements of key regulatory groups, and they should also be based on information gleaned from incident reporting trends and the facts underlying malpractice cases. The active participation of clinicians is critical to success.

············

CONCLUSION

The technological advances in radiology will continue at an incredible pace. The risk management professional can do much to increase the benefit and reduce the risk associated with this important clinical area.

Endnotes

1. "Radiology: A Brief History" at [www.rad-i-ology.co.uk/radsite/historical.htm].

2. "Medicine's Malediction." *Imaging Economics*, April 2004. Page 2.

3. "Rediscovering Radiology." *RT Image*, Vol. 17, no. 46, November 16, 2004.

4. Brateman, Libby, Ph.D. "The AAPM/RSNA Physics Tutorial for Residents: Radiation Safety Considerations for Diagnostic Radiology Personnel," *Radiographics*, 1999.

5. *Ibid.*

6. CT (computed tomography), sometimes called CAT scan, uses special x-ray equipment to obtain image data from different angles around the body and then uses computer processing of the information to show a cross-section of body tissues and organs. CT imaging is particularly useful because it can show several types of tissue—lung, bone, soft tissue, and blood vessels—with great clarity. Using specialized equipment and expertise to create and interpret CT scans of the body, radiologists can more easily diagnose problems such as cancers, cardiovascular disease, infectious disease, trauma, and musculoskeletal disorders. Available at RadiologyInfo at [www.radiologyinfo. org/content/ct_of_the_body.htm]. Accessed December 29, 2005.

7. Hampton, T. "Full-body CT scans scale up cancer risk," *Medical News and Perspectives, The Journal of the American Medical Association*. 292: 1669.

8. Shively, Christopher, "Quality in Management Radiology." *Decisions in Imaging Economics*, November 2003. Page 6.

9. The American College of Radiology. "ACR Practice Guideline for Communication: Diagnostic Radiology," effective January 1, 2002.

10. ACR White Paper on Magnetic Resonance (MR) Safety (Combined Papers of 2002 and 2004). Available on the American College of Radiology Web site at [www. acr.org/]. Last accessed December 21, 2005.

11. *Ibid.*, Page 23.

12. *Ibid.*, Page 3.

13. "Credentialing Guidelines for Practitioners Who are Not Anesthesia Professionals to Administer Anesthetic Drugs to Establish a Level of Moderate Sedation," Approved by the House of Delegates October 25, 2005. Available on the ASA Web site at [www.asahq.org]. Last accessed December 21, 2005.

14. "Being Extra Safe When Providing Anesthesia for MRI Examinations," The ASA Newsletter, published on the American Society of Anesthesia Web site June 2002, Volume 66 at [www.asahq.org]. Last accessed December 22, 2005.

15. [www.asahq.org/news/propofolstatement.htm].

16. "Sedation With Propofol: A New ASA Statement." *American Society of Anesthesia Newsletter.* Available on the ASA Web site at [www.asahq.org/Newsletters/2005/02-05/whatsNew02_05.html]. Last accessed December 21, 2005.

17. The American College of Radiology "Technical Standard on Teleradiology." January 1, 2003.

18. [www.sirweb.org/clinical/cpg/S219.pdf].

19. The American College of Radiology Statement on "Informed Consent," 2000.

20. "JCAHO Teleradiology Standards Open Door For Alternative Credentialing Pathway." Available on the American College of Radiology Web site, April 2005 at [www.acr.org]. Last accessed December 21, 2005.

21. Picture Archiving and Communications System, more commonly known as PACS, enables images such as x-rays and scans to be stored electronically and viewed on video screens, so that doctors and other health professionals can access the information and compare it with previous images at the touch of a button. Information available at NHS at [www.connectingforhealth.nhs.uk/pacs/whatispacs/]. Accessed December 29, 2005.

18

Risk Management Considerations in Home Health Care

Kelley Woodfin

Several unique characteristics of delivering health care services in the home setting exacerbate liability risk. These include:

- Lack of supervision for home care providers
- Use of technology traditionally used in the hospital setting
- Limited interface with physicians
- Intermittent nature of scheduled visits
- Unpredictable level of compliance that can be expected from the patient and family or friends who care for patients on a daily basis

Providing care in a patient's home also has significant workers' compensation exposures. Specific issues include potential staff involvement in automobile accidents as they drive to and from patients' homes, the risk of slipping and falling, and sprains and strains. The risk of slips and falls occurs when staff visit patient homes where there is ice on the driveway or walkway, construction is taking place in the home or area, or when working in rooms that are often filled with patient equipment and misplaced furniture. Staff risk strain or sprain injuries as they attempt to move patients without assistance. Finally, working alone in remote locations or high-crime areas, and the possible presence of weapons among patients, family, and friends in any location, clearly increase the chance that a home care provider will be the victim of violence.

This chapter discusses the rapid evolution of home care services, identifies specific risk management issues, and recommended strategies to manage those risks. The goal is to enhance the quality of care rendered, reduce exposure to liability, and ensure patient and worker safety.

....

THE RAPID EVOLUTION OF HOME CARE

At its inception, home care services involved periodic home visits by visiting nurses and private physicians. Nurses generally performed such tasks as blood pressure, wound monitoring, and patient education. Clearly the home care industry has changed significantly since those times. Home care now provides a full spectrum of services, including skilled nursing care, home respiratory care, infusion services that include total parenteral nutrition and chemotherapy, wound management, full rehabilitation services, cardiac care and monitoring, full-scope dialysis services, high-risk newborn care, early maternal and infant discharge programs, and high-risk obstetrical care.

Steady growth in the nation's senior population has also increased demand for home health care services. Although there has been an increase in the number of continuing care retirement communities, assisted living, and dementia facilities, seniors and their families usually desire that the older person remain at home maintaining independence for as long as possible. There are risks inherent in caring for an elderly person in the home. Greater cognitive and physical frailty result in the inability to follow simple directions and comply with treatment plans and less physical reserve to overcome self-care mistakes. There is also risk related to unrealistic expectations on the part of patient and family, including the assumption that patients are safe in the home as long as they are under the care of a home health services agency.

An evolving area of home health care is telemedicine. Telemedicine allows the physician to "visit" the home and monitor the patient electronically through the use of equipment such as video and integrated peripheral devices such as an electronic stethoscopes. One project that evaluated the efficacy of telemedicine in home care was a pilot study by Kaiser Permanente Medical Center in Sacramento, California, in the late 1990s. This work showed promising results regarding care delivery costs, patient satisfaction with videoconferencing, and successful use of integrated peripheral devices that transmit biological data to the physician.[1] The standards of care for telemedicine in home health care are still evolving; therefore it is not possible to address those issues completely in this chapter. However, it is reasonable to assume that this aspect of home care will become more common in the near future. So home care providers and risk management professionals should stay abreast of changes.

....

STAFFING

The primary types of home care providers are identified in Table 18.1.

In some situations, a home health agency may provide licensed nurses and home caregivers in addition to pharmaceutical, durable medical equipment, and DME technicians; respiratory therapists; chemotherapy certified licensed nurses; ostomy, wound, and

TABLE 18.1   Types of Home Care Providers

- Home health agencies
- Hospice agencies
- Home infusion and pharmaceutical services
- Durable medical equipment services
- Independently contracted licensed nurses and nursing assistants

TABLE 18.2   Common Home Health Services

- Nursing assessment
- Bathing and other personal care
- Catheter insertion/care/changes
- Case management
- Enteral/parenteral therapies
- Hospice care
- Infusion therapies
- Medication instruction
- Monitoring of acute/chronic conditions
- Nutrition counseling
- Pain control
- Patient education
- Rehabilitation therapies (P.T., O.T., speech)
- Ostomy management
- Wound care

pain consultants; hospice workers and rehabilitative services professionals, including physical therapists, occupational therapists, and speech therapists. In other cases, the home health agency might simply contract with ancillary services and provide only nurses and home care aides.

Hospice services are also sometimes provided, by physician order, for terminally ill patients. These services often include the skills of social workers, psychotherapists, clergymen, and licensed nursing personnel. Refer to Table 18.2

Although the types of services provided by an agency might differ, several important similarities affect the practice of home care providers:

- All services, from the drawing of venous blood samples to ventilation management, are provided in the home environment, over which the home care worker has limited control.

- Caregivers, nurses, rehabilitation therapists, and other types of home care workers are unsupervised while providing services in the home and have limited access to collegial support and professional resources, which are readily available in a hospital environment.

- The scope of resuscitative equipment readily available in a hospital setting, including emergency medical services, is not available in the home environment.

- Home care providers must rely on the patient or caregiver to comply with instructions or directions when a home care worker is not in the home. This means that non-health care providers are often responsible for suctioning, medication administration, turning and positioning, wound and ostomy care, and other elements of a treatment plan.

- A public that is very concerned about medical error can observe all provider interactions closely in the home care environment.

- The home care provider must consider the potential for community and domestic violence in every setting.

The risk management considerations discussed in this chapter are applicable to any type of health care services delivered in the home environment.

············
RISK MANAGEMENT CONSIDERATIONS

The home health care environment raises significant issues for risk management professionals, including but not limited to the broad categories of standard of care and duty; corporate liability; employment and supervision; safety and security; contracts, antitrust, fraud, and abuse; and marketing and advertising considerations.

Standard of Care and Duty

General negligence and professional malpractice are the most prevalent legal actions that arise in home health care. Although specific tort law approaches vary from jurisdiction to jurisdiction, it is generally accepted that home health providers owe patients admitted to any of their services a duty to render the degree of care that any health care professional with the same training would provide under the same or similar circumstances. Whether the standard of care has been met in an individual case is established by expert testimony based on current professional standards for the same or a similar condition, the agency's internal policies, procedures, and protocols, and standards established by federal and state agencies pursuant to statute.

On a national basis, Medicare regulations establish standards for all home health agency interactions with Medicare beneficiaries. Potentially relevant standards have also been published by professional associations, such as the National Association for Home Care and Hospice (NAHC),[2] a trade association that represents the interests of home care agencies, hospices, and home care aide organizations. This association reviews and approves home care standards for the industry. Standards for physicians, respiratory therapists, registered nurses, vocational nurses, mental health workers, rehab specialists, and other licensed professionals are also established by state regulations governing each profession.

As such requirements vary, and yet are the bases for a jury to determine whether there has been negligence, all home care providers should be aware of the regulations and private organization standards that might pertain to them. For example, all nurses should be familiar with their states' Nurse Practice Act, and the organizations that the nurses work for should keep their employees aware of any pertinent changes.

Policies and procedures of the organization should address the requirements of such regulatory or private standards. Such internal guidance documents must be reviewed routinely to ensure that they comprehensively address relevant requirements and that there are no inconsistencies. All new staff should be oriented to these approaches, and this orientation should be documented and regularly monitored by agency management.

A list of home care professional associations and federal regulations can be found at the end of this chapter.

Corporate Liability

The legal theory has grown that a company that provides health care services has an independent duty directly to clients to monitor the quality of health care and services provided to them. This is partly due to the perception that a health care organization is a "deep pocket" and has more assets than an individual. Another significant driver is the effort of plaintiff attorneys to avoid limitations imposed by caps on awards for professional malpractice, and at the same time strengthen the potential for punitive damages. In addition, in some states, plaintiff attorneys who file corporate negligence claims can avoid limits on the percentage of the award they will receive under state law-based contingency-fee requirements.

There are additional implications of corporate negligence or malpractice legal allegations for the risk management professional. One is that the plaintiff might have an opportunity to discover information about the corporation's business practices and finances that might not otherwise be available to them. Such information is particularly vulnerable during discovery related to common corporate liability allegations, such as negligent hiring and retention, negligent supervision, and negligent credentialing.

Another important implication of such actions, for the risk management professional, is that corporate liability claims require time-consuming review of company policies, procedures, financial statements, financial audit reports, and other documents, which might have applied during the timeframe alleged in the lawsuit. The potential need to produce these items at a much later date illustrates the importance of a well-organized approach to maintaining key organizational documents.

Employment and Supervision Issues

As previously noted, it is incumbent upon a home care agency to interview, orient, train, and supervise health care workers in a way that promotes proficiency and knowledge. Because home care providers function unsupervised in a setting which is not part of the health care organization, they must be particularly trustworthy and it is essential that they demonstrate reliable skills.

Basic competencies for each level of worker must be established by the home care agency and used to assess a candidate during interview. For example, before an interview, the candidate might be asked to complete a checklist indicating the number of times a skill or task has been performed in the past year and in the past five years. This document should also contain a provision that states that the information provided by the candidate will be used in the determination to hire.

Regulations that establish hiring requirements in specific areas, such as long-term care, should be followed to the extent that they apply. In at least one area, however, the home agency might be well served to exceed these requirements. For example, whether a specific state requires criminal background checks or not, health care employers risk charges of negligent hiring and retention if there is no record of performing such checks. Criminal and background checks should be performed on each candidate. The candidate should be advised orally and in writing that employment is contingent on passing this related screening. Common checks performed by health care providers are shown in Table 18.3. It is also necessary to check the driving record of candidates, when employees will be using their own vehicles.

The ability to work without supervision, solve problems effectively, and use good judgment in decision-making are critical skills for home care workers. These skills can best be facilitated via a mentoring program. No new employees, regardless of their role, should work alone in the home environment until a qualified mentor has directly observed their work and confirmed that they have the skills necessary to perform their duties without direct supervision. The home care agency may facilitate the hire of qualified individuals by stating a preference in their advertisement for candidates with at least one year of experience in a medical-surgical acute care

TABLE 18.3   Pre-Employment Background Checks Common in Health Care

- Criminal background checks, including fingerprint checks, on applicants for positions involving direct patient care or as required by state statute
- Verification of current residence address and phone number
- Verification of professional licenses and certifications
- Contact of references for personal testimonial
- Contact of previous employers for a period of at least 10 years
- Verification of education credentials
- Review of Board "Hot Sheets" and other professional board notices on problematic professionals

environment, and at least five years of experience in home health care. During the interview, it is important to consider the reasons why the person left the most recent job and to ask questions designed to reveal their decision-making and communication skills and their clinical judgment. Vignettes can be very helpful in assessing provider judgment.

Finally, a post-hire, pre-employment physical examination pertinent to the worker's job description and essential functions, such as lifting and moving patients and equipment, should be performed after the job offer is made, and again, the candidates must be advised orally and in writing that their employment is contingent on passing this examination, unless reasonable accommodations can be made for any existing disability, according to the Americans With Disabilities Act (ADA).[3] For this reason the physical exam must never be cursory. It should be thorough and should take into consideration the essential job functions that the worker will be required to conduct safely. The exam should also be specific enough to allow the employer to determine whether the person is physically capable of performing the job, or to determine reasonable accommodations that might be needed. If the person is deemed unable to perform the essential functions of the job for which they applied, and no accommodations are possible, employers would be within their rights to rescind the job offer.

Once a home health worker is hired, the next step should be a thorough orientation to policy and procedures, the company compliance plan, privacy and confidentiality in the home care environment, and so on. The range of subjects that should be covered in new hire orientation can be found in Table 18.4. Periodic assessment of documentation and case outcomes should be conducted by supervisors, as should periodic home visits with employees to observe their skills. Educational in-service programs and attendance at external continuing education programs for professional staff should be supported by management as a means of maintaining and improving skills and knowledge among staff. In addition, a "Back to Basics" in-service program should be conducted annually for certified and non-certified home health workers to ensure that they keep their skills current. Documentation of courses attended and any related skill checklists should be kept for at least seven years in the personnel file of each employee, although the retention period may be longer according to state law or provider agency policy.

TABLE 18.4   Suggested Subjects: Home Care New Hire Orientation

- Company information; company organization chart
- Supervisory structure; communication with and responsibility of supervisors
- Corporate Compliance Plan requirements
- Quality Improvement Plan requirements
- Risk Management Program requirements
- Privacy and Confidentiality in Home Care
- Company Employment Practices and Policies
- Company Operations Policy/Procedure Manual
- Injury and Illness Prevention Program
- Workplace Violence Prevention Policy
- Patient Safety
- Standards of Care and scope of practice—professional staff
- Standards of Care and scope of responsibility—non-professional staff
- Documentation Standards in Home Care
- Providing Care in the Private Home—idiosyncrasies and considerations
- Essential reporting: incidents, elder and dependent adult abuse, equipment failure

The U.S. Department of Labor has established employment standards for the home health care industry under the wage and hour standards in the Fair Labor Standards Act (FLSA).[4] These standards apply to persons employed in domestic service in households. In particular, they affect nurses, certified nurse aides, home health care aides, and other individuals who provide home health care services. Domestic service employees who reside in the patient's house where they are employed are entitled to the minimum wage, but may be exempt from the Act's overtime requirements. There are also wage and hour requirements for people who perform "companionship services," such as housework, meal preparation, bed-making, clothes-washing, and other similar personal services. Patients and families should be made aware of these requirements and any exceptions allowable by law. Copies of wage and hour publications may be obtained by contacting the nearest office of the Wage and Hour Division listed in most telephone directories under U.S. Government, Department of Labor. Note, however, that registered nurses are exempt from the FLSA wage requirements where their time is spent in the performance of duties of a nurse and they are paid on a salary or "fee basis" as defined by Regulations, 29 CFR, Part 541.

Safety and Security of the Home Environment

According to the Bureau of Labor Statistics, the injury rate for home health workers is 50 percent higher than that of hospital workers and 70 percent higher than the national average.[5] The majority of these injuries arise from automobile accidents while driving to or from a work assignment. However, lifting and workplace violence also contribute to worker injury in this setting.

As of the early 1990s, the Bureau of Labor Statistics reflected that more assaults occur against workers in the health care and social services industry than in any other employment category.[6] Home health care workers are particularly at risk because they provide services at multiple sites and in locations where safety hazards exist that are unique to this care environment.

It is essential that the safety and security of the home care worker and any associated issues that might affect the worker during provision of care in the home be identified in the pre-admission assessment. However, even after the patient is admitted for services pursuant to a "clean" home safety and security assessment, the situation should be reassessed periodically and documented in the patient's home care record. A non-hospital-based home health agency should not rely upon a previous hospital home assessment, even if it is fairly recent. Instead, the new provider should perform its own home safety, security, and clinical assessments before admitting a new patient to the service.

Where possible, the home safety and security assessment should be performed by a supervisor in the agency so that if unsafe situations are noted, the supervisor will have firsthand knowledge and can work with the patient, family, caregiver, or physician, as appropriate, to determine whether these issues can reasonably be overcome. Refer to Table 18.5.

If deficiencies cannot be corrected, it might be possible for the home care supervisor to construct a workaround plan, which should be discussed with the physician and the patient or caregiver. The elements of this plan will depend on the medical condition of the patient and the effect that the identified concern has on the patient's safety and recovery. In the final analysis, it might be that the only safe environment for the patient is in a skilled nursing or other type of care facility. Medical record documentation of all pertinent discussions is important to support the approach taken.

TABLE 18.5   Home Safety/Security Elements to Consider

- General condition of the home environment
- Presence and type of heating, such as wall, space, or central heating
- Presence of air conditioning or installed and/or free-standing fans
- Presence of throw rugs and their condition; condition of floors in all living areas
- Presence or absence of hot running water and working toilets
- Presence and condition of stairways
- Size and location of patient room within the house
- Adequacy of electrical sockets and source if health care equipment is to be used
- Presence or absence of smoke and carbon monoxide detectors; fire extinguishers
- Type and adequacy of lighting in and around the home

In addition to the home safety assessment identified in Table 18.5, security of the home and surroundings should be assessed, including but not limited to the following elements:

- Behavioral history of the patient and family members to ascertain whether there have been any past violent behaviors

- Presence and type of locks on doors and windows

- Presence of a working telephone with a listing of emergency numbers for fire, police, physician, hospital, poison control center, and pharmacy

- Presence of firearms in the house, and the ability or non-ability to secure them

- Adequacy of outdoor lighting, such as street lights, porch lights, and alcove lights

- Parking availability adjacent or close to the patient's house or apartment, and lighting in parking areas

- Characteristics of the neighborhood: high crime, multiple neighborhood gangs, known drug houses

- Proximity of shrubs and bushes where people might hide

If the area is determined to be unsafe, a similar approach to that delineated for management of in-home hazards should be taken, including discussion among the home care agency supervisor, the patient's physician, and the patient and caregiver. If an adequate workaround plan is not possible because of the extent of safety and security issues, the patient's physician and patient must be advised that the patient cannot be admitted to home care services. Potential alternative arrangements should then be identified, such as a skilled or assisted living facility, or a licensed board and care facility. It may be possible to provide home care services in those settings, until they are no longer needed.

Common sense dictates that, in addition to evaluations and interventions to make sure the environment is safe for a home care worker, it is desirable to share specific guidelines with any new patient or caregiver. These guidelines should particularly address the requirement that firearms not be allowed in the home while the home care worker is on the job, and the principle that any verbal or physical abuse toward the worker will not be tolerated. The home care worker should also make clear that it is desirable to have others, in addition to the patient, present during the visit.

All health care providers should ensure that their employees receive comprehensive initial orientation and annual retraining in personal and patient safety, and that they demonstrate proficiency after education and before being sent into the workplace. Part of this ongoing education should include providing employees with a personal safety risk assessment tool and teaching them how to react if they are confronted with a hazardous situation. It is reasonable to develop a threat analysis for some locales, with a response plan for the employee and agency to follow if a personal safety issue arises. Home health workers should be provided by their agency with a means of contacting the agency in an emergency, such as a cell phone, and a code to alert management to the situation so that the proper immediate intervention and assistance can be provided. It is also recommended that any and all events of a personal threat nature, or actual violence, be reported by the worker to the agency promptly so that adequate management and psychotherapeutic support can be provided and a determination made as to how or if the agency can continue to provide services to the patient.

From both and employee and patient loss control standpoint, cell phone availability for home care providers can be an important piece of equipment if properly used in the home setting. Having a cell phone will allow the health care worker to call the office or the physician when medically necessary in a timely manner and not necessitate the worker using the patient's phone. A cell phone will allow for confidential conversations away from the necessary equipment, as the health care worker has the flexibility to call from outside the house, his or her own car, or other location. From an employee perspective, having a cell phone is thought of as not only a time-saver but as a safety outlet. Since they are often not able to choose the location of their patient population, many find themselves in less than desirable neighborhoods. Although they should not rely on a cell phone as a protective device, it can nonetheless give them a means to call for needed assistance if and when necessary. Workers should be encouraged to call the agency before and after visits in neighborhoods that are risky or where the patients and families are difficult. Patient safety is important in home care but worker safety is equally important. Protocols for the use of cell phones should be developed and implemented.

Although their focus is on the larger societal problem of crime, local law enforcement agencies can also be a source of information for home care providers about safety. Specifically, the community liaison officer may be available to provide related education.

Home care supervisors should also have an open door policy, to ensure that workers feel comfortable expressing concern about their personal safety, either in a patient's home or going to and from their work assignments. Even with all these systems in place, the agency should rigorously analyze all incidents, and analyze trends for any patterns concerning existing or potential hazards that might result in harm to patients and workers, so that corrective action can be taken.

Defensive driving and driver safety instructions should also be provided to home health workers. In addition, home health workers should notify their automobile insurers if their private cars are to be used for business purposes. Many carriers require that the agency develop and implement a Business Automobile Safety Program to reduce the potential for accidents and injuries on the job. As a condition of employment, the agency should require all workers to provide a copy of their driver's licenses and certificates of insurance, with limits that meet predetermined requirements for coverage. As previously noted, each worker's driving history should be reviewed prior to employment and periodically thereafter. Reports to facilitate this process can be obtained from the state or local department of motor vehicles or similar agency. Most state laws permit employers to obtain and use this information to determine whether workers can use their own autos for business, or to provide such information to the employers' auto liability carriers for underwriting purposes.

If home health workers must transport patients in their private autos for any reason, their auto policies should cover both driver and any passengers for bodily injury and medical claims. Or, as most private auto insurance policies do not include significant limits for bodily injury, a preferable approach is for the agency to purchase its own auto liability coverage, including such limits. This strategy can help the agency avoid becoming the "deep pocket" in a lawsuit that might arise from an accident in which a third party was injured. Such coverage should also apply to company-owned vehicles that workers use to transport patients or conduct other business.

All home care workers should be aware that they must contact their supervisors immediately if they are injured on the job, and they must be aware of what initial paperwork to complete and how to submit that paperwork. They should also be required to carry all initial injury reporting paperwork with them in the field, so that it is readily available for them to complete. The agency should also be prepared to pick injured workers up and transport them to a designated provider for evaluation and treatment, if the circumstances of the injury indicate this is called for.

Home health managers should also orient staff to the applicability of Workers' Compensation benefits in the state, to report an injury, and how to access related services.

Policies and Procedures

It is important that home health services that are part of a larger institution individualize all policies and procedures to address the unique characteristics of the home health care environment. These policies and procedures must be routinely updated with the input of the clinical staff.

There continues to be some misperception among providers that it is better not to have procedures, because if there are no procedures, it will be harder for a plaintiff to prove a case. In reality, reasonable care must be rendered, even in the absence of policies, and it is much harder to achieve consistency of approach without them. Also, courts *expect* that there will be internal policies and procedures relevant to the case under their consideration, and a jury might be instructed to find corporate negligence if there are none.

The following are recommended processes to ensure that policies, procedures, and protocols are current:

- Have a system in place for multilevel and multidisciplinary review of newly drafted documents before they are implemented. This review can be as in-depth or cursory as the content requires. It is nonetheless a vital step to ensure that the new policy or procedure or protocol reflects current standards and is easy to understand and follow. Review should also assure that a monitoring and accountability process is written into the policy.

- Ensure that there is at least a bi-annual review process for all policies, procedures, and protocols, both administrative and operational.

- If possible, establish an electronic database of retired, new, and existing policies, procedures, and protocols. Even if an electronic database is used, all original policies, procedures, and protocols must be retained according to the agency's record retention policy so that they are retrievable for regulatory review or in the event of a lawsuit.

- Ensure that all policies, procedures, and protocols have the most recent review date noted on the document.

- Ensure that outdated policies are archived separately from those that are current, to prevent staff confusion. Archiving is also important because it helps to establish in litigation that the staff members were not using outdated protocols.

- Ensure that new or revised documents are distributed to all applicable workers for review and that there is a mechanism for identifying who has received a copy. A governing policy should require any employee who receives a policy, procedure, or protocol to document that they have read and understand it. They should also confirm in writing that they agree to follow it and to advise management when they are unable to follow it for any reason.

- Implement a mechanism for new hires to become familiar with all existing administrative and operational policies, procedures, and protocols.

- Ensure that monitoring is carried out to determine whether policies, procedures, and protocols are being followed, and involve the staff in this monitoring activity. Such involvement of the staff enhances their understanding of the rationale for policies, and they can be credible advocates to promote enforcement.

- Implement a mechanism for alerting employees to policies, procedures, or protocols that have been revised. Ensure that there is a training session to familiarize them sufficiently with the changes.

- Ensure that there is a process for attaching an applicable policy, procedure, or protocol to an incident report so that the document can be reviewed for relevance and proper action taken where necessary.

Contracts, Antitrust, Fraud, and Abuse Concerns

The home health care industry has been scrutinized by federal agencies for fraud and abuse in referral and billing practices for many years. Refer to Table 18.6. It is an important part of corporate responsibility to develop and implement a corporate compliance plan, and having such a plan is a condition of participating (CoP) in federal reimbursement programs.[7] To minimize exposure of the agency to federal and state fraud investigation, fines, sanctions, and federal lawsuits, the agency must:

- Develop standards of conduct, about which all staff are trained and that are a basis for monitoring compliance.

- Implement a conflict of interest statement that each employee of the agency (including executive management) signs, subsequently placing the original in their personnel files.

- Develop and implement a compliance program that sets forth acceptable, legal, and accurate practices for billing and referrals.

- Keep accurate records of billing disputes and corrective actions.

TABLE 18.6   Potential Antitrust Exposures for Home Health Agencies

- Exclusive contracts
- Hospital referral arrangements
- Monopolization of home care services in a particular locale
- Certain mergers and acquisitions
- Network price fixing or market allocations
- Predatory practices
- Deep discounts to health systems
- Management contracts

● Keep accurate records of patient referrals from referral sources and to, for example, laboratories, dialysis services, infusion services, pharmaceutical services, and durable medical equipment companies.

● Ensure that no outside services are used where an agency director, officer, physician, or staff member has any financial interest in the service.

● Have all contracts and affiliation agreements reviewed and approved by legal counsel before they are executed.

● Ensure that all contracts between the agency and other entities include provisions that require that entity to bill separately, and to provide evidence of adequate liability coverage, as defined by the agency. Other important contractual provisions include hold-harmless and indemnification provisions, which make clear that contractors are responsible for the actions of their employees, directors and officers, agents, and sub-contractors.

● Ensure that there is a process for obtaining and reviewing the utilization plan, including preauthorization requirements, of the managed care companies that contract with the home health agency.

● Develop and implement a comprehensive process for identification and reporting of false claims to the applicable governmental agency and to prevent billing errors on the part of the home health agency.

● Develop a process for prompt, thorough investigation of alleged illegal or unethical misconduct by corporate directors, officers, employees, independent contractors, consultants, and licensed professionals.[8]

Marketing and Advertising

In an effort to avoid allegations of fraudulent misrepresentation, breach of contract, breach of the covenant of good faith in advertising, or other related claims, the home health agency must establish a process requiring legal or risk management review and approval of any advertisements and promotional materials generated by marketing and public relations representatives, whether employed or independently contracted. Fraudulent advertising and fraudulent misrepresentation are legal claims that, in many states, are associated with the potential for punitive damages. It is also important that punitive damages are rarely covered by liability insurance carriers and must therefore be paid out of the defendant's "pocket."

It is not unusual for friction to develop between marketing and legal counsel or risk management when changes to templates are recommended, but the potential exposure makes it imperative that risk management or legal counsel be the ultimate decision-maker regarding propriety of advertising-related language and phrasing. (Refer to Chapter 9 on Advertising Liability in Volume III of this series for other related considerations).

············

CLINICAL CONSIDERATIONS

The acuity of patients discharged home for post-hospital care has increased in conjunction with emphasis placed by Medicare, Medicaid, and most private insurers on the importance of decreasing lengths of stay in the acute setting. It is therefore vital to take reasonable steps to ensure that each patient is a suitable candidate for home health care services and to consider the other clinical issues of home health care that have risk management implications.

Admission Process

Intake criteria pertaining to patient selection are essential and should include an assessment of the patient, the home environment, and the ability of a family member or friend to care for the patient in the home worker's absence. Refer to Table 18.7. A review of physician orders for home health care, and an assessment of the patient's care needs and level of acuity are also essential.

This approach will help the home health provider determine whether or not the patient is suitable for home care, and if so, what level of worker is needed. For example, if a family has a brain-damaged infant on a ventilator, a registered nurse with pediatric and ventilator experience will be needed to provide services, and periodic visits by a

---

TABLE 18.7   Checklist for Patient Referral to Home Health*

General Information:

Patient name, date of birth, and medical coverage

Diagnoses for home care

Other diagnoses

Anticipated length of care

In-home relatives or friends

Significant others, including DPOA-HC

Personal Care Needs:

Ambulation

Hearing/sight impairment

Bathing

Housework/meals

Dressing

Medication adherence

Feeding

Toileting

Transport for appointments

Requested Ancillary Care:

Registered Nurse

Physical Therapist

RN Specialist

Occupational Therapist

Licensed vocational nurse

Speech Therapist

Home health aide

Nutritionist/dietician

❖ Meal delivery Social Worker

❖ Wound Care Specialist Stoma Specialist

❖ Dialysis Specialist

❖ Enteral/parenteral Nutrition Therapy Specialist

Situations in Which Physician wants to be called:

Parameters for calling re: vital signs, test results, change in condition, non-compliance

Reasons specific to diagnosis

Non-compliance or abusive behavior

Injury the patient may have incurred in an unusual event

Contact Information for Physician:

Physician name, phone number, and specialty

Office hours

Pager #

Office and fax #

After-hours phone #

Coverage when physician unavailable

Orders for Care:

• Medication dosage, route of administration, frequency, start date, and stop date if applicable

• Diet; nutritional counseling

• Necessary tests and date due

• Infusion therapy, if needed, with specifics on type of IV fluid and rate, any agent to be infused, with dosage and frequency, start date, and, if applicable, stop date

• Rehab services, if needed; type and frequency

• Care specific to diagnoses, such as wound care, ostomy care, catheter care, etc.

---

*Adapted from: Table 5, "Home Health Care", *American Family Physician* (53/7, Nov 1988), S.L. Montauk, MD.

TABLE 18.8   Prerequisites for Medicare Entitlement for Home Health Care

- The patient is under the care of a physician, and a plan of care is rendered under the guidance of this physician.
- The patient requires skilled nursing, occupational therapy, physical therapy, or speech therapy on an *intermittent* basis and their needs can be met on this basis (defined as no more than 28 hours/week or 8 hours in a given day and occurring at least every 60 days).*
- The patient qualifies for Medicare.
- Care is medically necessary and reasonable.
- The patient is homebound.
- The patient resides in a home or facility that does not provide skilled care.

*These elements can be extended in some cases, but only with Medicare fiscal intermediary review and acceptance.

respiratory therapist might be necessary to maintain the equipment or to change settings as ordered by the physician.

Before accepting a patient, the provider must obtain information about the pertinent diagnoses, prognoses, and current condition, including clinical and psychological needs. To determine this information, a record of previous hospitalization, the treatment plan, and the physician orders must be reviewed carefully. Physician orders must specify exactly what health care services are to be provided, the duration of treatment, and the most suitable professional to provide the treatment, for example, RN, LVN, occupational therapist, physical therapist, and so on. In addition, the home health provider should ensure that the orders for service meet Medicare, Medicaid, managed care plan, or insurer requirements for reimbursement. Refer to Table 18.8. Home care organizations should also make every effort to work with managed care plans that allow denial of services to enrollees who are unsuitable for home care.

The patient's home health record should reflect whether there is an advance directive or living will, and if so, should contain a copy of it. Every home worker who provides services must be aware of the patient's wishes as expressed in an advance directive or living will. In addition, if there is a durable power of attorney for health care (DPOA-HC), a copy should be placed in the patient's home care record with names and contact numbers for all the agent(s) that hold the power of attorney or serve as designees for an advance directive.

Once a patient has been accepted, the home health provider has a duty to follow the attending physician's orders and communicate any changes in the patient's condition to the attending physician. If the orders are not clear, or if the service provider or the professional staff have any questions or concerns about applicability of an order to the home environment or to the patient after an assessment of needs has been performed, these must be communicated to the physician and resolved before home care service is initiated.

It is essential that the service providers who accept the patient for home care can provide the services ordered. If they cannot, the service providers must not accept the patient into their service. Refer to Table 18.9 for Sample Admission Criteria. Admitting a patient who does not meet the basic admission criteria increases the exposure of the health care provider to liability if an adverse outcome results.

Denial of Admission

Denials of admission to home care services should not be undertaken lightly, as they could result in allegations of discrimination or wrongful denial of service. Denial might also anger the family or patient enough to bring a malpractice suit alleging negligence regarding an unrelated clinical matter.

TABLE 18.9   Sample Admission Criteria

- Location of the patient's home must be within the service provider's geographic service area as approved by their licensing authority.
- Availability of clinical staff and expertise to meet the patient's needs.
- Availability of capable family support if the patient is unable physically, mentally, or emotionally to provide for his or her own care needs.
- Ability of family/caregiver to comprehend and follow instructions for home care and/or to operate any medical devices that might be in use.
- Available working utilities (gas, electric, phone), and evidence that the utility companies have been advised of any equipment the patient needs that must remain operative during a utility interruption.
- Evidence that emergency transport services in the patient's locale have been notified if the patient is using any life-support equipment in the home.
- Safe and reasonably secure home environment that is adaptable to the patient's needs.

By providing clear information about assessment and denial processes, orally and in writing, to new referrals, with a copy to the physician, the organization may limit this exposure. If a pre-admission denial becomes necessary, it must be criterion-based and not subjective. It must also be communicated to the patients, their families, the referral source, and the patient's physician, if that physician is not the referral source. The notice should be both oral and in writing, identifying the reason(s) for denial and recommending any viable alternatives.

Every reasonable effort should be made to work through issues that might give rise to a pre-admission denial before one is issued. To the extent possible, the admission assessment and determination of suitability for service should be performed within one business day of case referral, and denial issued within seventy-two hours of that assessment. Timeframes beyond that period might be construed as producing a delay in service, which could expose the home health provider to a lawsuit. A grievance and complaint process should be in place to handle any appeal of a pre-admission denial, but those appeals should be few and far between if there has been effective communication with the patient and family, and the reasons for the denial are applicable to the specific case.[9,10]

Withdrawal of Home Health Services for Cause

Before initiation of home care services, the patient or family should also be provided with information on the agency's policy regarding discontinuing care for cause, such as non-compliance, abusive behavior, drug or alcohol use, or other behaviors adverse to the patient's health and welfare, presence of weapons in the home, creating or allowing barriers to home access by home health workers, unresolved safety hazards, non-payment of invoices, change in services level where the agency does not have such services available, and so on. In addition, the patient and family should be advised of and given a copy of the patient rights and responsibilities, and the agency procedures for withdrawal of home health services, including notification of the patient's physician.

Before withdrawing services, except in those circumstances where a home care worker would be in immediate jeopardy, services should continue until the home health provider discusses the issues of concern with the patient, patient's family, and physician, and cooperates with all reasonable actions to resolve the issues before withdrawing care. Should the need for termination of services arise despite remedial actions, steps should be taken to avoid allegations of abandonment or other malfeasance. These include working with the patient's physician to ensure continuity of care through referral to another home health provider as evidenced by a letter of acceptance and obtaining a release from the patient or patient representative. Discussions with the physician, patient, responsible party, and pertinent family members regarding the withdrawal of services should be thoroughly and objectively documented in the patient record.

Confidentiality and Privacy

Both state and federal laws protect the confidentiality of medical records and protected health information (PHI). These laws restrict the use and release of certain health information and contain safeguards and restrictions regarding the disclosure of medical records. Home health providers should obtain the advice of a qualified attorney regarding compliance with state and federal laws that cover patient privacy and confidentiality. Home health workers should be aware of the use and disclosure requirement contained within the Health Insurance Portability and Accountability Act (HIPAA) Privacy and Security Rules. To mitigate exposure to fines, sanctions, and criminal or civil actions related to improper use and disclosure of protected health information, the agency must:

- Develop confidentiality and privacy policies and procedures.
- Educate staff about HIPAA and state laws relative to privacy and confidentiality of patients and patient records.
- Have each home health worker, regardless of level, sign a confidentiality statement.
- Monitor for staff compliance with confidentiality policies and procedures by periodic random concurrent and retrospective auditing.
- Obtain consent to allow for disclosures.
- Establish documentation, record management, and record release procedures that are designed to protect patient records, including the requirement not to transport patient records back and forth in a worker's private auto, and protection of patient records from unauthorized use or disclosure while in the home.

Informed Consent and Informed Refusal

Most experienced health care professionals understand the importance of informed consent; however, it is important to distinguish between two important types of consent. First, home health providers must have established policies and procedures and forms related to obtaining *general consent* for routine home care services such as medication administration and ostomy, wound, and catheter care. The second type of consent, *informed consent,* must be obtained for non-routine or specialized risk-prone services such as blood transfusions, renal and other dialysis services, and chemotherapy.

A responsibility matrix for obtaining informed consent is particularly critical, to help home workers remember who is to inform the patient of the risks, benefits, indications, and contraindications of the procedure, and who is to obtain the patient or legal representative's signature. Informed consent is considered by judges and juries to be a *process* and not simply a piece of paper. The informed consent form is used to memorialize the information given and the consent provided. Before signing the consent form, the responsible person must be given all necessary information with which to make an *informed* consent. The designated legal representative, who is responsible for giving consent when the patient cannot give it, or when the patient is a minor, must be clearly identified in the patient record. That person must receive the same information on risks, benefits, indications, and contraindications for the procedure that the patient would receive if they were of age or competent and capable of doing so.

The authorized agency person may give such information for the general consent for treatment by the agency staff, but the physician or related service provider (if not the agency) must obtain informed consent. It is the depth and clarity of the information provided that is questioned in a court of law, not just whether a signature was obtained. Informed consent is generally considered to be the following:

- The type of and purpose for the treatment
- The general and specific risks and benefits of the treatment
- Alternatives to the treatment and the associated risks and benefits of alternative therapies
- Risk of refusal

Note that any adult has the right to refuse a treatment without intending to refuse all services. For example, home health services should not be withdrawn because the patient refuses a recommended placement of a catheter or some other aspect of treatment. However, this refusal should be informed, meaning that there is a disclosure to the patient or the patient's legal representative of the possible consequences of not allowing the recommended treatment. If the patient's physician is not already aware, the agency should ensure that the physician is notified and that any alternative is discussed with the patient or the patient's legal representative.

There might be occasions when a patient's informed refusal will interfere with the agency's duty to provide care. When all reasonable efforts have been made to help the patient understand the possible risks associated with refusing, and to assess possible alternatives with the patient and physician, it might be clear to the agency that there is no reasonable way to continue care and that services must be withdrawn. This should be an action of last resort, with clear documentation in the home health record of the agency's actions to avoid withdrawal. Associated interventions and follow-up documentation should reflect the principles previously discussed concerning withdrawal of services.

Finally, all activities related to consent or refusal to consent must be objectively documented in the patient's home health record. Please see Chapter 4 in this volume for more information on informed refusal and consent.

Medical Equipment

Equipment for use in home care, as prescribed by the patient's physician, might be provided by the home health agency or by a durable medical equipment supplier. Any time a supplier is involved, a written contract for services must be completed, including provisions that address the equipment being supplied and the respective responsibilities of the agency and of the supplier with regard to issues such as equipment maintenance and training. Other contract provisions should of course be included as per Chapter 12 on Contract Review in Volume I of this series.

An important consideration for both supplier and home care agency is that each must have written procedures on the reporting of medical equipment-related patient injury or death pursuant to the provisions of the federal Safe Medical Device Act of 1990 (SMDA) and tracking processes for equipment as required by the SMDA.[11,12] Those workers who use medical devices and home care equipment as part of the patient's treatment plan must be thoroughly trained in the use, handling, cleaning, and adjusting of the equipment. This training is usually provided by the supplier. As noted, one element of the written contract between agency and supplier must delineate the responsibility for supplier training of home health workers and the patient or family in the proper use of the equipment they supply. Retraining should be addressed when new techniques or equipment become available.

To determine the safety and efficacy of having the patient or family be responsible for equipment during the absence of home health workers, patients and their families must receive a periodic evaluation of their knowledge and ability to operate the equipment. As noted, this training should preferably be administered by the equipment vendor. The medical record should contain documentation of training and assessment of provider and caregiver skills in using the equipment, and any follow-up action indicated, such as another training session.

The supplier must also provide preventive maintenance and have professionals experienced with the equipment available to answer questions and assist home health workers, as well as the patient and family as required. There should also be support to troubleshoot equipment problems, even after hours and on weekends. The process for these activities must be worked out and identified in the contract before it is signed.

In the pre-admission home assessment, the home must be evaluated for safe use of any medical equipment. Refer to Table 18.10 for a list of Common Durable Medical Equipment. It is important to inform the local utilities if life-sustaining equipment is to be used. There should also be a request for protection in the event of rolling blackouts or other utility interruption. Grounded electrical outlets should be available, as medical equipment must always be connected to this type of outlet. The amount of electricity being supplied into the household must be adequate; otherwise plugging it in and turning it on will result in a blown fuse. No major piece of equipment should ever be plugged into an extension cord with other electrical equipment, such as lamps, fans, televisions, irons, and so on. The home health worker assigned to the case should check to ensure that there is no fraying, splitting, or other damage to medical equipment cords, even though this is primarily the responsibility of the equipment vendor.

In the event of an equipment incident in which the patient is injured or dies, several things must take place in the immediate aftermath:

- Contact agency management by phone to report the incident and follow their instructions.

- Do not touch any dials or change any settings, attempt to continue using the equipment, or "test" the equipment to see if it actually failed.

TABLE 18.10   Types of DME Common to Home Health Care

Ambulation aides	Intravenous & TPN infusers
Apnea monitors	Lift chairs and stand-left machines
Bedside commodes & other toilet aides	Liquid oxygen and oxygen concentrators
Bed triangles	Wheelchairs
CPAP machines	Shower aides
Glucose monitors	Suction machines
Hand-held nebulizers	Oximeters
Hospital beds, including pressure-reducing mattresses	TENS units

- Ensure that the equipment and all cables, cords, or other pieces are sequestered as evidence for the agency. Arrange for their immediate removal.

- Gather and sequester all preventive maintenance documentation. This information must be maintained with the incident report by the agency's risk management professional or legal counsel.

- If necessary and if a camera is available, take photographs.

- Complete an incident report in which the settings and other characteristics of the equipment at the time of the adverse event are documented, and ensure that the report is routed to the agency's risk management professional or legal counsel no later than the following business day.

- Complete an SMDA report form and route it according to procedure.

- Arrange replacement of the equipment with the equipment vendor or other approved vendor unless death has resulted.

If serious injury or death has resulted, the family will likely demand to know what happened, and they will likely be in significant distress. For the purpose of responding to these requests for information, the agency should use its disclosure policy. (Refer to Chapter 3 for more information on disclosure) The home care worker should not attempt to answer specific questions, but instead should assure the family that the circumstances will be investigated by the agency and the equipment vendor. The physician should be involved, as required under the policy, and obtaining assistance from an agency social worker or mental health worker might help deal with the family's distress. However, no information about possible cause is to be released until a determination can be made, and then only by the agency risk management professional or other designated agency manager, as addressed in the disclosure policy. The agency and equipment vendor should cooperate with each other in the investigation; however, the agency must take action to sequester the equipment so that the vendor representatives may view it but not manipulate or repair it. (Refer to Chapter 7 on Biomedical Technology.)

Another question that often arises is whether cell phones or other wireless communication devices can interfere with the proper operation of medical devices and equipment. The answer is that the electromagnetic energy that emanates from such devices has the potential to interfere with equipment operation, resulting in malfunction with potential for patient harm, including inaccurate diagnostic results.[13] All three types of cell phones (analog, digital, and personal communication service) should be treated the same in agency policies and procedures related to cell phones, as should two-way pagers, which function similarly. Walkie-talkies, which generally operate at higher power and lower frequencies when in the "talk" mode, might pose a greater risk of interference with patient equipment.[14] As many others over whom the agency has no control could bring cell phones into the home care environment, it is recommended that home health agencies encourage equipment suppliers to provide equipment with a low degree of susceptibility to related interference.

Medications and Infusion Therapy

In most states, certified nursing assistants may apply topical ointments and help a patient open a vial of prescribed or over-the-counter (OTC) medication so that the patient may take the medication. However injections and administration of intravenous fluids are generally the province of a licensed nurse. Commonly, intravenous fluids are used in the home environment to facilitate intravenous administration of antibiotics, anticoagulants, and chemotherapeutic agents. Administration of the latter should be performed only by a registered nurse or a certified registered nurse specialist who has received specific training in administering chemotherapy. In some circumstances, chemotherapeutic agents are administered by a professional from an independently contracted infusion therapy provider.

When anyone other than the home health agency staff is to administer intravenous medications to an agency client, the agency must establish a contract with the specific organization, such as the infusion vendor. Note that the use of peripherally inserted central catheters (PICC) lines is now a common method for infusing medications and chemotherapy in the home. There are many advantages to the use of PICC lines, but there are also numerous associated risks, including catheter-related infection, accidental arterial cannulization on insertion, nerve injury, embolism, cardiac dysrhythmias, and extravasation of fluids and medications. In all states, it is legal for a licensed physician to insert the catheter; in some states, it may be the expanded role of licensed registered nurses who have been specifically trained and certified in PICC line insertion. Because of the risks inherent to insertion and maintenance of PICC lines, only RNs who have been trained and credentialed should insert or maintain a PICC line.[15,16] If these individuals are the employees of an independently contracted vendor, it is proper for the agency to ask for documentation of their training.

To the extent that home health workers assist with or administer medications, whether oral, injectable, parenteral, topical, suppository, or inhalation, the agency must establish competency through a medication training program. This approach should require demonstration of technique and written examination before a worker is released to perform a medication task in the home environment. Recognition of medication reactions and proper interventions, communication, and documentation of such events must be addressed in the training program. Obviously the extent of training will depend upon individuals' certification or licensure and the length of their experience. Registered nurses who specialize in chemotherapy might merely complete a competency list indicating how many times they have administered specific agents in the past five years, and a home health aide would be trained to help a patient self-administer certain medications.

Withholding Care and Other End-Of-Life Issues

This aspect of home health care has received significant attention over the recent past as a result of precedent-setting litigation such as the Terri Schiavo case. The salient issue in the Schiavo case was that the patient did not have a written living will or advance directives to guide caregivers in determining her end-of-life wishes, and this ultimately led to a vehement disagreement between her husband and parents about what Ms. Schiavo would have wanted done for her.

Numerous publications and resources containing information about advance directives, use of durable power of attorney for health care, and do-not-resuscitate orders are now readily available. With continued growth and evolution of high-technology options available for use in home health care, home health agencies must be increasingly cautious to ensure that patient wishes and desires related to continuation of care, resuscitative intervention, life-sustaining equipment, referrals to an acute care hospital, organ donation, and maintenance of food and fluids are documented and followed. The federal Patient Self-Determination Act (PSDA) also requires that home care providers ascertain whether advance directives exist "in advance of care provided"[17] and to inform patients in writing of the agency's policies on advance directives and applicable state law.[18]

As noted in the section on admission, all home care workers assigned to the patient must be aware of the specific contents of advance directives, of the presence of do-not-resuscitate orders, and of the names and contact numbers for proxy decision-makers identified in a durable power of attorney for health care. A copy of all advance directive documents and the DPOA-HC must be inserted in the patient's home care record. However, because the entire record might not be in the home at the time the information is needed, the originals must be readily accessible to the home care worker in the patient's home. In addition, the presence of such documents and relevant current orders should be incorporated in the patient's care plan, so that each assigned worker is aware of and follows the patient's wishes.

It is essential that if patients indicate on admission that they do not have advance directives and do not wish to have them, this information must be documented in the medical record. It is necessary to reevaluate this position periodically throughout the agency's contact with patients and their families. All discussions should be supported by documentation in the home care record.[19]

To proactively address bioethical dilemmas that arise in the home care environment, it is recommended that each home health agency have contractual arrangements with bioethics consultants and legal counsel available to provide advice and direction.

Initial orientation followed by periodic updates should be provided to each employee to ensure that staff are following the agency's PSDA policies and procedures. Random record reviews should be conducted, as should staff interviews, to validate ongoing staff awareness of and compliance with PSDA requirements.

Cultural Issues in Home Care

Cultural competence is an essential skill set for all home health workers, as it enables them to understand the various cultural perspectives and communications of diverse patient populations. Such skills also facilitate individualized care plans including, where necessary, language interpretation services. Education is critical to attaining and maintaining such skills.

This is particularly the case because home care providers and programs that receive federal funds are bound by the provisions of Title VI of the Civil Rights Act of 1964 which prohibits discrimination based upon a person's national origin. The law also requires reducing or eliminating cultural barriers that restrict a person from receiving effective, individualized social and health services.[20,21] To avoid fines and sanctions, it is recommended that home health agencies develop and implement related policies and procedures. All staff must be educated on these policies and procedures, and subsequently monitored for compliance. One of the processes put in place to ensure compliance should be a contract with a language interpreter service to ensure that interpreters for non-English-proficient patients are available when needed.

The National Center for Cultural Competence has available through its Web site a cultural competency enhancement series that can be downloaded and used to foster cultural awareness and competency of home care workers.[22] The Center can also refer home health agency administrators to other cultural competency resources where additional tools and publications can be obtained.[23]

Patient and Caregiver Education

Family involvement in a home care patient's life is crucial in helping patients maintain optimal mental functions and feel as though they are still a part of the family. In addition, because home care is by nature intermittent, the patient usually cannot remain at home unless there is an available friend or family caregiver who can perform certain tasks for them, when a home health worker is not in the home.

Despite the importance of family and caregiver involvement, however, there might be times when these individuals express discomfort with care procedures, or with seeing blood, or with handling equipment. Home health workers can ease this discomfort through teaching and mentoring activities. By demonstrating procedures, obtaining return demonstrations from caregivers, and being sensitive to their concerns, the home care provider can help them reach a point at which they are comfortable with performing the procedure themselves. The same principles, of course, apply to patient teaching.

It is important for assigned home care workers to continue supporting patients and their caregiver families or friends, until they have demonstrated their ability to perform essential care tasks independently. Many of these tasks relate to personal care, suctioning, wound care, hanging new intravenous fluids when a unit has been completed, and administering medications. Written materials on handling specific equipment or performing a specific procedure are very helpful teaching aides and also serve as the basis for documenting teaching activities in the medical record. Such documentation should include what was taught, and to whom, an assessment of subsequent ability to perform the task, and whether a return demonstration shows that the patient or caregiver is competent to perform the task in the home care workers' absence.

Transporting Patients

In addition to previously discussed business automobile liability coverage that specifically covers the transport of patients in employee cars, the agency should have written policies and procedures governing how to transport patients safely. If ambulatory assistive devices also are to be transported, the employee must be oriented as to how to embark and disembark patients and their equipment from the car safely. In any case, no home care workers should transport a patient unless they have been cleared to do so by the agency management, based on approval by the agency's business automobile liability carrier and a violation-free driving record.

•••••••••••

INFECTIOUS AND HAZARDOUS WASTE MANAGEMENT

Every home health agency should have a comprehensive infection control program that addresses surveillance, prevention, identification, reporting, and control of infections among home care employees and patients. Home health workers must be able to properly and safely handle regulated medical waste and other contaminated items, including soiled patient sheets and clothing, dressings or bandages that are contaminated with blood or other infectious materials, in accordance with applicable local, state, and federal laws. Any receptacle for the safe disposal of medical waste, including red bags and sharps containers accompanied by hazard labels, must be available on the job site for use by the home health worker. The agency should have a policy that prohibits employees from taking a patient's soiled clothing and linen to their own private homes to launder.

In addition, the agency's infection control plan should address preventing spread of infection through universal precautions and use of personal protective equipment (PPE) and should address managing exposures to blood and other infectious materials. Other points that are important to address in the infection control plan include use of engineering controls to prevent sharps injuries; safe use and disposal of sharps containers; tuberculosis testing, identification, and treatment; HIV testing and prophylactic treatment; and verification of employee immunity to mumps, measles, and rubella, tetanus, and diphtheria. All home care workers should know how to identify and report infections and exposures to infection control-related hazards and take proper action in the home care environment to prevent illness and injury. Provision of hepatitis B vaccine should also be provided free of charge to workers who have never had it, and any employees who defer the immunization should be approached periodically about reconsidering their decision.

Training on safety and infection control issues should be provided in terms that are applicable to the language and literacy of the workers and to their job functions. Documentation should be maintained in personnel records, with pertinent program materials, so that these items are readily available for audit by agency management and regulatory entities. Any issues associated with infections and illness or injury, whether patient or worker, must be addressed under the auspices of the agency's quality improvement and risk management plans, with corrective action directed at prevention of the same or similar incident in the future.

Finally, compliance with all requirements of the agency's infection control program must be monitored for effectiveness. Such monitoring specifically addresses reported illnesses and injuries and incident reports from employees.

Emergency Preparedness

The home care worker will be faced with important challenges in the event of a disaster that affects the household while the assigned worker is present. The hurricanes that affected the United States gulf region this year have illustrated that the "three-day food and water" standard no longer applies. In fact, it might take much longer for local and national emergency resources to get to the affected area. As it is human nature to relegate disaster planning and emergency preparedness to a lower priority because of the relative infrequency of disasters, it is recommended that all health care providers, including home health agencies, ensure that adequate emergency preparedness and disaster response plans are implemented and tested at least annually.

For home care patients who are using life sustaining equipment (ventilators or oxygen dependent patients) it is important that local and county disaster planning professionals know of the patient's needs, so that arrangements can be made ahead of time for transportation and equipment if a natural disaster does occur. Planning is critical to ensure that the necessary services are available.

In the home care environment, the emergency preparedness plan must be designed to ensure that care continuity occurs in a disaster. This means that the assigned worker on duty at the time might well be the person who stays in the patient's home to continue the care if roadways and communications are affected. The plan should address care prioritization, equipment management in a power failure, and communication between home care workers and the home or branch office. Specific attention should be paid to major disasters, and to the more common issues of fires, equipment and utility failures, and civil disturbances that might affect the particular home and locale.

Finally, the agency emergency preparedness plan must address business recovery after a major disaster or a situation that adversely affects home and branch office operations. Insurance carriers often have disaster, emergency preparedness, and business recovery staff or consultants available who can assist the agency to develop emergency preparedness and disaster plans.

Discharging Patients When Home Health Care Is No Longer Necessary

Discharging a patient from care must be undertaken with a rational approach and thoroughly documented to mitigate any allegation of abandonment or delay in service. The discharge criteria for hospice facilities are generally straightforward. When the patient dies, the care is terminated. For home health and private duty, the discharge process is more complex. Most home health discharges result from physician certification that the need for home health services no longer exists, such as when antibiotic IV therapy is discontinued or ends, when patients have returned to their pre-illness conditions and there is no longer a medical need for home health care, or when family or independently hired caregivers can take over the personal care needs of the patient.

As discussed earlier in the section on withdrawal of services, it is imperative that the home health provider ensure that patients and their families understand why they are no longer candidates for home care and that they are capable of providing for the patient's needs when home health care ends. Clear and realistic written discharge criteria for the agency to follow are important. Providing the patient with a description of the discharge process on admission to the home health service will minimize misunderstanding when the time for discharge arrives. It is also recommended that after-care instructions be written for the patient and family to help them understand what, if anything, they need to do once home health care ends. Such instruction should be signed by the patient or legal representative and a copy maintained in the patient's home care record.

Incident Identification and Reporting

If an adverse event regarding patient safety or employee injury occurs, staff should know who to contact for immediate assistance. Subsequent reporting of such circumstances is critical to a proactive loss prevention and control program. More specifically, such a program is dependent upon early incident identification, documentation, confidential reporting, and investigation. All home health care workers must be trained about the procedures and tools that support these activities. Reportable incidents in home health care include but are not limited to the following events, in no particular order of importance:

- Incorrect procedure performed, or correct procedure performed incorrectly
- Treatment provided without a physician order
- Prescribed treatment not followed
- A treatment or procedure performed is outside the scope of practice of the individual performing it
- Complaint about care or services (including billing) by patient or family
- Medication error or adverse drug reaction
- Development of infection not related to the original home health diagnoses
- Complication of treatment or procedure
- Cardio-respiratory arrest
- Exposure to blood or other potentially infectious materials
- Unscheduled admission to the hospital
- Failure to obtain proper consents
- Injury to patient or family member resulting from malfunctioning equipment

- Development of pressure ulcer or progression to stage III after care initiated
- Loss or damage to personal property
- Unsafe environment for the employee (exposure to criminal activity or weapons, verbal or physical assault by family members during visits, and so on)
- Unsafe environment for the patient (suspected abuse by employees, inadequate caregivers, patient fall, and so on)

The proper protocol for maintaining confidentiality of the documentation must be understood and followed. Incidents not witnessed by the home care worker must still be reported as soon as the worker has knowledge of their occurrence.

Risk management professionals can facilitate incident reporting by making sure that staff members understand that timely reporting is in the best interest of the patients, employees, and the organization, and that there will not be punishment or retribution for reporting an incident according to established policy. It is also important that staff understand:

- Why reporting of incidents is important
- What to report and required reporting timeframes
- How to report an incident and to protect confidentiality of a report and investigation notes
- To whom each type of incident report should be given, for example, Risk Management or Human Resources

Other Reporting

Staff must understand the need for mandatory incident reporting that is required of the risk management professional by such oversight agencies as the Department of Health and the FDA (for medical device reporting where a death has occurred or when significant injury has occurred and the manufacturer is not known). Education of home care providers as to their role, the required timeframes in which to report, and their assistance in reporting are vital for them to understand if the agency is to be in compliance.

Particularly important with regard to external reporting requirements are any instances of suspected or actual child abuse to the applicable state agency. The same is true for suspected or actual elder or dependent adult abuse. Failure to report such circumstances could result in loss of the agency license to operate, or in fines and sanctions. Refer to Chapter 14 on Pediatrics for more information on child abuse.

All home care workers must be aware of their abuse reporting requirements under the law, how to report, and when to report, and they should sign a document for their agency that states that they are aware of and understand their abuse reporting responsibilities. The home health agency should conduct annual retraining to ensure that each worker has had an opportunity to review legal requirements for reporting suspected and actual abuse situations, and to review applicable reporting responsibilities.

Medical Record Documentation

Documentation in the home health care record is a tool to communicate to others on the care team what care and services patients have received and how they responded. It is also a basis for audit to ensure that care meets standards in the industry and as established by internal policy and procedure. Documentation also plays a significant role at trial. It becomes the "script" in a negligence or malpractice lawsuit, at which time the documentation can either assist significantly in the defense of the case if it adequately reflects what was done for the patient, or be detrimental to the case and substantiate a breach in the standard of care. In addition, sloppy and incomplete documentation, while not always specific to a complaint at hand or contributing to allegations in a lawsuit, certainly sets the stage for the plaintiff's attorney to impugn the professionalism of the care provider and makes everyone spend needless time explaining issues that might have been easily corrected.

For these reasons, documentation must be clear, concise, legible, thorough, and descriptive of events that transpire in the patient's care.

············

CONCLUSION

This chapter has presented many of the risks associated with delivery of health care and services in patient homes and techniques to help the risk management professional and staff minimize the risk.

As the field of home care evolves, it is essential for home care providers to remain abreast of changes in regulations, standards, and guidelines in home health care, and to network with other agencies to identify best practices that can reduce liability and enhance safety.

Endnotes

1. Jerant, M. D. *Home Telemedicine: Merging the Old and New Ways.* UC Davis, September 1999.

2. National Association for Home Care and Hospice (NAHC). Available at [www.nahc.org].

3. Americans with Disabilities Home page. [www.usdoj.gov/crt/ada/adahom1.htm].

4. U.S. Department of Labor Employment Standards Administration.

5. U.S. Dept. of Labor, Bureau of Statistics, Summary 97-4, February 1997.

6. U.S. Dept. of Labor, Bureau of Statistics (1991). Occupational Injuries and Illness in the United States by Industry, 1989. Bulletin 2379.

7. Office of the Inspector General, Department of Health and Human Services: Compliance Program Guidance for Home Health Agencies, August 1998.

8. ECRI Quality and Risk Management 6. Overview of Home Healthcare Risks and Liability, Part II: Employee and Business Risk Management May 1996; 10.

9. Montauk, S. L. "Home Health Care" *American Family Physician.* November 1, 1998; (58/7).

10. Health Care Financing Administration HM-11; Medicare Standards for Home Care, Washington, D.C., I.S. Department of Health & Human Services, 1983.

11. Safe Medical Device Act of 1990 (SMDA), 21 U.S.C. §519(3) (i) as amended November 21, 1997.

12. 21 C.F.R. part 821 Medical Device Tracking Requirements. Available at: [www.washingtonwatchdog.org/documents/cfr/title21/part821.html].

13. Cell Phones and EMI: Frequently Asked Questions. Equipment and Technology 11.1: Continuing Care Risk Management, ECRI; 2002 Nov (1–3).

14. *Ibid.*

15. Position Paper: Peripherally Inserted Central Catheters. *Journal of Intravenous Nursing.* 1997, July–Aug; 20(4):172–4.

16. Position Paper: Use of Unlicensed Assistive Personnel in the Delivery of Intravenous Therapy. *Journal of Intravenous Nursing.* 1997 Mar-Apr; 20(2); 75–6.

17. Living Wills or Durable Powers of Attorney; Advance Directives. Fed Reg 1995 Jun 27; 60(123): 33262–98.

18. *Ibid.*

19. Gates, M. F., I. Schins, A. S. Smith. "Applying Advance Directives Regulations In Home Care Agencies." *Home Health Nursing.* 1996; 14(2):127–33.

20. Gorrie, Jan J. "Legal Review and Commentary: Failure to Provide Back-up Power Results In Death and a $450,000 Massachusetts Settlement." *Healthcare Risk Management.* 2005 Aug 27(8), 1–4.

21. Title VI, Civil Rights Act of 1964.

22. U.S. Dept of Health and Human Services, Office of Minority Health. National Standards for Culturally and Linguistically Appropriate Service in Health Care: Final Report. Washington D.C. 2001.

23. Nardi, D. A., and S. Siwinski-Hebel. "Cultural Issues in Home Care" *Advance for Nurses.* May 2005; pp. 21–25.

Suggested Readings

Home Care Subject to Employee Safety, Workers' Comp Risks. *Hospital Risk Management* 1993 Dec; 15(12):176–81.

"Overview of Workers' Compensation." *Continuing Care Risk Management.* 1993 Nov. (1–18).

A Workplace Violence Prevention Program—An Investment with a Great Yield, Commentary in IRMI Risk Management, James Madero, Ph.D. (Sept 2003).

Lyncheski, J. E. Esq. & Anne M. Lavelle Esq. "Facing Workplace Violence in the Health Care Industry." *ASHRM Journal.* 2002 Summer; (13–15).

Focus on Home Health Care Worker Safety, STAT (16:2001:6,8), published by Chubb Health Care.

Montauk, S. L., MD. "Home Health Care." *American Family Physician*, 1998 Nov.1 :(58:7)

Criminal Background Checks Continuing Care Risk Management Risk Analysis, ECRI 2003 Mar; 1–11.

Criminal Background Reports; A Survey of Fifty States. American Health Lawyers Association, Washington D.C.: AHLA; 2002.

Equal Employment Opportunity Commission (EEOC) Policy Guidance on Consideration of Arrest Records, Title VII of the Civil Rights Act as amended, 42 USC §2000 et seq.1982; EEOC Compliance Manual, Vol. II, Appendices 604-A and 604-B.

Rozovsky and Rozovsky. *Home Health Care Law: Liability and Risk Management.* New York: Little, Brown & Company, 1993.

Sherwin, Anne P. "Legal Issues Of Concern To Home Care Providers" in Harris, M (Ed.) *Handbook of Home Care Administration.* Gaithersburg, Maryland: Aspen Publishers, Inc. 1994.

Office of Inspector General, Department of Health and Human Services: Compliance Program Guidance for Home Health Agencies, August 1998.

Marrelli, T. M. *Handbook of Home Health Standards and Documentation Guidelines for Reimbursement.* 2nd. Ed. St. Louis: Mosby 1994.

Home Care Subject to Employee Safety, Workers' Comp Risks Hosp Risk Management 1993 Dec; 15(12):176–81.

19

Long-Term Care

Kathryn Hyer
Brenda K. Johnson

In 1860, half the population was under age twenty; in 1994, half were age thirty-four or older. By 2030, at least half could be thirty-nine years or older.[1] The population of the United States is aging rapidly. America's population, estimated at over 282 million in 2000, is growing older at a rapid pace. The number of Americans age sixty-five and older, estimated at 35 million in 2000, is expected to grow to 71 million by 2030 and to about 86 million in 2050, according to the Bureau of Census projections.[2] Census projections also indicate that the fastest-growing segment in the older population is individuals eighty-five and older. This group, estimated at about 4.2 million in 2000, is expected to grow to about 21 million by 2050.[3] The increase for seniors eighty-five years and older from 2000 to 2050 represents an increase of 388.9 percent (16.6 million).[4] This demographic shift increases liability- and compliance-related exposure for health care organizations. This chapter provides an overview of the regulatory environment, patient safety issues, and applicable risk management strategies.

THE REGULATORY ENVIRONMENT

By 2020 it is estimated that 54.6 million Americans will be older than age sixty-five (16.3 percent of the total population) and 7.3 million (2.2 percent) will be over age eighty-five.[5] Because older persons have the greatest incidence of disability and chronic illness and need substantially more health care services than younger populations, the health care system is evolving to meet these needs.

Long-term care services, which are expected to grow as the numbers of elders increase, are defined by the U.S. Department of Health and Human Services as the "range of medical and/or social services designed to help people who have disabilities or chronic care needs." Services can be short or long term and can be provided in a person's home, in the community, or in residential facilities, such as nursing homes or assisted-living facilities. Federal and state Medicaid programs have encouraged growth of home- and community-based care because elders do not want to enter nursing homes, and many home and community-based care services are cheaper than institutional care.

The demand for long-term care services and new housing arrangements means that medical providers must be familiar with the medical and nursing services available to arrange adequate support for elders who need assistance upon discharge from the hospital. Economic issues are of concern, as many residential settings provide very limited nursing service, unless the resident purchases help. Even those with assistance may have paraprofessional or personal care services available, rather than skilled services. There is also a wide range of home- and community-based residential services available.

Following is a brief review of issues and risk management strategies applicable to the long-term care setting.

Skilled Nursing Facilities

Approximately 17,000 certified nursing homes with 1.6 million beds in the United States served more than 1.4 million Americans in 2003.[6] The number of nursing home beds has decreased slightly over the past ten years while the acuity of residents admitted continues to increase. The risk management professional should be aware of the numerous federal requirements that pertain to quality of care in this environment.

The Nursing Home Reform Act of 1987 specifies that a facility "must provide services and activities to attain or maintain the highest practicable physical, mental, and psychological well-being of each resident in accordance with a written plan of care."[7]

Centers for Medicare and Medicaid Services (CMS) regulations provide that "residents have the right to be free from verbal, sexual, physical, or mental abuse; corporal punishment; and involuntary seclusion, and to be free from any physical or chemical restraints imposed for purposes of discipline or convenience." Under federal regulations, facilities must:

- Develop and implement written policies and procedures that prohibit mistreatment, neglect, abuse, and misappropriation of resident property.

- Report to the state's nurse's aide registry or licensing authorities any knowledge of actions by a court of law against an employee that would indicate unfitness for services.

- Ensure that all alleged violations involving mistreatment, neglect, or abuse—including injuries from unknown sources—are reported immediately to the facility administrator, to the state survey or certification agency, and other officials as required by law.

- Be able to provide evidence that all alleged violations are thoroughly investigated and that further potential abuse is prevented.

- Report findings of the facility's investigation to the administrator, to the state survey and certification agencies, and to other officials in accordance with state law within five working days of the occurrence; if the violation is verified, corrective action must be taken.

Operational and Clinical Risk

The facility should anticipate annual inspections by the state. These inspections usually result in citations and required corrective plans of action.

Survey and Surveyors Issues

Unlike other health care settings, the government does not accept accreditation by the Joint Commission on Accreditation of Healthcare Organizations (JCAHO) or other recognized agencies in lieu of inspection by the state, as evidence that a Medicare skilled nursing facility or a Medicaid nursing facility complies with program participation standards (deemed status). The Centers for Medicare and Medicaid Services (CMS) define the Federal Requirements of Participation that nursing homes must meet to participate in the Medicare and Medicaid programs. The requirements are detailed. They establish specific care standards in several areas that affect residents' functional health status, including quality of care, quality of life, and the facility's management practices.[8]

CMS contracts with the individual states to certify that homes meet these standards. Any violation of the standards is cited as a deficiency with a range of sanctions attached to the violation. All Medicare and Medicaid facilities must undergo an annual inspection or survey with qualified nursing home surveyors who have passed the surveyor minimum qualification test (SMQT). The annual survey occurs on average every twelve months but to avoid predictability in the survey, the window for the annual survey is from nine to fifteen months after the prior survey. In a further effort to ensure that facilities provide adequate care during nights and weekends, the federal government recently mandated that at least 10 percent of all surveys begin on "off-hours," in the evening or on weekends.

During the annual survey, a team of surveyors, including at least one registered nurse, spends several days in the nursing home to determine the quality of care and services rendered to residents, the food preparation, and the fire and general safety of the facility. The results of these annual surveys are entered into the Online Survey Certification and Reporting (OSCAR) database. The OSCAR results are made available to the public through the CMS Web site.[9]

Survey Citations

Citations for violations of federal regulations are determined through the annual survey process. Surveyors are required to follow procedures and protocols established by CMS. Federal law includes 185 separate regulations based on quality of residents' care and rights, referred to as F-tags, which are the basis for survey citations. Life and safety regulations, known as K-tags, also fall under the federal regulations and are part of the annual inspection.[10]

For each deficient practice in any of these regulations, the severity and scope of the violation is determined on a case-by-case basis.

Severity is determined by how much actual or potential harm there is to the resident(s). Severity is further defined as having one of four levels of harm:

1. No actual harm with potential for minimal harm

2. No actual harm with potential for more than minimal harm but not immediate jeopardy to patient

3. Actual harm with potential for more than minimal harm but not immediate jeopardy

4. Immediate jeopardy to resident health or safety

The scope of a violation is determined by how many residents of the facility were (or could have been) affected. Scope is classified into one of three categories:

- Isolated event
- A pattern of violation
- Extent

Remedies required of the facility for each violation are linked to the severity and scope of the violation. They range from closing the facility to plans of correction.

When a deficiency is found, the state may recommend and CMS can impose several sanctions including monetary penalties, increased state monitoring, ban on payment for Medicare admissions, or, in rare cases for serious violations, loss of the right to participate in the Medicare and Medicaid programs.[11]

The Guidance to Surveyors provides information that can help determine whether and how a particular deficiency might be scored depending on the scope and severity of the violation.

When investigating a potential risk event, managers should refer to all applicable standards, regulations, and survey protocols to assess whether a potential violation might have occurred. Consideration of the following requirements may facilitate investigation of a risk event.

- Quality of Care: Prevention of pressure ulcers, pain management, facility responses to resident changes in condition, management of nutrition or hydration problems, and medication errors.[12]

- Resident Rights and Facility Practices: Prevention of abuse, neglect, and mistreatment, use of physical and chemical restraints, especially use of anti-psychotic drugs, resident freedom of choice, advance directives, and informed consent.[13]

- Administration: Injury investigation and reporting requirements, provision of physician services, supervision of medical care, and quality assurance committee.[14]

- Quality of Life: Activities or programs to promote the resident's highest practicable level of physical, mental, and psychosocial well-being.[15]

- Resident Assessment: Functional assessments, establishment of the interdisciplinary plan of care, and timing and management of changes in condition.[16]

- Investigation and Reporting Obligations: A facility must investigate any injury to a resident and make a report to the facility administrator within five days.[17] Findings of these investigations must also be forwarded to the state survey agency. State law may also establish separate reporting obligations under a vulnerable adult statute.

Complaint Survey

State surveyors may conduct a complaint investigation in response to a reported risk event, or as part of a regularly scheduled inspection. Generally, complaint surveys require a review of clinical records and surveyor interviews with the resident, employee, and family. These interviews are conducted to determine whether an event constitutes a deficiency. It is best to advise staff to provide documentation and evidence that frames a particular event or complaint as dissatisfaction, but not as a deficiency.

············

RISK MANAGEMENT PROGRAM

Risk management in long-term care is best implemented as a facility-wide program.[18] The goal is to foster those aspects of risk management that aim to improve the quality of care for residents.

Risk management has become an important aspect of day-to-day patient care. A culture of teamwork will play a critical role in any successful program. An effective risk management program includes a comprehensive written description of the governing body's accountability for risk identification, risk control, and risk financing that is communicated throughout the organization. The program must contribute to conserving the financial assets of the facility and reducing accident and injury claims while monitoring areas of high litigation risk. The top litigation targets in long-term care remain pressure ulcers, malnutrition, dehydration, falls, elopement, adverse drug events, burns, delay in diagnosis or treatment, and improper discharge. Claims also can allege several violations of residents' rights. The following components are essential to include in any effective risk management program:

- Goals and objectives to include governing body approval of the program
- Designated individual responsible for developing, implementing, and monitoring all aspects of the risk management program
- Governance and committee structure to include the integration of risk management information into the management of the organization, through activities such as credentialing, contracting, performance reviews, quality improvement, resident satisfaction, standards of care, and investigations of legal allegations
- Resources for managing data from the incident reporting system
- Risk identification and tracking methodologies
- Documentation of findings and actions
- Annual program review with the governing body's input
- Loss control techniques identified and implemented
- Data analysis to identify trends
- Claims management
- Coordination of facility insurance and risk financing

Risk management should be a major goal for the administration, physicians, nurses, consultants, and all those who work in the long-term care setting. With the industry's increase in regulations, and the public's concern about patient safety, it is essential that adverse outcomes be followed up quickly and thoroughly. The first step that follows notice of any such event should be an initial risk management investigation. Any related documentation should be labeled "Privileged and Confidential/Attorney Work Product/Completed in Anticipation of Litigation," and any specific statutory protection provisions should be cited if they are available.

Information documented should include the resident's name, date of occurrence, location, a brief description of the incident, witness identification, and location. Specific areas that are commonly investigated in following up an adverse event include: environment of care, equipment management, communication between provider, patient, and family, medical record documentation, staffing, policies and procedures, and any identified barriers in the organization. Refer to Exhibit 19.1 for a sample form to capture specifics in each of these areas.

EXHIBIT 19.1 **Summary of Event Follow-Up**

Environment of Care:

1. Safety issues identified?   No _____   Yes _____
   Actions taken: _____

2. Environmental hazards?   No _____   Yes _____
   Contribution to incident?   No _____   Yes _____
   If yes, how: _____

3. Chemical product, waste, or medication involved?   No _____   Yes _____
   Explain: _____

Equipment:

1. Was a piece of equipment involved in the incident?
   No _____   Yes _____

2. Equipment is in good working condition?   No _____   Yes _____
   If no, explain: _____

3. Equipment immediately sequestered under lock and key?
   No _____   Yes _____
   Location: _____

4. Copy of the maintenance and service records obtained and secured?
   No _____   Yes _____
   Location: _____

5. Independent testing?   No _____   Yes _____
   Who: _____

6. Brand Name: _____
   Type of Device: _____
   Name and address of manufacturer: _____
   Model #: _____   Catalog #: _____ Serial #:_____
   Lot #: _____   Other #: _____

7. Safe Medical Device Report completed?   No _____   Yes _____
   Copy attached.

8. Purchase agreement on file and available?   No _____   Yes _____

Communication:

1. Initial response to occurrence timely and appropriate?
   No _____   Yes _____
   Explain: _____

2. Steps taken to avoid incident or complication?   No _____   Yes _____
   Explain: _____

3. Injury or adverse outcome.   No _____   Yes _____
   Reportable injury: No _____   Yes _____

4. Delays in diagnosis and/or implementation of treatment?
   No _____   Yes _____
   Explain: _____

5. Resident or family advised of the incident?   No _____   Yes _____
   Explain: _____

6. Resident or family reaction to the incident: _____

Medical Record Documentation:

1. Documentation discrepancies?   No _____   Yes _____
   Explain: _____

2. Facts of the incident documented in the medical record?
   No _____   Yes _____
   Explain: _____

3. Informed consent as appropriate?   No _____   Yes _____
   Time/date/by whom? _____

(Continued)

EXHIBIT 19.1   Summary of Event Follow-Up *(Continued)*

4. Resident monitored?   No _____   Yes _____
    If no, explain: _____

5. Inconsistencies or alterations in the medical record?
        No _____   Yes _____
    State inconsistencies and location in the medical record: _____

Human Capital:

1. Staffing adequate?   No _____   Yes _____
    Explain: _____

2. Staff competent and performing within the parameters of their job descriptions?
        No _____   Yes _____
    Explain: _____

3. Policies and procedures for deviation from standard of care?
        No _____   Yes _____
    Explain: _____

4. Policy and procedure protocol followed?   No _____   Yes _____
    Explain: _____

5. Physician's order adequate?   No _____   Yes _____
    Explain: _____

6. Patient rights issues present?   No _____   Yes _____
    Explain: _____

7. Organizational barriers: System Design?   No _____   Yes _____
    Explain: _____

8. Cultural tolerance?   No _____   Yes _____
    Explain: _____

Third-Party Involvement

   (1) Is there a third-party contractor involved in the event, e.g. agency nurse, medical director, maintenance
        staff, contractor?
   (2) Is there a contract available to review for responsibilities?
   (3) Is there a current certificate of insurance of the third party?

Improving Organizational Performance

It is generally accepted that integrating risk management and quality improvement programs facilitates improvement of care and minimizes risk. Key to this integration is the regular focused consideration of high-risk areas by a committee of facility representatives, including the medical director, clinical administration, safety and environmental representatives, direct patient care staff, and indirect care givers from dietary and housekeeping. It is also important to evaluate whether the following specific approaches have been implemented to promote the effective sharing of risk management and quality improvement information.

- Participation of the risk manager on the quality improvement committee
- Participation of the risk manager in clinical chart review activities
- Quality improvement review of clinical incidents or unusual occurrences reported to risk management
- Risk management review of trends, patterns, or clinical incidents identified through quality improvement monitoring

Additionally, there should be a regular review of the current status of changes that facilities are implementing and information that indicates management of high-risk areas with potential for exposure to loss. Specific long-term areas to assess for adequacy and suitable loss control initiatives are:

- Number of nursing personnel
- Food, supplies, equipment, and medication
- Trained personnel performing duties consistent with their level of competency

In this regard, note that regulations that govern provision of care include minimum staff-to-resident ratios. Compliance with these requirements is measured by inspections and surveys to ensure that the care provided meets or exceeds statutory and regulatory requirements.

- Care planning
- Policies and procedures, especially those that pertain to litigation-prone issues such as decubitus care
- Supervision and monitoring of nursing personnel to ensure that the health care plan, physician's orders, and policies and procedures have been implemented
- Nursing and medical assessment and evaluation of each resident on admission and on a frequent basis

Where nurses have questions about physicians' orders, or there are high-risk issues that staff perceives are not being addressed, it is imperative that the facility culture support efficient access of the chain of command so that resolution can be achieved.

Refer to Table 19.1 for specific risk management areas that are generally important to assess.

Prioritizing and Ensuring Best Practices in Care

Maintaining functionality, safety, and dignity in older adults is important to the maintenance of the standard of care and should be a goal for all long-term care facilities.

Functionality is a determinant of an older adult's quality of life, living arrangements, and the services that the resident needs. The activities of daily living are considered to be those everyday personal-care activities that have a direct effect on quality of life and independence. The activities of daily living (ADLs) are those activities that a resident can perform independently or with little assistance. They include taking food or nourishment, dressing, bathing, using the toilet, transferring (from bed to chair), and walking.

Physical or mental disabilities can affect a resident's ability to perform the ADLs. The inability to perform one or more of these activities necessitates that the resident or patient seek assistance from others.

As residents seek to maintain their ADLs, they can encounter safety issues. Falls and fall-related injuries of long-term care residents remain among the most common risk management concerns for nursing facilities. The incidence of falls in nursing homes is 1.6 falls per bed per year. Fall-related injuries frequently lead to major disability and mortality. Therefore, prior to admission, a facility must assess the resident's ADL functionality, cognitive disability, psychosocial, and medical concerns, and the need for assistance and supervision. The facility should be confident that it can safely meet the current needs of the resident. Developing satisfactory entry criteria which include a fall risk assessment can help ensure this result. Refer to Appendix 19.1 for more information related to falls.

TABLE 19.1   Specific Areas of Risk Management Program Evaluation

Knowledge Evidenced By Comments

Priority Evaluation

1) Has every service area defined and implemented a systematic way to conduct initial resident assessment to include the information gathered and the physical examination conducted upon admission to the area? Is there also a plan for regular reassessment? How is this information communicated among staff and caregivers?

2) Is there a comprehensive informed consent process in place to ensure that residents are actively participating in diagnosis and treatment decisions?

3) Is there a medical record policy and procedure to ensure the accuracy, completeness and consistency of medical record documentation?

4) Is there a consistent method by which residents are identified prior to diagnostic and therapeutic interventions?

5) Are there policies and procedures that address the process for medication administration?

6) Is there a process to ensure that proficiency to perform procedures is maintained?

7) Is there a process to ensure that privileging guidelines will be developed and implemented for new technologies and procedures?

8) Is there a process to ensure that all equipment is subject to infection control measures, safety checks, and preventive maintenance?

9) Are there policies and procedures that specify how the following will be accomplished?
   a) Informed consent or refusal
   b) Pertinent regulatory issues
   c) Resident communications
   d) Resident identification
   e) Advance directives
   f) Follow-up to violence or abuse
   g) Resident ambulation
   h) Skin care monitoring, evaluation, and treatment
   i) Documentation of ongoing care and following incidents such as a fall
   j) Admission and discharge
   k) Preservation of resident rights
   l) Elopement prevention

In general, residents have a fundamental right to considerate care that safeguards their personal dignity and respects their cultural, psychosocial, and spiritual values. This means that both the resident's rights to informed consent and right to refuse care are of paramount importance. Refer to Chapter 4 in this volume for more information on informed consent. A facility that seeks to improve resident perception by respecting the rights of each individual and conducting business in an ethical manner will positively influence the perception of residents and families, reducing litigiousness and enhancing the organization's reputation.

An assessment of the clinical environment might be helpful in meeting these three basic goals of functionality, safety, and dignity. These include the resident admission process, informed consent (including the resident's right to refuse treatment), regulatory compliance, residential family communications, documentation of care, and development of resident programs to include fall safety, restraints, elopement prevention, and skin care. The risk management professional can help managers evaluate these areas.

Refer to Table 19.2 for a tool to assist in evaluating whether the standard of care is met in key risk areas.

TABLE 19.2   Standard of Care and Resident Safety

Knowledge Evidenced By Comments

Priority Evaluation

1) Fall prevention program consists of:
   a) Fall profile assessment
      i) Do all new residents undergo a fall profile assessment upon admission?
      ii) Follow-up assessments are made at least quarterly or following a fall incident?
   b) Fall prevention program inservice is given to employees at least annually?
      i) component to educate resident
      ii) component to educate family
   c) The fall assessment program is included in the quality improvement reviews?
   d) There is ongoing monitoring of care plans and physical therapy notes to detect inadequacies.
2) Resident lifting or transfer
   a) General lifting
      i) A formal resident lifting or transfer program is established that provides for the assessment of all residents to determine the level of assistance required for transfer?
   b) Mechanical lifting
      i) Mechanical lifts are mandatory for lifts and transfers involving obese and non-ambulatory residents?
   c) Lifting and transfer belts
      i) The use of belts with handles are required for all residents not able to complete independent transfer?
3) Equipment inspection
   a) All equipment used for resident lifting and transfer is inspected at least quarterly?
4) Resident restraints
   a) A formal progressive restraint reduction program is established and monitored to ensure resident independence while at the same time preventing resident injury?
5) Elopement screening
   a) Elopement screening is done for all residents immediately following admission and at least annually thereafter?
6) Exterior control
   a) All access to the exterior of the facility is adequately controlled and monitored to prevent unauthorized access to the outside or any public areas?
7) Interior elopement control
   a) Environment designed to maximize resident comfort and provide freedom from anxiety?
   b) Increased supervision or alert staff?
   c) Exit door alarms?
   d) Individual elopement alarms?
8) Elopement response procedures
   a) Elopement response procedures are developed, posted at each nursing station, and maintained in the event of an elopement incident?
9) Elopement control and inservice drills
   a) Employees attend inservice training at least annually on various aspects of the elopement control program?
   b) Elopement response drills are held at least semi-annually?
10) Equipment testing
    a) Elopement systems (alarms and individual units) are tested weekly to confirm they are in proper working condition?
11) Water temperatures
    a) To prevent burns due to excessively hot water, the following control program is maintained:
       (1) Temperature alarm to activate at 105° F?
       (2) Weekly inspection and logging of water temperatures with proper corrective action taken as necessary? All testing and inspection documentation to be maintained on file.
12) Stairwell alarms
    a) Any stairwell normally accessible to moderate- and high-dependency care residents has doors equipped with keypad access to prevent unauthorized access by residents?
13) Risk management of skin integrity
    a) Admission assessment—every resident is assessed for skin fragility at admission using a profile with a trigger capability, and photos if possible?
    b) Weekly wound monitoring?
    c) Photographic documentation—photos taken on admission, change in condition, at discharge, readmission, quarterly?
    d) Weekly reports discussed with director of nursing and quality improvement?

....

FUTURE DIRECTION OF LONG-TERM CARE

The fear of frail elders and their families about nursing home placement has also stimulated a new form of living arrangement, assisted living, which provides more health and social services than is generally available at home, but not as many services as provided in skilled nursing facilities. Assisted living residences (ALRs), also known as assisted living facilities (ALFs), cover a range of housing and residential settings for elders within the broad array of community-based residential models in long-term care.

The rapid growth of this industry stems from escalating numbers of elders who can no longer live completely independently in the community and are willing to pay for additional services. Their interest is based in large part on the belief that autonomy, privacy, and personal and health care needs can be met outside the institutionalized setting of the nursing home.

States vary considerably in the regulation of the services and the settings. In some states the settings are thought of as part of the "hospitality" industry and are treated more as hotel rooms than as health care residences. In other states, ALFs are highly regulated by the state, as they are seen as health care facilities.

Still other approaches to meet the needs of the elderly are continuing care retirement communities (CCRCs), which incorporate independent living, assisted living, and skilled nursing on one campus; home care programs, adult day care, and various forms of managed care programs such as Program for the All-Inclusive Care for the Elderly (PACE).

Although parameters defining the standard of care in these settings are still very much in flux, their development will be important for the risk management professional and others in long-term care to monitor.

Financial Risk

Unfortunately, liability claims in long-term care outpace other industries. A 2005 ASHRM audio conference on long-term care warned that many providers were at high financial risk for such claims due to heavy regulation in an environment with limited reimbursement, increased levels of technology in long-term care settings, regulatory and accreditation issues, and a hostile legal environment that seeks to identify any violations of clinical practices and procedures.

Insurance Crises in Long-Term Care

This section discusses the access, availability, and affordability of insurance and other risk financing options.

Availability or affordability of insurance coverage for long-term care practitioners and facilities is affected by many issues, not the least of which are:

- Heightened awareness of medical errors with nursing homes as key targets
- Increase in frequency and severity of claims; loss cost and trends in excess of 25 percent
- Chronic staffing shortages
- Declining or inadequate reimbursement
- Large multi-state providers exiting high-cost states

These issues are exacerbated by the intensifying role of regulators, such as the Office of the Inspector General (OIG); fines and increased criminal and civil complaints;

EXHIBIT 19.2   Countrywide Severity per Claim

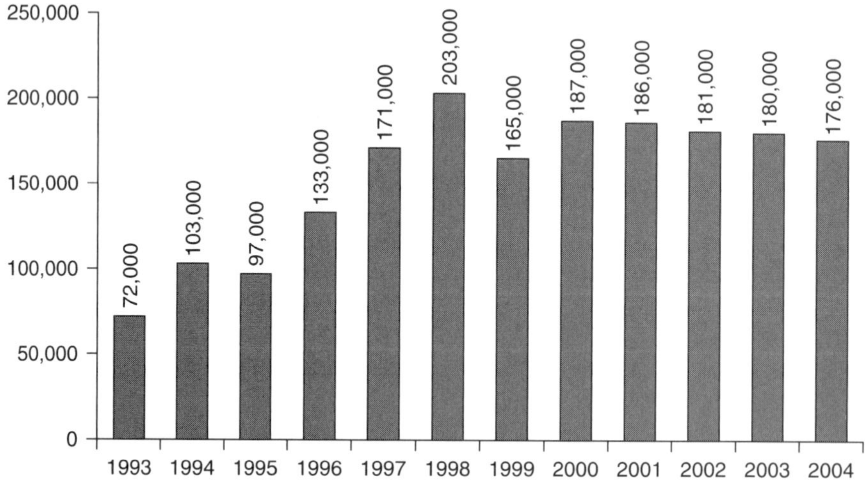

Source: Aon Risk Consultants, Actuarial and Analytics Practice, 2005. Reprinted with permission.

settlements, and verdicts. Some physicians have actually lost their professional liability coverage due to practice in nursing homes.

Aon Risk Consultants—Actuarial and Analytics Practice's report titled "Long-Term Care 2005 General Liability and Professional Liability Benchmark Analysis"[19] includes a database of 23 percent of long-term care beds in the country. The participants combined currently operate 445,000 long-term care beds, consisting primarily of skilled nursing facility beds, but the database also includes several independent living, assisted living, home health care, and rehabilitation beds. This report reveals that the loss cost per occupied bed has risen nationwide from $430 in 1993 to $2,310 in 2004. Refer to Exhibit 19.2 for a graphical depiction of nationwide loss cost. At the same time, the annual number of claims per 1,000 occupied beds has risen from 6.2 in 1996 to 13.1 in 2004 (see Exhibit 19.3). The nationwide average cost per claim in 2004 was $176,000.

Almost half (49 percent) of the compensation dollars paid went to the cost of litigation. Defense cost, which included attorney fees and the cost of investigation, represented 22 percent of the total compensation dollars, and plaintiff attorney fees equaled 27 percent. Only 51 percent of the compensation dollars went to the patient or family.

According to M. S. Reeves in Nursing Home Litigation 2005, "It was once thought that nursing home claims were low risk and low exposure. The life expectancy of the typical nursing home resident is not very long; therefore, it was thought that the pecuniary value of the case was lower. While that logic prevails in some cases, some juries are persuaded that the time remaining to the resident and her loved ones is important and the loss of those last few months or years may have substantial value. Couple this theory with evidence of abuse and neglect and the result can be explosive."[20,21]

Allegations against nursing homes often extend beyond what is typically alleged under medical malpractice in the acute-care setting. They include additional allegations under elder abuse laws and criminal neglect or patient protection statutes. Nursing home residents, in addition to medical malpractice, can also have a potential cause of action for premises and facility liability and breach of contract.

EXHIBIT 19.3   **Countrywide Annual Number of Claims per 1,000 Occupied Beds**

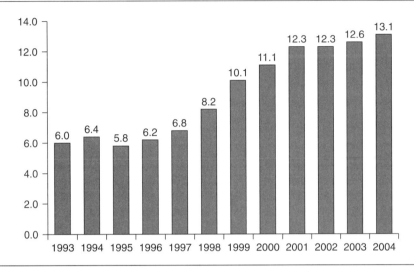

Source: Aon Risk Consultants, Actuarial and Analytics Practice, 2005. Reprinted with permission.

Much of the problem with insurance coverage availability and affordability seems to pit society's expectations against the quality of care that can be delivered under the present funding structure. As the risk management professional seeks to implement satisfactory loss control measures in the rapidly changing long-term care setting, there also should be a constant awareness of new entities that require coverage and new types of coverage that may apply.

Coverage Issues in an Evolving Setting

Of particular note, business plans and organizational goals must address whether there is coverage for the medical director; whether the credentialing process should include requirements that physicians and other independent providers maintain malpractice coverage, in addition to any availability issues, and proposed expansion of the organization, including new services, and mergers, acquisitions, or joint ventures. Risk management professionals are often responsible for working with consultants or actuaries to predict loss frequency and severity for the facility. The objective of such activity should be in part to educate senior management concerning the current insurance market and, in return, gain information about the organization's goals and critical issues that might otherwise increase facility risk. For more information on risk financing alternatives, please refer to Volume III, Chapter 12 in this series.

Negotiated Risk Agreements

Nursing home and assisted living residents (and their families) want to maintain independence for as long as possible and want to preserve their right to self-determine the role of the service provider in their need for continuing care. The judicious use of negotiated risk agreements (contracts) (NRAs) is one way to support resident independence while protecting the facility from liability. NRAs, negotiated between the resident and facility, identify activities that the residents will engage in and the autonomy that they will exercise over their care. In many cases, these activities might be outside the scope of what would normally be permitted or tolerated in the absence of such an agreement. The resident has negotiated an accommodation or an exception to facility policy for a trade-off. This trade-off may be the forfeiture of residents' right to sue the facility and the facility is (by contract) held harmless should residents become injured due to their negotiated activities (for example, smoking, walking unassisted, or other activities in which the risks outweigh the benefits).[22] For further information on contract review refer to Volume I, Chapter 12 in this series. Exhibit 19.4 highlights other types of contracts in long-term care and offers guidelines for required documents.

Personnel in Long-Term Care

Participation in Medicare and Medicaid programs requires long-term care facilities to query state nurse's aide registries for criminal history, specifically felonies, as this history puts residents at high risk. Facilities must check for findings of abuse, mistreatment, negligence, or misappropriation of property before allowing staff to work with residents. It is also important to verify employees' driver's licenses and to review their driving records before allowing anyone to use a facility vehicle to transport residents. It is important to be familiar with your state's specific requirements for the transportation of residents. Depending on state specific laws, type of vehicle being used to transport residents, and the number of passengers being transported will determine the class of license that will be required. On an annual basis, the driving record of all known drivers should be accessed and reviewed. Policy and procedures should address:

- Who can drive a facility vehicle and under what circumstances.

- Position description for employees that clearly defines what a "good driving record" is and what the ramifications are if one's record does not meet the standard. Ensuring that the maintenance of a good driving record is an "essential element" of the position description.

- Duty of employees who drive to notify human resources personnel when their licenses have been suspended, revoked, or amended in any way.

- Investigation of DUIs (driving while under the influence of substances) as quickly as possible.

According to Charlene Harrington of the University of California, San Francisco: "Poor staffing levels are the single-most important contributor to poor quality of nursing home care in the United States. Over the past twenty-five years, numerous research studies have documented the important relationship between nurse staffing levels, particularly RN staffing, and the outcomes of care. The benefits of higher staffing levels, especially RN staffing, can include lower mortality rates; improved physical functioning; less antibiotic use; fewer pressure ulcers, catheterized residents, and urinary tract infections; lower hospitalization rates; and less weight loss and dehydration."[23]

Increasingly, states are mandating staffing levels required to care for nursing home residents. Recent Congressional hearings and reports have recommended much higher staffing levels in nursing homes and have linked patient outcomes to the number of staff and to the level of nurse's training for staff who are caring for residents.[24] Experts have recommended minimum staffing levels of 4.55 hours per patient day.[25] Facilities that care for chronically ill residents are staffed primarily by paraprofessional nursing aides who are responsible for providing the majority of personal care for residents. The aides are supervised by the licensed nursing staff and the level of nursing supervision varies by state law. In some states nursing aides can be supervised by LPNs. The majority of nurses in

EXHIBIT 19.4   Contracts—Clinical Support Services Guidelines for Required Documents

Knowledge Evidenced By Comments

Priority Evaluation

1) Agreement with laboratory defining elective and emergency services available, to include pathology if appropriate, should include:
   a) Copies of current license and certificates
   b) Medicare provider number of laboratory
   c) Method and policies regarding transport of specimen, blood samples, and so on
   d) Procedure to obtain emergency services
   e) Procedures for payment and timely submission of reports to the facility
   f) Professional Liability and Workers' Compensation Insurance
2) Agreement with radiology group defining elective and emergency services available, to include:
   a) Medicare provider number of radiology service
   b) Procedure to obtain emergency services
   c) Procedures for payment and timely submission of reports to the facility
   d) Professional Liability and Workers' Compensation Insurance
3) Contract with medical records consultant, if appropriate, and/or transcribing service to include:
   a) Method for billing
   b) Method for obtaining dictation and for timely submission of transcription
   c) Professional Liability and Workers' Compensation Insurance
4) Contract with consulting pharmacist to include:
   a) Copy of current consultant license
   b) Professional Liability and Workers' Compensation Insurance
5) Agreement with security alarm service should:
   a) Written report
6) Agreement with fire safety systems monitoring service to include:
   a) Certification number
      i) Responsibility for annual inspection and test of entire system, quarterly sprinkler flow test for sensitivity of smoke detectors
   b) Written reports
7) Contract biomedical testing, at least quarterly, should include:
   a) Written reports
8) Contract with biohazardous waste disposal services to include:
   a) Documentation of certification number
   b) Documentation as to responsibility and manner of collection within the facility, how transport will take place, and what final disposition will be. (The latter must be in compliance with local regulations.)
9) Contract with laundry service to include:
   a) Documentation that all personnel are in compliance with OSHA standards for exposure to bloodborne pathogens
   b) Documentation as to manner in which the facility's laundry will be transported, processed, and inventoried
10) Contract with housekeeping service to include:
    a) Documentation requirement that personnel are bonded
       i) Documentation that all personnel are in compliance with OSHA standards for exposure to bloodborne pathogens and hazard communication
    b) Documentation of training and inservice requirements for personnel
11) Contract with pest control service should include:
    a) Written reports
12) Transfer procedure agreement with area hospital:
    a) Since medical staff members may not have admitting privileges at the hospital, the transfer agreement should describe procedures regarding the transfer to another physician, records requirements, and responsibility for payment
13) Agreement with local ambulance service for availability for non-life-threatening transport (such as patient transfer for observation):
    a) Medicare provider number
    b) Responsibility for payment

long-term care facilities are LPNs who are frequently charged with medication management. Medicare requires a registered nurse (RN) be on staff for a twenty-four-hour period. Usually the director of nursing and assistant director of nursing are RNs. Increasingly, the level of registered nursing staff is of concern. Studies suggest that the skill level of nursing staff affects the quality of patient care.[26] There remains, however, many open issues related to the suitability and level of staffing for nursing home care. Current studies do not fully address important related issues such as: the relative importance of other factors, such as management, tenure, and training of staff, in determining nursing home quality; the reality of current nursing shortages; and other operational details such as the difference between new nurses and experienced nurses, staff mix, retention and turnover rates, staff organization, and so on.[27]

The required medical director is usually part-time and reports to the administrator. Medical directors vary considerably in their responsibility for oversight of the medical care of residents; however, regulations require this oversight, and surveyors can cite a facility for inadequate medical supervision.

Credentialing and Recredentialing Staff

It is important that all clinical staff, including medical, rehabilitation, and nursing staff, be credentialed. When credentialing their practitioners, long-term care facilities often struggle with obtaining the needed documents from the primary or secondary sources. The correct method entails calling the state board, finding out whether the applicant holds an active license, and requesting written verification while cross-referencing the information to check for license restrictions. The purpose of primary sourcing is to reduce the possibility of forged credentials. Accepting photocopies of licenses does not meet the standard. Secondary source verification is confirmation of a health care practitioner's credentials based upon information from a credentialing verification organization or from another recognized and approved authority.

A secondary source should be a recognized independent authority. Do not rely upon a hospital's process of privileges and verification of sources. When recredentialing, look at additional training that practitioners might have received since the original verification. Organizations must credential all staff and contract employees who come into contact with residents. Organizations have the right to limit a practitioner's provision of care, regardless of what state law allows. The delineation of specific clinical tasks that a practitioner may carry out is called privileging.

Facility Maintenance and Safety Issues

Regular assessment of the safety and environmental aspects of the facility will assist in risk identification and acknowledgment of the current policies and procedures. A sample assessment tool is shown in Exhibit 19.5.

The Safe Medical Devices Act (SMDA) of 1990 identifies nursing homes as device users and therefore subject to the medical device reporting (MDR) requirement. A medical device is any item that is used for the diagnosis, treatment, or prevention of a disease, injury, illness, or other condition, and that is not a drug. In nursing homes this would include pressure manometers, thermometers, oxygen administering apparatus, infusion pumps, cardiac monitors, and the more recognizable long-term care staples such as walkers, canes, wheelchairs, crutches, hospital beds, and physical therapy equipment. A medical device also includes bandages, heating blankets, tongue depressors, and cotton swabs.

EXHIBIT 19.5   **Facility Maintenance and Safety**

Knowledge Evidenced By Comments

Priority Evaluation

1) Does the safety committee meet monthly to review all accidents, accident investigation reports, inspection reports, training, and other safety issues?
2) Are quarterly (or more often) accident or incident analysis (es) noting trends and corrective actions conducted?
3) Are monthly safety inspections completed?
4) Is annual training conducted? Contain safety requirements? Contain areas of accident frequency?
5) Annual safety report to risk manager? Is this report a framework for goals?
   a) Safety accomplishments for the past year?
   b) Continuing loss trends?
   c) Objective action plans to address loss trends or significant safety issues?
   d) Inservice schedule for the coming calendar year?
6) Does the safety committee address:
   a) The development and enforcement of safety policies and procedures? Specific safety programs?
   b) Safety training and awareness activities?
   c) Hazard surveillance or facility inspections? Monthly?
   d) Security procedures and programs?
   e) Disaster planning and drills?
   f) Accident or unusual occurrence review and analysis?
   g) Inspection results and findings?
   h) Comprehensive infection control program?
7) Training requirements: The following classes should be completed at least annually for all employees and physicians:
   a) Exposure control plan (bloodborne pathogens standard)
   b) Hazard communication
   c) Biomedical waste management
   d) Fire safety and evacuating plan, including use of fire extinguishers
   e) Risk management including the Safe Medical Device Act
   f) Infection control including hand washing, isolation procedures, and medication and supplies storage
   g) Medical gas shut-off procedures
8) Labor law posters:
   i) Is the poster describing all labor laws including minimum wage, OSHA, Workers' Compensation, Child Labor Laws, and the Family Leave Act displayed in the work area?
9) Facility maintenance requirements:
   i) Fire testing records?
   ii) Automatic sprinkler system?
   iii) Emergency generator and emergency lighting?
   iv) Fire drills?
   v) Fire alarm testing?
   vi) Fire plan with exit schematic?
   vii) Smoking regulations?
   viii) Carpet-flame spread test?
   ix) Drapes and curtains—flame retardant?
   x) Fire extinguishers and kitchen hood?
   xi) Evacuation plan—is it posted'?
   xii) Disaster drills?
   xiii) Fire department inspection reports?
   xiv) Preventative management plan?
   xv) Biomedical equipment grounding tests?
   xvi) Smoke detector testing?
   xvii) Garbage and trashcans—fire retardant?
10) Material safety data sheets (MSDS)?
11) Master list of chemicals?
12) Labeling of chemicals?
13) Biomedical waste compliance?
14) Biomedical equipment management?

(Continued)

EXHIBIT 19.5   Facility Maintenance and Safety *(Continued)*

15) Door stops removed?
16) Boiler room: shut-off marked and protected?
17) "No food or drink" policy for patient care areas and in areas that contain blood and body fluids?
18) Dumpster secured in order to prevent vandalism and dumping of hazardous materials and trash?
19) Generator maintenance?
20) Outside oxygen storage?
21) Employee Health Requirements:
    a) OSHA 300 and 300A Log Incident Report Form:
        i) Annual PPDs provided for all employees performing patient care? The CDC and OSHA guidelines for health care workers require a two-step PPD for new employees and involves a PPD at initial employment and a PPD 3–5 weeks later.
        ii) BCG: For employees who have been vaccinated with BCG and never had a PPD or have not converted, a PPD must be given. The PPD is given every year until they are reactive. For BCG employees that have a positive PPD, initiate the TB questionnaire and require a check x-ray every two years.
    b) Employee health and vaccine records:
        i) Vaccination records are created for each employee exposed to blood and body fluids and/or risk for infection?
        ii) Employees show proof of the following vaccinations:
            • Mumps
            • Measles
            • Rubella
            • Influenza
            • Varicella (for employees exposed to children)
    c) Medical follow-up after exposures:
        i) Written agreement made with an independent medical provider or practitioner for follow-up after an employee exposure incident has occurred
    d) Needlestick and sharps reporting?
    e) Hepatitis B vaccine records?
22) Fire safety and disaster preparedness requirements:
    a) Disaster drill?
    b) Fire alarm and sprinkler testing requirements completed?
        i) Annual smoke detector "sensitivity" testing?
        ii) Sprinkler systems (flow and dampers) testing?
        iii) Quarterly fire drills completed and documented?
        iv) The local fire department checks and approves fire plan annually?
23) Fleet safety:
    a) Basic fleet safety program consisting of proper driver selection procedures, driver training vehicle use and maintenance procedures, and accident investigation and review programs?
    b) Driver selection based upon:
        i) Providing a copy of driver license, information on driving experience, type of vehicle qualified to operate, and accident and traffic conviction record?
    c) Initial and periodic MVR (every three years) obtained?
    d) Commercial driver's licenses (CDL) required to provide results of medical examination, prior to start of work and after a job offer?
    e) Driving training:
        i) Role of the driver in resident safety, including assisting residents as they get on or off any transport vehicles?
    f) Vehicle maintenance:
        i) Inspected at least monthly?
    g) Vehicles are equipped with the insurance carrier's accident reporting kit?
    h) Internal accident review?
    i) Annual safety report to the risk manager to include:
        i) Safety accomplishments?
        ii) Continuing loss trends?
        iii) Action plans?
        iv) Education calendar?

Nursing homes must have written procedures for internal MDR systems and documentation and recordkeeping. Adverse event files must also be kept. Reportable adverse events include only those incidents or reports that the nursing home "has received or otherwise becomes aware of that reasonably suggest that a device has or may have caused or contributed to death or serious injury."[28]

1. IF: A user facility becomes aware of information that reasonably suggests that a device has or may have caused or contributed to a death.

   THEN: The facility must report to both the manufacturer and FDA.

   WHEN: Within ten working days of becoming aware of a reportable event.

2. IF: If a user facility becomes aware of information that reasonably suggests that a device has or might have caused or contributed to a serious injury.

   THEN: The facility must report to the manufacturer. If the manufacturer is unknown, a report is filed with the FDA.

   WHEN: Within ten working days of becoming aware of a reportable event.

3. IF: If a user facility submitted any reports to the manufacturer or the FDA during the year.

   THEN: The user facility must send a annual summary of reports submitted to the FDA.

   WHEN: By January 1st of each year.

Refer to Volume III, Chapter 16 in this series for more information on the SMDA.

Employee Health

Employee injuries can occur from several sources in long-term care facilities. The identification of high-risk work procedures should be a major function of the aspect of the risk management program that addresses employee health. The U.S. Department of Labor, Occupational Safety and Health Administration (OSHA) mandates documentation of work-related injuries and illnesses that require medical care on the OSHA Form 300 and Form 301 to report supplemental information for injuries and illnesses already reported. Form 300 A is a summary of reportable injuries and illnesses that requires posting yearly at the worksite from February 1–April 30. OSHA incorporates standards from the American National Standards Institute (ANSI) and National Fire Protection Association (NFPA).

According to the 2004 Bureau of Labor Statistics, U.S. Department of Labor, the injury and illness incident rate[29] for nursing and residential care facilities was 9.7 per 100 full time equivalents (FTEs) as compared with a 6.2 rate for health care and social assistance as an industry and 4.8 for all of private industries. Fourteen industries reported 100,000 or more cases in 2004 for a total of 2 million cases, or 43 percent of the total reported cases. The same fourteen industries, although ranked differently, all had at least 100,000 injuries and illnesses in 2003. Hospitals (NAICS[30] 622) led this group with 284,600 cases, with nursing and residential care facilities (NAICS 623) following with 215,200 cases. The health care and social assistance industry sector for 2004 was second only to manufacturing (20.9 percent) with the highest percent of nonfatal workplace injuries at 15.9 percent. The incidence of nonfatal illness in 2004 for the health care and social assistance industry sector, at 18.4 percent, again came second to manufacturing at 42.2 percent. Four out of ten injuries and illnesses were sprains and strains, with most of these stemming from overexertion or falls on the same level. Twenty percent of sprains and strains occurred in three occupations, of which nursing aids, orderlies, and attendants were one. The occupations also had the greatest number of injuries and illnesses, accounting for over 16 percent of the total days away for work cases.[31]

Employers have certain responsibilities under OSHA. Under the general duty clause 5(A)(1), an employer shall furnish to each of its employees employment, and a place of employment, that are free from recognized hazards that cause or are likely to cause death or serious physical harm to its employees. The general duty clause is used only where there is no specific OSHA standard that applies to the particular hazard involved.

For nursing homes, the general duty clause allows citations for high back-injury rates. As the standards of care evolve to include medical equipment to reduce back injuries by using lifts, nursing homes must recognize their liability. At a minimum, all long-term care providers should increase training about ways to prevent injuries for workers. Lack of tuberculosis surveillance and workplace violence prevention can be the basis for citation, as well.

The top ten OSHA standards currently cited for the health services industry are:

1. 1910.1030 Bloodborne Pathogens—the exposure control plan must be updated annually

2. 1910.1200 Hazard Communication—requires that the hazards of all chemicals produced or imported are evaluated, and that information concerning their hazards is transmitted to employers and employees by various means, including container labeling and other forms of warning, material safety data sheets, and employee training

3. 1910.0147 Control of Hazardous Energy, Lockout/Tagout—requires a program with procedures for affixing required lockout and tagout devices to energy isolating devices

4. 1904.0029 Recording and reporting occupational injuries and illnesses

5. 1910.0305 Wiring Methods—the design and installation of electrical equipment must meet ANSI and NFPA requirements

6. 1910.0132 Personal Protective Equipment, General Requirements—requires criteria for using personal protective equipment and the requirements for its actual use

7. 1910.303 General Requirements—requires installation and use of electrical equipment

8. 1910.0134 Respiratory Protection

9. 1910.0151 Medical Services and First Aid—requires medical services and first aid

10. 1910.0037 Means of Egress, General

Every nursing home has the potential to be inspected by OSHA. Advance notice of these inspections will not be given. Top priority for OSHA inspectors are those facilities in which imminent danger may be an issue. This may be defined as any condition where there is reasonable certainty that a danger exists that can be expected to cause death or serious physical harm immediately or before danger can be eliminated. Potential examples of imminent danger are prevalence of back injuries that inhibit normal function of the workers or bloodborne pathogen exposure.

To ensure employee safety and be prepared for an OSHA inspection, the facility must develop a plan that describes employees and employee procedures to ensure employee safety. This is usually best accomplished by a safety or risk management committee to address and develop an emergency management plan for such occurrences as electrical failures, chemical spills, gas leaks, bomb threats, radiation exposures, smallpox exposures, anthrax exposures, and tuberculosis exposures.

Regular assessment of the safety and environmental aspects of the facility will assist in workers' compensation risk identification and in acknowledging the current status of implemented policies and procedures.

Staffing shortages in health care are expected to escalate over the next ten to twenty years. These shortages are even more apparent in long-term care where the average caregiver is female, over forty years of age, non-professional, making minimum wage, and generally working alone with little to no mechanical assistance. It is therefore critical that risk issues relating to staffing resources are identified and addressed. Having a limited workforce is one issue. Having that limited workforce unavailable because of absenteeism, turnover, or a workers' compensation injury is unacceptable.

Workers' Compensation

The Bureau of Labor Statistics supports, through its statistical reporting and comparison with other industries, that long-term care is a "high risk" from a workers' compensation standpoint. OSHA, has developed regulations that are meant to protect employees. Several factors lead to workers' compensation claims:

- The nature of the job is conducive to losses. Lifting, transferring, bending, stooping, pushing, pulling, and so on all can cause injury if not done properly.

- The industry turnover rate is high. This makes training difficult. Untrained or improperly trained employees injure themselves, which can lead to lost time or modified duty and add to staffing shortages.

- The commitment of time, staff, and resources to reduce losses might not be a priority.

Employees must be made aware of their responsibility to work safely by following policies and procedures and attending safety in-service education, which includes how to complete the accident form and what the expectation is if there is lost time or modified duty.

Modified duty is a physician-approved temporary duty assignment, which gets the employee back to work as soon as medically possible. A modified duty program should include:

- Communication with the physician and employee about the modified duty program and what the expectation is with regard to the employee returning to work

- Temporary job duties based on the restrictions, which should be reviewed with the employee

Exhibit 19.6 is an example of a loss control risk assessment with an emphasis on employee injuries.

Ergonomics

Ergonomics is best defined as the relationship between people's bodies and their work activities. Repetitive stress injuries such as carpal tunnel syndrome, and certain neck, back, and leg disorders due to poor fit of office furniture are among the most common worker health problems that fall into the ergonomics category.[32] The increasing

EXHIBIT 19.6   **Loss Control Risk Assessment of Employee Injuries**

Knowledge Evidenced By Comments

Priority Evaluation

  1) Is there a loss control program consisting of two key elements:
    a) Safety loss prevention?
    b) Claims management?
  2) Are safety and loss prevention efforts coordinated by the safety committee?
  3) Are claim management efforts coordinated through the personnel department and the administrator or risk manager?
  4) Does the risk manager or administrator oversee and coordinate both functions?
  5) Employee selection
    i) Do all employees go through the appropriate application, interview, and prior reference checks as dictated by policy?
    ii) Are all employee selection procedures reviewed at least annually to ensure compliance with the Americans with
       Disabilities Act and other applicable civil discrimination laws?
  6) New Employees—Physical Examination
    a) Are necessary physical examinations conducted, both post-offer and post-hire, as needed?
    b) All documentation is reviewed and maintained on file?
  7) Specific Safety Programs
    a) All programs are in the facility safety manual and posted where necessary?
    b) Programs are reviewed and updated at least annually to ensure quality, effectiveness, and compliance with any
       applicable codes?
  8) Documentation
    a) Is documentation of all training and attendance kept and maintained on file? (Note trainer, content of training, and
       participants.)
  9) Claim management
    a) Is the goal of the claim management program to take an active role in minimizing both the financial and personal impact
       of a work-related incident?
    b) Does the program rely on active participation of the facility, employee, physician, and insurance carrier?
10) Medical attention
    a) Do employees report to the designated physician following an incident?
    b) Are all medical limitations clearly outlined and documented by the treating physician?
    c) Based on progress, are action plans revised as necessary to ensure a timely return to work?
11) Claim file reviews
    a) Loss runs:
      i) Are loss runs reviewed when received for accuracy, changes, open claims, and loss trends?
    b) Claim file review meetings:
      i) Are claim file review meetings held semi-annually to ensure claims and associated costs are properly managed?

---

number of injuries in nursing homes has focused OSHA attention on the need for ergonomics, the science of fitting the job to the worker, in long-term care settings. OSHA issued Guidelines for Nursing Homes on Ergonomics for the Prevention of Musculoskeletal Disorders on March 13, 2003. Although the guidelines are not mandatory, nor do they represent a new standard or regulation and impose no new legal requirements, it is felt that they will assist the nursing home industry with guidance in the prevention of employee injuries through the identification of ergonomic stressors and the development of control methods.

There is tremendous opportunity, and need to provide training, for nursing home administrators, nursing supervisors, risk management professionals, front line patient care providers, and staff development coordinators in controlling the risks associated with manual handling of residents. The OSHA Guidelines for Nursing Homes can assist the industry with that goal. The full (draft) report is available on OSHA's Web site.

Work-related musculoskeletal disorders (MSDs) often result when there is a mismatch between the physical capacity of workers, patient needs, and the physical demands of their jobs. This is exacerbated when workers do not have the training or equipment to perform routine activities. Repetitive actions, force, awkward positions, contact stress, and vibration can cause an MSD. Many routine activities have risk, such as transferring patients from one height to another and working in small spaces. Not only can repeated strain endanger the worker, it can result in patient injury.

Common MSDs are carpal tunnel syndrome, trigger finger, rotator cuff syndrome, muscle strains and tears, ligament strains, joint and tendon inflammation, pinched nerves tendinitis, and herniated spinal disc. MSDs are caused by several reasons, not all of which are work related. The condition can develop gradually over time, may result from an accident or injury, and be related to age, genetic causes, or other factors.

Employers need to provide basic information about common MSDs, how to avoid injury, what signs and symptoms workers need to recognize, and how to report them. Once an MSD has been reported, the employer must review the injured worker's job to determine if it routinely involves exposure to ergonomic risk factors.

Components of an ergonomics program should include:

- Management leadership and employee participation to:

  Assign and delegate responsibilities

  Designate persons with authority, resources, and the information to meet responsibilities

  Report MSDs, their signs, symptoms, and hazards; respond promptly to these reports

  Involve employees in program development, implementation, and evaluation

  Make a financial commitment to allocate adequate resources to prevent or reduce patient or employee injury

- Supervisor responsibilities:

  Identifying conditions that could cause or contribute to MSD

  Implementing recommendations to reduce or eliminate risk factors

  Encouraging staff to report MSDs

- Job hazard analysis and control:

  Include all employees who perform the same job where an MSD exists and observe them at work

  Develop a job hazard analysis tool incorporating the risk factors

  Rethink the job and make necessary changes

- Training:

  Provide initial training for employees and supervisors to include the purpose of the program

  Put safety measures in place for actions such as the purchase and use of mechanical lifts

  Conduct risk factor evaluations and provide education for the proper use of equipment lifting alone, with assistance, and with mechanical devices[33]

Public Relations and Media Relations: Strategies to Address the Negative Image of Long-Term Care

To foster a positive perception by the public of the quality of care provided in long-term care facilities, each organization should consider developing public relations and media relations plans. Personnel designated to design a public relations program should work closely with the risk management professional to ensure that wording of any related press releases or advertisements is objective and realistic.

Media relations are, of course, particularly important in a time of litigiousness, when average damage awards are increasing dramatically and punitive damages are sometimes awarded. As media coverage can affect the organization long after the professional liability case is resolved, it is critical that the facility assess its plan for working with the media during the aftermath of a clinical crisis.

In particular, the media relations plan should designate someone to speak to the press for the facility. The respective roles of public relations, legal counsel, risk management, administration, board representatives, and medical staff involvement should also be delineated. Additionally, a media relations consultant might be helpful if the facility or organization has a serious risk management incident. The professional liability carrier, if pertinent, should be involved in such circumstances, and it must be remembered that HIPAA generally requires the patient or resident to give consent for release of any protected health information (PHI). Please see Chapter 3 in this volume for more information on crisis management.

············

CONCLUSION

As America ages, the role and number of long-term care options for services and care will continue to grow. As the variety of these services proliferates, risk management professionals must be certain that loss prevention and patient safety measures are in place to enhance care, liabilities for each new venture are addressed, measures to comply with regulatory mandates are implemented, and that adequate risk financing is obtained.

Endnotes

1. U.S. Bureau of the Census. Current Population Reports, Special Studies, P23-190, 65+ in the United States. U.S. Government Printing Office, Washington, DC, 1996.

2. U.S. Census Bureau, 2004, "U.S. Interim Projections by Age, Sex, Race, and Hispanic Origin," [www.census.gov/ipc/www/usinterimproj/]. Internet Release Date: March 18, 2004, Table 2a.

3. *Ibid.*

4. *Ibid.*, Table 2b.

5. *Ibid.*, Table 2a.

6. Nursing Facilities, Staffing, Residents and Facility Deficiencies, 1997–2003. University of California San Francisco, August 2004.

7. Federal Nursing Home Reform Act from the Omnibus Budget Reconciliation Act (OBRA 1987), Federal Regulation 42 CFR 483.25, U.S. GPO.

8. 42 C.F.R. Part 483.

9. Centers for Medicare and Medicaid Services. "Nursing Home Compare." [www.hcfa.gov/medicaid/nhcomp.htm].

10. Medicare State Operations Manual, HCFA Pub-II, Chapters 2, 3, 7, Apps. p, and pp.

11. 42 C.F.R. Part 488.

12. 42 C.F.R. Part 483.25.

13. 42 C.F.R. Part 483.13.

14. 42 C.F.R. Part 483.90.

15. 42 C.F.R. Part 483.15.

16. 42 C.F.R. Part 483.20.

17. 42 C.F.R. 483.

18. ASHRM, *Risk Management Pearls for Long-Term Care and Skilled Nursing Facilities*. Chicago, Ill.: American Hospital Association, 2002.

19. Bourdon, T. W., S. C. Dubin. *Long Term Care: 2005 General Liability and Professional Liability Benchmark Analysis*. Aon Risk Consultants, Actuarial and Analytics Practice, March 1, 2005.

20. See e.g. *Horizon/CMS Healthcare Corporation v. Auld*. 34 S.W.3d 887 (Tex. 2000) (Tex.) (affirming remittitur of jury award of $2.371 million in compensatory damages to $1,541,203.13 and punitive damages from $90 million to $9,483,766.92 due to statutory caps in case involving negligent treatment and failure to treat pressure sores in nursing home); See also *In Re Conservatorship of Gregory*, 80 Cal.App.4th 514, 95 Cal.Rptr.2d 336 (Cal. App. 2000) (reducing a jury award of $365,580.71 in compensatory and $94.7 million in punitive damages to $124,480.57 in compensatory and $3 million in punitive damages).

21. Reeves, M. S., "Nursing Home Litigation 2005." available at [www.gorbyreeves.com/pdf/Reeves-NursingHomeLit.pdf]. Accessed May 26, 2006.

22. Duval, N. M., and C. Moseley. Negotiated risk agreements in long-term support services: A technical assistance paper of the national project, Self-Determination for Persons with Developmental Disabilities. Durham, NH: University of New Hampshire, National Program Office on Self-Determination, Institute on Disability, 2001.

23. Harrington, C., "Saving Lives Through Quality of Care: A Blueprint for Elder Justice," *Alzheimer's Care*. 2004; 5(1):24–38.

24. Health Care Financing Agency, "Appropriateness of Minimum Nurse Staffing Ratios in Nursing Homes, Report to Congress," December 2000.

25. Harrington, C., et al. "Experts recommend minimum nurse staffing standards for nursing facilities in the United States." *Gerontologist*, 2000, Vol. 40(1), 5–16.

26. Nursing Facilities, Staffing, Residents and Facility Deficiencies, 1994–2000. University of California, San Francisco, 2002, 58.

27. "Appropriateness of Minimum Nurse Staffing Ratios in Nursing Homes: Phase II Final Report" (2001), [63.240.208.147/medicaid/reports/rp1201home.asp]. HHS Secretary. Tommy Thompson, CMS Phase II Transmittal Letter as reported in "Staffing Levels in New York Nursing Homes: Important Information in Making Choices," Eliot Spitzer, Attorney General. Office of the Attorney General, Medicaid Fraud Control Unit, January 2006.

28. Shepard, M., M. A. Wollerton. "Applying the Safe Medical Device Act to Nursing Homes." *Food and Drug Administration User Facility Reporting Bulletin*, Issue No. 17, Fall 1996.

29. The incident rate represents the number of injuries and illnesses per 100 full-time workers and are calculated as $(N/EH) \times 200,000$.
    Where N = number of injuries and illnesses,
    EH − total hours worked by all employees during the calendar and
    $200,000$ = base for 100 equivalent full-time workers (working 40 hours per week, 50 weeks per year).

30. NAICS North American Industry Classification System replaced SIC the Standard Industry Code.

31. U.S. Bureau of Labor Statistics, Washington, DC. Workplace Injuries and Illnesses in 2004 USDL 05-2195, releases November 17, 2005 site accessed January 25, 2006.

32. Definitions, Acronyms, Idioms, Jargon available at [www.chem.purdue.edu/chemsafety/definitions.htm]. Accessed January 26, 2006.

33. Drawn from the Risk Management Pearls for Long-Term Care and Skilled Nursing Facilities. Chicago, Ill.: ASHRM, pp. 1–42.

Suggested Readings

Allen, J. E. "Effective Risk Management in Long-Term Care," *Journal of Long-Term Care Administration*, 1991, 19, 43–46, 49.

ASHRM, *Risk Management Pearls for Long-Term Care and Skilled Nursing Facilities*. Chicago, Ill.: American Hospital Association, 2002.

Best Nursing Practices in Care for Older Adults Curriculum Guide. (3rd ed.) Hartford, Conn.: Hartford Institute for Geriatric Nursing, 2001.

Brennan, T. A., et al. "Incidence of Adverse Events and Negligence in Hospitalized Patients: Results of the Harvard Medical Practice Study I." *New England Journal of Medicine*, 1991, 324(6), 370–376.

Carroll, R. (ed.). *Risk Management Handbook for Health Care Organizations* (3rd ed.). San Francisco: Jossey-Bass and the American Society for Healthcare Risk Management, 2000.

Comprehensive Accreditation Manual for Long-Term Care, Management of the Environment of Care. Oakbrook Terrace, Ala.: Joint Commission for Accreditation of Healthcare Organizations, 2002–2003.

Gurwitz, J. H., et al. "The Epidemiology of Adverse and Unexpected Events in the Long-Term Care Setting." *JAGS*, 1994, 42, 33–38.

John A. Hartford Foundation Institute for Geriatric Nursing, New York University, Division of Nursing.

National Fire Protection Association, Fire Prevention Code (2000 ed.); NFPA 101 Life Safety Code (2000 ed.); NFPA 99-222 Health Care Facilities (2002 ed.).

Omnibus Budget Reconciliation Acts (OBRA) of 1987, 1989, 1990 and 1995. Health Care Financing Administration, as published in the Federal Register.

Risk Management: A Technical Assistance Brief—A Guide to Risk Management. Hartford, Conn.: Hartford Loss Control Department and The American Association of Homes and Services for the Aging, 2000.

Risk Management Pearls for Medication Error Reduction. Chicago, Ill.: American Society for Healthcare Risk Management, 2001.

The Safe Medical Devices Act of 1990, Pub. L. No. 101-629, 104 Stat. 4511 (1990). The user reporting provisions are contained in section 2(a).

Shapiro, J. P. "Doctoring a Sickly System: Deadly Medical Mistakes Are Rampant. One Expert Thinks They Can Be Avoided." *U.S. News*, December 13, 1999.

Thomas, E. J., et al. "Costs of Medical Injuries in Utah and Colorado." Inquiry, 36, 1999.

"Top Claim Concerns: Falls, Wandering, Delayed Treatment," *Nursing Home Update*. St. Paul, Minn.: St. Paul Fire and Marine Insurance Co., 1994.

Weinberg, A. D. *Risk Management in Long-Term Care: A Quick Reference Guide*. New York: Springer Publishing Company, Inc. [www.usnews.com/usnews/issue/991213/errors.htm]. 1998. (Last visited December 24, 2001.)

Appendix 19.1

⋮ CONSUMER INFORMATION

Check for Safety (National Center for Injury Prevention and Control, U.S. Center for Disease Prevention) [www.cdc.gov/ncipc/pub-res/toolkit/checkforsafety.htm]

A Patient's Guide to Preventing Falls (American Geriatrics Society) [americangeriatrics. org/news/pdf/consumer_pamphlet.pdf]

Falls Prevention Guide for Seniors (North York Coalition for Seniors) [www. sunnybrook.utoronto.ca/~csia/ Falls&Mobility/NYCSFP Guide.pdf]

Protecting the Elderly from Falls (National Safety Council) [www.nsc.org/news/ bj032902.htm]

Falls Pose a Serious Threat to the Elderly (National Safety Council) [www.nsc.org/issues/ ifalls/falthreat.htm]

Falls in the Home (National Safety Council) [www.nsc.org/issues/fallstop.htm]

Tips to Help You Care for Your Elderly Parents (National Safety Council) [www.nsc.org/ issues/ifalls/faltips.htm]

Preventing the Fall: Designs on Building Safe Homes for the Elderly (National Safety Council) [www.nsc.org/issues/ifalls/falfalls.htm]

Don't Let a Fall be Your Last Trip (American Academy of Orthopedic Physicians) [orthoinfo.aaos.org/brochure/thr_report.cfm?Thread_ID=21&topcategory=About%20O rthopaedics&searentry=don%27t%20let%20a%20fall]

Preventing Falls Among Seniors—Tips (National Center for Injury Prevention and Control) [www.cdc.gov/ncipc/duip/spotlite/falltips.htm]

Tips to Prevent Falls in the Elderly (Wright State University) [www.nursing.wright.edu/ practice/falls/]

Preventing Injuries from Slips, Trips and Falls (Center for Disease Prevention) [www.cdc.gov/ nasd/docs/d000001-d000100/d000006/d000006.html]

Falls in the Home (National Agriculture Safety Database) [www.cdc.gov/nasd/docs/ d000101-d000200/d000131/d000131.html]

Falls Responsible for Many Injuries, Deaths (National Agriculture Safety Database) [www.cdc.gov/na sd/docs/d001501-d001600/d001556/d001556.html]

············

STATISTICS AND PREVALENCE

American Geriatrics Society: Falls and Balance Problems [americangeriatrics.org/education/forum/falling.shtml]

National Center For Disease Prevention And Health: Falls among Older Adults—Fact Book for the Year 2001–2 [www.cdc.gov/ncipc/fact_book/15_Falls_Among_Older_Adults.htm]

Falls and Hip Fractures among Older Adults [www.cdc.gov/ncipc/factsheets/falls.htm]

Falls in Nursing Homes—How Serious is the Problem? [www.cdc.gov/ncipc/factsheets/nursing.htm]

The Costs of Fall Injuries among Older Adults Fact Sheet [www.cdc.gov/ncipc/factsheets/fallcost.htm]

American Academy of Family Physicians: The Changing Approach to Falls in the Elderly [www.aafp.org/afp/971101ap/steinweg.html]

Other Countries

Falls by the elderly in Australia Trends and data for 2001 (Flinders University) [www.nisu.flinders.edu.au/pubs/reports/2001/eldfalls.php]

············

PREVENTION

National Resource Center on Aging and Injury: Preventing Falls Among Seniors [www.cdc.gov/ncipc/duip/spotlite/falls.htm]

National Safety Council, National Alliance to Prevent Falls As We Age [www.nsc.org/fallsalliance.htm]

National Center for Injury Prevention and Control U.S. Fall Prevention Programs for Seniors—Selected Programs Using Home Assessment and Modification [www.cdc.gov/ncipc/falls/default.htm]

Publications on Fall Prevention [www.cdc.gov/ncipc/duip/spotlite/ fallpub.htm]

Partnerships on Falls Prevention [www.cdc.gov/ncipc/duip/spotlite/fallpart.htm Aging] Internet Information Notes Page 3 of 5

The National Resource Center for Safe Aging [www.safeaging.org/]

Chapter 20: Falls (Merck Manual of Geriatrics) [www.merck.com/mrkshared/mm_geriatrics/sec2/ch20.jsp]

Falls and Fall Prevention. Since You Care: A Series of Guides (MetLife and National Alliance for Caregiving) [www.metlife.com/WPSAssets/11908483431050333861V1FFalls and Fall Preventtion 3–03.pdf]

Household Hazards Not Leading Cause of Falls by Elderly (Doctor's Guide) [www.pslgroup.com/dg/1ec9ae.htm]

The Fall Prevention Project (Temple University) [www.temple.edu/older_adult/]

The Elderly and Fear of Falling (International Herald Tribune) [www.iht.com/articles/88833.html]

Safe Aging [www.safeaging.com/]

Other Countries

Promising Pathways—Falls Prevention Programs for Older Canadians Living in the Community—A Handbook of Best Practices (Health Canada) [www.hc-sc.gc.ca/seniors-aines/pubs/best_practices/promising/pdf/PromisingPathwaysE.pdf]

············

RESEARCH AND REFERENCE

Falls—Medline Plus (U.S. Library of Medicine) [www.nlm.nih.gov/medlineplus/falls.html]

Falls Among Older Persons and the Role of the Home: An Analysis of Cost, Incidence, and Potential Savings from Home Modification (Public Policy Institute, AARP) [research.aarp.org/il/ib56_falls.html]

Association Between Falls In Elderly Women And Chronic Diseases And Drug Use: Cross Sectional Study (September 2003) (British Medical Journal) [bmj.bmjjournals.com/cgi/content/full/327/7417/712]

Why Do the Elderly Fall? (Locomotion Research Laboratory, Virginia Tech University) [www.research.vt.edu/resmag/sc2003/whyfall.htm]

Fear of Falling: An Emerging Health Problem (Boston University Center for Enhancement of Late Life Function) [www.applied-gerontology.org/BUBrief.pdf]

Tai Chi Helps Prevent Falls in Elderly (Massey University) [masseynews.massey.ac.nz/2003/masseynews/aug/aug11/stories/taichi.html]

Household Hazards Are not, as Commonly Believed, The Leading Cause of Falls By the Elderly (Yale University) [www.yale.edu/opa/newsr/00–11–30–02.all.html]

Falls in the Elderly (University of Pittsburgh) [www.pitt.edu/~kaf24/]

National Resource Center on Aging and Injury Falls Among Older Adults ~ Summary of Research Findings [www.cdc.gov/ncipc/duip/SummaryOfFalls.htm]

Assessment of Fall-Related Deaths and Hospitalizations for Hip Fractures Among Older Adults [www.cdc.gov/ncipc/duip/SummaryOfFalls.htm]

Source Information:
Available at:
Aging Internet Information Notes; Falls and Hip Fractures, pp. 1–5
Center for Communications and Consumer Services
U.S. Administration on Aging
Tel. 202-619-0724
FAX 202-357-3523
Internet: [www.aoa.gov]
E-mail: aoainfo@aoa.gov

Glossary

Sources

The terms and definitions listed in this glossary have been compiled from the following sources:

1. ASHRM Barton Certificate in Healthcare Risk Management Program;
2. Iowa Hospital Association, "Common Health Care Abbreviations & Terminology";
3. Farmers Insurance Group, "Risk Management Definitions";
4. Risk Management Handbook for Health Care Organizations, Third and Fourth Editions

AAAASF	American Association for Accreditation of Ambulatory Surgery Facilities, Inc., http://www.aaaasf.org
AAAHC	Accreditation Association for Ambulatory Health Care, Inc., http://www.aaahc.org
AABB	American Association for Blood Banks, http://www.aabb.org
AAHP	American Association of Health Plans
AAHRPP	Association for the Accreditation of Human Research Protection Programs, Inc., http://www.aahrpp.org
AAMC	Association of American Medical Colleges, http://www.aamc.org
AANA	American Association of Nurse Anesthetists, http://www.aana.com
AAP	American Academy of Pediatrics, http://www.aap.org
AARP	American Association of Retired Persons
Abd.	Abdominal
ABMS	American Board of Medical Specialties, http://www.abms.org
Abuse	The willful infliction of injury, unreasonable confinement, intimidation, or punishment with resulting harm, pain, or mental anguish
	Definition (fraud and abuse) describes practices that result in unnecessary costs to the Medicare/Medicaid program and other payor sources. Patient abuse is deliberate, non-accidental contact or interaction that results in significant psychological harm, pain or physical injury.
"Access" problem	Issues relating to impediments that restrict or limit persons in need of specific healthcare services from receiving them, e.g., lack of health insurance
Accident (medical)	An unintended occurrence resulting in injury or death that is not the result of willful action. Generally an accident means that it resulted in some degree of injury or harm to the person(s) involved. In the medical field, the term "accident" is generally not used to describe an event associated with clinical care, but refers to other types of events.
	An event that involves damage to a defined system that disrupts the ongoing or future output of the system.
ACEP	American College of Emergency Physicians, http://www.acep.org
ACGME	Accreditation Council for Graduate Medical Education, http://www.acgme.org
ACHE	American College of Healthcare Executives, http://www.ache.org
ACLS	Advanced cardiac life support
ACS	American Cancer Society
ACOG	The American College of Obstetricians and Gynecologists, http://www.acog.org
Acquired Immune Deficiency Syndrome (AIDS)	Fatal, incurable disease caused by a virus that can destroy the body's ability to fight off illness resulting in recurrent opportunistic infections or secondary diseases afflicting multiple body systems

Acquisition	A business transaction in which one corporation or entity purchases or otherwise acquires all of the assets or stock of another entity or organization
ACR	American College of Radiology, http://www.acr.org
ACS	American College of Surgeons, http://www.facs.org
ACU	Ambulatory care unit
Active error	An error that occurs at the level of the frontline operator and whose effects are felt almost immediately
Actuarial analysis	A study performed by a professional known as an actuary aimed at predicting the frequency and severity of claims for a specific line of insurance coverage for a future time period. Such an analysis includes both an estimation of the ultimate value of known claims and an estimation of the number and value of claims that have occurred but have not yet been reported.
Actuarial study	An analysis performed by a recognized actuary that determines appropriate funding levels required for operation of a selfinsurance trust
Actuary	A person who uses statistics to compute loss probabilities to establish premiums for insurance companies and self-insurance trusts
Acuity	Degree or severity of illness
Acute Care Hospital	Typically a community hospital which has services designed to meet the needs of patients who require short-term care for a period of less than 30 days
ADA	See Americans With Disabilities Act
	Also American Diabetes Association
Additional insured	A person or entity added to an insurance policy by endorsement at the request of the named insured, often after the inception of the policy. Frequently required by contracts in order to give one contracting party the benefit of insurance coverage maintained by the other
ADE	Adverse Drug Event
ADEA	See Age Discrimination in Employment Act
Admission	An out of court statement made by a person who is a party to the action. Admissions are normally admissible into evidence at trial.
ADR	Alternative dispute resolution
Ad testificandum	Used to require recipient to give testimony
Advance Directives	A legal document that outlines a person's wishes concerning health-care services should the person be unable to communicate those wishes
	Written instructions recognized under law relating to the provision of health car when an individual is incapacitated. An advance directive takes two forms: living wills and durable power of attorney for health care
Adverse Drug Reports (ADRs)	A known or unknown, undesirable side effect or reaction to a medication. "An unintended act (either an omission or commission) or an act that does not achieve its intended outcome" (Lucian Leape)
Adverse event	A negative or bad result stemming from a diagnostic test, medical treatment or surgical intervention
	An injury resulting from a medical intervention

Adverse medication event	An unintended deviation from how one or more steps in the routine/regular medication prescribing, dispensing or administration processes is carried out. Under this definition, the patient may or may not have been harmed, and there may or may not be some degree of provider or system "fault" or negligence associated with the adverse medication event.
Adverse outcome	A clinical outcome that, while neither desirable nor necessarily anticipated, may still have been a known "possibility" associated with the treatment or procedure. Under this definition, using the term "adverse outcome" does not imply that any provider was negligent or any "error" in process or system factors contributed to the adverse outcome.
AED	Automatic External Defibrillator
AERS	Adverse Event Reporting System
Affidavit	A written statement made under oath, without notice to the adverse party. A written or printed declaration or statement of facts, made voluntarily, and confirmed by the oath, or affirmation of the party making it, taken before an officer having authority to administer such oath
Age Discrimination	The denial of privileges as well as other unfair treatment of employees on the basis of age. Age discrimination is prohibited by federal law under the Age Discrimination in Employment Act of 1978 to protect employees between the ages of 40 and 70 years of age
Age Discrimination in Employment Act	29 U.S.C. Section 621 et seq. The federal statute prohibiting certain types of employment discrimination on the basis of age
Agency by *estoppel*	See Ostensible Agency Doctrine
Aggregate limit	The maximum amount the insurer will pay during the policy period, irrespective of the policy's limit of liability
AHA	American Hospital Association, http://www.aha.org
	American Heart Association
AHCA	American Health Care Association, http://www.ahca.org
AHERA	Asbestos Hazard Emergency Response Act
AHRQ	Agency for Healthcare Research & Quality, http://www.ahrq.gov
	A component of the Public Health Services (PHS) responsible for research on quality, appropriateness, effectiveness, and cost of health care
AICPCU	American Institute for Chartered Property Casualty Underwriters, http://www.aicpcu.org
AIDS	Acquired immune deficiency syndrome
Allegation	The assertion, declaration or statement of a person setting out what the party to an action expects to prove. Made in a pleading.
Allied Health Professional	A specially trained non-physician health care provider. Allied health professionals include: paramedics, physician assistants (P:A), certified nurse midwives (CNM), phlebotomists, social workers, nurse practitioners (NP), and other caregivers who perform tasks that supplement physician services
Allocated Loss Adjustment Expense (ALAE)	Money paid in the claims resolution process. Includes defense attorney fees, court costs, expert witness fees and photocopy costs attributed directly to an individual claim.

Alternative Delivery Systems	Health services provided in other than an inpatient, acute care hospital, such as skilled and nursing facilities, hospice programs, and home health care
Alternative Dispute Resolution	Any method of resolving a dispute other than formal civil litigation. May include arbitration, mediation or "black box."
Alternative Risk Financing (or Funding) (ARF)	Any of a number of mechanisms employed by individuals or organizations to pay for claims other than through the use of traditional insurance programs, including various types of captive insurance companies, risk retention groups, self-insurance trust funds, etc.
Alternative Treatment Plan	Provision in managed care arrangements for treatment usually outside of a hospital
AMA	American Medical Association, http://www.ama-assn.org
AMAP	American Medical Accreditation Program
Ambulatory	Not confined to a bed—capable of moving
Ambulatory Care	Medical care provided on an outpatient basis
Americans with Disabilities Act	42 U.S.C. Section 12101 et seq. A federal statute aimed at prohibiting discrimination against individuals with certain mental and physical disabilities in the areas of employment and public accommodation
ANA	American Nurses Association, http://www.nursingworld.org
Ancillary	A term used to describe services that relate to a patient's care such as lab work, x-ray, and anesthesia.
Annuity	A fixed sum payable periodically, subject to the limitations imposed by the grantor
ANP	Advanced Nurse Practitioner
Answer	A document filed with the court in response to a Complaint or Petition. The Answer must generally (1) admit that the plaintiff's allegations are true; (2) deny that the plaintiff's allegations are true; or (3) state that the defendant does not have information regarding the truth or falsity of the allegations.
Anti-kickback statutes	Medicare-Medicaid Antikickback Statute (42 USC §1320a-7b)
	"Knowingly and willfully" seeking or receiving a bribe, rebate or kickback for a referral for a program, reimbursable item or service
	"Knowingly or willfully" seeking or receiving a bribe, rebate or kickback with the intent to induce a referral for a program, reimbursable item or service
Antitrust Laws	Generally, any law that is designed to discourage or prohibit restraints of free trade, to unfairly reduce or eliminate competition, or to unfairly prevent entrance into a marketplace
Any willing provider laws	Statutes in some jurisdictions prohibiting managed care organizations (MCOs) from discriminating among licensed providers of healthcare services and requiring that the MCO reimburse any licensed provider willing to accept the MCOs reimbursement schedule for the provision of covered services to a plan beneficiary
AOA	American Osteopathic Association, http://www.aoa-net.org
AONE	American Organizations of Nurse Executives

AORN	Association of Perioperative Registered Nurses, http://www.aorn.org
Apparent agency	See Ostensible Agency
Appeal	An action that is taken after the trial of a matter, or after a dispositive motion has been entered in a matter. An appeal may be taken for the purpose of correcting an error made by the trial court or to obtain a new trial.
	A resort to a higher court for the purpose of obtaining a review of a lower court decision and a reversal of the lower court's judgment or granting of a new trial
Appellate Court	A court that is empowered to hear appeals. There are normally two tiers of appellate courts: an intermediate appellate court (e.g., U.S. Circuit Courts of Appeal) and a supreme court (e.g., U.S. Supreme Court, New York Court of Appeals). Some states have only one tier of appellate court.
Arbiter	A neutral third party who issues a decision binding on the parties in a formal or informal hearing on a disagreement
Arbitration	The hearing and determination of a case in controversy by a person either chosen by the parties in opposition or by a person appointed under statutory authority
	A method of dispute resolution used as an alternative to litigation
	Submission by the parties of a dispute to one or more individuals who then decide the controversy. May be binding (final) or nonbinding (aggrieved party may appeal or pursue conventional civil litigation)
Arbitration Clause	A clause in a contract providing for arbitration of disputes arising under contract. Arbitration clauses are treated as separable part of the contract so that the illegality of another part of the contract does not nullify such agreement and a breach of repudiation of the contract does not preclude the right to arbitrate.
ARC	American Red Cross
Archiving	Retaining and organizing expired insurance policies or revised policies and procedures to facilitate the determination of provisions in place at a specific past point in time
ARM	Associate in Risk Management
ARM-P	Associate in Risk Management for Public Entities
ART	Accredited Record Technician
ASA	American Society of Anesthesiologists, http://www.asahq.org
ASC	Ambulatory surgery center
ASCP	The American Society for Clinical Pathology, http://www.ascp.org
ASHE	American Society for Healthcare Engineering, http://www.ashe.org
ASHP	American Society of Health-System Pharmacists, http://www.ashp.org
ASHRM	American Society for Healthcare Risk Management, http://www.ashrm.org
ASRS	Aviation Safety Reporting System
Assault	An intentional act that is designed to make the victim fearful and that produces reasonable apprehension of harm

Assignment	The act of transferring to another all or part of one's property, interest, or rights
Association	An unincorporated group of persons assembled for a specific purpose or to complete a specific project. Unless the state has a specific statute governing the liabilities of the members, each member may be liable for the debts and obligations of the association.
Association or Group Captive	Jointly owned by a number of companies that are usually affiliated through a trade, industry or service group
Assumption of Risk	Understanding the risks associated with a particular course of action and agreeing to accept those risks.
	An affirmative defense in a negligence case which alleges that the plaintiff knew of the danger involved in what he was doing, did nothing to prevent his own injury and therefore, as a result, must bear the consequences of the action and cannot ask for the defendant to pay for his injury.
ASTM	American Society for Testing and Materials, http://www.astm.org
ATLS	Advanced trauma life support
Attorney-client privilege	A legal doctrine recognized by both common and statutory law protecting certain confidential communications between an attorney and his or her client from discovery in a legal proceeding unless the privilege is waived by the client
	A confidential communication between an attorney and a client in the course of a professional relationship which cannot be disclosed without the consent of the client
Attorney work product privilege	A legal doctrine recognized by both common and statutory law protecting the documents generated, theories devised, legal strategies formulated, etc., by an attorney on behalf of a client from discovery in a legal proceeding unless the privilege is waived by the client
Automatic Dispensing Cabinet	A cabinet that by its design has certain controls and documentation features that dispense medications pursuant to individualized patient drug profiles, ordered by a physician, and confirmed by a pharmacist
AVP	Assistant Vice President
AWHONN	Association of Women's Health, Obstetric, and Neonatal Nurses
BAA	Business Associate Agreement
Back pay	In employment practices liability claims, a demand for or award of damages asking the defendant to pay the employee's wages from the time of the alleged improper act (such as wrongful termination) to the time of the settlement or judgment by the court in the employee's favor. In cases in which it is alleged that the employee was improperly denied a promotion or salary increase, back pay represents the difference in the wages actually earned by the employee and those that would have been earned had the promotion or salary increase not have been denied.
Bad outcome	Failure to achieve a desired outcome of care
Bar Code Technology	A computer identification system that uses unique bar-stripe code to identify specific items, medications or patients. Most often used with a scanning device to read, or verify, each code

Battery	The touching of one person by another without permission. See Medical Battery
BBA	Balanced Budget Act of 1997
BBRA	Balanced Budget Relief Act of 1999
BCAA	Blue Cross Association of America
Benchmarking	A comparative process used by organizations to collect and measure internal or external data that may ultimately be used for the purpose of developing, implementing, and sustaining quality improvements
	A process, which identifies best practices and performance standards, to create normative or comparative standards (benchmark) as a measurement tool. By comparing an organization against a national or regional benchmark, providers are able to establish measurable goals as part of the strategic planning and Total Quality Management (TQM) processes
Benevolent gesture	Actions taken to communicate a sense of compassion or compensation arising from humane feelings, when there is no implication (direct or implied) as to "fault" for having contributed to or caused the outcome
BI	See Business Interruption Insurance Coverage
BIPA	Benefits Improvement & Protection Act of 2000
BLS	Basic life support
BLS	Bureau of Labor Statistics
Board Certified	Describes a physician who is certified as a specialist in his/her area of practice. To achieve board certification, a physician must meet specific standards of knowledge and clinical skills within a specific field or specialty. Usually, this means completion of a supervised program of certified clinical residency and the physician passing both an oral and written examination given by a medical specialty group.
Board Eligible	Describes a physician who has graduated from a board-approved medical school, completed an accredited training program, practiced for a specified length of time, and is eligible to take a specialty board examination within a specific amount of time.
Boiler & Machinery Coverage	Provides protection for explosion of boilers and other pressure vessels and accidental damage to equipment
	Covers resulting damage to other property, including property in your care, for which you are liable
	Covers the cost of temporary repairs as well as the additional cost incurred to expedite repairs
	Coverage is written on a "cost to repair or replace" basis and is not subject to depreciation
Borrowed Servant	A person whose services an original employer loan, with his/her acquiescence or consent, to a second employer to whose control and direction he/she becomes wholly subject, free during the temporary period from the control of the original employer
BP	Blood pressure
Brain death	Total irreversible cessation of cerebral function, as well as spontaneous function of the respiratory and the circulatory systems

Breach of contract	Failure, without legal excuse, to perform any promise that forms the whole or part of a contract. Also, hindrance by a party regarding the required performance of the rights and duties identified in the contract
Broker	A person who represents a buyer of insurance in negotiations with the underwriter and who serves as a consultant on various aspects of the buyer's insurance program
BTLS	Basic trauma life support
BUN	Blood urea nitrogen
Business interruption insurance coverage	Insurance coverage typically provided as a part of a property insurance policy covering the lost revenues and extra operating expenses associated with a covered loss such as a fire Attempts to replace revenues lost due to covered loss
C-Section	Cesarean Section
CAA	Clean Air Act
CAAS	Commission on Accreditation of Ambulance Services
CABG	Coronary artery bypass graft
CAHPS	Consumer Assessment of Health Plans
CAMTS	Commission on Accreditation of Medical Transport Systems
CAP	College of American Pathologists
Capitation	In managed care contracts, a payment methodology in which a provider is paid a set fee, often per member per month, to provide designated healthcare services to individuals covered by the managed care plan. The fee remains constant regardless of how much or how little healthcare service is actually provided.
Captain of the Ship Doctrine	Doctrine that imposes liability on a surgeon in charge of an operation for the negligence of his assistants during the period when those servants are under the surgeon's control, even though those servants are also employees of the healthcare entity
Captive insurance company	An insurance company established to provide insurance coverage to a sponsoring entity as opposed to marketing and selling policies commercially to insureds. The sponsoring entity may be a parent corporation and its related subsidiaries, a professional association or other group.
CARF	See Commission on Accreditation of Rehabilitation Facilities
Cardiac Catheterization	A procedure used to diagnose disorders of the heart, lungs, and great vessels
CARME	Center for the Advancement of Risk Management Education
Case management	See Utilization Management.
	A managed care technique in which a patient with a serious medical condition is assigned an individual who arranges for costeffective treatment, often outside a hospital
CAT	Computerized axial tomography
	Diagnostic equipment which produces cross-sectional images of the head and/or body

Catastrophic protection	Protects against the adverse effects of large losses from natural forces or man-made disasters
Cause of Action	The fact or facts that give the plaintiff the legal grounds to seek damages from another person. It is necessary to have a cause (or causes) of action in order to bring and sustain a lawsuit.
CBC	Complete blood count
CBRN	Chemical, Biological, Radiological and Nuclear (countermeasures)
CCAC	Continuing Care Accreditation Commission
CCHSA	Canadian Council on Health Services Accreditation
CCRN	Certification in critical care nursing
CCU	Cardiac care unit
CDC	See Centers for Disease Control
Census	The number of inpatients who receive hospital care each day excluding newborns.
Centers for Disease Control	The arm of the U.S. Department of Health and Human Services, U.S. Public Health Service responsible for tracking mortality and morbidity statistics among the U.S. population and for making recommendations for a variety of public health measures, often focused on communicable diseases
Centers for Medicare and Medicaid Services	Formerly Health Care Financing Administration (HCFA) The federal agency responsible for administering Medicare, Medicaid and the State Children's Health Insurance Program (SCHIP)
CEO	See Chief Executive Officer
CERCLA	Comprehensive Environmental Response, Compensation and Liability Act
CERT	Centers for Education and Research in Therapeutics
Certificate of insurance	A standardized form, usually produced by the insurance agent or broker who arranged for the coverage, evidencing specific insurance in place, the insurance carrier, policy period, policy number, etc.
CFO	See Chief Financial Officer
CGL	See Commercial General Liability
CHAP	Community Health Accreditation Program
Chain of command	Mechanism approved by appropriate bodies (i.e.: administration, medical staff and nursing) that allows staff members a forum or process to air concerns and deal with difficult situations. It typically defines the route or hierarchy for pursuing such concerns.
Chain of evidence	Procedure to insure that the location and integrity of evidence (blood, clothing, weapons, etc.) collected is at all times accountable from when it is collected to when it is turned over to the police or court.
Charitable Immunity Doctrine	A doctrine that relieves a charity of liability in tort; long recognized, but currently most states have abrogated or restricted such immunity
Chemotherapy	In the treatment of disease, the application of chemical reagents which have a specific and toxic effect upon the disease-causing microorganism

Chief executive officer	The corporate officer charged with responsibility for the financial and operational performance of the company. Often the CEO also carries the title of president.
Chief financial officer	The corporate officer charged with responsibility for overseeing the finance and accounting functions of the company, including reporting financial information to the public and to regulatory agencies, and interfacing with independent financial auditors
Chief Operating Officer	The corporate officer charged with responsibility for the operations of the company
Chief risk officer	The corporate officer charged with responsibility for identifying and managing a variety of financial, legal, strategic and hazard risks faced by the organization. Distinguished from a traditional risk manager, whose role is generally confined to identifying and managing hazard risks
CICU	Cardiac intensive care unit
CISM	Critical incident stress management
Civil False Claims	Enables lawsuits by government or any individual ("qui tam relator") against one who submits a false claim to the government
Civil Law	The system of laws by which one person may bring an action against another person seeking compensatory or punitive damages, or injunctive relief. Also refers to the predominant theory of laws established by the governments of most western European countries (with the exception of the United Kingdom)
Civil Rights Act of 1964	42 U.S.C. Section 2000 et seq. Broad federal statute prohibiting discrimination on the basis of race, color, creed or national origin in a variety of settings, including employment
Claim	The amount of damage for which an insured seeks reimbursement from an insurance company. Once the amount has been determined, it becomes a loss.
Claimant	Someone who brings a claim for alleged injuries.
Claims-made insurance policy	An insurance policy covering claims that are made during the policy period and that occurred since the policy retroactive date. Although policy definitions vary somewhat, most claims-made insurance policies consider a claim to be made when it is first reported to the insurance company, subject to certain terms and conditions. Claims-made policies are common for professional liability and directors and officers liability insurance.
Claims management	A systemized approach to reducing the financial loss and negative community image of a healthcare organization in situations where prevention fails and injury occurs
Class actions	Lawsuits, frequently liability lawsuits, including a number of similarly situated plaintiffs whose cases are factually almost identical. Joining all of the plaintiffs into a single lawsuit expedites pretrial discovery and prevents multiple trials on the same issues and can provide a forum for plaintiffs whose individual damages may be quite small. Seen most frequently in products liability and employment practices litigation
CLIA	Clinical Laboratory Improvement Act
	Certification standards for laboratories established to consolidate the requirements for Medicare participation with rules for laboratories

	engaged in interstate testing under the CLIA '67 program; standards contain new quality control and quality assurance, proficiency testing, and personnel requirements
Clinical Practice Guidelines	Also known as Clinical Pathways
Clinical research trials	Use of experimental drugs, devices or protocols on human subjects in a clinical setting under a set of prescribed procedures as part of the FDA approval process
CMP	Civil monetary penalties
CMS	See Centers for Medicare and Medicaid Services
CNM	Certified Nurse-Mid Wife
CNS	Central nervous system
COB	Coordination of benefits
	Designates the anti-duplication provision designed by the group health insurance to limit benefits where there is multiple coverage in a particular case to 100 percent of the expenses covered, and to designate the order in which the multiple carriers are to pay benefits
COBRA	See the Consolidated Omnibus Budget Reconciliation Act of 1986
Co-defendant	A defendant who has been joined together with one or more other defendants in a single action.
Code Blue	Indicates an emergency situation has occurred and mobilizes staff to respond
COI	Certificate of Insurance
COLA	Commission of Office Laboratory Accreditation
Collateral-source benefits	Amounts that a plaintiff recovers from sources other than the defendant, such as the plaintiff's own insurance
Collective bargaining	Collective bargaining consists of negotiations between an employer and a group of employees so as to determine the conditions of employment. The result of collective bargaining procedures is a collective agreement. Employees are often represented in bargaining by a union or other labor organization.
Combined ratio	A measure of insurance company profitability calculated by adding the ratio of losses incurred/premium and the ratio expenses incurred/ premium
Commercial Auto Coverage	Protects against loss arising out of the ownership, maintenance, and use of automobiles and their equipment, both those you own, hire, or borrow, and those you don't own but may be responsible for, such as the personal car of an employee used to run a company errand
Commercial General Liability	Protects against financial loss resulting from liability to third parties arising out of the premises you own or occupy, acts of independent contractors hired by you, products you sell when they leave your premises and liability you assume under contract, subject to exclusions of the policy
	Coverage applies to Bodily Injury, Property Damage and Personal Injury
Commission Error	Incorrect action performed, or an intended action that was improperly performed
Common cause	Factor that results from variation inherent in the process or system

Common Law	A system of laws in which the building blocks of the substantive law must be gleaned from decided cases, as opposed to statutory law
Compensatory damages	Damages sought or awarded to a plaintiff in a liability action to compensate him or her for losses, such as lost wages or medical expenses and for pain and suffering
Complaint	One of the initial filings with a court to begin a lawsuit. The Complaint normally recites all of the allegations against the defendant and theories upon which the plaintiff seeks to recover damages. May be called a Petition in some jurisdictions
Complementary medicine	Any of a number of therapies and treatment modalities, alone or in combination, utilized for the treatment or alleviation of specific symptoms or disease, which fall outside of those traditionally employed by physicians, surgeons and dentists, including acupuncture, massage therapy, herbal medicine, etc. Sometimes referred to as complementary and alternative medicine. Complementary and alternative medicine treatments often take a holistic approach to care and treatment and may include an emphasis on the spiritual dimensions of healing.
Complication	Undesired, unintended but often known negative clinical symptoms or physical injury that resulted from medical treatment. Also known as Clinical Complication
Computed Tomography Scan	The gathering of anatomical information from a cross-sectional plane of the body, presented as an image generated by a computer synthesis of x-ray transmission data obtained in many different directions through a given plane
Computer-aided Decision Support System	Computers with embedded knowledge (through software applications) that enhances clinicians' use of scientifically based patient care information
Computerized Practitioner Order Entry	A computerized system for prescriptions (or other orders) to be directly entered by the provider, thereby eliminating the transcription process. May or may not have CDSS embedded therein
CON	Certificate of need
Conditions of Participation	Requirements that hospitals must meet to participate in the Medicare and Medicaid programs
	Intended to protect patient health and safety and to assure that high quality care is provided to all patients
Confirmation Bias	The human tendency to prematurely form a conclusion based on a preconceived expectation
Consideration	In contract law, something of value exchanged for the promised performance of the other contracting party. Contracts frequently call for monetary consideration to be exchanged for the promise to provide specified goods or services.
The Consolidated Omnibus Budget Reconciliation Act of 1986	It provides in part for continuation of health coverage applicable to group health plans. Federal law thatrequires employers with more than 20 employees to extend group health insurance coverage for at least 18 months after employees leave their jobs. Employees must pay 100 percent of the premium
Constitution	A relatively short document enacted by a state or federal government that specifies the essential nature of governance by the elected legislature, and which generally restrains the actions of military or police forces, and the power exercised by regulatory agencies

Constructive termination	In employment law, a situation in which, even though an employee is not formally terminated from his or her position, the conditions of employment become so manifestly untenable that the employee had no choice but to quit and thus are treated by the court as a termination
Contingency fee	A fee for service, collectable only if the outcome is favorable to the payee
Contract	An agreement, either written or oral, involving an offer, the acceptance of the offer and an exchange of consideration
	An agreement between two or more persons that creates an obligation to do or not to do a particular thing. A promise or set of promises for the breach of which the law gives a remedy, or the performance of which the law in some way recognizes as a duty
Contributory Negligence	Conduct on the part of the plaintiff that falls below the standard to which he/she should conform for his/her own protection which is a legally contributing cause in addition to the negligence of the defendant
	If the claimant is himself negligent, and his negligence concurs with that of the health care provider to cause the injury, claimant cannot recover
COO	See Chief Operating Officer
COPs	See Conditions of Participation for Hospitals in Medicare and Medicaid. This term also applies to Skilled Nursing Facilities and Nursing Facilities.
Copayment	A type of cost sharing whereby a specified flat fee per unit of service or unit of time is charged to an enrollee for a service or supply. Many HMO's charge their members a nominal fee for all non-emergent ambulatory patient visits or for prescription medications
COR	Cost of Risk
Corporate compliance	As relates to healthcare fraud and abuse, any of number of programs and initiatives undertaken by providers to avoid civil and criminal investigations and charges related to improper billing procedures, inappropriate referrals, kickbacks and other prohibited activities under federal statutes such as the Anti-Kickback Act and the Stark I and Stark II amendments to the Medicare Act. Many healthcare providers have taken corporate compliance programs beyond these specific legislative and regulatory requirements to encompass broader corporate business ethics concerns.
Corporate liability	Holds the healthcare entity liable for the failure of administrators and staff to monitor and supervise properly the delivery of healthcare in that entity (i.e.: negligence in hiring, training, supervising, or monitoring).
Corporation	A legal entity that may be created by one or more persons or entities to carry out a business purpose. Corporations are persons in the eyes of the law and may sue and be sued. Except in extraordinary circumstances, the owners of the corporation—shareholders or members (in not-for-profit corporations)—are shielded from the liabilities of the corporation.
Cost benefit analysis	A method comparing the costs of a project to the resulting benefits, usually expressed in monetary value

Cost containment	Control or reduction of inefficiencies in the consumption, allocation or production of health care services
Counter-claim	A claim presented by the defendant in opposition to the claim of the plaintiff
CPA	Certified Public Accountant
CPCU	Chartered Property Casualty Underwriter
CPG	See Clinical Practice Guidelines or Critical Paths
CPHQ	Certified Professional in Healthcare Quality
CPHRM	Certified Professional In Healthcare Risk Management
CPI	Consumer price index
	An inflationary measure encompassing the cost of all consumer goods and services
CPOE	See Computerized Practitioner Order Entry
CPR	Cardiopulmonary resuscitation
CPT	Current procedural terminology
CQI	Continuous Quality Improvement
	An approach to organizational management that emphasizes meeting (and exceeding) consumer needs and expectations, use of scientific methods to continually improve work processes, and the empowerment of all employees to engage in continuous improvement of their work processes
Credentialing	The process of verifying and reviewing the education, training, experience, work history and other qualifications of an applicant for clinical privileges conducted by a healthcare facility or managed care organization. Typically performed for independent contractors such as physicians and allied health practitioners who are frequently not employed by the credentialing entity but who are granted specific clinical privileges to practice
Credentialing and Privileging	Process by which hospitals determine the scope of practice of practitioners providing services in the hospital; criteria for granting privileges or credentialing are determined by the hospital and include individual character, competence, training, experience, and judgment
Criminal False Claims	"Whoever makes or presents to any person or officer in the civil, military or naval service of the United States, or any department or agency thereof, any claim upon or against the United States, or any department or agency thereof, knowing such claim to be false, fictitious or fraudulent, shall be imprisoned not more than five years or shall be subject to a fine or both."
Criminal Law	The system of laws by which the state or federal governments may bring suit against an individual, which suit may result in the loss of freedom or the person's life
Critical Access Hospital (CAH)	Part of the Medicare Rural Hospital Flexibility Program created by BBA97. A critical access hospital is a limited service small rural hospital that receives cost based reimbursement for inpatient and outpatient care
Critical paths (CPG)	Clinical pathways, CareMaps, clinical path guidelines, and other variants
	Any of a number of processes employed to define the generally accepted course (or courses) of treatment for a specific medical

condition or illness. Generally deviations from the prescribed critical paths must be explained by existing co-morbidities, failure of prescribed treatments, etc.

CRNA   Certified Registered Nurse Anesthetist

CRO   See Chief Risk Officer

Cross-claim   A claim brought by a defendant against a plaintiff in the same action or against a codefendant concerning matters related to the original petition. Its purpose is to discover facts that will aid the defense.

CSO   Chief Security Officer

CT   See Computed Tomography Scan

CVA   Cerebrovascular accident, a stroke

CWA   Clean Water Act

Cycle Time   The time it takes to complete a defined process—for example, the length of stay for a patient in the ED from triage to final disposition (transfer to unit; discharge or transfer out) is the ED service cycle time

D&C   Dilation and curettage

Damage cap   A legislatively imposed upper limit on the amount of a specific type of damages that may be awarded to a plaintiff in a specific type of lawsuit. State tort reform legislation frequently places a cap on the non-economic damages that may be awarded to a plaintiff in a medical malpractice action.

Damages   Monetary compensation for an injury

                          The injuries for which the plaintiff/claimant seeks compensation from the defendant/health care provider. May include economic losses, emotional distress, pain and suffering, disability, etc.

DBA   See Doing Business As

DDS   Doctor of Dental Surgery

DEA   Drug Enforcement Authority

Declaration   A "declaration" is a statement made out of court. An unsworn statement or narration of facts made by a party involved in a transaction or by someone who has an interest in the existence of the facts recounted. Recounts of statements made by a deceased person are admissible as evidence in some cases contrary to the general rule.

Deductible   In insurance, the amount of loss that must be paid by the insured before the insurer starts to pay. The use of deductibles allows entities to avoid paying for coverage for smaller claims that it is capable of paying for itself.

Default judgment   A judgment entered by the court in a civil case in favor of the plaintiff and against the defendant when the defendant has failed to file some appearance in response to a summons. Defendants failure to so file is deemed to be an admission that the demands of the plaintiff's complaint are valid.

Deemed status   In order for a health care organization to participate in and receive payment from Medicare or Medicaid programs, it must be certified as complying with the Conditions of Participation, or standards, set forth in federal regulations.

Deep pocket	In claims, an informal term for the defendant having the most assets and/or available insurance coverage which becomes the target of the plaintiff. The "deep pocket" may have less responsibility for the plaintiff's injuries than other co-defendants but may be pursued more aggressively because of its financial resources.
Default judgment	May be entered for failure to plead (e.g., answer)
	May be entered on any claim in action
	May be set aside upon motion for good cause
Defendant	The person defending or defying; the party against whom relief or recovery is sought in an action or suit. In common usage, this term is applied to the party put upon his defense or summoned to answer a charge or complaint.
Defense	A denial, answer, or plea opposing the truth or validity of the plaintiff's case. This may be accomplished by cross-examination or demurrer. It is more often done by introduction of testimony of the plaintiff's case.
Demurrer	A generally archaic term (although still used in some jurisdictions) that essentially admits the truth of the allegations asserted by the plaintiff, but which seeks their dismissal due to legal insufficiency to state a cause of action. Has been largely replaced in the federal court system, and in jurisdictions following the federal court rules of civil procedure, by the Motion to Dismiss
Deposition	Testimony (under oath) of a witness taken upon interrogatories reduced to writing and used to support or substantiate testimony offered at trial. Depositions are a very important phase of the discovery process.
	A question and answer session in which the witness is interrogated, under oath, and the testimony is transcribed
DFASHRM	Distinguished Fellow of the American Society for Healthcare Risk Management
DHHS	Department of Health and Human Services (Federal)
Diagnosis-related Group	Methodology for establishing reimbursement to healthcare providers under federal Medicare programs, based on clinical diagnosis. Adapted for use by some managed care plans
	A resource classification system that serves as the basis of the method for reimbursing hospitals based on the medical diagnosis for each patient. Hospitals receive a set payment amount determined in advance based on the length of time patients with a given diagnosis are likely to stay in the hospital. Also used as the basis of the Medicare inpatient prospective payment system (PPS).
DIFF.	Differential blood count
Direct Insurance	A contractual arrangement involving the purchase of insurance by an "Insured" from an "Insurer"
Direct liability	Imposed upon party as a result of party's acts or omissions
Disclosure	Communication of information regarding the results of a diagnostic test, medical treatment or surgical intervention
Discovery	The process in litigation by which each party to the action seeks to learn all relevant facts that either: (1) support the plaintiff's cause(s) of action; or (2) support the defendant's asserted defenses or denials

	That period of time following the filing of a complaint during which the parties to the litigation attempt to gain information about all facts relevant to the litigation
	The process by which parties learn and disclose information about the facts and issues in a case
Dismissal with Prejudice	A dismissal of a defendant in a suit which bars any future action by the plaintiff
Dismissal without Prejudice	A dismissal that affects no right or remedy of the plaintiff to rejoin the dismissed party in the cause of action
DMAT	Disaster Medical Assistance Team
DME	Durable medical equipment
DNR	Do not resuscitate Do not report Department of Natural Resources
D.O.	Doctor of Osteopathy: a doctor who employs the diagnostic and therapeutic measures of ordinary medicine in addition to manipulative measures. This approach is based upon the idea that the normal body when in "correct adjustment" is a vital machine capable of making its own remedies against infections and other toxic conditions.
D&O	Directors & Officers (insurance coverage)
	Policies contain a two-part wrongful act definition: 1) any actual or alleged error or misstatement or misleading statement or act or omission or breach of duty by directors and officers while acting in their individual or collective capacities; 2) any matter claimed against them solely by reason of their being directors or officers of the company.
DOC	Date of closure
Documentation	The recording of pertinent facts and observations about an individual's health history including past and present illnesses, tests, treatments and outcomes The legal evidence of professional account-ability. See Legal Health Record
DOE	Department of Education
DOI	Date of incident
Doing Business As	An entity organized under one name but carrying on a trade or business under another
DOJ	Department of Justice
DOL	Date of loss
DOL	Department of Labor
DOR	Date of report
DOT	Department of Transportation
DPM	Doctor of Podiatric Medicine
DPT	Diphtheria, pertussis, tetanus
DRG	See Diagnosis-Related Group
DRS	Designated Record Set
DSM-IV	Diagnostic and Statistical Manual of Mental Disorders—Fourth Edition
Dual capacity	In employer's liability, an individual or entity serving as both an injured party's employer in a workers' compensation claim and in some other role in which it is alleged to have caused injury, such as the manufacturer of a defective piece of equipment involved in the injury or as the provider of improper medical treatment for the injury

Duces tecum	Used to require production of documents and things
Due diligence	The review of an entity targeted for acquisition by the acquiring party to ascertain pertinent information about its financial and operating history and current status. Corporate staff are generally held to the legal standard of having performed the review with due diligence before making a recommendation to the board of directors as to whether to proceed with the acquisition.
Due Process	A procedural requirement that may be met by providing the affected party with: (1) adequate notice of the proceeding; (2) the right to be represented by counsel; (3) the opportunity to be heard; (4) the right to call and cross-examine witnesses; and (5) the right to a written transcript of the proceeding
Durable Power of Attorney for Health Care	Allows an individual to designate in advance another person to act on his/her behalf if he/she is unable to make a decision to accept, maintain, discontinue, or refuse any health care services
DVM	Doctor of Veterinary Medicine
DX	Diagnosis
EAP	Employee Assistance Program
ECF	Extended care facility
Economic damages (specific damages)	Damages sought by or awarded to a plaintiff to compensate for out-of-pocket expenses, such as medical treatment or housekeeping services and lost wages resulting from the injury, as distinguished from non-economic damages, such as pain and suffering and loss of consortium, for which a dollar value is more speculative
	Funds to compensate a plaintiff for the monetary costs of an injury, such as medical bills or loss of income
ECRI	Formerly the Emergency Care Research Institute
ED	Emergency Department
EEG	Electroencephalogram
EENT	Eye, ear, nose and throat
EEOC	See Equal Employment Opportunity Commission
"800"	Federal and State regulatory body toll free numbers for registering quality of care complaints
EKG, ECG	Electrocardiogram
EMC	Emergency Medical Condition
Emergency-prudent layman's definition	The determination by a reasonably prudent individual medical training that he or she (or a person for whom he or she is seeking medical care) has a medical condition requiring immediate care. In some jurisdictions, emergency evaluation and treatment must be covered by a health plan if a reasonably prudent layman would have determined that it was necessary, even if the medical condition is determined not to have been a true emergency based upon the evaluation performed by trained medical personnel.
Emergency Medical Treatment and Active Labor Act	See EMTALA
EMF	Electric and Magnetic Fields
EMG	Electromyogram

Employee Polygraph Protection Act	29 U.S.C. Section 2001 et seq. Federal statute limiting most employers' ability to use polygraph testing in applicant screening processes
Employers' liability	Any of a number of causes of action related to the employment relationship but falling outside of workers' compensation and employment practices liability insurance coverage, including dual capacity claims, spousal claims and third-party over claims
Employment-at-will	Legal doctrine in most jurisdictions that an employer may discharge an employee for any reason, unless specifically prohibited by law
Employment practices liability	Any of a number of violations by an employer, based on statute or common law, giving rise to damages outside of those covered by workers' compensation or similar statutes, including wrongful termination, discrimination and sexual harassment
Employment Retirement Income Security Act (ERISA)	42 U.S.C. Section 1002 et seq. Federal statute pertaining to protection of certain qualified employee pension and benefit plans
	A federal law that regulates retirement plans and health insurance plans. If a lawsuit is brought under ERISA against a health insurance plan, it may be removed to federal court and damages will include the value of services wrongfully withheld.
EMS	Emergency Medical Service
EMT	Emergency Medical Technician
EMTALA	42 U.S.C. Section 1395 et seq. The Emergency Medical Treatment and Active Labor Act. Federal statute prohibiting the "dumping" of patients presenting to the hospital with an emergent medical condition or in active labor and limiting a hospital's ability to transfer them to other facilities. EMTALA specifies when and how a patient may be: 1) refused treatment; or 2) transferred from one hospital to another when the patient is in an unstable medical condition.
ENT	Ear, nose and throat
Enterprise liability	Shift liability from individual physicians to the enterprise at which they practice
EOB	Explanation of benefits
EOC	Environment of Care
EPA	Environmental Protection Agency
EPL	See Employment Practices Liability
EPLI	Employment Practices Liability Insurance
Equal Employment Opportunity Commission	Federal agency charged with responsibility for enforcing several federal statutes prohibiting various types of employment discrimination. Under some statutes, administrative hearing procedures before the EEOC must be exhausted before an employee has access to the court system.
Equal Pay Act	29 U.S.C. Section 206 et seq. Federal statute requiring equal pay for equal work without regard to the gender of the worker
Equity	Cases brought in equity are cases in which the court has the power, without a jury, to determine the facts of the matter and to decide the case. The decision is less affected by precedent than are cases brought at law; it is generally based upon principles of fairness to the parties. Examples of actions in equity include most domestic

relations cases and cases for injunctive relief (restraining orders). Courts of equity have been merged with courts of law in the federal and most state systems.

ER/ED	Emergency room/emergency department
ERISA	See Employee Retirement Income Security Act
ERISA preemption	A provision of ERISA that preempts state law governing qualified pension and benefit plans and makes the remedies provided for by ERISA exclusive. Generally interpreted as preempting malpractice actions against managed care plans which are governed by the Act
ERM	Enterprise Risk Management
ERP	Extended reporting period
Error	Failure of a planned action to be completed as intended or use of a wrong plan to achieve an aim. The accumulation of errors results in accidents.
Errors and Omissions (E&O) insurance	A type of insurance policy providing coverage for negligent advice or business services provided by an individual or entity not eligible for professional liability insurance coverage, such as medical billing companies, insurance brokers and managed care organizations
Essential job functions	Under the Americans with Disabilities Act, those functions of a particular job that an applicant must be able to perform, either with or without accommodation, in order to perform the job
Ethics Committee	Multi-disciplinary group which convenes for the purpose of staff education and policy development in areas related to the use and limitation of aggressive medical technology; acts as a resource to patients, family staff, physicians, and clergy regarding health care options surrounding terminal illness and assisting with living wills.
Event	A happening or occurrence that is not part of the routine care of a particular patient or the routine operation of the healthcare entity
Event reporting	A system in healthcare institutions by which employees use a standardized form to report any occurrence outside the routine so that the information can be used for loss prevention and claims management activities
Evergreen clause	In contracts, a clause which makes the agreement perpetual and on-going unless terminated by one of the parties. Contracts with an evergreen clause have no set expiration date.
Evidence	Evidence may be testimony, documents, things, pictures, recordings of sounds or other items that may prove that an occurrence did, or did not, occur. Such things may only be considered at trial if admitted into evidence by the court. Evidence may be excluded if it would unduly inflame the passions of the jury, if it is irrelevant, if it does not appear to be credible or probative, or for other reasons.
Evidence-based	Recommended practices that are based on the best available scientific knowledge, that has generally gone through a rigorous review process by leading medical specialists
Excess and surplus lines carriers	Insurance companies that specialize in providing cover-age over primary insurance policies or significant self-insured retentions. Under the insurance regulations of most states, such insurers may

write coverage in the state according to certain specified conditions without going through the licensing provisions applicable to admitted insurance carriers.

Excess capacity

The difference between the number of hospital beds being used for patient care and the number of beds available

Excess insurance policy

An insurance policy providing coverage above the limits provided by a primary insurer or a self-insurance program. Some insurance programs feature multiple layers of excess insurance policies.

Expense

Costs incurred associated with the generation of revenues

Expenses within policy limits

A provision in some insurance policies that allocated loss-adjusting expenses paid by the insurer are included when determining the applicable limits of coverage. For example, if $900,000 is paid to a claimant to settle a claim, and expense costs total $300,000, and the occurrence is covered by an insurance policy having limits of $1 million that includes a provision for expenses within policy limits, the insurer will only pay $1 million. If the policy indicates that expenses are covered in addition to policy limits, the insurer will pay a total of $1.2 million. Expenses covered within policy limits are said to erode the limits.

Exposure

Term synonymous with risk: chance of loss and that potential for liability that is covered by insurance

A percentage, calculated by the attorneys and claims adjusters, which estimates the likelihood of losing a trial

Extended reporting endorsement (tail coverage)

An endorsement added to a claims-made insurance policy, generally for additional premium, extending the period of time that claims can be made under the policy past the policy expiration date, either for a specified time period or indefinitely

Extra expense

Attempts to replace additional expenses incurred due to covered loss

FAA

Federal Aviation Administration

Face value

A perception that the level of validity of a concept is high, even when there is no scientific evidence to support that hypothesis

FACHE

Fellow of the American College of Healthcare Executives

Factitious disorder by proxy

See Munchausen syndrome by proxy

Facultative

Usually covers a single transaction handled directly with a reinsurer

Failure Mode

Different ways that a process or sub-process can fail to provide the anticipated result (i.e. think of it as what could go wrong)

Failure Mode Cause

Different reasons as to why a process or sub-process would fail to provide the anticipated result (i.e. think of it as why it would go wrong)

Failure Mode Effects Analysis or Failure Mode Effects Criticality Analysis (FMECA)

A prospective assessment that identifies and improves steps in a process, thereby reasonably ensuring a safe and clinically desirable outcome

A systematic approach to identify and prevent product and process problems before they occur

A systematic process often used by engineers to identify the steps of a process that may be subject to failure, in order to design measures to either prevent or control such failures. If a Criticality phase is used in this process, the perceived level of criticality of each type of potential failure is identified, to aid in setting priorities for establishing control mechanisms.

Fair hearing plan   A document, either freestanding or part of the bylaws of a medical staff, describing the procedures applicable to denial, revocation and suspension of clinical privileges and other medical staff disciplinary issues. Such plans specify due process requirements such as the right to notice, hearings, representation by counsel, appeals, etc.

Fair Labor Standards Act   29 U.S.C. Section 201 et seq. Federal statute establishing the authority for the Department of Labor to promulgate wage and hour regulations and providing the framework for collective bargaining by employees

False Claims Act   Two separate statutes: 18 USC §287; [31 USC §3729(a) and 31 USC §3730 (a)-(b)]. See Civil False Claims and Criminal False Claims

Family Education Rights & Privacy Act   [20 U.S.C. § 1232G; 34 CFR Part 99] Federal legislation designed to protect the privacy of student education records. It is applicable to all schools that receive funds under designated U.S. Department of Education programs.

Family Medical Leave Act   29 U.S.C. Section 2611 et seq. Federal statute requiring certain employers to provide a period of unpaid leave to employees meeting specified criteria in order for them to receive medical treatment or to provide care to designated family members

FASHRM   Fellow of the American Society for Healthcare Risk Management

Fatigue factors   The degree to which a person's physical or mental fatigue contributed to an adverse event or outcome

Fault tree analysis   A total quality management technique in which a complex process is broken down into a series of simpler steps and then particular areas of vulnerability for system breakdown are identified in an effort to anticipate and thereby avoid problems

An engineering tool designed to identify potential errors in a process

FDA   Food and Drug Administration

Federal Deemed Status   In order for healthcare organizations to participate in and receive payment from Medicare or Medicaid programs, it must be certified as complying with the Conditions of Participation, or standards, set forth in federal regulations.

Federal Emergency Management Agency (FEMA)   An independent response organization that reports directly to the President of the United States

Fee-for-service   A reimbursement mechanism that pays providers for each service or procedure they perform; opposite of capitation

FERPA   See Family Educational Rights and Privacy Act.

Fiduciary duty   A duty to act for someone else's benefit while subordinating one's personal interests to that of the other person. It is the highest standard of duty implied by law (e.g., trustee, guardian).

First-dollar coverage   Commercial insurance providing protection against the entire loss covered by the policy—without requiring the insured to pay a deductible

First party	Provides coverage for the insured's own property or person so that the insured will be restored to the same financial position that they had been in prior to the loss
Float staff	Hospital staff, either generally assigned to a specific patient care unit or not, made available to work on other units as required to yield appropriate staffing levels for a given patient volume and acuity
FLV (full liability value)	An estimate of the jury award if the plaintiff prevails on all issues.
FMEA	See Failure Mode Effects Analysis
FMLA	See Family Medical Leave Act
FOIA	Freedom of Information Act
Force Majuere	A clause found in some contracts making the contract, or specific provisions of the contract, inapplicable in times of natural disasters, such as earthquakes, hurricanes, etc., and sometimes other crises, such as war, riot and civil commotion
Forcing Function	A technological design feature that forces the user to conform to a certain process, usually for a safety reason (e.g., a car is designed to not permit ignition if the gear is in reverse)
Formulary system	A planned restriction on the inventory of medications stocked in a pharmacy, in order to limit the choice to essential drugs, in order to promote safety by virtue of increasing staff familiarity with a more limited range of stocked medications
For-profit hospital	A hospital operated for the purpose of making a profit for its owner(s); the initial source of funding is typically through the sale of stock; profits are paid to stockholders in dividends (also referred to as a proprietary or an investor-owned hospital)
Formulary	The list of prescription medications that may be dispensed by participating pharmacies without health plan authorization. The formulary is selected based on effectiveness of the drug, as well as its cost. The physician is requested or required to use only formulary drugs unless there is a valid medical reason to use a non-formulary drug. Formularies may be open or closed. Closed formularies are restricted by the number and type of drugs included in the list.
Forum non Conveniens	A forum that is not convenient for the parties for some reason. Such a forum will normally have jurisdiction over the matter, and the venue of the action is appropriate, but hearing and deciding the matter there will work a hardship upon the parties or the witnesses. Determining that a particular forum is not convenient is an exercise of the court's discretion.
FP	For Profit
FPO	Facility Privacy Official
Fraud	Making false statements or representations of material facts in order to obtain some benefit or payment for which no entitlement would otherwise exist
Fraud and abuse	Informal term for the various federal statutes and regulations regarding inappropriate billing, kickbacks, referrals, etc., related to the federal or state Medicare/Medicaid programs
Free Flow	The unrestricted flow of a fluid through an IV line
Freestanding Ambulatory Surgery Center	A medical facility which provides surgical treatment on an outpatient basis only

FTC	Federal Trade Commission
FTE	Full-time equivalent
Gag rule	An informal term for a provision found in some managed care contracts with physicians prohibiting the physicians from discussing treatment alternatives, such as experimental procedures, with managed care plan patients when such treatments are not covered by the plan
Garage Liability Policy	Covers loss resulting from premises exposure of parking areas, but excludes property in your care, custody and control
Gatekeeper	Term used to describe the coordination role of the primary care provider (PCP) who manages various components of a member's medical treatment, including all referrals for specialty care, ancillary services, durable medical equipment, and hospital services. The gatekeeper model is a popular cost-control component of many managed care plans because it requires a subscriber to first see their PCP and receive the PCP's approval before going to a specialist about a given medical condition (except for emergencies).
General liability insurance	Coverage for liability arising out of the hazards of the premises and operations
GI	Gastrointestinal
GL	General liability
GMP	Good manufacturing practice
GP	General practitioner
GU	genitourinary
Hard insurance market	Insurance market conditions characterized by rising premiums and shrinking availability of coverage. Hard markets typically prompt insureds to accept larger deductibles or self-insured retentions, reduce coverage limits and/or seek out alternative risk financing alternatives.
Hazard	A condition that increases the possibility of loss
Hazard Analysis	The process of collecting and evaluating information on hazards associated with the selected process. The purpose of the hazard analysis is to develop a list of hazards that are of such significance that they are reasonably likely to cause injury or illness if not effectively controlled.
Hazard Communication Standard	Also called the Employee Right-to-Know Rule
Hazardous Condition	"Any set of circumstances (exclusive of the disease or condition for which the patient is being treated) which significantly increases the likelihood of a serious adverse outcome" (JCAHO)
HAZWOPER	Hazardous Waste Operations and Emergency Response Standard
HCCA	See Health Care Compliance Association
HCFA	Health Care Financing Administration (currently known as the Centers for Medicare and Medicaid Services)
HCO	See Health Care Organization
HCQIA	See Health Care Quality Improvement Act
Health Care Compliance Association	The professional society for healthcare corporate compliance officers

Health Care Organization	Entity that provides, coordinates and/or ensures health and medical services for people
Health Care Quality Improvement Act	A federal law that requires reports to the National Practitioner Data Bank and which protects the confidentiality of peer review materials. 42 USC §11101et seq.
The Health Insurance Portability and Accountability Act of 1996	42 U.S.C. Section 201 et seq. Amendments to ERISA addressing a variety of healthcare-related issues including fraud and abuse and the portability of group healthinsurance benefits as well as mandating specific patient privacy protections.
	A federal law that resulted in the promulgation of several regulations including the HIPAA Privacy Rule. Full compliance with the privacy requirements is expected for covered entities by April 2003 with a one year extension for smaller health plans
Hearsay	An out-of-court statement made by a person not a party to the action, and who is not available to testify, that is offered to prove the truth of the matter asserted. Normally subject to numerous exceptions but, if not precluded by an exception to the rule, will act to preclude the admission of statements into evidence
HEDIS	Health Plan Employer Data and Information Set A standard data reporting system developed in 1991 to measure the quality and performance of health plans. A main goal of HEDIS is to standardize health plan performance measures for consumers and payers. HEDIS concentrates on four aspects of healthcare: (1) quality, (2) access and patient satisfaction, (3) membership and utilization, and (4) finance. Within each focus area is a specific set of HEDIS data measures (e.g., number of immunizations for pediatric enrollees, etc.). The National Committee for Quality Assurance (NCQA) is responsible for coordinating HEDIS and making changes each year.
H.E.I.C.S.	Hospital Emergency Incident Command System
HFAP	Health Care Facilities Accreditation Program (through the AOA)
HFMA	Healthcare Financial Management Association
Hgb.	Hemoglobin
HHS	The federal Department of Health and Human Services
HIAA	Health Insurance Association of America
Hierarchy Effect (steep hierarchy)	The effect that a perceived "pecking order" or relative stature/status differences have on the lower person's level of willingness to question a higher person's actions or decisions
High/Low Agreements	An agreement made between the plaintiff and defendant. The plaintiff will be entitled to at least the low amount and the defendant will be obligated to pay at least the low amount. The plaintiff will not be entitled to more than the high amount and the defendant will not be obligated to pay more than the high amount. If the jury returns a verdict between the low and high amounts, the case will settle for the amount of the verdict. A high/low agreement settles the case and no appeal may be taken.
HIM	Health information management
Hindsight bias	The tendency for a reviewer to focus most heavily on facts learned after an event and/or only the most obvious contributing factors, thereby failing to consider other, more subtle, contributing factors

HIPAA	See The Health Insurance Portability and Accountability Act of 1996
HIPDB	Health Integrity and Protection Data Bank
HIV	Human Immunodeficiency Virus
HMO	Health Maintenance Organization

A health care payment and delivery system involving networks of doctors and hospitals. Members must receive all their care from providers within the network

➤ *Staff Model HMO.* Physicians are on the staff of the HMO and are usually paid a salary

➤ *Group Model HMO*. The HMO rents the services of the physicians in a separate group practice and pays the group a per patient rate.

➤ *Network Model HMO.* The HMO contracts with two or more independent physician group practices to provide services and pays a fixed monthly fee per patient

Hold Harmless Provision	A contractual clause providing that one party agrees not to pursue a tort claim for vicarious liability against the other. Hold harmless provisions are usually found with indemnification provisions and are usually mutual.
Home Health Care	Health care services are provided in a patient's home instead of a hospital or other institutional setting; services provided may include nursing care, social services, and physical, speech, or occupational therapy
Hospice	An organization that provides medical care and support services (such as pain and symptom management, counseling, and bereavement services) to terminally ill patients and their families; may be a freestanding facility, a unit of a hospital or other institution, or a separate program of a hospital, agency, or institution
Hospitalists	A physician whose practice is caring for patients while in the hospital. A primary care physician (PCP) turns their patients over to a hospitalist, who becomes the physician of record and provides and directs the care of the patient while the patient is hospitalized and returns the patient to the PCP at the time of hospital discharge
HPL	Hospital Professional Liability (insurance)
HR	Human Resources (Department)
HRSA	Health Resources and Services Administration
Human Factors	Study of the interrelationship between humans, the tools they use, and the environment in which they live and work
Iatrogenic	Caused by medical treatment
IBNR	See Incurred But Not Reported
ICD-9-CM	International Classification of Diseases, 9th revision

The classification of disease by a diagnostic codification into sixdigit numbers. ICD-10, is under development and will use alphanumeric codes

ICF/MR	Intermediate care facility for the mentally retarded
ICS	Incident command system

ICU	Intensive Care Unit
I.D.	Identification
IDS	See Integrated Delivery System
IIA	Insurance Institute of America
IM	Intramuscular
IME	See Independent Medical Examination
Immediate Jeopardy	A situation in which the provider's noncompliance with one or more requirements of participation has caused, or is likely to cause, serious injury, harm, impairment or death to a resident
Immigration Reform and Control Act	8 U.S.C Section 1324 et seq. Federal legislation requiring employers to verify immigration status of prospective employees during hiring process
Improperly performed procedure or treatment	The appropriate procedure or treatment is done but is performed incorrectly. This is not to be confused with choosing the wrong procedure or treatment.
Inappropriate procedure or treatment	An incorrect procedure or treatment is provided. This usually involves medical judgment versus skills or techniques. This is not to be confused with performing the procedure incorrectly.
Incident	Any happening not consistent with the routine operations of the facility or routine care of a particular patient; an unexpected occurrence; an occurrence which leaves a patient, visitor or other person feeling, either rightly or wrongly, that he had been mistreated, neglected or injured in same manner.
Incident reporting	An early warning reporting system intended to identify risk situations or adverse events in a timely manner to trigger prompt investigation from a claims management perspective as well as corrective action to prevent similar future events
Incurred But Not Reported	Insurance and actuarial term for claims that have occurred but for which notification has not yet been received
Indemnification provision	A contractual clause in which one party agrees to accept the tort liability and legal defense of another. Indemnification provisions are usually found with hold harmless provisions and are usually mutual
Indemnify	To secure against loss, damage or expenses which may occur in the future; to insure.
Indemnity	An assurance or contract by one party to compensate for the damage caused by another; shifting an economic loss to the person responsible for the loss; the right which the person suffering the loss or damage is entitled to a claims; compensation given to make a person whole from a loss already received; settlements or awards made directly to plaintiffs as a result of the claims resolution process
	In regards to health care services: benefits in the form of cash payments rather than medical services.
Independent medical examination	Medical examination of a claimant by a practitioner other than the claimant's treating practitioner at the request of a defendant to verify the claimant's diagnosis and prognosis
Independent practice association	A group of independent physicians who have formed an association as a separate legal entity for contracting purposes. IPA physician providers retain their individual practices, work in separate offices, continue to see their non-managed care patients,

and have the option to contract directly with managed car plans. A key advantage of the IPA arrangement is that it helps its members achieve some of the negotiating leverage of a large physician group practice with some degree of flexibility for each provider. Also referred to as independent physician association.

Indicator	In quality improvement, a measurable objective standard against which performance is measured. Designed to be indicative of whether other care processes are also meeting established standards
Informed consent	Legal doctrine that patients generally have a right to be informed regarding proposed medical and surgical treatments, including anticipated benefits, risks and alternatives and to accept or reject such proposed treatments
Injunction	A court order prohibiting someone from doing some specified act or commanding someone to undo some wrong or injury
Insolvent	In reference to an insurance company, an insurer without the available financial resources to pay covered claims
Institute of Medicine	A division of The National Academy of Sciences, a private nonprofit organization of scholars dedicated to research and publications related to engineering and the sciences. Noted for its 1999 publication "To Err is Human: Building a Safer Health System," which focused in medical errors
Institutional review board	The body within a healthcare organization charged with establishing protocols for and overseeing clinical research trials and human experimentation
Insurance	Losses paid for with funds external to the organization
	A contractual relationship which exists when one party (the insurer), for consideration (the premium), agrees to reimburse another party (the insured) for loss to a specified subject (the risk) caused by designated contingencies (hazards or perils)
Insurance schedule	A document or graphic showing all of the insurance coverages in place for a given insured, usually including the names of insurers, policy limits, deductibles and retentions, policy numbers, inception and expiration dates
Insured versus insured exclusion	A provision common in insurance policies excluding coverage for claims in which one insured makes a claim against another
Integrated care	A comprehensive spectrum of health services, from prevention through long-term care, provided via a single administrative entity and coordinated by a primary care "gatekeeper"
Integrated Delivery System	A healthcare system made up of various types of providers, including hospitals, ambulatory care centers, surgery centers, home health agencies, physician practices, etc., and frequently a managed care organization, such as a health maintenance organization or a preferred provider organization
	An entity (corporation, partnership, association or other legal entity) that enters into arrangements with managed care organization; employs or has contracts with providers; and agrees to provide or arrange for the provision of health care services to members covered by the managed care plan
Intentional acts	In insurance policies, an exclusion for injuries caused by the intentional acts of an insured

Interrogatories	A written set of questions that is served upon the other party in litigation. All questions must be answered under oath and returned to the party that served the interrogatories.
Intravenously	Within the veins
IOM	See Institute of Medicine
IP	Internet Protocol
IPA	Independent practice association
IRB	See Institutional Review Board
IRMI	International Risk Management Institute
IRS	Internal Revenue Service
ISMP	Institute for Safe Medication Practices
IV	See Intravenously
IVP	Intravenous pyelogram (urogram)
JCAHO	See Joint Commission on Accreditation of Healthcare Organizations
JD	See Juris Doctor
Joint and Several Liability	A sharing of liabilities among a group of individuals collectively and also individually
	Liability in which each liable party is individually responsible for the entire obligation. Under joint-and-several liability, a plaintiff may choose to seek full damages from all, some, or any one of the parties alleged to have committed the injury. In most cases, a defendant who pays damages may seek reimbursement from nonpaying parties
Joint Commission on the Accreditation of Healthcare Organizations (JCAHO)	A voluntary nonprofit accreditation body which sets standards for hospitals and other types of healthcare organizations and conducts education programs and a survey process to assess organizational compliance
	The organization which evaluates and monitors the quality of care provided in hospitals based on standards established by the Joint Commission
Joint defense	Requires a defense of all defendants (e.g., physician and hospital) in an integrated response
Joint Venture	An undertaking by two or more entities to pursue business or other ventures. In many jurisdictions, entities cannot form partnerships; hence they are deemed to be joint venturers. Each joint venturer may be liable for the debts and obligations of the joint venture.
	An organization formed for a single purpose or undertaking which makes its membership liable for the organization's debts.
JUA	Joint Underwriting Agreement
Judgment	The official decision of a court that determines the relative legal rights and obligations of parties to a legal proceeding
Juris doctor	The educational degree awarded by law schools
Jurisdiction	The power of a court or other tribunal to hear and decide a legal matter. In common parlance, jurisdiction is often referred to as the physical locations from which courts are permitted to hear and decide cases.

Jury	A group of persons impaneled to hear a legal matter and to render a verdict. The jury typically finds the facts of the matter and the court applies the law to the facts. The number of jurors necessary to form a jury varies by jurisdiction and, possibly, by type of case.
Latent Error	Errors in the design, organization, training or maintenance that lead to operator errors and whose effects typically lie dormant in the system for lengthy periods of time
Law Courts	These are the courts that have jurisdiction to hear most civil lawsuits, such as suits for personal injury, breach of contract, etc. For almost all practical purposes, law courts have been merged with courts of equity, but differences in actions based in law versus actions based in equity still remain.
LCF	Loss Conversation Factor
LCL	See Lower Control Limit
LDF	Loss Development Factor
Leapfrog Group, The	A private business consortium for healthcare interests
Legal health record	The legal health record is the documentation of the healthcare services provided to an individual in any aspect of healthcare delivery by healthcare provider organizations. The legal health record is individually identifiable data, in any medium, collected and directly used in and/or documenting healthcare or health status. The term includes records of care in any health-related setting used by healthcare professionals while providing patient care services, for reviewing patient data, or documenting observations, actions or instructions.
Legally cognizable injury	An injury for which the law can provide redress
Length of stay	The period of hospitalization as measured in days billed; average length of stay is determined by discharge days divided by discharges.
LEP	Limited English Proficiency
Letter of intent	Formal notice to an organization that another organization is seeking to acquire or merge with it, setting due diligence in motion
Libel	Defamatory language expressed in print, writing, pictures or symbols tending to injure another's reputation, business or means of livelihood.
Limited Liability Companies	A limited liability company (LLC) may be formed by one or more persons or entities to carry out a business purpose. The LLC shields its owners (members) from liability but enjoys certain tax advantages not available to corporations.
Limits (policy limits)	In insurance, the maximum the insurer will pay, typically expressed either per occurrence (occurrence limit) or as an annual aggregate (the maximum insurer will pay for all claims covered under policy)
Living will	Document generated by a person for the purpose of providing guidance about the medical care to be provided in the person is unable to articulate those decisions (see Advance Directive).
LLC	See Limited Liability Companies
Long tail	An informal term for lines of insurance coverage in which there is frequently an extended period of time between the time an incident giving rise to a claim occurs and the time that the claim is reported.

	Medical professional liability is generally considered to be long tail insurance business.
Long term care	A continuum of maintenance, custodial, and health services to the chronically ill, disabled, or mentally handicapped
LOS	Length of stay
Loss	The reduction in the value of an asset
Loss control	Any of a number of programs and initiatives undertaken to prevent losses from occurring (loss prevention) or to decrease the severity of losses that do occur (loss reduction), including education and training, policy and procedure development, equipment maintenance, use of personal protective equipment, installation of sprinkler systems, etc.
Loss of consortium	Claim for damages relating to the loss of companionship, advice and sexual relationship with an injured party, typically filed by the injured party's spouse
Loss frequency	A measure of how many times a particular loss occurs or can be expected to occur in a given period of time
Loss prevention	Reduces an organization's losses by lowering their frequency
Loss reduction	A method to manage loss exposures. Actions taken to decrease severity of a loss
Loss run	A listing, usually generated by computer, of claims brought against an insured for a specific line of insurance coverage, that typically includes the name of the claimant, the date of occurrence, the date the claim was made, the status of claim (open or closed; suit, claim or occurrence), amounts paid and reserved for both indemnity and loss adjustment expenses, and a description of the facts giving rise to the claim
Loss severity	A measure of the size of an actual or expected loss; how much a loss will cost
Lower Control Limit	Used in statistical process control run charts
LPN	Licensed Practical Nurse
LPT	Licensed Physical Therapist
LTC	Long-term care
LTD	Long-term disability
LVN	Licensed Vocational Nurse
M. A.	Medical Assistant
M&A&D	Mergers, acquisitions and divestitures
Magnetic Resonance Imaging	Technology that utilizes magnetic fields to image the body's tissue
	A non-invasive diagnostic technique used to create images of body tissue and monitor body chemistry; uses radio and magnetic waves instead of radiation
Malfeasance	The wrongful or unjust doing of an act which the doer had no right to perform or which he had stipulated by contract not to do
Malpractice	Improper professional actions or the failure to exercise proper professional skills by a professional advisor, such as a physician, dentist, or healthcare entity. Also, professional misconduct, improper

discharge of professional duties, or failure to meet the standards of care of a professional, resulting in harm to another

Failure on one rendering professional services to exercise that degree of skill and learning commonly applied under all circumstances in the community by the average prudent reputable member of the profession with the result of injury, loss or damage to the recipient of those services or to those entitled to rely upon them

Managed care   A term that applies to the integration of health care delivery and financing. It includes arrangements with providers to supply health care services to members, criteria for the selection of health care providers, significant financial incentives for members to use providers in the plan, and formal programs to monitor the amount of care and quality of services

A healthcare organization, such as a health maintenance organization, that "manages" or controls what it spends on health care by closely monitoring how doctors and other medical professionals treat patients.

Managed care organization   Any of a number of organizations, such as health mainte-nance organizations and preferred provider organizations, which arrange for the provision of and payment for healthcare services with an eye toward reducing costs through managing access to specific providers

Mandatory Settlement Conference (MSC)   A court ordered meeting of the plaintiff and defendant held under the judges direction with the goal of resolving a claim. This meeting is not voluntary and the opposing parties must participate

MAR   See Medication Administration Record

Market-hard   See Hard Insurance Market

Maximum medical improvement (MMI)   In workers' compensation, the point in which the injured employee has recovered to the maximum extent medically expected (also called permanent and stationary, or P and S). When an employee reaches MMI, any residual disability, pain, etc., is expected to be permanent.

MBWA   Management by Walking Around

MCO   See Managed Care Organization

M.D.   Medical Doctor

MDR   Medical Device Reporting

MedPAC   Medicare Payment Advisory Commission

Mediation   Intervention between parties in conflict to promote reconciliation, settlement or compromise

Medicaid   A federal public assistance program enacted into law on January 1, 1966, under Title XIX of the Social Security Act, to provide medical benefits to eligible low income persons needing health care regard-less of age. The program is administered and operated by the states which receive federal matching funds to cover the costs of the program. States are required to include certain minimal services as mandated by the federal government but may include any additional services at their own expense

Medical battery   Traditionally, a battery that occurs during the administration of med-ical care and procedures. May also include actions against medical care providers for prolonging the lives of patients who had previously requested for no "heroic measures" to be undertaken when faced with a medical emergency

Medical Malpractice Review Panel

A panel consisting of two lawyers, two health care providers, and a circuit court judge which, upon the request of any party, passes non-binding judgment on claims of alleged medical malpractice. May conclude that there was negligence, no negligence, or question of fact which must be decided by a jury.

Medical services

The furnishing of professional healthcare services, including the furnishing of food, medications or appliances, the postmortem handling of bodies or arising out of service by any persons as members of a formal accreditation review board

Medical technology

Techniques, drugs, equipment, and procedures used by healthcare professionals in delivering medical care to individuals and the systems within which such care is delivered

Medicare

A federally administered health insurance program for persons aged 65 and older and certain disabled people under 65 years old. Created in 1965 under Title XVIII of the Social Security Act, Medicare covers the cost of hospitalization, medical care, and some related services for eligible persons without regard to income. Medicare has two parts. Medicare Part A: Hospital Insurance (HI) Program is compulsory and covers inpatient hospitalization costs. Medicare Part B: Supplementary Medical Insurance Program is voluntary and covers medically necessary physicians' services, outpatient hospital services, and a number of other medical services and supplies not covered by Part A. Part A is funded by a mandatory payroll tax. Part B is supported by premiums paid by enrollees.

Medication Administration Record

The record of all medications ordered and when each has been administered, maintained by nursing staff

Medication Error

"A medication error is any preventable event that may cause or lead to inappropriate medication use or patient harm while the medication is in the control of the healthcare professional, patient, or consumer. Such events may be related to professional practice, healthcare products, procedures, and systems, including prescribing; order communication; product labeling, packaging, and nomenclature; compounding; dispensing; distribution; administration; education; monitoring; and use." Source: National Coordinating Council for Medication Error Reporting and Prevention

"An unintended act, either by omission or commission, or an act that does not achieve its intended outcome" (JCAHO)

MEq.

millequivalent

MER

Medical Error Reporting (system)

Merger

A combination of business entities in which two or more organizations join assets and stock if applicable

Union of two or more organizations by the transfer of all assets to one organization that continues to exist while the other(s) is (are) dissolved.

MERS-TM

Medical Event Reporting System for Transfusion Medicine

MHA

Master of Hospital (Health) Administraton

MHSA	Master of Health Services Administration
MO	Myocardial infarction
	Mitral insufficiency
	Mental institution
Micro-system	Organizational unit built around the definition of repeatable core service competencies. Elements of a micro-system include: 1) a core team of healthcare professionals; 2) a defined population of patients; 3) carefully designed work processes; and 4) an environment capable of linking information on all aspects of work and patient or population outcomes to support ongoing evaluation of performance.
Misrepresentation	Any manifestation by words or other conduct by one person to another that, under circumstances, amounts to an assertion not in accordance with the facts. An untrue statement of fact
M&M	Morbidity and mortality
MOB	Medical office building
Morbidity	Associated negative consequences relating to a clinical treatment or procedure, e.g., complication
	Incidence and severity of illness and accidents in a well-defined class or classes of individuals
Mortality	Death rate
	Incidence of death in a well-defined class or classes of individuals
Motion	A filing with a court or other tribunal that requests that the court perform some function. The party seeking the relief in question "moves" the court to perform the act.
Motion for Judgment Notwithstanding the Verdict	In a trial process, the court normally enters judgment on a jury's verdict, and thus gives effect to the verdict. This motion seeks to have the jury verdict set aside and judgment entered by the court that is not in accord with the verdict. Usually granted for the appearance of bias, prejudice, or possible misconduct by the jury
Motion for New Trial	A motion that seeks to invalidate the original trial and declare that the matter must be re-tried. Usually granted when the verdict is contrary to the manifest weight of the evidence, or when there is a scant amount of evidence to support the jury's verdict
Motion for Summary Judgment	A motion that seeks to have a lawsuit decided (have judgment rendered) because there are no genuine issues of material fact for the jury to decide
Motion *in Limine*	A motion to preclude the admission of certain facts, testimony, items or proofs at trial. May be granted on the grounds that the evidence is not relevant, is redundant or duplicative of other evidence, will unduly arouse or inflame the jury, etc.
Motion to Dismiss	A motion that seeks to have a lawsuit dismissed because the Complaint or Petition fails to state a cause of action upon which relief may be granted. The filing of a Motion to Dismiss often stays the period in which an Answer must be filed.
Motion to Strike	Motion to eliminate a cause of action in the Complaint or Petition or to preclude the defendant from mounting a defense based upon a certain theory
MPA	Master of Public Administration

MPH	Master of Public Health
MQSA	Mammography Quality Standards Act
MRI	See Magnetic Resonance Imaging
MSN	Master of Science in Nursing
MSO	Management service organization
MSW	Master of Social Work
MT	Medical Technologist
Multi-hospital system	Two or more hospitals owned, leased, contract managed, or sponsored by a central organization; they can be either not-forprofit or investor-owned
Munchausen syndrome by proxy	A form of factitious disorder where one person, usually a parent, exaggerates or feigns illness in a child or deliberately causes or exacerbates actual medical problems the patient is experiencing
NASA	National Aeronautics and Space Administration
National Center for Complementary and Alternative Medicine	An agency of the National Institutes of Health developed to study and provide information about complementary and alternative medicine treatments and therapies
National Committee for Quality Assurance	A private nonprofit accrediting body for managed care organizations
National Labor Relations Act	The main body of law governing collective bargaining Explicitly grants employees the right to collectively bargain and join trade unions
	Originally enacted by Congress in 1935 under its power to regulate interstate commerce
National Practitioner Data Bank	A data bank maintained by the federal government containing reports on certain individual practitioners. A report must be made by any entity that pays money on behalf of a practitioner to settle a legal claim asserted against the practitioner. Reports must also be made by hospitals that restrict, suspend or terminate a practitioner's privileges to examine or treat patients at the hospital.
NB	Newborn
NBC emergencies	Disaster scenarios involving nuclear, bioterrorism or chemical warfare agents
NCC-MERP	National Coordinating Council for Medication Error Reporting and Prevention
NCI	National Cancer Institute
NCQA	See National Committee for Quality Assurance
NCVIA	National Childhood Vaccine Injury Act, U.S. Code 42 U.S.C. 300, established the National Vaccine Injury Compensation Program
NDS	National Disaster Medical System
Near Miss	"Used to describe any process variation which did not affect the outcome, but for which a recurrence carries a significant chance of a serious adverse outcome. Such a near miss falls within the scope of the (JCAHO's) definition of a sentinel event, but outside the scope of those sentinel events that are subject to review by the Joint Commission under its Sentinel Event Policy" (JCAHO)

Neglect	Failure to provide goods and services necessary to avoid physical harm, mental anguish or mental illness
Negligence	A legal conclusion that is reached when it has been determined that: (1) the defendant owed a duty of care to the plaintiff; (2) the defendant breached the duty of care; (3) the plaintiff was injured as a result of the breach of the duty of care; and (4) legally cognizable damages resulted from the injury
	Carelessness, failure to act as an ordinary prudent person or action contrary to that of a reasonable party. Or failure to use such care as a reasonably prudent and careful person would demonstrate under similar circumstances
	A violation of a duty to meet an applicable standard of care
Neonatal	The part of an infant's life from the hour of birth through the first 27 days, 23 hours and 59 minutes; the infant is referred to as newborn throughout this period
NESHAP	National Emission Standard for Hazardous Air Pollutants
Network	Self-contained, fully integrated system of providers
NF	Nursing Facility
NFP	Not-For-Profit
NICU	Neonatal intensive care unit
NIH	National Institute for Health
NIMH	National Institute of Mental Health
NIOSH	National Institute of Occupational Safety and Health
NLRA	See National Labor Relations Act
NLRB	National Labor Relations Board
NMHPA	Newborns' and Mothers' Health Protection Act
No-fault system	A system of compensation for injured parties that is not based on the fault or negligence of the party causing the injury. Examples include the workers' compensation system and the personal injury protection (PIP) automobile insurance mandated or available in some jurisdictions.
Nomenclature	A naming classification system, e.g., FDA's choice of new medication names
Non-economic damages (general damages)	Damages asserted by or awarded to a claimant for pain and suffering, loss of consortium, loss of enjoyment of life, etc., for which no objective dollar value exists Damages payable for items other than monetary losses, such as pain and suffering. The term technically includes punitive damages, but those are typically discussed separately
Non-Insurance transfer	The transfer of the financial obligations to pay for defense, expenses, verdicts, awards and settlements
	Reduces the transferor's loss exposure by contractually shifting legal responsibility for a loss through leases, contracts and agreements (exculpatory clauses)
Nonsuit	A privilege granted to plaintiffs in Virginia that allows them to withdraw a civil lawsuit at any time before decision, without prejudice to their right or ability to bring it one more time
NORA	National Occupational Research Agenda
Nose coverage	See Prior Acts Coverage

Nosocomial infection	A type of infection acquired during treatment/admission within a healthcare facility
	Infection acquired in a hospital
Notice of Claim	A letter from or on behalf of a claimant, addressed to a health care provider, which puts the health care provider on notice that a claim of alleged medical negligence is being made, and which triggers certain rights of the parties to request a medical malpractice review panel
NPDB	See National Practitioner Data Bank
NPSF	National Patient Safety Foundation
NPSG	National Patient Safety Goals (JCAHO)
NQF	National Quality Foundation
NRC	Nuclear Regulatory Commission
NTSB	National Transportation Safety Board
Nuclear medicine	The use of radioisotopes to study and treat disease, especially in the diagnostic area
Nurse practitioner	A licensed nurse who has completed a nurse practitioner program at the master's or certificate level and is trained in providing primary care services. NPs are qualified to conduct expanded health care evaluations and decision making regarding patient care, including diagnosis, treatment and prescriptions, usually under a physician's supervision and, generally, they provide services at a lower cost than PCPs. NPs may also be trained in medical specialties, such as pediatrics, geriatrics, and midwifery. Legal regulations in some states prevent NPs from qualifying for direct Medicare and Medicaid reimbursement, writing prescriptions, and admitting patients to hospital. Also called advance practice nurse (APN).
OASIS	Outcomes and Assessment Information Set
OBE	Occupied Bed Equivalent
OBRA	Omnibus Budget Reconciliation Act
OBS	Office-based surgery
OB-GYN	Obstetrics and gynecology
Obstetrics (OB)	The medical specialty concerned with the care of women during pregnancy and childbirth
Occupational Safety and Health Act/ Administration	29 U.S.C. Section 651 et seq. Federal statute (and agency created by it) charged with responsibility for promulgating standards and enforcement mechanisms governing worker safety for most industries
Occurrence insurance policies	Insurance policies for which coverage is provided for claims which occur during the policy period, regardless of when the claim is made
Occurrence reporting	An unexpected patient medical intervention, intensity of care or healthcare impairment
Occurrence Screen Reports	A systematic review of medical records/cases (either retrospectively or concurrently conducted) using predetermined screening criteria, conducted for the purpose of identifying cases that may warrant

closer PI review. Example criteria: unplanned returns to the ED within 72 hours of admission or prior treatment for a similar condition

OCR   Office of Civil Rights

OD   Doctor of Optometry

O.D.   Right eye

OIG   Office of Inspector General, www.oig.hhs.gov

Older Workers'   29 U.S.C. Section 621 et seq. Amendments to the Age Discrimination
Benefit Protection Act in Employment Act restricting employers from making certain age-based distinctions in employee benefits plans

OMB   Office of Management and Budget

Omission Error   Failure to carry out an intended action, or failure to recognize that an action should have been carried out

OPDRA   Office of Post Marketing Drug Risk Assessment

Operating margin   Margin of net patient care revenues in excess of operating expenses

Operating Room   Surgical suite

OPO   Organ Procurement Organization

OR   See Operating Room

Ordinance   A legislative enactment typically enacted by the elected legislative body of a city, town, county or other such minor political subdivision

ORYX™   The trademarked terms JCAHO used for its approach to integrate performance measures into the accreditation process. A key component of ORYX is the use of standardized core measures.

O.S.   Left eye

OSCAR   Online Survey Certification and Reporting Database

OSHA   See Occupational Safety and Health Act/Administration

OSHA general duty clause OSHA's general requirement that employers maintain a safe work environment. OSHA inspectors may cite the general duty clause whenever an unsafe workplace condition or work practice is identified, but no specific OSHA regulation applies.

Ostensible agency doctrine The doctrine of ostensible agency, sometimes referred to as apparent agency, permits a finding of liability on a hospital where there is the appearance of an employment relationship with an independent contractor.

In the absence of employer-employee relationship, a managed care organization (MCO) may still be held vicariously liable for the acts of provider physicians if the patient had a reasonable belief that the physician was the MCO's agent and that this belief was based upon representations made by the MCO to that effect. The burden is on the plaintiff to prove that he or she detrimentally relied on the fact that the MCO held the physician out as its agent.

OT   Occupational therapy

OTC   Over-the-counter

Out-of-plan   In managed care, healthcare services required by a plan
(or out-of-network)   participant which are either not provided for by the plan
services   (such as most experimental procedures) or which must be provided for outside of the plan network (such as an emergency department visit for a participant who is traveling out of town)

Outcomes	The end result of medical care, as indicated by recovery, disability, functional status, mortality, morbidity, or patient satisfaction
Outcomes measurement	The process of systematically tracking a patient's clinical treatment and responses to that treatment using generally accepted outcomes or quality indicators, such as mortality, morbidity, disability, functional status, recovery, and patient satisfaction. Such measures are considered by many health care researchers as the only valid way to determine the effectiveness of medical care
Outpatient care	Treatment provided to a patient who is not confined in a health care facility. Outpatient care includes services that do not require an overnight stay, such as emergency treatment, same-day surgery, outpatient diagnostic tests, and physician office visits. Also referred to as ambulatory care.
Over-the-counter	Drugs that may be obtained without a written prescription from a physician
Overuse	A healthcare quality problem involving the application or performance of unnecessary procedures or the provision of unnecessary services for patients
PA	Physician Assistant also posterior-anterior
PALS	Pediatric advanced life support
Paradigm	A conceptual framework that aids in the explanation of a complex phenomena or field of inquiry
Parallel processes	Two or more processes being performed simultaneously
Partnership	An entity formed by two or more persons to undertake a business purpose for profit. Each partner is liable for the obligations and liabilities of the partnership. Income to the partnership is considered income to the partners; there is no taxation at the level of the partnership.
Patient safety	Freedom from accidental injury. Ensuring patient safety involves the establishment of operational systems and processes that minimize the likelihood of errors and maximizes the likelihood of intercepting them when they occur.
Patient Self-Determination Act	42 U.S.C. Section 1395 et seq. Federal statute requiring certain healthcare organizations, including hospitals and HMOs, to provide patients with information regarding advanced directives
PC	See Professional Corporation
PCA	Patient Controlled Analgesia
PCE	See Potentially Compensable Event.
Peer review	A process whereby possible deviations from the standard of patient care are reviewed by an individual or committee from the same professional discipline to determine whether the standard of care was met and to make recommendations for improving patient care processes. Most jurisdictions provide at least a limited protection from discovery in civil actions for peer review activities.
	An evaluation of the appropriateness, effectiveness, and efficiency of medical services ordered or performed by practicing physicians or professionals by other practicing physicians or clinical professionals. A peer review focuses on the quality of services that are performed

	by all health personnel involved in the delivery of the care under review and how appropriate the services are to meet the patients' needs.
***Per diem* staff**	Staff of a healthcare provider called in to work on an "as needed" basis depending on patient volume and acuity, as opposed to having their work schedules determined in advance
Peril	The cause of the loss
Perinatal	The care of a woman before conception, of the woman and her fetus through pregnancy, and of the mother and her neonate until 28 days after childbirth
PET	Positron emission tomography
Petition	See Complaint. Also used to denote the written instrument that initiates certain proceedings, such as bankruptcy
Pharmacy patient profile	The specific record created for each patient in the pharmacy that typically notes the patient's name, diagnoses, weight, allergy history and medications prescribed and dispensed
PHI	See Protected Health Information
PHN	Public health nurse
PHO	Physician hospital organization
PHRP	Program for Human Research Protection
PHS	Public Health Services
Physician Hospital Organization	A type of integrated delivery system that links hospitals and a group of physicians for the purpose of contracting directly with employers and managed care organizations. A PHO is a legal entity which allows physicians to continue to own their own practices and to see patients under the terms of a professional services agreement. This type of arrangement offers the opportunity to better market the services of both physicians and hospitals as a unified response to managed care
Physician's assistant	A specially trained and licenses allied health professional, who performs certain medical procedures previously reserved to the physician. PAs practice under the supervision of a physician
PI	Performance Improvement (also known as process improvement)
PIAA	Physician Insurers Association of America
PICU	Pediatric intensive care unit
PIP	Personal injury protection
PL	Professional liability
Plaintiff	A person who brings a civil lawsuit
Pleadings	The formal allegations by the parties involved in a lawsuit that delineate the claims and defenses of each party and that request judgment by the court prior to resolution
PM	Preventive maintenance
PMA	Pre-market approval application
Policy	A predetermined course of action established as a guide toward accepted business strategies and objectives
	The formal, approved description of how a governance, management, or clinical-care process is defined, organized and carried out (JCAHO CAMH Manual, 2002)

POS	Point of service
Positron Emission tomography	An imaging technique, which tracks metabolism and responses to therapy. Used in cardiology, neurology, and oncology; particularly effective in evaluating brain and nervous system disorders
Post-loss damage control	Any of a number of initiatives taken after a potentially compensable event to build rapport with the patient and family and to decrease the likelihood or severity of a subsequent claim
Potentially Compensable Event	An occurrence of the type for which a claim can be reasonably anticipated but for which no claim has yet been asserted
	An adverse event for which there are grounds or contributing factors found after investigation, worthy of compensation being awarded the patient
P&P	Policy and procedure
PPE	Personal protective equipment
PPO	Preferred provider organization
PPS	Prospective payment system
Practice guidelines	Formal procedures and techniques for the treatment of specific medical conditions that assist physicians in achieving optimal results. Practice guidelines are developed by medical societies and medical research organization, such as the American Medical Association (AMA) and the Agency for Health Care Policy and Research (AHCPR), as well as many HMOs, insurers, and business coalitions. Practice guidelines serve as educational support for physicians and as quality assurance and accountability measures for managed care plans.
Precedent	A previously decided case that turned upon the same facts, circumstances or legal theory as presented in the case under consideration. Lower courts are bound to follow precedents set by higher courts in the jurisdiction in which the lower court is located. Cases decided by courts in other jurisdictions may be considered "persuasive authority" by the court rendering judgment in a given case. In this case the court may follow the decision of the other court, although not legally required to do so. The doctrine requiring the binding effect of precedent is called *stare decisis.*
Preemption	Doctrine adopted by the U.S. Supreme Court holding that certain matters are of such a national, as opposed to local, character that federal laws preempt or take precedence over state laws
Preexisting condition	A physical or mental condition that an insured has prior to the effective date of coverage. Policies may exclude coverage for such condition for a specified period of time
Preferred provider organization	A plan that contracts with independent providers at a discount for services. Generally, the PPO's network of providers is limited in size. Patients usually have free choice to select other providers but are given strong financial incentives to select one of the designated preferred providers. Unlike an HMO, a PPO is not a prepaid plan but does use some utilization management techniques. PPO arrangements can be either insured or self-funded. An insurerspon-sored PPO combines a large network of providers, utilization management programs, administrative sponsored PPO combines a large network of providers, utilization management programs,

	administrative services, and health care insurance. A self-funded PPO generally excludes administrative and insurance services from the plan package. However, employers can purchase these services separately.
Preventable Adverse Event	An adverse event that could have been avoided, if actions were taken prior to the final step of the process
Primary care	Basic care including initial diagnosis and treatment, preventive services, maintenance of chronic conditions, and referral to specialists
Prior acts coverage	In insurance, coverage that extends a claims-made policy to claims that occurred before the inception date of the policy but subsequent to a specified retroactive date for which a claim is made during the policy period. Sometimes referred to as "nose coverage"
Privileged communication	Communications, which occur in the context of legal or other, recognized professional confidentiality. Privileged communication allows participants to resist legal pressure to disclose its contents. A breach in such communication can result in a civil suit or tort.
Privileging (delineation of clinical privileges)	The process of granting specific clinical privileges, based on training, experience and current competence, for individuals credentialed to provide healthcare services under medical staff bylaws
PRN	"On an as-needed basis"
PRO	Peer Review Organization. See Quality Improvement Organization
Procedure	A method by which a policy can be accomplished; it provides instructions necessary to carry out a policy statement
Professional Corporation	A corporation formed by professional persons to undertake their profession (e.g., by physicians to practice medicine). The professional corporation (PC) is typically licensed to practice the profession of the owners. Only members of the profession can be owners (shareholders) of the professional corporation.
Professional liability insurance	Coverage for liability arising from the rendering of or failure to render professional services
Promulgation	The process for creation of rules or regulations. The process typically involves the announcement of the proposed regulation by the agency, allowance of a reasonable public comment period, consideration of the comments received, and the announcement of the final regulation.
Property Coverage	Covers your buildings, contents, attached equipment and building service equipment used for cleaning and maintenance
Prospective payment system	Also called prospective pricing; a payment method in which the payment a hospital will receive for patient treatment is set up in advance; hospitals keep the difference if they incur costs less than the fixed price in treating the patient and they absorb any loss if their costs exceed the fixed price.
Protected concerted activity	A group activity that seeks to modify wages or working conditions
Protected health information	Medical record information and other individually identifiable information for which privacy protection is afforded under HIPAA

Provider sponsored organization	Public or private entities established or organized and operated by a health provider or a group of affiliated health care providers that provide a substantial proportion of services under the Medicare+Choice contract and share substantial financial risk
PSA	Prostate specific antigen
PSDA	See Patient Self-Determination Act
PSO	Provider sponsored organization
PT	Physical therapy
PTO	Paid Time Off
Punitive damages (exemplary damages)	Damages sought or awarded to punish or deter the defendant or to deter others from similar conduct rather than to compensate the injured party. Generally require a showing of gross negligence or willful and wanton misconduct. Not insurable in some jurisdictions and may be excluded by insurance policies
	Damages awarded to the plaintiff over and above what will barely compensate him for his property loss, where the wrong done to him was aggravated by circumstances of violence, oppression, malice, fraud or wanton and wicked conduct on the part of the defendant and are intended to solace the plaintiff for mental anguish or to punish the defendant or make an example of him
	Damages awarded in addition to compensatory (economic and noneconomic) damages to punish a defendant for willful and wanton conduct
QA	Quality assurance
QAPI	Quality Assessment and Performance Improvement Program (Conditions of Participation)
QI	Quality improvement
QIO	See Quality Improvement Organization
QS	Quality System regulation for medical devices (21 CFR Part 820)
Quality assurance	Term that describes attempts by managed care organizations to measure and monitor the quality of care delivered
Quality Improvement Organization	Successor name for PROs. The Centers for Medicare and Medicaid Services (CMS) administers the Peer Review Organization (PRO) program that is designed to monitor and improve utilization and quality of care for Medicare beneficiaries. The program consists of a national network of fifty-three PROs (also known as Quality Improvement Organizations) responsible for each U.S. state and territory and the District of Columbia
	Federally funded physician organizations, under contract to the Department of Health and Human Services, that review quality of care, determine whether services are necessary and payment should be made for care provided under the Medicare and Medicaid programs
Quality of care	The degree to which health services for individuals and populations increase the likelihood of desired health outcomes and are consistent with current professional knowledge
	A desired degree of excellence in the provision of health care. The health care delivery processes which are thought to be determinants of

quality include: structural adequacy, access and availability, technical abilities of practitioners, practitioner communication skills and attitudes, documentation of services provided, coordination and follow-up, patient commitment and adherence to a therapeutic regimen, patient satisfaction, and clinical outcome

QuIC	Quality Interagency Coordinating Committee
Quid pro quo	"This for that"
***Qui Tam* Plaintiff**	A plaintiff in an action under the False Claims Act that is brought on behalf of the federal government. The False Claims Act prohibits the presentation of false claims for remuneration to the federal government.
Qui Tam Relator	One who brings an action on behalf of the government (originally on behalf of the king)

RAC	See Rent-A-Captive
RBC	Red blood count
RCA	See Root Cause Analysis
RCRA	Resource Conservation and Recovery Act
Release	A document executed by the plaintiff, usually in exchange for a monetary settlement, which releases the defendant from any further obligation or threat of suit
Reasonable accommodation	Under the Americans with Disabilities Act, those actions required by an employer to allow an otherwise qualified individual with a disability to perform a specific job. Reasonable accommodations include modifications to work processes and schedules and to physical facilities that are not "unduly burdensome."
Reconstruction Civil Rights Acts	42 U.S.C. Section 1981 and 1983. Post-Civil War federal legislation prohibiting certain types of racial discrimination
Regulation	An enactment issued (promulgated) by a regulatory (non-elected) agency. Regulations must be promulgated pursuant to a statute that gives the agency the authority to do so and typically must go through a promulgation process
Rehab Act	Section §504 of this 1973. Federal law prohibiting discrimination on the basis of handicap
Reinsurance	A contractual arrangement involving the purchase of insurance by an "Insurer" from "Another Insurer"—i.e., insurance for the insurance company
	A type of insurance purchased by providers and health plans to protect themselves from extraordinary losses. Types of reinsurance coverage include: individual stop loss, aggregate stop loss, out-of-area protection, and insolvency protection. Reinsurance is a transaction between and among insurers for the assumption of risk in exchange for a premium. Usually, a primary insurer will cede only a portion of its total risk and premium payments to a reinsurer, either as a percentage of total premiums or only for losses above a particular threshold
Release	A written instrument that normally concludes a legal proceeding and precludes the initiation or re-initiation of a further legal proceeding against the released party(s) with respect to the released claims

	A document executed by the plaintiff, usually in exchange for a monetary settlement, which releases the defendant from any further obligation or threat of suit
Rent-A-Captive	Owned by investors rather than insureds and organized to insure or re-insure third-party risks
Request for Admission	A set of questions served upon a party in litigation during discovery that requests the party served to admit or deny the truth of the requested question
Request for Production	A written set of requests served upon a party in litigation during discovery that asks the party to produce tangible things (e.g., records, photographs, equipment, etc.)
Reserves	Estimates of the amount ultimately required to settle a claim or pay a judgment (indemnity reserve) and to provide for a defense and pay other allocated expenses related to managing a claim (expense reserve)
	The amount of money the insurance company sets aside to satisfy a claim, based on the insurance company's estimate of what it will take to satisfy a settlement or verdict
Res Ipsa Loquitur	"The thing speaks for itself"; arises upon proof that the instrumentality was in defendant's exclusive control and that the accident was one which ordinarily does not happen in absence of negligence.
	A legal theory, which translated from Latin means "the thing speaks for itself" which applies in situations where the fact that a particular injury occurred allows an inference of negligence
Respondeat superior	Legal doctrine that the employer is responsible for the act and omissions of employees in the course and scope of employment. While the employee is also generally liable for his or her own negligence, the employer remains vicariously liable.
	"Let the master answer"—a doctrine of law under which the employer is responsible for the legal consequences of the acts of the servant or employee who is acting within the scope of employment
Restraint, chemical	A drug used as a restraint is a medication used to control behavior or to restrict the patient's freedom of movement and is not a standard treatment for the patient's medical or psychiatric condition.
Restraint, physical	A physical restraint is any manual method or physical or mechanical device, material, or equipment attached or adjacent to the patient's body that he or she cannot easily remove that restricts freedom of movement or normal access to one's body.
Retrospective premium plans	In insurance, a policy for which an initial deposit premium is paid with the ultimate premium determined based on the loss experience of the insured. Some plans adjust the premium based on losses incurred (which include reserves for claims not yet settled), while others make adjustments based on paid losses only. Common in workers' compensation insurance programs
Reuse	Most often used in the context of processing a single use device (SUD) in order to permit it to be used again
Reviewable sentinel event	The event has resulted in an unanticipated death or major permanent loss of function not related to the natural course of the patient's illness or underlying condition.
RFP	Request for Proposal

Risk	The chance of loss. Pure risk is uncertainty as to whether loss will occur. Speculative risk is uncertainty about an event that could produce loss. Pure risk is insurable, but speculative risk usually is not.
Risk acceptance	The decision not to transfer an identified risk but instead to assume its financial consequences
Risk adjusted (data)	The process of matching different groups in a manner that takes into account significant differences and equalizes them prior to performing comparisons. For example, prior to comparing mortality rates of different physicians, the patient population groups are "risk adjusted" to equalize for age and other clinical status differences.
Risk analysis	The process used by the person or persons assigned risk management functions to determine the potential severity of the loss from an identified risk, the probability that the loss will happen, and alternatives for dealing with the risk
Risk avoidance	The decision not to undertake a particular activity because the risk associated with the activity is unacceptable
	The only risk control technique that completely eliminates the possibility of loss from a given exposure. This technique reduces the possibility of a loss to zero by the conscious choice not to engage in or avoid a specific activity or operation.
Risk control techniques	Those techniques designed to prevent the likelihood of an occurrence or reduce the frequency of occurrences that give rise to losses or to minimize at the least possible cost those losses that strike an organization
Risk financing	Any of a number of programs implemented to pay for the costs associated with property and casualty claims and associated expenses, including insurance, self-insurance, captive insurance companies, etc.
Risk identification	The process of identifying problems or potential problems that can result in loss; recognizing the potential for loss
Risk Management	The process of making and carrying out decisions that will assist in prevention of adverse consequences and minimize the adverse effects of accidental losses upon an organization. Making these decisions requires the five steps in the decision process. Carrying out these decisions requires the risk management professional to perform the four functions in the management process. These include planning, organizing, leading and controlling.
	A systematic and scientific approach in the empirical order to identify, evaluate, reduce, or eliminate the possibility of an unfavorable deviation from expectation and, thus, to prevent the loss of financial assets resulting from injury to patients, visitors, employees, independent medical staff, or from damage, theft, or loss of property belonging to the healthcare entity or persons mentioned. The definition includes transfer of liability and insurance financing relative to the inability to reduce or eliminate intolerable deviations. Originally defined by the American Hospital Association as the "science for the identification, evaluation, and treatment of the risk of financial loss." Risk management now also encompasses the evaluation and monitoring of clinical practice to recognize and prevent patient injury.

Risk purchasing group	Any group that decides to buy, on a group basis, liability insurance in compliance with the Federal Risk Retention Act
	Domestic organization formed to purchase commercial market liability insurance on a group basis for members engaged in similar activities
Risk reduction	Reduces the severity of those losses that other risk control techniques do not prevent
Risk Retention Group	Liability-only domestic insurance captive for group whose members are engaged in similar activities
Risk transfer	The procedure of shifting risk of loss to another party who agrees to accept it
RMIS	Risk management information system
RN	Registered Nurse
Root Cause Analysis	A multi-disciplinary process of study or analysis that uses a detailed, structured process to examine factors contributing to a specific outcome (e.g., an adverse event)
	A process for identifying the basic or causal factors that underlie variation in performance, including the occurrence or possible occurrence of a sentinel event
RPG	See Risk Purchasing Group
RPLU	Registered Professional Liability Underwriter
RRG	See Risk Retention Group
RX	Prescription
Safe Medical Devices Act	21 U.S.C. Section 360 et seq. Federal statute governing the tracking of certain implantable medical devices and requiring reporting of patient deaths and serious injuries involving the use of medical devices or equipment
Sarbanes-Oxley Act	Applies to public companies that are required to file periodic Securities and Exchange Commission (SEC) Reports under Sections 12 or 15(d) of the Security Exchange Act of 1934 or if the public company has filed a registration statement that has not yet become effective under the Securities Act of 1933
SBS	Sick building syndrome
SC	Subcutaneous
SCCM	Society of Critical Care Medicine, www.sccm.org
SCHIP	State Children's Health Insurance Program
SE	Sentinel event
SEC	Securities and Exchange Commission
Segregation	Segregation of exposure units reduces the uncertainty of losses by increasing the predictability of both loss frequency and severity
Self-governing	As pertains to the hospital medical staff, a requirement contained in JCAHO standards that the medical staff elect its own officers and approve its own bylaws and rules and regulations
Self-insurance trust fund	A mechanism for funding claims and related expenses under a program of self-insurance whereby the insured establishes a segregated fund, administered by a trustee, which is replenished from time to time according to actuarially determined estimates of future loss costs

Self-insured retention	In insurance, that portion of a claim that the insured is required to pay before the insurer begins to pay. Similar to a deductible, but frequently funded through a mechanism such as a self-insurance trust fund and larger than a deductible. The insured generally manages claims falling entirely within the SIR (or contracts with a third party to do so), so that the insurer is only involved if the amount of the claim exceeds or is anticipated to exceed the amount of the retention. Common in hospital professional liability programs
Sentinel event	The JCAHO term for an unexpected occurrence involving death or serious physical or psychological injury or the risk thereof, including loss of limb or function. The phrase "or risk thereof" includes any process variation for which a recurrence would carry a significant chance of a serious adverse outcome.
	The JCAHO has a policy to encourage the voluntary self-reporting of sentinel events by accredited organizations in order to gather and publish information about the relative frequencies and underlying causes of such occurrences.
Settlement	An agreement between the parties in which consideration is passed and the matter is concluded as to those parties. Settlement may occur at any time.
	A compromise achieved by the adverse parties in a civil suit before final judgment
Severance agreement	A contract between an employer and a terminated employee. Generally severance agreements provide a lump sum payment or a period of salary continuation in return for the employee's agreement not to make certain claims against the employer.
Sexual harassment	Any of a number of statutorily prohibited kinds of sexually oriented and unwanted contact, remarks and comments or conditions of employment. In quid pro quo sexual harassment, participation in sexual activity or performance of sexual favors is made an explicit or implicit condition of employment. In a hostile environment, sexual harassment, jokes, comments, cartoons or touching of a sexual nature permeate the workplace, interfering with an employee's ability to perform his or her job comfortably.
SICU	Surgical intensive care unit
SIDS	Sudden infant death syndrome
Single Payer System	A financing system such as Canada's in which a single entity-usually the government-pays for all covered health care services
Single Point Weakness	A step in the process so critical that its failure would result in system failure or in an adverse event
SIR	See Self-Insured Retention
Skilled Nursing Facility	A facility, either freestanding or part of a hospital, that accepts patients in need of rehabilitation and medical care. To qualify for Medicare coverage, SNFs must be certified by Medicare and meet specific qualifications, including 24-hour nursing coverage and availability of physical, occupational, and speech therapies.
Slander	The speaking of base and defamatory words tending to prejudice.
Slips	Unintended human errors, usually during an activity that the person is proficient in and is performing on an "automatic mode" basis
SMDA	See Safe Medical Devices Act

SNF	Skilled Nursing Facility, a certain level of care provided to nursing home residents
SOB	Short of breath
Special cause	Factor that intermittently and unpredictably induces variation over and above that inherent in the system
Specials	Those elements of a plaintiff's damages which can be computed with relative precision. Includes lost wages, medical expenses, future expenses, etc.
SSA	Social Security Act
SSI	Supplemental security income, also ServiShare
SSN	Social security number
Standard	A minimum level of acceptable performance or results or excellent levels of performance or the range of acceptable performances on results. The American Society for Testing and Materials (ASTM) defines six types of standards: 1) standard test methods—a procedure for identifying, measuring, and evaluating a material, product or system; 2) standard specification—a statement of a set of requirements to be satisfied and the procedures for determining whether each of the requirements are satisfied; 3) standard practice—a procedure for performing one or more specific operations or functions; 4) standard terminology—a document comprising terms, definitions, descriptions, explanations, abbreviations, or acronyms; 5) standard guide—a series of options or instructions that do not recommend a specific course of action; 6) standard classification—a systematic arrangement or division of products, systems, or services into groups based on similar characteristics.
Standard of Care	In medical malpractice cases, a standard of care is applied to measure the competence of the professional. The traditional standard for doctors is that they exercise the average degree of skilled care and diligence exercised by members of the same profession, practicing in the same or similar locality in light of the present state of medical and surgical science. With increasing specialization, however, certain courts have disregarded geographical considerations holding that, in the practice of a boardcertified medical or surgical specialty, the standard should be that of a reasonable specialist practicing medicine or surgery in the same specialty.
	In a legal proceeding, the standard against which the defendant's conduct is measured. The defendant is expected to act as an ordinary, prudent person with similar training and skill would have acted in a similar situation. If the defendant's conduct falls below this standard, the defendant may be determined to have acted negligently.
Standing	The right or authority by which a person may bring and sustain a legal proceeding. It is normally conferred upon a person who has suffered an injury. It may also be possessed by someone who has been given the legal right to bring suit on behalf of someone who has suffered an injury.
Stark (#)	Physician referral laws-part of OBRA '89 ("Stark I") and '93 ("Stark II")
Stark I	Enacted initially in 1989 and took effect in 1992. Focus was on referrals involving provision of clinical laboratory services

Stark II	Broadened scope of prohibited designated health services
Stat.	Immediately
Statement of fault	A statement acknowledging responsibility for a specific event or outcome
Statute	A legislative enactment that has typically been enacted by the elected legislature of a state or the federal government
Statute of limitations	The time period defined by law in which a claimant must file a claim for damages or be barred from so doing. Most jurisdictions extend the allowable time period for individuals who are injured as minors, and many include a discovery rule extending the time period for individuals whose injuries were not readily discoverable.
	A statute that requires, absent good cause for delay, that a person bring suit within a certain period of time. The running of the statute may be stayed (tolled) for a number of reasons, such as incompetence, infancy, disability, etc. The effect of a statute of limitations may also be stayed if the plaintiff can prove late discovery of the injury, a continuing course of treatment, or active misrepresentation of the plaintiff's condition.
	A statute specifying the period of time after the occurrence of an injury or in some cases, after the discovery of the injury-or of its cause-during which any suit must be filed
Statute of Repose	A statute that sets a maximum period of time in which a suit may be brought. This statute is always longer than the statute of limitations, and generally is subject to fewer, if any, exceptions or tolling provisions.
STD	Short-term disability
	Sexually transmitted disease
Stop loss	Insurance coverage for healthcare and managed care organizations that have agreed in advance to accept financial risk for the provision of healthcare services under capitated managed care contracts. Stop loss policies limit the losses experienced by such entities when utilization of services exceeds estimates.
Sub-acute care	A level of care that is between acute care and long-term care
Subpoena	"Under penalty"
	A process to cause to cause a witness to appear and give testimony, commanding him to lay aside all pretenses and excuses and appear before the court named at a time mentioned to testify for the party named or experience a penalty.
	A document, issued by the court at the request of a party, which compels an individual to produce documents and/or attend a deposition or trail and give testimoney
Subpoena duces tecum	A process by which the court commands a witness who has in his possession or control some document or paper that is pertinent to the issues of a pending controversy, to produce it at the trial.
Subrogation	The process of collecting from the person responsible for damages. Allows the insurer making a payment to the insured to assume the insured's right of recovery against the third party responsible for the loss.
SUDs	Single Use Devices

Summary judgment	Procedural device available for prompt and expeditious disposition of controversy without trial when there is no dispute as to either material fact or inferences to be drawn from undisputed facts, or if only a question of law is involved
Summons	Usually a brief (one-page) document commanding defendant(s) to appear and answer before a court
Supreme Court	The highest appellate court within a given jurisdiction. Appeals taken from the trial of a lawsuit are ultimately heard by this tribunal.
Surety bonds	A three-part contract in which two parties, the surety and the principal (or obligor), agree to be bound by a promise to a third party, the obligee. If the principal defaults on the promise, the surety, for a premium paid in advance by the principal, steps in and fulfils the obligation. Surety bonds typical in the healthcare setting include patient trust fund bonds (to ensure that patient funds and valuables held by hospitals and nursing homes are appropriately safeguarded), performance bonds (to ensure that construction projects are completed as agreed upon) and various license bonds (to ensure appropriate performance of the licensee's duties). Once the surety fulfills the obligations to the obligee, it may seek reimbursement from the principal.
Surge capacity	Reserve capacity in terms of staff, space, equipment and supplies built into a healthcare provider's operations to accommodate emergency situations in which the demand for services may be greatly increased over normal levels
Surgicenter	A health care facility that is physically separate from a hospital and provides prescheduled surgical services on an outpatient basis, generally at a lower cost than inpatient hospital care. Also called a Free-Standing Outpatient Surgery Center
Swing beds	Acute care hospital beds that can also be used for long-term care, depending on the needs of the patient and the community; only those hospitals with fewer than 100 beds and located in a rural community, where long-term care may be inaccessible, are eligible to have swing beds.
System	Set of interdependent elements interacting to achieve a common aim. These elements may be both human and nonhuman (equipment, technologies, etc.).
Systemic or system-related issue	An issue that arises due to some design, process or any other operational aspect of a complex, multiple entity "system" or multistep process
T&A	Tonsillectomy and adenoidectomy
Tail	The delay between an actual incident of malpractice or alleged action and the filing of a claim is called the long tail. An insurance company underwriting occurrence policies will be covering claims for many years after the policy has expired due to this long tail. In contrast, the claims-made policy covers only those claims that are actually made during tenure of the policy. Therefore, if you cancel your claims-made policy, and wish to have continued coverage, you must purchase an extended reporting endorsement or tail coverage.
Tail coverage	See Extended Reporting Endorsement.
TB	Tuberculosis

Teaching hospitals Hospitals that have an accredited medical residency training program and are typically affiliated with a medical school

Telehealth See Telemedicine

Telemedicine The use of telecommunications to provide medical information and services

The provision of healthcare consultation and education using telecommunications networks to communicate information; medical practice across distance via telecommunications and interactive video technology (American Medical Association's Council on Medical Education and Medical Services)

The use of electronic information and communications technologies to provide and support healthcare when distance separates the participants (Institute of Medicine)

Tertiary care Refers to highly technical services for the patient who is imminent danger of major disability or death

Therapeutic Privilege A decision by a doctor that a patient should not have access to certain parts of the patient's medical records, out of a concern that the patient will not be able to cope with the information contained therein

Third party Provides coverage to a party other than the insured to make that person whole for loss or injury caused by the insured

Third-party administrator An independent organization that contracts to provide claims management services to a self-insured entity

A firm outside the insuring organization, which handles the administrative duties such as collecting premiums, claims processing, claims payment, membership services, utilization review, for employee health benefit plans and managed care plans. Third party administrators are used by organizations that actually fund the health benefits but find it not cost effective to administer the plan themselves. If claims payment is one of the services, the TPA is considered a third party payer. Unlike insurance carriers, TPAs do not underwrite the insurance risk.

Third-party over claim A claim by an injured employee against a party other than his or her employer, such as the manufacturer of a machine involved in the injury, in which the third party brings in the employer as an additional defendant, such as for failure to properly maintain the machine. Third-party over claims are a type of claim by an injured worker against his or her employer that fall outside of workers' compensation coverage and are generally covered by employers' liability policies.

Threat envelope In disaster planning, the analysis of those types of occurrences most likely to occur, as well as those less likely but having particularly serious consequences for a community or organization for which it determines it must prepare

Tight coupling An engineering term to describe when the steps of a process follow so closely to one another that a variation in the first step cannot be recognized and responded to or corrected, prior to a variance or adverse consequence resulting from the first step thereby affecting the second step, and the entire, desired outcome

Tomography A diagnostic technique using x-ray photographs which do not show the shadows of structures before and behind the section under scrutiny

Tort	A private or civil wrong or injury for which the court will provide a remedy in the form of an action for damages
Tortfeasor	Party to direct liability as a result of party's acts or omissions
Total Quality Management	A systematic set of processes and tools designed to improve quality on an ongoing basis
	A philosophy and system for achieving constant performance improvement at every level. Key elements of TQM include company wide continuous quality improvement (CQI) efforts (sometimes called a quality improvement program), self-directing work teams, employee involvement programs, flexible service delivery processes, quick change over and adaptability, customer focus, supplier integration, and production cycle time reduction. Many health care organizations implement TQM programs as a competitive strategy
TPA	See Third-party Administrator
TPO	Treatment, payment and operations
TQI	Total quality improvement
TQM	Total Quality Management
Transitional duty (alternative duty, light duty, modified duty)	The assignment of an injured employee to work differently than what he or she ordinarily performs in terms of duties, work environment or duration during a period of recovery
Transparency	A practice of full disclosure to the consumer/patient, as opposed to providing limited information or a policy of secrecy
Treaty	The reinsurer agrees in advance to accept certain classes of exposures as outlined in a "treaty." The insurer assumes underwriting authority on behalf of the reinsurer.
Triage	Evaluation of patient conditions for urgency and seriousness and the establishment of a priority list in order to direct care and ensure the efficient use of medical and nursing staff and facilities. Triaging patients occurs in situations with multiple victims
Trial Court	Usually the lowest level court within a given jurisdiction and the court in which the actual trial of the matter will be conducted
TSCA	Toxic Substances Control Act
TX	A charting abbreviation for "treatment."
UCL	See Upper Control Limit
Ultrasound	Refers to sound that has different velocities in tissues which differ in density and elasticity from others; this property permits the use of ultrasound in outlining the shape of various tissues and organs in the body
UM	See Utilization Management
Umbrella	In insurance, an excess insurance policy providing limits above more than one type of primary policy, such as professional and general liability and auto liability. Umbrella policies may also include some specific coverages not found in the underlying policies.
Unanticipated outcome	A result that differs significantly from what was anticipated to be the result of the treatment or procedure
Under use	A quality problem involving the failure to provide a healthcare service or procedure for persons for whom it was clinically indicated or needed

Underwriter	An insurance company employee who makes determinations regarding the acceptability of a given risk for insurance coverage and for specific terms, conditions and pricing of such coverage
Underwriting	The process of identifying, evaluating, and classifying the potential level of risk represented by a group seeking insurance coverage, in order to determine appropriate pricing, risk involved, and administrative feasibility. The chief purpose of underwriting is to make sure the potential for loss is within the range for which the premiums were established. Underwriting can also refer to the acceptance of risk
Universal access	The provision of coverage for health care services to all citizens
Upper Control Limit	Used in statistical process control run charts
UR	Utilization review
URAC	Utilization Review Accreditation Commission, also known as American Accreditation HealthCare Commission
URL	Uniform Resource Locator (also known as web address)
Urgent Care	Care for injury, illness, or another type of condition (usually not life threatening) which should be treated within 24 hours. Also refers to after-hours care, and to a health plan's classification of hospital admissions as urgent, semi-urgent, or elective
USC	U.S. Code
USERRA	The Uniformed Services Employment and Reemployment Rights Act
USP	U.S. Pharmacopeia, a non-governmental organization that promotes the public health by establishing standards to ensure the quality of medicines and other healthcare technologies
U.S. Patriots Act	Federal legislation that enhances the ability of law enforcement to deter and detect acts of terrorism, including cyber-intelligence gathering, wire-tapping and other means of gathering needed information from designated privacy records
USPHS	United States Public Health Service
Utilization	Patterns of usage for a particular medical services such as hospital care or physician visits
Utilization Management	The function of monitoring the utilization of healthcare resources by individual patients, e.g., to verify that surgical cases justify criteria for performing that procedure; to verify that the length of stay in a hospital is justified, etc. Also referred to as case management
Utilization review	An evalution of the care and services that patients receive which is based on pre-established criteria and standards
VAHRPAP	Veterans Administration Human Research Protection Accreditation Program
VBAC	Vaginal Birth After Cesarean Section
VDRL	Serology
Venue	The physical location, or the tribunal within such location, in which a legal proceeding may be brought. Usually the place in which the injury is alleged to have occurred
Verdict	The formal decision or definitive answer of a jury impaneled to hear and decide the facts of a legal proceeding, which is reported to the court

VHA	Veterans Health Administration
Vicarious Liability	The imposition of liability on one person for the actionable conduct of another, based solely on a relationship between the two persons. Indirect or imputed legal responsibility for the acts of another, e.g., the liability of an employer for the acts of an employee. A principle for torts and contracts of an agent
VIP	Very important person
Voir Dire	The process of questioning jurors, prior to seating them, to determine if any jurors have knowledge of the case, personally know or know of the parties, or may otherwise have preconceptions that would prevent them from hearing and deciding the case impartially
Volume-outcome relationship	The theory that for certain procedures, higher volume (by either a specific provider or a hospital) is associated with better health outcomes
Waiver of subrogation	A contractual provision in which one party agrees not to seek indemnification by the other in the event of a subsequent loss for which the second party may bear responsibility
War risk exclusion	A exclusion found in many types of insurance policies excluding losses caused by acts of war or military action
WC	Workers' compensation
Whistleblower	An individual, frequently an employee or former employee, who reports unlawful activity, such as healthcare fraud and abuse or OSHA violations, to the government or an administrative agency. Some statutes provide for the whistleblower to receive a share of fines levied against the organization for making the report. Most statutes prohibit retaliatory discharge or other discriminatory actions against an employee who makes such a report.
WHO	World Health Organization
WIC	Women and Infant Children Program
Withholds	A provision in some managed care contracts withholding a portion of a healthcare provider's reimbursement until the end of a specific time period. If certain utilization targets are met for the period, the provider then receives the withheld reimbursement payments.
WBC	White blood count
WMD	Weapons of mass destruction
Workers' compensation	Statutory obligation requiring employers to provide compensation to employees for injuries arising out of, and in the course of, their employment
Working memory	The concentrated short-term memory used by persons when learning any new task, process
Worried well	Individuals who, in a disaster, contact healthcare providers for information or present at treatment sites for reassurance, even though they have no specific injuries or symptoms, inhibiting the provider's ability to assess and treat those truly in need of medical services

Name Index

Subject Index